An A To Z of On The Buses

Compiled by

Craig Walker

First Published in Great Britain 2014 by Mirador Publishing

Copyright © 2014 by Craig Walker

First edition: 2014

A copy of this work is available through the British Library.

ISBN : 978-1-910104-20-0

Mirador Publishing
Mirador
Wearne Lane
Langport
Somerset
TA10 9HB

Dedicated to Lewi Walker
1933-2013

Introduction

The book you are about to read was inspired by my lifelong love of the hit sitcom On The Buses and results from the culmination of several months of research followed by two years of writing. It is hoped that, like the subject material, it will cater for various generations. The hit sitcom On The Buses and its three spin-off films still attract fans young and old and this book will hopefully meet the needs of these generations.

It will bring back many happy memories for those fortunate enough to have watched On The Buses when it first aired on television. The younger fans who were brought up on the repeats and the highly successful spinoff films will find elements of this book very useful as it covers all aspects of On The Buses and sheds light on various popular figures of that time mentioned in the television series and films that the younger generation may not have recognised.

Personally, the appeal of On The Buses is that it stemmed from an age in comedy that relied on saucy innuendo and double entendres laced into well-written scripts supplied by Ronald Wolfe and Ronald Chesney. This coupled with a cast laden with talent and great comedic chemistry between the characters meant the recipe was there for a comedy classic. Its comedy had a seaside postcard feel much like the Carry On series of films which were hugely popular from the late 1950s through until the mid-1970s and On The Buses also relied on a stable cast. Reg Varney as bus driver Stan came into the series already as a star from his roles in The Rag Trade and Beggar My Neighbour and learnt his trade on stage before that. For Bob Grant, who played toothy-grinned and randy conductor Jack, On The Buses really brought him his fame but this would later weigh heavily against him later in life as typecasting really stinted his growth as an actor more especially on television. Michael Robbins was to play know-it-all brother-in-law Arthur and he possessed a great talent for dead-pan humour and he really excelled in the role. The part of his wife Olive, a down-trodden and unglamorous woman went to South African-born actress Anna Karen and she was to find stardom in the role and is still best remembered today as Olive. Doris Hare took up the role as Mrs Butler (the mother of the family) from Series Two of the television series onwards and came with many years of experience as an actress and made the part her own on taking over from Australian actress Cicely Courtneidge. Finally, the role of Inspector Blake was played by Stephen Lewis. Better known for stage roles he had not long broken in to television work and he was to mould the character of the put upon and harassed inspector of the bus depot superbly. Many of his traits were his own invention and were not part of the scripts but they became part and parcel of a great character.

On The Buses ran from 1969 to 1973 and contained references, phrases, characters, buses and a whole host of other minor details that will be covered in this book. This will contain over 1,000 entries and includes career details of everyone that worked in On The Buses whether in front of the cameras or behind them with some including their personal memories of working on either the television series or the spin-off films. This will give you a chance to learn more about those you may not remember or have known about but who played their own part, however large or small, in creating the comedy masterpiece that is On The Buses.

When reading this book it is worth considering that you may spot inconsistencies in some facts. These are merely a result of the difference in plotlines between the television series and the spin-off films which is purely because the films were based on the TV series and not a direct continuation of the story between the two formats. The biggest difference being that the green-liveried buses of the Luxton and District Bus Company on the small screen were instead red-liveried buses of the Town and District Bus Company in the spin-off films. Another noticeable difference was the differing fortunes of the relationship of Arthur and Olive Rudge. In the TV series,at the beginning of the seventh series, their marriage ends in divorce with Olive having produced no more than chilblains. On the big screen though their marriage remained intact and they were to have a son affectionately known as little Arthur. Other plotline differences between the small and big screen forms of On The Buses are evident as you will note and recall when reading this book.

All that remains for me to say is that I hope that On The Buses fans around the world and of all age groups thoroughly enjoy the book. A trip down memory lane for some and a learning experience for others. Enjoy.

A Night In Paris

This is the name of a perfume that is worn by Olive in the Series Six episode 'Love Is What You Make It'.

She adorns the scent as part of a plot created by Jack to make husband Arthur jealous by having him find her with another man in a bid to stop their marriage from falling apart. The unfortunate Inspector Blake is lured to the Butler house under false pretences and as Olive attempts to make a pass at him he describes her perfume as 'a bit of a pong'.

The perfume name was fictional though it was probably based on a highly popular Paris perfume created in 1929 by Monsieur Bourjois which was called 'Soir de Paris' which translates into English as 'Evening In Paris'. The perfume has been discontinued for a number of years.

ABC Rail Guide

A book that Inspector Blake can be seen reading in bed as Stan attempts to smuggle clippie Doreen into his new lodging's bedroom by carrying her on his back in the Series Five episode 'Stan's Room'.

This ABC Rail Guide was first published in its earliest form in 1841 and aside from a few years in the 1960s has been an annual publication listing every timetable on the British railway network. Sadly, in 2006, Network Rail ended the long tradition to replace it with an internet and telephone-based inquiry service.

Abide With Me by The Luton Girls Choir

A vinyl record picked up by Stan from the Butler collection when he brings Iris home and she asks him to put on some mood music in the Series One episode 'The New Conductor'. Her reaction to Abide With Me by The Luton Girls' Choir is: 'Oh my gawd.'

In reality there was a great tradition and history behind the Luton Girls' Choir. They were one of the most renowned choirs of an era spanning from the 1930s until 1977. The choir performed at the 1948 Royal Command Performance at the London Palladium with recording contracts and radio appearances following as well as television appearances in the 1960s. It is doubtful that the Luton Girls' Choir actually ever recorded a version of Abide With Me though.

Accident Form

This is a form that has to be filled in following accidents at work by employees of the Luxton and District Bus Company.

In the Series Four episode 'The Injury', Inspector Blake has an accident that had been set-up for Stan when he falls through a flight of wooden steps at the depot breaking his big toe. As a result he asks Stan and Jack to sign an accident form that he hands them and tells them to get the nurse to fill it in afterwards. On realising Stan is unfit for work after an earlier accident at home, Blakey hands him another accident form to fill out.

Accident Pay

Accident pay is paid by the Luxton and District Bus Company but only when an employee has an accident and is injured whilst on duty as seen in the Series Four episode 'The Injury'.

When Stan faces the prospect of having to report sick for work after having an accident at home he is warned by Jack that he will only receive sickness benefit from the company unless Stan can get to the depot and have an arranged accident there and so earn accident pay. This proves difficult as Stan has a suspected broken toe and dislocated shoulder and cannot put on his own shoes and so borrows a pair of Olive's plimsolls.

On arrival at the depot Jack urges Stan to sign on to make the accident official whilst maintenance worker Joe has arranged for Stan to have his accident by removing the side bolts from a flight of wooden steps and replacing them with matchsticks. However, the ploy is set to fail when Inspector Blake goes up the steps first and has the accident breaking his toe and so earning full accident pay whilst all Stan gets is sent home with his wages being stopped.

Ackers Street

With a newly-fitted radio control system aboard his bus in the Series Three episode 'Radio Control', Stan uses it to report to the depot that they are stuck in a traffic jam at Ackers Street and won't arrive at the Cemetery Gates for another twenty minutes. In all truth Stan and Jack's bus had already arrived at their destination but intend to use the time to get to know two clippies called Edna and Joyce better who have been put on their bus to learn how to use the new radio control system.

Later in their shift, Stan's bus is boarded by Inspector Blake just as Stan receives a message from control about a burst water main on his route and is advised to take a diversion. It is then that Blakey tells Stan to turn left into Ackers Street to avoid the problem and to be quick as the bus is already late. The worried driver points out that he doesn't know that area well so is not going to rush but the diversion is still destined to end in disaster.

Acting Inspector

A rank that Jack is promoted to from conductor at the Luxton and District Bus Company in the Series Five episode 'Vacancy For Inspector'.

When Inspector Blake admits that he is run off his feet with the depot being short of an inspector he reveals the manager has asked him to promote one of the men. Jack though is vehement that nobody wants the job and will use his influence as shop steward to make sure none of the staff take on the role. However, his attitude soon changes when he is told by Blakey that the manager suggested Jack for promotion. To Stan's horror, Jack quickly warms to the idea of becoming Acting Inspector but he hopes to appease Stan by promising to give him all the overtime as he will be making up the time sheets as well as putting attractive clippies on his bus.

On becoming Acting Inspector, Jack undergoes a personality change. His promises of overtime to Stan are soon forgotten and to his best mate's horror he bids to better himself with Blakey by revealing a number of Stan's rule-breaking tricks to him. This includes how Stan manages to be clocked-in for duty without being in the depot, parking his bus around a corner to avoid picking up passengers and taking stock from the canteen via one of its broken window panes. Jack's mannerisms and attitude mirrors that of Inspector Blake and it would seem that his friendship with Stan is at an end as he reveals more of Stan's indiscretions.

Jack's spell as Acting Inspector comes to a sudden end though when he resigns from the post telling Stan that he wasn't having any fun in the role. Stan feels that Jack is a 'born layabout' which is why the role wasn't for him whilst Inspector Blake has the view that he knew Jack wasn't inspector material all long.

Ada

Played by Eunice Black

One of a group of women employed as bus drivers by the Town and District Bus Company in the film On The Buses.

Ada is well-built, with dark-hair and is a middle-aged woman whose arrival leaves the men at the depot feeling threatened. A campaign of dirty tricks towards her and her colleagues follow but Ada and her friends launch a fight back against Stan. They subject him to a painful experience when they corner him in the depot and put a tyre pump up his trouser leg blasting air up to Stan's most personal regions leaving him in agony whilst Ada and her friends are in stitches. But she does suffer at Stan's hands herself. She has a diuretic pill put in her tea prior to a shift which leaves her forced into parking her bus mid-route and rushing to a public toilet. Ada also falls foul of a false diversion sign placed strategically by Stan and Jack. She has Inspector Blake aboard her bus which is diverted onto a motorway and after he stops the bus he asks what she is doing but is told: 'I was diverted I saw a sign.' It is a diversion that sees them arrive back at the depot two hours late much to the anger of the manager.

When Inspector Blake is later forced to concede defeat and stop using women bus drivers things look glum for Ada. However, she and three of her former bus driver colleagues are made up to rank of inspector and soon set about upsetting Stan and Jack.

Ada

Played by Sue Walker

A middle-aged, well built clippie who can be heard screaming inside the women's toilet in the depot in the Series Two episode 'Late Again'.

Ada exits the toilet shouting: 'You nasty little peeping tom.' She explains to a waiting Inspector Blake that she was putting her make-up on when Stan came through the window of the women's toilets in a bid to make a discreet entrance into the depot. Ada claims that seeing him in the mirror gave her a nasty shock but Stan retorts that it wasn't nice for him either when he saw her which leaves Ada outraged. She calls him a cheeky lout and tells the stunned inspector that women aren't safe with men like Stan around but he tells her that she is which infuriates her but Inspector Blake diffuses the situation by urging her to get on her bus and that he'll handle the matter. She exits the scene in a huff.

Adam the Gardener

Inspector Blake is dubbed 'Adam the Gardener' by Jack as the depot's gardening competition begins to get competitive in the Series Seven episode 'Gardening Time'.

It is likely to be a reference to a character of the same name seen in a long-running weekly cartoon strip which appeared in the Sunday Express newspaper offering gardening tips in the 1940s. The character was a creation of writer Morley Adams who passed away in 1954.

Adams, Mr

A bespectacled middle-aged man who is a general manager at the Luxton and District Bus Company's depot who appears in the Series Three episode 'Busmen's Perks'.

It is insinuated by Jack that Mr Adams is squandering the company's profits by having his Jaguar car sprayed metallic bronze, filling it up with diesel meant for the buses and having maintenance worker Nobby spend hours fixing the car's cigar lighter all free of charge. Mr Adams also has an attractive secretary who is often doing overtime and Jack feels he knows what they are up to but it is Mr Adams who has the last laugh as he orders a spot check to be done on the maintenance department's stock levels just a day after Stan has obtained two tins of paint for some home decorating.

Ahmed

Played by Ishaq Bux

An ageing, bearded busman of Indian origin is seen at a social event in the depot in the Series Three episode 'The Snake'.

Ahmed who wears a turban courteously welcomes Stan and Jack on their arrival into the depot's canteen for an Indian Dance event. He tells them he has kept a place for them and that Fatima, a canteen employee that Stan and Jack are attracted to, will be bringing them refreshments before entertaining them with a special Indian dance. He later introduces Fatima's dance in his native tongue and at the end of the evening, prior to Stan leaving for home, Ahmed gives him a plateful of an Indian sweet mix to take home to the family.

Airline Pilots

Stan and Jack get mistaken for airline pilots in the Series Three episode 'The New Uniforms'.

When dining in a cafe wearing their new prototype uniforms, Stan and Jack are mistaken for airline pilots by two young and attractive Swedish women called Ingrid and Birgit. Seeing it as an opportunity to date the falsely impressed women they decide to play along with the masquerade with Jack claiming he is the navigator and Stan is the pilot. When asked if they fly to Sweden, Jack tells them they are on the New York route but Stan has misgivings about the charade as he knows nothing about planes although Jack is not to be put off and introduces Stan to the women as Captain Butler. A date is arranged with the women but after just one night the busmen's secret is soon discovered.

The following day, Ingrid and Birgit turn up at the depot looking to catch a bus to the museum. As Inspector Blake offers advice the two young women see Stan and Jack who are back in their old uniforms with the prototype uniforms scrapped and they soon realise that their dates are not airline pilots at all much to the watching Inspector Blake's glee.

Albert Hall, The

The famous London landmark and music venue is referred to by Arthur in the Series Three episode 'The Cistern'.

As Stan is about to demonstrate how quiet the newly-fitted toilet cistern flushes a watching Arthur blows his nose. Mrs. Butler urges him to keep quiet whilst Stan demonstrates but Arthur retorts: 'It's not a symphony concert. We're not at the Albert Hall.'

The Albert Hall is a world famous venue opened in 1871 by Queen Victoria and has seen the greatest musicians of all-time performing on its stage. Located in Knightsbridge, London the venue has an approximate seating capacity of 5,500 and is best known for staging the annual Proms concerts.

Aldershot

A town in Hampshire referred to in the Series Six episode 'The Prize'.

It is revealed that Stan was based in Aldershot during his national service and according to Arthur that is where he did his 'last spud bashing' when Stan offers to peel the potatoes for his mother as he tries to get in her good books as she has just won a holiday for two which he hopes to accompany her on.

Aldershot is a small town steeped in a military background so much so that its town signpost boasts it as 'The Home of The British Army'.

Alf

Played by Albert Moses

This is an Indian busman who is seen in the Series Seven episode 'Friends In High Places'.

Wearing a turban, Alf is dining in the depot canteen. He is to push the plate away from himself after tasting some of the cook Mrs. Webb's food saying: 'Oh blimey.' As Jack is about to complain vehemently as shop steward about the cook and threaten strike action, Alf urges him to tell Mrs. Webb that they can stand her cooking no longer.

Allen, Mrs

An unseen character referred to in the Series Five episode 'The Busmen's Ball' who lends a dressmakers dummy to Olive. It is needed as she attempts to make alterations to her dress for the upcoming Busmen's Ball event to be staged at the bus depot.

Allen, Stuart

Producer (On The Buses TV Series 1, 2, 3 and 4)

Stuart Allen was the first producer of the On The Buses television series. He was to produce the first four series of the classic sitcom which was a total of thirty nine episodes. It is fair to say that Allen produced a large majority of the best-loved On The Buses episodes between 1969 and 1971.

Allen is renowned for producing a whole host of top quality British sitcoms spread over three decades. These included All Gas And Gaiters, Love Thy Neighbour, Yus My Dear, The Rag Trade, Mind Your Language and Yes Minister to name but a few. Without a doubt he will always be remembered for his behind the camera contribution to On The Buses and the great job he did in casting the parts for the hit sitcom.

Producer Stuart Allen at the 2009 On The Buses Event

Here are some of Stuart Allen's memories of On The Buses whilst talking at the 40th Anniversary On The Buses event staged at Elstree Studios in Borehamwood in June 2009.

Memories

'London Weekend Television had just started as a television company and the Head of Programmes at London Weekend Television thought that he wanted to have a better style of comedy. Fortunately, the audience, our television viewers weren't that keen on very sophisticated middle-class comedy and I said to Frank (Muir): 'I think we ought to do something which appeals to the majority of people and not just a few'. And so he said: 'Well I've got this script here. It's been rejected by the BBC. What do you think of this?' We read it and we thought this is the sort of show we need to do at London Weekend Television and we set about casting it.

Reg Varney was available and had been in The Rag Trade and very successful he was too and he was very keen and both the Ronald's (Wolfe and Chesney) thought that he was the man for the job so that's the start. Having got the star we needed mum. I approached various actresses and the first actress I approached was Doris Hare because Reg liked her and I liked her and we thought she would be ideal so I went to see her, she lived by Putney Bridge and said: 'Doris will you come and be the mum in On The Buses?' I told her all about it and she said: 'Yes I'd love to Stuart but my husband's job is a phrenologist and he's in a conference in South America and I've promised to go with him and so I'm not available'. We couldn't put the show off because television companies had to have the show when they wanted it not when you could do it and so she couldn't do it. I tried various actresses and in the end I asked Dame Cicely Courtneidge, as she was then, if she would do it and she did, as you know, the first series. But she didn't gel with the others. She was a big star in her own right and the thing about On The Buses it was a team show everyone helped everyone else and we couldn't have people who wanted to do their own thing and Cicely Courtneidge's idea was to sit around the piano and sing songs. Anyway then we had to cast the bus conductor and also the inspector and I had fortunately been asked by London Weekend Television to do a show called Mrs Wilson's Diary that had run successfully in the West End for some time. It was based on a private eye who ran this sort of diary every week and they made a stage show of it and in the cast there were two actors Bob Grant and Stephen Lewis. Stephen funnily enough played an inspector looking after Harold Wilson in the story of Mrs Wilson's Diary. I thought he's a great actor and Bob Grant with his great big teeth he played George Brown. He was a drunken foreign secretary at the time and was quite notorious but anyway Bob was very amusing playing this character so I suggested that the Ronnies (Wolfe and Chesney) have a look at these two and they agreed with me that they were right for those two (parts).

Michael Robbins, he's no longer with us now, I worked with him at the BBC when I was producing at the BBC and I thought he was quite talented and ideally suited. But I was stumped when it came to Olive and so I said to the Ronnies: 'I don't know a girl who is sort of plain and fat'.

Stuart credits Ronald Chesney and Ronald Wolfe with casting Anna Karen for the part of Olive and he offered this memory.

'Another amusing story about Anna was that when the show became successful after the second series when people were watching in their millions she started to get a little glamorous and she started to slim a bit and of course this wasn't good. She was a very sensitive girl and I found that if I upset her enough in rehearsals and said rather nasty things to her she'd rush off to the canteen, eat a lot of cream buns and come back with a figure that we required.

That's the casting for you and we've went through all of them. It was the fact that they worked so well together that I think has ensured that the show continues to be successful today.'

Angry Passenger

Played by Dervis Ward

An angry passenger is berating Jack and later Inspector Blake in the second spin-off film Mutiny On The Buses.

In the opening scene he can be seen complaining to Jack as he is stopped from boarding the bus as it waits at the stop. He says: 'Why can't we get on?' Jack can't let the passengers on as Stan is kissing his girlfriend and clippie Suzy on the upper deck but tells the angry passenger that the driver is carrying out an inspection. When the passenger asks how long he is going to be Jack tells him he the driver won't stop until he is satisfied. Moments later, Inspector Blake arrives on the scene to resolve the issue.

In the final scene of the film a demoted Blakey is the conductor aboard Stan's bus and the same angry passenger tries to board the bus saying: 'I've had enough of this'. Blakey blocks the entrance onto the bus and he is told: 'It's a disgrace.' The uncomfortable ex-inspector explains: 'I can't let you get on until my driver says so.' Again Stan is involved in a romantic clinch upstairs on the bus with a different clippie.

Anstiss, Rodney

Camera Operator (Holiday On The Buses)

Rodney (also known as Chic) Anstiss was an experienced camera operator who had a lengthy career working on films and television series.

His career in the industry spanned over forty years starting in 1948 where he was to work his way up through the ranks. He finally worked on his first film as camera operator in 1966 with the much-loved film Born Free. Anstiss went on to work on many classic films such as The Battle Of Britain, Lust For A Vampire, Nearest And Dearest, That's Your Funeral, Love Thy Neighbour and a host of classic Hammer films as well as the multi-Oscar winning 1982 film, Gandhi. He was also to work on successful television series such as Jeeves And Wooster and the Hammer House Of Horror series.

Antonioni Film

The new depot nurse called Mary, who is to lodge with the Butlers in the Series Five episode 'The New Nurse', is a big fan of the Antonioni films.

Mary tells Arthur and Olive that she will be going to the cinema to watch an Italian film that she describes as 'one of Antonioni's masterpieces' adding: 'They say it's a spiritual experience.' In stark contrast Arthur and Olive are planning to go and watch Dracula Meets The Apeman but Arthur's interest in Mary sees him suggest that they all go to watch the Antonioni film instead. Even though Olive declines it doesn't deter him as he gives her the money to go and see the film alone whilst he takes Mary to see the Antonioni film.

The evening out ends with Mary having thoroughly enjoyed the film and in a bid to impress Arthur agrees saying: 'All that stark realism, sheer power, primitive passion.'

The Antonioni referred to was the famous Italian film director Michelangelo Antonioni who was to direct a string of Italian and English films based on realism from 1947 up until his death in 2004. His films won critical acclaim but also were panned in other quarters.

Apex Corner

This is a destination that a disgruntled passenger aboard Stan's bus is travelling to in the Series One episode 'Olive Takes A Trip'.

The passenger complains about the bus service and rising fares to Stan as the ill trainee clippie Olive drinks a cup of tea. He moans: 'It cost me two bob from the garage to Apex Corner and by the time you get there I've no doubt the fares will have gone up again.'

Although the majority of street names used in On The Buses were purely fictional it is almost certain that the location mentioned in this scene was taken from the same Apex Corner located in Mill Hill, North London.

Appendix Three

A section quoted from the rulebook by Stan as assistant inspector to a clippie called Betty in the Series One episode 'The New Inspector'.

Stan feels that Betty's skirt is far too short as she boards her bus for her shift. He tells her: 'Appendix Three – Conductresses. Mini-skirts should not be more than two inches above the knee.' Stan's ruling counts for nothing though as Betty is in a relationship with the depot manager who likes her in her short skirt.

Aquarium

The inspector brings his aquarium filled with tropical fish around to the Butler house as Stan is to look after them whilst he goes on a fishing holiday in the Series Five episode 'The Inspector's Pets'.

It doesn't take long for disaster to strike as Olive trips over the electrical wire of the aquarium which causes it to short and puts the tropical fish's life in danger. In a panic Stan attempts to repair the aquarium but only succeeds in cracking the glass with a knife which starts a race to rescue the fish from the leaking tank using a chip pan.

The maintenance department at the bus depot come to Stan's rescue repairing the aquarium by replacing the broken glass with part of a bus windscreen which, if missed, is to be explained away as being smashed by hooligans on a Saturday night. All that remains is for the aquarium to be refilled with warm water from the depot's fire buckets and the tropical fish released back into the repaired tank from thermos flasks where they have been stored. And so Inspector Blake returns from holiday none the wiser about the mishap and is touched by Stan's gesture of good will.

Area Manager

A position held by Gerald Simpson at the Luxton and District Bus Company serving at the Luxton depot for a short period before his retirement in the Series Seven episode 'Friends In High Places'.

Aries

The star sign of Jack as revealed in the Series Seven episode 'What The Stars Foretell'.

As Olive and Sandra discuss their horoscopes as seen in a magazine they are reading, Jack who is sceptical takes the magazine and says: 'Let's see what is says for the old ram.' It predicts changes and that he will go on a journey but he still believes it is all nonsense. It also predicts that someone in authority may turn nasty as Jack's nemesis Blakey enters the canteen.

In reality actor Bob Grant who played Jack was born on the 14th of April 1932 was also Aries by birth. It would seem that this was factored in when the script was written for the episode.

Arthur at Town and District

After he is made redundant from his job Arthur, with the help of brother-in-law Stan, gains employment at the Town and District Bus Company as a bus driver in the film Mutiny On The Buses.

It is a come down for Arthur to work alongside Stan having always bad-mouthed busmen and the bus services. His first task in the job is to pick up his new uniform from the stores but is a poor fit with the jacket being far too long and before he has had his first shift his baby son leaves an unwelcome deposit in his new cap. Arthur is also put in an awkward position when the notorious Nymphy Norah is allocated as his clippie – a woman said to have worn out more men than the five 'o clock rush hour. It is amusing as Arthur's career at Town and District follows a similar path to which he had constantly berated Stan for taking. His flirting with Nymphy Norah at a social event at the depot leads to a brawl; he plays his part in messing up a fire drill and joins Jack in enjoying a laugh at Inspector Blake's expense.

We never see how Arthur's career ended at the Town and District Bus Company but it is clear that he is no longer a busman by the time of the third spin-off film Holiday On The Buses. He can be seen returning from work in a suit with no sign of a bus driver's uniform but what that new job is remains a mystery.

Arthur's Ambition

Arthur reveals it was always his ambition to take up medicine in a conversation with the family and the new depot nurse Mary who is lodging with them in the Series Five episode 'The New Nurse'. He gets encouragement from her when she remarks he would have made a very good doctor as he has the right manner.

Later in Series Five, in the episode called 'Boxing Day Social', Arthur's mother pays the Butlers a visit and mentions that her son was about to start studying medicine when he gave it up to marry Olive. It would seem that Arthur's ambition was never to be fulfilled.

Arthur's Injury

An injury sustained to Arthur's bottom after an accident during the night in his bedroom in the Series Three episode 'Busmen's Perks'.

Arthur has helped Stan paint his and Olive's bedroom but with no hardener mixed in, the paint takes even longer to dry. When Olive awakes in the middle of the night with the need to visit the toilet trouble is in store as she can't find the light switch. As Arthur gets out of bed in a bid to prevent Olive touching the wet paint he trips in the dark and falls into a drawer left out to dry on the floor having been painted earlier and is left with a backside blighted by splinters. With mum claiming Arthur might get lockjaw it is left to Stan to try to bring some relief to Arthur. Armed with a needle, Olive's tweezers and a reading glass Stan attempts to remove the splinters but only succeeds in aggravating Arthur's injury further which causes Arthur to promise to bring in decorators to decorate his bedroom properly.

Artificial Respiration

A part of the Luxton and District Bus Company's course of instruction on firefighting covered in the Series Six episode 'No Smoke Without Fire'.

It is Inspector Blake who briefs the employees giving instructions on how to give artificial respiration. He tells the staff that the patient has to be laid well back and pulling the chin down, open the mouth wide open, pinch the nostrils and placing their lips over the patient's mouth and then fill their lungs with air. After removing their lips he advises them to watch for chest movement. Stan and Jack do watch for chest movements but not of the patient but of clippies attending the course.

Ashton, Marcia

TV Role: Elsie (Series 6 Episode 5 'Union Trouble)

Born in Sheffield, Yorkshire on the 1st of July 1932, Marcia Ashton boasts an acting career spanning over fifty years on television, film and stage.

She has appeared in a string of classic television series through the decades. In the 1960s Ashton was to appear in No Hiding Place, Compact, Z Cars and Father Dear Father amongst others before taking parts in Upstairs Downstairs and mystery series Melissa in the 1970s. After appearing in classic sitcom In Sickness And In Health in the 1980s parts continued to roll in through the 1990s appearing in hit series such as Rumpole Of The Bailey, Brookside, The Bill and Men Behaving Badly. Into the new millennium Ashton has remained very active as an actress having appeared in a number of popular television series including Doctors, Footballers Wives, EastEnders, Holby City, Midsomer Murders and Spooks.

On the big screen her roles were much less prolific with her most notable roles coming in the Tommy Trinder comedy film You Lucky People in 1955, crime film The Green Buddha in the same year and Travelwise in 2000. She has also enjoyed a successful stage career having appeared in shows at both the West End and on Broadway in the USA.

Ashton, Pat

TV Role: Doreen (Series 5 Episode 2 'Stan's Room' and Series 5 Episode 11 'The Strain')
Film Roles: Sally (On The Buses) and Nymphy Norah (Mutiny On The Buses)

Pat Ashton was born in 1946 and was to have a very successful career as an actress that ran for twenty years.

Primarily, she was a comedy actress and appeared in numerous hit sitcoms such as Nearest And Dearest, Romany Jones, Yus My Dear, The Fosters, Only When I Laugh, The Gaffer and Tripper's Day to name but a few. She will also be remembered for her appearance as a Hills Angel in the legendary comedy television series The Benny Hill Show. Drama roles were also to come her way in Crown Court, Dixon Of Dock Green and Z Cars.

Her big screen career saw her land a small part in the smash hit musical Half A Sixpence in 1967 before her roles in the On The Buses and Mutiny On The Buses films in the early 1970's. She was also to appear in films such as The Optimists, Party Party and the horror film Bloodbath At The House Of Death in 1984. Shortly after this role Pat Ashton's career as an actress stalled coming to a premature end in 1985 but she has left us with the great characters she portrayed on the small and big screen in On The Buses which will always be loved.

Sadly, in June 2013, Pat Ashton passed away in Diss, Norfolk at the age of sixty seven.

Askew Road

A fictional street name mentioned in connection with an emergency diversion for Stan's bus in the Series Four episode 'Not Tonight'.

Inspector Blake informs Stan the diversion is before the High Street and he has to turn off the street before Askew Road. He has to be told more than once though as Stan is distracted by the attractive new canteen employee, Stella.

Assault

Inspector Blake and Stan are accused of assault in two separate incidents at the Luxton and District Bus Company.

In the Series Four episode 'The Injury', Stan reports for duty at the bus depot in agony after an accident at home where he has injured his shoulder and toe in a fall. He plans to fake an accident at work in a bid to earn accident pay so must appear fit prior to starting work. However, during a conversation with Inspector Blake who prods a finger at Stan's injured shoulder, is unaware of the agony he is inflicting even when Stan groans in pain. To divert any suspicion of an injury Jack accuses the inspector of assaulting Stan telling him it is a very serious matter. The flabbergasted Blakey hits back by threatening to take Stan up to see the depot's doctor and have him examined to see if he has broken his shoulder. Stan and Jack can't risk the inspector finding out the true extent of Stan's injury so any further talk of assault is dropped.

It is Stan that is to be accused of assaulting Inspector Blake in the Series Six episode 'Union Trouble'. This comes about when Stan begins a sit-in protest in the cab of his bus as he attempts to stop canteen employee Elsie from being sacked. In a desperate bid to stop Stan causing any disruptions Blakey tries to drag the troublesome driver out of the cab but only succeeds in having his head trapped in the door. He accuses Stan of assaulting him but the matter goes no further as Jack, who is watching, claims to have not witnessed the accident.

Assistant Inspector

This is a rank that Stan is briefly promoted to at the Luxton and District Bus Company in the Series One episode 'The New Inspector'.

It is a position seen as a poisoned chalice by all busmen, shown by the distinct lack of applicants when the job is advertised. Stan applies for the job purely for financial reasons. He needs the extra money so he can buy his beloved mum the coat of her dreams. His best friend and conductor Jack is shocked and his attitude towards Stan changes as he visits the Butler house to reclaim his dartboard and informs Stan he has been dropped from the depot's darts team.

Stan, distinctive in his new inspector's uniform, reports for duty on his first shift in his new post supplied with rulebook, clipboard and inspector's pencils but soon finds out that life is tough at the top. Labelled 'Hitler's Deputy' by Jack, Stan sets about his job by telling the conductor he is not to smoke in the depot, his lack of proper uniform and then reports a clippie for her skirt being too short which proves to be his downfall. After a day of reports and run-ins with Jack there comes an end to Stan's brief promotion as the depot manager is angry at Stan's report about the length of the clippie's skirt as he likes her dressed that way as he is in a relationship with her. He orders Inspector Blake to remove Stan from the post and it is a painful experience for Stan as he has to return his rulebook, clipboard and inspector's pencils. Within moments of being reduced in rank, Jack's attitude to Stan changes once more as he offers to come around to the Butler house with some mates for darts practice. All's well that ends well.

Assistant Traffic Manager

Played by Samantha Birch

This is a member of management staff who arrives at the depot where she is to be posted for a few months along with the traffic manager Mr. Nichols in the Series Four episode 'The Lodger'.

The Butlers, short of money take Mr Nichols in as a lodger but it turns out to be a nightmare experience for Stan and Olive which ends up with the lodger being asked to leave. However, Inspector Blake tells Stan that the assistant traffic manager is looking for lodgings but after the experience of the last lodger Stan is put right off the idea. When an attractive young woman pops into the canteen, she tells the inspector: 'Oh Mr Blake I managed to get fixed up this morning. Nice digs and there's a bachelor there so I'll be alright.' As Stan and Jack drool over her, Inspector Blake gleefully informs them that she was the assistant traffic manager and so Stan has missed out on a golden opportunity to get to know her better.

Atlas, Charles

Arthur is dubbed Charles Atlas by Stan in the Series Five episode 'A Thin Time'.

After Arthur tries to impress a clippie called Beryl at the depot with tales of his physical prowess, Stan says to him: 'Well come on Charles Atlas there's another bus goes in ten minutes.' In a bid to back up his false claims of an interest in fitness Arthur says that he'll walk home even though it is three miles away.

Charles Atlas was an iconic figure in the world of bodybuilding and was the best known muscleman in the world in the 1940s, 50s and 60s. He was to run a special fitness course which was to include a range of exercises designed to build muscles. These courses came in twelve lessons with the programme called Dynamic Tension. Atlas was also to produce instruction booklets for the courses and his advertisements were commonplace in magazines and newspapers from the 1940s onwards. Born in Italy in 1892, Charles Atlas passed away in New York in 1972 after suffering a heart attack following an early morning run.

Aunt Maud

Played by Betty Hare

The sister of Mabel Butler and aunt to Stan, Olive and Arthur who is referred to regularly and appears in the Series Two episode 'Aunt Maud'. She lived in the fictional town of Hickley Green which was almost thirty miles away from Luxton.

Aunt Maud can be seen paying her sister a visit bringing her large pet dog called Marcus with her which wreaks havoc aboard Stan's bus. Her stay with the Butlers sees her embarrass Arthur and Olive with questions about their marriage. She claims it is nine years since she saw Arthur at the wedding and touches on the delicate subject of his operation. Stan can't avoid Maud's cross-examination either and she displays surprise that he has never married. Maud's visit also means a change in sleeping arrangements which sees Stan forced into sharing a bed with Arthur and her departure doesn't go smoothly either as the taxi driver refuses to take Marcus in his cab and suggests a horsebox instead. It means trouble for Stan as he has to try to smuggle Marcus aboard his bus against Jack and Inspector Blake's wishes.

Maud's home cooking was not up to the same standard as her sister. In the Series Three episode 'Foggy Night' mum lauds her sister's rabbit pie but Arthur is less complimentary about it as he, Olive and mum prepare to travel back from a visit to Aunt Maud.

All three attempt to visit Aunt Maud again this time aboard Arthur's motorcycle combination in the Series Four episode 'Nowhere To Go' taking presents with them. A plant bought by mum loses its flower buds when Stan closes the roof of the sidecar and a cooked chicken is dropped by him and he wipes it down with an oily rag before wrapping it up again in its baking foil. A road accident is to prevent the Butlers from reaching Aunt Maud though.

Maud was kind-hearted as seen by her anniversary card and present to Arthur and Olive in the Series Four episode 'The Anniversary'. Along with the card she sends them a pet poodle which Olive adores but Arthur is allergic to the canine. Her kindness shines through again in the Series Six episode 'No Smoke Without Fire' as she brings back plenty of duty-free cigarettes from Majorca for Stan and Arthur but a lot of those ends up going to waste.

Health wise it is suggested that Maud has a liver complaint in the Series Five episode 'The Strain'. Olive offers Stan some green pills for his backache as she reveals she got them from Aunt Maud. Arthur backs this up saying they were left over from her liver.

Another visit to Aunt Maud by the Butlers is planned for her birthday. Olive tries making a birthday cake, without much success, for the occasion in the Series Six episode 'Private Hire'. Again the trip is curtailed but this time they are told by Inspector Blake that there is no room for them aboard a hired coach which they had intended to travel on to get to Aunt Maud's house.

We learn in the Series Seven episode 'Olive's Divorce' that mum always visits Aunt Maud on Thursdays. Olive declines an invitation to accompany her mum as she feels that her aunt will make her go through all the details of the divorce case again which she says would be too painful for her.

In summary, Aunt Maud's character was kind-hearted but could also be nosy and inquisitive. She did have a similar trait to her sister Mabel in that she could be bossy and forceful often getting her own way.

Aunty June

An unseen character that is the aunt of Inspector Blake and who is referred to in the Series Seven episode 'The Visit'.

We first hear Mrs. Blake (the inspector's mother) mention Aunty June to Mabel Butler whilst they play bingo at the social club. She says that her son gets more like his Aunty June every day and describes her sister as very like herself though not as nice. Later, when his mother is leaving Luxton, the inspector tells her he will phone Aunty June and get her to meet his mum at the station when she arrives. With his mother having departed after her short stat with the Butlers he excitedly tells Mrs. Butler he has received a card from his Aunty June saying he is coming to visit but she has other ideas and rules out any such visit after the inspector's mother had caused so much trouble during her stay.

Aunty May

This is an unseen character in the Series Four episode 'The L Bus' who is the aunt of Jack Harper.

On a visit to the Butler household Jack tells Arthur, who is looking to buy a new bed, that his Aunty May is selling her double bed and it is practically brand new and would cost half the price of a new bed that Arthur is thinking of buying from a bed store. Jack says that her husband passed away recently and so no longer needs a double bed. The problem proves to be delivery of the bed as Aunty May has a flat at Leeside Column which is on the other side of Luxton.

Austin Automatics Ltd.

This is the fictional manufacturer of the new automatic food dispenser that is installed by the Town and District Bus Company in the depot canteen. It is capable of issuing tea, coffee, hot chocolate, hot and cold fruit drinks as well as other cold snacks. A staff shortage forces the company to offer these alternative canteen facilities in the film On The Buses.

The bus crews soon grow restless with what they see as inadequate canteen facilities and Stan puts forward his sister Olive for a job in the canteen. Inspector Blake though insists that the food from the dispenser is quite alright. His attitude soon changes when he obtains a pie from the food dispenser and finds it unpalatable.

Autocar Magazine

A magazine that Arthur can be seen reading in bed in the film Holiday On The Buses despite his pride and joy being his motorcycle and combination. He reads the magazine after being shown up in a public display of old-time dancing at the holiday camp and is in no mood for conversation with Olive.

The Autocar magazine issue seen was actually dated the 6th of May 1971 and so was more than two years old considering Holiday On The Buses premiered on the 26th of December 1973. This particular issue of Autocar featured a full road test article on the Datsun 240Z. It also covered a two car test comparing the Morris Marina 1.8 Saloon and the Hillman Hunter as well as a road test of a Renault 16TL.

Published weekly the Autocar magazine is thought to be the longest running car magazine in the world. It was first published on the 2nd of November 1895 and is still a popular publication to the present day with its format remaining virtually unchanged as it covers road tests for all categories of automobiles, motorsport events and other news related to the car industry.

Automated Food Dispenser

This is the fictional name of the depot canteen's new food dispensing machine as seen in the Series Five episode 'Canteen Trouble'.

After a succession of corruptible canteen staff members are to be dismissed the Luxton and District Bus Company look to an alternative form of catering. An automatic food dispenser offering snacks such as sausage rolls, pork pies, meat pies, Cornish pasties, cheese sandwiches, egg and tomato sandwiches and a range of hot and cold drinks is installed and Inspector Blake is certain the machine can't be corrupted. He is for a shock though when Stan is unable to purchase a meat pie as the machine rejects his bent coin but a young woman from the vending machine company is on hand to offer Stan two complimentary meat pies. He and Jack are buoyed by this and plan to pay a visit to the depot's machine shop to start bending more coins in a bid to get more complimentary food from the vending machine company.

Avon, Roger

TV Role: Policeman (Series 4 Episode 5 'Christmas Duty')
Film Role: Policeman (Safari Park) (Mutiny On The Buses)

Roger Avon was born in 1914 in Jarrow, County Durham and went on to have a prolific acting career spanning well over forty years in mainly bit part roles.

His television roles were varied as he appeared in a number of classic sitcoms such as Hancock's Half Hour, The Likely Lads, Dad's Army, Steptoe And Son, For The Love Of Ada, Doctor In Charge, On The Buses, Sykes, Bless This House, When The Boat Comes In and Blackadder The Third. Drama roles were equally plentiful on television with roles coming his way in a host of classic series such as Danger Man, Doctor Who, Dr Finlay's Casebook, Department S, Randall And Hopkirk (Deceased), Upstairs Downstairs, Softly Softly, The New Avengers, Peak Practice and The Bill.

The most successful films that Avon appeared in came in the 1950s and 60s and those included A Night To Remember, A Hard Day's Night, Murder At The Gallop, Runaway Railway, Daleks Invasion Earth: 2150 AD and Quatermass And The Pit.

Avon carried on his acting career until he passed away in 1998 at the age of eighty four.

Baboons

A breed of animal seen during the Town and District Bus Company's trial run of its tour bus to Windsor Safari Park in Mutiny On The Buses.

With Stan driving the tour bus supervised by Inspector Blake they are to pass through an enclosure of baboons shortly after entering the safari park. The inspector mocks Stan telling him the baboons look just like him but Stan has the last laugh. As one of the animals turns around to reveal its red backside Stan claims it looks just like Blakey. Puzzled, the inspector wonders why their backsides are so red to which Stan replies it's because it is the mating season. The tour bus is to leave the enclosure without incident.

The baboons seen in the film were Hamadryas Baboons native to northern regions of Africa. They remained at Windsor Safari Park until its closure in 1992 and they were to be shipped out to their new home at the Beekesbergen Safari Park in the Netherlands in late 1993.

Babysit

Stan is to babysit for Arthur and Olive to allow them a night out in the bar whilst he looks after his nephew Arthur in the film Holiday On The Buses.

There is an ulterior motive for taking on babysitting on his night off as Stan sees it as an opportunity to entertain holiday camp employee Sandra with his interfering family out of the way. His hopes for an evening of passion are to be foiled though by a mischievous little Arthur. As soon as things are beginning to hot up between Stan and Sandra the infant appears from his bedroom and pesters his uncle to read him a story leaving Sandra frustrated. When Stan finally puts little Arthur to bed he gives him his water pistol to play with even though it was earlier confiscated by his dad and this proves to be a disastrous move. Stan's babysitting stint ends when his mum returns from her night out to discover that Stan was more interested in Sandra than babysitting and this has allowed little Arthur to wreak havoc in his bedroom with his water pistol.

Bachelor Party

Bridegroom-to-be and bus driver Bill is taken out on a bachelor party by Stan who is his best man, Jack and a group of drivers on the eve of his wedding to Sally, the niece of Inspector Blake in the Series Five episode 'The Best Man'.

Blakey is concerned to hear that Stan and Jack have planned a pub crawl for the bachelor party with drinking sessions with drivers, maintenance staff, and also the depot's darts team. It would seem that the inspector was right to be concerned when Stan, Jack and Bill stagger into the Butler house in the early hours of the morning. Stan and Jack sing boisterously whilst Bill is in a drunken stupor after being plied with whisky and gin throughout the evening. Their raucous behaviour awakens Arthur, who is none too pleased, and Olive who is in for a thrill. A drunken Bill mistakes her for his bride and pulls her on top of him kissing her as he does so. It is clear that he needs to be sobered up in order to get married without any mishaps.

Today bachelor parties are far more commonly known as a stag night or stag party.

Back Strain

What Stan is to suffer after attempting to lift a clippie and his girlfriend Doreen Smith in a bid to guess her weight in the Series Five episode 'The Strain'.

Stan doubles up in agony after trying to lift Doreen but to save face he tells Inspector Blake that it is nothing more than cramp. However, Jack believes Stan may have suffered a slipped disc but it is the diagnosis of the doctor that matters.

Bed-ridden and stiff, Stan is examined by Doctor Clark and a slipped disc is ruled out but he is diagnosed as having strained his back. He is prescribed some tablets to help combat the pain and is told that he should be moving more freely in a couple of days. Stan takes that to be good news and presumes he'll be able to return to work which is essential as he will receive no sick pay but his doctor rules that possibility out feeling that driving a bus in his condition may put too much strain on the back and ruin the healing process. However, hope is offered to a desperate Stan when Doctor Clark says that it may safe to drive his bus wearing a lumbo-sacral support or corset as it is better known.

Stan is to return to work wearing a corset with his back strain still handicapping him. He finds the slightest tasks cause him agony but he is determined to battle through the pain as he has a date with Doreen lined up. A date is fine but anything else has to be ruled out as Stan aggravates his injury as he frolics on the sofa with her. She insists on taking him up to bed but purely because he is in such discomfort. Once again Stan's hopes of romance are dashed.

Badgers Lane

This is a location where Stan and Jack's bus terminates in the film Mutiny On The Buses.

It is at Badgers Lane where Stan and Jack are to give Arthur his bus driving lessons aboard their bus. It sees the bus stop getting knocked over and the pair also using the secluded location to practice their darts by propping a dartboard on the bonnet of their bus. Inspector Blake becomes suspicious as every trip of theirs to Badgers Lane results in a late return to the depot. Stan attempts to blame the traffic for their unpunctuality but the inspector isn't fooled and is to try various methods to check up on Stan and Jack at Badgers Lane without having any real success.

Baker, Ken

Assistant Director (Mutiny On The Buses and Holiday On The Buses)

Ken Baker was the assistant director on Mutiny On The Buses and the best-loved of the three spin-off films, Holiday On The Buses. He was famed in the film and television industry with almost thirty years of experience and was to have a close affiliation with the famous Elstree Studios in Borehamwood, Hertfordshire where much of his best-remembered television series and films were made.

He was to work on a host of classic television series from the production company Incorporated Television Company (ITC) such as The Saint, The Baron, The Champions, Randall And Hopkirk (Deceased), Department S, Jason King, The Adventurer and Return Of The Saint. Away from ITC other hit series he worked on included cult classics UFO, Here Comes The Double Deckers, Space: 1999 and Hammer House Of Horror as well as The Professionals, Inspector Morse and the hit US series Hart To Hart.

On the big screen Baker was to work on a number of hit films such as Wonderful Life, Love Thy Neighbour, George And Mildred, Bloodbath At The House Of Death, Wild Geese II, Labyrinth and Willow.

Ken Baker who worked with successful production companies such as ITC and Hammer on both the small and big screen has now retired from the industry but resides in Borehamwood just a mile or so from the Elstree Studios which played such a big part in his life.

Ball, Sally

Continuity (Holiday On The Buses)

Sally Ball's career spanned over twenty years working on television and film productions working largely in the continuity department.

She was frequently employed by ITC and worked on a number of their television series including The Saint, The Champions, Randall And Hopkirk (Deceased), Jason King, The Adventurer and The Protectors.

Ball's big screen career saw her work on continuity in Hammer films Doctor Jekyll And Sister Hyde, Holiday On The Buses and Love Thy Neighbour with other films including Paper Tiger and Caravan To Vaccares.

Ballroom

This is a venue seen at the holiday camp in the Holiday On The Buses film.

The ballroom is where Inspector Blake is to hold his dance classes and also where the exhibition of old-time dancing is staged in front of a packed audience.

Bankipore

An area in India where Inspector Blake was stationed when in the armed forces during World War Two as referred to in the Series Three episode 'The Snake'.

As he, Stan and Jack listen to Indian music at a social event in the depot's canteen it causes Blakey to reminisce. 'Ah barmy nights in the mess at Bankipore,' says the inspector awash with nostalgia.

Bankipore is now a residential area in the town of Patna which is situated on the River Ganges in India.

Banks, Arthur

Construction Manager (Mutiny On The Buses and Holiday On The Buses)

As a construction manager Arthur Banks was to spend his entire career in the film industry at Hammer Films.

He was to work on classic horror films such as Paranoiac, Dracula Has Risen From The Grave, Frankenstein Must Be Destroyed, The Horror Of Frankenstein, Scars Of Dracula, Twins Of Evil, Vampire Circus and Frankenstein And The Monster From Hell amongst others. He was also to have credits in Hammer's comedy productions including Nearest And Dearest, Mutiny On The Buses, That's Your Funeral and Holiday On The Buses.

Baptiste, Austin

TV Role: Tabla Player (Series 3 Episode 6 'The Snake')

Austin Baptiste was a talented musician who did have a brief career as an actor. Aside from his bit-part role in On The Buses, Baptiste was to appear in the BBC drama series R.C.M.P – a series about the Canadian mounted police. His only other acting credit came on television in the adventure series Virgin Of The Secret Service.

Sadly, Austin Baptiste passed away in London in 2007.

Barley Common

This fictional location was referred to in the second spin-off film 'Mutiny On The Buses'.

When Inspector Blake contacts a policeman on his beat by mistake on the new radio control system the policeman tells him he is on his way back to the station. The inspector, who presumes he is talking to one of his bus drivers, tells him he should be on his way to Barley Common. Little does he know he is ordering around an officer of the law.

Barman, The

Played by Philip Dunbar

A character who is seen serving Stan, Jack and their dates Eileen and Sandra in the Series Five episode 'The Epidemic'.

The foursome are enjoying a night out in the Rose and Crown pub and call to the barman ordering a round of drinks and oysters. He brings the order over on a tray saying: 'Here you are gents,' collecting empty glasses from their table as he does so. Later in the evening, when Stan starts to display flu symptoms and decides to go home, Jack asks the barman if someone can phone for a cab for Stan but he replies:' I'm afraid they're not answering sir. All the drivers have got flu.' A polite barman but this is of no comfort to Stan.

Barry, Hilda

Film Role: Old Woman (On The Buses)

Hilda Barry, born in London in 1884, was to appear in a host of television and film roles in the second half of her life and was frequently used as a bit-part actress.

Her television career saw her appear in many hit drama series including TV adaptions of The Railway Children and Quatermass And The Pit as well as The Prisoner, Dixon Of Dock Green, Special Branch, Armchair Theatre and Z Cars.

She was also a familiar face in classic 1960s and 70s sitcoms appearing in Hancock, Steptoe And Son, Father Dear Father, The Fenn Street Gang and Whatever Happened To The Likely Lads.

On the big screen her most notable and best remembered roles came in Carry On Loving, On The Buses and Steptoe And Son Ride Again.

Sadly, Hilda Barry was to pass away in 1979 at the age of ninety four.

Basher

Played by Maurice Bush

Basher is a seemingly violent employee at the Luxton and District Bus Company who threatens Stan in the Series Six episode 'Private Hire'.

Employed as a maintenance worker at the bus depot, Basher also works as a part-time bouncer at a dance hall and Jack is to ask him to lend a penniless Stan some money. Basher growls: 'No. I'm sick of smashing blokes' faces in trying to get my money back.' He does finally change his mind when Jack promises he'll get his money back in a couple of days and Stan receives five pounds. However, Basher gives him a chilling warning threatening violence if he doesn't get his money back in time. This threat and a need for more money is enough to encourage Stan to use a bus as a removal van in an attempt to raise the extra cash needed.

Basildon

A town in Essex, Basildon was regularly referred to in On The Buses.

It was first to be referred to in the Series One episode 'The New Conductor' when Stan is to have a new clippie put aboard his bus called Iris who hails from Basildon. In the Series Two episode 'Bon Voyage', Stan prepares to drive a coach from the depot to the airport as the depot's charter holiday is about to get under way and he gets final orders from Inspector Blake. He tells Stan to go to Southend via Basildon. Finally, in the Series Seven episode 'The Football Match' the Basildon bus depot's football team takes on the Luxton depot team.

Basildon is located in Essex and is twenty five miles east of London and was to be established as a town in 1949. Coincidentally, Eastern National – the supplier of the fleet of buses used in the On The Buses television series were to cover the actual bus routes from North London to Basildon and beyond.

Basildon Bashers, The

The football team that represents the Basildon bus depot in the Series Seven episode 'The Football Match' is called The Basildon Bashers.

The Basildon Bashers are to be the opponents of The Luxton Lions – the team assembled by the Luxton depot. To the surprise of the Luxton Lions and their manager Inspector Blake, the Basildon Bashers turn out to be a ladies football team. Their team is a mixture of talent with players of varying sizes, build and ages that is captained by a woman from the Basildon depot's accounts department called Eunice Jones. She introduces some of her team to the Luxton Lions side starting with a couple of ageing, rotund and non-athletic looking players called Flossie Farmer and Polly Potter who play at outside-right and full-back. The Bashers forwards are younger, fitter and pleasingly to Stan and Jack are more attractive than the rest of the team. With Iris, Mary and Rita all introducing themselves as forwards the Bashers seem set for an attacking formation. And in the end the match result shows the men who the bosses are when it comes to football.

Bayntun, Amelia

TV Role: Woman (Series 5 Episode 9 'Lost Property')

Born in Bristol in 1919, Amelia Bayntun was to have a varied acting career on stage, television and films.

Her stage career began in the late 1930s and appeared in Stars In Battledress during the Second World War. Her most notable stage roles came in the late 1950s in Dry Rot and this was followed in the early 1960s with roles in hit productions in London's West End such as Sparrows Can't Sing and the musical Blitz.

On television in the 1960s she had drama roles in Dixon Of Dock Green, David Copperfield, Adam Adamant Lives and Z Cars. Her most notable comedy roles came in the sitcom Dear Mother Love Albert and the classic sketch show The Dick Emery Show.

Her best remembered film role was to come as Mrs Fussey in the memorable film Carry On Camping and she was also to appear in later films in the legendary comedy film series such as Carry On Loving, Carry On At Your Convenience, Carry On Matron and Carry On Abroad. She was also to have uncredited roles in smash hit films Thunderball and The Railway Children.

At the age of sixty nine Amelia Bayntun passed away in London in 1988.

Beatles, The

A legendary British pop band that was referred to in the Series Three episode 'The Snake'.

As Stan and Jack await the start of an Indian Dance event in the depot's canteen, Indian music softly plays in the background. Jack would rather listen to something he can recognise but Stan mockingly remarks: 'That happens to be one of The Beatles latest hits'.

When 'The Snake' was first transmitted The Beatles were on the verge of an acrimonious split but there is no doubt that the Fab Four, as they were also known, were one of the most successful and best-loved pop phenomena's of all-time. The band comprising of four Liverpudlian members called Paul McCartney, John Lennon, George Harrison and Ringo Starr had a massive global following recording a staggering amount of number one hit singles and albums which remain amongst the best-selling of all-time. Their plethora of chart topping hits ranged from 1962 to 1969.

The likely connection between Indian music and The Beatles as referred to in 'The Snake' episode comes from a spell between 1967 and 1968 when The Beatles were to become involved with an Indian guru called Maharishi Mahesh Yogi who was a teacher of spirituality. During this spell George Harrison was to learn to play the sitar, an Indian stringed instrument which along with tabla drums (another Indian instrument) were to be used on some of the band's later hits. Also their hit album The Beatles was largely written on a visit to Maharishi Yogi in India and was released in 1968.

Beauty Locks Products

Beauty Locks are a range of fictional products that Stan buys from the chemist in the Series Seven episode 'The Poster'.

The Beauty Locks products are recommended to Stan by the chemist's assistant and the range of products includes hair spray, setting lotion and shampoo. Stan purchases these items along with a number of other beauty creams and lotions as he prepares for a make-over in an attempt to improve his chances of winning a contest to appear on a promotional poster that is to be released by the Luxton and District Bus Company.

Ben and Bill

A name that Stan calls Inspector Blake and Acting Inspector Jack Harper in the Series Five episode 'Vacancy For Inspector'.

As the new duo of inspectors approach Stan and his new clippie Christine, Stan throws an insult at them saying: 'Here comes Ben and Bill'.

I would say that this was a reference to the hit 1950s BBC children's series about Bill And Ben – The Flower Pot Men. It featured two wooden puppets in the form of two little men made out of flower pots who speak a strange language and had a friend called Little Weed. Bill and Ben were the names of the flower pot men and I presume that, to avoid any copyright issues with the BBC, the writers opted to use the names in reverse in the episode.

Benton, Ron

Assistant Art Director (On The Buses)

Ron Benton worked as the assistant art director on the film called On The Buses and was to be the first credit of his career. However, he waited fifteen years for his next job in the industry. This came in the US production The Last Days Of Patton – a made-for-television film that won an Emmy award and was his final credited work in the industry.

Berlin Wall, The

An iconic structure built in Germany during the Cold War that is referred to in the Series Two episode 'Aunt Maud'.

Stan and Arthur are forced to share a bed to accommodate Aunt Maud. Arthur insists on sleeping on the right side of the bed pointing out that he has slept on that side of the bed for nine years whilst Olive sleeps on the other side. To Stan it sounds like the Berlin Wall and he presumes they do meet at times at Checkpoint Charlie.

The Berlin Wall was erected in 1961 by the government of what was then the German Democratic Republic (East Germany). It ran through the heart of the city of Berlin with the purpose being to stop people defecting from the communist-backed East Germany which was part of the Eastern Bloc to West Germany which was run by a federal government and had closer ties to the United States and United Kingdom. Checkpoint Charlie was a crossing point through the Berlin Wall and became a symbol of the Cold War. At this checkpoint was the entrance from West to East Germany where passage was only possible with a visa. Many people died trying to defect by either scaling the wall or by other means in an attempt to escape the oppressions they felt but in 1989 the first steps to the re-unification of Germany were taken which was to finally see the destruction of the Berlin Wall.

Bert

Played by Nosher Powell

Bert is a well-built busman at the depot who also worked as a physiotherapist for a football team having learnt the trade in the army. Bert was not the sort of person to argue with and he does make some decisions on Stan's behalf in regards of the running of the depot canteen.

When Stan is troubled with a stomach complaint, Bert is on hand to give him some physiotherapy in the canteen but his heavy-handed treatment leaves Stan in even more pain in the Series One episode 'Bus Driver's Stomach'. Bert completes the physiotherapy leaving the driver doubled up in pain but he tells Stan to have a nice, hot bath when he gets home.

In the next episode 'The Canteen', Bert and his fellow employees vote to let Stan run the depot canteen. However, when things don't go smoothly Bert leads the protests as Stan's new cook offers unpalatable Indian dishes and he takes it upon himself, on behalf of Stan, to sack the new cook. The replacements are Olive and Mrs Butler and when they struggle to operate the kitchen appliances Bert and his colleagues are affected. With no meals on the table the impatience grows until he finally gets his food which, unknown to him, has come straight from a local fish and chip shop. Bert is appeased and he is soon to see the canteen back under the control of the management.

Beryl

Played by Janice Hoy

Beryl is a clippie who flirts with Arthur in the depot canteen in the Series Five episode 'Boxing Day Social'.

As the Butler and Rudge families enjoy the festivities at the Boxing Day Social event in the depot canteen trouble brews. Beryl, a busty young scantily-clad off-duty clippie walks up to Arthur and in a posh voice says: 'Arthur love, you promised to buy me a drink earlier. What about it?' Sheepishly, he tells her he will but a little later in the evening. A drunken Olive watches and flies into a jealous rage as Beryl exits the scene.

Beryl

Played by Alex Marshall

A clippie that Arthur flirts with and in the process tells her a few white lies about himself in the Series Five episode 'A Thin Time'.

Beryl works aboard the bus that Arthur travels home from work on and the pair become friends. He tries to impress her as he claims to be interested in physical fitness but he is in for a nasty shock as he finds she is already dating a young long-haired busman. When she remarks how she likes men with a good head of hair, Arthur's hopes are dashed. Later, in a bid to impress her, he dons a wig but as he gets off the bus which is driven by Stan and has Beryl aboard as a clippie, his head gets trapped in the faulty door as it closes. He is pulled free but is revealed to Beryl in all his baldness as mum and Oliver arrive on the scene. Beryl is accused of chasing after Arthur and warned to stop but amidst laughs, she says: 'Me? Chase him? You must be joking.' And she walks away laughing. His pride shattered Arthur mutters: 'She should be so lucky.'

Bessie

Bessie is an unseen bus cleaner at the depot who is off work sick in the Series Five episode 'A Thin Time'. Stan, who describes her as 'little, old Bessie' whose 'knees are giving out' takes on her duties as he is so desperate for overtime.

Best, George

An iconic but controversial footballer famous in the 1960s and 70s who was referred to in a couple of episodes of On The Buses.

In the Series Five episode 'The New Telly', Olive is trying to persuade a sceptical Arthur that they should buy a new colour television. She tells him that their black and white television's picture is all grey leaving them unable to tell black from white to such an extent that he felt George Best looked like Father Christmas. At the time this episode was written and first aired George Best had grown a full black beard and with the Butler's telly making everything seem grey this explains why George Best was likened to the white-bearded Father Christmas. Later,

Blakey blasts Jack for not being able to leave the women alone in the Basildon Bashers side in the Series Seven episode 'The Football Match'. Stan remarks that neither could George Best leave women alone. However, the inspector points out: 'At least he waited 'til he got off the football field first, didn't he?'

George Best was, and in many people's eyes, still is the most talented player to have been produced by Britain. His superb ball skills and natural talent were a marvel to behold for football fans, especially those of Manchester United and Northern Ireland for whom he played for most notably. Sadly, off the pitch he was to lead a troubled life in which he battled alcoholism from an early age that led to liver problems later in life. This would lead to a controversial liver transplant carried out on the NHS but, at the age of fifty nine, Best sadly passed away in 2005 following multiple organ failure.

Best Man

Stan is to become a best man in the Series Five episode 'The Best Man'.

Stan is chosen to be best man to fellow bus driver Bill who is to marry Inspector Blake's niece, Sally. The inspector is disappointed by Bill's choice and feels the need to warn Stan of his duties and responsibilities in the role but for Stan the organising of a bachelor party for Bill and his colleagues is foremost in his mind which worries Blakey.

After a raucous bachelor party the day of the wedding arrives. Hung over Stan has another kind of headache as his best man's speech is mocked by Arthur when he recites it, the groom remains drunk and Stan is flustered and nervous. Although mum tries to calm her son telling him that all he has to do is get the groom to the church things aren't as simple as that as he soon finds out.

Bet, The

Stan indulges in a bet with both Jack and Arthur in the Series Six episode 'No Smoke Without Fire'.

When smoking is banned at the bus depot it leads to Jack betting Stan that he can't give up smoking. The bet is extended as Stan arrives home and is ridiculed by Arthur for trying to beat the smoking habit by eating sweets causing Stan to bet his brother-in-law he can't stop smoking either. To prove his strength of will Arthur insists that they both throw their cigarettes into the fire but Stan's resolve shows signs of weakening.

Later in the evening Stan is caught smoking by Arthur and despite having had a sly smoke himself he tells Stan: 'You owe me ten pounds mate.' Despite Stan protesting he hasn't got the money he is told to draw the money out at the post office the following morning. However, Stan has the last laugh though when he catches Arthur about to smoke himself and rules out paying him any money.

At work Stan isn't so lucky. A fire aboard a bus is started when he discards a lit cigarette into a used ticket bin and Inspector Blake has to be rescued from the upper deck as the bus is ablaze. Although Stan's job is not in danger due to lack of evidence he is forced to honour his bet with Jack paying him five pounds otherwise the cunning conductor threatens to explain to the management how the fire really started.

Betty

Played by Doreen Herrington

Betty is an attractive, busty clippie who is having an affair with the depot's general manager in the Series One episode 'The New Inspector'.

Betty sees herself as being in a position of power due to her relationship with the manager but she is not so popular with other female staff members. She places herself above the rules as she chooses to blatantly disregard the dress code according to the rule book and when Stan, in his new role of assistant inspector, says he is reporting her later in her shift he receives insolence and no respect. It is his reports about Betty that leads to his dismissal from the post.

Betty's Husband

Played by Nosher Powell

This is the suspicious, well-built husband of the character known as 'Turnaround Betty' in the film On The Buses.

Betty's husband arrives home in his removal van as Stan is being seduced by Betty in the bedroom. Her husband had grown suspicious of his wife when he finds Jack's PSV badge in the bedroom and comes home hoping to catch them in the act. Stan is almost caught instead but whilst Betty's husband searches the bedroom without success it gives Stan the chance to make a chaotic escape.

Bill

Played by John Lyons

Bill is a bus driver who is to share a last night drink with Stan and other colleagues in the Series Seven episode 'Goodbye Stan'.

Bill, a busman in his late twenties, is first seen telling Stan and Jack that Inspector Blake has not arrived for work yet. Moments later though, he laughs as Blakey has his hands full arriving at the depot carrying his possessions with Bill saying: 'Look here he comes.' Later in the evening, he can be seen next to Stan at the bar of the Luxton and District Social Club smoking a cigar. He shares a drink with Stan who is leaving Luxton for a new job and he leads a sing-song as the busmen burst into song singing 'For He's A Jolly Good Fellow.'

Bill

Played by Hugh Walters

The bus driver that is to marry a clippie called Sally who happens to be the inspector's niece in the Series Five episode 'The Best Man'.

Bill is a thin-faced man in his early thirties who is not looked at in a favourable light by the inspector who describes him as being 'dim' and matters aren't helped when he makes Stan his best man. Things get worse when at his bachelor party he drinks himself into a drunken stupor and stays overnight at the Butler house. He is so drunk that he mistakes Olive for his bride-to-be and pulls her on top of him kissing her passionately and his drunken state lasts well into his wedding day when even Olive's smelling salts don't bring him to his senses.

To cap it all Bill arrives late at the church for his wedding and his bride has to borrow Olive's ring in order that the service can be completed as the intended ring is stuck on Stan's finger. Finally, the couple are married and can head off on their honeymoon.

Bingo

Bingo is a popular game often played by Mrs Butler as referred to in several episodes of On The Buses.

We first learn of mum's habit in the Series One episode 'The New Conductor' when Stan lets his mother down as he takes his new clippie called Iris out on a date instead of escorting his mum to the bingo. Later, when Mrs Butler is dating bus conductor Wilf Phillips she has a night out at the bingo with him in the Series Three episode 'Mum's Last Fling' and borrows the house-keeping money to pay for her night out much to the families disappointment. Most notably, bingo features in the Series Seven episode 'The Visit' as Mrs Butler treats the inspector's mum Mrs Blake to a night out at the bingo at the Luxton and District Social Club with Blakey and Olive accompanying them. The evening is made interesting with Jack acting as the bingo caller and it ends on a high for Mrs Blake who wins the jackpot on a card paid for by Mrs Butler. The recriminations are to start when Mrs Blake refuses to split the winnings of ninety seven pounds and hostilities grow.

As a game, bingo's history dates back to 1530 and an Italian lottery called 'Lo Giuoco del Lotto D'Italia'. The game was gradually spread across Europe by travelling merchants and is now played all over the world almost five hundred years later.

Bingo Caller

Jack takes on the role of bingo caller in the Series Seven episode 'The Visit'.

As bingo caller at the Luxton and District Social Club, Jack is to invent his own array of number descriptions a lot of which are saucy in nature and earns him ridicule from Inspector Blake. When Mrs Blake claims the jackpot prize it is Jack's job to check the winning ticket and present the thoroughly loathsome Mrs Blake with the prize money. This causes a heated debate between Mrs Butler and Mrs Blake over who pays for the next round of drinks but thankfully Jack is on hand to act as a peacemaker and offers to buy the drinks himself.

Binney, Neil

Camera Operator (On The Buses and Mutiny On The Buses)

Neil Binney was to have a long and distinguished career as a cameraman. It spanned over forty years and he was to work on some of Britain's best-loved films and television series.

Aside from On The Buses and Mutiny On The Buses, Binney has worked on a wide range of films across many genres spanning the decades. In the 1960s his credits included I've Gotta Horse, Carry On Up The Khyber, Frankenstein Must Be Destroyed and Run a Crooked Mile. The 1970s brought credits in Taste The Blood Of Dracula, Blood From The Mummy's Tomb, Ooh…You Are Awful, Asylum, Steptoe And Son Ride Again and Carry On Behind. Into the 1980s he would work on George And Mildred, Rising Damp, Conan The Destroyer, A Fish Called Wanda and towards the end of his career in the 1990's in Nuns On The Run and Aliens 3. Binney was also to work on several classic television series spread across three decades with the pick of those being The Adventurer, Space: 1999, Return Of The Saint, Quatermass, Hammer House Of Horror, Jeeves And Wooster, Minder and Peak Practice.

Neil Binney retired from the industry towards the end of the 1990s.

Birch, Samantha

TV Role: Assistant Traffic Manager (Series 4 Episode 11 'The Lodger')

Samantha Birch has had an acting career that stretches over forty years in television roles in varying genres.

Debuting in 1969 in the ITV sitcom The Best Things In Life she would go on to appear in a host of other hit comedy roles in her career. The most notable of those being Doctor In The House, Hark At Barker, On The Buses, Dear Mother Love Albert, No Honestly and Bernard's Watch. Her drama roles on television were less frequent and came in Wicked Women in the early 1970s and the hit BBC medical drama Doctors in the early 2000s.

Bird Impressions

Inspector Blake is to display a talent for bird impressions in the Series Four episode 'The Kids Outing'.

With a number of restless and out of control children misbehaving in the depot's canteen as they await the bus that is to take them on their outing to be repaired a suggestion is made by the inspector's nephew, Harold. He reveals to Stan and Jack that his uncle does bird impressions and they see this as an opportunity to have a laugh at Blakey's expense and encourage him to give them an impression to entertain the children. Blakey begins with an impression of a canary and follows it up with what he calls the mating call of the black-headed gull. He is surprised to hear a reply to his call which turns out to be a mischievous prank by Jack who jokes that the inspector 'has clicked'. This brings an abrupt end to the inspector's impressions as he storms off in a huff.

Birgit

Played by Pauline Cunningham

Birgit is a young, attractive Swedish woman who, along with her friend Ingrid, mistake Stan and Jack for airline pilots in the Series Three episode 'The New Uniforms'.

She is a rather naïve student in her twenties who is in the country studying English. When she and her friend see Stan and Jack dining in a café wearing a prototype new uniform they mistake them for airline pilots. This attracts them to the ageing lotharios who decide to play along with the pretence as Stan jokes that flying a plane is just like driving a bus. Birgit disagrees though saying in broken English: 'Oh no busmen are, how you say, ignorant louts.' It isn't long before a double date is arranged between the devious Stan and Jack and the naïve Birgit and Ingrid for later in the evening. Although the date goes very well Birgit realises her mistake the following day. She arrives with her friend at the bus depot looking to catch a bus to the museum but see Stan and Jack there and realise they are busmen. As Inspector Blake watches on in glee, Birgit asks: 'Are you not Captain Butler?' Their worst fears are confirmed by the inspector and Birgit and Ingrid say a few choice words in Swedish angrily directed at Stan and Jack before turning their backs on them and storming out of the depot for the last time.

Birthday Cake for Aunt Maud

When Olive attempts to bake a cake she ends up failing miserably in the Series Six episode 'Private Hire'.

When she is left to bake a birthday cake for Aunt Maud disaster ensues. She adds milk to the cake mix before baking it and the cake exits the oven looking like 'a heap of old black porridge' according to Arthur and not a birthday cake. Although Stan tries to help Olive salvage the cake by icing it, the attempt ends in failure as they ice the cake with ready mixed tiling cement being used by Arthur who is re-tiling the kitchen using icing sugar. This spells the end for the cake and a replacement has to be bought.

Birthmark

Stan has a birthmark on his bottom which is referred to in a couple of episodes on On The Buses.

It is first mentioned in the Series Two episode 'Aunt Maud' when mum is asked by her visiting sister at the depot: 'Has he still got that little birthmark on his little botty?' Inspector Blake butts in saying: 'I should ask the clippies about that if I were you.' When he sees he has offended Mrs Butler with his witty remark he quickly apologises insisting no offence was intended. Later, in the Series Three episode 'Going Steady', Stan and his family entertain his fiancée Sally and her uncle Inspector Blake. Mum takes the opportunity to show them a photograph of Stan naked on a rug taken when he was six-months-old and Sally remarks: 'Oh look Stan I can see your birthmark. The one you've got on your bottom.' Her uncle is shocked that she should know about it but she puts his mind at rest by telling him that Stan told her about it.

Black, Eunice

TV Roles: Traffic Warden (Series 3 Episode 7 'Mum's Last Fling'), Rosie (Series 4 Episode 3 'Dangerous Driving' and Series 4 Episode 5 'Christmas Duty'), Gladys (Series 6 Episode 1 'No Smoke Without Fire') and Flossie Farmer (Uncredited) (Series 7 Episode 5 'The Football Match')
Film Roles: Ada (On The Buses) and Mrs Hudson (Holiday On The Buses)

Eunice Black was born in London in 1915 and was to go learn the acting trade on stage from the late 1930s but it wasn't until she reached her forties that her career began to take off with roles coming in films and television where she would become one of the most regularly used supporting actor or actress in On The Buses. She was also to become a fully qualified teacher of English and drama.

Her stage career began at the Unity Theatre, London in 1937 and she would spend years learning the trade in repertory theatre. Her most notable stage role came in Running Wild in 1956 at the Alexandra Theatre in Birmingham and she was a regular on the pantomime scene but she was more renowned for what was to come in films and on television.

Aptly enough, her film career began in the early 1960s where she played a schoolteacher in the BAFTA Award-winning film A Taste Of Honey. Her other film roles would come in Drop Dead Darling, On The Buses, Holiday On The Buses and her final acting role came in the 1990 film Bullseye. She also had an uncredited role in the classic musical Chitty Chitty Bang Bang as well as a range of adult films.

On television she was regularly seen in many hit British sitcoms such as Sykes And A..., On The Buses, Please Sir, The Liver Birds, Doctor At Large, Father Dear Father, George And Mildred, Last Of The Summer Wine and she was also to appear in the comedy sketch series The Benny Hill Show. Drama roles came her way most notably in Martin Chuzzlewit, Hunter's Walk and Crown Court.

In 2007 she wrote her autobiography called 'Nine Lives Of A Free Spirit' at the age of ninety two but sadly she passed away shortly afterwards.

Blackburn, Tony

This famous disc jockey and TV presenter of the 1960s and 70s is referred to in the Series One episode 'The Early Shift'.

Stan is amidst complaining to mum about the new schedules at work that mean earlier starts in the morning. As he prepares for breakfast he switches on the radio but there is only static. Stan moans: 'Look at that. Even Tony Blackburn ain't up.'

At the time this episode first aired on British television, Tony Blackburn was the presenter of the newly formed and popular BBC Radio One's flagship breakfast show. He remained in this post until 1973 when he moved to a mid-morning slot on the same station. Blackburn was also a presenter of the iconic BBC TV show Top Of The Pops which was at the height of its popularity. Finally, in 1984, he left Radio One but does still remain in the trade and has worked on many different radio stations and is still seen making guest appearances on a range of television shows.

Black-leg Labourer

Inspector Blake is called a black-leg labourer by Jack in the Series One episode 'The Early Shift'.

As Stan, Jack and George are on picket duty during a strike at the bus depot they hear a bus exiting the back of the depot. They race around to see Inspector Blake about to take a bus out as he bids to break the strike. This infuriates the shop steward Jack who amongst other things calls Blakey a 'black-leg labourer'.

This derogatory term is one given to employees who continue to work during a strike at their place of work. It is a term that has been in use for well over a hundred years.

Black Velvet

This is a drink that is ordered by Jack whilst he and Stan date two clippies in the Series Five episode 'The Epidemic'. He orders the round of drinks with a dozen oysters.

The drink Black Velvet consists of a dark stout beer such as Guinness which has either a sparkling white wine or champagne added to it. The cocktail originates from a bartender at the Brook's Club in London who, in 1861, created the first Black Velvet for the purpose of mourning the death of Prince Albert.

Blackwall Tunnel

This famous Central London tunnel is referred to in a couple of episodes of On The Buses.

In the Series Three episode 'Brew It Yourself ' a drunk Stan is being forced to eat large platefuls of mashed potatoes by Jack in a desperate bid to sober him up prior to having a breathalyser test. Jack feels even a large spoon isn't big enough to do the job and suggests Stan uses a saucer but he refuses saying: 'This is a mouth here mate not the Blackwall Tunnel.' Later, in the Series Five episode 'The Epidemic', Olive is feeling unwell with flu symptoms and so Arthur peers into her mouth in a bid to see if her tonsils are swollen. As he does so he says: 'Has anybody got a torch? It's like looking down the Blackwall Tunnel.'

The Blackwall Tunnel is a dual road tunnel that runs under the River Thames in East London. The first tunnel was built in 1897 using Victorian technology but it is likely that the second tunnel which was wider and far better lit was the tunnel the writers were referring to as it opened to much publicity in 1967, a year and a half before On The Buses first hit our television screens.

Blake, Inspector Cyril

Played by Stephen Lewis

A strict, but at times, gullible inspector who has his work cut out trying to keep the buses running to time with busmen Stan and Jack creating a lot of his problems. Life is lonely at the top for him with the job earning no friends amongst the busmen and although he shows the management great respect he is often to be chastised and harassed by various managers at the depot.

Cyril Blake, an inspector at the Luxton and District Bus Company, is often called a variety of cruel nicknames by busmen at the depot such as Hitler, Dracula and Frankenstein but most commonly is called Blakey. He does have a close relationship with his mother who he takes on holidays and his other relatives include a sister who bears a close resemblance to him, a brother who suffers back problems, a troublesome nephew called Harold and a niece called Sally who is to cause him a lot of stress as she contemplates marrying his greatest enemy, Stan.

His career at the Luxton and District Bus Company begins with him employed as a driver with Stan as his conductor. At that time he is seen as one of the lads at the depot but promotion to inspector soon changes all that and his attitude towards one-time close colleagues sees him adopt a tough stance and a line is drawn in the sand. A few years into this stint he considers leaving the post and moving to the countryside to run a farm with his fiancée Molly but those plans fall through at the last moment. A chance of further promotion a few months later sees him apply for another job but eventually he turns it down to remain as an inspector as he is touched by the seemingly emotionally affected colleagues but they mistakenly believe he is going to pass away instead of leaving for another job. His working relationship with Stan and Jack is strained to say the least. He sees them as the cause of his problems and is to try unsuccessfully on numerous occasions to get Stan sacked but is often thwarted by the shop steward who happens to be Stan's friend, Jack. He is forced closer to Olive and Mrs Butler when he moves into the Butler house as a lodger in 1973. Blakey often puts Olive down for her looks and woeful cooking much like her ex-husband Arthur and though he shows Mrs Butler more respect he does take advantage of her hospitality at times.

Blake's love life is very limited. He is to have a serious relationship with a canteen cook called Molly despite her being many years younger than him. However, with marriage on the cards, the relationship is cruelly sabotaged by Stan and Jack as they do not take to the even stricter inspector set to take Blakey's place. Although Olive and Mrs Butler briefly flirt with the inspector when he is a lodger he is adamant that he has no intention of marriage and absolutely no interest in romance with either of them.

In the spin-off films Cyril Blake is to hold the position of inspector at the Town and District Bus Company. Promotion to Chief Inspector is to come his way but this is to be followed by a fall from grace. When the company's new tour bus goes on a trial run to Windsor Safari Park, with Stan driving and Blakey aboard supervising, disaster strikes and the company are told they will not be allowed to visit the park again. For his part in the debacle the inspector is demoted to role of conductor and placed aboard Stan's bus – what a come down. He is re-instated as inspector by the time two buses are written off in an accident outside the depot and this sees him finally sacked after fourteen years of service. Blakey is soon to find employment at a holiday camp where he takes up a position of Chief Security Inspector where his role is 'to keep out all undesirables, louts and hooligans'. He also takes on the role of teacher in dance classes as he bids to form an old-time dance team. The job ends in shame though when camp manager Mr Coombs finds him in an uncompromising position with the camp nurse and is promptly sacked. He goes on to take a job at the labour exchange as clerk where he ends up having to deal with two familiar faces in the form of Stan and Jack looking for jobs.

His love life on the big screen offers one relationship for him. The holiday camp nurse Joan is to have a brief fling with him attending his dance classes and treating his big toe for gout. She is to be led astray by Jack leaving Blakey livid. He discovers Joan has been unfaithful and confronts her in an angry exchange which is to cost him his job and ends their relationship. Blakey is destined to live a lonely life as inspector on the small and big screen. His hobbies include fishing, tropical fish and he also has an interest in self-defence and keep fit classes. His position at the depot ultimately leaves him socially isolated – no friends amongst the busmen and looked down upon by the management. It is tough at the top.

Blake, Mrs

Played by Pat Nye

The mother of Inspector Blake who pays her son a visit staying at the Butler for a few troubled days in the Series Seven episode 'The Visit'.

Mrs Blake, whose Christian name is never disclosed, is generally a loathsome character. She makes a host of unreasonable demands whilst a guest at the Butler house and displays a selfish and mean streak when refusing to part with any of her prize money won at the bingo. Her strict demeanour even has an effect on her son who is afraid to defy her and he faces being chastised frequently by her. She also stoops to issuing threats to Mrs Butler when she is asked to leave. When her brief visit to Luxton ends it is only her son that is sad to see her leave.

Blake's Visit, Mrs

Mrs Blake's visit to Luxton is far from an enjoyable experience for Mrs Butler and Olive in the Series Seven episode 'The Visit'.

When Inspector Blake asks if his mother can stay with them on her visit to Luxton, Mrs Butler gives her consent. However, she is soon to find out she has made a grave mistake. On arrival Mrs Blake immediately begins moaning and treating her hosts as if they were her own personal servants. She complains about having to carry her suitcase from the taxi into the house, the chilliness of the living room, insults Olive and issues orders throughout her stay. Mrs Butler is soon running out of patience and does not like her guest treating her house like a hotel. The complaints and moaning continues though as Mrs Blake criticises Mrs Butler's cooking and has the nerve to ask for her to polish her shoes. At the end of her tether she cracks and tells the obnoxious Mrs Blake to leave but retracts this when she is warned Cyril will be upset when he hears what has happened hinting she may lose him as a lodger. In a grovelling bid to appease Mrs Blake she offers to treat her to all-expenses paid night out at the bingo which is accepted.

The bingo night out is to be a bitter event which ends in a heated debate between the two women. At least one good thing comes out of it as it affords Mrs Butler an opportunity to rid herself of her unwanted visitor. Mrs Blake leaves Luxton in the same way she arrived amidst moaning and complaining but at least Mrs Butler and Olive have finally rid themselves of perhaps the biggest battle axe to be seen in On The Buses.

Blakey's Accident at the Cemetery Gates

When the inspector suffers an accident in the Series Three episode 'First Aid' it is to have repercussions at the Luxton and District Bus Company.

Inspector Blake makes a routine check-up on Stan and Jack as they enjoy lunch aboard their bus at the Cemetery Gates. He berates them for another late departure and during an inspection of the bus the hapless inspector slips on Stan's chips aboard the bus injuring him and breaking his clipboard. In agony and prostrate he finds matters are made worse by the blundering first aid offered by Stan and Jack. The first aid book aboard the bus is incomplete and a series of errors by the bungling busmen see them move their patient before diagnosing the injury, put an unsterile plaster onto a cut on his shin and aggravates the injury further by mishandling him.

Relief is finally at hand for Blakey when he returns to the depot and a clippie with a first aid badge offers her assistance. It turns out to be a painful but, at the same time, pleasurable experience for him as the clippie offers a massage much to Stan and Jack's envy. The inspector is to suffer strained knee ligaments from the accident and has to use a walking stick for a few days. However, the whole incident leads to the bus company introducing a first aid test which all bus crews must pass or they will face demotion.

Blakey's Brother

Blakey refers to his brother in the Series Five episode 'The Strain'.

The inspector tells Stan, who unknown to him is wearing a corset after injuring his back, that when his brother injured his back he was in a corset for six weeks. It alarms Stan when Blakey says that the corset did his brother a lot of harm when he tightened it too much. This was to cut off the flow of blood to his vital organs and Blakey claims that 'he's never been right since'.

Blakey's Career as Bus Driver

The Series Six episode 'Stan's Worst Day' offers a glimpse of Blakey's career as a bus driver prior to promotion to rank of inspector.

As bus driver for the Luxton and District Bus Company, Blakey seems to have an amiable relationship with Stan who is his conductor. They are on first name terms, are generally much more civil to one another and even have nights out together socialising. Blakey's driving record wasn't unblemished as he suffers an accident damaging the bus on one of his final shifts as driver and with promotion beckoning he warns Stan who will take over the driver's role that he will have to foot the bill for the damage done.

Their friendship is further damaged when Blakey is caught being pushed around on a trolley as he larks about. The manager is none too pleased and warns him about his future conduct. Blakey blames Stan for endangering his promotion and vows to make his life a misery. Worse is to come when, after a night out with Stan and the new employee Jack, he returns with them to the Butler house for a drink but his new inspector's uniform that he is wearing is ruined when Olive spills a trifle over it. This infuriates Blakey and effectively ends the amiable relationship that had existed between Stan and himself.

Blakey's Injury

Blakey is to be injured in an accident outside the Town and District's depot in the film Holiday On The Buses.

With the inspector aboard Stan and Jack's bus as it leaves the depot disaster strikes. The bus is forced to break suddenly to avoid an on-coming car which causes Inspector Blake, Jack and a female passenger to fall from the back platform of the bus with the inspector injuring his foot. It turns out he has broken his big toe causing his foot to be bandaged and he is forced to use a walking stick whilst the injury heals. Although the fracture clears up after a few weeks he is struck down by gout in the toe as he takes up a new job in a holiday camp. The camp nurse who becomes romantically involved with the inspector treats the toe by rubbing ointment on it but the healing process isn't helped when his injured toe is trodden on by the well-built holidaymaker Wally Briggs during a dance lesson.

Blakey's Military Career

Inspector Blake's military career prior to employment with the Luxton and District Bus Company is referred to in a couple of episodes of On The Buses.

His military career was to see him leave a Liverpool quayside bound for Burma in 1941. Four of the five years in the Far East saw him stationed in Bankipore, India where he proudly served under Lord Louis Mountbatten and was involved in transport. In charge of the mules, it was Blakey's job to lead the mules over long distances, through rough terrain and severe weather battling through enemy lines. He is proud that he always made it to his destination on schedule but wonders, later in life, whether it was worth it when the likes of Stan and Jack benefit from the freedom enjoyed by Britain.

Blakey's New Uniform

The inspector's new uniform is to be ruined in the Series Six episode 'Stan's Worst Day'.

As Inspector Blake witnesses a painter attempting to paint over scratches on the side of Stan's bus which has been damaged in a collision with the Town Hall. As he awaits an explanation from Stan, the reckless driver rushes through the depot, bumping into the inspector who slides on a discarded trolley and collides with a step ladder. On this step ladder is the painter who is knocked off and spills paint over Inspector Blake's new uniform causing him to dub Stan 'the clumsiest driver that's ever been in the depot.' Futile efforts are made to clean up the uniform as Stan and Jack use cloths dabbed with paint thinner to wipe down the uniform but the damage has already been done.

Blitzkrieg

A word used by Jack to warn Stan that Inspector Blake is on his way in the Series Two episode 'Late Again'.

Stan has arrived late at the depot for another early shift and as Blakey rushes over to berate him Jack warns: 'Watch it... blitzkrieg.'

Blitzkrieg was a type of attack used in the Second World War. A German word meaning lightning war a blitzkrieg was a form of attack using all forms of armoured vehicles, infantry, aerial attacks and overwhelming forces attacking with great speed at enemy lines with real effect.

Bluebeard

Inspector Blake is dubbed Bluebeard by Jack in the Series Seven episode 'Hot Water'.

Arriving late at the depot for his shift, the inspector appears unshaven and dishevelled. He is not in the best of moods snapping at Jack who hits back saying: 'Alright, alright Bluebeard don't get your knickers in a twist. Just 'cos you got up late and didn't have time to shave.' Blakey explains that the immersion heater at home has broken down leaving him without hot water to shave hence his appearance.

In reality Bluebeard was a fearsome wealthy aristocrat that featured in a French folktale written in 1697 by Charles Perrault. Bluebeard had a frightening blue beard (hence the connection with the stubble-faced Inspector Blake) and was avoided by the women as his previous wives were presumed to have been killed by him.

Bob

Played by Bob McNab

Bob is a busman and talented footballer seen in the Series Seven episode 'The Football Match' and is star player of the Luxton depot's football team.

In his late twenties Bob is certainly the star player of the Luxton Lions side. He displays his talent during a training session for an upcoming match against The Basildon Bashers with an impressive display of ball-juggling skills and the rest of the team feel sure they can't lose with Bob in the side. However, Stan and Jack choose to clown around in the training and as they do Stan collides with Bob knocking him over. The team's talismanic figure is left writhing in agony and feels he has broken his ankle and is ruled out of the big match.

Bogeyman

Arthur is indirectly referred to as a bogeyman by Stan in the Series Four episode 'The L Bus'.

When Arthur and Olive's bed collapses they have to find alternative sleeping arrangements. He chooses to sleep downstairs on the sofa whilst Olive spends the night in her mum's bed. Mum later reminisces that it was just like when Olive was a child saying: 'She always used to come into my bed when she was little and afraid of the bogeyman.' Hearing this Stan quips: 'Being married to him I'm surprised she don't sleep with you every night.'

Bogeyman is a term used to describe a frightening figure with tales about the term varying from around the world. It was often used by parents telling their children that if they misbehaved the bogeyman would get them.

Bognor Regis

A factual town referred to in the Series One episode 'The New Inspector'.

Stan and Jack are having fun at the expense of a former inspector joking about his reason for leaving. Jack jokes: 'The old inspector went to Russia to carry out Stalin's purge.' Inspector Blake corrects him saying he went to Bognor to grow roses.

Bognor Regis (often abbreviated to Bognor) is a seaside town in West Sussex around fifty five miles to the south west of London. It began as a fishing village before gaining status as a town in the eighteenth century and gradually developed into a resort town by the end of the nineteenth century. It gained prominence in 1960 when the famous Butlin's Holiday Camp was opened and, until recent years, staged an annual 'Birdman of Bognor' competition.

Bolsheviks

A term used by Inspector Blake in response to remarks made by Jack in the Series Three episode 'Busmen's Perks'.

In the stores at the depot Jack is amidst persuading Stan that he is entitled to use the bus company's paint as perks of the job when Inspector Blake arrives on the scene. Jack tries to change the subject as they watch a car being spray-painted saying: 'I was pointing out to Brother Stan here as shop steward how the company's profits are being squandered on the governor's Jag.' Inspector Blake bids to stamp out any trouble and snaps: 'Now don't you start your Bolsheviks around here mate. Mr Adams, as general manager is entitled to use that car as and when he thinks fit on the company's business.'

The Bolsheviks were a political party that split from the Russian Labour Party in 1903 and was founded by Lenin. Their philosophy was based around bidding to overthrow the Tsar through a mass workers revolution. In this instance in On The Buses the Tsar would be Mr Adams with the shop steward Jack taking the place of the workers trying to start a revolution.

Bond, James

This famous fictional secret service agent is referred to in a couple of episodes of On The Buses.

In the Series Two episode 'Self Defence', Stan is displaying to the family some moves he picked up at the bus company's judo and karate classes which Stan likens to those used by James Bond in the films he featured in. Later, in the Series Three episode 'Mum's Last Fling', Stan has to stop off whilst on duty to pay a gas bill and his bus gets issued with two parking tickets. He thinks he has solved the problem when he screws them up and throws them away but they end up back in the inspector's hands when the traffic warden retrieves them. Jack tells Stan: 'You should have done like James Bond and swallowed them.'

James Bond was a fictional secret service agent created by novelist Ian Fleming in 1952. The character was to become a worldwide phenomenon on the big screen and the most renowned fictional spy of all-time. Bond features in twenty three official films to date starting in 1962 with Sean Connery, George Lazenby, Roger Moore, Timothy Dalton, Pierce Brosnan and Daniel Craig all playing the suave agent. When On The Buses originally aired on television the James Bond films were at the height of their popularity and very topical.

Bond, Roy

Gaffer (Mutiny On The Buses)

Roy Bond's career in the film and television industry was to see him based at Elstree Studios where he worked in the camera and electrical departments.

Towards the end of the 1960s he was to work on his only television credit. As an electrician he worked on several episodes of the hit ITC series The Avengers. His big screen credits were to come in the early 1970s where he worked as gaffer on Mutiny On The Buses. Bond also had credits as an electrician on the Amicus horror production Dr Phibes Rises Again which was to be his final project in the industry in 1972.

Bonus Money

A special payment paid by the Luxton and District Bus Company as mentioned in the Series Two episode 'Bon Voyage'.

When Stan has his uniform stolen from his bus as he sunbathes in the cemetery further bad news is to follow as he returns to the depot scantily dressed. Inspector Blake tells him that to pay for a new uniform the company will deduct the cash from Stan's bonus money.

Booking Clerk

The occupation of Arthur as mentioned in the Series One episode 'The Early Shift'.

Despite having ambitions to be a doctor, Arthur is to be employed by British Rail as a booking clerk at the fictional Crossley Junction railway station. Even though Stan mocks him for the lack of work that the job entails Arthur is proud of the job and the fact that he has been treasurer of the railway union for a number of years. However, he is also known to have helped himself to British Rail stock – that being their toilet paper.

Booth, Harry

Director (On The Buses and Mutiny On The Buses)

Born in London, Harry Booth was to have a prolific career from 1941 onwards in the film and television industry chiefly as a director which spanned fifty years.

His director roles began on television and his most notable credits came in dramas such as Sir Francis Drake, Man Of The World, The Pathfinders and The Protectors. He'd also direct episodes of hit children's series such as River Rivals and Here Comes The Double Deckers.

On the big screen his big successes were On The Buses and Mutiny On The Buses which he directed. Other films that he worked on were Go For A Take and The Flying Sorcerer.

In other capacities he worked on hit television series such as The Adventures Of Robin Hood, Fabian Of The Yard and The Avengers. His other film credits included the Goons film The Case Of The Mukkinese Battle- Horn, At The Stroke Of Nine, Penny Points To Paradise, The Final Test, The Sleeping Tiger and his career came to an end in 1991 with an editing role on Robin Hood: The Movie.

Boston Crab

A wrestling hold referred to by Stan in the Series Two episode 'Self Defence'.

Stan and Jack have no interest in attending the self-defence classes offered by the bus company until they see two attractive clippies sign up to attend. Jack changes his mind saying he'll attend as he wouldn't mind rolling about on a mattress with them. Stan agrees saying: 'Rolling about in the Boston crab eh?'

The Boston crab is a wrestling hold that involves the attacking wrestler sitting on the lower back of their opponent who is face down with the attacker keeping a firm grip on the opponent's legs. The hold was brought to prominence during the early 1960s through until the mid-1980s when British wrestling was at the height of its popularity and regularly pulled in millions of television viewers during its stint on the classic ITV sports series – World Of Sport.

Botany Bay

This is a historic penal colony that is referred to in the Series Seven episode 'On The Omnibuses'.

During a vivid dream of Stan's, which is to see Stan and Jack as busmen in the early part of the twentieth century with Inspector Blake present, Jack encourages Stan to take part in a strike. It is a move that infuriates the tyrannical inspector who urges Stan to get aboard his bus but when he refuses he is warned: 'You know what this means don't you? It means sedition and a clear revolution. It means that you will be sent to Botany Bay on a convict ship'.

Botany Bay was where Captain Cook aboard HMS Endeavour was to set foot in Australia for the first time in 1770. It was soon decided that Botany Bay would be the site of a new penal colony where criminals from Britain would be shipped. The location got its name because of the vast amount of plants found in the bay.

Bowerbank, Elaine

Hairdressing Supervisor (Holiday On The Buses)

Elaine Bowerbank had a lengthy career working in the make-up department on the film and television industry.

She was to begin her career working on low budget films in the UK in the early 1970s but her talents were to see her move onto bigger blockbusting productions in the 1980's. Her most notable credits of the 1970s were Holiday On The Buses, The Best Pair Of Legs In The Business and The First Great Train Robbery.

It was in the 1980s that smash hit films were to benefit from her hairdressing skills with credits in the Oscar-winning films A Passage To India, The Mission and Aliens as well as Santa Claus and Gorillas In The Mist. Further film credits followed in the 1990s in productions such as Shining Through, City Of Joy and 1492: Conquest Of Paradise which was to wrap up her big screen career in 1992.

Her television credits, although few and far between were successful. In 1988 she was to win a coveted Emmy award as a hairstylist on the hit series Jack The Ripper. She was to later have credits in made-for-television films The Return Of Sam McCloud and Diana: Her True Story.

Bowie, Les

Special Effects (Holiday On The Buses)

Les Bowie was born in Vancouver, Canada in 1913 but moved to the UK and was to become a pioneering figure in the film special effects industry. He began working on low budget films in the early 1950s and was renowned for his innovative techniques which would see him graduate on to work on many blockbuster films through until the end of the 1970s.

In the first few years in the industry in the 1950s his credits included classic films such as The Quatermass Experiment, Dracula and Quatermass 2. Into the 1960s more classic films on his impressive CV included The Curse Of The Werewolf, The Day The Earth Caught Fire, First Men In The Moon, The City Under The Sea, Quatermass And The Pit as well as an uncredited contribution to 2001: A Space Odyssey. The 1970s were to see Bowie's career continue apace as he worked on films such as Vampire Circus, Dracula AD 1972, Frankenstein And The Monster From Hell, Superman and another uncredited role in the ground-breaking science-fiction classic Star Wars. In Holiday On The Buses, Bowie was behind the effects that made the submerged double decker bus at the end of the film which was in fact made of plywood.

Les Bowie had the proud distinction of winning an Oscar in 1979 for his visual effects in the hit film, Superman.

Sadly, just a few months later, he was to pass away at the age of sixty six.

Boxing Day Social

An annual social event held at the bus depot canteen that features in a Series Five episode of the same name.

Although the Boxing Day Social is looked forward to by the busmen, Arthur has a differing opinion especially as he has his mother and sister staying with the Butlers over the festive period. He tells his mother: 'Well you know what these do's are like. Full of drunken louts making advances at women whether they are married or single.' He is confident that his sister Linda is above such things but he is in for a shock.

The Butler and Rudge families attend the evening event and Mrs Rudge seems to enjoy herself dancing with Inspector Blake as does Mrs Butler. However, Arthur is less comfortable as he watches Jack chatting up his sister and ends up threatening the lothario conductor unless he leaves Linda alone.

Arthur suffers more hassle when he is caught flirting with an off-duty clippie by a drunk Olive who has consumed a few too many vodkas. She embarrasses herself and berates Arthur causing a scene at the event. The evening is to end in more ill-feeling when Linda lures Stan onto an out-of-service bus in the depot and seduces him. However, the passion is soon dampened by the arrival on the scene of Inspector Blake and a shocked Mrs Rudge. Stan is looked upon as the villain of the piece but he has had no pleasure but takes all the blame as the Boxing Day Social comes to an end.

Boy Scouts Salute

This is a hand gesture made by Stan that Olive refers to in the Series One episode 'Olive Takes A Trip'.

Stan directs a rude gesture to Inspector Blake as he walks passed him in the depot. Olive who is training to become a clippie says: 'Oh, Stan you've given him the boy scouts salute.' Stan corrects her saying it was the busman's salute explaining: 'It's the same, two fingers you know but we don't bring 'em right up to the forehead. We stop in halfway in between like this.' He demonstrates but the inspector sees him leaving him in an awkward position.

The two-fingered salute generally belongs to either Cub or Wolf Cub Scouts. Mrs Butler does reveal in the same scene that Stan was a Wolf Cub when he was a boy.

Brady, Pete

TV Role: Disc Jockey (Series 3 Episode 9 'Foggy Night')

Pete Brady was born in Montreal, Canada in 1942 and was to have a notable career as a disc jockey and was to go on to have roles in television.

He was to have vast experience across the globe as a disc jockey where he began his career in his native Canada before moving to work in the same role in Jamaica and finally progressed on to the UK in the mid-1960s. He worked at Radio London and also BBC Radio One in its formative years and was to settle down to live in Britain.

On television he will be best-remembered as presenter from 1968 to 1972 on the hit ITV children's series Magpie. His acting roles were limited to his part in On The Buses where his voice is heard on Olive's radio and an appearance in the hit police drama Special Branch.

He has since progressed on to work in the film and video industry in the latter years of his life.

Braemar, Winifred

TV Role: Winnie (Series 4 Episode 7 'The Kids Outing', Series 4 Episode 11 'The Lodger' and Series 4 Episode 13 'Not Tonight')

Winifred Braemar was to begin her acting career on stage and would go on to have roles in films and on television.

Stage roles beckoned first for Braemar and she'd have roles in the late 1930s in George And Margaret and The Corn Is Green. Other notable roles included The Light Of Heart and Annie Get your Gun.

The mid-1940s were to see her make her first film appearance in Beware Of Pity. The remainder of her films roles came in the late 1960s in Work Is A Four-Letter Word and in the 1970s in the spin-off film For The Love Of Ada and Confessions From A Holiday Camp.

Braemar's television roles were largely comedic with a number of credited and uncredited appearances in On The Buses, Please Sir, Doctor In The House and For The Love Of Ada. Her solitary drama role on the small screen was to come in the highly acclaimed BBC series Roads To Freedom in 1970.

Brainsbury

A fictional town where Arthur's sister lives as mentioned in the Series Four episode 'The Other Woman'.

Arthur and Olive are suffering marital problems after a night out sees him flirt with the off-duty clippie Wendy. He walks out on Olive and spends the night sleeping in the sidecar of his motorbike though she fears he is with Wendy. The following morning Arthur returns to the house but he isn't planning on staying as he asks Jack: 'Excuse me Jack. Do you mind telling me when the buses leave your depot for Brainsbury?' He reveals that he intends going to stay with his sister whilst he reconsiders his position. As it turns out Arthur never gets to Brainsbury as he reconciles with Olive as it becomes clear that Wendy never had any romantic interest in Arthur.

Brambell, Wilfrid

Film Role: Bert Thompson (Holiday On The Buses)

Born in Dublin, Ireland in 1912, Wilfrid Brambell was to have a long, distinguished career as an actor. He will always be best remembered for playing one of the best-loved comedy characters on British television in the 1960s and 70s starring as Albert Steptoe in the long-running smash hit BBC sitcom Steptoe And Son. His acting career spanned over fifty years with roles on stage followed by film and television appearances.

Brambell started out as a stage actor learning his trade in the early 1930s at The Abbey Theatre in Dublin. He would go on to have notable stage roles in the UK in Blind Man's Buff, Happy As Larry, The Taming Of The Shrew, The Canterbury Tales, A Christmas Carol and The Ghost Train amongst others. In 1971 he also played a character called Rooksby in a stage play called The Banana Box written by Eric Chappell. This play was later adapted for television with Rooksby becoming Rigsby who was played by Leonard Rossiter in the smash hit sitcom, Rising Damp.

On the big screen his credits included a host of renowned films such as Dry Rot, Flame In The Streets, The Boys, In Search Of The Castaways, A Hard Day's Night, Crooks In Cloisters, San Ferry Ann, Witchfinder General, Steptoe And Son, Steptoe And Son Ride Again, Holiday On The Buses and The Terence Davies Trilogy. He was also to have uncredited roles in the 1930s Hitchcock classic The Thirty Nine Steps and Carry On Again Doctor.

Television credits came his way from the mid-1950s onwards with a string of drama roles in series such as The Quatermass Experiment, Quatermass II, The Black Brigand, The Adventures Of Robin Hood, William Tell, No

Hiding Place, Maigret and latterly in All Creatures Great And Small. Brambell's comedy roles most notably came in Life With The Lyons, The Larkins, Steptoe And Son, According To Dora, Never Say Die and Citizen Smith.

Sadly, in early 1985, at the age of seventy two after a battle against alcoholism and cancer, Wilfrid Brambell passed away.

Breathalyser Test, The

Stan has to take a breathalyser test at the depot in the Series Three episode 'Brew It Yourself' and it takes all of shop steward Jack's ingenuity and cunning to save Stan from the sack.

Stan turns up at the depot drunk after sampling his home-brewed beer before leaving for work unaware how strong his beer actually is. He makes unwelcome advances to a clippie and Inspector Blake is on hand to witness the driver's drunken behaviour and warns him that he could face instant dismissal for signing on for duty whilst under the influence of alcohol. However, Jack steps in to defend his mate saying: 'Hang about. As shop steward I cannot allow you to make unsubstantiated allegations about one of our members. You cannot prove he is intoxicated'. The inspector thinks otherwise saying he will get the company doctor to get Stan to take a breathalyser test. It is left up to Jack to try to sabotage the test in any way he can whilst Inspector Blake hunts down the doctor.

Jack believes he has 'the cure' in the canteen and asks fellow busman Chalkie to get Stan a big plateful of mashed potatoes. He tells Stan to eat it as, according to him, it'll get rid of the alcohol by soaking it up. However, it is all too much for Stan to eat and it appears that his time has run out when Inspector Blake arrives on the scene to declare that he'll carry out the breathalyser test himself. Prior to the test Jack has one last trick up his sleeve. He tells Stan that if he blows into the bag with a mouthful of smoke it messes up the test and so gets him to take a long puff on a cigarette before taking the test. It turns out to be a deeply uncomfortable exercise for Stan as he has to hold his breath as Blakey explains the rules and waits for the appropriate moment for the test to begin. Warned that he will be sacked if the crystals turn green, Stan blows his smoke into the bag. To the perplexed amazement of the inspector and much to Stan and Jack's relief the crystals turn brown, with Jack claiming this was because Stan is ill. Inspector Blake is forced to agree and sends Stan home with his job still intact.

The breathalyser test was introduced in Britain under The Road Safety Act of 1967 by the then Transport Minister Barbara Castle. It was an Act that caused great controversy at the time as people felt it was infringing their personal liberties. That attitude has changed through the years though as drink-driving offences have proven to be a major cause of accidents on the roads.

Breck, Julia

TV Role: Canteen Girl (Series 6 Episode 7 'The Prize')

Julia Breck was born in Newport on the Isle of Wight in 1941 and in a career as an actress that spanned over a decade with credits on television, stage and to a lesser degree in films.

Breck was to work alongside comedy legend Spike Milligan in a string of television series such as Curry And Chips, Oh In Colour, The Last Turkey In The Shop Window, Q5 and There's A Lot Of It About. She was also to appear in other classic comedy series in the 1970s such as The Liver Birds, On The Buses, Monty Python's Flying Circus, Some Mothers Do 'Ave 'Em and The Two Ronnies. Her drama roles included credits in Man At The Top and Thriller. On the big screen her solitary film role came in an adult comedy called The Love Box whilst she was also an accomplished stage actress appearing in an early 1970s Andy Warhol play called Pork amongst other things.

She retired from acting in the early 1980s to raise her three children and moved with her husband to live in France.

Bree, James

TV Role: Doctor Clark (Series Five Episode 11 'The Strain')

Born in London in 1923, James Bree was to have a prolific career as an actor that was spread over fifty years on stage, film and television.

His stage credits were plentiful and would perform with the Royal Shakespeare Company in the 1960s in productions such as Ondine, The Taming Of The Shrew, The Caucasian Chalk and A Penny For A Song. Other notable stage roles came his way in The Love Of Four Colonels, The Matchmaker, The Devil's Disciple, The Taming Of The Shrew, The Winter's Tale, As You Like It, The Tempest, The Importance Of Being Earnest and Gentlemen Prefer Blondes.

On the big screen he was to appear in films such as Never Let Go, A Matter Of Choice, On Her Majesty's Secret Service, The Odd Job, On The Black Hill and Without A Clue. Bree's television credits were extensive across the genres spread over five decades. His comedy roles came in a number of classic sitcoms including George And The Dragon, Doctor At Large, Please Sir, On The Buses, Nearest And Dearest, Rising Damp and sketch series The Dick Emery Show. Bree was also to appear in a whole host of hit British dramas the pick of those being No Hiding Place, Doctor Who, Sherlock Holmes, The Prisoner, The Avengers, Randall And Hopkirk (Deceased), Upstairs Downstairs, Z Cars, Hadleigh, I Claudius and Ruth Rendell Mysteries.

Sadly, after a long illness, James Bree was to pass away towards the end of 2008 at the age of eighty five.

Breeze, Olivia

TV Role: Janet Mould (Series 4 Episode 6 'The L Bus')

As an actress Olivia Breeze has worked on a number of stage productions in her career as well as having a handful of roles on television and in films.

Her stage credits include roles in The Matchgirls, Cowardly Custard, Annie, A Chorus Line, Side By Side By Sondheim and Some Enchanted Evening. She is also a highly accomplished choreographer and director of stage shows working on smash hit musical Joseph And The Amazing Technicolor Dreamcoat and the award-winning A Chorus Of Disapproval amongst others and remains involved in stage work to the present day. Breeze's television roles were to come in a made-for-television film A Winter's Tale in the early 1960s and later comedy roles included Doctor At Large, On The Buses and Maggie And Her.

Her solitary film role came in 1963 in a hard-hitting war drama called Reach For Glory.

Olivia Breeze.

Here are Olivia Breeze's thoughts about On The Buses and her experiences of working on the hit sitcom.

'It was just wonderful work because it was very much a family feeling. Reg and Bob and all the principals were just very kind. It only seems like yesterday actually. I'd been in the business for a little bit because I started off as a dancer and then went into acting and loved comedy. The whole thing felt right, you felt comfortable. You didn't feel 'oh god they're big stars, they're going to think I'm terrible' and all that. Although they were big stars they weren't grand. They were just lovely to us.

It is family orientated, these days everything is so crude and vulgar and On The Buses was double entendre – a bit like Max Miller. Max Miller was the most wonderful variety comedian. His timing was impeccable and he'd just get to the point and you just made up your mind what he was talking about and it was up to you, exactly the same with On The Buses, the same with the all the Carry On films.'

Brennan, Kevin

Film Role: Mr Jenkins (Mutiny On The Buses)

Born in Australia in 1920, Kevin Brennan was to move to the UK in 1959 and his acting career was to take off. He was to go on to have an impressive list of credits in films, on television and stage spanning over thirty years.

On the big screen his film career had begun in the late 1940s in Australia but his most notable roles came in the 1960s in Live Now – Pay Later, The Punch And Judy Man and The Small World Of Sammy Lee. These were followed in the 1970s with roles in the classic thriller Get Carter, Mutiny On The Buses and The Spaceman And King Arthur with latterly in the 1980s in Invitation To The Wedding. Brennan's television credits were extensive with credits in a host of hit British dramas in the 1960s, 70s and 80s. The most notable of those being Maigret, Richard The Lionheart, The Saint, The Avengers, Softly Softly, The Troubleshooters, Ivanhoe, Budgie, Emmerdale Farm, Z Cars, Crossroads, Colditz, Fall Of Eagles, Poldark and The Professionals. Comedy roles on the small screen were also plentiful with the pick of those coming in The Rag Trade, Albert And Victoria, Romany Jones, Bless This House, When The Boat Comes In and In Loving Memory.

His stage credits included the musical adaption of Geoffrey Chaucer's The Canterbury Tales in the late 1960s and a part in Amadeus in the early 1980s.

Towards the end of 1998, Brennan sadly passed away at the age of seventy eight.

Brian

Played by Keith Norrish

Brian is a long-haired bus driver employed by the Luxton and District Bus Company who is dating his clippie Sandra in the Series Five episode 'The Epidemic'.

Brian is seen sitting on a bench in the depot reading a newspaper when Sandra, his clippie and girlfriend, sits down next to him and they share a kiss and a chocolate bar. It is common knowledge in the depot that he spends every penny he has got on Sandra and as a jealous Stan watches on as they flirt he remarks that he doesn't spend money on a haircut. When Brian later falls victim of a flu epidemic sweeping through the depot it leaves the way open for a fully fit Stan to entertain Sandra.

Bridal Chorus, The

This famous piece of music is hummed by Jack in the Series Seven episode 'What The Stars Foretell'.

With the inspector being pressurised into an unwanted marriage by both Olive and Mrs Butler, Jack takes the opportunity to have a laugh at his expense. The inspector passes him in the depot and Jack jokes: 'Hello, here he comes…Casanova.' He is to then hum the Bridal Chorus song much to Blakey's displeasure. The Bridal Chorus is a classical piece of music written by the German composer Richard Wagner in 1850 and heard in his opera Lohengrin. It was finally to become popular around the world decades later being used to accompany the bride as she walks down the aisle of the church at weddings. At times lyrics, not penned by Wagner, are added to the song such as 'Here comes the bride, all dressed in white.'

Bride of Dracula, The

Both Jack and Olive are given this name in two separate episodes of On The Buses.

Firstly, in the Series Five episode 'Vacancy For Inspector', Jack in his new role as acting inspector, is becoming a clone of Inspector Blake in his mannerisms and attitude towards Stan. The miffed driver warns Jack of his partnership with Blakey: 'I'll tell you what they'll be calling you down the depot mate – the bride of Dracula. And for god sake don't you two start breeding 'cos there won't be enough blood to go around.' Later, in the Series Seven episode 'What The Stars Foretell', Olive believes she is going to marry Inspector Blake as that is what she reads into her horoscope. As Olive passes Jack in the depot he says: 'Hello. Here she is – the bride of Dracula.'

The Brides Of Dracula was a hit 1960 horror film starring Vincent Price which was a Hammer Films production.

Bridget

Played by Brenda Gogan

An Irish cook who, three weeks after Olive leaves the post, takes on the job in the Town and District's depot canteen. Bridget is to have a brief relationship with Stan in the first spin-off film, On The Buses.

The dark-haired Bridget becomes the new canteen cook replacing Olive. Her cooking is far more edible and Stan is impressed and falls for her good looks. Her specialities cooking-wise are her steak and kidney pies and treacle puddings but Stan is troubled by her deeply religious side. His cheeky charm is to win her over and things go well as Stan enjoys a heavy snogging session with Bridget on the settee at his house. However, any chance for a prolonged romance ends when a pregnant Olive interrupts their snogging to collect her knitting. Bridget's religious side kicks in and startled she gets to her feet saying: 'A pregnant woman. It's a message. It's the lord warning me. She was a messenger come down from heaven.' Despite Stan's plea that it was his sister who had come down from upstairs, Bridget is adamant Stan should stay away from her before she leaves the Butler house for good and ending the romance in the process.

Briggs, Johnny

TV Role: Window Cleaner (Series 6 Episode 2 'Love Is What You Make It')

Born in Battersea, London in 1935, Johnny Briggs graduated from the Italia Conti Academy stage school and went on to build a long career as an actor across the genres but he will be best remembered as Mike Baldwin in the hit soap Coronation Street whom he played from 1974 to 2006.

The early part of his acting career was dominated by stage roles which included parts in Sauce Tartar, La Boheme, Tosca, Rigoletto, Dial M For Murder, Boeing Boeing, Wait Until Dark and latterly in Doctor In The House, The Kitchen and Parcel Post.

Briggs career on the big screen has seen him appear in much-loved films such as Sink The Bismarck, The Bulldog

Breed, HMS Defiant, Doctor In The House, A Stitch In Time, 633 Squadron, The Intelligence Men, Carry On Up The Khyber, Bless This House and Carry On Behind. Other notable big screen roles came in Carry On England and Man About The House.

Television credits include drama roles in The Saint, No Hiding Place, The Troubleshooters, Department S, The Persuaders, Softly Softly, Crossroads, Echo Beach, Doctors and of course, Coronation Street. In comedy roles he was to appear in On The Buses, Bowler, Thick As Thieves, Doctor On The Go, Carry On Laughing and Yus My Dear amongst others.

In 2007, Briggs was awarded the MBE for his services to entertainment a year after receiving a Lifetime Achievement Award at the British Soap Awards. He remains active as an actor more than sixty years after his career began.

Briggs, Lily

Played by Lily Briggs

This is a holidaymaker at the holiday camp in the film Holiday On The Buses.

Lily Briggs is a middle-aged woman, dark-haired and rotund cockney woman who is married to the common and somewhat crude Wally Briggs. Her hobbies include knitting and though she strives to better herself she is often let down and embarrassed by her husband. She turns her hand to taking dance lessons learning old-time dancing and although Wally's lack of ability hinders her they do eventually make it into the dance team and let nobody down in front of a large audience in the ballroom at the holiday camp. Lily is constantly berating Wally for his crudeness and his seemingly high sexual appetite and does have a domineering streak in her as she keeps Wally in line with her put-downs of him with little retort from him. Their holiday comes to an end with the couple attending the farewell ball on their last night at the camp.

Briggs, Wally

Played by Arthur Mullard

Wally is a holidaymaker who attends the holiday camp with his wife, Lily.

He is a large, middle-aged cockney man who is married to Lily. Wally struggles to come up to his wife's standards. He is prone to innocent moments of crudity and his distinct lack of dancing ability does him no favours with his wife but it would seem that dance lessons do help as he dances without errors at an exhibition of old-time dancing later in front of a large audience. He is blamed, wrongly, when Olive minus her glasses gets into his bed by mistake with Lily calling him a sex maniac. It is clear he does have a much greater sexual appetite than his wife as she often has to dampen his ardour. This surfaces again when he describes Olive as 'a flashy bird' and he says that he could fancy her. His wife keeps him on a tight leash though not giving him the chance to stray even though he tries by making her take sleeping tablets. A marriage, in short, lacking romance but they do have fun together.

Bright Stores

This is a fictional bed store that is referred to in the Series Four episode 'The L Bus'.

Arthur and Olive are in the market for a new bed. Pointing out a newspaper advert Olive says: 'Here Arthur, look Bright Stores have got a bed sale on next week – a bed week.' Although Arthur had been contemplating buying two single beds for them, on studying the newspaper advert, he sees double beds are cheaper and so opts for that option. Bright Stores do not get his business though as he buys a second-hand bed from a relative of Jack's instead.

Brighton

A popular seaside resort referred to in the Series Three episode 'The Inspector's Pets'.

Inspector Blake is holiday-bound looking forward to a three day fishing trip to Brighton with his mother for company. It turns out to be a relaxing weekend for him with a few fish caught.

Brighton is a very popular seaside resort on the South Coast in East Sussex. Renowned for its pier it also has high quality beaches that are hugely popular with holidaymakers with other tourist attractions being the Royal Pavilion which at one time was a royal residence.

Bristow, Malcolm

Sound (Series 7 Episode 2 'The Perfect Clippie', Series 7 Episode 5 'The Football Match' and Series 7 Episode 6 'On The Omnibuses)

Malcolm Bristow was to work in the sound department in the film and television industry with a handful of credits spread over a decade.

His first project came on the big screen in 1970 as he worked on dubbing Love Is A Splendid Illusion. His last credit was to see him work in the sound department on the crime film The Orchard End Murder. Aside from On The Buses, which he worked on the sound during location shooting of three episodes, his only other notable television work was to be on the Oscar-winning short animated film – A Christmas Carol which premiered on television before gaining release at the cinema.

Bristow moved on from production to open his own studios where many up and coming production staff learned their trade.

British Museum, The

A famous tourist attraction referred to in the Series Two episode 'The Used Combination'.

As Arthur shows Stan and Jack the motorcycle combination he has just bought, Jack asks to see its handbook. Stan though mocks the age and condition of Arthur's pride and joy saying: 'You'll find it in the British Museum.'

The British Museum is located on Great Russell Street in Central London and was established in 1753. Amongst its prized assets is The Rosetta Stone and is home to the largest collection of artefacts from Ancient Egypt in the world.

British Rail

The ill-fated former company responsible for running national rail services across Britain is referred to in three episodes of On The Buses.

In the debut episode 'The Early Shift' it is revealed that Arthur is employed by British Rail working as a booking clerk. Later, in the Series One episode 'Olive Takes A Trip', Arthur supplies a toilet roll stamped with British Railways that he has stolen for Olive to use as a mock roll of tickets as she practices being a clippie at home. Stan says: 'Cor blimey no wonder the British Railways are going broke.' Finally, in the Series Four episode 'The Anniversary', it is revealed that Aunt Maud has sent them a present to be delivered by British Rail. Stan, who evidently has a low opinion on the rail service offered says: 'Cor blimey if it's coming by British Rail you won't get it 'til your golden anniversary.'

British Rail, known in its early years and occasionally in On The Buses as British Railways, was formed in 1948 when the UK rail network was nationalised by the Labour government of Clement Atlee. It took over from the main four railway companies of the time which were London Midland and Scottish (also known as LMS), Great Western Railways (GWR), London and North Eastern Railway (LNER) and Southern Railway in running the national rail services. As was the case in On The Buses, in real life the train services offered by British Rail were ridiculed as they were often blighted by industrial action, unpunctuality and perceived poor buffet service. However, it was to remain the national train operating company until the rail network was privatised by John Major's Conservative government in 1994. The rail network was then split into separate franchises and those were run by a number of train operating companies with these franchises going out to tender when the lease expires. Today though Unions and a growing amount of the public do now favour a return to the renationalisation of the British rail network feeling it would offer a better service.

Bronchitis

A medical condition that Olive and Inspector Blake suffer from as referred to in a number of episodes of On The Buses.

Olive's bronchitis is mentioned in the Series One episode 'The New Conductor'. She suffers a bout of coughing and feels she may be getting her bronchitis. The Series Five episode 'The Epidemic' sees Inspector Blake coming down with the flu and is treated by the depot nurse. Stan asks whether he has the flu and the nurse describes him as a borderline case saying: 'I suspect it's only a touch of bronchitis.' His bronchitis is again referred to in the Series Seven episode 'Goodbye Stan' when he contemplates becoming a lodger in the Butler house. He tells Mrs Butler: 'You know I suffer with a touch of bronchitis Mrs Butler. I couldn't stand a damp room you know.' However, the bronchitis that Olive and Inspector Blake suffer from does not affect their lives in anyway.

Bronchitis is an infection affecting the airways of the lungs and causes fits of coughing and can develop during colds or flu.

Brooks, Mr

An elderly bespectacled man wearing a bowler hat and equipped with a clipboard is chosen by the Town and District's insurance company to assess their driver Stan Butler in his skidpan test in the film On The Buses.

Mr Brooks begins by showing Stan the controls of the London Transport bus that is to be used for the test. He then proceeds to give the nervous driver instructions regarding the test telling him to make two circuits of the course ending with one left-hand skid and one right-hand skid before he allows Stan to get his test underway. Much to Inspector Blake's chagrin, Mr Brooks gives an unbiased assessment at the end of the test saying: 'Oh I thought he did very well. I'll pass him.' He makes his exit leaving Blakey miffed but Stan relieved.

Brown, Gaye

TV Role: Molly (Series 4 Episode 2 'The Canteen Girl')

Gaye Brown was born in Twickenham, London in 1941 and has had a long career on stage, television and in films.

Stage has played a big part in her career and can boast credits with the Royal Shakespeare Company in Once In A Lifetime, Look Out Here Comes Trouble, The Hang Of The Gaol and Cousin Vladimir. In London's West End she has appeared in productions such as The Sloane Ranger Revue, 42$_{nd}$ Street and Absolute Turkey. Other notable stage roles across the UK include Half A Sixpence, Hobson's Choice, The Secret Garden, Pygmalion, Oh What A Lovely War, Guys And Dolls, Romeo And Juliet and Gay's The Word.

Her credits in television span back to the mid-1960s with drama roles in hit series such as The Borderers, Z Cars, The House Of Eliott, All The King's Men and Emmerdale. She was also seen in a number of classic British comedy series including On The Buses, Nearest And Dearest, The Goodies, When The Boat Comes In, Shelley, Only Fools And Horses and Last Of The Summer Wine.

Brown's film roles have included parts in A Clockwork Orange, A Touch of Class, The Rocky Horror Picture Show and Sweeney Todd: The Demon Barber Of Fleet Street. Other notable film roles came in Up Pompeii, The Masque Of The Red Death, An American Haunting, Cheri and Into The Woods.

Her acting career continues to the present day after almost fifty years in the industry.

Brown Owl

This is a name that Stan calls Inspector Blake in the Series One episode 'Olive Takes A Trip'.

Stan and Olive talk about their youth when they were cubs and brownies in their uniforms but now they are in bus uniforms Olive feels it is quite different. However, when Stan sees Inspector Blake he says: 'Oh no it's not love – here comes Brown Owl.'

Brown Owl is a term used in the Brownies given to the adult leader of the group.

Brown's Baby Food

A fictional brand of baby food that is eaten by Stan and Jack in the Series Five episode 'The Nursery'.

When Stan and Jack are forced to spend their lunch break looking after babies in the depot's newly formed nursery after Olive smashes her glasses, trouble brews when the mischievous busmen become hungry. They help themselves to jars of baby food for lunch with Jack dining on mixed homogenised beef, mixed vegetables and gravy and he is forced to use a baby's pusher as a utensil.

Stan's choice of baby food consists of liver, chicken, spinach and bone broth with a dessert of stewed rhubarb, essence of figs and prunes for afters. However, Inspector Blake is to pay a visit to the nursery and finds that Stan and Jack have eaten food that was intended for the babies and tells them: 'Four new p's each them jars. Do you know that? You've been pinching. I've caught ya. I'm having yous two. I'm making out a complete report about this.' But first he has another problem to deal with as he is left to handle the babies in the nursery that need their nappies changing.

Bryant, Sandra

TV Role: Sandra Lumley (Series 7 Episode 1 'Olive's Divorce', Series 7 Episode 10 'What The Stars Foretell', Series Seven Episode 11 'The Allowance' and Series 7 Episode 13 'Gardening Time')
Film Role: Sandra (Holiday On The Buses)

Born in Edgware, London in 1945, Sandra Bryant's career as an actress saw her with a number of roles in films and on television. In 1959 her film career began with an uncredited role in the hit comedy film Carry On Teacher. She was later to have credits in Wuthering Heights, She'll Follow You Anywhere and Holiday On The Buses. On television she was much more active. Roles in hit dramas included Z Cars, Emergency-Ward 10, Doctor Who, Special Branch and Coronation Street. She also made appearances in the hit 1970s sitcoms On The Buses, Whatever Happened To The Likely Lads, The Fenn Street Gang and Not On Your Nellie. Her career spanned well over twenty years in which time she worked with a host of great actors and actresses prior to the end of her career in the early 1980s.

Brylcreem

Brylcreem is a hair-styling product which Stan applies to his hair when dating Sally in the Series Three episode 'Going Steady'.

Stan can't break the habit of using brylcreem and is chastised for it by Sally. She tells him: 'You've got some of that brylcreem on your hair. You promised you wouldn't. You look much less common with your hair all wind-swept.'

Brylcreem was first created in 1928 by the now defunct UK company County Chemicals and was made from a mix of water, mineral oil and beeswax in a cream-line substance. It is still used around the world as a hair-styling product well over eighty years after its invention.

BSA M21

License Plate: JVB 54

The type of motorcycle and combination that Arthur buys second-hand and is to be seen for the first time in the Series Two episode 'The Used Combination'. Incidentally, the same vehicle was used in an episode of the hit sitcom Dad's Army.

The motorcycle was a BSA M21 manufactured in Small Heath, Birmingham by the British Small Arms Company. The sidecar seen in On The Buses is unlikely to have been the one that originally came with the motorcycle. The BSA M21 used is believed to have been built post-Second World War between 1945 and 1948. Its engine consisted of a single cylinder and 591cc that produced 15bhp (brake horse power) with a four-speed gearbox. The top speed of the motorcycle with sidecar attached was approximately 55mph (miles per hour).

BSA was, at one time, the largest motorcycle manufacturer in the world but in the space of a decade the company suffered a spectacular fall from grace. In 1972 they went into bankruptcy and ceased manufacturing motorbikes despite a forced merger with rival company Norton Villiers. The company's collapse was largely due to increased competition from the mid-1960s with a sudden influx onto the European market of cheaper Japanese-manufactured motorbikes in the form of Honda, Suzuki and Yamaha. Sales dropped at BSA with losses growing and there was to be no reversing of the trend.

BSA has survived to this day as an operating company and today supplies spare parts for the many vintage BSA models still roadworthy today as well as manufacturing a limited number of retro-design motorbikes.

Bubonic Plague

A disease referred to by Arthur when Stan takes extreme precautions to stop himself catching the flu from Arthur, Olive and his mother in the Series Five episode 'The Epidemic'.

Stan is the only member of the family to avoid catching the flu and is left to look after the invalids by cooking, washing up and waiting on them hand and foot. He is desperate to avoid the flu as overtime for fit bus drivers is plentiful and he has a potential date lined up with a clippie. The lengths he goes to in an attempt to avoid the flu sees him wear rubber gloves, spray disinfectant on a cloth and covering his mouth with it before collecting dishes from Arthur who is gobsmacked. He says: 'My dear good man we have got the flu not the bubonic plague.' Stan refuses to take any chances though as he places the dishes into a basinful of water and disinfectant and when handling dirty laundry from the flu victim he sprays the clothes with more disinfectant and lifts them with tongs whilst wearing rubber gloves.

The bubonic plague is the disease behind the Black Death that swept through Europe in the fourteenth century wiping out half the continent's population. It resurfaced many times, most notably in the seventeenth century with what become known as The Great Plague of London which killed hundreds of thousands of people. The disease was spread by fleas from rodents passing infection onto humans. Without treatment bubonic plague proves fatal but today antibiotics are effective in treating the disease.

Bullseyes

A hard-boiled sweet referred to in the Series Six episode 'No Smoke Without Fire'.

When Arthur indulges in betting Stan that he won't be able to give up smoking Arthur is confident he can kick the habit and believes he has the answer to curbing the craving for a cigarette. He tells Olive: 'By the way sunshine I think you'll find some bullseyes in my raincoat pocket.'

Bullseyes are hard-boiled sweets with black and white stripes and taste of peppermint.

Bunter, Bessie

This is a name that Olive is called in the Series Seven episode 'Friends In High Places'.

Mrs Webb's canteen cooking is under attack as it is so bad that even Olive refuses to eat the food served up. The angry cook hears the complaints and says: 'Oh Bessie Bunter's reared her ugly mush has she?'

Bessie Bunter was a fictional character that was created in 1919 by writer Charles Hamilton and appeared in the Greyfriars School stories. She was the sister of the more famous Billy Bunter and shared similar traits to Olive having a large appetite, being obese and bespectacled.

Burntwood

The name of a another depot also run by the Luxton and District Bus Company which is referred to in the Series Seven episode 'The Poster'.

The Burntwood bus depot puts forward a candidate called McGregor for the promotional poster contest. It also supplies one of the judges that sit on the panel for the contest who is also a chief inspector at the Burntwood depot.

Burrows, Rosemary

Wardrobe Supervisor (On The Buses)

Rosemary Burrows carved out a hugely impressive career in the film industry that was to see her work in the wardrobe departments and in costumes in many classic films.

She was to begin her career in the late 1950s at Hammer Films and was to work on that company's best remembered films including The Revenge Of Frankenstein, The Phantom Of The Opera, Captain Clegg, The Nanny, Dracula: Prince Of Darkness, The Plague Of The Zombies, Quatermass And The Pit, The Devil Rides Out, Frankenstein Must Be Destroyed, On The Buses, Dr Jekyll And Sister Hyde and Hands Of The Ripper to name but a few. From the mid-1970s she moved on from Hammer to work on a range of films across the genres which had varying success. The most notable credits were At The Earth's Core, The Spy Who Loved Me, Death On The Nile and into the 1980s further credits in Krull, A Passage To India and Willow amongst others. The latter half of her career was to see her work on more hit films such as Shining Through, Immortal Beloved, Lost In Space, Gladiator, 102 Dalmatians, Harry Potter And The Philosopher's Stone, Master And Commander: The Far Side Of The World, The Hitchhikers Guide To The Galaxy and her final project in the industry V For Vendetta.

Burrows retired in the mid-2000s after almost fifty years in the industry to end a highly impressive career.

Bus Driver, The

Played by Philip Dunbar

This is a bearded busman who discusses with Stan and Jack in the depot in the Series Six episode 'Bye Bye Blakey'.

When the inspector is mistakenly believed to be dying, Stan and Jack discuss his demise with another bus driver who says coldly: 'Well I'm not surprised. I always said he was a sick man.' He is not impressed when Stan and Jack announce they are to have a whip-round to buy Inspector Blake a present and pours scorn on the idea saying: 'Well he's not going to be around long enough to enjoy it is he?' He also is to laugh at some of Jack's suggestions for the present. Later, the bus driver who remains unnamed attends the presentation of the gift – a basketful of fruit and applauds the arrival of Blakey but when it becomes clear the inspector is fit and well he joins in with his colleagues in pelting Blakey with the fruit.

Bus Driver

Played by Harry Fielder

This is a long-haired bus driver seen joining in a prank to embarrass Inspector Blake in the film Mutiny On The Buses.

He, along with his colleagues, strips down to his bare essentials in the depot when they take Inspector Blake at his word when they wear nothing but their uniforms as supplied by the company. Later, during a darts match between the busmen and management he acts as the scorekeeper wearing a bright floral shirt. The darts match ends up in a fight between Olive and Nymphy Norah and the bus driver can be seen keeping his distance from the fight cowering in the background.

Bus Driver's Stomach

A fictional medical complaint suffered by bus drivers and is referred to in depth in the Series One episode 'Bus Driver's Stomach'.

Stan suffers acute stomach pains which he says is an occupational hazard caused by sitting over the bus engine all day coupled with the stress and strain of the job and calls it bus driver's stomach. Arthur scoffs at this and blames Stan's unhealthy diet of greasy foods and quotes from a book that he runs the risk of death and this chilling warning is enough to see Mrs Butler put her son on a diet.

At the depot, Jack offers his advice for Stan telling him if he has got a pain then feed it. He feels the problem is caused by his posture with his vertebra pressing against his gastric nerve. Jack suggests that fellow busman Bert, who is also a physiotherapist for the depot's football team, tries some physiotherapy on Stan. It turns out to be a painful experience for him and when Inspector Blake announces that all bus drivers are to undergo medicals with those failing to pass being transferred to other duties Stan has problems.

His mother shows her cunning side when she arranges for the family doctor to visit the house to examine Stan without his knowledge. Doctor Clark diagnoses him as having an acute inflammation of the stomach and duodenum and places him on a strict diet of milk and slops. Also Mrs Butler gets a rubber ring from the chemist for Stan to sit on as he drives his bus in a bid to stop the vibrations from the engine upsetting his stomach. The medical leaves Stan nervous with his job hanging in the balance but to his relief he is to pass and he can continue as a bus driver.

Buses – The Mechanical Stars of On The Buses

Although Reg Varney, Bob Grant, Stephen Lewis, Anna Karen, Doris Hare and Michael Robbins were the big stars of On The Buses, the buses themselves were stars in their own right. Before the series went into production a fleet of buses had to be secured for filming and when London Transport refused the use of their fleet comprising largely of Routemasters at that time the producers had to look elsewhere. The Eastern National Omnibus Company were approached and were very co-operative and offered the use of their fleet of buses and depot in Lordship Lane, Wood Green in North London for filming. Their fleet consisted of Bristol Lodekka buses which were to be used throughout the entire seven series of On The Buses on the small screen.

By the time a spin-off film was lined-up On The Buses had become a massive television hit and London Transport were keen to be involved offering the use of their skidpan at Chiswick, London and their buses. A Routemaster is taken for a spin in more ways than one in the first spin-off film but it was chiefly Eastern National's Bristol KSW buses that were used and repainted red for the fictional Town and District livery.

A number of other buses and coaches were randomly seen in On The Buses on both the small and big screen. The details of each of these buses and coaches can be found in the following section.

Bristol Lodekka FLF (Flat-floor, Long, Forward entrance)

The Eastern National Omnibus Company was to supply a number of their Bristol Lodekka FLF's which were to feature in all seven series of On The Buses.

They were built in Bristol, England by the Bristol Commercial Vehicles Ltd. Company. Bristol Lodekkas were manufactured from 1949 to 1968 and the bodywork for the double-deckers was built separately by Eastern Coach Works in Lowestoft. The buses which were used in the hit sitcom were largely fitted with Gardner diesel engines. The six cylinder power unit produced 10,225cc and enabled a top speed of just over fifty miles per hour and was fitted in the front of the bus. It also boasted a semi-automatic transmission. With a total seating capacity of seventy the double decker stood at a height of thirteen feet six inches which was lower than other double decker models of the time, hence its given name of Lodekka.

The Bristol Lodekka FLF's were highly popular in the late 1960s and early 1970s but with the arrival on the streets of newer one man operated buses the writing was on the wall for the Lodekka. From the late 1970s to the early 1980s they were to be gradually phased out and put to other uses such as being used to train learner bus drivers. Today a number of Bristol Lodekka FLF's have been preserved by bus enthusiasts and many are seen at bus rallies, some are proud exhibits in transport museums across the UK and a handful have gone further afield around the world to be used in all kinds of novel ways. Of all the Bristol Lodekka FLF's used the most commonly seen was license-plated AEV 811F and was to appear in over twenty episodes of On The Buses.

The Bristol Lodekka (pictured over) is almost identical to those used in the filming of episodes of On The Buses. The bus design was ideal for filming the TV series according to producer Stuart Allen as the front loading doors as opposed to the then more common rear loading doors meant that Stan had shorter distance to travel from his driver's cab to the doors to indulge in the much-loved rapport with Jack aboard the bus. Built in 1966 and fitted with a six cylinder Gardner engine, the bus was finally retired from service in the 1970s and was all set to become a mobile bar in the Netherlands in the late 1980s when David Sheppard Senior and Junior, as fans of On The Buses, purchased the bus and set about a labour of love restoring the bus to its present condition.

In 2006 the bus featured in an ITV interview with Reg Varney and as a passenger aboard the bus in Exmouth, Devon he reminisced and answered questions about the hit sitcom. Sadly, Reg passed away almost three years later so it is virtually certain this would have been his final ever trip aboard a Lodekka. The bus also made the long trip up from Devon in 2010 to make an appearance at the Back On The Buses event in Borehamwood, Hertfordshire. The bus remains in pristine condition lovingly cared for by father and son of the Sheppard family and is the pride of their vintage bus collection.

Stuart Allen, Anna Karen and an in character David Sheppard Jnr poses in front of the restored Bristol Lodekka FLF at the 2010 Back On The Buses event.

London Bedford VAS/Plaxton

Presumably supplied by the Eastern National Omnibus Company, a London Bedford VAS/Plaxton coach was to be seen in the Series Two episode 'Bon Voyage'. The coach is used to transport employees of the Luxton and District Bus Company to the airport as their works holiday to Spain gets underway.

The small coach was built in Luton, England by Bedford (a subsidiary of Vauxhall Motors) in 1965. Bodywork for the coach was built by Plaxton in Scarborough, England and the coach itself was powered by a 3520cc engine and ran on diesel oil. This particular model was rare and larger seating capacities and more amenities aboard coaches was in demand and so this model had design changes made. The coach used in On The Buses is believed to have remained in service until 1972 and is now preserved and out of service in Scotland.

Leyland PD2/RTL 1557

An out of service ex-London Transport Leyland PD2 bus can be seen in the Series Six episode 'No Smoke Without Fire'. Despite the bus being in poor condition, Stan is ordered by Inspector Blake to take out the bus with Jack to train two clippies. The vehicle is to meet a sad end as a discarded cigarette end in an on-board used ticket bin sets the bus alight and it is soon left a burnt out shell. Logic dictates that the Leyland PD2 was destined to be scrapped and so was able to be used in the spectacular blaze scene.

The Leyland PD2 was built by Leyland Motors near Preston, England in 1954. The bodywork on the bus used in the episode was built by Park Royal in West London. Fitted with a Leyland six cylinder 9.8 litre diesel engine it came equipped with a four speed synchromesh gearbox. The bus was fourteen feet six inches high and had a seating capacity of fifty six (twenty six on the lower and thirty on the upper deck).

The final Leyland PD2's were built at the end of the 1950s and the last PD2 was withdrawn from service in 1968 by London Transport. In general the vehicle was deemed noisier than alternative models and more strenuous to drive. After being withdrawn from service some PD2's were retained and used to train drivers or transport staff up until the early 1970s whilst others were sold abroad or ended up with independent bus companies in the UK.

The particular bus used in 'No Smoke Without Fire' was numbered RTL 1557 with licence plate of OLD 666. It was no stranger to television appearances as, in its red London Transport livery it can be seen in episodes of The Avengers and The Monty Python Show.

Bristol RESH/Duple Commander IV

A coach supplied by Eastern National and seen in the Series Six episode 'Private Hire' is a Bristol RESH/Duple Commander IV. Stan and Jack are in desperate need of money and aim to use a coach in the depot to take pensioners out on an outing at a cost of course.

The Bristol RESH was an extremely rare model with only eleven being built by Bristol Commercial Vehicles in 1968. Its bodywork was built by Duple in Blackpool, England – a company who manufactured coach and bus bodywork from 1919 until its demise in 1989. The coach was fitted with a six cylinder Gardner diesel engine and had a seating capacity of thirty six. In 1971 the coach was withdrawn from service a few months prior to it being seen in 'Private Hire'. Sadly, the coach has since been scrapped.

Leyland Atlantean/Park Royal

A driver-only operated bus that was part of the London Country fleet at the time, which featured in the Series Seven episode 'The Poster'. Stan can be seen driving the bus, proudly admiring a promotional poster with his photo adorning it which is being put up by the roadside. Distracted he is to crash his bus into a garden and lands in trouble.

The Leyland Atlantean was a pioneering bus of its time as it was fitted with a rear-mounted engine and with its front entrance it enabled the introduction of driver operated only buses. This model was built in 1972 and fitted with a Leyland engine and the bodywork was manufactured by Park Royal. It was also to have a number of safety features installed including an alarm system to prevent the engine over-heating, introduction of a new safety braking system as well as added protection to the steering and brake controls in the event of a serious head-on collision.

The particular bus seen in 'The Poster', licence plated JPL 124K and fleet number AN64, was to remain in service with London Country until the early 1980s. It was transferred to the North Western Bus Company operating on routes in Lancashire until the early 1990s when it was withdrawn from service after almost twenty years of service in London and Lancashire.

AEC S-type

The oldest bus to be used in On The Buses belonged to the long defunct London General Omnibus Company that became part of the London Underground and ceased operating as a single company in 1933. The bus seen in the Series Seven episode 'On The Omnibuses' was an AEC S-type and featured heavily in Stan's dream about life as a busman many years earlier.

The AEC S-type was built by the Associated Equipment Company Limited in Walthamstow, East London in 1922. It was an open top double decker bus which had a seating capacity of fifty four and although the open top made it unpopular in the winter its increased seating capacity compared to other models of the time meant cheaper fares. Seats were uncomfortable being no more than wooden benches and the bus was powered by a four cylinder, 5.1 litre petrol engine producing thirty five horse power with a three speed gearbox and a fully manual brake system.

The AEC S-type licence-plated XL 8962 with fleet number S454 was in service with the London General Omnibus Company from 1922 to 1931. Aside from its appearance in On The Buses it also appeared in an episode of the classic costume drama Upstairs Downstairs and is now fully preserved under private ownership and can occasionally be seen in transport museums and bus rallies.

Bristol KSW

The three spin-off films were to use green-liveried Eastern National buses sprayed red for the fictional Town and District Bus Company's fleet with older stock of buses used in the form of Bristol KSW's. The films would demand more rigorous and dangerous stunts from the buses and so it is probable that the Bristol KSW's, built in 1952 and amidst being removed from public service at the time the first spin-off film went into production, were deemed more dispensable than the Bristol Lodekka's made famous in the television series.

Bristol KSW's were manufactured by the Bristol Tramways And Carriage Company (later to become Bristol Commercial Vehicles) with the bodywork built by Eastern Coach Works Limited in Lowestoft. Fitted with a seven litre Gardner diesel engine, the bus was twenty seven feet long with a rear entrance. In total there were 614 KSW's built between 1951 and 1957.

Ironically, the Bristol KSW's were to be withdrawn from service in the late 1960s and early 1970s to be replaced by Bristol Lodekkas. Today a small number of KSW's have been preserved and can be seen at bus rallies.

Leyland Atlantean/Metro Cammell

The bus liveried in a Union Jack and seen going on a trial run to Winsor Safari Park in the second spin-off film Mutiny On The Buses was a Leyland Atlantean. It was to be seen in the film being boarded by a lion and later by chimpanzees.

This particular Leyland Atlantean was built in 1960 near Preston, England and had its bodywork manufactured by Metro Cammell in Birmingham, England. With a rear-fitted Leyland 9.8 litre engine it also came supplied with a semi-automatic gearbox and had a seating capacity of sixty four.

The bus used in Mutiny On The Buses served as a sightseeing tour bus on the streets of London for the City Coach Line Company and is thought to explain the Union Jack livery seen in the film. In 1973 it was then exported to Hong Kong where it served with the Kowloon Motor Bus Company until it was withdrawn from service in 1976.

Bristol Lodekka LD6G

An open top bus that was to feature heavily in the final spin-off film Holiday On The Buses as the holiday camp bus driven by Stan was supplied by Crosville Motor Services. The Bristol Lodekka LD can be seen throughout the film and ends it bogged down in wet sand and via special effects is last seen under twelve feet of water in the Irish Sea.

The Bristol Lodekka of the LD series was built in 1956 by Bristol Commercial Vehicles in Bristol. The Eastern Coach Works Limited company built the bodywork. The bus was front-fitted with a six cylinder, 8.4 litre Gardner engine, a five speed gearbox and had a top speed of fifty two miles per hour. It was a convertible bus which had a removable roof enabling open top summer operation with a seating capacity of sixty and a rear entrance onto the bus.

The bus seen in Holiday On The Buses was licence-plated XFM 229 and was part of the Crosville Motor Services fleet serving North Wales where Holiday On The Buses was filmed. It went into service in 1956 and was finally withdrawn in the mid-1980s. Sadly, it is believed that the bus has since been scrapped.

Bush, Maurice

Role: Basher (Series 6 Episode 3 'Private Hire')

Maurice Bush was born in 1930 and was to have a long career as an actor and his stocky build was to often see him in roles as a tough character in films or on television.

His first acting roles came on the big screen in the early 1950s. His film credits came most notably in Laughing Annie, The Frightened City, The Creeping Flesh and Trial By Combat with an uncredited role also coming in the smash hit 1971 film A Clockwork Orange.

On television he would have drama roles in hit series such as Budgie, Dixon Of Dock Green, Doctor Who, New Scotland Yard, Target and Inspector Morse amongst others. He was to appear in many hit sitcoms of the 1960s and 70s such as Doctor In The House, Hark At Barker, The Fenn Street Gang, On The Buses Father Dear Father and Love Thy Neighbour.

After a lengthy career as an actor spanning five decades, sadly Maurice Bush passed away in 1999 at the age of sixty nine.

Busman

Played by Keith Norrish

A busman, in his thirties, comes looking for his Christmas Club money in the Series Five episode 'The New Telly'.

He walks up to Inspector Blake who is sat behind a desk in the depot dishing out the company's Christmas Club money. 'Come on Blakey let's have it,' he says as he rubs his hands together in anticipation. Jack warns him that the inspector is making some very crafty deductions and when Stan weighs in with a joke the fed-up Blakey tells everyone to clear off and the busman makes his way away.

Busman

Played by Kenneth Waller

An ageing busman wearing a paper Christmas hat that is seen in the Series Five episode called 'Boxing Day Social'.

The out-of-uniform busman is to make an announcement at the Boxing Day Social event in the depot's canteen during a break in the music. He says: 'Ladies and gentlemen, inspectors and other layabouts take your partners for another dance.' As the music starts up the busman blends into the crowd and is not seen again.

Busman's Code

A form of phonetic alphabet that Stan is forced to learn when the Luxton and District Bus Company decides to install a radio control system into every bus in the Series Three episode 'Radio Control'.

The code used for the new radio control system is known as 'The Busman's Code' and uses a number of entries from various other factual phonetic alphabets used by transport and armed forces. This mixture of terms coupled with invented entries was done purely to maximise the comedic effect. The Busman's Code is listed below and alongside is the phonetic alphabet or source that the entry stems from.

Letter Code For Radio Controlled Buses

A Able – British Forces 1952

B Bertie – German Phonetic Alphabet

C Charlie – International Aviation, British Forces 1952 and RAF 1924-56

D Delta – International Aviation

E Easy – British Forces 1952

F Freddy – RAF 1924-43

G Georgie (George was more commonly used) – British Forces 1952 and RAF 1924-56

H Hotel – International Aviation

I Idle – A fictional entry

J Juliette – International Aviation

K Katie – A fictional entry

L Love – British Forces 1952 and RAF 1942-56

M Mother – RAF 1942-43

N November – International Aviation

O Oscar – International Aviation

P Peter – British Forces 1952 and RAF 1942-56

Q Queenie (Queen was more commonly used) – British Forces and RAF 1924-56

R Romeo – International Aviation

S Sugar – British Forces 1952

T Tango – International Aviation

U Uncle – RAF 1924-56

V Victor – International Aviation, British Forces 1952 and RAF 1924-56

W William – British Forces 1952 and RAF 1924-56

X X-Ray – International Aviation, British Forces 1952 and RAF 1924-56

Y Yoyo – A fictional entry

Z Zulu – International Aviation

Busman's Gazette

A fictional magazine mentioned by Inspector Blake in the Series Two episode 'Bon Voyage'.

Stan and Jack have an instant camera at the depot which they tell the inspector they will be taking on the works holiday in a ploy to attract the women. They intend to pretend to be professional photographers conning the women into thinking their pictures will appear on magazine covers. Inspector Blake jokes: 'Which one? The Busman's Gazette?'

Busman's Grab

A term, thought to be based on the wrestling hold called the Boston crab, describing a hold Stan has on a clippie called Iris in the Series One episode 'The Darts Match'.

The inspector enters the canteen as Stan has Iris in a clinch as she struggles to get her darts back from him. Jack watches on and tells the bemused Inspector Blake that Stan is practising all-in-wrestling to which Blakey says: 'What's that? The busman's grab is it?' Stan, amidst laughter, says: 'No. The clippies clutch.'

Busmen's Ball

An annual social event held in the depot's canteen and the event features heavily in the Series Five episode of the same name. It is also referred to in the Series Seven episode 'The Ticket Machine'.

The Busmen's Ball, which Inspector Blake calls a 'dinner dance', sees the busmen get their choice of cabaret in the form of Sandra The Scandinavian Stripper for the event. It is the cabaret that encourages Arthur to change his mind and attends with Olive who is bedecked in a dress she has made especially for the event and Mrs Butler in tow.

It turns out to be a troubled event and Olive is to have her dress ripped with drinks spilt over it when the striptease act reaches its finale. Busmen scramble to catch Sandra's underwear and Olive is caught in the stampede and she is left to exit the event in tears, Stan though, is a little happier as he caught the underwear which means he gets the chance to meet Sandra afterwards to return her underwear to her. Later, in the episode called 'The Ticket Machine', Inspector Blake visits the Butler house in an attempt to sell tickets for the Busmen's Ball for fifty pence to Mrs Butler. When Stan mistakenly thinks the inspector is referring to tickets from a stolen ticket machine which he has in his possession he tells Blakey he only took it to stop his family from the shame of being penniless. Unaware of Stan's misunderstanding Blakey barks: 'Butler I know the Busmen's Ball is not exactly the Royal Garden Party but I fail to see how it could shame your family.'

Busmen's Benevolent Fund

A fictional charity for employees of the Luxton and District Bus Company which is referred to in a poster at the depot in the Series Five episode 'The Busmen's Ball'.

The Busmen's Benevolent Fund is a charity that is to benefit from proceeds gained at the Busmen's Ball social event.

Busmen's Perks

A term used by Jack as he encourages Stan to use paint from the depot's stores to decorate Arthur and Olive's bedroom in a Series Three episode of the same name.

Jack tells Stan that having access to the paint is no more than busmen's perks of the job pointing out that even the depot manager Mr Adams uses the paint on the company's executive car. The unsure driver takes the plunge and obtains hi-gloss paint, brushes, spirits and hardener from Nobby in the maintenance department all for the cost of two pints of bitter. Getting the paint and accessories out of the depot without Inspector Blake finding out proves difficult and is an uncomfortable experience for Stan. He smuggles the paint onto his bus by hiding the tins under a layer of sand in the depot's fire buckets, with the paintbrush hidden down the back of his trousers with the bristles causing him great irritation. Worse is to follow when a bottle of spirits gets smashed in his drivers cab with the fumes forcing him out of the confined space. Stan does succeed in smuggling everything out of the depot but Jack's claim that Stan was entitled to the paint as busmen's perks prove unfounded as the management are to carry out a spot-check of stock levels in the maintenance stores of the depot. To avoid the two tins being missed Stan is forced to pay five pounds to Nobby to replace the paint which, by this time, he has used.

Butch Cassidy and the Sundance Kid

Stan calls the first two female bus drivers to arrive at the Town and District Bus Company this name when he sees them for the first time in the film On The Buses.

Inspector Blake takes great pleasure in telling Stan he won't be doing his extra late shift anymore as the first two women drivers have arrived. Ruby and Vera are introduced and sarcastically Stan says: 'Blimey, Butch Cassidy and the Sundance Kid'.

Butch Cassidy and the Sundance Kid was a blockbuster film made in 1969 and would go on to win four Oscars in 1970. The film told the story of two bank robbers in the Wild West in the 1890s. Wanted for armed robbery the two men are hunted down by a posse and the film was to star Paul Newman and Robert Redford.

Butler, Albert

An unseen character often referred to who was married to Mabel Butler and was the father of Stan and Olive.

Albert Butler, with his balding head, but not as bald as Arthur according to Mrs Butler, had a good sense of humour which he passed onto his son Stan. A virile man, he wore false teeth but he only put those in when he ate his meals. When courting Mabel he bought a motorcycle combination similar to that owned later by Arthur. He and his wife would often both squeeze into the sidecar at the same time for heavy petting sessions. Their wedding hardly sounded romantic as Mrs Butler recalls that Albert turned up at the altar for their wedding smelling of carbolic soap as he had come to the wedding straight from the public baths. Married life was tough during the Second World War with Albert and Mabel working in the same munitions factory but they hardly saw each other as he was on night duty for five years. The only real time they spent together was in the air raid shelter where they slept on a camp bed as German bombers attacked. It is around these dark days of the war that Olive was conceived. Soon afterwards Albert was to go into active service in the army. Albert and Mabel were to share a marital double bed for twenty nine years after beginning married life sharing a three-foot wide single bed. Mabel firmly believes that married couples should always have double beds and passes this advice on to Olive and Arthur.

Albert is to have passed away in 1953 with the cause of death not known.

Butler, Mabel Ethel

Played by Cicely Courtneidge and Doris Hare

She is the mother of Stan and Olive who became a widow in 1953 when her husband Albert passed away. Mabel has a sister called Maud who she is close to and they frequently visit each other even though they live around twenty miles apart. Her interests include nights out at bingo, the cinema and knitting and is renowned for her great cooking.

Mabel Ethel Butler is more commonly referred to as mum or Mrs Butler. She is old-fashioned and has strict house rules that constantly thwart her son's efforts to court his girlfriends in the house. Her meddling and attitude destroys much of her son's relationships with her over-bearing manner coupled with smothering motherly love she refuses Stan the chance to pursue a serious love life. However, she depends on Stan to, at times, single-handedly financially support the family and so whenever he displayed an urge to leave home to further his personal life and career Mabel stands in his way using various methods to ensure he changes his mind.

She is also fiercely protective of her two children and is always ready to leap to their defence should they be criticised or insulted as they regularly are by son-in-law Arthur and Inspector Blake. Mabel also makes a point of not getting involved in the marital affairs of Olive and Arthur telling the couple who live in her house that she never interferes in a happy marriage.

Mabel spent the early part of her working life employed in a munitions factory before becoming a housewife. She was to retire but as a pensioner she did return to work briefly as canteen cook at the Luxton and District's bus depot on two occasions.

Although a widow for many years Mabel did still have isolated romances in her life. A relationship with bus conductor Wilf Phillips is to end in heartbreak for her as she discovers he is already married and seemed to be only interested in her assets. She also pursues Inspector Blake when he moves into her house as a lodger hoping briefly to marry the hapless inspector as her tea leaves ordain but romance is not what her new lodger is after. Mabel is also to have a brief relationship with an old flame who is the area manager at the bus depot. Gerald Simpson is a widow who also worked in the munitions factory with her in the Second World War and is to meet her many years later when he employs her as a canteen cook. He is soon wining and dining Mabel for a few weeks until he retires from his post and moves away from Luxton. In the final spin-off film Holiday On The Buses, Mabel is to have a holiday romance with an elderly, flirtatious Irishman called Bert Thompson who is also a widow. The pair are to date whilst at the holiday camp and although the romance is curtailed by the end of the holiday Bert promises to keep in touch.

Butler, Maharishi

This is a name given to Stan by Inspector Blake in the Series Two episode 'Bon Voyage'.

When Stan returns to the bus depot wearing no trousers after having his uniform stolen whilst sunbathing in the cemetery at the Cemetery Gates he lands himself in trouble. He clambers out of his driver's cab at the depot trouser less leaving a waiting Inspector Blake shocked. Stan is left open to ridicule when Jack tries to explain away the incident by claiming Stan is a guru. 'Maharishi Butler,' laughs the inspector. 'I suppose he sits in the cab up there contemplating his navel at the traffic lights waiting for it to go from red to green,' adds Blakey revelling at the chance to mock Stan.

When this episode was written there was a famed guru called Maharishi Mahesh Yogi who had come to prominence in 1968 when he was to become involved with the legendary pop band The Beatles, becoming their guru hence the term used by the inspector in 'Bon Voyage'. Maharishi Mahesh Yogi was to develop the technique called Transcendental Meditation and he led a full life before passing away in 2008 at the age of ninety four.

Butler, Stan

Played by Reg Varney

Stan Butler is a happy-go-lucky bus driver who frequently flouts the rules at work and although he has an eye for the women he is still a bachelor living at home as he approaches his forties. He is often expected to put his family first before his personal life by his over-bearing mother and it hinders any hopes he has of a lasting romance.

Stan Butler is known to his friends and family as Stan but referred to as Butler by Inspector Blake at the bus depot. He lives at home with his mother Mabel, his sister Olive and brother-in-law Arthur which is far from ideal. His mother often scuppers his relationships with her interfering mannerisms but through it all he remains very close and loyal to his mother. He is always quick to have a joke at his younger sister Olive's expense mocking her cooking, weight, appearance and her marriage amongst other things but in times of stress and alarm he does offer his support and love. His relationship with Arthur is largely bitter as he is offended by Arthur's know-it-all attitude, his personal insults, meanness and tendency to constantly meddle in his love life.

Stan was to be an employee of the Luxton and District Bus Company for a number of years where he began as a conductor before progressing on to become a bus driver. A very brief spell as assistant inspector ends abruptly and makes him unpopular with his colleagues but is soon happy to return to his role as bus driver. A cheery and popular member of staff at the bus depot, Stan's best friend is his conductor Jack Harper and both like to make Inspector Blake's life a misery with their antics. Jack has an annoying trait of pinching a lot of Stan's girlfriends but as shop steward he often uses his cunning to save Stan from the sack. There is one person at the depot that Stan doesn't get on with. Inspector Blake will not rest until he manages to sack Stan who he sees as unpunctual, troublesome and a constant thorn in his side. However, in 1973 Stan quits his job at the Luxton and District Bus Company for financial reasons and leaves home moving to the Midlands to work in a car factory.

Even though he is a bachelor nearing his forties he can boast a full love-life but most of his relationships fail to develop further than one night stands. The closest he comes to marriage is when he becomes engaged to clippie Sally Ferguson who happens to be the inspector's niece. The engagement though ends as Sally's upper class views and attitude doesn't go down well with Stan or his family. He later has an on-off relationship with another clippie called Doreen Smith which is destined to fail as she is left frustrated by Stan's inability to stand up to his mother.

In the spin-off films Stan is a bus driver for the Town and District Bus Company. He is to work alongside Jack and Inspector Blake for fourteen years in which time he briefly becomes the company's inaugural tour bus driver but a disastrous trial run to Windsor Safari Park brings an end to that lucrative position. He and Jack are finally sacked a few months later after crashing a bus writing it off and injuring the depot manager and damaging his car. After a few weeks of unemployment he lands a job driving a tour bus in a holiday camp but this is destined to last only a few weeks. Stan and Jack are sacked when they allow the tour bus to be submerged in the sea after a romantic double date with a pair of holidaymakers goes wrong. From another spell of unemployment Stan emerges to work in the demolition trade.

Stan's love-life on the big screen offers no marriage but more short relationships with clippie Sally, a canteen cook called Bridget, a passionate Italian holiday camp waitress called Maria and Sandra a holiday camp employee. In the second spin-off film Mutiny On The Buses, Stan does engage clippie Susy and they plan to rent a flat and get married. Financial problems brought on by family hardships mean Stan cannot afford to rent a flat and Susy grows impatient and fed-up waiting she calls off the engagement.

Ultimately, on the small or big screen, Stan is always left frustrated with his love-life but remains a cheery disposition. His hobbies and interests in life are darts, nights out with Jack and accompanying his mother to bingo. Stan fights for personal independence which he never achieves but remains devoted to his mother throughout.

Butler House, The

The Butler house is home to Mrs Butler, Stan, Olive and Arthur in the television series.

It has three bedrooms, a dining room, small kitchen and the front room downstairs is often referred to as the parlour with the house being owned by Mrs Butler. Upstairs are the bedrooms and a bathroom with a separate toilet whilst there is a small back garden and an even smaller front garden. The house is seen as a chance to make money by Mabel's boyfriend Wilf Phillips who suggests that once the family had left home she could earn a lot of money renting out the rooms, but these plans fail to materialise. However, the house is spacious enough for the Butlers to periodically take in lodgers though it is always Stan who has to give up his bedroom to accommodate them.

Butler House's Back Garden, The

The back garden at the Butler house is largely neglected but features heavily in the Series Seven episode 'Gardening Time'.
The Butlers and Rudges were certainly no gardeners and only ventured into the back garden to visit its shed where Arthur often worked on his motorbike. However, when Inspector Blake moves into the house as a lodger and enters the depot flower and vegetable competition at the bus depot he sets about giving the back garden a makeover but is it to have his work cut out as the garden resembles a rubbish tip. It is littered with a mattress, an old mangle, a rusty cylinder, a broken bicycle and a deckchair amongst other things.

The inspector is determined to transform the garden as his next door neighbour and rival in the competition is none other than Jack Harper who is confident of winning the contest himself. He sets about removing weeds from the garden after removing the rubbish and he is later to plant pansies, cabbage plants, spring greens, petunias and hydrangeas. On completing the makeover Inspector Blake proudly describes his back garden as 'a triumph of the gardener's art' to Jack.

Inspector Blake and Jack face an anxious wait to see who will prevail winning the competition and the bragging rights.

Bux, Ishaq

TV Role: Ahmed (Series 3 Episode 6 'The Snake')

Born in Kanpur, India in 1917, Ishaq Bux was to move to the United Kingdom and fashion himself an impressive career as an actor with numerous credits in both film and television.

His credits began as he entered his forties when he appeared on the BBC television drama English Family Robinson in 1957. Other drama roles on the small screen were to follow most notably in The Indian Tales Of Rudyard Kipling, Dixon Of Dock Green, Department S, Wicked Women, Softly Softly, Quatermass, Angels, The Jewel In The Crown, The Singing Detective and the Sherlock Holmes adventure The Sign Of Four. Bux was also to appear in a number of hit sitcoms aside from On The Buses including Oh Father, It 'Ain't Half Hot Mum, Metal Mickey and Minder.

On the big screen Bux was to appear in a string of films now widely regarded as classics and these were The Rocky Horror Picture Show, Raiders Of The Lost Ark, Octopussy and A Passage To India. Other film roles included parts in Nine Hours To Rama, Man In The Middle, Inadmissible Evidence, The Raging Moon, The Horsemen, The Vault Of Horror and The Missionary.

Sadly, in 2000, Ishaq Bux was to pass away in London after a period of ill health at the age of eighty three.

Caldicot, Richard

TV Role: Doctor Clark (Series 1 Episode 4 'Bus Driver's Stomach')

Richard Caldicot, born in London, England in 1908, was to have a prolific career as an actor on stage, film and television.

By his early twenties, Caldicot had learnt his trade in repertory theatre and was already appearing in West End roles on stage in 1928 in Journey's End. He'd go on to have a long stage career spanning the decades with his most notable roles including Ten Nights In A Bar-Room, Running Riot, No Sex Please We're British, Babes In The Wood, My Fair Lady, The Kidders, She Stoops To Conquer and Me And My Girl. His television career saw him in varying roles across the genres. Caldicot's notable drama roles came in The History Of Mr Polly, Oliver Twist, Ghost Squad, Richard The Lionheart, Z Cars, No Hiding Place, Danger Man, The Forsyte Saga, The Prisoner, Vanity Fair, The Avengers, Department S and Randall And Hopkirk (Deceased) in the 1950s and 60s. In the second half of his career came further drama credits in hit series such as Doomwatch, Catweazle, Paul Temple, UFO, Angels, Coronation Street, Crown Court, Casualty, Bergerac and The Memoirs Of Sherlock Holmes. He also appeared in a host of comedy roles on television with the pick of those being Sykes And A…, Steptoe And Son, HMS Paradise, The Beverley Hillbillies, On The Buses, All Gas And Gaiters, Hark At Barker, Please Sir, The Goodies, The Morecambe And Wise Show, Some Mothers Do 'Ave 'Em, Fawlty Towers and Clarence.

Film credits were also plentiful and the most notable of these were in the classic Norman Wisdom film One Good Turn, Dentist On The Job, You Must Be Joking, The Spy Who Came In From The Cold, The Rise And Rise Of Michael Rimmer, Firepower and Mountains Of The Moon.

Richard Caldicot's acting career spanned over sixty years and also included a large part in the long-running smash hit BBC radio sitcom The Navy Lark. He remained active until his death in 1995 at the age of eighty seven.

Cammish, Rodney

Designer (Series 7 Episode 1 'Olive's Divorce', Series 7 Episode 2 'The Perfect Clippie', Series 7 Episode 3 'The Ticket Machine', Series 7 Episode 4 'The Poster', Series 7 Episode 7 'Goodbye Stan', Series 7 Episode 9 'The Visit', Series 7 Episode 11 'The Allowance' and Series 7 Episode 13 'Gardening Time')

Rodney Cammish was a production designer who spent the majority of his career at London Weekend Television where he was to work on the best television series that they were to produce.

From 1970 onwards his LWT credits included a number of hit sitcoms such as Doctor In The House, Please Sir, On The Buses, Doctor In Charge, The Fenn Street Gang, Bowler, Romany Jones, Maggie And Her, Yes Honestly and Mixed Blessings. He was also to work on the pick of LWT's dramas in the 1970s and 80s including New Scotland Yard, Upstairs Downstairs, Within These Walls, Enemy At The Door, The Gentle Touch, Mitch and Dempsey And Makepeace. After becoming an art director, Cammish was to leave LWT after twenty five years to work on the BBC series Murder In Mind in the early 2000s as his career began to wind down after more than thirty years in the industry.

Campbell, Gavin

Film Role: Motorcycle Cop (On The Buses)

Born in Letchworth, Hertfordshire in 1946, Gavin Campbell was to appear on television, in films and on stage as an actor before progressing on to become a presenter of television series.

He debuted in the hit BBC Police drama Softly Softly in 1968 in what would be his biggest role as an actor playing PC William Digby in more than twenty episodes. He would go on to appear in other classic British dramas such as Department S, UFO, The New Avengers and Grange Hill. Campbell will probably be best remembered for his role as co-presenter of the highly successful BBC consumer series That's Life from 1982 through until 1994.

On the big screen his film credits came in an overseas production called Nicaragua, On The Buses and the X-rated thriller The Playbirds.

He was also an accomplished stage actor appearing in a number of Royal Shakespeare Company productions in the mid-1970s. These came most notably in Richard II, Summerfolk, King John and Love's Labour's Lost.

After his involvement in That's Life, Campbell's career took a new direction as he moved into production and would run courses teaching up and coming talents in areas of public speaking and effective communication where he still works to this day as well as presenting finance programmes on the Money Channel.

Can Can

A dance that Stan mockingly says Inspector Blake is doing in the Series Two episode 'The Used Combination'.

The inspector raises his leg to demonstrate an exercise that Stan should try in an attempt to cure his supposed bout of cramp which prompts Stan to turn to Jack and say: 'God blimey he's doing the Can Can'.

The Can Can (known in France as cancan) is an energetic music hall dance that has its origins in France in the 1830s. It is a dance performed by a line usually of female dancers wearing long skirts with black stockings that lift their skirts and carry out a series of high kicks and other movements often revealing their underwear. The dance grew to become popular around the world and it developed more flamboyant moves over the years. To this day it is still performed and has featured in hit stage musicals and films.

Canteen

The canteen at the Luxton and District Bus Company's depot is to feature heavily in several episodes of On The Buses.

In the very first episode called 'The Early Shift' new shift patterns deny Stan and Jack access to the canteen facilities. It leads to the employees going on unofficial strike as they battle to regain their canteen breaks. Later, in Series One, in the episode 'The Canteen', the bus company allow the employees to take over running the canteen.

Stan is elected the first chairman of the canteen sub-committee and has the task of hiring staff as well as running the canteen. Disaster strikes as he employs a cook who cannot speak a word of English and her dishes are not at all appealing to the busmen. She is replaced by Olive and Mrs Butler but unconventional pricing sees the canteen running at such a loss that the bus company takes control of the canteen once more.

More financial issues affect the canteen in the Series Five episode 'Canteen Trouble'. The canteen is running at a loss and this is exasperated by Stan who is helping himself to stock from the larder. Inspector Blake acts quickly by bringing in a new member of staff at the canteen who he believes will not be corruptible but he is in for a shock. The new canteen cook will part with the food but it comes at a high price for Stan. For Blakey it is the last straw and he introduces an automated food dispenser in the canteen but it doesn't stop Stan from getting a free meal.

It would seem that the canteen was only to be entered into by employees of the bus company. In the Series Seven episode 'Olive's Divorce', Mrs Butler comes into the canteen to tell Stan that Olive is unwell outside and he tells her: 'Now mum I've told you to wait outside. You mustn't come into our canteen.'

In the Series Seven episode 'Hot Water' the canteen is left with no hot water after Jack removes the immersion heater from the water tank. He sees it as a chance to make money by selling it on to Inspector Blake who is in the market for an immersion heater. Later, in the same series in 'Friends In High Places' the staff threaten to strike unless the cook is dismissed. Mrs Webb is upset by the criticism and resigns and is briefly replaced by Mrs Butler.

The canteen at the Luxton and District Bus Company's depot was a multi-purpose venue as it was to play host to a range of events such as darts matches, self-defence lessons, Indian social events, keep-fit classes, the Busmen's Ball and Boxing Day Social events. It was also in the canteen that Stan is forced to take a breathalyser test by Blakey when he turns up for work drunk in the Series Three episode 'Brew It Yourself'. Stan and Jack were also to stage an impromptu fashion show in the canteen using tables as a makeshift catwalk as they mockingly model their new uniforms in the Series Three episode 'The New Uniforms'.

The canteen at the depot of the Town and District Bus Company was beset by similar problems in the spin-off films. A staff shortage crisis force the canteen to offer only cold food and an automated food dispenser is installed. Olive is to become canteen cook but her employment is cut short when she becomes pregnant. The film On The Buses sees Stan and Jack put diuretic pills into the female bus driver's tea in the canteen which causes chaos on the roads. The second spin-off film Mutiny On The Buses is to see the canteen used as the venue for a Busmen V Management darts match and is to end in violence. Stan is hit on the head with a tray as he tries to stop a fight between Olive and Nymphy Norah.

Without a doubt the canteen was a key setting in On The Buses. Many hilarious scenes were set there and it was to be the stage for much of the banter between Stan, Jack and Inspector Blake.

Canteen Cook

This was a post taken on by Olive in the film, On The Buses.

During a staff shortage problem at the Town and District Bus Company, Stan manages to persuade Inspector Blake to take on his sister Olive as canteen cook. Despite her husband Arthur showing little faith that she'll be able to hold onto the job for any length of time, Olive does avoid the sack. However, her first shift is a catalogue of disasters. With an early start at 6 am to make tea for the early shift staff, Olive soon runs into trouble preparing lunch. Stan enters a smoke-filled canteen kitchen to find that the hapless Olive has mistaken the electric stove for a gas stove and has spent twenty minutes trying to light it. She also has trouble melting fat in a pan to fry fish but this is purely because she has placed it on the wrong ring which results in her melting a saucepan. To make matters worse she burns the beef joint in the oven and Inspector Blake arrives on the scene to investigate the lack of food being served up. He is in for a nasty shock when he tries removing pieces of melted saucepan from the electric stove and causes an explosion.

Olive is fortunate to avoid the sack and goes on to earn her first pay packet from the Town and District Bus Company. She proudly tells the family: 'My first week's money, canteen cook – twelve pounds eighty.' Of course this is before Arthur makes his deductions. The job though is destined to end when Olive is forced to quit the job as she discovers she is pregnant.

Canteen Girl

Played by Julia Breck

This is an attractive young woman who serves Stan and Jack in the canteen in the Series Six episode 'The Prize'.

Stan and Jack enter the canteen with Stan ordering stewed beef. He asks the canteen employee: 'You got any dumplings?' She turns around revealing herself to be a busty young woman which excites Stan with Jack having to hold him back from making advances to her. His ardour is dampened when she tells him: 'Now look love you can have fish and chips or cold pork pie.'

Canteen Girl

Played by Melanie Jane

This is a young blonde-haired woman who serves Stan and Jack tea in the canteen in the Series Seven episode 'The Football Match'.

During a football training session at the bus depot, Stan and Jack divert via the canteen for liquid refreshment during an exercise involving running backwards. They stop at the counter and are handed their teas and the canteen girl asks: 'Late for your shift are you?' Stan tells her they are running early and that's why they are running backwards before they make their way back into the depot.

Canteen Stock Losses

A problem that the canteen suffers from when Stan and Jack take advantage of canteen staff members Suzy and Gladys in the Series Five episode 'Canteen Trouble'.

The canteen is running at a loss as Stan and Jack get more food than they are paying for from Suzy. When asking for a bigger portion of steak and kidney Jack is about to be charged extra money but he reminds Suzy of all the vodkas he bought her the previous night and she relents charging him less money. Stan is also benefitting as Suzy helps him smuggle bacon hidden inside a newspaper, sausages hidden in the fingers of his gloves, steak and kidney puddings hidden in his scarf and a block of cheese hidden in Stan's cap, all of which is unpaid for. Inspector Blake though is determined to see the canteen run at a profit and dismisses Suzy who he feels was a little too generous with her helpings.

Suzy's replacement is called Gladys and although she appears charmless, Jack convinces her to part with more canteen stock free of charge for Stan but she expects him to show his appreciation in other ways. In return for a leg of lamb and sausages, Gladys is looking for romance but the idea fills Stan with horror. In a panic he tries to escape the stock room but Inspector Blake comes to his rescue and uncovers Stan's latest attempt to smuggle canteen stock out of the depot without paying for it. Although Stan escapes the sack Inspector Blake turns to technology in an attempt to run the canteen at a profit.

Canteen Tea

Canteen tea is a beverage that is held in such low esteem by employees of the Luxton and District Bus Company.

In the Series Three episode 'First Aid', Inspector Blake has an accident aboard Stan's bus injuring his knee. Stan attempts to treat the injury by applying a cold compress which is no more than a cloth soaked in cold canteen tea from his flask as there is no water available. 'You can't put that all over me,' pleads the inspector. 'It's canteen tea. Kills all known germs,' jokes Stan.

Even Inspector Blake doesn't rate the canteen tea as seen in the Series Seven episode 'What The Stars Foretell'. Olive is to take a cup of tea into his office and tells him: 'They say the way to a man's stomach is through his heart.' Blakey, unmoved replies: 'Yeah well if it's canteen tea it gives him heartburn.' Later, in the same series, in 'The Allowance', Jack and Sid complain about the tea. Jack drinks a cup of the canteen tea and pulls a face saying: 'Oh blimey I'm not drinking that rubbish I've got respect for my insides.' A passing Mrs Webb, the canteen cook, pushes her urn and Sid advises her: 'It's about time you sent that tea urn in for a de-coke.' She proudly replies that she scours her urn out twice a week with washing soda. Jack quips: 'Well in that case, do us a favour, next time leave out the washing soda before you put the tea in will you?'

Car Factory

Stan is to get a job in a car factory causing him to quit the Luxton and District Bus Company after several years of service in the Series Seven episode 'Goodbye Stan'.

When Stan applies for and gets a job working on a production line in a car factory in the Midlands the news stuns his mum, Olive and best friend Jack. He cites the need for a higher paid job as his reason for leaving. However, his mum tries to dissuade her son from leaving home without success. Stan leaves Luxton for pastures new a few days later in an emotional farewell though he does keep in touch sending his mother letters and money.

At the time this episode was written the Midlands was the centre of the British car industry with car plants offering a large percentage of jobs to people living in Birmingham, Coventry and surrounding towns in the area. Sadly, this is no longer the case with the demise of the likes of British Leyland (later to become MG Rover), Triumph and other great names of the past. Car plants do still operate in the area but are of much less size and numbers.

Carby, Fanny

TV Role: Gladys (Series 5 Episode 7 'Canteen Trouble')

Fanny Carby was born in Sutton, Surrey in 1925 and was a renowned stage actress who was to have a long and full career on stage, television and in films. She was also a founder member of the famous Joan Littlewood's Theatre Workshop.

She was to have one of her best-remembered roles in the stage production Oh What A Lovely War which was a big success and it migrated to Broadway where she also appeared. Other notable stage roles included The Shoemaker's Holiday, The Two Bouquets, Every Man In His Humour, Bartholomew Fair, Billy (the musical version of Billy Liar), The Threepenny Opera, Cabaret, Sparrows Can't Sing and Moll Flanders. Carby was to make prolific television appearances and these included parts in classic dramas such as Othello, Crossroads, Out Of The Unknown, Dixon Of Dock Green, Z Cars, Angels, The Sweeney, Juliet Bravo, David Copperfield, Coronation Street, The Bill, Middlemarch and Heartbeat. She was also a regular supporting actress to Spike Milligan appearing in Q9, Curry And Chips and Milligan In. Other comedy roles on television included credits in Pardon The Expression, Till Death Us Do Part, Nearest And Dearest, On The Buses, The Fenn Street Gang, Love Thy Neighbour, Sykes, In Sickness And In Health, Birds Of A Feather and Goodnight Sweetheart amongst others.

Her film career began to take off in the early 1960s. Carby would have roles most notably in The Kitchen, The Traitors, Some People, Sparrows Can't Sing, The Family Way, Oh What A Lovely War, A Day In The Death Of Joe Egg, The Elephant Man, Biggles and Mrs Dalloway to name but a few.

Carby's career as an actress spanned well over fifty years but sadly, in 2002 she passed away at the age of seventy seven in London.

Carnell, Mike

TV Role: The Milkman (Series 3 Episode 12 'The Squeeze')

Mike Carnell's acting career has offered roles in films, television and on stage over a period of over forty years.

In the late 1960s his film career began with a small role in the comedy Arthur! Arthur! His other notable big screen role came in 1988 in the smash hit film Little Dorrit. On television he was to appear in classic sitcoms such as On The Buses, Only Fools And Horses, Hi-de-Hi, You Rang M'Lord, In Sickness And In Health and The Brittas Empire. Drama roles came his way from the late 1970s in Dick Barton: Special Agent, Big Deal, Tales Of The Unexpected, The Bill, Jack The Ripper and made-for-television films Fools Gold: The Story Of The Brinks – Mat Robbery and Eskimo Day.

His stage career includes roles in Habeas Corpus (alongside the legendary Sir Alec Guinness), Raffles (The Amateur Cracksman) and Mad About The Musicals. Into the 2010s he still trod the boards on stage and was a regular on the pantomime scene.

Carpenter, Derek

TV Role: Joe (Series 4 Episode 3 'Dangerous Driving')

Born in 1948, Derek Carpenter's acting career spanning over five decades has seen him with roles on television, film and stage.

Television credits came in renowned dramas such as Crossroads, Geminal, Grange Hill and Tales Of The Unexpected. In comedy he appeared in Ours Is A Nice House and On The Buses. His solitary film role was to come in the early 1980s playing a clown in Captain Stirrick. Stage credits have played a large part in his career beginning with credits in Incident At Vichy and The Two Executioners. In recent years roles have come in As You Like It, Duchess Of Malfi, Ticket Of Leave Man, Prince Of Homburg and Danton's Death.

Another string to Carpenter's bow is that he is also well-versed as a circus entertainer capable of tightrope walking, stilt-walking, clown playing, uni-cycling and fire-eating.

Casson, Maxine

TV Role: Mary (Series 7 Episode 5 'The Football Match')

Maxine Casson had a fairly brief but hectic career as an actress on the big and small screen in the 1960s and 70s.

Her pin-up model looks saw her appear in a number of saucy roles on the big screen including Love Is A Splendid Illusion, Escort Girls, Confessions Of a Driving Instructor and The Bawdy Adventures Of Tom Jones as well as a part in the Disney film Digby The Biggest Dog In The World. On television her drama roles came most notably in Z Cars, Paul Temple and Hine. She was more active in comedy roles appearing in classic comedy series such as Doctor At Large, The Goodies, The Liver Birds and Bless This House.

Maxine Casson was to quit acting in the late 1970s.

Castle, Barbara

A powerful political figure of the 1960s and 70s who was referred to in a couple of episodes in the first two series.

In the very first episode of On The Buses called 'The Early Shift', Stan is on picket duty and as a TV crew show up to film a report and interview him Mrs Butler suggests: ' Don't you think you ought to have some make-up on? Well they all do – the Queen and Mr Wilson.' An uncomfortable Stan replies: 'Well he probably borrows Barbara Castle's powder puff.' Later, in the Series Two episode 'Self Defence', Stan tells mum that his work colleagues may go on strike because of the lack of protection given to them whilst on duty. Mum is worried about the lack of money coming in and says: 'Barbara Castle might come along and take all our furniture away.'

At that time Barbara Castle was one of the most powerful female politicians in British political history. As a Labour MP representing Blackburn in Lancashire since 1945 she was to rise to an elevated position of power in the Labour government under the leadership of Harold Wilson in the mid-1960s. She became Minister of State for Overseas Development in 1964 before progressing on to become Minister of State for Transport (1965-1968) and then on to the lofty position of First Secretary of State from 1968 to 1970 doubling as Deputy Prime Minister to Harold Wilson.

Castle remained a crucial part of the government until Labour lost the 1979 General Election but she did go on to be elected to the European Parliament from 1979-1989. A year later, in 1990 she was made a peer becoming Baroness Castle of Blackburn. In 2002, after a bout of pneumonia, Barbara Castle passed away at the age of ninety one.

Casualty Ward

Inspector Blake is to be treated in a casualty ward after he is injured when Stan's bus reverses into his office in the depot as new rules cause chaos in the Series Four episode 'Safety First'.

Catley, David

Designer (Series 1 Episode 1 'The Early Shift', Series 1 Episode 2 'The New Conductor' and Series 1 Episode 3 'Olive Takes A Trip')

David Catley was a production designer who was to work on several television series for over twenty years with the majority of those being London Weekend Television productions.

He began his television career working for Associated-Redifussion in 1961 and worked on dramas such as The Skewbald and No Hiding Place as well as the game show Don't Say A Word and the comedy series The Dickie Henderson Show. When London Weekend Television came into being in 1968, Catley was to work on classic comedy series such as On The Buses, Please Sir, Six Dates With Barker, Doctor In Charge, The Fenn Street Gang, Bowler, Thick As Thieves, Yus My Dear, Mind Your Language and Metal Mickey as well as some less successful sitcoms. He was also to work on a number of LWT's classic dramas including Manhunt, New Scotland Yard, Within These Walls, Seven Faces Of Woman and The Gentle Touch. An impressive career ended with his retirement in the mid-1980s.

Catwalk

A makeshift catwalk made from a line of tables in the depot canteen is used by Stan and Jack in the Series Three episode 'The New Uniforms'.

Stan and Jack are not happy at being chosen to be the guinea pigs by trialling the company's new prototype uniforms. They show their disdain by holding an impromptu fashion show in the canteen on the tables forming a catwalk. Both model and comment in camp voices on the uniforms in front of their mocking colleagues. They take the chance to poke fun at various aspects of their new attire with Jack vowing to take the matter up with the union and management as Inspector Blake breaks up the fashion show accusing Stan and Jack of 'performing like a couple of sissy's'. Jack retorts: 'Well what do you expect putting us in uniforms like this. It could change our personalities.' Their objections to the new uniforms soon melt away as they prove to be a hit with the women.

Cave, The

A fictional nightclub referred to in the Series Four episode 'Dangerous Driving' by a young clippie called Pat.

She discusses a date with Stan in the canteen saying: 'They've opened this new dance place on the High Street called The Cave. It ain't half nice. Can we go there?' Stan isn't so enthusiastic but replies: 'Yes of course we can.'

It is quite possible that The Cave was based on the world famous nightclub in Liverpool called The Cavern where the legendary pop group The Beatles were discovered by Brian Epstein in 1961.

Cemetery Gates

This was the famed destination for Stan and Jack's No.11 bus which features in a number of episodes of On The Buses.

In the Series Two episode 'Bon Voyage', Stan and Jack, in a desperate bid to get a suntan before they go on holiday to Spain, resort to sunbathing in the graveyard at the Cemetery Gates. However, Stan is to have his uniform stolen from the cab of his bus by a passing tramp leaving him in an embarrassing position. The Series Three episode 'First Aid' sees Inspector Blake have an accident aboard Stan's bus whilst it is parked at the Cemetery Gates. He twists his knee and cuts his shin but even worse is that he only has Stan, Jack and an inadequate first aid box to rely on for treatment. The Cemetery Gates appear again in the Series Three episode 'The Inspector's Niece'. Stan and Jack compete for the affections of trainee clippie Sally who, unknown to them, is Inspector Blake's niece and Stan bids to impress by buying her flowers from a stall beside the Cemetery Gates. Later in Series Three in 'Radio Control', Stan and Jack arrive at the Cemetery Gates with two clippies called Joyce and Edna aboard their bus learning how to operate the new radio control system. The two ageing lotharios see it as an opportunity for romance and Jack tells Stan to take Edna off somewhere to which Stan snaps: 'Hang on! Blimey you've got all the bus. This is a cemetery you know. What am I supposed to do? Snog her up against one of the tombstones?' He eventually entertains Edna in the cab of his bus. Finally, in the Series Seven episode 'The Allowance' it isn't only Inspector Blake who is fed up with the clippies delaying buses with their visits to public toilets. Bus driver Sid moans: 'Do you know I had to make fifteen emergency stops on that Cemetery Gates run? We were passed three times by funerals.'

Incidentally, the location for the famous Cemetery Gates is on Cedar Road and is the entrance to the Lavender Hill Cemetery in Enfield, North London.

Centenary Exhibition

A special event staged at the bus depot which features in the Series Seven episode 'On The Omnibuses'.

The event to celebrate one hundred years of the Luxton and District Bus Company is organised by Inspector Blake who sees himself as somewhat of a historian on the subject. The Centenary Exhibition has a series of old photographs from the late nineteenth and early twentieth century of buses and staff from that era as well as a display of uniforms that were worn at that time. The main exhibit is the antique first motor bus used by the Luxton and District Bus Company in the mid-1920s.

Central Control

The name given by Inspector Blake to the area in the depot where the new radio control system's call centre is based in the Series Three episode 'Radio Control'.

As the Luxton and District Bus Company decide to install their buses with a two-way radio control system Inspector

Blake explains the system to the employees. He tells them: 'There will be a central control in my office there manned by Miss Woodhall who will serve directly under me'. The central control is to see Inspector Blake receive some lewd messages from Stan across the airwaves purely by accident.

Central Station

A fictional unseen bus station referred to by Inspector Blake in the film Mutiny On The Buses.

The Town and District Bus Company have installed a new radio control system and Inspector Blake enjoys the feeling of control he has over his staff. As Stan attempts to give Arthur driving lessons whilst on duty the inspector contacts him on the radio control system. Blakey orders: 'The bus in front of you has just broken down. There's a queue about a mile long waiting at the Central Station. That'll keep you busy won't it?' A frustrated Stan responds by blowing a raspberry, which the inspector describes as 'a little interference' to depot manager Mr Jenkins who is by his side.

Chaffey, Nicolette

Film Role: Nurse (Mutiny On The Buses)

Nicolette Chaffey, born in England, has had a varied career in show business which has taken her from being an actress on film, television and most notably on stage in the UK before going on to work further afield. She ventured to the USA and went on to become an accomplished stage play director and partner in a highly successful production company as well as being a vocal coach.

On the big screen she was to have a small role in Mutiny On The Buses and over two decades later appeared in the US comedy film The Shot. Her television credits in the UK saw her appear in the early 1970s hit drama The Pathfinders and in children's series Hickory House. Further afield she has credits in the award-winning US drama The Practice and Australian soap Certain Women. Her stage career began in the mid to late 1960s with roles in the UK in Lady Windermere's Fan but perhaps her most notable role came in a production of As You Like It in the USA. In 1979, Chaffey settled in the USA and along with her husband were to become highly regarded at staging and producing their own stage shows with which they have had great success. This partnership continues to thrive to the present day.

Chairman of the Dance Committee

A position held by Inspector Blake which comes to prominence during the organising of the annual Busmen's Ball event in the Series Five episode 'The Busmen's Ball'.

The employees of the Luxton and District Bus Company are adamant on the cabaret they want for the event and it isn't the usual conjuror that the inspector hires. As spokesman for his colleagues, Jack confronts Blakey and asks him to book a stripper for the Busmen's Ball but the respectable inspector is repulsed by the idea. However, Jack won't be denied and threatens him that the busmen will boycott the event unless he hires the stripper. 'Don't you try blackmailing me mate I tell you,' barks Inspector Blake. Jack though promises to take the matter up with the dance committee and have it put to the vote but the inspector is confident in the knowledge he is the chairman of the dance committee. This time it is the busmen who win out as the dance committee vote in favour of hiring the stripper.

Chalet

The type of accommodation the Butler and Rudge family stay in at the holiday camp and in which they suffer many mishaps in the film Holiday On The Buses.

The chalet comprises of two bedrooms, a bathroom, a living room and a kitchen with mum remarking when she first sees it that it is all so clean. That changes when Stan spills the contents of a mud-filled suitcase onto the carpet and it is left to Arthur to scrub it clean. Another mishap befalls the chalet when Stan babysits for Arthur and Olive looking after their son, affectionately known as little Arthur. He allows the mischievous child to play with his water pistol against the parent's wishes. Little Arthur fills the pistol with various colours of ink and leaves the walls in the bedroom splattered in ink. To avoid the sack it is down to Stan and Jack to borrow paint from the camp stores to redecorate the bedroom. However, another coat of paint is needed as Olive leaves handprints in the wet paint as she searches for the light switch without her glasses on in the middle of the night. The mishaps don't end there as Arthur uses petrol to clean the paintbrushes and carelessly disposes of it down the toilet. When Stan pays a visit to the toilet and discards a cigarette down it there is an explosion that leaves the toilet basin smashed to pieces. Once more a visit to the camp stores is called for and Stan and Jack raid it at night for a new toilet and plumb it in to the chalet to end their worries.

Chalkie

Played by Glen Whitter and Jules Walter

Chalkie is a West Indian bus driver employed by the Luxton and District Bus Company. He is seen briefly in a number of episodes of On The Buses and is much in the same mould as Stan and Jack.

He is willing to help Stan and Jack when needed such as when Stan arrives for work drunk. Chalkie helps supply platefuls of mashed potatoes for Stan to eat as Jack claims it will help sop up the alcohol. He is always keen to have a laugh and pokes fun at the appearance of Stan and Jack in their new prototype uniforms and also joins them in winding up Inspector Blake. Also prone to moments of mischief he is warned not to take liberties by the inspector in the Series Six episode 'Private Hire'. He is always ready for overtime and even when Stan attempts to start an unofficial strike without union backing he is set to work an overtime shift for Inspector Blake. However, he really is just one of the lads at heart who owns a Mini that looks set for the scrap heap. Chalkie does attend events at the depot such as the Busmen's Ball and is a member of the Luxton Lions football team which is thrashed by the Basildon Bashers. He is also one of a handful of busmen who share a farewell drink with Stan who is to leave the bus company and is clearly a good friend of Stan's who tells him: 'I'll miss you Chalkie.' The West Indian busman was the most regularly used supporting character in On The Buses.

Chamber of Horrors

The Chamber Of Horrors is an attraction at Madame Tussauds in London which was also the title of a hit horror film in 1966 that is referred to in the Series Three episode 'Foggy Night'.

As passengers sleep aboard his bus which is fog-bound in the countryside in the early hours of the morning, Stan says to Jack: 'God blimey look at them all. It's like spending the night in the Chamber of Horrors.'

The Chamber of Horrors first appeared at the original home of Madame Tussauds in Baker Street, London in 1835. It was to feature wax figures of infamous murderers and criminals as well as victims of the French Revolution. Madame Tussauds relocated to its current location in Marylebone Road in 1884 including the Chamber of Horrors and the world famous waxworks museum has now become one of London's most popular tourist attractions.

Chambers, Garry

Scriptwriter (Series 7 Episode 4 'The Poster')

A scriptwriter who was to write material for legendary comedy stars from the early 1970s through until the 1990s. The vast majority of his scripts and comedy material were to appear on television.

Chambers was to write scripts and sketches for two of Reg Varney's variety style series those being The Reg Varney Revue and Reg Varney. His other notable writing credits saw him work on The Two Ronnies writing a number of their classic sketches as well writing material for The Les Dawson Show, The Faith Brown Show, Cannon And Ball, Russ Abbot's Saturday Madhouse, The Best Of The Lenny Henry Show and Noel's House Party. On the big screen he wrote the script for a 1975 comedy film called Side By Side and was to co-write scripts with the late, great Dick Vosburgh as well as working with Wally Malstan on a number of projects.

Champion the Wonder Horse

Jack is described as Champion the Wonder Horse by Inspector Blake in the Series Seven episode 'The Poster'.

The Luxton and District Bus Company is about to introduce a promotional poster and a contest is to be held to see which busman's photo will appear on it with a cash prize incentive. Jack is set to enter the contest but Inspector Blake interrupts saying: 'They're looking for a champion bus driver not Champion the Wonder Horse.' No doubt this was a direct reference to Jack's trademark toothy grin which bears resemblance to the teeth of a horse.

Champion the Wonder Horse was a smash hit US children's television series that ran for twenty six episodes from 1956 to 1958. It followed the adventures of Champion, a wild stallion befriended by a boy called Ricky in the southwest of the USA in the 1880s. It was also to be a big hit on British television with numerous re-runs being screened periodically in the 1960s, 70s and 80s ensuring a new generation of fans to the series.

Charlie the Cleaner

Played by Ian Gray

A middle-aged cleaner wearing brown overalls and a cloth cap who is employed by the Luxton and District Bus Company. He can be seen sweeping up in the bus depot late at night in the Series Four episode 'Nowhere To Go'.

The moustachioed cleaner, Charlie, can be heard moaning to Inspector Blake he's had a terrible night and asks him: 'Is all the buses in?' The inspector tells him they are but he just has to check his last way bills. Charlie continues to sweep up before going on to Stan's bus spraying it with disinfectant which brings a coughing and spluttering Jack and a clippie off the bus shortly after him. He calmly carries on with his cleaning chores around the depot.

Charlton, Bobby

This much-respected professional footballer of the 1950s, 60s and 70s is referred to by Stan in the Series Seven episode 'The Football Match'.

During a football training session at the bus depot Stan's clowning around sees him injure the Luxton Lions star player Bob, which rules him out of their big match against the Basildon Bashers. Stan's team-mates are angry as they see their chances of earning their bonus payment for winning the match disappear and they want to know what Stan intends to do about a replacement. He nervously jokes: 'I wonder if Bobby Charlton's free on Saturday?'

At the time this episode was written Bobby Charlton's long and distinguished playing career with Manchester United was coming to an end and he was set to join Preston North End as player-manager. He was, and still is, an iconic figure of British football whose career saw him survive the tragic Munich air disaster in 1958, win the World Cup with England in 1966, win three league titles with Manchester United as well as the European Cup in 1968 and went on to win the BBC Sports Personality of the Year Lifetime Achievement Award in 2008. He still holds the proud record as the record goal-scorer for England scoring forty nine goals for his country. Currently, Bobby Charlton is a director at his beloved Manchester United – a post he has held since 1984. His biggest personal honour was to come in 1994 when he received a knighthood and so become Sir Bobby Charlton.

Charring

An obsolete term used by Stan as he explains to Inspector Blake that his mother might have to get a job in the Series Seven episode 'The Perfect Clippie'.

Stan grovels to the inspector to give Olive a job as a clippie and when Blakey refuses he tries to weaken his resolve by telling him: 'We're skint at home and she's at her wits end and it's just that I don't want her to take in washing or have to go out charring.' It has the desired effect as the inspector relents and agrees to give Olive a chance to prove herself as a clippie.

Charring was a term used for a woman who was employed to do housework and general cleaning duties.

Chemist

Played by Kenneth Gilbert

A character who is seen serving Stan and later embarrasses Inspector Blake in the Series Seven episode 'The Poster'.

The chemist, who is called Mr Peabody, is a middle-aged man who takes Stan's shopping list but a phone call sees him called away and he asks his assistant to attend to the busman. The chemist returns later to find Inspector Blake in the shop and says to him: 'Oh Mr Blake it's arrived. It got here this morning. It's just under here under the surgical counter.' To the inspector's embarrassment and a watching Stan's amusement, Mr Peabody takes a corset out of a brown paper bag and holds it up for all to see. It sees Stan laugh out loud whilst Blakey tries to explain it is for his mum as he snatches the corset from Mr Peabody who soon exits the scene.

Chemist's Assistant

Played by Elaine Wells

The chemist's assistant who serves Stan on his visit to the chemist searching for beauty products for his makeover in the Series Seven episode 'The Poster'.

A blonde-haired woman in her late thirties who is called Miss Quiggly is left to serve an uncomfortable Stan when the chemist has to answer the phone and is called away. She takes his shopping list, recommends a number of products for him and enquires what type of skin the product is for increasing his discomfort. Thankfully, for Stan moments later the chemist returns to take over serving him as Miss Quiggly exits the scene.

Chesney, Ronald

Co-creator and Co-writer of On The Buses.
Producer (On The Buses, Mutiny On The Buses and Holiday On The Buses)

Born in England in 1922 of French parentage, Ronald Chesney was one half of the comedy writing team that co-created and co-wrote the comedy masterpiece On The Buses. However, long before he began concentrating on writing comedy scripts, Chesney was known as one of the greatest harmonica players in the world playing concerts around the world with musical greats such as Gracie Fields and Duke Ellington amongst others.

It was in the early 1950s when he began penning comedy scripts originally for radio shows and formed a long-running and fruitful partnership with Ronald Wolfe. They went on to write a host of classic sitcoms for television such as Educating Archie, The Rag Trade, Meet The Wife, On The Buses, Romany Jones, Yus My Dear and a number of other less successful sitcoms. He was also to write material with Wolfe that appeared in episodes of The Reg Varney Revue and 'Allo 'Allo.

Chesney was also to team up with Wolfe on the big screen writing the script for a musical comedy called I've Gotta Horse in 1965. They went on to write and produce the three On The Buses spin-off films in the early 1970s and also penned the scripts used for the stage productions of On The Buses which were to tour Canada and Australia in the 1970s and 80s.

He is now enjoying his retirement and spends it still involved in his overseas scripts and playing jazz on his grand piano. Chesney has also been a regular supporter of the annual On The Buses events staged in Borehamwood since 2008 where he has attended each event.

Ronald Chesney

Here are some of Ronald Chesney's recollections of working on the set of On The Buses as revealed at the 2010 Back On The Buses event in Borehamwood, Hertfordshire.

Memories

'Well I think one memory is when we were doing a show in front of a live audience. All of our television shows were in front of an audience and they laughed we didn't have dubbed laughter in those days but we had one show where we got so many laughs that Stuart (Allen) had to stop recording the show to stop the audience laughing.

It was the one called 'The New Uniforms' when Stanley went home because the inspector wanted them to have their measurements for their new uniforms so he got a tape measure out and then his brother-in-law said: 'Why does he always get a bigger breakfast than me?' So mum says: 'No you've got a sausage and an egg…' He says: 'His sausage is bigger than mine.' And they start measuring his sausage and he says: 'My sausage is curved and his isn't' and we went on like this and the audience couldn't stop laughing.'

Chief Inspector

Played by John Crocker

A character employed at Luxton and District's Burntwood depot seen in the Series Seven episode 'The Poster'.

The chief inspector is a balding, bearded middle-aged man who is on the judging panel that is to select from a shortlist which bus driver is to appear on a new promotional poster. He addresses the representative of his own Burntwood depot telling him: 'Thank you McGregor and even if you are from my depot I must say you put up a very creditable performance.' He himself is told by fellow judge Mr Lawrence that none of the contenders seen so far came across as conscientious with a safe driving record to which he agrees. He then asks to see the final contender who is Stan Butler, who suitably impresses the judges to win the contest with the chief inspector telling Inspector Blake: 'I must say you train your men very well inspector. You must be very proud of his responsible attitude.' Blakey is not as forthcoming with praise for Stan as the judging panel congratulate the winner. The chief inspector shakes Stan's hand and warmly says: 'Congratulations. You're just the sort of image that we need.' Blake would be quick to disagree with that but is forced to toe the line.

Chief Inspector at Town and District

This is a position that Inspector Blake is promoted to in the film On The Buses.

When the Town and District Bus Company discontinue the use of women bus drivers Inspector Blake refuses to sack them as Stan and Jack desire. Instead they are to take on roles as inspectors when he proudly announces that his promotion to chief inspector has come through and he shows off the braid on his cap to the busmen. However, Jack and Stan take the chance to have a joke at his expense as Jack says: 'Here Blakey I like your yellow braid. Suits him don't it Stan?' The bus driver adds: 'Yeah matches your teeth.'

The promotion is not to last for long though for a reason that is never disclosed as he is soon to be back in his inspector role in the second spin-off film Mutiny On The Buses.

Chief Security Inspector

This is a post taken on at a holiday camp by Cyril Blake shortly after he is sacked by the Town and District Bus Company in Holiday On The Buses. Even though the job offers less money and longer hours than his previous job he is delighted as he believes he'll never have to work with Stan and Jack again. This turns out to be a false hope as the troublesome duo later are to gain employment at the same holiday camp which spells trouble for Blakey.

The role as chief security inspector includes him being seen to keep undesirable characters out of the camp and keep a written log of all visitors entering and exiting the camp. He also has the task of briefing his security staff as well and advises them to welcome the holiday-makers with a nice, big smile. Although not part of his duties, Blakey spends his spare time giving dance lessons forming a dance team that is to perform in an exhibition event. Old habits die hard for him as he still feels the need to issue orders to Stan and Jack warning them: 'I want you to understand I don't want any hanky panky with the female staff right. They're here to work, the same as yous two.'

Blakey is to jeopardise his job though because of his obsession with creating trouble for Stan. He encourages Luigi, an Italian chef in the staff canteen, to threaten Stan as he tells him the driver has been dating his sister, Maria. A confrontation sees the stocky chef assault Stan but is stopped by the camp manager who is none too happy when he learns that his chief security inspector is responsible for spreading rumours and inciting trouble. Worse follows when Blakey falsely believes Stan is having an affair with his girlfriend, the camp nurse Joan. He chases after Stan in anger and when Joan tries to stop him and explain that he has made a mistake falls on top of her and rips her dress off by accident as he tries to push her off in full view of the camp manager. He is pulled off Joan and the manager queries his sanity before telling him: 'In the army we have pills for men like you but as we don't happen to have them here I have no alternative but to terminate your employment forthwith. Now get out!' It is a sad end to Cyril Blake's short career at the holiday camp.

Chimpanzees

These animals are seen gaining access to the Town and District's Special Tours bus driven by Stan at the Windsor Safari Park in the film Mutiny On The Buses.

As the tour bus makes its way to the exit of the safari park two chimpanzees' leap onto the banner on the back of the bus, clambering up it and enter the bus through the open window at the back of the upper deck of the bus. The chimpanzees make their way downstairs with one leaping onto the steering wheel causing the bus to swerve out of control sending a policeman scurrying out of the way before coming to a halt after exiting the park. The policeman opens the door of the bus saying: 'What's going on here? Can't you drive this...bus?' He is stunned to see a chimpanzee alone at the steering wheel with Stan and Inspector Blake sitting in a passenger seat with the other chimpanzee for company.

The chimpanzees seen in Mutiny On The Buses were residents of Windsor Safari Park and had originally been part of the famous travelling Billy Smart's Circus. They were to remain at the safari park until its closure in 1992 when they were relocated to Monkey World in Dorset, England. The colonies of chimpanzees have remained at that location to the present day.

Chimps

A reference is made to a famous television advert in the Series Seven episode 'The Football Match'.

During half-time of the football match between The Luxton Lions and The Basildon Bashers, Mrs Butler brings cups of tea made by Olive into the dressing room. One taste of the tea and Stan spits it out saying: 'Blimey I bet the chimps on telly make better tea than this.'

Stan's remark is a reference to the popular adverting campaign run by tea brand PG Tips. From 1956 through until the late 1990s, their adverts featured chimps dressed in clothes drinking tea, talking and taking part in a range of activities. The adverts are still fondly remembered today and one of the PG Tips ads featuring a chimp called Mr Shifter moving a piano still holds the world record as the most shown advert on British television. Incidentally, On The Buses star Michael Robbins was to provide voice-overs on one of the many PG Tips chimps' adverts.

Chit/Chitty

These documents were often referred to in On The Buses and were signed notes for staff due money or other services from the Luxton and District Bus Company.

In the Series Seven episode 'Goodbye Stan', Inspector Blake sacks Stan for calling him 'a fish-faced twit' and gleefully tells him: 'I'll give you a little chit Butler. You can take this up and get your money. And you don't need to come back on Monday.' The inspector's glee is short-lived though as Stan reveals he was set to hand in his resignation but being sacked means he will now receive a week's wages. Overtime at the Luxton and District Bus Company was paid by chitty. In the Series Five episode 'The New Nurse', Stan and Jack return to the depot after their shift and the toothy conductor says: 'We better get Blakey to sign our chittys. We don't want to lose our overtime.' Later, Stan is in need of a new uniform long before he is due to receive one in the Series Five episode 'Stan's Uniform'. Inspector Blake reluctantly agrees he needs a new uniform and tells Stan that he'll make out a chitty for twenty four pounds but Stan will have to pay the costs. However, Jack has a plan which sees the driver avoiding having to pay for a new uniform.

Christine

Played by Madeleine Mills

An attractive young, slim clippie with dyed blonde hair has an appetite for food and is never without a snack in the Series Five episode 'Vacancy For Inspector'.

When Jack becomes an inspector, Stan tells him he'd like Christine as his new conductress describing her as 'a smasher'. She is a gullible clippie who fails to see the wrong in Jack despite the fact that he lands his best friend in trouble with Inspector Blake. As far as she is concerned he is just doing his job and to Stan's amazement she describes Jack as being cuddly. Stan is besotted by Christine but sadly he is to find out that her first and only love is for food. He is finally turned off her when she visits the Butler house and eats at such a pace that even Olive doesn't get a look-in as Christine scoffs scampi and sliced bread. Amazingly, she remains ravenous and leaves to go on a date with Jack. A trip to a Chinese restaurant follows and three hours later Jack manages to stop her eating as his money runs out. She puts her healthy appetite down to her active glands which kills any romance for Stan.

Christmas Club

An arrangement at the Luxton and District Bus Company where employees contribute a portion of their weekly wage throughout the year into a fund receiving their saved money just before Christmas as seen in the Series Five episode 'The New Telly'.

Inspector Blake runs the depot's Christmas Club and makes the pay-outs. Inevitably, he is accused of short-changing the employees with what Stan and Jack describe as 'crafty deductions' but the inspector insists they are no more than 'out of pocket expenses'. The Christmas Club is usually spent at the depot canteen on a range of festive goods resembling a Christmas hamper though Stan has other plans for his money as well.

Christmas Duty

Stan and Jack are looking forward to having Christmas Day off when Inspector Blake drops a bombshell in the Series Four episode 'Christmas Duty'.

It is Christmas Eve and Stan and Jack are prepared for their Christmas celebrations until the inspector receives a phone call from his bus crew destined for a shift on Christmas Day. The clippie has the flu and the bus driver who is also her husband will have to stay at home to look after her. Next on the work's rota are Stan and Jack who, despite their protests, are now rostered to work on Christmas Day.

The shift begins at 8 am and ends at 2.30 pm meaning that the Butler household will have to delay their Christmas dinner to wait for Stan to finish work. In general, he and Jack view their festive shift as a waste of time and this is backed up when they finish their working day with very few passengers and meagre ticket sales. Inspector Blake is adamant their shift was worthwhile as he reminds them: 'We're running a public service 'int we?' Stan can't agree saying: 'Nobody goes to the Cemetery Gates on Christmas morning – alive or dead.' If working on Christmas Day wasn't bad enough Stan faces the prospect of no Christmas dinner when he gets home. It turns out to be a Christmas for him to forget.

Chubby Chops

A description given of Stan by Arthur as he tells him he is putting on weight in the Series Four episode 'Dangerous Driving'.

When a newspaper article claiming that bus drivers are prone to many illnesses due to the nature of the job it leads to know-it-all Arthur winding up Stan telling him he has put on weight and is unfit. He pulls at Stan's cheeks saying: 'Regular little chubby chops we're becoming.' Stan shrugs the comment off but it does push him into attending a keep fit class at the depot as he looks to get fit for a date.

Churchill, Winston

A historical figure that Olive was named after as referred to in the Series Seven episode 'The Perfect Clippie'.

As Olive gets set to apply to become a clippie at the Luxton and District Bus Company for the second time an application form is filled in by her brother Stan. He fills in her full name as Olive Winnie Butler as requested by his mum who reminds him she named her after Winston Churchill who was affectionately known as Winnie.

Winston Churchill is surely the most respected Prime Minister Britain has ever had. He rallied the British armed forces and raised public spirits in the dark days of the Second World War when he became Prime Minister in 1940. His leadership, famous steely speeches and military experience was to help tip the outcome of the war in favour of the Allied Forces. Churchill was to oversee the defeat of Germany despite bouts of ill health. Eight years later, in 1953 he was to be knighted at Windsor Castle but his health was deteriorating as he was to suffer from strokes and a heart attack. He passed away in 1965 at the age of ninety and was bestowed the honour of a state funeral which was attended by the greatest politicians and leaders across many eras and countries all over the world.

Clapton, Patricia

TV Role: Edna (Series 3 Episode 8 'Radio Control' and Series 3 Episode 13 'On The Make')

Patricia Clapton's career as an actress was to see her with roles in films, television and stage with credits spanning over half a century from the early 1960s.

Her first credits came on the big screen and was to have an uncredited role in the 1961 adventure The Hellfire Club and went on to have a small role in The Kitchen later that year and this would prove to be her last film appearance. Television credits began in the early 1960s and would include roles in a string of classic dramas spanning three decades. These were to include Z Cars, The Plane Makers, Ghost Squad, Sergeant Cork, Dixon Of Dock Green, The Gold Robbers, Danger UXB and The Bill. Comedy roles came most notably in On The Buses, Just Jimmy, Pardon The Expression and A Sharp Intake Of Breath. Clapton's stage career has seen her appear in Johnny The Priest, Fings Ain't Wot They Used To Be, Cato Street, High Street China, Billy Liar, Playboy Of The Western World, The Latecomers, The High Lady B, The Mole Catcher's Daughter, Naked Ambition, Clothe The Naked and Bruises.

From he 1990s onwards Clapton's acting career has been stage-orientated and she still treads the boards to the present day.

Patricia Clapton.

Clara the Clippie

The name of Stan's drag act as seen in the Series Four episode 'The Kids Outing'.

With Stan supervising an unruly children's outing run annually by the Luxton and District Bus Company, he is struggling to keep them entertained in the canteen when their bus needs repaired. He decides to perform his drag act last seen at the depot's Christmas party and borrows a clippie's uniform. Introduced to the children by Jack as 'Clara the Queen of the clippies', Stan makes his entrance in the uniform, with make-up, false eyelashes, a hairband and two balloons up his pullover. Amidst hoots of laughter and cheers he clambers onto a table in the canteen to sing a song with canteen employee Winnie accompanying him on the piano. Mum is impressed that her son looks 'just like a real girl'. Olive disagrees: 'Oh mum no real girl looks as awful as that.' 'Some of them do,' quips Arthur.

Stan as Clara proceeds to sing a song which is followed by a string of jokes. However, a maintenance worker informs Jack their bus has been repaired and on hearing the news the children rush out of the canteen cheering, leaving Stan alone still telling jokes unaware that he has lost his audience. As Jack tells him to get changed as the bus is ready, Inspector Blake arrives on the scene to berate Stan for his attire and accuses him of having 'gone kinky'. It cuts no ice when Stan explains he only did it to entertain the children. After quickly changing clothes Stan is ready to take out the bus filled with impatient children but not until he has removed his false eyelashes as the inspector warns him they infringe the Highway Code.

Clare, Elyse

TV Role: Clippie (Series 3 Episode 10 'The New Uniforms')

Elyse Clare's career as an actress in the UK was to see her appear in two classic early 1970s sitcoms in the form of On The Buses and Love Thy Neighbour on television. Stage roles also came her way until her career and life took a new twist.

After marrying Kerry Jewel (son of the great British comic Jimmy Jewel) in 1971 they were to immigrate with their sons to Australia in 1978. Clare was to have a small role in the hit Australian musical film Starstruck in 1982 before she and her husband went into the theatre productions trade in the mid-1980s.

They were to be something of a pioneering production company developing Australia's first dinner theatre and introducing a touring circuit for their stage shows taking in all the major cities in the country. Their productions were a big success, none more so than Pan – their stage adaption of Peter Pan. It was a smash hit at the box office taking record receipts in 2000. Their production careers continue apace to the present day with their total stage productions now totalling over one hundred and fifty.

Clare, Malcolm

Choreographer (Holiday On The Buses)

Malcolm Clare, a much-respected and highly talented dance choreographer, was to work on a range of television, film and stage projects. He was to choreograph the old-time dance sequences in Holiday On The Buses in 1973 and other big screen films he worked on included Tommy The Toreador and the musical starring Cliff Richard and The Shadows called Finders Keepers.

Clare choreographed a number of television series in the 1960s and early 1970s including The Black And White Minstrel Show, The Music Box, Scott On, The Melodies Linger On and was also to work alongside Reg Varney on his cabaret show The Reg Varney Revue as a dance director.

On stage Clare's expertise was much sought after and he choreographed hit stage show Oliver and The Young Visitors amongst others. He also formed his own dance troupe called The Malcolm Clare Dancers who were to make regular television appearances on 1960s music television series such as Cliff And The Shadows.

As an actor Clare also appeared in the 1960s comedy series Three Of A Kind and had a small role in the film The Frightened City. Obviously, Malcolm Clare was a man of many talents.

Clark, Doctor

Played by Richard Caldicot and James Bree

The family doctor of the Butler and Rudge family who examines Stan's stomach in the Series One episode 'Bus Driver's Stomach' and treats Stan for back strain in the Series Five episode 'The Strain'.

Doctor Clark is held in high esteem by Mrs Butler who sees him as 'very thorough' but her son holds a differing opinion describing the elderly doctor as 'a doddering old fool'. However, against his wishes, the doctor examines Stan's stomach and immediately finds where the pain is but his patient pleads it's only a twinge.

The diagnosis by Doctor Clark is that he has an acute inflammation of the stomach and duodenum and warns Stan to watch what he eats. Worryingly, he pours scorn on the idea of Stan passing his upcoming medical at the depot. In an attempt to rid him of his stomach pains the doctor prescribes Stan a painkiller and places him on a strict diet of milk and slops much to his displeasure.

When Stan injures his back after a prank at the depot, Doctor Clark is called upon to treat the bed-ridden patient who is eager to return to work as soon as possible. After checking his reflexes the doctor rules out a slipped disc and tells Stan he has strained his back warning him the pain will last a few days, prescribing tablets to take.

The tablets will kill the pain and enable Stan to be up and about in a couple of days according to the doctor. However, Stan returning to work is ruled out as the doctor recalls he is a bus driver and feels that driving such a heavy vehicle will put too much strain on the back and it may never heal. The only solution, if Stan wants an immediate return to work, is if he wears a lumbo-sacral support (a corset) to protect his back. The idea abhors him but as he has no choice he takes Doctor Clark's advice and before leaving the doctor advises Stan not to take any exercise without the corset for two weeks.

Clark, Nobby

Played by Patrick Connor

This is a middle-aged employee of the Luxton and District Bus Company who is a busman responsible for organising the depot's charter holiday to Spain in the Series Two episode 'Bon Voyage'.

Nobby hands Stan and Jack their tickets for the charter holiday asking them to sign for them and they contemplate taking unnecessary luggage with them. Nobby, however, warns them that they are only allowed thirty three pounds of baggage and if they exceed that then they will have to pay an excess baggage charge. He goes on to remind them that the coach leaves the depot at 10 pm on Saturday night. Later, on the night of the departure, as the coach loads Nobby has a clipboard and is checking everything is in order putting Stan's case in the boot of the coach shortly before it departs.

He obviously had a sense of humour which comes to light in the Series Three episode 'The Squeeze'. He writes a humorous comment at the bottom of the ad on the notice board for Arthur's motorcycle combination which is for sale. He writes 'Keep death off the road!'

Clippie

Played by Elyse Clare

A young brunette clippie wearing a hairband is to get a shock when the inspector drops a magazine as she passes in the Series Three episode 'The New Uniforms'.

Inspector Blake has just confiscated an adult magazine found in Stan's jacket pocket but when the clippie arrives on the scene asking the inspector to sign her way bill he drops the magazine. Picking it up she looks at it and believing it belongs to him says: 'Inspector! I never thought you...' As he tries to explain the presence of the offending item Stan interrupts pointing at a picture in the magazine as he does so he says to the clippie: 'I'll tell you what it is miss you see. You see we are going to have new uniforms and you see that bird there with the two beads and the fig leaf? That's gonna be yours.' Stan and Jack walk off laughing leaving the clippie stunned and giving the inspector a puzzled look.

Clippie

Played by Laura Graham

A ginger-haired clippie in her thirties who arrives in the depot and in a rush to drop off her son at the depot's newly formed nursery in the Series Five episode 'The Nursery'.

She rushes into the depot carrying her baby son in a cot with cuddly toys and a holdall asking Stan and Jack: 'Which way to the nursery?' Jack replies: 'Oh it's through that door love and along the corridor.' In a flustered state she says: 'Corridor? Oh dear I'm gonna be late on duty.' Stan offers to give her a hand carrying her baby into the nursery as she follows. Leaving her baby in the nursery with the nurse she tells Stan: 'I must dash I'm due out.' She then informs the stern nurse: 'I've put his feeding chart in the cot.' As she heads for the door Inspector Blake enters asking what Stan and Jack are doing there but the clippie tells him they helped bring her baby up, before she dashes off for her shift.

Clippie

Played by Juel Morrell

A somewhat naïve, blonde clippie who is seen asking a silly question and making a suggestion in the Series Four episode 'Safety First'.

She arrives on the scene with Inspector Blake precariously positioned with his head stuck between iron bars on his office door which has been knocked off its hinges when Stan reverses his bus into Blakey's office. As Stan and Jack attempt to free him the clippie says: 'Ooh inspector what have you got your head through that door for?' 'So he can see through the other side you silly...' replies an exasperated Stan. He explains the inspector has his head stuck through the door and they can't get it off. The clippie recalls that when her little brother got his head stuck they pulled his ear-lobes down and freed him. The inspector tells him he doesn't want his ear-lobes pulled but Stan and Jack attempt it in any case and fail. The clippie watches on as the inspector is finally freed with the help of a blow torch.

Clippie

Played by Petra Siniawski

An attractive brunette clippie who arrives for her medical a day early as several busmen await stripped to the waist in the Series Six episode 'Bye Bye Blakey'.

She arrives in the makeshift waiting room asking the men: 'Is this where the medical is?' Stan replies: 'The medical? Yes that's right so you better get stripped off to the waist,' The clippie, amazed, says: 'What? All of us?' Stan pretends the doctor will want to examine their chests and Jack urges: 'Come on get 'em off love.' However, Inspector Blake enters the room and tells the clippie her medical is not until the following day and orders her to leave. With that she puts her jacket back on as Stan berates the inspector for spoiling their fun to which the clippie shares a flirtatious moment with Stan before leaving.

Clippie in Canteen

Played by Jacqui Cook

This is a clippie with dyed-hair who catches Stan in an awkward position in the depot canteen in the Series Six episode 'Love Is What You Make It'.

She arrives in the canteen just after Stan has spilt his breakfast of beans, sausages, eggs and bacon down his trousers and he tries to scoop it back onto his plate. With a look of disgust she says: 'Aren't you a messy eater?' Stan snaps: 'Don't you start.' Jack butts in excusing Stan's behaviour claiming that the driver is in a rotten mood but Stan explains that Arthur and Olive's marital problems are responsible for his mood. After buying a cup of tea she sits down next to Jack who hugs her. It becomes clear that Jack has a date lined up with the clippie and he declines the chance of overtime so he can keep the date. She exits the canteen moments later with her date and Stan as another shift beckons.

Clippies

A clippie is a slang word for female bus conductress. It is thought to have come from when the conductress used to clip each ticket they sold. The term has become somewhat obsolete as from the early 1970s onwards buses became increasingly driver-only operated. Conductors of either sex are now a very rare sight aboard buses and only a few select Routemasters operating in Central London as well as buses operated by the Stagecoach Strathtay company in Tayside, Scotland still employing conductors. Thanks to On The Buses continued popularity though the term clippie lives on and remains fondly remembered.

Clothing Issue Form

A document filled in when employees at the Luxton and District Bus Company receive a new uniform as referred to in the Series Five episode 'Stan's Uniform'.

Stan requests a new uniform when his is left in a terrible condition after wearing it whilst unblocking drains at home but he is in for a disappointment. Inspector Blake is to tell him: 'I've checked the clothing issue form and you can have a new uniform – six and a half months' time.' Stan is left to concoct a plan to get a new uniform without having to wait that length of time for it.

Clothing Store

An area in the bus depot where items of uniform are stored and can be obtained from, which features in the Series Five episode 'Stan's Uniform'.

Stan has ruined his new uniform within hours of receiving it and is in desperate need of a replacement. He pays a visit to the clothing store but George, the staff member manning the store, refuses to issue Stan any clothes without a chitty. In desperation he asks George if he can patch up his shredded jacket but it is beyond repair and is put in the bin. George then offers Stan a dusty, old uniform handed in the previous day by retired busman Ernie which he gladly accepts and so the clothing store comes to Stan's rescue in his time of need.

Coach Hire

Stan is coerced into hiring a coach to raise cash when he is desperately short of money in the Series Six episode 'Private Hire'.

Owing money to fellow employee Basher who threatens violence if he doesn't receive his money on time he also needs money to buy Aunt Maud a birthday present and is penniless after gambling away his wages. Jack believes he has a solution that involves using a coach at the depot to take a group of old age pensioners on an outing to the seaside charging each passenger a fee which Stan will keep. The driver is not keen on the idea of taking the coach without permission but Jack tells him he'd just be borrowing it and in a bid to persuade Stan he reminds him of the consequences if Basher doesn't get his money plus he'd be doing the pensioners a favour. Stan finally agrees to go along with Jack's plan and feels better when he hears the inspector won't be in the depot on the day of the outing as it is his day off.

On the day of the outing though Stan and Jack are in for a shock as they arrive to borrow the coach without the bus company's permission. The inspector, working overtime, is wise to their ploy and catches them in the act of taking the coach promising them that they will both be sacked. Jack's quick-thinking though saves the day as he tells Blakey that Stan was not pinching the coach but hiring it as per regulations displayed in a notice in the depot. It saves them both from the sack but it means Stan is out of pocket as the money he received from the pensioners for the trip goes out of his pocket into the Luxton and District Bus Company's coffers and he is still ten pounds short of the total needed to hire the coach. The inspector insists that the ten pounds will be stopped out of Stan's next wages compounding his woe.

Coco

A large pet dog owned by a clippie called Edna which stands between Stan and romantic moments with her as she becomes a lodger at the Butler house in the Series Three episode 'On The Make'.

Coco, a Great Dane, is devoted to owner Edna and that causes problems for Stan. As he struggles with Edna's luggage he also gets lumbered with taking Coco back to the Butler house but Inspector Blake is adamant the dog can't travel on one of their buses as other passengers would object and so Stan and Coco face a three mile walk home.

The Butler household's occupants are far from enthused about Coco's presence. Arthur describes the dog coldly as 'an enormous great hound' whilst mum forbids Edna from keeping Coco in her bedroom and means her pet has to sleep downstairs with Stan. The dog, known to bark at intruders to the room, is placid enough in its new environment but Stan wants it to bark in the hope it will lure the attractive Edna downstairs enhancing his chances of romance. However, this does not happen so Stan resorts to mimicking Coco's bark and to his joy he hears someone answering his call. Delighted he says to the dog: 'Hey I didn't need you son. I did it on my own. I've got a better woof than you.' Unfortunately, for Stan it is Arthur that comes downstairs and not Edna. He is wise to Stan's ploy and Edna soon arrives on the scene remarking that Coco sounded different to which Arthur quips: 'Almost human.' The incident sees mum allow Edna to take her dog up to her bedroom ruining any hope of romance for Stan.

The following day Stan is assured of a night alone with Edna as the family have gone to the pictures. However, he is thwarted as Jack arrives at the Butler house to whisk Edna away on a date leaving Stan alone with Coco to watch television and share a bag of crisps. Stan is foiled again.

Cocoa

A hot beverage used by Mrs Butler in a ploy to dampen Stan's ardour as he entertains his girlfriends at home on two
separate occasions.

In the Series One episode 'The New Conductor', Stan has invited Iris, a new clippie aboard his bus, around to his house in hope of romance. He and Iris are beginning to get passionate in the back room when his mum interrupts offering a passionless snack of cocoa and kipper sandwiches. It annoys Iris who yells: 'I don't want your blasted cocoa!' Moments later, she grows fed up with the interruptions and storms off home in a huff. Later, Stan attempts to entertain Doreen another clippie as the family watch television in the front room, in the Series Five episode 'Stan's Room' but mum uses the cocoa routine again as she pops into the room during the commercial break with Doreen refusing the drink. A plethora of interruptions ruin Stan's night and the final nail in the coffin is when he tries to smuggle Doreen upstairs but is found out and she leaves in a rage.

Cocoa, a hot beverage made from hot water, cocoa powder, milk and sugar is now more commonly referred to as hot chocolate.

Cockburn, Peter

TV Role: TV Commentator (Series 5 Episode 12 'The New Telly')

Peter Cockburn had many strings to his bow. He had roles as an actor in films and on television as well as being a TV announcer and commentator.

On television he was to be an announcer on the now long defunct ATV London channel and also in the early 1960s he would commentate on ITV's wrestling coverage as a stand-in for the regular commentator Kent Walton. As an actor his credits came in dramas such as The Plane Makers and Paul Temple and the sitcom On The Buses.

On the big screen he was to have an uncredited role in the classic British comedy film Carry On Camping as a commentator. He also was to host corporate films throughout the 1960s and 70s.

Colour TV License

A license that the family will need to purchase as they plan to buy their first colour television set in the Series Five episode 'The New Telly'.

Before the family can buy a new colour television they need to overcome the cost of the license which Stan points out will cost twelve pounds. Mum is disgusted that it costs so much for a license that lasts only a year compared to a marriage license which lasts for life but Arthur, trapped in marriage feels that some things give you more pleasure than others. Stan is willing to pay the twelve pounds for the license but as Arthur refuses to pay for the aerial the wait for a colour television looks set to go on.

The Colour Television License was first introduced in the UK in January 1968 and was to cost ten pounds. When the episode 'The New Telly' was penned in 1971 the license was indeed twelve pounds and it has since continued to rise annually. As of April 2010 a Colour Television License cost one hundred and forty five pounds and fifty pence.

Commissionaire, The

Played by Frank Littlewood

The commissionaire is an official title of a uniformed doorman who is to give Stan directions in the Series Three episode 'Mum's Last Fling'.

Whilst on duty and mid-route Stan takes the opportunity to pay an overdue gas bill stopping his bus outside the offices of the North Thames Gas Board. He rushes into the building and is met at the door by the commissionaire. The elderly doorman tells Stan politely that to pay the gas bill he has to go to the first floor. 'There's a lift just going up,' he adds. Stan catches the lift but overshoots his floor delaying his return to his bus.

Committee Leader

A union role held by conductor Jack Harper as referred to in the first episode of On The Buses called 'The Early Shift'.

As a bus prepares to exit the rear of the depot, Stan, Jack and George are on picket duty as a strike hits the Luxton and District Bus Company. To prevent the bus leaving the depot Jack orders Stan to lie down in front of the bus. The driver protests asking Jack: 'Why don't you lie down there?' Jack's self-importance shines through as he tells his best pal: 'No. No. I'm the committee leader I've got to negotiate with 'em 'int I?' On that note Jack and George then physically force him to lie down.

Commonwealth, The

The long running conglomeration of nations is referred to by Inspector Blake in the Series Three episode 'The Snake'.

At an Indian social event at the depot, Inspector Blake is embarrassed when Stan and Jack arrive and sit down without removing their shoes as is the custom. He tells them to take off their shoes but Stan is reluctant saying: 'I can't. I've got a hole in my sock.' Disgusted the inspector says: 'Do you know they could leave the Commonwealth over you two. Properly let our side down eh.'

The Commonwealth (formerly known as the British Commonwealth) is a group of countries that were almost all under British rule historically. It currently has fifty four member countries and those are sovereign states with their own independence. India is part of the Commonwealth hence the inspector's remark at the Indian social event.

Competing for Blakey's Affections

A curious tug-of-love breaks out between Olive and her mother as they battle for the affections of the perplexed Inspector Blake in the Series Seven episode 'What The Stars Foretell'.

A combination of horoscopes and tea leaf reading leads Olive and Mrs Butler to believe they are destined to marry and both turn their attention to Inspector Blake who is lodging at their house. Although he insists he has no intentions of getting married, Olive and her mother are lining him up as their next husband. Olive attempts to flirt with the inspector in his office, adorns perfume to attract him, warms his slippers in the oven and plans a night at home alone with him. Mrs Butler, not to be outdone, lovingly cooks the inspector a full breakfast, a special casserole and undergoes a makeover donning a wig and gown in a bid to seduce him. Things come to a head with Olive and her mother arguing over who is going to marry him but he steps in insisting he has no intention of marrying either of them. The situation, much to his relief, is resolved when the horoscopes rule out marriage for both Olive and Mrs Butler and things can return to normal.

Complete Angler, The

Jack dubs Inspector Blake this name on his return from his fishing holiday in the Series Five episode 'The Inspector's Pets'.

As Stan and Jack finish filling up the inspector's fish tank with warm water in Blakey's office, the toothy conductor warns of Inspector Blake's arrival saying: 'Heads up here comes the complete angler.' It is likely that Jack's name for Inspector Blake is a reference to one of the most popular angling books of all-time. Izaak Walton wrote 'The Compleat Angler' in 1653 and was to add to the book in the coming years with five more editions being released up until 1676. To this day it is still a much sought after book.

Complexion Queen

A fictional brand of face mask recommended to Stan by the chemist's assistant in the Series Seven episode 'The Poster' when he feels the need to undergo a course of beauty treatment.

The Complexion Queen face mask is applied by Jack but when it is left on for too long Stan is left with a red complexion on his face as a result.

Conductors

A male employee aboard both Luxton and District and Town and District Bus Companies whose job it is to collect fares. It is also their duty to go through the stages of guiding the driver and bus in and out of the depot. Although Stan thinks otherwise it requires a modicum of intelligence as referred to in the Series Seven episode 'The Perfect Clippie'.

When Stan manages to get Olive a job as a clippie with Luxton and District he feels she will be up to the job. He makes a remark that offends Jack as he claims: 'You don't have to be too bright to be a conductor.' Angrily, the conductor replies: 'Listen mate before I joined here I had to take an IQ Test.'.

Connor, Patrick

TV Role: Nobby Clark (Series 2 Episode 6 'Bon Voyage')

Born in Margate, Kent in 1926, Patrick Connor had a long career as an actor appearing in many hit television series and roles on the big screen. He was also an adept stage actor before progressing into production of stage plays.

On television he was a versatile actor appearing in classic dramas from the mid-1950s through until the early 1990s. These included Fabian Of The Yard, The Buccaneers, Quatermass And The Pit, No Hiding Place, Dixon Of Dock Green, Crossroads, Danger Man, The Avengers, The Persuaders, Z Cars, The New Avengers, Poirot, Casualty and The Bill amongst others. He was also to have roles in a string of the best sitcoms of their era such as Doctor In The House, On The Buses, Please Sir, For The Love Of Ada, Dad's Army and Boon. His film career began in the mid-1950s and his most notable roles were to come in John And Julie, Kill Her Gently, The Strange Affair, Flame, Eye Of The Needle, Ragtime, Brazil and Lifeforce.

On stage he would have roles in productions such as Wedding In Paris, One More River, Donkeys Years, Troilus And Cressida and The Recruiting Officer. His stage career culminated in him moving into production of stage plays such as Romeo And Juliet and Trailing Arbutus.

Connor remained active until he passed away in July 2008 at the age of eighty two.

Convenience Bonus

A back-dated payment linked to the newly formed public convenience allowance that all clippies are to be paid by the Luxton and District Bus Company in the Series Seven episode 'The Allowance'.

It is agreed between all parties concerned that the clippies will receive a public convenience allowance to compensate them for having to pay to use the public toilets whilst they are on duty. Olive tells her mum the news about the bonus payment saying: 'Yeah and its back-dated to the beginning of the year so we get a convenience bonus as well.'

Convict 99

Inspector Blake is dubbed convict 99 by Jack in the Series Seven episode 'Gardening Time'.

The inspector, falsely arrested for attempting to break into the Butler house when he gets locked out late at night, arrives at the depot the following morning still wearing his striped pyjamas escorted by a policeman following his release. Jack revels in Blakey's predicament and quips: 'Hello. Here he comes…convict 99.'

Convict 99 was the title of a classic 1938 British comedy film starring Will Hay. He played school master Doctor Benjamin Twist who is disgraced and ends up taking on a new job that isn't in a school as he expected but as a governor in a prison. He celebrates his new job by getting drunk and on his way to the prison he gets confused as a new in-mate and dubbed convict 99 until the mistake is realised.

Cook, Jacqui

TV Role: Clippie In Canteen (Series 6 Episode 2 'Love Is What You Make It')

Jacqui Cook's career as an actress spanned through three decades and from the early 1960s up until the mid-1980s had roles on stage, television and in films.

In the early 1960s she made her acting debut on stage and had a role in Brush With A Body at the Theatre Royal, Bath before moving into television. Her television career saw her appear in dramas such as Monitor and Angels amongst others. Comedy roles were more prolific and she appeared in a string of hit 1970s sitcoms including On The Buses, Happy Ever After and Are You Being Served? She would also appear in less successful comedy series such as Turnbull's Finest Half-Hour and in the early 1980s in The Last Song. Cook's only notable big screen appearance came with a small part in the Hammer film Captain Kronos – Vampire Hunter in 1974 though she did appear in the made-for-television film The Knowledge in the late 1970s.

Coombs, George

Played by Henry McGee

A middle-aged man in the position of manager of the holiday camp that features in the film Holiday On The Buses.

George Coombs is an ex-military man who likes to keep fit and also plays golf. He lives close to the holiday camp with his wife and pet Alsatian dog. As the holiday camp manager he is strict but fair and makes it clear he will stand for no nonsense from his staff. This strict disciplinarian streak comes out in the ruthless manner he instantly dismisses his chief security inspector when he witnesses him taking his jealous rage out on camp nurse Joan. Blakey is ordered to 'get out' by the infuriated Mr Coombs. Likewise, Stan and Jack who had managed to flout the rules many times as busmen are quickly dismissed by him after their first indiscretion.

Coombs, Mrs

Played by Hal Dyer

Attractive middle-aged woman, wife of the holiday camp manager George Coombs in the film Holiday On The Buses.

Mrs Coombs is somewhat of an impatient woman who is prone to headaches. Her unwillingness to wait until her husband finds her shower cap sees her forego a shower and she also urges George not to be too long in the bathroom. Curiously, the married couple sleep in separate single beds perhaps going some way to explain why the Coombs have no children.

Coombs, Pat

Film Role: Vera (On The Buses)

Born in Camberwell, London in 1926, Pat Coombs was to go on to carve out a memorable career as an actress on radio, television and in films. Her career spanned over fifty years where she was to work alongside legendary comedy stars such as Arthur Askey, Bob Monkhouse, Tony Hancock, Dick Emery and Eric Sykes to name but a few.
Her career had begun in the late 1940s in the most popular form of entertainment of that time – radio. She was to perform alongside Arthur Askey in the smash hit Hello Playmates, Ted Ray in Ray's A Laugh and Charlie Chester in Stand Easy. Her future as an actress was to lie in the new emerging form of entertainment – television.

On television her roles were largely comedic and she appeared in classic sitcoms such as Hancock's Half Hour, Beggar My Neighbour, Sykes And A..., Up Pompeii, Till Death Us Do Part, You're Only Young Twice, An Actor's Life For Me, In Sickness And In Health and Birds Of A Feather. She was also to appear in a number of top comedy sketch shows including The Cyril Fletcher Show, The Dickie Henderson Show, The Roy Castle Show, The Reg Varney Revue, The Dick Emery Show and Noel's House Party. Appearances in children's series such as Here Comes The Double Deckers, Super Gran and Ragdolly Anna were included in her career as well as drama roles in Cranford, Bleak House, EastEnders and Doctors.

Coombs' big screen career was to see her have uncredited roles in British comedy classics Follow A Star, A Stitch In Time and Carry On Doctor. Amongst her recognised film roles were Till Death Us Do Part, Dad's Army, Ooh...You Are Awful, Carry On Again Doctor, Adolf Hitler – My Part In His Downfall and the classic Willy Wonka And The Chocolate Factory.

Sadly, Pat Coombs passed away in 2002 with emphysema having suffered from the debilitating disease osteoporosis since 1995. She died at the age of seventy five at the famous actors and actresses nursing home, Denville Hall. A comedy character actress much-loved and of great talent was lost to the world.

Corset

A garment that Stan is forced to wear when he strains his back in a prank at work in the Series Five episode 'The Strain'.

After straining his back Stan is left bed-ridden but financially he cannot afford to take any time off work despite being immobilised. His doctor offers a possible solution in that Stan wears a lumbo-sacral support, better known as a corset, enabling him to drive his bus. Arthur revels in Stan's predicament and says he can't wait to see him in his corset. However, he is so desperate to return to work and be able to date a clippie that he agrees to wear the corset.

The corset, which comes from Doctor Clark's surgery, is specially reinforced with steel bars and is laced up at the back. It proves to be very troublesome and uncomfortable for Stan to put on and to make matters worse he also has to put his uniform on as well. With the help of Arthur, Olive and mum he gets dressed but finds he cannot fasten his trousers due to the corset and has to resort to fastening them with a safety pin.

Stan arrives for his first shift at the depot in his corset he is still in agony and very stiff. Even bending down to pick up a pen is difficult but worse is to follow as he struggles to get into his cab to drive his bus. He needs the assistance of Jack and fellow busman George to lift him into his cab so he can fulfil his shift.

His chances of romance on his date at home with clippie Doreen is also hampered by the corset. When she discovers Stan is wearing a corset she finds it all very amusing and when he takes it off and prepares to get amorous with her his immobility comes back to haunt him. He ends up aggravating his back injury and any hope of romance, on a rare occasion when he had the house to himself for the evening is over. Doreen insists on taking the invalid Stan upstairs to bed and he muses: 'Innit marvellous eh? The first time a bird's ever insisted taking me to bed and I'm like this. I get all the pain but never the pleasure.'

Cosmo Club, The

A fictional nightclub where Stan and Jack see Sandra the Scandinavian Stripper perform and intend on getting the exotic dancer to replace the mundane conjuror as cabaret at the annual event in the Series Five episode 'Busmen's Ball'.

Costa Brava

A famous holiday resort in Spain that is referred to in a couple of episodes of On The Buses.

In the Series Two episode 'Bon Voyage' the depot's annual charter holiday is to be a two week vacation in the Costa Brava. Later, in the Series Six episode 'The Prize', a raffle is won by Mrs Butler and the prize is a holiday for two in the Costa Brava. It leaves Stan, Olive and Arthur vying to join her on her trip to Spain.

The Costa Brava has long been a popular holiday destination for Britons. It is located on the north eastern coast of Spain, just north of Barcelona and it was developed into a substantial holiday resort in the 1950s to target holidaymakers on package holidays. Its favourable summer climate and top quality beaches helped to transform the Costa Brava from a fishing community into a popular holiday resort especially with British, French and German holiday-makers.

Costello, Deirdre

TV Role: Molly (Series 4 Episode 13 'Not Tonight')

Deirdre Costello was born in Leeds, Yorkshire in 1948 and has had an extensive career as an actress from an early age with roles on stage, television and films in a career spanning well over forty years.

An active stage career began in the early 1960s and her most notable stage roles coming in Alibi, Halfway Up The Tree, Comfort And Joy, Daughters, Our Own People and Abigail's Party to name but a few. She has also gone on to become an accomplished play writer putting on shows in Derbyshire where she has now settled to live.

Her television credits are varied with the pick of her drama roles coming in classic series such as Paul Temple, Upstairs Downstairs, Hadleigh, Within These Walls, Dixon Of Dock Green, Crossroads, The Sweeney, Z Cars, The Professionals, Danger UXB, Angels, Juliet Bravo, Coronation Street, Hannay, Grange Hill, Jack The Ripper, The Bill, London's Burning, Peak Practice, Emmerdale and Doctors. In comedy roles on the small screen her most notable roles have come in On The Buses, Doctor At Large, Nearest And Dearest, Dad's Army, Whatever Happened To The Likely Lads, Love Thy Neighbour, Mind Your Language, I Didn't Know You Cared, Rosie and Big Deal.

On the big screen her most notable role came in the classic 1997 British comedy film The Full Monty which was to win an Oscar. Other film roles included Hammer film Demons Of The Mind, Valentino, The Great Riviera Bank Robbery, The Elephant Man, Looks And Smiles, The Doctor And The Devils and Grow Your Own.

Costello remains active as an actress and play writer to the present day.

Course of Instruction on Fire Fighting

The bus depot almost burns down after a fire in the paint shop which couldn't be put out quickly as the employees did not know how to use the fire-fighting equipment. The bus company decide to act on this in the Series Six episode 'No Smoke Without Fire'.

It is decided that the busmen will be put on a special course of instruction on fire fighting and also rule that anyone found smoking in the depot will be sacked. The course includes instructions on how to rescue unconscious persons using a technique called the fireman's lift, how to administer the kiss of life which Stan and Jack enjoy practising on a pair of attractive clippies and another technique known as the silvester method is demonstrated by a rotund clippie called Gladys on a less than enthusiastic Stan.

Courtneidge, Dame Cicely

TV Role: Mum (Series 1 Episode 1 'The Early Shift', Series 1 Episode 2 'The New Conductor', Series 1 Episode 3 'Olive Takes A Trip', Series 1 Episode 4 'Bus Driver's Stomach', Series 1 Episode 5 'The New Inspector', Series 1 Episode 6 'The Canteen' and Series 1 Episode 7 'The Darts Match')

Born in Sydney, Australia in 1893, Cicely Courtneidge came from a family with show business in its blood. She was renowned for her stage performances early in her career in both the UK as well as in her native Australia. Courtneidge was to marry comedian and actor Jack Hulbert and they moved to the UK where she continued her career as an actress on television, stage and in films.

It was on stage that she first made her bow and it remained her first love. She was to appear in a host of stage productions including The Arcadians, Lido Lady, Under The Counter, Gay's The Word, The Bride And The Bachelor, The Bride Comes Back, Dear Octopus, Move Over Mrs Markham and Once More With Music amongst many others. Her film career was to take off in the 1930s when she appeared in a host of films such as The Ghost Train, Jack's The Boy, Falling For You, Things Are Looking Up, Me And Marlborough and The Imperfect Lady. Later in her career big screen roles came in The Spider's Web, The L-Shaped Room, an uncredited role in the classic Those Magnificent Men In Their Flying Machines, The Wrong Box and Not Now Darling. Television roles were not so common in her career and all came in the 1960s. She was to appear in hit dramas such as Man Of The World and Sergeant Cork and roles came in sitcoms Before The Fringe and her biggest small screen role as mum in the first series of On The Buses.

Courtneidge, who was the Australian armed forced sweetheart in World War Two, has the distinction of being made a Dame in 1972. Sadly, she passed away in London in 1980 at the age of eighty seven and so the original Mrs Butler was lost to the world.

Cousins, Frank

A famous politician and trade union leader who is referred to by Stan in the first ever episode of On The Buses called 'The Early Shift'.

Mrs Butler is miffed that a bus strike meant she and Olive had to walk two miles home in the pouring rain and feels that Stan could have held the strike up for her. Her son though insists: 'They wouldn't hold it up for Frank Cousin's mum.'

Frank Cousins was a Labour politician who was to hold the post of General Secretary of the Transport and General Workers Union (TGWU). This post saw him run one of the largest trade unions in Britain from 1956-1969 and would have had the vast majority of busmen in his union at the time this episode was written. A man of great power and influence hence Stan's reference.

Cradock, Fanny

This was a famous television cook in the 1950s, 60s and 70s who is referred to by mum in the Series One episode 'The Canteen'.

Stan is hunting for a new canteen cook to work in the depot canteen which he is currently running. His mum tries to persuade him to give Olive the job saying: 'Now look. Olive can make all sorts of tasty dishes if she wants to. She always watches Fanny Cradock.'

Fanny Cradock regularly appeared on television in the 1950s, 60s and 70s with a host of cookery shows. She was also to write a number of cookery books and was a valued restaurant critic. Sadly, she passed away in 1994 at the age of eighty five.

Crawford, Jessie

Played by Yootha Joyce

A middle-aged bespectacled clippie new to the Luxton and District Bus Company who causes ructions at the depot when demanding an allowance for her fellow female colleagues who have to pay to use public toilets whilst on duty in the Series Seven episode 'The Allowance'.

Jessie, a headstrong character is described as an 'old boiler' by Jack who can't stop talking and is determined to stand up for women's rights at the depot. Although she initially ruffles shop steward Jack's feathers he warms to her way of thinking and uses her grievances to heap more problems on Inspector Blake's plate. She pressurises the inspector by threatening to bring the depot to a standstill with strike action until eventually the manage-ment introduces a public convenience allowance and with it a back-dated bonus payment to reimburse the clippies for having to pay to use public toilets. Jessie is also to get the male staff's backs up as her actions disrupt bus services but she has the full backing from the clippies which makes her a powerful new enemy of Inspector Blake. The inspector though has problems dealing with Jessie who refuses to be silenced until she gets her way. But get her way she does.

Crew

A term used for the full quota of staff to work aboard buses. The crew comprised of a bus driver and either a conductor or their female counterpart – a clippie.

Crocker, John

TV Role: Chief Inspector/2ₙₐ Judge (Series 7 Episode 4 'The Poster')

John Crocker was born in Streatham, London in 1925 and was involved in acting from an early age up until his seventies. His career saw him breakthrough on stage before working on television and in films.

At the age of twelve Crocker was to have his first acting role on stage and would go on to have many credits on stage and in repertory and pantomimes. His most notable roles included Mary Bonaventure, The Young Elizabeth, Doctor's Delight, The Representative, Slap In The Middle, Queen Of Hearts and Mother Goose.

He was to make his television debut in the early 1950s in the hit comedy series Billy Bunter Of Greyfriars School. Other classic comedy series he was to appear in were to include The Dickie Henderson Show, On The Buses, Whatever Happened To The Likely Lads, Waiting For God and The Naked Civil Servant. His main forte though was drama and he was destined for roles in a long list of classic series such as Emergency – Ward 10, No Hiding

Place, The Avengers, The Baron, The Saint, Softly Softly, Manhunt, Budgie, Upstairs Downstairs, Crown Court, Within These Walls, Bergerac, Poirot, Campion, The Bill, Lovejoy and Between The Lines.

His film roles were to be less numerous and came in varied roles in films such as The Moonraker, The Object Of Beauty and Blood Ring as well as uncredited roles in hit films such as Chitty Chitty Bang Bang and The Assassination Bureau.

In recent years he has also become a noted playwright having penned a number of tried and tested stage productions of pantomimes such as Humpty Dumpty, Aladdin, Cinderella and Robinson Crusoe.

Crufts

The world famous pedigree dog show is referred to in the Series Four episode 'The Anniversary'.

Stan buys a bag of dog biscuits for Olive's new pet poodle Scruffy and the inspector, not realising they were meant for dogs has one with his cup of cocoa at the depot. As he struggles to digest it, Stan wonders what effect they'll have on Blakey saying to Jack: 'Perhaps it'll make his moustache grow longer and silkier.' The conductor jokes: 'I tell you what; if it does we'll enter him for Crufts.'

Crufts is an annual dog show staged in Britain, the largest such event in the world, which got its name from its founder Charles Cruft. The first show was staged in 1891 in Islington, London and since then it has grown in size and popularity with entrants appearing from all over the world with many different categories and breeds of dogs on show which is also covered on television.

Cundell, Pamela

Film Role: Ruby (On The Buses)

Born in Croyden, Surrey in 1926, Pamela Cundell was to become a much-loved character actress on television, film and stage as primarily a comedy actress in a lengthy career.

The role she is perhaps best remembered for came on television in the classic sitcom Dad's Army playing Mrs Fox. She was also to appear in a host of classic sitcoms and comedy shows stretching over four decades and these included The Benny Hill Show, Doctor In The House, The Liver Birds, Pardon My Genie, The Train Now Standing, Bless This House, Are You Being Served, Only When I Laugh, Big Deal, In Sickness And In Health, Goodnight Sweetheart and The Detectives. Cundell has also had roles in hit dramas such as No Hiding Place, Dixon Of Dock Green, Z Cars, Minder, London's Burning, Casualty, children's series The Borrowers, A Touch Of Frost, Holby City, The Bill, EastEnders and Doctors.

Her film career afforded her a small role in the smash hit musical Half A Sixpence. Cundell went on to appear in films such as Mrs Brown You've Got A Lovely Daughter, Love Thy Neighbour, Memoirs Of A Survivor, Twenty Four Seven, Paradise Grove and The Jealous God.

On stage she has had a long and full career with roles in many productions which included The Rose And The Ring, Brimstone And Treacle, Something's Afoot, Faith Hope And Charity, Out Of Order, Plunder and also appeared in a stage adaption of Dad's Army. Cundell has long been a regular on the pantomime scene across the country as well.

Her career continues to this day – a veteran actress who has worked alongside a host of legendary actors and actresses.

Cunningham, Pauline

TV Roles: Birgit (Series 3 Episode 10 'The New Uniforms') and Frieda (Series 6 Episode 1 'No Smoke Without Fire')

Pauline Cunningham was to have a short but hectic career as an actress on television and stage from the late 1960s until the late 1970s.

She made her debut in an episode of the hit BBC sci-fi drama Out Of The Unknown in 1969. Other drama credits in her career came most notably in Z Cars, Man At The Top and The Sweeney. On the comedy front she was to have roles in Two In Clover, On The Buses and Love Thy Neighbour as well as a made-for-television comedy film Come Spy With Me (her final credit) in 1977.

Cunningham was also to appear on stage in a spin-off of On The Buses in 1973 alongside Stephen Lewis, Bob Grant, Anna Karen and Terry Duggan called Busman's Holiday.

Cure, The

A name Jack gives to a plate of mashed potatoes which he believes will help Stan to fool the breathalyser test in the Series Three episode 'Brew It Yourself'.

Jack ushers a tottering Stan into the depot's canteen and calls for Chalkie to get 'the cure' as a drunk Stan faces having to take a breathalyser test. Jack tells Stan that the mashed potatoes will sop up the alcohol according to an item he saw on television when the breathalyser first came out. As Stan sits down to eat 'the cure', Jack feels a spoon won't get the dish eaten quickly enough and suggests his best friend uses a saucer but he struggles to finish the plateful and admits he is surprised that one plateful would fool the test. However, he is told it will take at least three platefuls which leave him feeling quite sick at the thought of it. He refuses to eat any more so Jack has to resort to another cunning plan to ensure that Stan avoids failing the breathalyser test and avoiding the sack as well.

Curly Top Wigs

A fictional brand of wigs bought by Arthur as he attempts to impress a clippie in the Series Five episode 'A Thin Time'.

When Arthur takes a shine to Beryl, a clippie aboard the bus he travels on, he is disturbed to hear that she likes her men to have a good head of hair. In a bid to cover up his baldness he buys a set of wigs advertised in a magazine on seven days approval without telling the family as they are immersed in another financial crisis with an unpaid electric bill to add to their worries. However, his secret is uncovered by Jack, who as next door neighbour, takes in a parcel labelled Curly Tops that is addressed to Arthur and he reveals he has seen the wigs advertised as he hands them over to a sheepish Arthur.

In the hope of some privacy and to escape from family taunts, Arthur excitedly retires to his bedroom locking the door to open his parcel. He tries on the five wigs but Stan, puzzled by the locked door, peers through the keyhole to see his brother-in-law wearing a wig. Arthur is horrified that his secret is out but refuses to let Stan in until he shouts: 'Olive, there's a strange hairy man in your room.' The bedroom door is quickly opened and Stan is dragged inside leaving Arthur open to ridicule as the driver pokes fun at each wig as they look more like pot scourers, live animals and sporrans to him. It is therefore a shock to Stan when he discovers that each wig cost fifteen pounds and demands to know how Arthur can afford them whilst he is forced to clean buses to earn the money to pay the bills. Moments later, mum and Olive arrive on the scene to discover Arthur's secret purchase and are shocked and despite his protests he is pressurised into returning the wigs.

Much to the family's displeasure though, his determination to impress Beryl sees him keep one of the wigs wearing it to the bus depot. Disaster strikes though when Arthur stoops to pick something up for Beryl and gets his head trapped in the faulty doors on Stan's bus. When he is finally pulled free he is revealed in all his baldness to Beryl but Olive is on hand to pick up the pieces. The incident ends Arthur's experimenting with wigs and ends any hopes he had of romance with Beryl.

Curtis, Alan

TV Role: Mr Stewart/Inspector (Series 4 Episode 2 'The Canteen Girl')

Born in Coulsden, Surrey in 1930, Alan Curtis career as an actor spanned around fifty years with roles on television, film and stage.

His television career began in the mid-1950s with a host of drama roles. These would go on to include credits in classic series such as The Avengers, Coronation Street, Crossroads, The Saint, Doctor Who, Dr Finlay's Casebook, Z Cars, Paul Temple, Jason King and most recently Footballers Wives. The 1970s were to see Curtis turn more to comedy roles appearing in hit series such as Up Pompeii, On The Buses, The Morecambe And Wise Show, Six Dates With Barker, Whoops Baghdad, Last Of The Summer Wine, The Bounder and Duty Free amongst others.

On the big screen he was to have roles in drama and horror films such as Tomorrow At Ten, Die Screaming Marianne, The Flesh And Blood Show and children's adventure Professor Popper's Problem. There can be little doubt though that the highlight of his film career were to be his roles in the classic Carry On Henry and Carry On Abroad.

Curtis was also to make regular appearances on stage with roles coming in We Must Kill Toni, Nude With Violin, The House By The Lake, Verdict, Three Way Switch, A Guardsman's Cup Of Tea, This Happy Home and The Ghost Train amongst others. He'd also appear in pantomimes such as Peter Pan and Sinbad The Sailor.

He now resides in West London and has been an announcer for the MCC at Lord's for many famous cricket matches in recent times.

Dalby, Lynn

TV Role: Janet (Series 3 Episode 5 'Busmen's Perks')

Lynn Dalby was born in Harrogate, North Yorkshire in 1947 and was to go straight into acting on leaving school. She learned her trade at the Corona Acting School which was renowned for bringing through a host of actors and actresses that went on to become stars. Her career has seen her earn many roles on British television and on the big screen.

Her most notable role on television came in Emmerdale Farm (later to become Emmerdale) where she played Ruth Merrick in the early 1970s. Other drama roles came in Crossroads, The Gold Robbers, Crown Court, Budgie, Special Branch, 1990 and Return Of The Saint amongst others. In comedy roles she appeared in Never A Cross Word, The Gnomes Of Dulwich, Doctor In The House, On The Buses and Bowler most notably.

On the big screen her solitary film role came in the 1975 horror film Legend Of The Werewolf.

In the mid-1980s, Dalby emigrated to Australia where she has continued her acting career with her most notable roles coming in Tusitala, Water Rats, All Saints and Always Greener on Australian television.

Dance Committee

The dance committee is an organisation at the bus depot that deals with arranging events such as the annual Busmen's Ball.

In the Series Five episode 'The Busmen's Ball', Jack backed by his colleagues demand a change to the cabaret act lined up for the ball. They want a stripper hired but Inspector Blake refuses to replace the usual act – a conjuror. A boycott of the event is threatened but the inspector remains unmoved and so Jack promises to put it to the vote with the dance committee. Blakey remains unruffled as, being the chairman of the dance committee; he believes he has the power to influence the vote. However, as it turns out he loses the vote and the busmen get their stripper at the Busmen's Ball.

Dancing Team

Arthur and Olive are forced into join the dancing team at the holiday camp in Holiday On The Buses.

The dancing team is set to perform in front of an audience in the ballroom until a couple pull out and Blakey is left with no option but to cancel the exhibition but Stan suggests Arthur and Olive as replacements. He needs the exhibition to go ahead so that Blakey will be pre-occupied allowing himself and Jack to raid the camp stores for a new toilet to plumb in to the family's chalet to replace the toilet they blew up. He tells Arthur: 'Well you and Olive will have to make up the dancing team.' His reluctant brother-in-law declines but Stan reminds him of how he and Olive used to dance together regularly and insists he doesn't have a choice and so Arthur and Olive join the dancing team.

Darby and Joan Club

The famous clubs for the elderly is referred to by Jack in the Series Four episode 'Dangerous Driving'.

In the depot canteen, clippie Pat puts on a record and invites Stan to take part in the latest dance craze – The Shake. He is left exhausted with a stitch at the end of the dance and even though he is unfit he agrees to take her out to a nightclub. Jack though is on hand to warn him: 'You don't look fit enough to take part in a tiddlywinks match with the local Darby and Joan Club.'

Darby and Joan Clubs are for elderly people to join and partake in a range of activities aimed specifically at their age group. The term 'Darby And Joan' has its origins in a poem written in the eighteenth century by Henry Woodfall. It tells of an elderly married couple who live a quiet if somewhat drab life whose names are Darby and Joan.

Darts Match – The Battle of the Sexes

When clippies Iris and Jenny dare to play darts on the board in the depot canteen whilst Stan and Jack are looking to practice trouble brews in the Series One episode 'The Darts Match'. The clippies are infuriated when they are forced off the board by their male colleagues and end up challenging the over-confident Stan and Jack to a match and are willing to bet that they will win the match.

Stan's build up to the darts match though is hampered in various ways. Practice at home is not ideal and things get even worse when one of his cherished feather-flighted darts ends up in Olive's stew and is ruined. He is left to try to get used to a new set of darts as the match nears. It is also a distraction that one of his opponents is none other than old flame Iris who he is still attracted to and arranges a date with her for after the darts match.

The night of the darts match at the depot canteen arrives with Inspector Blake acting as referee and scorer. However, Stan is to be cunningly put off his game by Iris who plies him with beer and distracts him with her alluring perfume. It has the desired effect as he toils so much that the match ends up as an embarrassing and humiliatingly heavy defeat for Stan and Jack much to Inspector Blake's glee.

The night gets even worse when Jack, as the depot's darts team captain, drops Stan from the team replacing him with Iris who he escorts home to discuss the darts fixtures.

Darts Night

A social event staged in the depot canteen with busmen and their families invited features in the Series Four episode 'The Other Woman'.

It is a night for playing darts but Arthur seems more interested in playing away with voracious off-duty clippie, Wendy. As Stan and his family, with Jack and Inspector Blake playing darts Arthur flirts and enjoys a drink with the clippie leaving Olive feeling neglected and increasingly angry. Her mind isn't on the game and her comfort eating sees her leave jam all over the darts as she is more interested in Arthur's behaviour.

Meanwhile, Stan and Jack see the darts match as a chance to get one over on the inspector by defeating him at darts. They resort to skulduggery blunting his darts with a file and distracting him which helps them secure the win but the night ends up being dominated by Arthur and Olive's marital problems.

The event is to come to a head when Olive is fed up with her husband's flirting and leaves upset and with a headache but Arthur remains behind to continue his hopeful, but destined to be, forlorn pursuit of Wendy.

Davenport, Claire

Film Role: Peggy (On The Buses)
TV Role: Mrs Webb (Series 7 Episode 11 'The Allowance' and Series 7 Episode 12 'Friends In High Places')

Claire Davenport was born in Sale, Cheshire in 1933 with her acting career beginning on stage before progressing onto television and film roles. It was a career as an actress that spanned almost forty years.

Her debut role as an actress came in 1961 in Caesar And Cleopatra on stage. Other stage roles in her career included Tons Of Money, Hotel Paradiso, Hedda Gabler, Bartholomew Fair, Marco Polo, Frozen Assets and her final acting credit of her career came in the stage production On The Air in 1998.

On televsion she appeared in a string of classic sitcoms which included The Rag Trade, George And The Dragon, On The Buses, Billy Liar, Love Thy Neighbour, Fawlty Towers, Robin's Nest, George And Mildred, Mind Your Language and In Sickness And In Health. Other comedy roles came in Not The Nine O' Clock News, Frankie Howerd Strikes Again and The Smell Of Reeves And Mortimer. Davenport also appeared in dramas of the highest calibre such as Doctor Who, Crossroads, The Baron, Casanova, Z Cars, Angels and Remington Steele to name a few.

Her film roles, mainly small parts, came most notably in The Best Pair Of Legs In The Business, The Return Of The Pink Panther, Carry On Emmannuelle, The Tempest, The Elephant Man and Return Of The Jedi. She was also to appear in a string of sex comedies such as Adventures Of A Plumber's Mate and Rosie Dixon – Night Nurse amongst others.

Sadly, Davenport was to pass away in 2002 at the age of sixty eight after suffering renal failure. She was and still is a much-loved actress and familiar face on British television.

Davidson, Peter

TV Role: Tough Passenger (Series 7 Episode 2 'The Perfect Clippie')

Peter Davidson, born in Scotland, has had an acting career spanning forty years with roles on television, stage and in films and has gone on to work in the production side of the industry as well.

As an actor he was most active on the small screen appearing in a host of comic roles in the 1970s, 80s and 90s with parts in The Goodies, On The Buses, Doctor In Charge, Romany Jones, Doctor On The Go, Agony, Minder, Fairly Secret Army and Class Act amongst others. Davidson also appeared in dramas such as The Adventures Of Black Beauty, The Professionals, The Onedin Line, Secret Army, All Creatures Great And Small, The Gentle Touch, Juliet Bravo, Sons And Lovers, Inspector Morse, Casualty and Great Expectations.

His most notable stage role came in the 1972 adaption of Hamlet in a West End performance.

Davidson's film credits spanned from the mid-1970s and included roles in Adolf Hitler – My Part In His Downfall, Captain Kronos – Vampire Hunter, The Incredible Sarah, The Elephant Man, Under Suspicion and Best.

He also progressed into the production side of the entertainment industry forming his own production company called Magic Carpet Productions and has made tourist films which he has scripted and presented.

Dawkins, Paul

TV Role: Manager (Series 7 Episode 6 'On The Omnibuses')

Born in 1919, Paul Dawkins was a relatively late developer as an actor with his career finally taking off as he entered his forties. He was to fashion a career spanning across the genres on television, the big screen and stage.

Drama roles on television were numerous throughout the 1960s and 70s with credits coming in No Hiding Place, Crossroads, The Baron, The Avengers, Public Eye, Dixon Of Dock Green, Z Cars, Manhunt, Softly Softly, The Onedin Line, The Protectors, Wuthering Heights, All Creatures Great And Small and The Professionals to name but a few. He was also to have parts in hit sitcoms such as Pardon The Expression, On The Buses, The Worker and Nearest And Dearest.

Film roles were also plentiful and included a part in the classic romance Far From The Madding Crowd. His other big screen credits came in Lock Up Your Daughters, Walk A Crooked Path, Universal Soldier, Dad's Army and O Lucky Man amongst others.

His stage career was to see him with credits in Afore Night Come, The Jew Of Malta, The Merry Wives Of Windsor, The Changing Room, Plunder, Troilus And Cressida, Roots, The Rainmaker and A Man For All Seasons.

Sadly, Dawkins was to pass away in 1979 at the age of sixty.

Day Pass

Chief Security Inspector Blake is travelling on a day pass on the holiday camp's mystery tour in the film Holiday On The Buses.

Stan, who has a date lined-up for later in the day, rushes to get Blakey and the other passengers back aboard the tour bus so he can make his date in time. However, the inspector refuses to be rushed saying it is his first time as a passenger and he intends to take his time. Stan is in no mood for delays and tells Blakey: 'Oh yeah. Well you listen to me mate you're on a day pass so you get on that bus.'

Day Steamer Cruise

This activity at the holiday camp gives Stan a chance to date holidaymaker Mavis without her overbearing mother interfering in the film Holiday On The Buses.

The activity called the Day Steamer Cruise includes a trip aboard a ferry which is ideal for Stan as his date's mother can't stand boats as she gets seasick and so he can look forward to an uninterrupted date. With a cabin leased to entertain Mavis in he also orders a bottle of duty free champagne to add a romantic touch. She is in the mood for romance but sadly Stan isn't as he feels the full effect of seasickness and feels faint. It leaves Mavis frustrated as he exits the cabin in search of fresh air but Jack is on hand to step in and entertain Mavis himself.

De Rosa, Franco

Film Role: Luigi (Holiday On The Buses)

Franco De Rosa was born in Viareggio, a coastal resort in North West Italy in 1944. He was to make a career in acting from an early age and quickly broke into British television and films as well as productions made in his native Italy with varying success. Television credits came in drama series such as Armchair Theatre, Mystery And

Imagination, Paul Temple, Dixon Of Dock Green, Jason King, Spy Trap and Q.E.D. His most notable comedy role came in the controversial hit sitcom Love Thy Neighbour.

De Rosa made a number of big screen appearances in hit films including Return From The Ashes, Yankee, Drop Dead Darling, The Miniskirt Murders, Journey To The Far Side Of The Sun, The Stud and Richard's Things.

Dearnaley, Doreen

Continuity (On The Buses and Mutiny On The Buses)

Born in London in 1929, Doreen Dearnaley was to work on the production of a host of films and also made a rare foray into television working in continuity.

She was to work in the trade for a quarter of a century and her credits included a range of classic Hammer films such as The Camp On Blood Island, Dracula, The Revenge Of Frankenstein, The Snorkel, Further Up The Creek, Hell Is a City, Quatermass And The Pit, On The Buses, Frankenstein Must Be Destroyed, Dracula AD 1972 and Mutiny On The Buses. Away from Hammer she was also to work on some of the best films of the 1950s, 60s and early 1970s including The Navy Lark, Up The Junction, Carry On Camping, Spring And Port Wine and Get Carter.

Her sole television credit came in the classic 1960s drama series The Baron.

Decimal System

The new decimal currency system that had just been introduced is referred to in the Series Four episode 'The Lodger'.

Stan and Jack are suffering from the inflated prices of the canteen leading Stan to claim: 'Since they've done this decimal system, since they've rounded the figures up we're all swindled. It's a swindle.' It is also hitting food prices elsewhere as Stan has to resort to bringing sandwiches to work to eat as he cannot afford the new canteen prices. Inspector Blake is also to suffer when hunger gets the better of Stan in the canteen when he pinches food from the inspector's plate burning his mouth in the process and the troubled bus driver has more to worry about. He is troubled by the family's financial crisis caused by decimalisation and the Butlers are forced to take in a lodger which is destined to cause distress for Olive.

Britain was to move on to a decimal system for their currency on Monday the 15th of February 1971, just over a week after 'The Lodger' was first transmitted on British television. The old system of pounds, shillings and pence was to be replaced with a pound that contained one hundred pence. Just as was portrayed in the episode the general public felt shops used decimalisation as an excuse to inflate prices but the high inflation rate in Britain at the time was probably the real reason for the price increases.

Demarcation

A ruling that is referred to by Jack in the Series Four episode 'Safety First' and one that is to save Stan and Jack's jobs.

Inspector Blake is hospitalised after his office is demolished by Stan's bus which was reversing in the depot. Amidst writing out a lengthy and detailed report he tells a visiting Stan, concerned for his job, that he and Jack will be sacked insisting it was dangerous driving, attempted manslaughter and wilful damage of company property. However, after a visit to see the union secretary, Jack brings news that exonerates them from all blame.

He tells the inspector that if anyone gets the sack it will be him as it was him that ordered Stan to manoeuvre the bus in the depot. Jack explains to a bemused Blakey: 'According to the union mate a bus driver is not allowed to manoeuvre a bus in a depot. That is the job of the shunter. It's the rule mate its demarcation 'innit.' The disbelieving inspector is told by Jack to look it up in the rule book under section six paragraph four.

Demoted

A punishment that befalls Inspector Blake for his part in the disastrous trial run of the Town and District Bus Company's new tour bus to Windsor Safari Park in the second spin-off film Mutiny On The Buses.

He is demoted to rank of conductor and put aboard Stan's bus much to Jack's amusement and his horror as Blakey explains: 'Things weren't going too well. They demoted me I'm afraid.' Jack rubs salt in the wounds by telling him it's a bit of a come-down. The downcast but proud ex-inspector promises him: 'I'll show you lot how to do this conductoring job mate.' At this point Stan starts up his bus only to be chastised by his new conductor who reminds him he isn't due out for another two minutes. However, the thoroughly fed up driver puts his former superior in his place saying: 'Look mate I'm the driver and I'm the boss and I go when I say.' But Blakey, not used to taking orders from Stan, claims they'll go when he rings the bell to which the bus starts to head out of the depot leaving him to run along and jump aboard the moving bus to cheers from the watching busmen.

It is soon clear that Blakey as conductor holds no power over Stan. He, like Jack before him, has to cover for his driver who is kissing a clippie on the upper deck at the turnaround point, by not allowing the impatient and disgruntled passengers to board the bus. How the mighty have fallen.

Denton, Geoffrey

TV Role: Old Gentleman (Series 1 Episode 3 'Olive Takes A Trip')

Born in 1904, Geoffrey Denton was to first make his name on stage before progressing onto big screen roles at the end of the 1940s before working on television from the mid-1950s.

Denton's stage career began in the early 1920s and would include roles in The Cat And The Canary, Something In The Air, Dry Rot and Afore Night Come amongst others. His film credits came in Adam And Evelyne, Appointment With Venus, Horrors Of The Black Museum, Life Is A Circus, The Snake Woman and Nothing But The Night amongst others. He was also to have a number of uncredited roles spanning from the late 1940 s through until the late 1960s.

On television Denton was to appear in classic dramas such as The Vise, Emergency – Ward 10, The Saint, No Hiding Place, The Troubleshooters, The Forsyte Saga, Z Cars, Softly Softly, Public Eye, Jason King and the award-winning War And Peace. Comedy credits were fewer and further between with parts in The Army Game, Three Live Wires, The Valiant Varney's, On The Buses and in And Mother Makes Three.

He was to retire from acting in the mid-1970s before sadly passing away in 1977 at the age of seventy two.

Department of Employment

This is a department that Stan and Jack are forced to visit when they are sacked by the Town and District Bus Company along with Inspector Blake in the film Holiday On The Buses.

As Stan and Jack queue in the rain outside the Department of Employment for the first time they meet their old nemesis Blakey exiting the building. He tells them that he has found a better job which puzzles them as it has lower wages and longer hours than those he had as inspector. What makes the job better as far as he is concerned is that he'll never have to work with them again but he is to be in for a shock later.

The Department of Employment is seen again with Stan and Jack visiting again after they are sacked from their jobs at the holiday camp. As Stan arrives at the counter and demands service he finds that now in employment there is none other than Blakey. Stan pleads for a job as a driver and Mr Blake says he has just the job for him for someone who is always smashing things up – working in demolition.

Depot Crash

An accident in the bus depot sees Stan reverse his bus into Inspector Blake's office trapping Blakey amongst the debris in the Series Four episode 'Safety First'.

Stan is ordered by Inspector Blake to turn his bus around in the depot and he warns him: 'Watch out for those pillars 'an all I don't want any wings scraped.' Jack is on hand to guide Stan but is not watching where the bus is heading as it crashes into the inspector's office with Blakey still inside. A panicked Stan and Jack rush into what is left of the office to find Inspector Blake with his head trapped between the bars on his office door which has been knocked off its hinges and rescue attempts are soon under way. Joe from the maintenance department aids in the rescue as he brings a grease gun as Stan and Jack bid to grease Blakey's ears and pull the bars up over his ears but this is destined to fail. Next Joe brings a pair of cutters to cut through the bars but Stan says they'll never do as the bars are too thick. A naïve clippie arrives on the scene and suggests they try pulling the inspector's ear lobes down and lift the bars over the lobes as she points out that it worked when her little brother was in a similar position. However, the inspector gets highly agitated at this suggestion but, thankfully for him, at last Joe comes up with the solution bringing a burning plant to burn through the iron bars and finally free Inspector Blake.

Depot Doctor

An unseen character referred to in a number of episodes of On The Buses.

In the Series Three episode 'Brew It Yourself', Inspector Blake tells a drunken Stan he will get the company doctor to give him a breathalyser test. However, when the doctor can't be found Jack casts aspersions on the doctor's character saying he'll be over in the pub getting drunk. The test, therefore, is left to be carried out by the inspector. The depot doctor is referred to again in the Series Four episode 'Cover Up' when Stan, with yards of material wrapped around his waist under his overcoat starts sweating profusely and the inspector becomes suspicious. Jack tells Blakey Stan has a shocking cold but the inspector is so concerned he suggests the driver comes up with him to see the doctor. But Stan avoids an examination and manages to escape the depot with the concealed stolen material. Finally, in the Series Four episode 'The Injury', Stan struggles into work with injuries sustained at home and he bids to have an arranged accident at work which will see him receive full sick pay. However, he runs into the inspector at work who is unaware of Stan's agony and pokes him in the shoulder causing the driver to yell in pain. To cover up the injury Jack accuses Inspector Blake of assaulting Stan but when Blakey threatens to take the pained driver up before the doctor to be examined to see if he has broken his shoulder Jack declines to take the matter further.

Depot Flower and Vegetable Competition

The depot flower and vegetable competition is run by the Luxton and District Bus Company and features in the Series Seven episode 'Gardening Time'.

There is no interest in the competition at the depot until the manager points out to the inspector it was his wife's idea and he will be judging the competition. Always eager to impress the management, Inspector Blake promptly enters the contest and sets about working on the back garden at the Butler house. Jack's lies force him into entering the competition after he tells clippie and girlfriend Sandra that he has a lovely garden in which she can sunbathe and so is reluctantly pushed into entering the contest even though his knowledge about gardening is negligible.

The rivalry between Jack and Blakey as they prepare their gardens is intense and sees them both waging a campaign of dirty tricks as both intend to win at all costs believing it to be a two horse race. They are in for a shock though when they learn that neither has won the competition and the first prize of twenty five pounds. All they achieve is to draw for last place and in fact it is none other than the manager's wife who wins the competition. The inspector is miffed and feels that isn't fair but the manager explains: 'No you're quite right Blake it's not fair but I've got to live with her and that's not fair either is it?'

Depot Manager

Played by Michael Sheard

This is a strict disciplinarian of a depot manager at the Town and District Bus Company who finally sacks Inspector Blake, Stan and Jack in the film Holiday On The Buses.

An impatient man, he berates Inspector Blake for having to wait for a mechanic to look at his car and blasts him for the unpunctuality of Stan's bus ordering the inspector to do his job properly and go out with Stan's bus to ensure it runs to time. Seconds later, the manager is in for a nasty shock when he becomes trapped under the bonnet of his car after Stan's bus reverses into it and closes the bonnet as he examines the engine. He struggles to free himself and holding his injured back he yells: 'Get that bus away from my car. Get it out of here.' Stan follows orders and drives his bus forward but fails to see an on-coming bus which smashes into the side of his bus causing serious damage. The depot manager, not one for leniency, sacks Inspector Blake, Stan and Jack from the Town and District Bus Company after many years of service.

Depot Nurse

Played by Patricia Shakesby

This was a young, attractive nurse with a strong Irish accent who treats Inspector Blake after he has an accident in the depot in the Series Four episode 'The Injury'.

With the inspector in agony with a foot injury, aided by Jack, he limps over to sit down on a bench. The depot nurse rushes to his side saying she saw the accident and begins to take off the inspector's boot. Telling her his ankle hurts she examines his foot and announces to Stan and Jack: 'I'm afraid he's broken his big toe. Oh you'll be off for a long time with this inspector.' The nurse then has the task of dealing with the accident form which has been signed by Stan and Jack which closes the matter.

Depot Team

The Luxton and District Bus Company try to recruit its employees for the depot's football team in the Series Seven episode 'The Football Match'.

Such is the need for players in the depot team, known as The Luxton Lions that a cash incentive is offered if they win their next match against a rival depot team called The Basildon Bashers. The five pounds win bonus offered is enough to lure Stan and Jack to put their names down for the team especially when they learn that Bob, a busman and highly-talented footballer is in the side. With his presence they feel the match is as good as won and Stan begins planning to spend the five pounds to pay overdue rental fees on their television.

Inspector Blake, who is also team manager, feels there is no place in the team for them as they are both unfit. He points to Jack's chain-smoking and Stan's poor eating habits as evidence to back up his claim. However, the inspector finally relents allowing them in the team but tells them that they must attend training in their own time. He warns Stan: 'No training – no playing. No playing – no winning. No winning – no fiver. No fiver – no telly.'

Depot Wedding

The marriage of bus driver Bill and clippie Sally who is the inspector's niece features in the Series Five episode 'The Best Man'.

Inspector Blake is not best pleased with his niece's choice of future husband. He describes Bill as being 'dim' and feels he must be dim to have chosen Stan to be his best man. The inspector is also disturbed to hear that Stan has planned a bachelor party for Bill on the eve of his wedding and fears the worst envisaging the bridegroom getting blind drunk.

The wedding day arrives and Inspector Blake, who is giving Sally away, waits with her at St Barnabas Church. They have a long wait though as Stan and Bill are so hung-over from the bachelor party it takes them so long to get ready. On arriving at the church the bridegroom is still the worse for wear whilst Blakey berates Stan saying: 'I might have known you'd be late. I've been waiting outside the front of the church with my niece like an idiot. She thought she'd been jilted.' Although Stan claims they aren't all that late the flustered vicar butts in saying: 'Late? Late? The organist has played your music three times.' The ceremony is delayed even further when Stan has trouble removing the wedding ring he had placed on his little finger so he wouldn't lose it. Arthur knowingly tells him: 'It is a well-known fact that one's joints swell up in the morning especially after excessive drinking.' He suggests Stan tries lubricating it but this fails to work. It is Olive who saves the day though when she lends her wedding ring for the ceremony so that it can finally go ahead.

With the wedding finally complete the newlyweds and guests board a Luxton and District bus hired out for the day by Inspector Blake and prepare to head for the reception at the Red Lion pub. However, the day has a sting in its tail for Stan as he manages to lubricate the ring from his finger and has it in his mouth when Jack pats him on the back causing him to swallow it. Instead of enjoying the reception Stan faces a trip to the hospital and misses the newlyweds departing on their honeymoon to Spain.

Diamond

A precious stone inside an innocuous brown envelope lost board Stan's bus is to give the fraught driver a sleepless night and fears of the sack in the Series Five episode 'Lost Property'.

A late shift ends with a brown envelope being found aboard Stan's bus. Instead of handing it in to lost property as per regulations Stan takes the envelope home intending to hand it in the next day. However, he is unaware of its valuable contents and leaves it on the sideboard at home only for Arthur to take it up to bed to use it to work out his pools permutations. It is not until he receives a late night phone call from Inspector Blake that Stan discovers the importance of the envelope as it contains a diamond left on the bus by a jeweller and to his horror he discovers the envelope is missing.

When Stan tracks the envelope down to Arthur and Olive's bedroom he is in for another shock as he finds the envelope ripped in half with no sign of the diamond. It leads to Stan conducting a full scale fingertip search of the bedroom stripping the bed of its covers and sheet with a number of false alarms along the way finding toenail cuttings, biscuit crumbs and pills but no diamond. It is all very uncomfortable for Arthur whilst Olive suffers cramp when she is told not to move a muscle. With the bed searched thoroughly with no success Stan fears the sack and in desperation contemplates widening the search by pulling up the floorboards. But as hope wanes Stan's prayers are answered as he finds the diamond stuck in Olive's corn plaster on her toe much to his relief.

With a reward of ten pounds in place for the diamond's safe return, which Stan is unaware of, he does not want the management to know he took the envelope home knowing that was an infringement of the rules so asks the inspector for his name to be left out of the incident. This leaves the way open for Inspector Blake to accept the reward himself claiming he found the diamond and so Stan's job is safe. The inspector is sure that Stan has learnt something from the whole affair but the driver doesn't agree saying he always knew he couldn't trust inspectors, as he feels he should have had a share of the reward.

Diet

A worry about Stan's health sees him being put on a strict diet in the Series Four episode 'Dangerous Driving'.

A newspaper article paints a depressing picture on bus driver's lifespan claiming that they are prone to many illnesses. Arthur takes great delight in teasing his brother-in-law labelling him chubby chops and describing fat around Stan's waist as double chin. Despite being told it is muscle, Arthur insists it is fat and that he needs to go on a diet. He goes on to quote an excerpt from a book he owns that warns that obesity can prove fatal taking years off of one's life. It is enough to see Stan forced onto a diet by his family.

The diet means Stan's favoured fried food is to be replaced by a hard-boiled egg and two dried apricots under the instructions of Arthur. To wash it down Stan asks for a cup of cocoa but is instead given a lemon juice which Arthur explains will break down the fatty cells and cleanse the stomach. The harried bus driver though is soon fed up with dieting and threatens to treat himself to a snack of bread and dripping but his mother's pleas and worrying changes his mind. Instead of a traditional English breakfast at the depot canteen he has what he calls a four-course breakfast consisting of yoghurt and three prunes. Relief though is soon at hand for Stan as Jack tells him of a new report in the morning newspaper which states that the previous day's worrying article was inaccurate. This is enough for Stan to put an end to his diet returning immediately to his preferred unhealthy eating habits.

Dimples

Dimples is a pet name given to Stan by his short-term fiancée Sally in the Series Three episode 'Going Steady'.

When Sally calls Stan by a pet name 'Dimples' it amuses a listening Jack greatly. Amidst hysterics he says to Stan: 'Well you haven't got any dimples on your face. What else have you been showing her?' Although it is never confirmed it is almost certainly a reference to the birthmark on Stan's bottom that Sally mentions later in the same episode.

Dior, Christian

An iconic fashion designer referred to by Arthur in the Series One episode 'Olive Takes A Trip'.

Olive has become a clippie for the Luxton and District Bus Company and proudly shows off her new uniform to Arthur and Stan. However, an unimpressed Arthur feels it hadn't exactly been styled by Christian Dior. Stan chips in: 'More like it's been bashed out by Leyland Motors.'

Christian Dior, born in Granville, France in 1905 was to become one of the most famous fashion designers of the twentieth century. Establishing his own fashion house in 1946 his designs were to be daring, imaginative and innovative. The New Look clothing line was iconic as it changed women's dress designs forever. Sadly, in 1957, Christian Dior suffered a heart attack (his third) and died at the age of fifty two. Despite this his name lives on to this day and his fashion house has expanded to become one of the largest and most respected clothing producing companies in the world renowned for its product's style and quality.

Disc Jockey

Played by Pete Brady

The disc jockey is a character heard but not seen in the Series Three episode 'Foggy Night'.

Stranded aboard Stan's fogbound bus, Olive listens to her radio and hears a newsflash about the thick fog engulfing the area. The disc jockey doesn't relay any good news as he reports the fog won't lift until the morning. He urges the listeners to pull off the road and listen to his show introducing the next song on his playlist. Deflated by this news the radio is turned off and the passengers settle down for what promises to be a long and uncomfortable night.

Diuretic Pills

This type of tablet is used by Stan and Jack to discredit the newly recruited women bus drivers who threaten their livelihood in the film On The Buses.

When a pregnant Olive reveals that she is taking diuretic pills that help her keep her weight down by causing her to lose liquid by increasing her visits to the toilet it gives Stan and Jack an idea. They borrow some of the pills and their ploy sees them pretend to befriend six of the women drivers in the depot canteen offering them cups of tea to show their goodwill. However, the tea has had diuretic pills added to it but unaware the women and Inspector Blake are thankful for the drink. As far as Stan and Jack are concerned the pills have the desired effect as the Town and District bus services are soon in chaos. The women drivers are forced to abandon their buses in mid-route in desperate search of toilets or the nearest bush. Inspector Blake is also affected and spends large parts of his shift in the depot toilet. The general manager is fuming and berates the inspector about the women drivers saying: 'You're responsible for these women. In future you ruddy well see to it that they take their precautions before they leave the depot.' The incident is a blow to the inspector and the women drivers' credibility.

Divorce

Arthur and Olive's rocky marriage ends in divorce in the Series Seven episode 'Olive's Divorce' with the Butler family appearing in court with a strategy to ensure Olive receives her maintenance money.

The divorce case held at a county court is to see Stan give evidence, mum make a court statement describing Arthur as a 'sadistic, perverted beast' and Olive claiming that he threw a tin opener at her piercing her stomach and leaving a scar. However, the real truth of that story is that she had cooked one of her special stews and Arthur took a look at it and threw her the tin opener saying: 'Here open a can of beans.' The scar was actually from when Olive fell off a scooter when she was a child.

The other strategy is put forward by the Butler's family solicitor who suggests that Olive wears a veil to impress the judge and Jack jokingly advises her to keep the veil over her face whilst in court or the judge will feel Arthur had every justification asking for a divorce.

On the other side of the case, Arthur is cross-petitioning the divorce on the grounds of cruelty which Stan refutes as nonsense as he lived with them for ten years. On hearing this Inspector Blake feels it is a clear case of cruelty if Arthur had to live with Stan for ten years.

A distraught Olive enters court and is even more distressed on her exit as it proves to be a long six hour wait in court for her case to come up and so she misses her tea. It comes to light that Arthur does not attend the court case and that he left Olive for another woman. Mum though, attempts to lift her daughter's spirits by telling Stan: 'Now she's got her divorce. She's got her freedom.'

Doctor

Played by Frederick Peisley

The doctor is an elderly, grey-haired doctor at the bus depot who is seen giving Olive a medical examination in the Series Seven episode 'The Perfect Clippie'.

Before Olive can begin her second spell as clippie at the Luxton and District Bus Company she must first undergo a medical in the first aid room at the depot. With her mother attending, Olive has her hearing tested by the doctor who declares: 'You have excellent hearing.' He goes on to ask Olive to undress to her underwear which shocks her but is encouraged to do as she is told by her mum. Mrs Butler is concerned, puzzled and suspicious of the request but the doctor reassures them both saying: 'Rest assured I have sworn the Hippocratic Oath'. He becomes impatient waiting for Olive to undress behind the screens and after a struggle with her corset she emerges wearing a pair of baggy knee-length knickers and vest causing the doctor to look away in stunned disbelief. There is, in the end, no danger of Olive failing her medical such is the desperation for staff as indicated by the inspector. She passes the medical and so begins her second and more successful stint as clippie for the Luxton and District Bus Company.

Doctor's Certificate

A document referred to by Jack in the Series Four episode 'Christmas Duty'.

When he and Stan are forced to work on Christmas Day as a clippie falls foul of the flu, Jack who is desperate to avoid working on the festive occasion, asks Inspector Blake if she has a doctor's certificate. The inspector confirms she has and the illness is legitimate meaning Stan and Jack have to work on Christmas Day.

Donkey

Little Arthur, son of Arthur and Olive, uses a donkey in a mischievous prank in the film Holiday On The Buses.

As Blakey lounges in the sun, having an afternoon nap in a deckchair, little Arthur ties a rope, attached to a donkey, to the chair. He then fires his cap gun in the donkey's ear causing it to break into a trot, collapsing the deckchair with the inspector still in it being pulled along behind the startled beast. Donkey Derbies were frequently held at the Pontins Holiday Camp where the film was shot. It is virtually certain that the donkey used in this scene would have been based on site and a regular in their Donkey Derbies.

Donoghue, Carolae

Film Role: Doreen (Holiday On The Buses)

Carolae Donoghue was to have a short career as an actress with a couple of roles on television and one film credit. Her television roles came in the late 1960s in the BBC drama mini-series Point Counterpoint and this was followed by an appearance in an episode of the classic comedy sketch series Monty Python's Flying Circus. Donoghue's solitary film credit came in 1973 in Holiday On The Buses following which her acting career petered out.

Doreen

Played by Carolae Donoghue

This blonde-haired holidaymaker who, along with her friend Joyce is to go on a moonlight mystery tour with Stan and Jack aboard their bus in Holiday On The Buses.

Doreen, who is in her mid-thirties, is a decisive, opinionated woman and more vocal than her friend. When they agree to a late night trip aboard Stan's bus she pairs off with him. As they share a snog on the upper deck of the bus they are unaware the bus is sinking in wet sand. A visit to his driver's cab sees Stan realise their predicament and whilst he tries to move the bus, Jack, Joyce and Doreen try pushing the bus free of its sand trap but with no success. When Jack says they'll have to walk home a fed up Doreen says: 'Oh thanks very much. That's very nice I must say. Come on pet we'll thumb a lift.' Despite Stan's pleas the two holidaymakers storm off.

Doreen

Played by Kate Williams

A clippie who is dating Stan in the Series Two episode 'Late Again' but their chances of romance are affected by their differing shift patterns at work.

Doreen's dates with Stan are late night affairs as she is on late shifts and has to make do with snogging sessions on her own doorstep. She finds Stan's sexual appetite overpowering labelling him 'a naughty boy' when he asks to come into her house. He is refused entry and reminded that he has an early shift in the morning.

Opinions at home and at work are varied on Doreen. At home Arthur feels it is not right for her to keep a man in her house until the early hours of the morning and that she gives Stan love bites. At the depot Jack can see that Doreen is wearing Stan out and calls him a lucky blighter. Stan does point out that she is not the sort of woman to be rushed into things but Jack rubbishes this opinion as he prefers the more direct approach when dealing with women.

Stan's romance with Doreen is to hit the rocks though when the sleepy driver arrives late again for work and is caught by Inspector Blake and is forced to admit he slept in. He is promptly sent home and put onto a night shift which ruins his plans for another late night date with Doreen. He makes another mistake when he asks Jack to pop round to Doreen's house to tell her he can't make the date. The devious conductor uses the opportunity to win his way into her affections and spends the night there. As Stan visits the following morning he realises Jack has taken his place as Doreen can be heard calling him 'Jacky darling' and as Jack tells his friend it's not his fault she calls out that his breakfast is ready. The crestfallen driver heads home leaving Doreen and Jack to their breakfast with another of his potential relationships in tatters.

Douglas, Sally

TV Roles: Eileen (Series 2 Episode 6 'Bon Voyage') and Susie (Series 3 Episode 4 'Brew It Yourself)

Sally Douglas was born in 1942 and shortly after leaving school was to realise her ambition becoming an actress. She was also to try her hand at modelling and went on to appear in a number of the best adult magazines in the 1960s. As an actress she was to have many roles on the small and big screen throughout the 1960s and into the early 1970s.

Her television credits included classic dramas such as Man Of The World, No Hiding Place and Danger Man. Comedy roles came in legendary sitcoms such as Dad's Army, Doctor In The House and On The Buses. On the big screen she was to appear in a string of classic comedy films in uncredited roles such as Doctor In Love, The Pure Hell Of St Trinian's, Carry On Jack, Carry On Spying, Carry On Cleo, The Intelligence Men, That Riviera Touch, Carry On Follow That Camel and Up Pompeii. Credited roles were also to come in Carry On Cowboy, Carry On Screaming, Genghis Khan and Witchfinder General.

In the early 1970s her acting career was halted when she became a mother for the first time and signalled the end of her acting. Sadly, in 2001, Sally Douglas lost a battle with cancer and passed away at the age of fifty nine.

Dowdeswell, Caroline

Film Role: Sandra (On The Buses and Mutiny On The Buses)

Born in Oldham, Lancashire in 1945, Caroline Dowdeswell was to attend theatre school as a child and on leaving school she fashioned a career as an actress that spanned almost twenty years on British television and in films.

Primarily seen on television she was to appear in dramas such as Softly Softly, Z Cars, Hadleigh, Casanova, Murder

Must Advertise and Crossroads. In comedy roles she was to appear in hit sitcoms Dad's Army, Billy Liar, Man About The House and more prolifically in Ours Is A Nice House. On the big screen her film roles came solely in the two spin-off films On The Buses and Mutiny On The Buses. In 1978, at the tender age of thirty three she was to retire from acting and is now employed in the book publishing industry.

Dracula

This is a far from complimentary nickname Stan and Jack call Inspector Blake throughout all seven series of On The Buses. The first such reference comes in the Series One episode 'The New Inspector' when Stan tells Blakey he could have made a fortune in the films playing Dracula. The nickname was never used in the three spin-off films.

Dracula, one of the most famous characters in horror film history, was a vampire that preyed on attractive women and was created by the Irish writer Bram Stoker in 1897. Many decades later the character of Dracula struck fear into millions of cinema goers around the world appearing famously in a number of Hammer Films productions who, coincidentally produced the three On The Buses films. Dracula has been portrayed by a host of legendary actors such as Christopher Lee, Bela Lugosi and Jack Palance and the many films about the vampire still strike fear into viewers.

Dracula Meets the Apeman

Dracula Meets The Apeman was a completely fictional film that Olive tells the new lodger Mary that she and husband Arthur are going to watch at the pictures in the Series Five episode 'The New Nurse'.

Drake, Sir Francis

A historical figure referred to by Stan in the Series Seven episode 'On The Omnibuses'.

Amidst a dream, Stan is to be first to drive the Luxton and District Bus Company's first motor-powered omnibus in the 1920s. He proudly tells his mum and sister the news and says he feels like a pioneer similar to Sir Francis Drake. When Olive is ignorant to who Stan speaks of he explains he was a sailor who sailed around the world. Vacantly Olive queries: 'What? In a bus?' Stan gives up remarking that she is 'dead ignorant'.

Sir Francis Drake was a hugely-respected Vice Admiral who held a position high in command in the English fleet that went into battle against the Spanish Armada in 1588. He was also the first Englishman to circumnavigate the world in his ship called Pelican (later renamed Golden Hind) between 1577 and 1580. A year later, in 1581, he was to be knighted and passed away in 1596 after a bout of dysentery at the age of fifty five.

Dressmaker's Dummy

An aid used to complete alterations on Olive's dress in the Series Five episode 'The Busmen's Ball'.

With Stan and Arthur toiling to alter the dress as Olive wears it, mum suggests borrowing a dressmaker's dummy from her friend, Mrs Allen. It proves troublesome getting the dummy home aboard Stan's bus as the inspector looks to board the bus mid-route to find the dummy blocking the doorway. After a piece of cunning from Stan he manages to dissuade Blakey from removing the dummy from the bus and the offending item gets to the Butler house. However, more problems arise when Olive finds her dress doesn't hang properly on the dummy. Mum points out that the dummy is too small and needs padding out to resemble Olive's figure ordering Stan and Arthur to help. With the dummy wearing a brassiere stuffed with tea towels and a girdle with a towel wrapped around the waist, the dummy's measurements, after much struggling, began to match Olive's figure. She can finally set about her dress alterations with Stan assuring her that she would look the 'belle of the ball' in her altered dress.

Driving Lessons

Stan is to give Arthur driving lessons as he seeks employment as a bus driver with the Town and District Bus Company in the film Mutiny On The Buses.

After being made redundant Arthur is seeking a new job and with the Town and District Bus Company looking to recruit new bus drivers it seems an ideal opportunity but first he must take driving lessons. These lessons come at some risk and as Stan has to give lessons whilst on duty he risks being caught by Inspector Blake. He teaches Arthur about the bus controls, clutch and gears but over-confidence sees Arthur lose control of the bus with Stan perched precariously, hanging from the driver's door and he eventually lands in a pile of manure and with it trouble. He is left with a uniform unfit to wear and when he arrives back at the depot without his trousers on he is left open to ridicule from the inspector.

Three weeks later and the driving lessons and mishaps continue. Know-it-all Arthur disregards more advice from Stan and reverses the bus into a bus stop knocking it over. But, of course, it wasn't his fault as he claims the gear slipped. It leaves them with a felled bus stop to explain away with Jack suggesting: 'Oh we'll say some hooligans did it. Lots of stupid louts doing things like that these days.' With the lessons complete another accident befalls Arthur and Olive as they are forced to be towed home after the starter lever is snapped off the bike by Olive. The journey home proves to be destined for disaster.

Droopy Drawers

This is a name that both Inspector Blake and Stan are called in separate episodes of On The Buses.

In the Series Four episode 'Dangerous Driving', Inspector Blake hosts the depots keep fit classes and appears wearing a t-shirt and knee-length shorts. Amidst laughter, Jack says to Stan: 'Get a load of old droopy drawers.' It is Stan's turn to be ridiculed in the Series Seven episode 'The Football Match'. He is forced to don a pair of knee-length shorts that he wore many years earlier whilst on national service for football training at the depot. The shorts cause great hilarity amongst his fellow busmen and the inspector. The leg-pulling is all too much for Stan who turns to walk out on the training session when Inspector Blake says: 'Oh come back here droopy drawers. Don't get your knickers in a twist.' This brings more laughter at Stan's expense.

Duggan, Terry

TV Roles: Irate Passenger (Series 1 Episode 3 'Olive Takes A Trip'), Shopkeeper (Series 3 Episode 2 'The Cistern'), The Passenger (Series 4 Episode 8 'The Anniversary'), The Taxi Driver (Series 5 Episode 4 'The Inspector's Pets') and Norman (Series 6 Episode 4 'Stan's Worst Day').
Film Role: Nobby (On The Buses)

Born in Hoxton, London in 1932, Terry Duggan was to have a long and varied career as an actor on television, film and stage that spanned well over thirty years. He was also to marry Anna Karen who, of course, played Olive in On The Buses.

On stage, Duggan performed in cabaret and had a much-renowned act as a drunk which he perfected over the years. He was also a regular on the pantomime scene and appeared in the stage production Busman's Holiday which starred Anna Karen, Bob Grant and Stephen Lewis and the 1982 stage production Steaming.

His television roles saw him appear in classic dramas such as Adam Adamant Lives, The Gold Robbers, Randall And Hopkirk (Deceased), Manhunt, Dixon Of Dock Green, Return Of The Saint, The Bill and Poirot. Duggan was also to appear in the best of British comedy including On The Buses, Please Sir, The Fenn Street Gang, Are You Being Served, Mind Your Language, Only Fools And Horses and Just Good Friends. Film credits in his career included roles in Poor Cow, Touch Of Leather, A Nice Girl Like Me, The Horror Of Frankenstein, Family Life,

Schizo, What's Up Nurse, Murder By Decree, Riff-Raff and Beautiful Thing. Duggan also appeared in the classic Oscar-winning sci-fi 2001: A Space Odyssey playing an ape attacked by a leopard in the opening scene of the film.

Terry Duggan finally retired from acting in 2001 and in the latter part of his life was struck down with ill health before passing away in 2008 at the age of seventy six.

Duke Of Windsor, The

An alternative title given to King Edward VIII after his abdication and this historical figure was referred to by Stan in the Series Five episode 'Boxing Day Social'.

With Arthur's mother and sister paying a festive visit to the Butler's, discussions turn towards Arthur's lost opportunity to become a doctor when younger. Mrs Rudge says to the Butlers: 'He was just about to start studying for medicine then he chucked up his whole career for love of your Olive.' Stan is flabbergasted and remarks: 'God blimey this is a Duke of Windsor all over again.'

The Duke of Windsor was a title given to King Edward VIII when he abdicated the throne in 1936. His abdication came after less than a year as King as he was to fall in love and proposed marriage to a divorced woman from the United States called Wallis Simpson. There was such political pressure applied by the British government led by Stanley Baldwin who felt Mrs Simpson would never be accepted as Queen by the British public that King Edward VIII abdicated and finally wed Wallis Simpson on the 3rd of June 1937.

Dunbar, Philip

TV Roles: Barman (Series 5 Episode 5 'The Epidemic') and The Bus Driver (Series 6 Episode 6 'Bye Bye Blakey').

Philip Dunbar's career as an actor has spanned across six decades with roles across the genres on television, film and stage and continues acting to the present day.

His television roles have included drama roles in No Hiding Place, The Avengers, Paul Temple, New Scotland Yard, Country Matters, Z Cars, The Chinese Detective, Mitch, Call Me Mister, Tales Of The Unexpected, The Bill and Devices And Desires amongst others. In comedy roles his credits include On The Buses, Holding The Fort, Now And Then, Mann's Best Friends and Never The Twain. Dunbar's film roles have come in the latter part of his career coming in The Testimony Of Taliesin Jones, Mike Bassett: England Manager, The Foreigner, The Football Factory, Song Of Songs, Amazing Grace, Thr3e and Love's Kitchen. On stage he has appeared in a number of productions for the Royal Shakespeare Company such as Henry VI, Coriolanus, The Jail Diary Of Albie Sachs and The Changeling. Away from that famous company he had credits in Richard II.

Duncan, Juliet

Film Role: Gladys (Mutiny On The Buses)

Juliet Duncan's solitary acting credit came with her bit-part role as Gladys in Mutiny On The Buses in 1972.

Duty Free Cigarettes

Aunt Maud is to give Arthur and Stan a supply of duty free cigarettes on her return from a holiday in Majorca in the Series Six episode 'No Smoke Without Fire'.

Both Arthur and Stan receive a large boxful of duty free cigarettes from their Aunt Maud which Stan shares with

Jack and a pair of clippies. However, when he gets involved in a bet with Jack and Arthur who wager that he can't quit smoking, Stan is forced to prove his seriousness to quit by throwing all of his duty free cigarettes into the fire along with Arthur's supply. Cunningly, Arthur has emptied his cigarettes into Olive's knitting bag unnoticed by Stan and so Arthur throws what is no more than an empty box onto the fire at the Butler house. He also takes it upon himself to throw Stan's cigarettes into the fire and as they burn Stan tries to retrieve them leaving Arthur to scoff at his brother-in-law's lack of self-control.

The wager seems to have been lost for Stan when Arthur later catches him having a smoke and demands that Stan pays up on his bet. Feeling at ease to have a cigarette himself Arthur sneaks to the toilet where he has hidden his supply of duty free cigarettes on top of the cistern but his secret is uncovered when the family investigate his strange behaviour. He is found standing on the toilet but claims there is a problem with the chain and when mum shows him how to pull it Arthur's hidden supply of cigarettes come raining down on his head. It is revenge for Stan as he has a chance to laugh at Arthur and discovering that his brother-in-law was smoking as well he declares he won't be honouring their bet.

Dyer, Hal

TV Role: Mary (Series 5 Episode 8 'The New Nurse')
Film Role: Mrs Coombs (Holiday On The Buses)

Born in 1935, Hal Dyer's career as an actress saw her with roles on television, film and stage. She was also to wed Michael Robbins who, of course, went on to play Arthur in On The Buses.

Dyer's television credits varied from classic dramas to the cream of British sitcoms and children's series. Her drama roles included Beauty And The Beast, Z Cars, First Night, The Baron, Within These Walls, Ruth Rendell Mysteries and The Bill. Comedy credits came in On The Buses, Doctor At Large, Bowler, The Fuzz, Robin's Nest, George And Mildred, Butterflies and Executive Stress amongst others. She also appeared in a string of hit children's TV series in the late 1970s and early 1980s including Just William, Grandad and most notably in Rentaghost.

Aside from Holiday On The Buses, Dyer's other big screen credit came in the late 1970s romantic drama The Stud.

Stage was close to Hal's heart and stage roles were to include parts in Coriolanus, The Critic After The Rain and Afterplay. She was also to go on to open her own stage production company called the Green Room Company in 1992. The company would begin by putting on stage shows with performances in a room above a coffee shop which she ran before expanding to perform in other venues. She remained active on stage until she tragically suffered a brain haemorrhage late in 2011 and passed away at the age of seventy six.

Hal Dyer in costume after another stage production.
(Picture courtesy of Gillian Bryant)

Here are some of the late Hal Dyer's views and memories on her career, her husband and his time in On The Buses and other roles shared in 2009.

Memories

Speaking of her first meeting with Michael – 'I was a drama student at Birmingham and he (Michael Robbins) was in the company. We were doing a Christmas show and I had to teach him how to dance because I had been trained as a dancer first. He had two left feet I have to admit so that is how I met him. And he took me out to dinner once I remember and then I really didn't see much of him because I think I came back to London and my course had finished and then he came back to London to do something then I went back to Birmingham for a couple of productions at the rep which Michael wasn't in. So we kind of crossed over rather a lot and then eventually we were both in London together and we got married in 1960.'

On Michael (pre-On The Buses) – 'He was very out of work when we first got married and then he did a series with Hylda Baker which was glorious because it was a real money series (wages) and then we both worked at cinemas. I worked at The Empire, Leicester Square and he worked at The Odeon opposite. He was very smart with gloves, long-tails and I was just an ice cream girl so that was rather good and then well we used to do all sorts of funny things. We used to pretend to do private things with badges you know and eventually he got some good work and I went to rep in Felixstowe so that was my first full-time rep job after Birmingham which was weekly so that was quite hard work and I didn't see Michael an awful lot.'

Michael in On The Buses – 'You have nothing for years and then two major series were offered to him – one was On The Buses and one was The Dustbinmen which was fairly successful but not as successful as On The Buses of course and it just went from strength to strength and obviously led to wonderful things.'

On her role in On The Buses – 'The episode was a lovely one. They kept saying: 'Basically Hal you're not On The Buses material you know. You sound a bit posh and you've not got much at the front you know.' In the end Derrick Goodwin said: 'We've got a lovely episode called The New Nurse.' So I played a posh nurse who wanted digs and she moved into the Butlers and of course Michael being the character he was leapt onto this snobbery sort of bandwagon.'

Michael's opinion of his time in On The Buses – 'He loved it. Sometimes old ladies would hit him on the head and say: 'I'm married to a b*****d like you', or something like that you know. Most people loved him. He was very good with people; he did lots of charity stuff. He was just good with people. He had a very nice speaking voice of course which he didn't totally use in On The Buses and they'd say: 'What are you talking all posh for?' (when he chatted at do's you know).

On Michael's role in The Pink Panther Strikes Again – 'He was playing a drag queen in that you see and he said it was extremely difficult for him because (nothing against being with a lot of gay boys) but he was so nervous. On the first day he had to come in the pink ball gown and everything and there was all these lovely boys sitting around looking very pretty and gorgeous and then he had to sing. Blake (Edwards), a few days before, sent a special message – a tape and said: 'This is the voice you are dubbing to – a woman's voice she's not bad.' Of course it was Julie Andrews's voice so when you see The Pink Panther Strikes Again it's Julie singing.'

Easi Order Catalogue

A company Olive and her mother sign up to become agents for in the Series Seven episode 'The Ticket Machine'.

The pair are naively to buy goods from the Easi Order catalogue for themselves such as a tea set, guitar and dress but Stan explains that, as agents, they are supposed to sell goods to other people and not themselves. Even though they remain excited about earning commission on the goods that they sell they are soon brought back down to Earth with a bump as Stan points out how much they'd need to sell to make a sizeable amount of money out of the venture. On hearing the goods have been bought on seven days approval Stan tells Olive and his mum: 'Right well I've seen them and I don't approve. It's going back tonight.' However, before he gets his way, the goods suffer a series of mishaps leaving the tea set smashed, the dress ripped and the guitar broken with another financial crisis left to overcome for the Butlers.

East, John M.

TV Roles: Lofty (Series 1 Episode 1 'The Early Shift') and The Mechanic (Series 6 Episode 4 'Stan's Worst Day')

Born in London in 1932, John M. East came from a family with the theatre in its blood. He followed his grandfather into acting performing on television, film and stage and would go on to work as a script writer and producer.

On television he was to appear in drama series such as Motive For Murder, No Hiding Place and Doctor Who. Comedy roles were more commonplace on the small screen and included appearances in The Dickie Henderson Show, On The Buses, The Morecambe And Wise Show, Romany Jones, The Fosters, Mind Your Language and Jack Of Diamonds.

On the big screen he appeared in Shoot To Kill in the early 1960s. In the late 1970s he moved into the genre of adult films with roles in The Playbirds, Confessions From The David Galaxy Affair and Emmanuelle In Soho which he also co-wrote and produced.

After retiring from the industry he suffered a serious stroke in 1999 and sadly passed away four years later at the age of seventy.

Eastern Bus Company, The

A fictional bus company which takes over Jack's No.11 route in the Series Seven episode 'What The Stars Foretell'.

With the Luxton and District Bus Company amidst a takeover with the National Bus Company, Inspector Blake warns Jack that his job is in danger. He tells the cockily confident conductor: 'I might inform you Harper that your No.11 route to the Cemetery Gates has been taken over by the Eastern Bus Company so I should start looking for another job if I were you mate.' However, there is to be a reprieve for Jack when staff go on strike at the Eastern Bus Company in protest and will only return to work when all staff at Luxton and District are reinstated and so Jack's job along with other colleagues are saved.

Purely fictional in their own right the Eastern Bus Company and National Bus Company referred to in this episode were merely taken from the Eastern National Bus Company – the factual bus company which were to supply their fleet of buses and its depot in Wood Green, London which made the filming of On The Buses possible.

Eau de Cologne

This is a famous brand of perfume that is referred to in a couple of episodes of On The Buses.

Olive, on her first shift as clippie in the Series One episode 'Olive Takes A Trip', complains that the fumes from the engine of Stan's bus are making her feel sick. Frustrated, Stan tells her she will have to get used to it saying: 'This bus runs on diesel oil not Eau de Cologne.'

In the Series Three episode 'The Inspector's Niece', Stan is so eager to impress his new trainee clippie Sally that he rushes home during his lunch break to tidy himself up. He asks his mother to iron his trousers and as she does so Arthur remarks: 'The fragrant odour of hot busman's trousers makes cabbage water smell like Eau de Cologne.'

Eau de Cologne is a famous perfume first created in Cologne, Germany in 1709 by an Italian called Giovanni Maria Farina. Its scent was a hit and was to be sent to royalty all over Europe and production was to see various other forms of Cologne perfumes released. The factory where it was first produced at Obenmarspforten in the German city of Cologne is the oldest such factory in the world and to the present day Eau de Cologne is still in production.

Edna

Played by Patricia Clapton

A diminutive curly-haired clippie, who first flirts with Stan, goes on to date him and later becomes a lodger at the Butler house.

Edna and her friend Joyce are placed aboard Stan and Jack's bus in order to learn how to operate a new radio control system in the Series Three episode 'Radio Control'. She is a quiet and nervous woman who is to pair off with Stan at the Cemetery Gates where he takes her into the driver's cab to show her how to operate the radio control system. He takes the opportunity to have a snog with Edna but she is worried that the inspector can hear what they are up to via the radio control system. Although Stan puts her mind at rest she is to lean on the button opening a channel to Inspector Blake who hears the pair getting amorous over the airwaves. Furious, the inspector joins the bus mid-route but a calamity waits. A diversion sees the inspector order Stan to take a route back to the depot that he is unfamiliar with and the bus crashes into a low bridge. Edna is left shaken up and offended when Stan remarks that Jack was alright as he fell on something soft – Edna.

Edna features heavily in the final episode of Series Three 'On The Make'. She has been dating Stan who has been keeping her out until midnight which leads to her landlady throwing her out of her flat. Left homeless Edna is in tears at the depot and it is up to Stan to come up with a solution as she blames him for her predicament. He invites her to become a lodger at the Butler house paying a meagre three pounds of rent per week, which she is delighted to accept and believes all her worries are over. Arthur though, is far from enthusiastic with the idea but feels better when he realises that her massive pet dog Coco will be staying as well deterring Stan from taking advantage of the situation. It is clear that Edna adores her dog and enjoys his company at night as she confesses to being nervous living away from home and the dog and Arthur both combine to thwart any chance of romance developing between Edna and Stan. It is made worse for Stan as she flaunts herself in a skimpy dressing gown but he is powerless to make a move. Evidently, she grows frustrated waiting and she has a shock for Stan the following evening. Just as he thinks he has arranged a quiet night in alone with Edna as the rest of the family go out to the pictures he finds that she has lined up a date with Jack who will be entertaining her at his house leaving Stan crestfallen and left to look after Coco and so he is foiled again.

Edna

Played by Ursula Mohan

This dark-haired clippie is to date Jack in the Series Four episode 'Nowhere To Go'.

She is to have a snogging session with Jack aboard Stan's bus which is parked in the depot late at night. However, they are disturbed by Charlie the cleaner when he enters the bus spraying it with disinfectant causing Edna to exit coughing with Jack following she complains to a nonplussed Inspector Blake: 'It's made all my mascara run.' With nowhere else to go they call it a night but arrange a romantic night at the Butler house for the following evening with Stan and his date Suzy as Arthur, Olive and mum will be away visiting Aunt Maud for the weekend.

Things aren't to go to plan though for the foursome as they arrive at the Butler house after their date and have all their romantic thoughts banished. The rest of the family are at home and recovering from a motorbike accident ending any hopes of a night of passion for Edna leaving her frustrated along with Suzy, Jack and an exasperated Stan.

Edwards, Percy

TV Role: Bird Impressionist (Series 4 Episode 7 'The Kids Outing')

Born in Ipswich, Suffolk in 1908, Percy Edwards was an animal lover, who from an early age, was to show a great talent for bird and animal impersonations. He would go on to make a career in show business with his rare talent and was to appear on radio, television and in films providing his impressions.

He was to start his career in the entertainment industry early in the 1930s on radio. He performed on BBC radio shows Vaudeville, Ray's A Laugh alongside comedy great Ted Ray and A Life Of Bliss amongst others.

Later in life he worked on a range of television series spanning almost thirty years. Drama series such as UFO and the cartoon series The Ark Stories intermingled with comedy series such as A Life Of Bliss (the television adaption), The Morecambe And Wise Show, On The Buses, The Good Life, Ripping Yarns, The Goodies, Just William, Hi-de-Hi and Sorry made for an impressive career on the small screen.

Edwards was also to have a number of film credits where he again provided his impressions and voice overs. In the early 1980s and up until the end of his career in The Island Of Adventure, The Plague Dogs and the much-acclaimed Jim Henson productions The Dark Crystal and Labyrinth.

He was to retire in 1989 and was awarded an MBE for his services to entertainment in 1993. Sadly, Percy Edwards passed away three years later at the age of eighty eight.

Efficiency Bonus

A payment paid out to its staff by the Luxton and District Bus Company and referred to in the Series Seven episode 'The Ticket Machine'.

With the Butlers amidst another financial crisis Stan is banking on receiving his efficiency bonus payment a month early to pay off family debts but Inspector Blake has other ideas. Stan is told mockingly by the inspector that he won't be getting the bonus as he is not efficient. Desperate for cash, Stan is given a solution by Jack who suggests they use a stolen ticket machine he has obtained to issue tickets keeping the money from the ticket sales. Although Stan isn't keen on the idea his financial plight leaves him with no choice. With the scam under way, it looks like his luck has changed for the better when he finally receives his fifty pounds efficiency bonus after all from the manager but he is in for a nasty shock. Inspector Blake, who on a visit to the Butler house earlier had found a used ticket from the stolen ticket machine uncovering Stan's dishonesty, confronts the driver with the evidence. He offers to sell the used ticket to Stan for fifty pounds and with the other option being the sack he has no alternative but to part with his bonus money. Blakey takes great pleasure in donating the money to the busman's benevolent charity box leaving Stan back in financial difficulty but at least he still has his job.

Eileen

Played by Sally Douglas

Eileen is an attractive, young and busty dark-haired clippie who is to pose for a photograph taken by Jack in the Series Two episode 'Bon Voyage'.

As Stan and Jack tell Inspector Blake of their ploy to pose as photographers with their instant camera to impress the women as they prepare for the works holiday in Spain, Eileen passes by in the depot. To demonstrate their plan, Jack asks her if she wants her picture taken and she is happy to oblige taking off her jacket before posing much to Stan and Jack's excitement. After the photo is taken she asks Jack: 'Can I see it now?' She is told it will take a few minutes so she takes the opportunity to fetch her way bill promising she'll be back.
She appears later in the episode with another clippie as she bursts out laughing when she sees Stan standing trouser less in the depot which also amuses Jack.

Eileen

Played by Cheryl Hall

She is a young blonde-haired clippie who is to date Jack in the Series Five episode 'The Epidemic'.

Eileen is first seen sharing a laugh with Stan and Jack at Inspector Blake's misfortune when he scalds himself when he accidently tips a bowlful of boiling hot water over himself. She goes on to accompany Jack, Stan and his date Sandra on a night out at the pub. Whilst there she remarks the pub does some nice sandwiches but Jack promises her oysters even though they are expensive as he has earned plenty of money through overtime. Oysters are served and eaten by Sandra and an ill Stan first with Eileen commenting that the oysters are alive when they swallow them which makes Stan feel even worse. However, she enjoys the round of oysters and drinks but Stan's night ends in disappointment as he has to go home after coming down with the flu, leaving Jack to entertain Eileen and Sandra alone.

Eileen

Played by Doreen Herrington

She is a busty dark-haired clippie who lends Stan her uniform in the Series Four episode 'The Kids Outing'.

Eileen, wearing a hair-band in her long hair, enters the canteen where children from the kids outing are waiting. One of them cheekily asks her to give them a strip. In a cockney accent she replies: 'You must be joking.' She then agrees to lend Stan her uniform as she goes off duty so that he can perform his drag act Clara the Clippie in a bid to keep the unruly children entertained.

Eileen

Played by Anna Michaels

This attractive, young blonde-haired clippie struggles with her ticket machine at the start of the film On The Buses.

As Jack and Stan pass by she asks the toothy conductor: 'I can't adjust my ticket machine. Can you give me a hand?' Both of the randy busmen move to help the busty Eileen and she enjoys their attention laughing hysterically as they fumble with her straps around her waist. Inspector Blake is soon on the scene though to end their fun by offering Eileen his assistance. As he helps adjust her diagonal straps he is left open to ridicule from the troublesome busmen before they depart laughing raucously.

Eileen

Played by Shirley Steedman

This young and somewhat naïve clippie is seen receiving her Christmas club money in the Series Five episode 'The New Telly'.

Eileen collects her club money from Inspector Blake and when Stan and Jack playfully accuse him of dishonesty, with regards to the Christmas club pay-outs of which he is in charge, she comes to his defence. She claims: 'If it hadn't been for the inspector I wouldn't be in the club.' The naïve remark leaves Blakey open to ridicule from Stan and matters are made worse when Eileen adds: 'He said all I had to do was give him a little bit each pay day.' Jack laughs and labels Blakey 'a dirty old man' to which he explains he just wanted to give her a surprise for Christmas. Stan and Jack joke that he's made Eileen pregnant and the inspector is angered.

She is later seen plotting with Stan and Jack to con the inspector into buying the Butler's old black and white television set when she pretends that she and her friend Edna want to buy it for fifteen pounds. It leaves Inspector Blake miffed that he wasn't offered the chance to buy it but his hopes are later raised when Eileen tells Stan she can't buy it as her friend has bought a coat instead. She pretends to feel terrible about letting Stan down but is given a hug by him and he tells her not to worry. The ploy works and the inspector demands to be allowed to buy the television set which turns out to be an error and a painful experience for him.

Electric Light Company

This is a fictional company that Stan refers to in the Series Five episode 'A Thin Time'.

Stan talks to Jack about another financial crisis at home saying: 'I had the final demand notice in from the Electric Light Company. They're coming in to cut my lights off.' Such is his need for instant cash to settle the bill Stan pleads with Inspector Blake to give him some overtime but the inspector only has overtime for conductors. Stan though, is determined to cut down on future bills and when he returns home from work to find the house brightly lit with all of the lights on he tells the family: 'I'm gonna start by economising. Look at this place – it's like the Blackpool Illuminations.' He switches off lights but mum wants another solution and orders Stan to get some overtime.

The fictional Electric Light Company was likely to have been based on the City of London Electric Lighting Company which served many areas of the capital city. It was to be merged into the London Electricity Board in 1948 as the electricity industry was nationalised and which in turn became London Electricity Plc. when the industry was privatised by a Conservative government in 1990.

Elephant

This is an animal that Olive is likened to on a number of occasions in On The Buses.

Firstly, in the Series Two episode 'Bon Voyage', Stan is having trouble shutting his packed suitcase claiming he'd need and elephant to shut the case. Arthur turns to his wife and dryly says: 'Olive sit on the case.' Similarly, in the Series Four episode 'The Injury', Stan is to find that two plastic tiles meant for the bathroom wall have somehow been stuck together. He exclaims: 'Blimey you'd need an elephant to pull these apart.' Arthur, who fears his money has been wasted if the tiles can't be separated, tells Olive to get hold of one end of the tiles.

Finally, in the film Mutiny On The Buses, Arthur whilst taking driving lessons reverses Stan's bus into a bus stop knocking it over. Stan tells Jack that it would take an elephant to lift the bus stop as they contemplate what to do about the felled bus stop. Arthur butts in saying: 'Olive give them a hand.' However, Stan is not in the mood for his brother-in-law's cheeky comments and tells him to stop being funny.

Elsie

Played by Marcia Ashton

A middle-aged canteen employee at the depot who looks set to lose her job until Stan intervenes in the Series Six episode 'Union Trouble'.

A new rule brought in by Inspector Blake means the canteen has to close for two hours in the afternoon as a cost-cutting measure. A worried Elsie tells Stan and Jack: 'They're cutting down on the staff an' all. I've got the push at the end of the week.'

Immediately, a strike is called by Jack but he is to back down when offered a cash incentive by the management leaving Stan to carry on the fight to save her job alone. Elsie doubts that Stan's efforts will save her job but is grateful when he pledges not to return to work until she has got her job back. However, he is forced to eat humble pie when he calls off his one-man strike but Elsie gets a reprieve. As soon as Jack has received his cash incentive from Inspector Blake he reverts to type and calls a strike which brings about an immediate capitulation from the inspector who abolishes the new canteen opening hours and is also forced to re-instate Elsie rather than risk a strike.

Elsie

Played by Wendy Richard

A young, blonde Cockney clippie who is to have her opinion altered of Inspector Blake changed in the Series Five episode 'The Busmen's Ball'.

Elsie arrives in the inspector's office looking for her way bill as Stan and Jack try to persuade Blakey to hire a stripper for the Busmen's Ball. A photo of the proposed stripper lies on the desk which the inspector tries to hide from Elsie. However, she not only finds her way bill but the photo as well to which she says: 'Ooh Inspector. Oh so you're one of those. Fancy.' The inspector is left open to ridicule and a series of falsehoods from Stan and Jack who pretend the photo is of a clippie that the inspector has taken. Elsie falls for their tale and says to Inspector Blake: 'Here just you wait 'til I tell the other girls about you.' As she storms out of the office, Stan and Jack share a laugh at the inspector's expense who is infuriated.

Elsie – Blakey's Young Love

An unseen girlfriend of a young Cyril Blake that he had a relationship with during World War Two and is referred to in the Series Five episode 'The Epidemic'.

As the inspector is forced to roll up his sleeve by the nurse so he can have his flu jab a tattoo is revealed on his left arm. A heart emblazoned with 1941 and the words 'Cyril loves Elsie' are seen by Stan and Jack. The inspector explains that Elsie was his sweetheart who saw him off from a Liverpool quayside as a young soldier sailing to the Far East in 1941. She told him she'd wait for him but she didn't leaving him heartbroken. He had been away for five years but Stan jokes that five years is a long time for somebody to wait on a Liverpool quayside.

Elsie the Bus Cleaner

Elsie is an elderly woman wearing a headscarf and dirty green overalls who is seen in the Series Five episode 'A Thin Time'. She carries a mop and bucket being told by Inspector Blake to clean the number fourteen buses.

Emergency Duty

This is a type of shift that a financially-strapped Stan signs up for in the Series Four episode 'Cover Up'.

Emergency duty was a shift for bus crews put in place by the Luxton and District Bus Company which puts on extra buses in times of emergency. On this occasion in 'Cover Up' a train failure at a junction throws rail services into chaos and it is up to the bus company to implement a shuttle service carrying rail passengers to their destination beginning late at night with ten buses allocated for the task in hand. However, Stan is destined not to earn any money from his emergency duty as Inspector Blake discovers that the desperate driver has helped himself to company property in the form of bus seat material and promptly charges him for it.

Emery Paper

A type of paper referred to by Stan when Inspector Blake ridicules his legs in the Series Two episode 'Bon Voyage'.

Whilst sunbathing at the Cemetery Gates, Stan has his uniform stolen and is forced to drive his bus trouser less back to the depot. When he arrives he is seen by Inspector Blake who is stunned and describes the bare legs of Stan as a 'ghastly, horrible, disgusting' sight. The driver replies: 'Well if I'd known you'd have felt like that I'd have given my legs a rub down with emery paper.'

Emery paper is a substance very similar to sandpaper and is used for rubbing down rough surfaces or polishing smooth surfaces.

EMI – MGM Studios

The EMI – MGM film studios in Borehamwood, Hertfordshire were to produce all three On The Buses spinoff films from 1971 to 1973.

The studios, formerly owned by the Associated British Picture Corporation, were to become EMI – MGM Elstree Studios in 1970 and remained in this guise until MGM (Metro Goldwyn Mayer) pulled out of the studios late in 1973 when the studios were renamed the EMI Elstree Film Studios.

Films to be produced at the EMI – MGM studios included the classic A Clockwork Orange, a range of Hammer horror films such as The Horror Of Frankenstein, Blood From The Mummy's Tomb and Dr Jekyll And Sister Hyde as well as comedy and adventure films Henry VIII And His Six Wives, Up The Front, Not Now Darling and Digby The Biggest Dog In The World amongst others.

To this day the studios remain operative although their size has diminished greatly since the late 1970s and they are now known as Elstree Film Studios Limited.

It is now better known for its television productions with series such as Big Brother, Who Wants To Be A Millionaire and Dancing On Ice being the best known of these. Films are also still produced there with recent hit productions including Batman Forever, Watch That Man and Star Wars: The Return Of The Sith.

On The Buses returns to Elstree Studios in 2009 as part of an anniversary event.

Emmerton, Ivy

Hairdressing Supervisor (On The Buses and Mutiny On The Buses)

Ivy Emmerton made her name as a hair stylist in the film industry. She was to work on dozens of films in her career which spanned a quarter of a century from the late 1940s.

She worked in the make-up department as hair stylist on noted films such as Your Witness, Time Without Pity, Seven Thunders, Carve Her Name With Pride and Serious Charge in the 1950s. Her credits in the following decade included the war classic Sink The Bismarck, Tarzan The Magnificent, The Two Faces Of Dr Jekyll, The Rebel, The Young Ones, The Quare Fellow, On The Beat, The Wild Affair, Genghis Khan, Sky West And Crooked, The Trap, Far From The Madding Crowd and Goodbye Mr Chips. Into the 1970s and Emmerton was to work on horror films Crescendo, Cry Of The Banshee and Blood From The Mummy's Tomb. Her final credits were to come in the first two On The Buses spin-off films before her retirement from the industry.

Encyclopaedia Britannica

A famous book referred to by Jack in the Series Three episode 'Foggy Night'.

As Arthur sleeps next to Olive aboard Stan's fog-bound bus he clasps a newspaper across his chest as if protecting himself. Jack is puzzled as to why he sleeps like that and Stan asks the curious conductor what he would do if he were married to Olive. 'I'd go to bed with the Encyclopaedia Britannica,' laughs Jack.

The Encyclopaedia Britannica is the oldest encyclopaedia printed in English in the world. It first went into print in 1768 with three volumes and it has since expanded to now being printed in the USA since 1901 with the latest edition containing a massive thirty two volumes. The Encyclopaedia Britannica is also now available in computer software format and via a website.

Engagements

Stan is to be engaged twice – once in the television series and once in the film Mutiny On The Buses.

In the Series Three episode 'Going Steady', Stan is to become engaged to a clippie who happens to be Inspector Blake's niece – her name is Sally Ferguson. Having been dating for a few weeks they announce their engagement but not everyone is pleased. Inspector Blake is furious and even though he is only Sally's uncle he says he'll forbid them from marrying. Equally, Stan's mum is far from happy and is reduced to tears by the news as she laments Stan leaving home. Even his best friend Jack is not in favour of Stan marrying as he feels he is too young to get wed and feels there are many clippies in the depot all willing and ready for a relationship for Stan to enjoy.

In the relationship, Sally is keen to change Stan as she forces him to give up smoking and berates him for continuing to wear brylcreem in his hair. She urges him to dress more fashionably and encourages him to restyle his hair. Their relationship runs into trouble when Sally and her uncle are invited to tea at the Butler house. Sally's snobbish attitude towards Mrs Butler's home cooking doesn't go down well and when Sally starts correcting Stan grammatically and criticising how his new hair-style and tie looks he doesn't like these traits of his fiancée. When his family come to his defence an argument ensues and as a result the engagement is called off.

The film Mutiny On The Buses sees Stan engage a clippie called Suzy. It is her wish for them to move into a flat on marrying which greatly upsets Stan's mum who feels his fiancé is being very unreasonable. However, finances rule out that option for the couple when the flat's rental costs rise. More pressure is put on the relationship as Stan is pressurised by his family to stay at home when Arthur is made redundant leaving them in desperate need of Stan's income. As Suzy becomes impatient waiting for marriage, Stan suggests they can marry straight away and stay at the Butler house. As they discuss the possibility with Stan's mum, Olive and Arthur arrive home to drop a bombshell when they reveal their second child is on its way. This is the final straw for Suzy who gives Stan her engagement ring back and calls off the wedding. And so another engagement ends in disappointment for Stan.

Entertainments Manager

An unseen employee at the holiday camp referred to by Stan in the film Holiday On The Buses.

Arthur tells Stan he and Olive cannot dance in the inspector's old-time dancing team as they do not have the outfits. Stan replies: 'Look the entertainments manager can give you the fancy gear.' Although Arthur is reluctant to do as Stan asks he and Olive are kitted out in ballroom dancing outfits and are part of the exhibition of old-time dancing.

English, Shirley

Film Roles: Third Canteen Lady (On The Buses) and Woman Getting Off Bus (Mutiny On The Buses) (Both uncredited roles)

Shirley English was a bit-part actress whose career peaked in the 1970s. She was to appear in a handful of film and television roles and also worked as a double. Comedy roles were her forte and aside from her uncredited roles in the first two On The Buses spin-off films she had the distinction of appearing in three Carry On films, those being Carry On Matron, Carry On Girls and Carry On Emmannuelle. Television roles were to see her appear in the classic sitcoms Some Mothers Do 'Ave 'Em, Are You Being Served and Mind Your Language. Also, in an uncredited role, she appeared in the hit soap EastEnders.

Within the last few years she has retired from acting and resides in the West Country.

Eskimo Nell

This is a bawdy character from a lewd ballad that is likened to Stan by Inspector Blake in the Series Three episode 'Foggy Night'.

When Stan turns up for duty on a chilly day at the bus depot wearing a scarf, his cap and a large pair of earmuffs the inspector is irritated. He asks his driver: 'What are you made up for? Eskimo Nell?' He has to repeat the question as the earmuffs hinder Stan's hearing and this leads to the inspector urging him to take them off. The character Eskimo Nell stems from a crude ballad thought to have originated from Canada in the late nineteenth/early twentieth century. The lyrics from the ballad went on to be a basis of a script for a 1975 bawdy film called Eskimo Nell as well as appearing in comedy sketches performed by The Goodies and later by Benny Hill.

Ethel

An elderly woman who is a pianist for Inspector Blake during his old-time dance classes in Holiday On The Buses. This character was uncredited in the film.

Excess Baggage

Stan looks to avoid an excess baggage charge as he packs his suitcase for his holiday trying not to exceed thirty three pounds in weight in the Series Two episode 'Bon Voyage'.

In looking to avoid the excess baggage charge for the works holiday to Spain, Stan enlists the help of Olive. He methodically lists and weighs every item packed but his efforts to keep the weight down are hindered as his mum insists he takes a range of medicines. Help is at hand as Arthur lends his assistance adding up the weights as he remarks that if that job is left to Olive they will get the answer in furlongs. When Stan finally feels he has successfully packed his suitcase avoiding the dreaded excess baggage charge, Arthur points out that he has forgotten to include the weight of the suitcase. It is soon to become clear that in order for him to take all of his essentials he will have to come up with another solution. He does this by going on holiday wearing a raincoat whose pockets are stuffed full of items that won't fit in his case which enables him to avoid the excess baggage charge.

Exhibition of Old Time Dancing

A dance team trained and assembled by Chief Security Inspector Blake performs an old-time dance routine in front of a packed audience in the ballroom of the holiday camp in Holiday On The Buses.

The team consisting of nine couples including Arthur and Olive, Mrs Butler and Bert Thompson and Mr and Mrs Briggs take to the dance floor to a round of applause. However, just as the dance gets under way there are problems for Olive as her girdle snaps hindering her movement and the dance has to be started again. Much to Inspector Blake's pleasant surprise the dance begins very well but problems arise again to turn the exhibition into a comedy of errors. Olive's bracelet gets tangled in Arthur's cufflink and she drops her spectacles before stepping on and smashing them. In his desperation to escape the embarrassing predicament and untangle himself the sleeve of Arthur's shirt gets ripped off causing hysterics amongst the audience and humiliated he walks out on the dance which ends in disaster.

Exploding Toilet

Stan and the family have to contend with an exploding toilet in their holiday chalet in the film Holiday On The Buses.

After hastily repainting their chalet after an earlier mishap, Arthur cleans the paintbrushes using petrol and orders Olive to empty the pot of petrol down the toilet which she does flushing it in the process. However, when Stan pays a visit to the toilet he discards a lit cigarette down it which reacts with the petrol causing an explosion that smashes the toilet to smithereens and causes a series of explosions in the drains across the holiday camp but thankfully the inspector naively believes the explosion to have been caused by an accumulation of marsh gas. And so the family narrowly avoid the inspector finding out but once more the family are faced with a predicament of having to replace the toilet without being discovered by the management.

F

Faithfull, Marianne

This famous pop singer and actress at her peak in the 1960s is referred to by Jack in the Series Three episode 'The New Uniforms'.

With new prototype uniforms on their way to the Luxton and District Bus Company, Stan and Jack are shown the designs chosen with the sketches of two busmen in the new uniforms standing in a camp pose. Whilst Stan feels the driver looks like Mick Jagger, Jack claims: 'That's nothing I shall look like Marianne Faithfull.' He remarks, in a camp voice, that the uniform could change his personality.

Marianne Faithfull was a multi-talented figure of the 1960s. Born in London in 1946, she was to become a pop star in the Swinging Sixties and also an actress performing on stage, television and films as well as being a respected songwriter. In the late 1960s she was to have a well-publicised affair with the legendary Rolling Stones singer Mick Jagger before falling on hard times in her personal life in the 1970s. She was to rekindle her pop career late in the 70s and she continues to tour the world performing pop concerts and her acting career has seen her appear in hit sitcom Absolutely Fabulous amongst other things.

Family Man

Played by Michael Slater

This is a balding middle-aged man who boards Stan's bus in the Series One episode 'Olive Takes A Trip'.

The man boards the bus with his wife and two children and it is left up to Mrs Butler to issue him a ticket as her daughter Olive is incapacitated with travel sickness on her first shift as a clippie. Unable to work out the rudimentary working of the ticket machine, Mrs Butler struggles to complete the task and manages to spill Olive's float sending coins rolling all over the floor of the bus as the family man waits for his tickets.

Family Planning Clinic

Olive can be seen paying a visit to a family planning clinic in the film On The Buses.

As she makes her way to the clinic it is said by Stan that Olive is hoping to get the contraceptive pill from the clinic free on the NHS. Jack, however, points out that she'd only get it if she were aged under fifteen or over sixty five. Stan bemoans the government for this saying that one way is illegal to get pregnant and the other is impossible. Following her visit to the family planning clinic though Olive has some startling news for the family – she is expecting her first baby.

Farewell Ball, The

A dance event staged at the holiday camp's ballroom for holidaymakers prior to their departure in the film Holiday On The Buses.

The farewell ball sees Mabel Butler enjoying herself with the flirty Irishman Bert and perhaps Olive's luck is in at last. As she dances with a drunken Arthur he remarks: 'Here sunshine. I can't think why but I quite fancy you.' Olive smothers him in kisses and the pair head back to their chalet and the bedroom. However, applying perfume and body deodorant to prepare for a night of passion she is to find Arthur in a deep sleep. Foiled again Olive bursts into tears.

Farewell Drink, The

Stan is to leave the Luxton and District Bus Company after a number of years of service in the Series Seven episode 'Goodbye Stan' and to mark the occasion he has a farewell drink with his workmates after his final shift.

Although promising his mother he'd spend his last night in Luxton at home with her, Stan agrees to have one drink at the social club with his long-time friend and conductor Jack and fellow busmen Bill, Harry, Bert and Chalkie. However, he is coerced into more than just one drink and it turns into a lengthy drinking session rounded off by a boisterous drunken rendition of 'For He's A Jolly Good Fellow' by Stan's colleagues in honour of him. Stan finally staggers home drunk later in the evening to be met by mum and Olive who are waiting to surprise him with a special meal but that is the last thing he needs at this time after a heavy drinking session.

Farmer, Flossie

Played by Eunice Black

A stocky, dark-haired woman in her fifties who works at the Basildon bus depot and plays for The Basildon Bashers against The Luxton Lions in the Series Seven episode 'The Football Match'.

Flossie Farmer, an outside-left for The Basildon Bashers is unlike most members of her team in that she is not very appealing to Stan and Jack. Kitted out in a figure-hugging football tracksuit and chewing gum she is not the sort of woman they want to meddle with. Later, during the football match she is seen taking part in a team tactic where her team surround the ball protecting it from the opponents until they get near the goal when they break ranks and score. She also goes on to foul Stan leaving him writhing in agony clutching his shin. Worse is to follow for him when he accuses the Bashers team of cheating which isn't taken kindly to and their team mob Stan with their team captain emerging and holds up his shorts which they have removed. Screaming triumphantly she and Flossie parade his shorts around the football pitch which proves that Flossie Farmer was not a woman to be crossed.

Fatima

Played by Julia Mendez

An attractive canteen employee who Stan and Jack are attracted to in the Series Three episode 'The Snake'.

Fatima, with long dark hair is in her late twenties and of Indian origin and speaks in broken English. She is a highly-talented dancer who performs a snake dance at an Indian social event in the depot canteen which entrances Stan and Jack. The snake she dances with is her pet which she looks after with great love and care. This is displayed when Jack wins the battle to date Fatima but she insists on bringing her pet on the date. However, Jack's cunning sees him offload the snake into his laundry bag for Stan to take home so that he can enjoy his date with Fatima in the pub. Later though, she has to use her talents at the Butler house as she and Jack call round to find the family trapped in the toilet with the snake on the loose on the landing. She returns the snake to the laundry bag and makes a hasty retreat from the house with Jack fearing the wrath of Stan.

Ferguson, Sally

Played by Madeleine Mills and Sandra Miller

A young and attractive clippie who is a trainee clippie that attracts the attention of Stan and Jack but she holds a dark secret and she is to appear in three episodes of On The Buses.

Sally is a red-headed clippie in her twenties who is to be trained by Jack aboard Stan's bus in the Series Three episode 'The Inspector's Niece'. Her naivety and flirtatious nature is to have Stan and Jack vying for her affections but her high standards in how she likes her men mean the two scruffy busmen must smarten up to stand a chance of winning her over. It is Jack's choice of a garish floral shirt with matching tie and sense of humour that wins her over but little do the randy busmen know that Sally is, in fact Inspector Blake's niece. This does not stop a romance blossoming later between Sally and Stan which develops into a serious relationship in another episode later in Series Three called 'Going Steady'. The couple announce plans to marry despite objections from relatives and friends but Sally's upper class attitude turns out to be a passion-killer for Stan. Not satisfied with making him give up smoking, urging him to dress more fashionably and restyling his hair she corrects his every mispronunciation and grammatical mistake he makes in front of his family and Inspector Blake. To cap it all Sally upsets Stan's mum by belittling her cooking. The short-lived engagement is brought to an abrupt end and Sally is to move onto her next conquest.

In the Series Five episode 'The Best Man', Sally is to marry a bus driver called Bill much to her uncle's displeasure as he describes him as being dim. Her wedding, although blighted by a series of mishaps, including being kept waiting at the altar and having to borrow Olive's wedding ring for the ceremony, is completed. Sally and Bill head for the wedding reception via a bus hired by Inspector Blake before flying out to Spain on their honeymoon.

Ferris, Roger

Lyricist (On The Buses)

Roger Ferris is a talented musician, songwriter and lyricist with a varied musical career spanning over forty years.

The memorable theme song from the film On The Buses was called 'It's A Great Life On The Buses' and was composed by Geoff Unwin with Ferris supplying the catchy lyrics. Just a few months earlier he had the distinction of working as a sound engineer in the Abbey Road studios as The Beatles had their last ever recording session together. Later, in the 1970s, he was to compose hit songs for the band The Arrows before going on to co-write the Racey hit Boy Oh Boy which reached number twenty two in the UK charts and co-wrote an album track for the band, Smokie.

Later in life, in the 1990s, Roger Ferris was to become a guitarist and song-writer for a blues band called Smokestack and remains a member of the band to the present day.

Fertility Pills

Mum's boyfriend Wilf Phillips suggests that Olive tries taking fertility pills to get pregnant in the Series Three episode 'Mum's Last Fling'.

Wilf, in the midst of suggesting Olive and Arthur will soon be starting a family, hints that they will have to move out of the Butler house. Arthur has other ideas and remarks: 'We've been married nine years mate all she's produced so far are chilblains.' Wilf is not to be deterred and turns to Olive saying: 'Well you want to take one of those fertility pills, you can have five in one go.' Naively, she says she doesn't want to have babies by taking pills as she wants Arthur to be involved. It is left up to Stan to point out she doesn't only take the pills to have a baby.

Fielder, Harry

Film Role: Bus Driver (Mutiny On The Buses)

Born in Islington, London in 1940, Harry Fielder was to go on to become one of the most active bit-part actors in show business appearing in hundreds of roles on television and films spanning well over thirty years.

On the big screen his lengthy career was to see him appear in comedy films such as The Magnificent Two, Carry On Follow That Camel, Carry On Up The Khyber, Carry On Henry, Bless This House, Steptoe And Son, Go For A Take, Carry On Abroad, Carry On Dick, The Likely Lads, The Pink Panther Strikes Again and 101 Dalmatians are the pick of those. He was also to work on films across the other genres many of them much-loved. In the 1960s his career began with roles in Quatermass And The Pit, Billion Dollar Brain, The Charge Of The Light Brigade, Oliver, Where Eagles Dare, Chitty Chitty Bang Bang, Frankenstein Must Be Destroyed and Battle Of Britain amongst others. The 1970s were to offer bit-part roles in classics such as Frenzy, Voyage Of The Damned, The Eagle Has Landed, The Sweeney, Star Wars, The Thirty Nine Steps, Superman, Quadrophenia and more were to follow. Into the 1980s and parts came in The Elephant Man, The Long Good Friday, Superman II, Raiders Of The Lost Ark, Reds, Who Dares Wins and Highlander to name but a few. The 1990s saw no let up with Fielder appearing in hit films such as Wilde, Incognito, Mission Impossible, The Jackal, The Man Who Knew Too Little, Diana And Me and Entrapment which was to wrap up his screen career in 1998.

Fielder was equally active on television and has appeared in a whole host of classic British sitcoms. These were to include Steptoe And Son, Fawlty Towers, Citizen Smith, Yes Minister, Hi-de-Hi, It Ain't Half Hot Mum, Terry And June, The Young Ones, In Sickness And In Health, Chance In A Million and Brush Strokes as well as roles in comedy sketch series such as The Two Ronnies, The Norman Wisdom Show, Not The Nine O'Clock News, The Les Dawson Show, The Kenny Everett Television Show and Smith And Jones. He was also to appear in the best of British dramas including a range of ITC (Incorporated Television Company) series such as Man In A Suitcase, The Saint, The Champions, Randall And Hopkirk (Deceased), The Persuaders, The Protectors and Space: 1999. Away from ITC, Fielder also appeared in Z Cars, Poldark, Softly Softly, The Sweeney, The Duchess Of Duke Street, Shoestring, Secret Army, The Professionals, When The Boat Comes In, Doctor Who, Minder, Hart To Hart, Juliet Bravo, Big Deal, Dempsey And Makepeace, EastEnders, Grange Hill, Bleak House, Casualty, London's Burning and The Bill are the pick of his television career.

Harry Fielder, known to many affectionately as Aitch, has now retired from acting and has just released his autobiography of his career called Extra, Extra Read All About It. He remains active attending fans conventions and events whilst working on his own website.

Harry 'Aitch' Fielder meets the late Ronnie Wolfe at The Bafta Theatre.

Here is Harry Fielder talking about working on Mutiny On The Buses at the 2010 Back On The Buses event in Borehamwood, Hertfordshire on Saturday the 26th of June 2010.

Memories

'I came up here (Elstree) in '71. I was an extra and had some scenes and that was fun too. It was a lovely crew as well, lovely cast because they made you feel welcome. You weren't just an extra you were part of the furniture.

I thought I was smart with a flowery shirt and I looked terrible. When I look at it now it was so bad and the hair was down the back and it was dark. I dye it grey now just to tell people I'm getting old.

I was a bus crew and also I was the chalker on the dartboard in the canteen where there was quite a big scene. Olive and another girl had a fight but when I see the fight coming I went to the back of the crowd because, I thought, I don't want to be in this but it's all on film.

It's wonderful to see all fans of On The Buses because it was such a good show in its day. I never worked on the black and whites for London Weekend but when they made the films I was asked to come down for a few days and done it. It was just a job but because they were so nice – the company and the actors I done it. No problems.'

Finalist

Played by Folker Hendrix

This character is a tall, dark-haired bus driver with a small, neatly trimmed moustache in his twenties who is an unnamed finalist in the promotional poster competition in the Series Seven episode 'The Poster'.

We learn from Inspector Blake that as well as a bus driver he plays football for Melwood depot's team and attends the selection event wearing a gaudy yellow shirt with his uniform. The judging panel deem him and two other finalists called McGregor and Perkins unsuitable to appear on the company's recruitment poster with Stan winning the contest. As the unnamed finalist congratulates Stan he slyly kicks him in the shin before exiting the depot.

Fire

A blaze aboard Stan's bus endangers life and his job in the Series Six episode 'No Smoke Without Fire'.

A smoking ban in the workplace sees Jack bet Stan that he won't be able to give up smoking. However, it is no surprise that Stan cannot resist smoking and tries to smoke a cigarette covertly on the bus but is almost caught by Inspector Blake discarding his lit cigarette in a used ticket bin aboard the bus. As the bus gets back underway with only Stan, Jack and the inspector aboard they are all unaware that a fire has started in the bin. The fire begins to grow in intensity and Jack tries to put out the blaze with a fire extinguisher but his incompetence sees him drop it and it falls off the bus. With Inspector Blake trapped upstairs drastic action is needed. Parking his bus in a remote field Stan rushes to put out the fire with the extinguisher from the driver's cab but as the fire rages he finds his extinguisher all but empty. Meanwhile, Inspector Blake cuts a desperate figure on the upper deck yelling for help from the rear window with the lower deck engulfed in flames. It is up to Stan and Jack to act fast if they are to rescue their old nemesis. Using old fencing found next to the bus the pair use it as a makeshift ladder enabling the inspector to clamber to safety but as he does so he is to fall into a pond as the ladder tips backwards adding to his misery.

In the aftermath of the incident Stan fears the sack but he gets lucky as the bus company prefer to put the fire down to faulty wiring which ensures that the insurance company pays for a new bus. To compound the inspector's frustrations he is ordered by the management to thank Stan and Jack for saving his life which he finds very hard to do.

Fire at the Depot

A blaze at the Town and District bus depot causes havoc in the film Mutiny On The Buses.

131

Stan and Jack attempt to use the engine to heat up fish and chips aboard their bus which almost sees them caught by Inspector Blake. They are forced to drive the bus back to the depot with the chips burning on the engine causing smoke to bellow out of it. On arriving at the depot Stan leaps from his cab and rushes to remove the chips from the engine which are now alight throwing them into an inspection pit. That proves to be a bad mistake as the burning chips set fire to a bundle of rags in the pit. A shocked Inspector Blake exclaims: 'Oh my god…look. There's a fire in the inspection pit.' He orders Stan to get the fire extinguisher and the bus driver reads its instructions step-by-step. However, this proves futile as the extinguisher is virtually empty. The stressed Blakey orders the fire alarm to be sounded as flames begin to leap from the pit dangerously close to Stan's bus and the inspector yells: 'Get the hose quick and turn the water on.' Another mishap prevents this though as the tap has rusted up and the inspector, by now at the end of his tether shouts: 'Don't panic! Don't panic! I'll phone the fire brigade.' At this point the livid general manager Mr Jenkins arrives on the chaotic scene and orders Stan to reverse his bus away from the fire and although that prevents an even more serious fire developing it sees Inspector Blake's new Minivan being crushed as Stan's bus reverses into it.

The depot is saved from burning down but staff incompetence, poor training and inadequate firefighting appliances sees Mr Jenkins introduce new measures.

Fire Buckets

Positioned hanging on the walls in the bus depot these fire prevention aids are used in a couple of episodes of On The Buses.

In the Series Three episode 'Busmen's Perks', Stan uses two fire buckets painted red to smuggle pots of paint onto his bus past Inspector Blake who is on the prowl. The paint pots are hidden in the bottom of the buckets under a layer of sand which conceals them. Later, in the Series Five episode 'The Inspector's Pets', Stan and Jack are amidst refilling the repaired aquarium of the inspector's in his office prior to his return from holiday. They are to use the fire buckets filled with warm water to refill the aquarium before adding the fish which are stored in thermos flasks.

Fire buckets, still used to this day, mainly in government-controlled buildings, are filled with sand. They can be used on oil fires where water is non-effective and also used to sprinkle over spillages of flammable liquids and reducing the risk of fire or explosion.

Fire Drill

An exercise carried out at the Town and District's bus depot after an earlier fire caused chaos in the film Mutiny On The Buses.

The idea of a fire drill doesn't go down well with the staff as Jack points out that they are busmen not firemen but he is put firmly in his place when Mr Jenkins says it has all been agreed with the union. The drill is to be supervised by Inspector Blake and it is to be used to train the staff on how to operate newly-purchased firefighting appliances.

However, Stan and Jack decide to use it as a chance for more tom-foolery. As the inspector bids to keep everyone on their toes, Stan fools around with the fire extinguisher and in an act of revenge sprays it into brother-in-law Arthur's face but worse is to follow. When the inspector is called away he puts Stan and Jack in charge of the foam-making machine with trouble sure to brew. They try to increase the amount of foam it is producing with Jack turning the handle up so much it comes off in his hand and inexplicably he throws the handle into the inspection pit as it begins to fill up with foam. The machine is now out of control and foam soon begins to engulf the depot as the gobsmacked Blakey returns to find his drill in chaos. In remonstrating with Stan and Jack he falls into the inspection pit which is now hidden beneath a sea of foam. Hoots of uncontrollable laughter ring out from the busmen with only Stan showing concern for the inspector's well-being. As he goes to his rescue he loses his balance and joins Blakey in the pit. It is up to an enraged Mr Jenkins, who arrives on the scene, to try to restore order but suddenly Olive aboard an out of control motorbike and sidecar enters the depot and forces him to also fall into the pit.

The fire drill ends with foam-covered Inspector Blake wheelchair-bound ready for treatment from a nurse. However, when the infuriated general manager emerges from the pit he blames the inspector for the fiasco and pushes him in his wheelchair back into the foam-filled pit.

Firefighting Appliances

The Luxton and District Bus Company's fire equipment are referred to by Inspector Blake in the Series Six episode 'No Smoke Without Fire'.

When a fire starts in the depot's paint shop after an employee drops a lit cigarette in a can of paint thinner it is left up to the inspector to put the blaze out. He later tells Stan and Jack that there was no problem with the firefighting appliances it was just that none of the staff knew how to use them apart from him. It causes the bus company to introduce training for its staff with a course of instruction on firefighting.

Fireman's Lift, The

This is a technique that is taught during the course of instruction on fire fighting in the Series Six episode 'No Smoke Without Fire'. Inspector Blake demonstrates the fireman's lift on Jack.

The fireman's lift is still taught today as a method to carry either injured or unconscious people in a fire to safety. It is better known today as the firefighting lift as, of course, the fire brigade does now employ both men and women.

First Aid Book

A manual stored in the first aid boxes aboard the Luxton and District buses which feature in the Series Three episode 'First Aid'.

When Inspector Blake slips and falls aboard Stan's bus injuring himself in the process Jack has to refer to the first aid book as he and Stan look to treat the inspector. The book contains a section on how to treat people injured in a fall that Jack refers to but it is of no use as one of the key pages of the manual has been ripped out. The first aid book is used later in the episode by Stan as he uses it to revise for his first aid test in his bedroom. He studies a section on suspected fractures and the treatment required before enlisting the help of Arthur. Also covered in the book are sections on haemorrhages and bleeding as well as on dizzy spells.

First Aid Clippie

Played by Suzanne Vasey

This is a clippie who has a first aid badge and treats the injured Inspector Blake in the Series Three episode 'First Aid'.

A long-haired blonde clippie with a posh accent called Eileen helps Stan carry the limping inspector over to a bench in the depot and offers her assistance as she holds a first aid badge. She examines his leg and declares it is swollen and starts to massage it much to the inspector's pleasure but the envy of Stan and Jack. Eileen has to tick the conductor off when he offers to help the inspector saying: 'If you put your hand in the wrong place it could lead to trouble.' Instead she and a fellow clippie help the inspector to the first aid room with great care as Jack curses as he feels they are fussing over nothing more than a strain.

First Aid Room

An area at the Luxton and District bus depot manned by either a nurse or doctor and used to treat ill or injured staff members and carry out medical examinations which is referred to and seen in three episodes.

In the Series Three episode 'First Aid', Stan and Jack help the limping Inspector Blake off of the bus after his accident. 'Come on mate, we'll get you over to the first aid room,' says Stan. The inspector is met by a clippie with a first aid badge who treats him as he sits on a bench in the depot before she helps him to the first aid room. The depot's first aid room appears in the Series Five episode 'The New Nurse'. Inspector Blake has an upset stomach and is treated on the treatment table of the first aid room by the company's new nurse. She examines his stomach and feels his pains are caused by stress and worry with which he agrees. The nurse gives him a medicine to drink but he is still troubled with pains. He is later to obtain medicine, pills and yoghurt from the first aid room. The Series Seven episode 'The Perfect Clippie' sees Olive being examined by the company doctor in the first aid room. She has to pass a medical before she can become a clippie for the Luxton and District Bus Company and is accompanied by her mother. Her hearing is described as excellent by the doctor and after a thorough examination she passes her medical.

First Aid Test

An examination of the busmen's first aid skills are arranged after Inspector Blake injures himself in a fall aboard Stan's bus and incompetent treatment by Stan and Jack worsens his injuries in the Series Three episode 'First Aid'.

The price of failure is high for Stan and Jack as they are warned by the inspector that if they fail their first aid test they will be transferred to other departments such as cleaning or maintenance. This is enough to worry Stan into revising for the test using the company's first aid book and even enlists the help of Arthur to assist in the revision.

The following morning, to his relief Stan is to pass his test but Inspector Blake pours scorn on this saying he only passed because it was another inspector testing him. Jack also passes but not quite so comfortably as he later tells Stan to go and help a nurse when a pregnant woman goes into labour on their bus pointing out that Stan did better than him in the first aid test.

First Chairman and Treasurer of the Canteen Sub-Committee

A post Stan is elected to against his wishes in the Series One episode 'The Canteen'.

When the Luxton and District Bus Company's management allow the employees to run the depot canteen themselves, Jack nominates Stan to become first chairman and treasurer of the canteen and fellow employees back his nomination. Stan reluctantly is left in charge and the post means it is up to him to employ a new canteen cook and finance the running of the establishment.

It turns out to be a disastrous post for Stan as he makes a string of costly mistakes. He employs an Indian cook without the grasp of either the English language or the ability to cook traditional British dishes for the busmen and he is soon pressurised into dismissing her which costs him money to pay her off. Stan's next error comes when he is persuaded to give Olive the job despite her legendary lack of cooking ability but he is comforted when his mother offers to lend a hand. However, things don't go to plan as Mrs Butler toils with working the electric stove putting a saucepan on the wrong ring burning a hole in it. As the waiting busmen grow impatient waiting for their food, Stan is forced to take desperate measures. He pays a visit to a local fish and chip shop to buy the busmen's lunch without their knowledge. However, his mum and sister make the error of charging less for the fish and chips than Stan has paid for them leaving him drastically out of pocket. The inevitable sacking of Olive sees Stan having to fork out more money out of his own pocket to pay her wages which is his last act in the short-lived role.

The short spell of the employees running the canteen ends just two days after it has begun with Stan losing more money in those two days than the bus company had lost in six months. And so the canteen ends up back in the hands of the Luxton and District Bus Company.

First Judge

Played by Michael Sheard

A man who sits on the depot's judging panel for the promotional poster contest in the Series Seven episode 'The Poster'.
The middle-aged bespectacled man with a moustache is not overly impressed by the first three candidates to appear before the judges as he sees them as too clean cut and not at all like the typical bus driver type which they are looking for. When Stan appears in front of the panel with an oil-smeared face and uniform in a bid to present himself as a caring, responsible and conscientious bus driver the first judge is won over. After a brief conference with his fellow judges he announces Stan as the winner of the promotional poster contest much to Inspector Blake's obvious disappointment.

First Policeman

Played by Ivor Salter

This is a policeman who settles a dispute between Inspector Blake and a housewife in the film On The Buses.

The policeman in his mid-forties arrives on the scene of a heated confrontation as Inspector Blake tries to confiscate a young housewife's laundry as he wrongly believes it belongs to Stan. The fiery housewife tells the policeman: 'He pinched my laundry.' In a bid to settle the matter the policeman holds up a pair of black frilly pants from amidst the laundry bag and asks Blakey: 'Are these yours?' When the inspector claims they are his driver's, Stan lands him in deeper trouble telling the policeman: 'No I can truthfully say officer I've never seen those before in my life.' The policeman proceeds to take down the inspector's details whilst Stan mocks Blakey saying in a camp voice: 'See you in court darling.'

Fish-Faced Twit

An insult aimed at Inspector Blake by Stan in the Series Seven episode 'Goodbye Stan'.

As Stan is about to hand in his resignation for a new job he has lined up, cunning Jack points out that he should get himself the sack thus earning a week's pay in lieu of notice. Stan takes the advice and uses the opportunity to insult the inspector calling him a 'fish-faced twit'. Blakey demands an apology which isn't forthcoming and so Stan is sacked. However, the inspector's glee is short-lived as he discovers that Stan has tricked him out of a week's pay as he had planned to resign anyway.

Fit and Beautiful

This was the name of a fictional health magazine read by Arthur in the Series Five episode 'A Thin Time'.

He reads the Fit and Beautiful magazine at the Butler house hiding it behind his newspaper until it is discovered by Stan. He labels his brother-in-law a 'filthy old man' as the magazine is full of pictures of naked women. This repulses Olive and mum but Arthur argues that there are naked men in the magazine as well and that it is purely a scientific magazine. It is from this Fit and Beautiful magazine that he orders a set of expensive wigs despite the family being immersed in another financial crisis.

Flat Feet

A medical condition that Arthur suffers from that is to prevent him from doing his national service as referred to in the Series Six episode 'The Prize'. However, Stan refuses to believe this and accuses Arthur of being cowardly claiming he has a yellow streak down his back.

Flower Display at the Bus Depot

A floral arrangement is set up at the bus depot by Inspector Blake in the Series Seven episode 'Gardening Time'.

The inspector has caught the horticultural bug and sets up a flower display consisting of chrysanthemums, begonias, hydrangeas and pansies in flower pots on the window ledge of his office. Jack though, has no respect and sees the flowers as free to pick to give to his girlfriend Sandra. However, the inspector is determined to catch the villain that his destroying his display. He sets a trap that sees him catch Jack red-handed and he exacts painful retribution until the manager puts a stop to his fun and to make matters worse he ridicules Blakey's flowers as 'feeble specimens'. The inspector, however, does get the chance to prove his prowess as a gardener when the manager announces there is to be a depot flower and vegetable competition with a cash prize of twenty five pounds for the winner.

Flynn, Kenneth

TV Role: Child (Series 4 Episode 7 'The Kids Outing')

Born in London, Kenneth Flynn's solitary acting role came as a mischievous schoolboy in an episode of On The Buses. He was never to appear in front of the cameras again and on leaving school took up a career away from acting.

Fogbound

A fate that is to befall Stan's bus and to make matters worse the family and Inspector Blake are aboard in the Series Three episode 'Foggy Night'.

The Luxton and District's number fourteen bus service from Gibbet Hill is on its way back to the depot making its way through the remote countryside when thick fog brings a halt to the journey late at night. Despite Inspector Blake's statement to the concerned passengers that all of the bus company's drivers are highly trained, Stan enters the bus from his drivers cab exclaiming that he is lost as he can't see where he has been or where he is going. There is no better news to relay as Olive listens to her radio with a newsflash forecasting the dense freezing fog not to lift until the following morning.

The stranded passengers and bus crew settle down for a long night aboard the bus. Whilst mum knits herself to sleep and Blakey snoozes, Stan and Jack use the opportunity to alleviate their boredom. Using peanuts he finds in his pocket, Jack bets Stan he can throw them into Blakey's mouth as he sleeps and is to succeed but wakens the inspector who swallows the nut only to mistake it for a tooth. The night is to take a turn for the worse for Olive when she needs to go to the toilet. It means a trip outside and to ensure she doesn't get lost in the fog mum gives her a piece of wool with mum holding onto the ball on the bus. However, Olive loses the wool and gets pushed into nettles by a cow but by following Stan's voice she finds her way back to the bus in a distressed state and covered in mud. The same cow threatens to invade the bus frightening the passengers but is chased off by Jack with Stan joking that with his teeth the cow probably thought he was the farmer's horse. By this time the passengers are growing restless and Arthur urges the inspector to find a phone box and phone the depot to report their predicament. Although Blakey is not keen on the idea all of the passengers insist he makes the effort. He ventures out into the foggy night allowing Stan and Jack to raid his snack box which contains two bags of crisps which are eventually shared out amongst the passengers. They are disturbed though by the inspector's return who has walked into a ditch losing his boots in the process leaving his feet covered in mud. It is to be a messy end to the night for a fed up Inspector Blake.

The following morning brings an end to their ordeal as the fog lifts allowing them to complete their journey. The bus arrives back at the depot after a trip which has lasted over twelve hours.

Folkestone

A factual seaside town that the inspector has visited on a fishing trip that is referred to in the Series Five episode 'The Inspector's Pets'.

Prior to a fishing holiday in Brighton the inspector takes from his wallet a faded photograph of himself and shows it to Stan saying: 'That's me at Folkestone holding the catch.' Stan mistakes the fish being held up in the photo for a kipper only to be told by Blakey that it is a sole.

Folkestone is a small town on the Kent coast which is seventy one miles to the south east of London. With a population of just over 50,000 it was once a popular seaside resort but with a decline in holidaymakers it has been forced to re-invent itself in recent years. It is now, of course, renowned as the passenger terminal for the Eurotunnel which opened in 1994.

Foot, Moira

Film Role: Katy (On The Buses)

Moira Foot, born in Nottingham in 1953, was to go straight into acting on leaving school. She was to fashion a career that included roles in films, television and on stage.

On the big screen her film roles came in the early 1970s in One Brief Summer and On The Buses. Stage credits included appearances in Suddenly At Home and A Bit Between The Teeth but it was on television that she was most active. Primarily, her best work came in a string of classic British comedy series such as Hark At Barker, Six Dates With Barker, Doctor At Large, Billy Liar, Are You Being Served, The Benny Hill Show and The Dick Emery Show in the 1970s. The 80s saw Foot have a role in the hit David Croft and Jeremy Lloyd-written 'Allo 'Allo which she is perhaps best remembered for. Drama roles included parts in Quiller and The New Avengers.

Her acting career spanned over twenty years and she has since quit acting and now runs a farm in the south east of England with her husband.

Football Match – The Luxton Lions V The Basildon Bashers

The Luxton and District Bus Company's football team lines up in a match against a team from the nearby Basildon depot in the Series Seven episode 'The Football Match'.

With a cash incentive of five pounds promised to The Luxton Lions players if they win, Stan and Jack are keen to be involved. However, the team manager Inspector Blake feels they are unfit and insists they must take part in training if they want to play in the match. Reluctantly, they agree but in any case they feel the match is already won with their highly-talented star player Bob in the team. Training though proves to be disastrous for Stan.

His clowning around sees him collide with Bob who injures his ankle ruling him out of the big match and leaving Stan with the job of finding a replacement to appease his team-mates. With their star player side-lined and no replacement forthcoming things look bleak.

Match day arrives and in desperation Stan recommends Olive for a place in the team but the inspector won't allow it until he meets the captain of The Basildon Bashers in embarrassing circumstances discovering the opponents are a ladies team. It lifts the hopes of The Luxton Lions and Olive is allowed to play as goalkeeper so the match can go ahead.

With Olive taking to the pitch in red high-heeled shoes and minus her glasses which she removes fearing she might break them as goalkeeper, the match refereed by Inspector Blake gets under way but soon degenerates into farce. The Basildon Bashers are better organised and have game plans whilst The Luxton Lions have a short-sighted goalkeeper and Jack who is not interested in playing football spending the entire match chatting up attractive members of the Bashers team.

By half-time, Stan has been booked for dissent, Olive has scored an own goal and flattened the ball when falling on it and The Basildon Bashers lead 5-0. A half-time ear-bashing from the manager has no effect and The Luxton Lions day gets worse when they are served a disgusting half-time cup of tea made by Olive which is no tonic.

The second half doesn't get any better for The Lions as their opponents use a cunning game plan to score yet again and also resort to breaking the rules to score at will. Even Stan's bid to counter with his own game plan where he hides the ball up his jersey and runs the length of the pitch unchallenged to bring the ball out and smash it into the net doesn't change the end result.

The match ends in high embarrassment for Stan when he accuses the Bashers of cheating. He is surrounded by their captain and the rest of the team and they rip his shorts off and parade them around the pitch. Despite his team getting thrashed Inspector Blake revels in Stan's embarrassment telling him: 'You not only lost the game, you lost your fiver and you lost your trousers as well.'

Football Pools

A game that Arthur plays religiously which is referred to in episodes and a spin-off film of On The Buses.

In the Series Three episode 'The Snake', Arthur can be seen discussing matches with Stan as he works out his football pools coupon. Later, Arthur uses an envelope containing a diamond to work out his pools permutations on in the Series Five episode 'Lost Property' which causes Stan problems. On the big screen, in the first spinoff film On The Buses, Arthur sits doing his pools and winds up Stan who is concerned about the new influx of women bus drivers at the depot. Stan warns him: 'I tell you something mate. You'd better start getting your football pools up 'cause I'm gonna end up losing all my overtime.'

Football pools came into being in the early 1920s through the Littlewoods Company with other companies soon introducing their own coupons. The purpose of the game is to predict results from the weekend's fixtures lists. It was a very popular game in the 1950s through until the early 1990s but since the introduction of the National Lottery in 1994 its popularity has waned somewhat but is still played by great numbers.

For He's A Jolly Good Fellow

A song that is sung boisterously by Stan's friends and colleagues as they share a farewell drink with him as he prepares to leave Luxton for pastures new in the Series Seven episode 'Goodbye Stan'.

The traditional song, written in 1709, is frequently sung on special occasions and is one of the most popular songs in the English language. According to the Guinness Book of World Records only 'Happy Birthday To You' is sung more frequently in English.

Francis, Eric

TV Role: Joe (Series 4 Episode 1 'Nowhere To Go' and Series 4 Episode 9 'Cover Up')

Eric Francis was born in Manchester, Lancashire in 1917 and was to break into acting in his mid-thirties and cemented a career as an actor that spanned almost forty years with an abundance of roles in films and television.

His first big break came on the big screen in the early 1950s appearing in Valley Of Song, Trouble In The Glen, Make Me An Offer, Indiscreet and I Was Monty's Double amongst others. The 1960s brought further big screen roles in Hand In Hand, The Flesh And The Fiends and The Amorous Prawn. His best remembered role on the big screen came in the 1970s in the classic horror film Theatre Of Blood and that decade also saw him appear in The Private Life Of Sherlock Holmes and Confessions Of A Pop Performer. Into the 1980s, Francis was to appear in The Shillingbury Blowers, The Boys In Blue and the award-winning films The Meaning Of Life and Little Dorrit.

On television he was to appear in a long line of classic British drama series such as Doctor Who, Z Cars, The Troubleshooters, Dixon Of Dock Green, Van der Valk, Secret Army, Danger UXB, Shoestring, Minder, Big Deal, Casualty and The Bill. Comedy roles were also plentiful coming most notably in Some Mothers Do 'Ave 'Em, On The Buses, Love Thy Neighbour, Going Straight, Terry And June, That's My Boy, Don't Wait Up and May To December.

Eric Francis continued acting up until passing away in 1991 at the age of seventy four.

Frankenstein

This is a derogatory name given to Inspector Blake by Stan and Jack in several episodes of On The Buses.

The first occasion they refer to Inspector Blake as Frankenstein is in the Series Four episode 'The L Bus'. Jack warns Stan that the inspector is approaching by saying: 'Heads up. Here's Frankenstein.' Similarly, in another Series Four episode called 'Safety First', as Blakey nears them in the depot wearing a scarf, Stan says to Jack: 'Heads up here comes Frankenstein.' Puzzled, the toothy conductor asks: 'What's he got that scarf 'round his neck for?' Stan jokes: 'So you can't see where his head's bolted on.' In the final episode of Series Four, 'Not Tonight' the new canteen employee Stella introduces herself to Stan. In return Stan introduces her to the inspector saying: 'You recognise this? This is Frankenstein.' Finally, in the Series Five episode 'Lost Property', Inspector Blake who is keen to avoid ridicule again, rules that lost property forms must be completed by the bus crews instead of inspectors. 'Old Frankenstein's getting crafty,' says Jack.

Frankenstein is one of the most famous horror novels ever written. Mary Shelley was to write the book in 1818 about a terrifying constructed monster created by a scientist. Her novel was to be adapted into numerous films with the first being made in 1910 with films up to the present day having included legendary actors such as Boris Karloff, Christopher Lee and Robert De Niro playing the fearsome monster.

Frankenstein Meets The Ape Woman

This is a fictional film's theme song about to be played on Olive's radio in the Series Three episode 'Foggy Night'.

As fogbound passengers aboard Stan's bus have just heard that the thick fog is not to lift until morning they hear the disc jockey on Olive's radio say: 'Coming up next – the great theme song from Frankenstein Meets The Ape Woman'. Stan mocks Arthur by telling him they are playing his song.

It is likely the classic 1943 horror film Frankenstein Meets the Wolf Man starring Lon Chaney Jnr and Bela Lugosi inspired Wolfe and Chesney's fictional title with Ape Woman replacing Wolf Man for comedic value at Olive's expense.

Fraser, Helen

TV Role: Linda Rudge (Series 5 Episode 15 'Boxing Day Social')

Born in Oldham, Lancashire in 1942, Helen Fraser was to attend dance classes from an early age before progressing on to drama school in her teens. She ventured down to London on leaving school to attend RADA (Royal Academy of Dramatic Art) where she was to graduate. She has since gone on to have a long and successful career as an actress in film, television and on stage.

Her best-remembered role in her big screen career came in the award-winning 1963 comedy film Billy Liar. She also appeared in other film roles such as A Kind Of Loving, Repulsion, The Birthday Party, Start The Revolution Without Me, Something To Hide, From Beyond The Grave and Gorillas In The Mist.

Fraser's television credits are just as impressive with appearances in classic British dramas such as Z Cars, No Hiding Place, Dixon Of Dock Green, Crown Court, Tales Of The Unexpected, The Box Of Delights, Coronation Street, Casualty and most notably a starring role in the long running and award-winning series Bad Girls. She has also had numerous roles in quality comedy series such as Pardon The Expression, Six Of The Best, The Likely Lads, Doctor In The House, The Dustbinmen, Never Mind The Quality Feel The Width, On The Buses, Man About The House, Doctor In Charge, Rising Damp, The Dick Emery Show, Sorry, Duty Free, In Loving Memory, One Foot In The Grave and The Royle Family amongst others.

She has also had an active stage career, a genre she has great fondness for, with roles in a musical based on the life of On The Buses star Dame Cicely Courtneidge called Vitality. Fraser also appeared in Belcher's Luck in the 1960s. In recent years she has appeared on Broadway in The Beaux Stratagem before returning to the UK with roles in Absolute Hell and The Vagina Monologues. She remains active on stage having performed in Bad Girls: The Musical and the stage adaption of Billy Liar.

Fred

Played by David Lodge

This busman is in his mid-forties and is often seen in conflict with Stan and the inspector in the film On The Buses.

Fred is a moustachioed busman who is first seen complaining to Inspector Blake when it is announced that the canteen will only serve cold food in the future. As he smokes a pipe he moans about there being no chips and later is one of the first to read the inspector's notice about the introduction of women bus drivers to the Town and District Bus Company. He angrily tells the inspector that it is a diabolical liberty and feels sure that the union will do something about it. Sadly, he is to be disappointed. He also shows an impatient side when Olive is employed in the canteen and the food is not ready on time. He bangs on the closed serving hatch yelling: 'Now come on. How much longer are we gonna wait? We want our grub.' When Stan enters the canteen Fred turns to him and says: 'Stan, what is your sister doing in there? We want our lunch.' Later, he is agitated once more when he sits in the canteen watching Stan flirting with Sally – a woman bus driver. Fred turns to shop steward Jack and says: 'As union representative you go over there and tell him to cut it out.' On the whole, he is an angry and often disgruntled character with Stan being a thorn in his side throughout.

Fred

Played by Larry Martyn

Fred is a dark-haired busman in his mid-thirties who is the bus driver that replaces Stan aboard Jack's bus on joining the Luxton and District Bus Company.

He is an unmarried bus driver who, in the Series Seven episode 'What The Stars Foretell', tells Olive that he has never married as he has never been caught yet and makes it clear he has no intention of marrying. He is in for a shock later when Inspector Blake warns of redundancies as the National Bus Company is to take over a number of Luxton and District Bus Company routes with Fred being made redundant as they are made on a last in first out policy. 'Gawd blimey I've only been here a week and I've got the bullet already,' says a disappointed Fred. However, his job is saved when the employees of the rival bus company who are taking over a number of Luxton and District's routes go on strike and won't return to work until all redundancies are dropped with all staff being re-instated. In the final Series Seven episode 'Gardening Time', Fred is indifferent to the gardening competition at the depot and says to Jack from the drivers cab: 'Oi Oi. When you've finished your gardening club. I thought you wanted to get out early.' Fred takes out the bus and it is to end up with more plants on it than passengers as Jack uses it to transport stolen plants for his garden. Fred is a bus driver in the same mould as his predecessor Stan. He is a bachelor who is willing to use his bus for dubious purposes whilst on duty and gets pleasure from the inspector's misfortunes.

Free Passes

Free passes are an item which staff and their families are given to travel aboard Luxton and District buses free of charge. These are referred to in the Series Four episode 'The L Bus'.

Stan and Jack are to use their bus to transport a bed bought by Arthur to save on delivery costs despite having four trainees aboard. However, mechanical problems force them to return to the depot where Inspector Blake is to discover a mattress aboard the bus and is determined to charge Stan for what he deems as a parcel. The miffed driver is quick to protest saying: 'What are you talking about? We get free passes for us and our families.'

Blakey is unmoved on his position and replies: 'Yes well a mattress is not a relative is it?' To his glee the trainees let it slip that there is more than just a mattress on the bus and he charges Stan for each item with cost varying depending on their size.

Freudian Slip

Arthur accuses Stan of making a Freudian slip in the last episode of Series Six called 'The Prize'.

As Stan, Arthur and Olive compete to accompany mum on a holiday for two to the Costa Brava which she won in the depot raffle, they are bending over backwards to be nice to her. Stan errs when he says: 'He doesn't realise the Costa Brava's going up all the time,' but meant to say the cost of living. Arthur pounces on Stan's mistake and declares: 'Did you hear that mother-in-law? What a Freudian slip.' Stan doesn't want his mum to know that all of his helpfulness is due to having a possible holiday on his mind and so tries to claim it was a slip of the tongue.

A Freudian slip is a term used to describe a verbal or memory mistake and thought to be linked to the unconscious mind. It was discovered by the neurologist and later renowned psycho-analyst Sigmund Freud at the beginning of the twentieth century.

Friday Night Social

A social event to be staged in the depot canteen and seen advertised on a poster in the Series Four episode 'The Canteen Girl'.

The Friday night social event is to start at 8.30 pm in the depot canteen with sausages and beer on the menu. Inspector Blake arranges to meet his new fiancée Molly at the event and sees it as the last such event he'll attend at the depot before he and Molly leave Luxton to start a new life in the country. However, Stan and Jack are to lead her astray and she arrives late for the event with a shock for the inspector as she displays a flirtatious and carefree attitude that Blakey does not like. The Friday night social therefore ends up being a heart-breaking event for Inspector Blake as his brief engagement to Molly ends.

Frieda

Played by Pauline Cunningham

Frieda is an attractive clippie with fair hair in her late twenties who, along with her friend Susy, is to be placed aboard Stan's bus and trained by Jack in the Series Six episode 'No Smoke Without Fire'.

Although Frieda is not as out-going and flirtatious as her friend she isn't inhibited. She is to attend the inspector's course of instruction on fire fighting and as he shows them how to administer the kiss of life Stan tries to share a kiss with her but is stopped by Blakey. Later, she and Susy are trained aboard Stan's bus which is constantly breaking down with the two ageing busmen using the opportunity to flirt with their trainees. Frieda is to pair off with Stan enjoying a snog and a cigarette on the lower deck until the inspector arrives on the scene. He orders Frieda and Susy to get on the bus waiting behind them ending their fun as he vows to stay with Stan and Jack until they return to the depot.

Frisky Bics

A fictional type of dog biscuit that Stan buys for Olive's new pet in the Series Four episode 'The Anniversary'.

Frisky Bics are described as containing everything needed to keep a dog healthy including Woofo, a special dog conditioner that is guaranteed to make its coat shiny. As Stan stands in the depot with a paper bag containing the biscuits, Inspector Blake arrives on the scene when Jack urges a reluctant Stan to give the inspector a biscuit. Blakey finds the biscuit very tough to bite into and Stan claims that is because they are hard-baked and suggests he dips them in his cocoa to soften them up. Unaware of what he is eating the inspector warms to their taste claiming they are savoury with an unusual flavour. He considers getting some of the biscuits for his mum and asks to see the bag. The penny drops as he looks at the bag and realises he has been eating dog biscuits leaving him furious but Stan and Jack highly amused.

From Here To Eternity

This is a classic 1950s film that is referred to by Arthur in the Series Six episode 'Love Is What You Make It'.

Another argument is to break out between Arthur and Olive. They debate which film they watched whilst courting at The Gaumont many years earlier with Arthur insisting: 'They were showing From Here To Eternity'.

From Here to Eternity was made in 1953 and starred Burt Lancaster, Deborah Kerr and Montgomery Clift. A romantic wartime drama which was to win an amazing eight Oscars and it was also a box office smash for Columbia Pictures.

Fry, Iris

TV Role: Maisie (Uncredited Role) (On The Buses Series 1 – 7)

Iris Fry was a much-used but seldom credited actress seen on our television screens from the mid-1960s through until the 1980s. Her television credits came in classic comedy series such as Doctor In Charge, Seven Of One, The Two Ronnies, Fawlty Towers and The Liver Birds as well as uncredited appearances in On The Buses, Steptoe And Son and Father Charlie. Drama roles also came her way in Doctor Who, Play For Today, Upstairs Downstairs and The Bretts being the pick of those. She was also to appear on the big screen in the late 1970s in the musical drama Jubilee and the award-winning Murder By Decree.

Fuhrer

This is a derogatory name that Stan and Jack call Inspector Blake in a couple of episodes of On The Buses.

Firstly, in the Series Two episode 'Self Defence', Blakey is calling for silence in the canteen as he wants to make an announcement. Stan mockingly says: 'Hang on. Hang on. The Fuhrer talks.' The Series Three episode 'Radio Control' similarly sees bus crews assembled in the depot awaiting another announcement from the inspector and they grow impatient. As Blakey urges the restless crowd to be quiet, Jack shouts: 'Silence. The Fuhrer wants to speak.' Miffed, the inspector asks for some respect.

The word fuhrer is German for leader and is a word associated most exclusively with the dictator Adolf Hitler. He was to give himself the title just before the outbreak of World War Two.

Fuller, Tex

Film Roles: Harry (On The Buses and Mutiny On The Buses)

Tex Fuller can boast a career as not only an actor on film and television but also as a renowned stuntman on a number of memorable films in a career spanning well over thirty years.

His television career was to see him appear chiefly in bit-part roles in classic dramas such as The Avengers, Z Cars, Adam Adamant Lives, Blake's 7, The Agatha Christie Hour and The Professionals. He was also to have roles in top quality comedy series including The Likely Lads, The Two Ronnies, Citizen Smith and The Goodies. As a stuntman on television he worked on Doctor Who, Sorry, In Sickness And In Health and Last Of The Summer Wine.

On the big screen, Fuller had an uncredited role in Carry On Constable and went on to appear in The Marked One, No Blade Of Grass, On The Buses, Mutiny On The Buses, Blood From The Mummy's Tomb and Nuns On The Run. As for roles as a stuntman he worked on three classic James Bond films – those being From Russia With Love, You Only Live Twice and A View To A Kill. Other films he has performed stunts on include Casino Royale, Where Eagles Dare, Superman II, The Company Of Wolves, Brazil and Willow.

Fuller retired from the trade in the late 1990s after a lengthy and packed career.

Fullerton, Shiranee

TV Role: Mrs Sharma (Series 1 Episode 6 'The Canteen')

Shiranee Fullerton's career as an actress consisted solitarily of her role as Mrs Sharma in an episode of On The Buses. She was a rare case of an actor or actress appearing in the hit sitcom following which their acting careers never took off.

Galloping Gourmet, The

Arthur calls Stan the galloping gourmet in the Series Six episode 'The Prize'.

As Stan rushes into the kitchen in a rush to make mum's breakfast he slips and falls on some broken eggs. A watching Arthur laughs saying: 'The galloping gourmet.'

Clearly a reference to the hit cookery show of the same title. British chef Graham Kerr presented The Galloping Gourmet from 1969 until 1971 in the United States and was to make him a star around the world. The series was renowned for incorporating light-hearted humour into the show and it is still repeated on television to the present day.

Gandhi

A historical political figure referred to in the Series Three episode 'The Snake'.

Stan and Jack are competing for the affections of an Indian canteen employee called Fatima with Jack being confident of arranging a date with her. Stan mocks his over-confidence telling him: 'I suppose you think if she sees you in your y-fronts she'll think you're Gandhi.'

Mohandas Gandhi (better known as Mahatma Gandhi) was a legendary figure who struggled to gain independence for India over three decades. He was an idealist whose belief in a non-violent stance and philosophy was much-respected. He was determined to free India from what he saw as oppressive British rule which was finally achieved on the 15th of August 1947. Sadly, a few months later he was to be tragically assassinated at the age of seventy eight. To this day he remains one of the most iconic figures not only in India but also world political history. Stan's remark about Jack in y-fronts is a reference to Gandhi preferring to dress in the traditional Indian garment of a dhoti and shawl with the lower garment remotely resembling y-fronts.

Garden Crash

Stan has an accident when he crashes one of Luxton and District's newest buses into a garden in the Series Seven episode 'The Poster'.

As Stan drives his bus down a quiet side street with Jack and Inspector Blake aboard he gets distracted as, by the roadside, a promotional poster containing his photograph is plastered onto a billboard. Excitedly, he points out the poster to the inspector but takes his eyes off the road which causes him to crash his bus into a garden, smashing through a small wooden fence and ending up on a lawn.

The impact sees Jack and the inspector tumble out of the door of the bus as it grinds to a halt inches away from crashing into a house. On his hands and knees Blakey says: 'Right your poster's coming down for a start.' The hapless driver is also called a 'stupid, great twit' by Jack. Although nobody is injured and the damage to the bus is superficial the incident signals the end of Stan Butler's moment of fame on the promotional poster as the inspector rips down the roadside poster in frustration.

Gardner, Andrew

Designer (On The Buses TV Series 1, 2 and 3)

Andrew Gardner was to work on production crews for various television series to be made by London Weekend Television. His association with LWT spanned twenty years and he worked on some of that company's best-remembered programmes in the 1960s, 70s and 80s.

Aside from his role as a designer on the production crew of On The Buses where he worked on a total of twenty one episodes, his other early credits included comedies Hark At Barker and several episodes of Please Sir. In the 1970s his credits came in dramas such as New Scotland Yard, Within These Walls and Enemy At The Door. However, comedy series that were to benefit from his involvement included The Fenn Street Gang, Bowler, The Top Secret Life Of Edgar Briggs, Romany Jones, the spin-off sitcom of On The Buses called Don't Drink The Water and Yus My Dear. The first half of the 1980s saw him work on a number of hit series such as romantic drama We'll Meet Again, dramas The Gentle Touch and Mitch as well as sitcoms A Fine Romance and Me And My Girl.

On his departure from LWT, Gardner was to direct for Scottish Television before retiring from the industry in the late 1990s.

Gardner, Inspector

An unseen character referred to by Inspector Blake in the Series Three episode 'First Aid'.

Stan and Jack are pleased and somewhat relieved that they have passed their mandatory first aid test at the depot. Inspector Blake pours scorn on their achievement though as he tells them: 'You were very lucky it was that Inspector Gardner that tested you. I can tell you that much.'

Garrod, Keith

TV Role: Child (Series 4 Episode 7 'The Kids Outing')

Keith Garrod's acting career was to consist only of a role as a mischievous schoolboy who sabotages Stan's bus prior to it leaving on a children's outing. It was only to be a brief flirtation with acting as on leaving school Garrod pursued a career away from show business.

Gasworks

A location visited by buses from the Luxton and District and Town and District Bus Companies and referred to in a number of episodes and two spin-off films.

Stan indicates, in the Series Three episode 'Radio Control' that the number fourteen bus goes to the gasworks. As he uses the newly-fitted radio system he talks to what he believes to be a bus driver. However, it is an airline pilot who tells him he is Delta Tango14 going to Chicago via London, New York and Boston. Stan replies: 'You can take my advice mate you go to the gasworks via the High Street.' The gasworks are referred to again in the Series Five episode 'A Thin Time' when Inspector Blake finds Jack and tells him: 'Oh there you are Harper. You can do your overtime on the twenty four to the gasworks mate.' It's a blow to Stan though as there is no overtime available for drivers.

In the first spin-off film On The Buses the gasworks are referred to by Inspector Blake as he re-arranges his bus crews. The inspector tells a disgruntled Jack: 'I'm putting you on the number twenty to the gasworks.' Despite the conductor moaning he doesn't want to go to the gasworks Blakey insists he'll go where he is told adding: 'I'm putting you with Ruby over there. I want you to give her the benefit of your experience.' In Mutiny On The Buses, Inspector Blake orders what he thinks is a bus driver on the radio system to go to the gasworks. He is unaware that he is in fact ordering a police sergeant who on discovering the error confiscates all of the bus company's radio equipment after the mix-up and severely reprimands the inspector.

Gatti, Gigi

Film Role: Maria (Holiday On The Buses)

Born in Cagliari, Italy in 1935, Gigi Gatti was to spend the first half of her working life as an actress and was to appear in a number of British television series and made one big screen appearance.

Aside from a sizeable role in Holiday On The Buses her credits were television-based. Drama roles came in the much-acclaimed 1960s series Public Eye, The Carnforth Practice, Dixon Of Dock Green, Survivors and Take Three Women amongst others. She was also to appear in the classic sitcom The Liver Birds.

After around twenty years as an actress Gatti's career took a new turn in the 1980s when she was to study psychotherapy and graduated from Regent's College, London in 1991. She worked in that field in the UK until 2000 when she returned to Italy to carry on her work. Shortly afterwards she was diagnosed with cancer which she battled until her death in 2003 at the age of sixty six.

Gaumont, The

A fictional cinema referred to by Stan in the Series Six episode 'Love Is What You Make It'.

As mum and Stan discuss the troubled marriage of Arthur and Olive, mum rather fancifully feels that marriages are made in heaven. Stan disagrees: 'This one wasn't. This was made in the back row of the stalls of The Gaumont.'

It is likely that The Gaumont referred to was based on the famous Gaumont State Cinema in Kilburn, London near to Ronnie Wolfe's home in Golders Green. The cinema opened in 1937 and was one of the largest in the world. Noted for its grandeur and lavish fittings as well as being fitted with an impressive Wurlitzer Organ which remains the largest of its kind in working order in Britain today. The Gaumont State Cinema is now a luxurious bingo hall which is still in use to the current day.

Gaynor, Avril

TV Role: Joyce (Series 2 Episode 3 'Self Defence')

Avril Gaynor was to go straight into acting on leaving school and went on to have roles in television, film and on stage.

On television she was to appear in a range of series including drama Katy and The Des O'Connor Show early in the 1960s. She was later to have roles in the hit sci-fi Adam Adamant Lives, Comedy Playhouse, On The Buses and more recently The All New Harry Hill Show. On the big screen her roles included appearances in Mini Weekend and in recent years the comedy romance Confetti.

Gaynor was also very active on stage with roles in the smash hit musical My Fair Lady in the early 1960s. She ventured to Italy and was to appear in Federico Fellini and Franco Zeffirelli's production of Romeo And Juliet before returning to the UK for further stage roles in Company and the original adaption of Joseph And The Technicolor Dreamcoat followed by a role in Two Gentlemen Of Verona amongst others.

In recent years she has remained active in show business working on the production of stage shows as well as acting as a devisor on similar projects. She is also associated with, and a proud patron of the world famous Bluebell Railway where she works as their press officer.

Avril Gaynor.

General Inspector

The position held by Blakey at the Luxton and District in Stan's vivid dream of life on the buses in the 1920s in the Series Seven episode 'On The Omnibuses'.

General Inspector Blake is a somewhat intimidating and tyrannical figure who does not think twice about threatening Stan and Jack with severe retributions if they did not carry out their duties. He benefits from the lack of a union to protect the employees but when Jack moves to create such a union, Blakey sees it as a threat to the control he holds and is determined to stamp it out. When Jack mentions going on strike in a protest against the long work schedules the general inspector warns the conductor and his driver that by going on strike they would be sacked and face six months hard labour. Later, when Stan and Jack try to protest about their work conditions by refusing to take a bus out they are soon put in their place. General Inspector Blake warns Stan: 'You know what this means don't you? It means sedition and a clear revolution. It means that you will be sent to Botany Bay on a convict ship.' It's a chilling warning that sees both men return to duty immediately. Unlike real life, Blakey holds all the power over the busmen but he still has to contend with being constantly put down by the strict general manager who belittles his efforts in the job.

General Manager

The title of the position of Inspector Blake's immediate superior, sometimes abbreviated to manager, at the Luxton and District Bus Company on the small screen and the Town and District Bus Company in the spin-off films.

George

Played by Brian Grellis

An employee of the Luxton and District Bus Company who works in the clothing store at the depot who comes to the aid of Stan in the Series Five episode 'Stan's Uniform'.

George, wearing brown overalls and in his late twenties, is visited by Stan who is in need of a replacement uniform to replace his shredded new jacket and trousers. Although he would like to help the troubled driver he tells him he can't give out any items of uniform without a chitty as he would land himself in trouble. He points out, that in any case, he doesn't have anything in Stan's size. In desperation Stan asks if George can patch up his new jacket which is in tatters but is told that all it is fit for is the dustcart. However, George is to come to Stan's rescue as he hands him a dusty old uniform saying: 'You can have old Ernie's. He retired yesterday.' Although the uniform is in an awful state Stan is relieved as, at least he has a uniform to wear for duty.

George

Played by Keith Norrish

A conductor in his early thirties at the Luxton and District Bus Company who revels in the inspector's discomfort and also moves to help an injured Stan.

In the Series Five episode 'The New Nurse', Stan and Jack are looking for the inspector in the depot as they need their chitty signed. George is on hand to tell them that Blakey has had to go to the sickroom as he has got stomach pains. He laughs along with Stan and Jack at the inspector's ill health. George appears again in the Series Five episode 'The Strain' as he helps Jack to lift an injured Stan into the driver's cab of his bus. They finally succeed by putting him in his cab backwards but only after the inspector catches them in the act and puzzled he asks: 'What's going on here then?' Jack replies: 'We're chairing him.' A bemused Blakey is not impressed but a phone call takes him into his office allowing George to help lift Stan into his cab before he scurries off.

George

Played by David Richardson

George is a blonde-haired bespectacled conductor who, along with an unnamed busman, carries two boxes of Christmas goods bought by Stan and Jack in the Series Five episode 'The New Telly'.

George tells Stan and Jack: 'Here you are lads we've got your orders from the canteen. You owe us what's written on the side.' He also embarrasses the inspector by revealing that Blakey has also put in an order as well and brings out a smaller box with his goods in it which earns the inspector merciless leg-pulling from Stan and Jack. George laughs along with them before departing the scene.

George

Played by Rudolph Walker

A West Indian bus conductor in his thirties at the Luxton and District Bus Company who stands alongside Stan and Jack on picket duty at the bus depot in the Series One episode 'The Early Shift'.

George is first seen ridiculing Stan who arrives in the depot riding Olive's bicycle. He says: 'Why don't you ride side saddle eh?' Stan replies: 'Why don't you belt up mate?'

Later, George is amongst a group of busmen rallied together by Jack who vote to go on strike over them being deprived of their canteen facilities. He is to join Stan and Jack on early morning picket duty outside the depot where he holds a placard and is quick to spot a television crew arriving on the scene to report on the strike. Shortly afterwards he yells: 'Hey listen they've started up one of the buses. Hey they're going to take it through the back gate.' The three busmen rush around to the back of the depot where they see Inspector Blake preparing to take a bus out in a bid to break the strike. 'Scum,' shouts George.

They make a move to prevent the bus leaving the depot with Jack and George forcing Stan to lie down in front of the on-coming bus. The plot yields results as the bus company ends up meeting the busmen's demands but they are in for a shock as canteen staff go on strike for better pay. Jack is miffed and promises that no buses are going to leave the depot until they get their food. He orders Stan to lie down in front of a bus again with George, once more, helping Jack to force the struggling driver to lie down as the credits roll on the episode.

Gestapo, The

This is a title often given to the strict disciplinarian Inspector Blake by Stan and Jack in a couple of episodes of On The Buses.

In the Series Two episode 'Family Flu', Stan is unloading his shopping from his bus in the depot, against company policy, when Jack warns of the inspector's approach. 'Watch out. Here comes the Gestapo,' he says. Similarly, in the Series Four episode 'The Injury' an injured Stan plans to have an arranged accident in the depot so he can claim accident and sick pay with Jack urging him to sign on for duty to make it official. As they prepare to put their plan into action Inspector Blake approaches and Stan warns his conductor: 'It's the Gestapo.'

The Gestapo were the feared secret police force of Nazi Germany that was formed in 1933 and remained in existence until the fall of the Nazi movement in 1945 at the end of World War Two. The feared force was closely linked with the protection of the Nazi Party and Germany of that time. It would investigate any treason, sabotage or acts against the Nazi government and often it would freely act outside the law without any danger of prosecution as long as the Nazi regime was protected. During World War Two the Gestapo expanded its number of members and were to carry out countless executions of any sect members daring to oppose Nazism as well as being responsible for a number of the most notorious concentration camps where mass executions were carried out. The Gestapo was a feared organisation responsible for a range of heinous crimes.

Gibbet Hill Run, The

This is a fictional name given to the number fourteen bus route operated by the Luxton and District Bus Company in the Series Three episode 'Foggy Night'.

The Gibbet Hill run is referred to by Stan as being the worst route in the depot and Inspector Blake gleefully agrees saying that Stan and Jack will stay on that route until he can find a worse one. The route to Gibbet Hill is a two hour long journey through the countryside stopping only at limited stops via Little End and Hickley Green and is renowned for the road having potholes en route as well as being hilly.

Gifts for Blakey

A convalescing Inspector Blake recovers at home after an accident of Stan's making at the depot but things go downhill when he receives unwanted visitors bearing gifts in the Series Five 'The New Telly'.

The inspector suffers injuries when he buys the Butlers' television set which is to explode in his office. As he rests at home in his sick bed Stan, Arthur and Jack pay him a visit with a range of gifts in a bid to appease Blakey. Stan buys him a new portable television set complete with a six month guarantee however the inspector is adamant he will be taking legal action over his injuries. Jack is also to bring a boxful of goods for Blakey which has been bought by the worried busmen as they fear the sack over the incident. The box contains bottles of beer, chocolates, cigars and crisps. However, Stan and Jack are cheekily to make themselves at home by watching a football match on Blakey's new television despite his protests and also drink and spill his beer whilst perched on his sick bed. Somehow though, the troublesome busmen avoid the sack despite the inspector's injury claims.

Gilbert, Kenneth

TV Role: Chemist (Series 7 Episode 4 'The Poster')

Kenneth Gilbert's career as an actor spanned over half a century and was to see him appear in all genres on television, film and stage.

His television career included credits in a range of classic dramas beginning in the 1960s with roles in Sir Francis Drake, No Hiding Place, Crossroads, Z Cars, Softly Softly and Callan. The 1970s brought more drama roles in series such as Crown Court, The Protectors, The Adventures Of Black Beauty, Edward The Seventh, Doctor Who, The Sweeney, The New Avengers and Shoestring amongst others.

The following decade saw him make appearances in The Gentle Touch, The Chinese Detective and Dempsey And Makepeace. Into the 1990s and roles came his way in award-winning dramas House Of Cards and To Play The King as well as Cracker. Although his acting career neared its end he was to appear in hit dramas Poirot and Midsomer Murders in the 2000s. Aside from his role in On The Buses, Gilbert's comedy credits were rare.

As for his career on the big screen he was to appear most notably in Tomorrow At Ten, Twins Of Evil, Ivanhoe, God's Outlaw and The Lady And The Highwaymen amongst others.

Gilbert could also boast a great stage career where he appeared in a number of Shakespearean plays such as King John, The Card, A Midsummer's Night Dream and Hamlet. Also on stage his credits included parts in Trouble With Father, Rebecca and The Mousetrap.

In the mid-2000s he was to retire from acting after a full and varied career.

Gillies, Carol

TV Role: Eunice Jones (Series 7 Episode 5 'The Football Match')

Born in Keighley, Yorkshire in 1941, Carol Gillies was to break into acting in her twenties developing a career that would bring roles on the small and big screen as well as on stage.

Gillies television career as an actress was to gain her credits in the best of British dramas such as I, Claudius, Crown Court, Within These Walls, Angels, The Sandbaggers, Shoestring, Widows, Jane Eyre, The Jewel In The Crown, C.A.T.S Eyes, The Black Tower, Campion and Casualty. Her comedy roles on the small screen came most notably in On The Buses, Yes Honestly and Metal Mickey.

She was to have numerous film roles in her career beginning with the comedy A Nice Girl Like Me. The pick of her other big screen credits were to come in The Hiding Place, From A Far Country, Praying Mantis, Secrets, Florence Nightingale, Anastasia: The Mystery Of Anna, Baby Boom, Madame Sousatzka and Back Home. On stage she was to appear in a range of productions including The Beggars Opera, Aliens and Orpheus Descending.

Sadly, Carol Gillies was to pass away at the age of fifty in 1991.

Gladys

Played by Eunice Black

A rotund, dark-haired clippie in her fifties employed by the Luxton and District Bus Company and who demonstrates a rescue technique on Stan in the Series Six episode 'No Smoke Without Fire'.

Gladys attends the depot's course of instruction on fire fighting and is called upon by Inspector Blake to demonstrate the Sylvester method on Stan. Despite the protests from the worried driver he is told to lie down as she takes her jacket off and lies down on top of him to perform the technique. However, the demonstration doesn't go to plan as Stan feels her weighty build too much to bear and pushes her off. He gets to his feet remarking he'd need a kiss of life after Gladys' demonstration on him.

Gladys

Played by Fanny Carby

A canteen employee at the depot brought in by Inspector Blake to cut down on the theft of stock and to run the canteen at a profit in the Series Five episode 'Canteen Trouble'.

Gladys, a dark-haired woman in her late forties, comes to the job with excellent references. She was a prison wardress at Holloway Prison for ten years and although she comes across as charmless and incorruptible she does have underlying passions.

The inspector feels comfortable that she is the right woman for the job but Jack sets out to prove him wrong. He leads Gladys to believe that Stan has feelings for her and arranges for the unsuspecting driver to meet her to collect a leg of lamb and sausages free of charge in the back room of the canteen later in the day. Stan has no idea what he is in for though as on arrival Gladys bolts the door so they won't be disturbed. He is to hide the food in his overcoat but things become complicated as Gladys looks to become amorous with him.

Somewhat sex-starved she explains she left her last job as she had nothing but women to work with and urges Stan not to be shy. He is very reluctant to co-operate but he is pulled on top of her as she refuses to be put off. However, the inspector is to arrive on the scene and not only catches Stan and Gladys in an uncompromising position labelling Stan a sex maniac; he also uncovers the driver's attempt to steal more food. Although caught in the act Stan is relieved in some ways as his ordeal with Gladys is over. The incident is to see Gladys being sacked leaving the inspector to look for another solution to the canteen problem.

Gladys

Played by Juliet Duncan

A plump, long curly-haired clippie employed by the Town and District Bus Company and is seen in a state of undress on a couple of occasions in Mutiny On The Buses.

Gladys is one of a number of clippies who come to work in nothing but their supplied uniforms and display their compliance with the ruling to a gobsmacked Inspector Blake. It lands him in trouble with manager Mr Jenkins and Gladys makes things worse when she jokes in a northern accent: 'Ooh I think he must be lusting after my body.' Later, as a fire drill is underway at the depot, Stan and Jack enter the women's changing room telling a number of clippies in their underwear that everyone has to get out. Gladys, wearing a turquoise undergarment and nothing else, leaps excitedly on Jack saying: 'Save me.' She knocks him over in the process before the mischievous busmen are flung out of the room.

Gladys

Played by Parnell McGarry

Gladys is a blonde-haired and overweight trainee clippie who is trained by Jack in the Series Three episode 'The Inspector's Niece'.

Although she is keen to impress and eager to learn, Jack is glad to see his shift with her end. He is far from complimentary about Gladys to Stan as he moans about the standard of trainees deteriorating and feels she must weigh at least twenty stone. He later reports to Inspector Blake that she is 'a dead loss'. As she leaves the bus in the depot she says cheerfully: 'Cheerio dearies. Thanks for the ride. Bye bye cutie,' stroking Stan on the cheek as she passes him. Later though she has useful information for Stan as she tells him that their new trainee Sally is actually Inspector Blake's niece.

Gladys

Played by Maggie McGrath

This is a red-haired woman bus driver in her fifties newly employed by the Town and District Bus Company in the film On The Buses.

Gladys accepts a cup of tea in the depot canteen from Stan unaware that it has had a diuretic pill added to it as he and Jack bid to discredit the woman drivers.

Glamour Bath

A type of bath that Olive takes prior to looking for a night of passion with her husband Arthur in the Series Three episode 'First Aid'.

She hopes to make herself more desirable and has a bath using a special soap and scented bath oil. On entering the room she proudly tells Arthur: 'I've had a glamour bath. It's made my skin all soft and smooth.' Unimpressed he replies coldly: 'Yes it's brought out all the exotic radiance of your chilblains.' Once again Olive's hopes are dashed.

Gloria

Played by Jan Rennison

This attractive young blonde-haired clippie is new to the Town and District Bus Company and is to share a passionate kiss with Stan in Mutiny On The Buses.

Gloria is mistakenly thought to be Stan's new clippie and he flirts with her when he learns she is unattached prior to going on duty at the bus depot. However, he is in for an unpleasant surprise when he finds out that his new conductor is none other than the demoted Blakey whilst Gloria is whisked away to the canteen for a cup of tea by the new inspector. Later though, Stan has his way with Gloria as he enjoys a passionate kiss with her on the upper deck of his bus and she asks: 'You do love me don't you? You do love me?' Between kisses he replies that he does and Gloria asks if he will marry her one day. Excitedly, Stan says yes in an attempt not to dampen her ardour but she takes this to mean that they are now engaged. He isn't as enthusiastic about another engagement and he protests amidst her kisses as the camera pans away and the closing credits roll.

Godfrey, Tommy

TV Role: Wilfred Phillips (Series 3 Episode 7 'Mum's Last Fling')

Tommy Godfrey was born in Lambeth, London in 1916 and his acting career begun on stage as a comic appearing in music hall productions. He was to go on to become a familiar face on British television with numerous credits on film and stage as well.

His first big break came with a small role in the classic Ealing comedy film Passport To Pimlico in 1949. Other film roles included Hide And Seek, Work Is A 4-Letter Word, Till Death Us Do Part, Bless This House, Straight On Till Morning, From Beyond The Grave, The Vault Of Horror, Love Thy Neighbour and ending with The Great Muppet Caper in 1981.

Godfrey was most active on television and was regularly seen in comedy roles in hit 1960s and 70s sitcoms. These were to include Till Death Us Do Part, Never Mind The Quality Feel The Width, On The Buses, Steptoe And Son, Sykes, Love Thy Neighbour and Mind Your Language. He was also to have comedy roles in sketch and variety series such as The Dick Emery Show, The Goodies, The Tommy Cooper Hour and The Howerd Confessions. Drama roles were also numerous and he was to appear in 60s hit series such as The Avengers, The Saint, Nicholas Nickleby, Z Cars, Dixon Of Dock Green and Special Branch. He was equally as active in the 70s with roles in Department S, Softly Softly, Follyfoot, The Persuaders, Jason King, Crown Court and his last drama role came in the 1980 detective series Sherlock Holmes And Doctor Watson.

His acting career had begun on stage in the early 1940s and his forte was musicals where he appeared in Beyond Compere and High Button Shoes. Towards the end of his career he had a role in Underneath The Arches as well.

Tommy Godfrey sadly, was to pass away in 1984 at the age of sixty eight.

Gogan, Brenda

Film Role: Bridget (On The Buses)

Brenda Gogan's acting career began in her native Ireland in the 1960s with a number of stage roles before progressing on to film and television roles.

On the small screen her credits came in dramas that had varying success in the form of The Sinners and smash hit Budgie. A short-lived BBC sitcom called Tales From The Lazy Acre is also amongst her credits. Gogan's solitary big screen role was to come in the spin-off film On The Buses. It offered her a sizeable role and was to be a smash hit at the box office. Her career as a stage actress was to see her appear in countless Irish productions in the late 1960s and the UK into the 1970s and her credits included a part in Table Manners. She was also to go on to direct and produce stage productions. In recent years she has returned to Ireland and in 1997 set up the Drogheda School of Performing Arts based at The Little Duke Theatre in Drogheda, County Louth where she has worked as a director and teacher.

Gold Digger

A term Arthur uses to describe Nymphy Norah in the film Mutiny On The Buses.

As Stan and Suzy's engagement threatens to fall apart, Arthur comments that women cause all the trouble to which Jack agrees: 'Yeah your dead right. You stick to Nymphy Norah at least you know where you stand with her.' Arthur laments: 'Norah? Right little gold digger she turned out to be. Hardly ever talks to me now.'

A gold digger is a term used to describe a person who uses their charm to get money or gifts from others. The saying was first used in 1915 to refer to a mercenary woman but it is thought to originate from a humorous song from the Wild West dating back to the gold rush in 1830.

Goldfish

Inspector Blake has two pet goldfish which he brings with him when he moves into the Butler house.

His pet goldfish are called Gordon and Mary and are originally kept in a chamber pot beneath his bed in the Series Seven episode 'Hot Water'. He is later to be chastised for his treatment of the fish by the depot's area manager

Gerald Simpson in the Series Seven episode 'Friends In High Places'. He berates the inspector for keeping his goldfish in a bowl as he feels it is cruel to keep them in captivity as having to swim around in circles all day must drive them mad. The inspector has to bite his tongue as he realises this is his superior talking.

Goodwin, Derrick

Producer (On The Buses TV Series 5 and 6)

Born in 1935, Derrick Goodwin's career began in stage management working on stage productions before going on to become an acclaimed producer who worked on a number of hit television series spanning over twenty years.

He was to join the BBC drama department before becoming freelance. Goodwin debuted as a producer on the sitcom Dear Mother, Love Albert and went on to work on a host of sitcoms which were to have varying success. These included eighteen episodes of On The Buses, The Train Now Standing, Bowler, Thick As Thieves, Oh No It's Selwyn Froggitt, Mixed Blessings, Holding The Fort, Mann's Best Friends, Running Wild and Ffizz. He was also a director of a number of classic drama series having worked on Coronation Street, Z Cars, Doctor Who, New Scotland Yard and Within These Walls amongst others. Goodwin's stage credits saw him produce productions such as Naked, No Road, Call Of The Drum and Abiding Passions.

In recent years he has been involved with writing scripts for a range of television and stage shows. He also teaches the skills of producing and directing television and stage productions to up and coming directors of the future.

Gorgeous Girlies

A fictional adult magazine that Stan and Jack find in the possession of the inspector's young nephew Harold in the Series Four episode 'The Kids Outing'.

Harold, who cunningly has the Gorgeous Girlies magazine hidden behind a comic, drops it and it is picked up by the stunned busmen. Stan hands it back to the schoolboy saying: 'Don't let your uncle see you with that otherwise he'll do his nut.' Unaware to him though, Inspector Blake overhears this and catches Stan giving his nephew an adult magazine and angrily labels him a 'filthy beast'. The Gorgeous Girlies magazine was purely fictional and, in fact can clearly be seen in the episode as actually being called Man. The Man magazine originated in Australia, the idea of Kenneth Murray in 1936 and featured fiction and non-fiction articles, cartoons and images. It continued in this guise until the late 1960s when it had become dated with an influx of risqué adult magazines flooding the market. Man magazine followed suit and was to re-invent itself as an adult magazine with male-orientated material but this was not enough to prevent its demise in 1974.

Graham, Laura

TV Role: The Clippie (Series 5 Episode 1 'The Nursery')

Laura Graham left school and studied at The London Academy of Music and Dramatic Art for two years before going on to build a career that was to offer many credits in television, film and on stage.

A range of television roles spanned over two decades in the 1960s and 70s. Drama roles came in classic series such as Dixon Of Dock Green, Z Cars, Spy Trap, Love For Lydia and the highly-regarded The Eagle Of The Ninth. Fondly remembered children's series Just William and Worzel Gummidge are also amongst Graham's credits as well as, of course, the classic sitcom On The Buses. Her solitary big screen appearance came in the 1966 multiple Oscar-winning film A Man For All Seasons. Her stage career was to see her perform at classic theatres such as the Old Vic, Royal Court and Young Vic. Credits were to come in A Midsummer Night's Dream, The Balcony, Rosencrantz And Guildenstern and Creditors to name but a few in the 1970s.

Laura Graham started a new chapter in her life in the 1990s when she moved to Tuscany in Italy. She is now an author of romantic novels and enjoying the tranquillity of life in Tuscany.

Grainer, Ron

Composer (Mutiny On The Buses)

Born in Atherton in Queensland, Australia in 1922, Ron Grainer was to learn music from a very early age learning to play the piano and violin by the age of four! It was clear that he had a talent for music and he would go on to become a legendary composer of some of British television's most iconic theme tunes as well as film and stage musical scores.

Grainer was to compose themes for British television series from the early 1960s up until his death in 1981. His best-loved iconic themes came in Maigret, Doctor Who, Steptoe And Son, The Prisoner, Man In A Suitcase, Shelley and Tales Of The Unexpected with the wonderfully haunting Doctor Who theme still unchanged and still heard regularly on television to this day. These scores were just the tip of the iceberg though with his compositions heard on countless television series from all genres which are fondly remembered to this day.

On the big screen Grainer had composed film scores for films such as A Kind Of Loving, Some People, The Caretaker, Nothing But The Best, To Sir With Love, Only When I Larf and The Assassination Bureau in the 1960s. The following decade saw him provide musical scores for smash hit cult film The Omega Man and also Hoffman, Mutiny On The Buses, Steptoe And Son, Steptoe And Son Ride Again and The Bawdy Adventures Of Tom Jones were the pick of those.

His scores have also been heard in a string of stage musicals including Robert And Elizabeth, On The Level and Sing A Rude Song.

Tragically, Ron Grainer was to be struck down by spinal cancer and passed away in 1981 in Suffolk, England at the age of fifty eight. He leaves behind a lifetime of classic musical scores that are still loved to this day and will never be forgotten.

Grant, Bob

TV and Film Role: Jack Harper (On The Buses Series 1 – 7) (On The Buses, Mutiny On The Buses and Holiday On The Buses)

Bob Grant was born in Hammersmith, London in 1932 and left school before training at the Royal Academy of Dramatic Art for two years. After a spell of national service his career as an actor begun on stage and he later progressed on to work on television and in films.

He debuted as an actor in Worm's Eye View in 1952 at the Court Royal Theatre, Horsham. Grant went on to appear on stage in The Good Soldier Schweik joining the famous Joan Littlewood Theatre Workshop in the process. Other theatrical credits were to include Sparrows Can't Sing, Everyman In His Humour, a starring role in the Lionel Bart musical Blitz, Twang, Mrs Wilson's Diary and he also wrote and performed in his own stage plays Instant Marriage and Package Honeymoon. Later in his acting career came stage appearances in No Sex Please We're British, Stop It Nurse, Darling Mr London, Oh Calcutta and Hobson's Choice amongst others.

Grant's television career was to see him begin in drama roles and his credits included Quatermass And The Pit, Sir Francis Drake, No Hiding Place, Softly Softly, Z Cars, Mrs Wilson's Diary (the television adaption) and The Borderers. Of course his role in On The Buses is what he will always be best remembered for and in addition he also co-wrote a number of the classic sitcom's scripts. Other comedy roles offered themselves in a Comedy Playhouse offering called The Jugg Brothers which he co-wrote and co-starred in with fellow On The Buses star Stephen Lewis and a pilot comedy called Milk-O which he also penned and played a milkman with Anna Karen playing his wife.

On the big screen he was to appear in the highly-acclaimed comedy Sparrows Can't Sing, an uncredited role in The Beatles film Help and Till Death Us Do Part in the 1960s. He would, of course, go on to co-star in all three On The Buses spin-off films in the early 1970s. Sadly, roles gradually dried up on television by the 1980s as he had been somewhat typecast by his memorable role in On The Buses. Stage roles also became rare and manic depression blighted his later years and tragically, at the third attempt, took his own life in 2003 at the age of seventy one. It was a tragic end to his life for a man who had lit up millions of people's lives and continues to do so to this day.

Bob Grant backstage during one of his many pantomime performances.

The tragic end to Bob Grant's life means it is difficult to gather his memories but with two radio interviews he gave early in the 1980s, one with VRN Radio in Kirkcaldy, Scotland with John Murray interviewing and the other on Isle of Wight Radio with John Hannam, he shared these memories.

Memories

Bob Grant speaks about joining the Joan Littlewood Theatre Workshop to John Murray in 1981:- 'Well that was curious actually because in those days she wasn't really known outside of a very small circle. I didn't know anything about her at all. My agent said that I'd got an audition down in Stratford East down in the East End of London. I didn't really know where that was; anyway I caught the train down there. There I was all dressed up in my best audition suit, my bowler hat, my rolled umbrella and I arrived in this very scruffy theatre in the backstreets of the East End and I didn't like the look of it at all. I thought this is very off, very scruffy I didn't like this. This was the old Theatre Royal. I thought I don't want to work here at all. She (Joan Littlewood) made me do all sorts of improvisations and things. I didn't fancy it a bit and eventually she said: 'Can you sing?' And I said: 'No.' I thought that would clinch it, she definitely won't want me now. She said: 'Well you must be able to sing something?' I said: 'I don't know any songs.' She said: 'Well you must know the national anthem?' I said: 'Well I just about know that.' I sung that and said: 'Thank you very much for giving me your time and I shall go now.' Thinking that I'd blown the whole thing completely which is what I wanted to do and she said: 'You start Monday.' And I worked there on and off for I suppose about twelve to fifteen years and enjoyed it enormously. Actually it was terrific.'

On his stage career he told John Hannam this:- 'I was very lucky. I worked with the Joan Littlewood Theatre Workshop in Stratford East and from there got into shows in the West End and did a whole run of successes – very nice indeed. I was very young at the time and was suddenly pitch forked in to the West End and enjoyed it enormously and that gave me a big break very early. I always remember with great affection Sparrows Can't Sing which was a very good film made and I enjoyed my musical Instant Marriage which we had a very good run with which I wrote and played in as well. Blitz was tremendous – that was a magical experience. The scenery was so marvellous but I suppose one always looks back at these shows with a certain amount of nostalgia.'

On how he got his part in On The Buses he told Murray:- 'That, again, like most things was sheer chance that I happened to be doing a show called Mrs Wilson's Diary which was on in London for about a year and it was subsequently televised. The producer of that was looking around for likely people for this series which nobody thought would run at all. We were booked for just seven episodes and really everybody thought that would be about it so we did our seven episodes and then we did another six, then another thirteen and so it went on. Six years later we were still doing it and three feature films and of course it was an enormous success. It was rather interesting actually as originally the writers (Ronnie Wolfe and Ronnie Chesney) took that series to the BBC and the then Head of Light Entertainment said that 'this will never make a series'. And then of course the rest is history'.

From television to the big screen, how well did On The Buses transfer onto film asked Murray:- 'The films were extremely successful. Particularly the first and third. They all made money and they played all over the world very, very successfully. I think it was probably one of the only TV series that did transfer successfully to the big screen. It certainly was the only one to have three films made of it and three that made money – a lot of money.'

Bob tells Hannam of a funny story on the first day of filming On The Buses:- 'We were filming, of course nobody really knew what we were doing and we were in a bus garage in North London and of course they were running a bus service as per normal. I was dressed up there in my bus conductor's uniform waiting for a take, waiting for the cameras to roll and a little old lady came up to me. She said: ''ere,' she says, 'does this bus go to Southend? And I said: 'I'm terribly sorry madam. I really don't know you see I'm filming so I really don't know.' She said: 'Well you bloody well ought to,' and hit me over the head with her umbrella. I thought well that's a great start so I have felt a certain sympathy with bus conductors ever since. You see that's the sort of treatment they get.'

Bob reveals to Murray the circumstances of On The Buses ending:- 'We all agreed we wanted to quit while we were ahead. The series was still very, very successful and we didn't want to just go on to the point when people were saying: 'Oh gosh not that boring old rubbish again,' so we quit while we were ahead. I think after six years anyway we'd all run out of ideas as much as anything.'

Bob relates an amusing story to Murray regarding the power of television:- 'A couple of years ago I was in Bombay and a ragged little urchin, I suppose he was only about five or six-years-old just dressed in a loin cloth was staring at me very intently for a very long time and eventually he said: 'On The Buses, On The Buses,' (in an Indian accent). And where this little urchin could ever have seen it I don't know but I suppose he must have seen it in a shop window or something like that. But it was quite astounding to be standing in a street in Bombay and know that you were known even by a scruffy little street urchin like him. It was really very touching and very heart-warming and very funny.'

Did Bob worry about being typecast? He told Murray:- 'No I don't think so. I don't think that's something one really considers. If something like that (On The Buses) comes up you do it and worry about it afterwards. Though it was difficult for all of us afterwards for a time because people tend to only think of you as that character but no it doesn't bother me.'

Grant, Tiberius

TV Role: Tibbles (Series 7 Episode 13 'Gardening Time)

Tiberius, the pet cat of Bob Grant and his wife Kim Benwell, was to be credited for his appearance in the last ever episode of On The Buses. A white Persian cat this was, of course, to be Tiberius only credit of the cat's career.

Gray, Ian

TV Role: Charlie the Cleaner (Series 4 Episode 1 'Nowhere To Go')

Ian Gray's career as an actor saw credits spread over a quarter of a century most notably on television and in films.

Comedy roles on television were plentiful for Gray and he was to appear in classic sitcoms such as Please Sir, Doctor In The House, On The Buses, Doctor In Charge and the highly regarded Clochemerle. Alongside the comedy legend Ronnie Barker he was to appear in Hark At Barker, Seven Of One and in a number of sketches in The Two Ronnies. The pick of his drama roles were to come in Dr Finlay's Casebook, King Of The River, Strange Report, Roads To Freedom, Dixon Of Dock Green and Life Of Shakespeare.

On the big screen his credits were to include the musical Just For Fun, the sitcom spin-off film The Lovers and he then went on his travels for a series of films made in Australia in the first half of the 1980s. These included the award-winning war film Breaker Morant, prison drama Stir and Robbery Under Arms. He was to return to the UK in the late 1980s to complete his career on the small screen.

Green Lane

A fictional street referred to by Jack in the Series Three episode 'First Aid'.

When a woman goes into labour on the upper deck of Stan's bus Jack feels it is the driver's fault. He tells Stan: 'You went too fast down Green Lane over that hump-backed bridge.'

Green Man, The

A fictional public house referred to by Stan in the Series Five episode 'The Best Man'.

Amidst planning Bill's bachelor party, Jack and Stan plan a pub crawl much to Inspector Blake's horror. Stan tells the inspector: 'At 10 o'clock we are meeting the darts team down at The Green Man.'

Green Pills

Mum describes Olive's tablets as green pills which they contemplate giving to Stan after he injures his back in the Series Five episode 'The Strain'.

As Doctor Clark prepares to prescribe a bed-ridden Stan some tablets mum says: 'Ooh perhaps some of Olive's green pills will do him some good?' Olive agrees: 'Oh yes they did my back a lot of good.' She adds she got them from Aunt Maud but Arthur insists their aunt had been taking them to treat a liver complaint. Stan though refuses to take the green pills making it clear he'll take whatever the doctor prescribes him.

Green Stamps

This popular shopper's loyalty scheme is referred to in a couple of episodes of On The Buses.

In the Series Three episode 'Mum's Last Fling', Mrs Butler undergoes a makeover in a bid to impress her boyfriend Wilf. She wears a short skirt and what she calls a fun wig and when she is quizzed as to how she could afford them she tells the family that she bought them with green stamps. Later, for Christmas, Stan and mum buy Arthur and Olive a single-bed size electric blanket as a present in the Series Four episode 'Christmas Duty'. Olive grumbles about it not being a double blanket but Stan explains: 'We didn't have enough green stamps for a double.'

The green stamps referred to were actually called Green Shield Stamps and though the scheme originated in the United States at the end of the nineteenth century it arrived in the UK in 1958. Supermarket chain stores of the time such as Tesco, Fine Fare and Co-op amongst others were involved in the scheme which saw shoppers awarded stamps for their shopping and on filling collector booklets with these stamps they could claim gifts from either a catalogue or special Green Shield Stamps shops. The scheme proved highly popular in the 1960s and 70s but the writing was on the wall for the stamp system when inflation and new discount stores such as Kwik Save devalued the stamps. In 1983 the stamps were abolished and despite briefly being resurrected a few years later the scheme finally ended in 1991.

Greene, Bill

Construction Manager (On The Buses)

Bill Greene was to work on the sets of a number of Hammer films and classic television series from the famed ITC stable as a construction manager. He worked entirely at Elstree Studios in the mid-1960s through until the early 1970s.

His television credits came in a string of memorable series such as The Baron, The Saint, The Champions, Department S and Randall And Hopkirk (Deceased). In total he worked on well over a hundred episodes of these series. In the same role Greene's credits on the big screen were all Hammer productions. These included horror films The Vampire Lovers, Lust For A Vampire, Blood From The Mummy's Tomb, Dr Jekyll And Sister Hyde, Dracula AD 1972, Demons Of The Mind and his sole comedy spin-off film On The Buses.

Grellis, Brian

TV Role: George (Series 5 Episode 10 'Stan's Uniform')

Brian Grellis acting career consisted of primarily television and film credits though he has been involved in stage work.

His first big break came on television in a role he is best remembered for as Detective Sergeant Bowker in the long-running hit police drama Z Cars.

His other notable small screen roles came in classic dramas such as Softly Softly, Jason King, Doctor Who, the award-winning War And Peace, Survivors, The Onedin Line, The Gentle Touch, Minder, Bergerac and the BBC's terrifying drama Threads. Grellis was also to appear in a number of highly-regarded sitcoms including The Fenn Street Gang, On The Buses, Whatever Happened To The Likely Lads, Last Of The Summer Wine, The Good Life and Get Some In. On the big screen his credits began in the late 1960s with roles in Submarine X-1, comedy Only When I Larf, war dramas Mosquito Squadron and Battle Of Britain and James Bond film On Her Majesty's Secret Service. These were followed by roles in 70s horror films Trog and Fear In The Night.

He was to go on to be co-founder of The Living Theatre company in the 1980s which is still active to this day churning out a range of stage productions.

Gretna Green

This small town in south west Scotland is referred to by Stan in the film On The Buses.

When Inspector Blake and woman driver Ada's bus gets diverted onto a motorway via false diversion signs placed strategically by Stan and Jack they arrive back at the depot two hours late. Stan enjoys ridiculing the inspector and jokes: 'I tell you what. You had us worried I thought you two had nipped off to Gretna Green.'

Gretna Green, a town on the border of Scotland and England, has long been seen as an ideal location for quick and easy weddings owing to far more liberal marriage laws that exist in Scotland compared to those in England. It has seen many runaway couples marrying there and this tradition has existed since 1753 when laws were toughened up in England with regards to marriage with changes to the age limit and consent being needed from parents.

Griffiths, Lucy

TV Role: Old Lady (Series 7 Episode 6 'On The Omnibuses')

Born in Birley, Hertfordshire in 1919, Lucy Griffiths was to go on to have a long and full career as an actress spanning around thirty years with prolific work on television and films integrated with stage work.

Her career on the big screen was to include roles in a number of classic British comedy films in the 1950s, 60s and 70s. These included One Good Turn, The Ladykillers, Carry On Nurse, Carry On Constable, Murder She Said, Carry On Regardless, Murder Ahoy, Carry On Doctor, Carry On Again Doctor and Carry On Behind. Other film roles were to come in Doublecross, Gideon's Day, Jack The Ripper, The Two Faces Of Dr Jekyll, Frankenstein And The Monster From Hell and Disney's One Of Our Dinosaurs Is Missing amongst others. She was also to appear in a plethora of hit television series. Comedy roles included credits in The Likely Lads, Please Sir, Doctor At Large, The Fenn Street Gang, On The Buses, Doctor In Charge and Mind Your Language. Griffiths was also to have roles in successful and much-acclaimed dramas Emergency-Ward 10, Z Cars, Adam Adamant Lives, The Prisoner, Sherlock Holmes, Dixon Of Dock Green, Within These Walls, Secret Army and All Creatures Great And Small.

Sadly, shortly after retiring from acting, Lucy Griffiths passed away in 1982 at the age of sixty two.

Griffiths, Terry

Graphics Designer (Opening Titles Sequence of On The Buses TV Series 2-6)

Terry Griffiths worked as a graphics designer for London Weekend Television from the late 1960s until the mid-1980s. He was responsible for designing the opening titles sequence seen in On The Buses from Series Two until the end of Series Six.

He is also credited with designing the iconic London Weekend identity graphic seen at the start of their productions from 1971 and was also to design the revamped identity graphic in 1978. Griffiths was also to create many title credit sequences for a range of LWT series. Memorable series such as The Adventures Of Black Beauty and Upstairs Downstairs benefitted from his designs. He was also behind the credit sequences for Maggie And Her, Just William, Me And My Girl, Another Banquet, Lillie and Dempsey And Makepeace to name but a few.

After around fifteen years at LWT as a graphic designer he was to move on to pastures new in the mid-1980s.

Grimsby

This is a seaside town which is referred to by Stan in the Series Five episode 'Canteen Trouble'.

When Arthur objects to eating food that Stan has taken from the canteen saying it would be against his principles he is labelled a hypocrite by his brother-in-law. Stan reminds Arthur of a piece of cutlery that he stole from a hotel in Grimsby which Olive claims was a souvenir from their honeymoon. Arthur blames his wife for the theft claiming it was her idea. Grimsby was founded as a town by the Danes in the twelve century and is situated on the Lincolnshire coast. It is renowned for its fishing industry and was to be heavily bombed by the Luftwaffe in World War Two as it was a major British port at that time.

Gripe Water

A cure given to babies with stomach complaints is used incorrectly by Olive in the film On The Buses.

Her son Arthur is unwell and she is given a bottle of gripe water by her mum for the baby's stomach. Husband Arthur and her brother Stan look on in stunned amazement as Olive proceeds to rub the water onto her son's bare stomach. 'You stupid great lump. What on earth do you think you are doing?' asks Arthur. Stan adds: 'You're supposed to put it in through his mouth not his belly button.' It is an incident that displays Olive's naivety and inexperience when it comes to raising babies.

Guineas

A now defunct unit of British currency referred to by Mrs Butler in the Series Four episode 'The Lodger'.

She is livid that traffic manager Mr Nichols, who is lodging with them, has made a pass at Olive. She rants to the family: 'I told him he could have a room, a bed and two meals a day for ten guineas a week. I think he's paying ten guineas a week and all found!' Mr Nichols is promptly told to leave the Butler house.

Although a long defunct part of British currency replaced by the pound, a guinea was still used in quoting prices for land, horses or up-market goods until decimalisation in 1971. A guinea was equivalent to one pound and five new pence in decimal value.

Guvnor

A slang term often used to describe the depot manager in a number of episodes of On The Buses.

In the Series Three episode 'Busmen's Perks', Jack is amidst encouraging Stan to help himself to paint from the depot's stores when the inspector arrives on the scene in the mechanical stores room asking what they are doing there. 'I was just pointing out to Brother Stan here, as shop steward, how the company's profits are being squandered on the guvnor's Jag'. He is lambasted for his remark by the inspector who points out that the manager only uses the car for company business.

Inspector Blake uses the term in the Series Six episode 'Private Hire'. He storms over to Stan and Jack in the depot with a handful of letters saying: 'They're complaints. The guvnor sent me out to give you a rocket about these.' They are then told of the nature of the complaints from various passengers with bad experiences aboard their bus.

Jack tries to persuade Stan to use a surplus ticket machine to earn money to pay off debts in the Series Seven episode 'The Ticket Machine'. He reminds his driver: 'We wanted the guvnor to back date our pay rise to a year before, didn't we? But he refused didn't he? Well it's just another way of taking it 'innit.'

Guvnor is a slang term for a boss, leader or person in power. It dates back to the early nineteenth century and was later used by the legendary writer Charles Dickens in his books.

Guy, Jennifer

TV Role: Iris (Series 7 Episode 5 'The Football Match')

Jennifer Guy was born in Carshalton in Surrey and has had a long career as an actress spanning five decades with credits on television, film and stage.

The majority of her roles have come on television in varying genres. She has appeared in a host of classic sitcoms with the pick of those being in the 1970s with roles in Sykes, On The Buses, George And Mildred and Are You Being Served? These were followed in the 80s with appearances in The Cuckoo Waltz, Chance In A Million, Room At The Bottom and in the 90s with Birds Of A Feather. In drama she had credits in A Horseman Riding By, Cribb, Number 10, Bergerac, Prospects, Harry And Cosh, Nelson's Trafalgar and also children's series such as Rainbow, Cavegirl and Billie: Girl Of The Future.

Her film career saw her appear in Up The Front, Persecution, Side By Side and Cruel Passion amongst others in the 1970s. The following decade saw her gain roles in hit films Biggles, the award-winning fantasy adventure Willow, Without A Clue and The Phantom Of The Opera. Other film credits include B-horror movie Razor Blade Smile and her career on the big screen has continued on into the 2010s.

Guy's career on stage is equally impressive. Her credits include roles at the famous Young Vic Theatre in Much Ado About Nothing and Tom Thumb The Great. Other roles came in A Funny Thing Happened On The Way To The Forum, A Midsummer Night's Dream, Pommies, The Hollow Crown (directed by her and staged in the USA) and A Comedy Of Errors.

Her acting career continues to the present day on various fronts.

Hall, Cheryl

TV Role: Eileen (Series 5 Episode 5 'The Epidemic')

Born in London in 1950, Cheryl Hall has had a long career as an actress which began soon after she had left school.

She is best remembered for her role as Shirley in the hit BBC sitcom Citizen Smith in the late 1970s. Other comedy roles on television came in much-loved series such as On The Buses, The Fenn Street Gang, Sykes, Bless This House, Lucky Feller, In Loving Memory, A Gentleman's Club, As Time Goes By and William And Mary. She has also appeared in some of the best British dramas starting in the 1970s with credits in Callan, Public Eye, Doctor Who, Z Cars, Love Story, Within These Walls, The Sweeney, Crown Court, Dixon Of Dock Green, Softly Softly, Survivors and Danger UXB. The 1980s brought roles in Tales Of The Unexpected, The Gentle Touch, EastEnders and Poirot with the 90s seeing her appear in Inspector Morse, London's Burning, Casualty, Wycliffe, Bramwell and the award-winning Silent Witness. The 2000s saw further quality drama roles for Hall as she went on to have roles in Waking The Dead and The Bill. She can also boast credits in classic children's series such as Rainbow, Grange Hill and Woof.

On the big screen her roles include parts in the highly-acclaimed Deep End, Villain, the star-studded comedy The Magnificent Seven Deadly Sins, No Sex Please: We're British and The 14. Her stage credits include roles in Men's Beano and The Loud Boy's Life.

Although, in recent years acting has taken something of a back seat in Hall's life, she has had a busy time. She works as a teacher and also, in 1997 she stood unsuccessfully as a Labour candidate for the seat of Canterbury in the General Election. Her career as an actress is on-going with occasional roles still coming in more than forty years after it began.

Hall, Frederick

TV Role: The Manager (Series 6 Episode 4 'Stan's Worst Day')

An actor with a career spanning over five decades, Frederick Hall's credits predominantly were television-based though he was to make his breakthrough initially on the big screen.

An Italian film called Il fornaretto di Venezia kick started a long television career with his other film role coming in the 1987 comedy film Wish You Were Here in which he had a small part. Television credits dominated his career with drama series appearances being plentiful. The pick of those coming in No Hiding Place, A Tale Of Two Cities, Public Eye, Roads To Freedom, Softly Softly, Doomwatch, The Adventures Of Black Beauty, Emmerdale, Hadleigh, Z Cars, Survivors, The Gentle Touch, Bergerac, Doctor Who and Boon. In comedy roles Hall appeared in hit sitcoms such as The Worker, Doctor At Large, On The Buses, Doctor In Charge, The Fenn Street Gang, Bowler, Beryl's Lot and The Top Secret Life Of Edgar Briggs.

Sadly, Hall passed away in 1996.

Hall, Roger

Production Designer (Series 3 Episode 1 'First Aid' and Series 3 Episode 2 'The Cistern')

Roger Hall can boast an enviable career as a production designer. He began on British television productions in the 1960s, 70s and 80s and was to progress on to big screen projects in the latter part of his career.

As a production designer Hall worked for London Weekend Television on a number of hit series such as The Gold Robbers, On The Buses, Hark At Barker, The Fenn Street Gang, New Scotland Yard, Not On Your Nellie, the multi-award winning Upstairs Downstairs, Within These Walls, Love For Lydia, Lillie and The Goodies. He went on to work on the hit Thames Television series Reilly: Ace Of Spies, the award-winning Jim Henson production The Storyteller and the US production Merlin which was to earn Hall a coveted Emmy award. His big screen credits include Dreamchild, Highlander II: The Awakening, The Power Of One, Jane Eyre, Gulliver's Travels for which he won another Emmy, The Odyssey, Alice In Wonderland, A Christmas Carol and Don Quixote to name but a few. He was also to work on the Oscar-winning 1981 film Chariots Of Fire.

Roger Hall's career has taken him from London Weekend Television to Hollywood and seen him win the highest awards for his quality of work on television and in films. It was indeed a career that reached the greatest heights.

Hallows, Ted

Gaffer (Holiday On The Buses)

Born in Twickenham, London in 1913, Ted Hallows was to work in the electrical department at the illustrious Elstree Studios working primarily for the famed production company ITC as well as having credits on a handful of Hammer films.

On television he was to work on several ITC classics from the mid-1960s through until the early 1970s. These included The Saint, The Baron, The Champions, Department S, Jason King and The Adventurer. His film credits included Hammer films Holiday On The Buses, Man About The House and To The Devil A Daughter. Other films he has worked on are And Soon The Darkness and the acclaimed The Raging Moon.

Hammer Films

The famous and much-loved production company was behind On The Buses, Mutiny On The Buses and Holiday On The Buses all of which brought healthy returns at the box office.

Hammer Film Productions were founded in 1934 and are renowned for their numerous low budget horror films that they produced from the mid-1950s until the mid-1970s. The pick of those being The Quatermass Experiment, The Curse Of Frankenstein, Dracula, The Hound Of The Baskervilles, The Curse Of The Werewolf, Quatermass And The Pit, The Plague Of The Zombies and Demons Of The Mind. The early 1970s also saw them produce a series of spin-off comedy films based on smash hit sitcoms of that time. Although Hammer ceased film productions in the mid-1980s it has since been resurrected some twenty years later under new ownership and has begun its film productions once more in the horror genre.

Happiest Days Of Your Life, The

This is a film that Arthur and Olive are to go to the pictures to see in the Series One episode 'The Darts Match'.

After watching Stan and Jack lose at darts against two clippies in the depot canteen, Arthur tells his brother-in-law: 'Here Stan, see ma home will you? Olive and me are going to the pictures to see The Happiest Days Of Your Life.'

The Happiest Days Of Your Life was a hit British comedy film made in 1950. It was to tell the humorous tale of two schools merged together causing chaos as the schools concerned were an all-boys and all-girls schools. The film starred Alastair Sim, Margaret Rutherford, Joyce Grenfell and Richard Wattis.

Harding, Mrs

Mrs Harding is an unseen character that tells Mrs Butler that the tea in Spain is like hot water with a sun-tan and three bob a cup in the Series Two episode 'Bon Voyage'.

Hardings Ltd.

The name of the fictional painting and decorating company that Arthur and Olive plan to bring in to decorate their bedroom in the Series Three episode 'Busmen's Perks'.

The company are set to charge him thirty pounds for the job but Stan has other ideas. He is not willing for the family to pay that sort of money for a job he feels is unnecessary. Eventually though, he is encouraged to come up with another option and offers to get paint from the bus depot and decorate the room himself. However, after he makes a mess of the job leaving Arthur in agony, his maimed brother-in-law promises he will bring in the decorators. They up their charge to forty pounds as they now have to scrape Stan's paint from the walls and then redecorate the room.

Hare, Betty

TV Role: Aunt Maud (Series 2 Episode 4 'Aunt Maud')

Betty Hare came from a family with acting in its blood and was the sister of Doris Hare who, of course, played Mabel Butler in On The Buses. She was neither as famous nor as prolific an actress as her sister but still had a number of credits on stage, television and in films.

Stage was where her acting career began and where she was to be most active. Hare appeared in the Cole Porter musical Nymph Errant in the West End in 1933 and later in the Noel Coward musical Pacific 1860. She was also to appear in Lights Up, Waiting In The Wings, My Place and Sail Away to name but a few. On television she was to have drama roles in Nicholas Nickleby and the highly-regarded Roads To Freedom. She was also to be seen in a string of hit LWT sitcoms such as On The Buses, Doctor In The House, Please Sir, Doctor At Large and Doctor In Charge.

Her big screen credits saw her debut in the 1952 crime drama Tread Softly. The spin-off film of the hit sitcom For The Love Of Ada offered her a role with her final appearance in films coming in the 1977 sex comedy Confessions From A Holiday Camp.

Hare, Doris

TV and Film Role: Mabel Butler (On The Buses Series 2-7) (On The Buses, Mutiny On The Buses and Holiday On The Buses)

Doris Hare was born in Bargoed, Monmouthshire in Wales in 1905 and like her parents, brothers and sisters she was to pursue a career in acting. Stage roles were to be followed by big screen credits and then television roles in an acting career that spanned virtually all of her life.

She was to make her stage debut at the age of three and went on to appear in countless stage roles throughout her lengthy acting career. With a role in the hit musical Words And Music written by Noel Coward other notable stage appearances came in The Show's The Thing, Lights Up, Night Must Fall, Fiddlers Three, Birds Of Paradise, No Sex Please We're British, Romeo And Juliet, Waters Of The Moon, It Runs In The Family and Forty Years On amongst many others. She reached the pinnacle as a stage actress working for the coveted Royal Shakespeare Company and National Theatre as well as appearing in the West End and on Broadway in many hit productions.

Hare progressed on to big screen roles in the 1930s with appearances in Opening Night, Night Mail, Luck Of The Navy and the musical Discoveries. The 1940s brought roles in the comedy film She Couldn't Say No, Here Comes The Huggetts and The History Of Mr Polly with her film career continuing on into the 1950s. In that decade she was to appear in Dance Hall, Thought To Kill, Double Exposure, Tiger By The Tail and the star-studded war drama Another Time Another Place. In the 1960s she was to have credits in the classic comedy film The League Of Gentlemen and quality drama A Place To Go. Aside from her roles in all three On The Buses spin-off films she was also to appear in three of the Confessions sex comedy films. Her film career came to a close in the 1990s with parts in the hit British comedy film Nuns On The Run and a small part in the award-winning drama Second Best.

She could also boast a career on television that offered roles in hit dramas such as Colonel March Of Scotland Yard, Douglas Fairbanks Jnr Presents, The Avengers, No Hiding Place, The Saint, Dixon Of Dock Green, Coronation Street, Randall And Hopkirk (Deceased) and Nanny amongst others. Comedy roles spread over three decades came in classic series such as The Benny Hill Show, On The Buses, The Secret Diary Of Adrian Mole Aged 13 ¾, The Growing Pains Of Adrian Mole, Never The Twain and Stuff.

Her career also included roles in several hit comedy series on radio and in 1941 she was to be awarded an MBE. She finally retired from acting in 1995 before passing away in 2000 at the care home for retired actors and actresses Denville Hall in Northwood, Middlesex at the age of ninety five.

Doris Hare
(Photo kindly supplied by the Hare family).

Doris Hare – the second Mrs Butler

During the height of the huge popularity of On The Buses Doris lived with her husband John in a flat overlooking the Thames at Putney Bridge. Although she would normally be chauffeur-driven around in a Rolls Royce, Doris loved to travel aboard buses and then the Underground to get to the LWT Studios at Wembley. She found those journeys very heart-warming as she would mingle with Cockney women that she had modelled her character Mrs Butler on and enjoyed the fact that they were able to identify with her and her screen character.

Doris held a great deal of respect for Reg Varney and his work ethic which allowed his fellow co-stars to be funny as well. She also valued the On The Buses code of conduct that there was no swearing in the series. It was her belief that there was too much swearing on TV and in films at that time which she found unnecessary. Doris could always lay claim to being a specialist in double entendre but this was far removed from the bad language she hated.

Harold

Played by Sheridan Earl Russell

A curly-haired, bespectacled boy who is Inspector Blake's nephew who attends the bus depot's outing organised by Stan in the Series Five episode 'The Kids Outing'.

Although the inspector claims his nephew is a sensitive and well-behaved boy this is clearly not the case. Harold aggravates Jack by continually ringing the bell aboard the bus in the depot with Jack describing him as a liberty taker and 'a shifty-eyed lout'. The boy also has an adult magazine which he hides behind his comic until dropping it and his uncle refuses to believe it belongs to Harold blaming Stan for trying to corrupt him. Later, Harold boasts that he knows his biology feeling he knows why Olive is feeling unwell when she rushes off the bus to be sick. He mischievously claims that Olive is pregnant but Arthur puts him in his place telling him: 'You might know your biology son. You certainly don't know Olive.'

Harper, Jack

Played by Bob Grant

Jack is a bus conductor with an eye for the women and alongside his driver and friend Stan, enjoys the chance to make Inspector Blake's life difficult. He is a middle-aged bachelor living with his family and holds the position of the depot's union representative.

Jack Harper is known to his friends as Jack whilst the inspector often refers to him as Harper. He lives at home with his family who we never see, as the Butler's next door neighbours and he has a pet cat called Tibbles. Jack is a popular figure at the bus depot except with Inspector Blake but he often shows a nasty, selfish side to his nature when poaching Stan's girlfriends but does repay his friend by frequently saving him from the sack using his influence as the union representative to great effect. He is a bad influence on Stan often encouraging him to break rules at work which usually ends up with the hapless driver shouldering much of the blame. Jack treats Mrs Butler largely with respect and much like Stan he is always keen to have a joke at the expense of Arthur and Olive.

His career at the Luxton and District Bus Company begins with him as a trainee conductor replacing Stan who progresses on to become a driver following Cyril Blake's promotion from driver to inspector. Jack is to be promoted to acting inspector a few years later in 1971 where he displays a heartless side to his nature as he looks to better himself by landing Stan in trouble with Inspector Blake by revealing some of his friend's most notable indiscretions. However, he finds that he misses the banter and opportunity to wind up the inspector and resigns from the post to return to his role as conductor. Jack's job comes under threat in 1973 when the Luxton and District Bus Company is absorbed by another company with Inspector Blake adamant that Jack faces redundancy as bus routes are lost to other companies. However, the union rules out that possibility as busmen strike demanding there will be no job losses due to the merger and their demands are met.

Jack's love life consists almost entirely of flings with clippies although none of them blossom into long-term relationships. Clippies called Joyce and Sandra afford him his longest flings on the small screen and he was also to enjoy a date with a young Swedish passenger called Ingrid.

On the big screen Jack is a conductor under the employment of the Town and District Bus Company with Stan as his driver. He revels in his role as shop steward and the sense of power it gives him over Inspector Blake and frequently uses this to his advantage. However, even he is powerless to stop the introduction of women drivers by the inspector as there can be no sexual discrimination in who the company employs. A new hard-line manager called Mr Jenkins arrives at the depot and is determined to run a tight ship and the balance of power swings to the management forcing Jack to resort to blackmailing him to wrestle back the power. He is finally to be sacked from the Town and District Bus Company for his part in writing off a bus in an accident that sees the new depot manager injure himself and damages his car. Jack and Stan face a few weeks of unemployment before taking on a job working aboard a tour bus at a holiday camp. They feel they have landed on their feet but the job proves to be only short-term as they break rules by borrowing the tour bus for a late night date and end up submerging it in the sea and lose their jobs in the process.

His big screen romances were to see him have an affair with a housewife called Betty who lives in a house on his bus route and uses his time at the turnaround point for romantic moments with her. Any chance of the affair developing is dented when Inspector Blake moves Jack onto another bus route denying him the opportunity to meet the married Betty whilst her husband is at work. He later enjoys an affair with a holiday camp nurse called Joan despite the fact she is dating Blakey. Jack charms Joan and leads her astray visiting her in her treatment room for moments of passion but when Blakey unearths her infidelity he is enraged and confronts her and it leads to the inspector being sacked.

On both the small and big screen Jack is a confident, middle-aged lothario who possesses a filthy laugh and has a toothy grin. He is of questionable character but as union representative he is a powerful ally for Stan. He often threatens to carry out strikes to get concessions from the management and this ploy is largely successful. His hobbies are darts for which he is captain of the depot darts team and on the small screen works as a bingo caller at the depot's social club. Many years before becoming a conductor he served his national service studying radio systems and tides during this time. In short a mischievous character with a sense of humour that makes him a hit with the women.

Harper, Mrs

An unseen character referred to by Arthur in the Series Three episode 'Mum's Last Fling'.

When Mrs Butler dresses up for a night out she explains she is going out for a drink with a friend. 'Not that Mrs Harper again?' asks Arthur. She surprises Arthur, Stan and Olive when she replies that she is going out on a date with bus conductor Wilf Phillips.

It is not made clear whether the Mrs Harper mentioned is in anyway related to Jack but considering the Harpers lived next door it would seem likely that they were.

Harper's Back Garden

The back garden of the Harper house features in the final episode of On The Buses, the Series Seven episode 'Gardening Time'.

Although not a keen gardener, Jack's back garden is not as neglected as the Butler's next door prior to the depot's flower and vegetable competition. His garden does have the advantage of a small trimmed lawn and a small tree which has grown from a conker planted by Jack. However, with Inspector Blake next door overhauling the Butler's garden he feels impelled to improve his garden in a bid to ensure he wins the gardening competition.

Jack is to use his bus to transport a range of flowers and plants that he has stolen from flower beds and plant pots on his bus route. The stolen floras which include pansies are re-located in his garden along with a set of garden gnomes for decoration. Whether these improvements will sway the opinion of the judge only time will tell.

Harris, Max

Composer (On The Buses Film)

Max Harris was born in Bournemouth, Dorset in 1918 and was to study at the Royal Academy of Music. He would go on to compose a number of much-loved themes and soundtracks for films and television series.

His compositions were most prominent on television beginning in 1960 with the theme for the hit comedy series The Strange World Of Gurney Slade which was to reach No.11 in the UK pop charts. The 60s also saw him compose themes for popular series such as dramas The Indian Tales Of Rudyard Kipling, Sherlock Holmes and The Gold Robbers amongst others. Into the 1970s and he supplied the theme music for hit series that included Doomwatch, Seven Of One, Carry On Laughing, Porridge, Open All Hours and Mind Your Language. He continued his impressive array of credits into the 1980s composing themes for What A Carry On, A Gentleman's Club and Blackeyes. On the big screen Harris was to compose the theme for the 1968 film Baby Love. He also wrote the soundtrack music heard in the first On The Buses spin-off film in 1971 and later in the 70s the theme for Carry On England. His final credit on the big screen came when he composed the theme for the US film The Christmas Wife.

Max Harris was a masterful composer and accomplished conductor who was to win two Ivor Novello awards as well as an award from the British Academy of Songwriters, Composers and Authors (BASCA) for his contributions to music. He retired in 2002 before sadly passing away in 2004 at the age of eighty five.

Harrison, Albert

Played by John Lyons

Albert is a bus driver in his late twenties with fair wavy hair who joins the Luxton and District Bus Company as a trainee driver.

In the Series Four episode 'The L Bus' he is to be one of four trainees placed on the training bus with Stan and Jack left in charge of the training. Stan, who calls him Bert, gives him the task of driving the bus out of the depot and onto the easier circular route as training begins. The following day of his training sees Stan and Jack use the training bus to deliver a bed and all of its fittings bought by Arthur. However, as Albert drives he brings the bus to a halt when it suffers an oil leak and has to be towed back to the depot with the bed still aboard. Although reluctant he helps the other trainees to move the bed onto a replacement bus without the inspector's knowledge. However, he reports trouble to Stan when the mattress gets stuck on the stairs and when they finally free it Inspector Blake is on hand to catch them in the act. Blakey gleefully charges Stan for carrying the mattress on the bus rating it as a parcel. The naïve Albert asks Stan: 'Where do you want the mattress? By the headboard or the spring base?' This is music to the inspector's ears who promptly charges Stan for the extra items as well.

Albert is to appear again in the following episode 'The Kids Outing' when he asks Inspector Blake who is going to drive the bus for the outing. The inspector is very happy knowing that his nemesis Stan Butler has the difficult task of not only driving the bus but also organising the whole event and catering for the many children.

Harry

A middle-aged, dark-haired busman wearing a t-shirt and trainers who, along with another busman, demonstrates an exercise called 'the see-saw' by Inspector Blake at a keep fit class at the depot in the Series Four episode 'Dangerous Driving'. This was an uncredited character in the episode.

Harry

Played by Tex Fuller

A balding, middle-aged conductor employed by the Town and District Bus Company who later is to become a driver.

In the film On The Buses, Harry replaces Jack as Stan's conductor after Inspector Blake swaps Jack onto another route. Harry is to find it an uncomfortable experience though. With their bus parked at the turnaround point he enjoys a cup of tea sitting on the rear platform of the bus whilst Stan enjoys a visit to Betty's house across the road where he is seduced. However, Stan is disturbed by the arrival home of Betty's suspicious husband. He manages to escape from the house and rushes to his bus, starting it up to make his getaway. As the bus reverses, Harry still drinking his tea is flung backwards spilling his tea and as the bus moves forward he falls from the back of the bus onto the road.

Harry also appears as a driver at the beginning of Mutiny On The Buses. When Stan is kissing Suzy on the upper deck of his bus, his conductor Jack wants him to hurry up as passengers are getting impatient as they wait to board the bus. Harry, who is the driver of the bus parked behind Stan's, sees another bus approaching and says to Jack: 'Here comes one behind. We've only got twenty minutes to get back to the depot. Stan will never make it.' The bus arriving behind has Inspector Blake aboard intent on investigating the delays to the bus services but of course he is powerless to prevent the hold-up.

Harry

Played by Arthur Lovegrove

Harry was an ageing bus driver in his fifties who, like the rest of the drivers at the Luxton and District Bus Company, has to undergo a medical in the Series One episode 'Bus Driver's Stomach'.

The balding Harry, a bus driver for twenty years, realises that the complaint known as bus driver's stomach is something that he has learnt to live with. He, like most of the busmen at the depot has a diet centring on greasy chips and it is a worry when the bus company orders all bus drivers to take medicals. Those failing the medical are to be transferred to other duties such as cleaning confirms Inspector Blake. Three drivers fail their medicals, one of those being Harry but he benefits as he is transferred to a higher paid post at the depot as an inspector.

Harry

Played by Don McKillop

A fair-haired conductor in his early forties at the Luxton and District Bus Company who is to take over as inspector whilst Blakey goes on a fishing trip in the Series Five episode 'The Inspector's Pets'.

Harry has a laugh at Stan's misfortune when he sees the damage to the side of his bus following a collision with a bollard. 'Hello. What have you been doing? Stock car racing?' he laughs. He does sympathise with Stan agreeing that the offending bollard in the High Street is a proper menace. The troubled driver contemplates the inspector's reaction who is not in the best of moods after having to cancel his fishing holiday. However, Harry offers hope saying: 'It's a pity he didn't go. You know I'm in charge when he goes off but now if he had I could have been looking the other way whilst the boys in maintenance fix that up for you. Blakey need never have known.' As Stan rushes to find the inspector to offer a solution that will see him able to go on his fishing trip, Jack and Harry use a sign to cover up the damaged section of the bus. The generous gesture to turn a blind eye from Harry perhaps saves Stan from the sack.

Hayman, Damaris

Film Role: Mrs Jenkins (Mutiny On The Buses)

Born in Kensington, London in 1929, Damaris Hayman began her career as an actress in repertory theatre before progressing on to television and film roles in a career that spanned around fifty years.

Hayman's television career included roles in classic drama series such as Crossroads, No Hiding Place, Z Cars, Doctor Who, The Onedin Line, The Sweeney, The Bill, the award-winning The House Of Elliott and Screen Two amongst others. She was primarily to appear in comedy roles such as those in classic 1960s sitcoms Citizen James and Steptoe And Son. The 70s saw her appear in The Liver Birds, Doctor At Large, Sez Les, Robin's Nest and Mind Your Language to name but a few. On into the 1980s came credits in hit sitcoms Keep It In The Family, The

Young Ones, Duty Free, Filthy Rich And Catflap, Clarence and in the 90s in If You See God Tell Him and One Foot In The Grave. Other comedy roles saw her gain credits in memorable comedy sketch shows such as The Dick Emery Show, The Morecambe And Wise Show, The Tommy Cooper Hour and The Little And Large Show. Also she was to have roles in cult children's series Here Comes The Double Deckers, The Basil Brush Show, Jackanory and Super Gran.

She was very active as well on the big screen appearing in hit films such as The Belles Of St Trinian's, Greyfriars Bobby, Bunny Lake Is Missing, The Pink Panther Strikes Again and The Missionary. Hayman also had roles in sitcom spin-off films Love Thy Neighbour, Mutiny On The Buses and Man About The House as well as a host of other film roles spanning four decades.

Hayman was also an accomplished stage actress with her roles including parts in East Lynne and A Little Bit Of Fluff to name but a few. She retired from acting early in the 2000s and has become a patron of a stage school and is now enjoying her retirement after a memorable career.

Here are Damaris Hayman's memories of working on Mutiny On The Buses.

Memories

'Mutiny On The Buses was filmed during a period of power cuts. These always came at the most inconvenient moment and at home we soon learned to have torches and candles always at the ready. These, however, were not much use in the studio.

Everyone who was ever involved with 'On The Buses' will remember the huge standing set of the bus depot, which included an office and a service area with inspection pits. The sequence in which I was involved took place in the office.

We had been working happily and I was enjoying myself for the regulars were welcoming and friendly – not always the case! And then the lights went out. A quick switch to a generator restored the lights in the office set, but left all the rest of the studio in deep darkness, and we were urged not to stray for fear of accidents. But you've guessed it – one rash soul wandered and fell into an inspection pit, fortunately emerging unhurt. This unscripted drama has blotted out my memory of the rest of the day!'

Heath, Suzanne

TV Role: Suzy (Series 4 Episode 1 'Nowhere To Go')

Suzanne Heath was to go into acting after leaving school in what was to be a short-lived career at the start of the 1970s with a handful of roles on television and one film credit.

On the small screen she was to appear in hit dramas such as Wicked Women and The Pathfinders. Her comedy roles came in a string of London Weekend Television productions including Doctor In The House, Please Sir, On The Buses and The Fenn Street Gang. A solitary film role was to come in 1971 in the comedy film The Magnificent Seven Deadly Sins which had a star-studded cast.

After a brief flirtation with stardom Heath would take a career change away from acting.

Helper

This is a job that becomes available at the depot's newly opened nursery in the Series Five episode 'The Nursery'.

The nurse in charge of the nursery needs a helper and lets Inspector Blake know in no uncertain terms. 'Where is that helper? I told you I wanted a helper now where is she?' snaps the nurse. The rattled inspector tells her they can't get the right woman for the job as they don't want it but he promises to put a notice up advertising the part-time job which offers wages of ten pounds a week.

With Stan's help it is Olive who gets the job but it doesn't take long for things to go wrong. The bossy nurse leaves Olive in charge of babies as she takes her lunch break. She orders Olive: 'The feeds are all ready and I'll be back at two o'clock and also dear number six wants changing. Will you see to that at once?' No sooner has the nurse left than Olive loses her glasses, stepping on them and they end up smashed rendering her 'as blind as a bat' according to Stan.

She has to go home to get her spare pair of glasses leaving her brother and Jack to look after the babies. It's a move that spells trouble as the hungry busmen help themselves to baby food and milk and when Inspector Blake finds out it is sure to cost Olive her job.

Henrix, Folker

TV Role: Finalist (Series 7 Episode 4 'The Poster')

Folker Henrix solitary credit as an actor came on television in an episode of On The Buses. His working life though was to be away from acting.

Herrington, Doreen

TV Roles: Betty (Series 1 Episode 5 'The New Inspector') and Eileen (Series 4 Episode 7 'The Kids Outing')

Doreen Herrington was to have a career as an actress from the mid-1960s through until the mid-1970s with credits on television and in films.

On the small screen she was to have roles in hit drama No Hiding Place and episodes of The Wednesday Play series. Her two roles in On The Buses were to be her solitary comedy roles on television.

Herrington's film roles came in the late 1960s in two highly-acclaimed big screen productions. The gritty award-winning drama Poor Cow in 1967 was followed by a bigger role in a similar type film called Up The Junction in 1968.

Hickley Green

This was a fictional town which is home to Aunt Maud. Hickley Green was served by Luxton and District's number fourteen bus route in what was a two hourly service and was twenty eight and a half miles away from Luxton.

High Street

A street often referred to in both episodes and a spin-off film of On The Buses.

The High Street has a notorious bollard which is difficult to negotiate with Stan bumping into it and damaging his bus in the Series Five episodes 'The Nursery' and 'The Inspector's Pets'. It was in the High Street that a passenger gets off Stan's bus leaving two portions of fish and chips aboard in the Series Five episode 'Lost Property'.

Once more the High Street features in another Series Five episode called 'Vacancy For Inspector' when Jack encourages Stan to wait around a corner with his bus before continuing the journey back to the depot. He explains: 'We don't want to pick up all them passengers. Look the High Street will be packed this morning.' Stan fails to understand until Jack says: 'Look the number twenty four joins us here don't they, all the way to the depot. Well let him pick 'em up.' It is a ploy that later lands Stan in trouble.

In the first spin-off film On The Buses, diversion signs are being prepared to be placed in the High Street. Stan and Jack obtain these diversion signs from maintenance worker Nobby and are to use them to confuse and discredit the women bus drivers.

Highway Code

An important set of standards to ensure safe and competent driving that is essential learning for drivers which is referred to in both the small and big screen versions of On The Buses.

In the Series Four episode 'The Kids Outing', Stan has just performed his drag act called 'Clara the Clippie' in the depot canteen in a bid to keep a rowdy group of children entertained. However, on exiting the canteen back in his uniform and about to take the children on their outing in his repaired bus he still has his false eyelashes on. Inspector Blake orders him to take them off as they are impairing his vision and infringing the Highway Code.

On the big screen in Mutiny On The Buses, Arthur is about to take his driving test to become a bus driver. Although Stan believes him to be studying the Highway Code, Arthur is to fall in sleep in bed reading it but there is no need to panic as he passes his driving test.

The Highway Code has been the official road users' guide in the United Kingdom for well over seventy years. It covers all aspects of road safety and knowledge of it is necessary prior to learning to drive. Around a million copies of the Highway Code book are sold per year and it is still in publication to this day with new and relevant material being added to each new edition.

Hill, Fanny

A Swedish adaption of a film which the Butlers once went to see at the pictures as referred to in the Series Three episode 'The Inspector's Niece'.

As mum, Arthur and Olive prepare to go to the pictures to watch a Swedish film, mum insists on taking her glasses to read the subtitles. She recalls when they went to watch the Swedish film Fanny Hill and in it there was a couple in bed and when she looked down at the subtitles by the time she looked back up again they had done it.

The Swedish adaption of Fanny Hill was released late in 1968 and tells the story of a woman called Fanny Hill and her love life's ups and downs. It starred Diana Kjaer in the lead role and co-starred Hans Ernback and Keve Hjelm in what was an adaption of a John Clelland novel written in 1748.

Hippy

Stan likens himself to a hippy in the first ever episode of On The Buses called 'The Early Shift'.

Stan, Jack and George are on picket duty when they hear a bus being started up as it attempts to exit the depot to break the strike. Jack and George try to prevent this by forcing Stan to lie down in front of the bus. Amidst protests Stan says: 'I feel like a hippy.'

A hippy was a member of a popular culture that was at the height of its popularity at the end of the 1960s. It was a culture that was renowned for its desire to break clear of social ties and hippies embraced peace movements and stylised their clothes and cars etc. in bright, vibrant colours. They also had a reputation for protesting against movements that challenged their beliefs but these were non-violent protests hence Stan's feeling of affinity with a

hippy.

Hitchcock, Claude

Sound Recordist (Holiday On The Buses)

Claude Hitchcock could boast a long career working in the sound department on a string of classic films and was also to go on to work on a host of television series.

His career began on the big screen and he was to work on several memorable films such as Quatermass 2, Zulu, The Blue Max, Vampire Circus, Holiday On The Buses and Oscar-winning films Born Free and The Dirty Dozen amongst others. Many other film productions were to see him work for Hammer Films and Walt Disney Productions to name but a few.

On television, Hitchcock was to work on hit ITC series such as The Avengers, The Champions, The Persuaders, Space: 1999 and Return Of The Saint. Other credits included the classic children's series The Adventures Of Black Beauty and the award-winning romantic drama The Far Pavilions.

After over fifty years in the industry Claude Hitchcock finally retired at the end of the 1980s.

Hitler

A cruel nickname Stan and Jack often call Inspector Blake in several episodes and the spin-off films of On The Buses. The inspector has a toothbrush moustache and is in a position of power much like the dictator Adolf Hitler.

Leader of the Nazi Party and Chancellor of Germany from 1933 to 1945, Adolf Hitler was the architect of World War Two when he was to invade a number of neighbouring countries. He was also to lead a shameful bid to exterminate the Jewish race interning millions of Jews in concentration camps where they were to be executed.

World War Two raged across the globe from 1939 to 1945 but, as it neared its conclusion, with the Russian army converging on Berlin from the east and British and American forces doing the same from the west, Hitler could see the war was lost. To prevent capture and trial for his war crimes he took his own life alongside his new wife, Eva Braun.

Hobbs, Nicholas

TV Role: McGregor (Series 7 Episode 4 'The Poster')

As an actor Nicholas Hobbs may not be a household name but he can boast a long, packed career as a bit-part actor and stuntman on television and in films.

His first break came on the small screen in the early 1970s as an actor and that aspect of his career continues into the 2010s. Drama roles have included small parts in hit series such as Z Cars, Doctor Who, Space: 1999, Dick Turpin, Dempsey And Makepeace, Lovejoy, Between The Lines and Inspector Morse. He was also to appear in classic sitcoms The Fenn Street Gang, On The Buses, The Darling Buds Of May and the comedy series The Comic Strip Presents.

As an actor his big screen roles were to include an uncredited part in the James Bond film Octopussy and more recently credits in the acclaimed horror film Below, comedy San Antonio and the award-winning 2004 romantic drama Closer. Hobbs was destined to be more sought after as a stuntman especially on the big screen. He has worked in that role in a string of James Bond films such as The Spy Who Loved Me, Octopussy, Never Say Never Again, A View To A Kill, Goldeneye and Tomorrow Never Dies. Also other notable films he has acted as a stuntman on include Carry On Girls, The Eagle Has Landed, A Bridge Too Far, Superman, An American Werewolf

In London, Indiana Jones And The Temple Of Doom, The Company Of Wolves, Brazil, Willow, Batman, Braveheart, Billy Elliott and Robin Hood.

On television he also worked as stuntman in dramas such as Blake's 7, London's Burning, Taggart, The Bill, Boon, Ivanhoe, Merlin, Messiah, Heartbeat, Rebus and Ashes To Ashes. Comedy series such as Sleepers, The High Life and One Foot In The Grave have also had Hobbs perform as a stuntman.

He has now racked up forty years of experience in the industry and is still in demand today.

Hodges, Mr and Mrs

An elderly, well-dressed couple that Inspector Blake calls upon to demonstrate the military two step during his dance class in the film Holiday On The Buses. The couple perform the dance impeccably and are praised warmly by the inspector.

Holden, Ruth

TV Role: The Lady Passenger (Series 4 Episode 10 'Safety First')

Born in 1929, Ruth Holden attended stage school from the age of sixteen before developing a career as an actress on television, film and stage that was to span more than fifty years.

Her best remembered television roles came in classic soaps such as Coronation Street, Crossroads, Emmerdale and Brookside. Other drama roles included parts in Z Cars, Follyfoot, Sam, Juliet Bravo, the feature length Threads, How We Used To Live, All Creatures Great And Small, Cracker, Earthfasts, Medics and Heartbeat. Comedy roles were to come in Doctor In The House, The Dustbinmen, On The Buses, The Fenn Street Gang, Billy Liar, No Honestly, Bless Me Father, A Bit Of A Do and Last Of The Summer Wine amongst others.

Big screen roles were to come in a Children's Film Foundation production called Cup Fever in 1965 and the US romantic comedy Just Tell Me What You Want. She was also to appear in a number of made-for-television films throughout her career. Holden had also toured appearing in the stage production called Coronation Street On The Road in the mid-1960s.

She continued in acting until she sadly passed away towards the end of 2001 at the age of seventy two.

Holiday Accident

Arthur and Olive with their son and Mrs Butler aboard the motorbike and sidecar are involved in an accident on their way to a holiday camp in the film Holiday On The Buses.

As the holiday-bound family near their destination and cross a hump-backed bridge they are overtaken by Stan driving his bus but in greeting them he is distracted. He fails to see an on-coming car until the last moment and swerves to avoid a collision which forces the motorbike and sidecar to swerve into the side of the bridge. The family's suitcases are catapulted off the sidecar, over the side of the bridge and into the river below sending Arthur and Olive scurrying to retrieve the cases. Although, he manages to get one of the cases back, the other floats out into deeper waters and he forces Olive into a desperate attempt to fetch it. She fails miserably leaving her muddied and upset. Not an ideal start to their holiday and though there were no injuries in the accident the Rudge family find themselves short of clothes to wear.

Holloway Prison

A prison in which the new canteen employee Gladys used to work in as a prison wardress as referred to in the Series Five episode 'Canteen Trouble'.

Inspector Blake is really pleased with his new recruit feeling that she will be beyond corruption. He points out to Jack and Stan that she used to work in Holloway Prison so they won't be able to charm her and acquire food without paying for it.

Holloway Prison is an infamous women's prison located in Islington, London and opened in 1854. The prison's most distinguished inmates include Myra Hindley (for a short time) and Ruth Ellis who was to be the final woman to be executed in the United Kingdom in 1955.

Home-Brewed Beer

Stan is to try his hand at making home-brewed beer in the Series Three episode 'Brew It Yourself'.

Amidst a financial crisis it would seem the time is right for Stan to attempt to brew his own beer in turn saving him money on expensive beer at the pub. Using ingredients including hops, malt extracts, sugar and yeast he sets about the task but his competency is called into question by Arthur especially when Stan insists on adding plaster of Paris to the water that makes his beer but explains that is because the family live in a district with soft water. The ingredients are left in an insulated bucket to ferment for four days and soon it is time for Stan to taste his best bitter.

Of course, Arthur is very sceptical of Stan's effort and refuses to sample the beer as, in appearance; it looks like Olive's soup. However, after scooping off a layer of yeast from the top of the beer, Stan tastes his beer and declares it to be smashing. Olive and mum are reluctant to drink their sample so Stan drinks it for them despite knowing he has another shift at the depot to complete that afternoon. It is after he has left for work that the family discover the beer to be a lot stronger than Stan thinks. Arthur tries some of the beer and is pleasantly surprised but on checking its gravity with a hydrometer finding it to be very strong he declares: 'Blimey that's not beer! It's firewater.' Mum also discovers its strength as some of the spilt beer takes the varnish off of her table.

Later that night, Stan returns home, having almost lost his job and having undergone a stressful breathalyser test, to find the family have drunk the remainder of his homebrew. He is shocked to see Arthur and Olive drunk and getting passionate in an armchair whilst mum needs escorting up to bed. Initially, the fear of nearly losing his job leaves Stan adamant he'd make no more beer but if it can breathe passion into Arthur and Olive's marriage then he and Jack believe it will be a hit with the clippies and so set about brewing more beer.

Home Decorating

This is a task that Arthur and Stan are to undertake as the bedroom of Olive and Arthur needs decorating in the Series Three episode 'Busmen's Perks'.

Budget dictates that the room will be painted and although Olive would like it painted red as it makes a woman appear sexier and mum suggests a pale pink or mauve colour, Stan has the final say insisting it will be painted in green and yellow as that is the colour of the Luxton and District's buses. With the paint coming from the bus depot and costing him nothing Arthur is happy with the colour scheme.

They find the home decorating more challenging than they thought with several mishaps. Paint is spilt over a chest of drawers forcing them to paint it as well, Arthur forgets to add hardener to the paint which prevents it from drying as quickly as it should and he is later to suffer a painful injury in the night falling into a drying drawer. He is left with a backside riddled with splinters and he is so fed up with his predicament that he insists on bringing in professional decorators to do a proper job on the bedroom.

Hong Kong Flu

A variety of flu that breaks out at the bus depot depleting the Luxton and District Bus Company of fit bus crews in the Series Five episode 'The Epidemic'.

Hong Kong flu, according to newspaper reports, lasts for two weeks which Stan can understand as his radio made in Hong Kong also only lasted that long.

Hopkins, Beryl

An unseen clippie that Inspector Blake feels is abusing the company's public convenience allowance in the Series Seven episode 'The Allowance'.

The inspector is fed up with the rash of fraudulent allowance claims and reels off a list of offenders saying: 'And listen to this one. Beryl Hopkins. For phoning her mother – three pounds.' Olive claims it was an emergency as Beryl needed the toilet but didn't have her handbag and purse. 'Well where does her mother live? Australia?' asks Blakey. 'No she was on holiday in Majorca at the time,' replies Olive. This stuns the inspector who is intent on making sure the troublesome allowance gets cancelled.

Hospital Porter

A job held by Arthur prior to moving in as a lodger at the Butler house and referred to in the Series Six episode 'Stan's Worst Day'.

Arthur, a hospital porter who pretends to be a doctor, arrives at the Butler house for the first time looking to rent a room he has seen advertised in a shop window. He is greeted with competition for the room from new bus conductor Jack who is also looking for accommodation at the Butler house after being encouraged by his new friend Stan. Arthur uses his profession to his advantage saying: 'These people are busmen aren't they? The card did state that the room was for business and professional people. As I happen to be in the medical profession I, of course, will be taking the room,' Arthur tells Mrs Butler. It is a decision he will later regret.

Hot Water

The Butler house has to do without the valuable commodity of hot water for a brief time in the Series Seven episode 'Hot Water' much to the new lodger Inspector Blake's displeasure.

It is the inspector who makes the discovery whilst shaving and complains to Olive: 'The hot water's freezing cold. How am I supposed to shave in freezing cold water? My bristles'll all frizzle up.' He takes his complaint to Mrs Butler who blames him and her daughter Olive for using up all of the hot water leaving her without any to do the washing up. However, he is not happy as he points out: 'I am paying for hot water you know…not a basinful of ice. I'm not a bloomin' penguin you know.'

It later becomes clear that Inspector Blake had earlier altered the settings on the thermostat and Mrs Butler feels that he has broken the heater by fiddling with it and so he will have to pay to have it repaired.

As it turns out, despite being against all his moral beliefs, he is coerced by Jack into obtaining a stolen immersion heater and with the toothy conductor's help looks to plumb in the new system and return hot water to the Butler household.

Housewife

Played by Wendy Richard

This attractive young woman in her late twenties is to accuse Inspector Blake of trying to steal her laundry in the film On The Buses.

When Stan mistakenly picks up the wrong laundry bag from the launderette and rushes back to board his bus he is caught in the act by the inspector who confiscates the laundry saying he'll keep it as evidence as Stan will be going up to see the general manager. However, the housewife and her friend rush from the launderette onto the scene and try to retrieve her bag.

She accuses a baffled inspector of stealing her washing and wrestles to get it back as a policeman arrives on the scene. The angry housewife tells the policeman: 'He pinched my laundry.' Although Inspector Blake claims a pair of black lace panties belong to his driver this leaves him open to ridicule from the housewife and Stan and Jack revel in his discomfort as the policeman prepares to take down his details.

Howard, Charlotte

TV Role: Stella (Series 4 Episode 13 'Not Tonight')

Charlotte Howard's career as an actress has spanned well over forty years primarily in television roles but also has worked in films and on stage.

On the small screen her career began late in the 1960s in comedy series Cold Comfort Farm. Other comedy roles would follow in hit sitcoms such as Nearest And Dearest, On The Buses, Father Dear Father, Love Thy Neighbour, Bless This House and Robin's Nest. She would also appear in dramas such as Nana, Z Cars, Crown Court, I Claudius, For The Love Of Albert, Angels and Ruth Rendell Mysteries. Her film roles were somewhat limited. A small role in the acclaimed war drama The Hiding Place and a made-for-television film called Jekyll And Hyde in 1990 were the pick of her film career. Howard has also gone on to appear in stage roles up to the 2010s with roles in Rebecca and Robin Hood And His Merry Men.

Hoy, Janice

TV Role: Beryl (Series 5 Episode 15 'Boxing Day Social')

Janice Hoy was to have a short career as an actress on television from the mid-1960s until the early 1970s. She debuted in the hit drama The Power Game in 1966, before going on to appear in an episode of the classic sci-fi series Doctor Who. Her final credit came in On The Buses in 1971 after which her career in acting wound down.

HP

A term used by Stan when referring to household goods in the film On The Buses.

Stan is stunned when his mother has a new washing machine delivered even though the family are amidst a financial crisis after he loses vital overtime at work. He says: 'Mum this is absolutely ridiculous. We've got enough on the HP already. No I'm sorry that'll have to go back.' He goes on to remind her that they are already paying HP for their television, fridge and vacuum cleaner. When Arthur says he can't afford to pay any more money as he hasn't finished paying off his new bed yet. Stan reminds him: 'You don't pay as it is. I pay all the HP.' As it turns out the washing machine is returned to the shop with the family having to resort to using the launderette.

The term HP is an abbreviation for hire purchase. This was, and still is, a frequently used method for a financially struggling person or family to buy goods. The goods are gradually paid for in a series of instalments at the end of which time the goods are then owned by that person.

Hudson, Mavis

Played by Maureen Sweeney

This attractive young holidaymaker in her late twenties arrives at the holiday camp with her bossy and overbearing mother in the film Holiday On The Buses.

On arrival at the camp Mavis immediately gets propositioned for a date by Stan when he learns she has no boyfriend. Although keen for romance Mavis and Stan are constantly thwarted by her over-protective mother. Even whilst relaxing at the swimming pool with her mother nowhere to be seen Mavis has no peace as Stan tries to court her. Her mother suddenly surfaces from beneath the water and growls: 'Mavis! Bring my towel.' And so another potential romantic moment is broken up for the couple. Mavis finally gets her chance to date Stan when they go on a boat cruise without her mother who can't stand boats as they make her seasick. It is much to her frustration though that she is to be denied again. Despite hiring a cabin, ordering duty free champagne and about to have a romantic kiss with Stan he himself suffers a bout of seasickness leaving him unable to satisfy Mavis. 'Well a dead loss you are and on my last day as well,' she moans as she helps him out of the cabin on to the deck for some fresh air.

Moments later, she does manage to pair off with Jack though. He pays Mavis a visit in her cabin and ends up alleviating her boredom as he shares the champagne with her before they share a kiss and cuddle on the bunk bed whilst her original date recovers from his seasickness outside.

Hudson, Mrs

Played by Eunice Black

The ageing mother with dark hair in her fifties accompanies her daughter Mavis on holiday in Holiday On The Buses.

Mrs Hudson is a dislikeable character who is always meddling in her daughter's private life and often speaks to her in a bullying manner treating her like a servant at times. Her constant interference between Mavis and Stan leads the fed-up bus driver to suggest Jack takes Mrs Hudson on a date to distract her but the conductor is horrified and flatly declines. Later, Stan calls to see Mavis just as Mrs Hudson returns from the bingo. She interrupts as they kiss, saying coldly: 'What's going on?' When he claims he was asking Mavis if she'd like to come for a drink, Mrs Hudson replies: 'Good idea. We can all go together.' She takes Stan by the arm, an indication she has romantic inclinations in that direction herself. The holiday does see her manage to keep Stan and Mavis apart until a boat cruise which she can't attend as she suffers from seasickness but there is no romance to be had between the couple as the holiday ends.

Hunchback of Notre Dame, The

This is a character from a famous book that Stan likens to Arthur in the film Mutiny On The Buses.

Arthur's snoring annoys Olive to such a degree that she sews tennis balls onto the back of his pyjama jacket to stop him sleeping on his back which in turn will stop him snoring. However, after putting the jacket on Arthur discovers the balls and as he is doubled over reaching back to try to remove them Stan enters the bedroom saying: 'You look like the Hunchback of Notre Dame.'

The Hunchback of Notre Dame was a novel written by Victor Hugo in 1831 about a deformed bell-ringer called Quasimodo who had a hunched-back and walked in a stooped manner hence Stan's comment.

Hunter-Craig, Alan

Designer (On The Buses TV Series 4, 5, 6 and 7)

Alan Hunter-Craig was to work as a production designer on a total of forty three episodes of On The Buses from Series Four onwards from late 1970 through until 1973. He was also to work on a variety of classic television series in the same role in a career that spanned a quarter of a century. His career began at the BBC in the mid-1960s and was to work on classic sitcoms Sykes And A … , The Likely Lads, Dad's Army and the police drama Softly Softly. In 1970 he went on to become an employee of London Weekend Television where he worked as a designer on hit sitcoms On The Buses, The Train Now Standing and Bowler before moving on to end his career working on the award-winning drama Rumpole Of The Bailey and the classic soap Crossroads.

He has since moved on to work as an architect and is still using his skills as a designer in his seventies.

Hussy

A derogatory term often used in On The Buses on both the small and big screen versions and describes a woman who is thought to have committed adultery.

In the Series Five episode 'Boxing Day Social', Inspector Blake is showing Arthur's mother Mrs Rudge around one of the buses parked in the depot. When he encounters Stan kissing a woman on the bus he says: 'Who's that hussy with you there?' It soon becomes clear to the inspector that the woman is Arthur's sister Linda.

On the big screen, in Holiday On The Buses, Olive mistakenly enters the wrong chalet on her way back from the toilet and ends up in bed with holidaymaker Wally Briggs. However, as the chalet light is switched on by him, Olive realises her mistake and scrambles out of the bed as Mrs Briggs exclaims: 'You brazen hussy.' Later, in the same film, as camp nurse Joan enjoys a snog with Jack in her treatment room they are disturbed by the arrival of Inspector Blake. He is incensed to hear Joan with another man but by the time he gets into the room Jack has made his escape. Convinced it was Stan, the inspector is livid and even though Joan insists it wasn't him he shouts: 'Don't you lie to me you…you hussy.'

Hyde, Roy

Sound Editor (Holiday On The Buses)

Roy Hyde's career revolved chiefly around the film industry where he worked in the sound department for over thirty years.

The vast majority of his credits came for the famed Hammer Films production company beginning in the late 1950s with Ten Seconds To Hell, the classic war film Yesterday's Enemy and the acclaimed horror film The Mummy. The 1960s saw him work on a number of Hammer horror films with the pick of those being The Evil Of Frankenstein, The Gorgon, Fanatic, Frankenstein Created Woman and Quatermass And The Pit. Other films away from Hammer in that decade that Hyde worked on included the award-winning drama A Taste Of Honey, The Mouse On The Moon, Doctor Terror's House Of Horrors, Doctor Who And The Daleks and The Virgin Soldiers. The 1970s brought more credits working on Hammer productions of a comedy and horror variety. Most notable of those were The Vampire Lovers, Scars Of Dracula, Vampire Circus, Love Thy Neighbour, Holiday On The Buses, Frankenstein And The Monster From Hell and Man About The House.

On television he did work in the sound department on the hit war drama The Pathfinders in the early 1970s. His final credit of his long career came in the mid-1980s in the sci-fi series Terrahawks which was created by the legendary Gerry Anderson.

If You Were The Only Girl In The World

This is a popular song that is sung drunkenly by Stan and Jack in the Series Five episode 'The Best Man'.

After taking him out on a last night bachelor's party, Stan and Jack arrive home at the Butler house carrying a comatose Bill who is to be married the following day. The inebriated pair give a loud rendition of 'If You Were The Only Girl In The World' before dropping Bill into an armchair where he falls into a drunken sleep.

The song 'If You Were The Only Girl In The World' was written in 1916 by Nat D. Ayers with lyrics added by Clifford Grey. It would first appear in a musical revue stage show in London called The Bing Boys Are Here and came to the fore in the hit 1953 musical film starring Doris Day called By The Light Of The Silvery Moon.

Immoral Behaviour

A clippie called Wendy is accused of immoral behaviour by Mrs Butler at the depot in the Series Four episode 'The Other Woman'.

When Mrs Butler and Olive come to the depot in search of Arthur who has walked out on Olive they confront Wendy who had flirted with him at a darts night event. Mrs Butler turns to a present Inspector Blake and says: 'Sack that woman for immoral behaviour.' The inspector points out that if he were to do that there wouldn't be a clippie left in the depot. In any case Wendy dispels such an idea of having an affair with Arthur. 'Just because he bought me a few gins he spread it around. Who'd fancy him? I wouldn't be seen dead with him. Shrivelled up little weed,' scoffs Wendy.

Income Tax

The renowned tax on wages is referred to in the Series Three episode 'Mum's Last Fling'.

Inspector Blake unknowingly gives Stan some news that cheers him up as he tells him that the bus conductor Wilf Phillips, who is dating Mrs Butler despite Stan's dislike of the fellow busman, is actually married. The inspector tells him Wilf has been claiming for his wife on his income tax and has been married for twenty years. It kills off the budding romance between Wilf and Mabel so things can return to normal in the Butler household.

Income tax was first introduced to the United Kingdom in 1798 by the youngest Prime Minister in Britain's history, William Pitt the Younger. In that instance it was introduced to pay for guns and other military equipment for the Napoleonic Wars. Since then income tax has become a part of every government's budget.

Indian Dance

A social event at Luxton's bus depot canteen organised by Indian busmen that features in the Series Three episode 'The Snake'.

The event attended by Stan, Jack, Inspector Blake and a number of Indian busmen, is to see exotic Indian sweet mix offered to the guests with traditional Indian music as entertainment. The main attraction for Stan and Jack comes when canteen employee Fatima, scantily clad, performs an Indian Fertility dance with a snake. Both of the randy busmen have intentions of dating Fatima and at the end of the evening it is Jack who wins the spoils but has to deal with the prospect of going on a date with Fatima and her pet snake. It takes all of Jack's cunning to lumber Stan unknowingly with the snake, hiding it in his laundry bag which he asks Stan to take home with him. It is an event that goes well for Jack whilst Stan and his family are left in peril in its aftermath.

Indian Fertility Dance

A dance performed by the canteen employee Fatima at the Indian Dance social event in the depot canteen in the Series Three episode 'The Snake'.

The Indian Fertility dance is performed with a live snake to an accompaniment of traditional Indian music played on Indian instruments. As the dance gets under way, Inspector Blake tells Stan the fertility dance is artistic. As he watches, enthralled by Fatima's movements, Stan remarks that it is no wonder India has such a big population with such a fertility dance. The dance sees Fatima bedecked in jewellery and wearing a scanty costume, wrap the snake around her body and then approaches Stan putting the snake, with its tongue spitting out, in the busman's face before taking it away. He remarks: 'I tell you what mate that's put me right off my jellied eels.' There is to be a jaw-dropping finale to the dance as the Indian drum beats increase in tempo. She places the head of her snake in her mouth but the snake is unharmed on removing it and she receives an enthusiastic round of applause from Stan, Jack and Blakey at the end.

Indicators

A part of Stan's bus that Inspector Blake picks fault with in the Series Four episode 'Safety First'.

After lambasting Stan and Jack about the amount of complaints the company has received about them, the inspector then spots another fault, this time with their bus as it is about to leave the depot. 'Your indicators are all wrong. It's only the back half going to the Cemetery Gates, the front half is going to the General Hospital,' snaps Blakey. He goes on to tell Stan: 'We're trying to run a bus service here not a bloomin' mystery tour.'

An indicator is an abbreviated term for a destination indicator which is the panel at the front of the bus which gives details of the bus service's final destination. Such an indicator is also situated at the rear of the bus. These destination indicators were to first start appearing on buses in Britain in the 1920s and have now evolved to electronic displays with more route information details being made available.

Ingrid

Played by Yutte Stensgaard

Ingrid is a beautiful young Swedish student who, along with her friend Birgit, mistake Stan and Jack for airline pilots in the Series Three episode 'The New Uniforms'.

In her mid-twenties with long blonde hair, Ingrid is in a café with her friend when she points out Stan and Jack in their new prototype uniforms. As she eyes them up she sexily sweeps her long hair back behind her and goes to chat up the ageing busmen. She believes them to be airline pilots and it doesn't take long for Stan and Jack to carry on the pretence and ask the Swedish couple out on a date. Ingrid is cautious at first saying they'd been told to be careful with airline pilots but finally agrees to a date when Stan promises they are not like other airline pilots – and how right they are. Naively, as Stan and Jack leave the café the young Swedes think they are onto a good thing.

After a date that goes well, Ingrid and Birgit are in for a shock the following day. They turn up at the depot looking to catch a bus to the museum and see that Stan and Jack are no more than busmen and scruffy ones at that. Much to Inspector Blake's glee he informs the two shocked young women that they don't fly 'a yumbo yet' and can't even drive a number eleven bus to the Cemetery Gates and back. Ingrid and Birgit speak a few choice words in Swedish and march away ending Stan and Jack's fun.

Inhaler

A medical device used by Olive as referred to in the Series Three episode 'The Inspector's Niece'.

As Arthur, Olive and mum get ready for a night out at the pictures, Olive rummages through her handbag saying: 'I can't find my inhaler.' Arthur wonders why she needs it but she explains: 'Well you know what sitting in a hot cinema does to me.' On receiving the inhaler from mum, Arthur warns her: 'Here and you try and remember where you put that in your bag. Last time we were in the cinema you shoved the lipstick up your nose.'

Inspection Pit

An area in the Town and District's bus depot that features in the film Mutiny On The Buses when a fire breaks out in it and later a fire drill that goes wrong sees Inspector Blake fall into a foam-filled inspection pit.

The inspection pit was a recess built into the floor around six feet deep that was for buses to be parked above. Maintenance crews and mechanics positioned in the inspection pit could then get access to and repair damage to the under-carriage of the vehicle. It remains an essential part of bus depots and garages to the present day.

Insurance Company

Two insurance companies are to bring Stan good news on the small screen but bad news when he crashes his bus on the big screen.

When Stan discards his cigarette end in a used ticket bin aboard his bus resulting in the bus being burnt down he fears the sack in the Series Six episode 'No Smoke Without Fire'. However, the Luxton and District Bus Company's insurance company are willing to pay for a brand new bus as they accept the bus company's explanation that the fire was caused by faulty wiring. This ensures that Stan will not lose his job as he had feared.

On the big screen, in On The Buses, Stan in his haste to escape from an angry husband reverses his bus into a public telephone box and bus shelter destroying both. The accident causes over two hundred pounds worth of damage but Stan claims the bus got into a skid and he couldn't control it. The general manager is not impressed and tells him: 'Well the insurance company aren't satisfied. They say its incompetent driving and they're withdrawing your cover until you've passed a test.' The test in question is to be carried out by the Town and District Bus Company's insurance company with Stan's driving skills being tested thoroughly on London Transport's skid pan.

Interpol

Interpol is a famous foreign police organisation which was referred to by Stan in the Series Four episode 'The Lodger'.

Stan is forced to economise by eating sandwiches for lunch in the depot canteen but he cannot resist pinching a Brussels sprout and a handful of chips from Blakey's plate who has been called away to answer a phone call. However, the inspector returns and notices the missing sprout and accuses the cheeky driver of stealing his food. Stan turns to Jack and says: 'I'll tell you what Jack ring up Interpol.' He does later confess to Blakey that he did take the sprout but only because he can't afford proper meals.

Interpol, otherwise known as the International Criminal Police Organisation was formed in Austria in 1923 but headquarters moved to France at the end of World War Two in 1945. It is an organisation that works to assist police forces from all over the world to combat crime. Interpol is the second largest global government-run organisation in the world – only the United Nations is bigger.

IQ Test

This is a test that Jack claims to have taken prior to becoming a conductor in the Series Seven episode 'The Perfect Clippie'.

Jack is offended when his driver and friend Stan informs him Olive is going to become a clippie and should have no problems claiming: 'You don't have to be too bright to be a conductor.' Jack hits back: 'Listen mate before I joined here I had to take an IQ test.' Both men show their ignorance though as Stan asks: 'What's that?' To which Jack replies: 'I don't know.'

An IQ (Intelligence Quotient) test is used to rate ones intelligence through a series of tasks and questions. Such a test was indeed used when bus companies recruited bus conductors and clippies with a pass mark needed to succeed. Tests such as these remain in place to this day in public transport-related jobs and are now more commonly known today as psychometric tests.

Irate Passenger

Played by Terry Duggan

A disenchanted man who is far from satisfied with the bus service offered by Stan and Olive's bus in the Series One episode 'Olive Takes A Trip'.

The irate passenger is in his mid-thirties and unhappy with the delay to the bus service. He comes down from the upper deck when the bus stops to complain and finds Olive sitting on the platform of the bus as she tries to overcome a bout of travel sickness and when he returns later as he grows increasingly impatient she is drinking a cup of tea brought to her by a considerate elderly gent from a nearby café. Angrily, the passenger says: 'Oh no I've seen the lot now. Five minutes from the depot and you stop for a tea break. No wonder the country's ruined.'

Stan grows fed up as the man goes on to moan about the rising fares and tells him to get on the bus behind refunding his fare. As the passenger leaves content Stan is pleased with how he dealt with the situation but Mrs Butler, on the journey to support her daughter, points out that the passenger hadn't bought a ticket yet.

Iris

Played by Jennifer Guy

Iris is an attractive young woman in her twenties who is a player in the Basildon Bashers football team in the Series Seven episode 'The Football Match'.

A busty blonde woman wearing a green and black striped football top, she emerges from the dressing room and introduces herself to Stan and Jack saying: 'I'm Iris. I'm one of the forwards.' Stan jokes that she looks like two of the forwards in a reference to her busty build to which she laughs.

Iris ends up having a mixed game as she is felled by Olive and gets covered in mud but she does end up on the winning side as the Basildon Bashers thrash the Luxton Lions.

Iris

Played by Ursula Mohan

A receptionist for the depot manager who has black, curly hair and needs help moving house in the Series Six episode 'Private Hire' and turns to Stan and Jack.

Iris, a woman in her mid-twenties, is fed up as she and her mother are amidst moving house but have no removal van. Financially-strapped Stan and Jack have an idea to solve her problem and earn money at the same time. They are to use a bus they are meant to be taking out on tests as a removal van which will earn them five pounds from Iris. However, she doesn't tell them a piano needs moving and it is this that gets them in trouble as Blakey sees their bus passing him in the street with the piano sticking precariously out of the door. Although her furniture does get moved she is later to voice her concern about the fate of an old folks outing at the depot which is in danger of being cancelled. Her concern is to give Stan and Jack another idea of how to make money.

Iris

Played by Gwendolyn Watts

A saucy cockney woman who is to become a clippie aboard Stan's bus and dates him in the Series One episode 'The New Conductor'.

From Basildon, Iris is a busty, dark-haired woman in her thirties who has a reputation at the depot for wearing out many bus drivers. She is also rebellious with little respect for the inspector and has a talent for darts.

Placed aboard Stan's bus as his clippie the pair get on together so well that they arrange a date in the evening. After a drink at the Red Lion they return to the Butler house where their romantic mood is spoilt by a combination of things. Iris spots a pair of mum's bloomers hanging up to dry in the living room which she finds hilarious and when she asks Stan to put on some romantic music he can't oblige as the Butlers record collection has no such music.

Finally, as things begin to heat up between them; Mrs Butler breaks the pair up offering a snack of cocoa and kipper sandwiches dampening the couple's ardour. Further interruptions by the interfering mother leaves Iris fed up. Frustrated she walks out and leaves the Luxton depot the following day after asking for a transfer.

A few weeks later though, Iris returns and soon gets embroiled in a battle of the sexes sporting contest against Stan and Jack in the Series One episode 'The Darts Match'. Iris and her friend Jenny show an aptitude for darts but are prevented from playing on the dartboard in the canteen by Stan and Jack leaving Iris infuriated by their sexism.

She feistily challenges the two busmen to a darts match putting Stan in an awkward position. He still holds a flame for Iris and she uses her charms to distract him in the match. The contest ends sweetly for Iris as she and Jenny win with Iris being invited to join the depot darts team by Jack but sadly for Stan his romance with her cannot be rekindled.

Iris's Mum

Played by Mary Maxted

This is a dark-haired middle-aged woman and mother of the bus depot receptionist Iris who were both moving house in the Series Six episode 'Private Hire'.

She is briefly seen being told by Jack to open the door of their new house and put the kettle on as he and Stan prepare to move a piano into the house.

Iron Cross

A medal that was awarded to German soldiers is referred to by Stan in the Series One episode 'The Canteen'.

As Inspector Blake reflects on his military career in India he is mocked by Stan and Jack. He points out that he earned a medal for his services. 'Did you? What was it? The Iron Cross?' jests Stan amidst laughter.

The Iron Cross is a medal awarded for gallantry to soldiers in the German Army. Introduced in 1813 it was first awarded in the Napoleonic Wars to soldiers of the Kingdom of Prussia (later to become part of Germany) and later in the First and Second World Wars. The Iron Cross is no longer awarded and despite various lobbies to have it revived the medal is no more – to be replaced by the Cross of Honour for Bravery.

Izzard, Bryan

Producer (On The Buses TV Series 6 and 7) (Holiday On The Buses)

Born in Dorking, Surrey in 1936, Bryan Izzard cut his teeth in the broadcasting industry as a trainee producer at the BBC on radio and then television before moving on to London Weekend Television where his career took off. He would go on to become the third producer to work on the On The Buses television series.

He became renowned as a producer of many hit comedy series such as The Fenn Street Gang, The Reg Varney Revue, eighteen episodes of On The Buses from the sixth and seventh series and Not On Your Nellie all of which were LWT productions. He would go on to work on other notable comedies such as The Allen Stewart Tapes, Charles Endell Esq, Take A Letter Mr Jones, Rep and An Actor's Life For Me.

Bryan Izzard outside The South Bank Studios in the early 2000s.

Izzard had a spell as an independent producer in the early 1980s forming the Bright Thoughts Company producing series for newly-formed Channel Four such as a tribute show to musical artists from yesteryear called The Green Tie On The Little Yellow Dog and a short-lived comedy called Interference.

On the big screen he was to produce Holiday On The Buses which is widely regarded by many to be the best of the three spin-off On The Buses films. He would later go on to direct a musical film called Julie And The Cadillacs towards the end of his career in 1999. His career also saw him work as a director of many more hit series predominantly in the 1970s.

Sadly, Bryan Izzard passed away in 2006 at the age of sixty nine but his work is still fondly watched to this day on television.

J

Jack's First Day at the Luxton and District Bus Company

Jack arrives at the Luxton and District Bus Company as a new conductor as recalled in the Series Six episode 'Stan's Worst Day'.

He begins his new job as conductor aboard Stan's bus in the early 1960s with Stan himself starting his career as a bus driver after years of work as a conductor. Jack is to reveal he is looking for new accommodation saying: 'My landlady won't let me take birds up to my room. I might as well leave I'm never there.' Stan's first act as a friend to Jack is to suggest he moves into the Butler house as they are looking for a lodger but Jack is warned by inspector-to-be Blakey that the Butlers are really looking for someone to marry Stan's sister Olive. As it turns out Jack visits the Butler house but is keen to allow hospital porter Arthur, who is also looking for accommodation, to take the room as he is scared off by the attention of Olive.

Jack's Teeth

Jack Harper has a trademark toothy grin but it leaves him open to ridicule on a number of occasions in both episodes and a spin-off film.

His teeth are poked fun at frequently by friends and colleagues. Stan reckons that Jack's teeth remind him of a horse he once knew as well as likening them to a piano – an observation later made by Olive. As far as Arthur is concerned, when the randy conductor flirts with his sister Linda he threatens to thump him unless he stays away from her claiming that Jack's teeth make a good target. In the spin-off film Holiday On The Buses, Jack is to try to justify his ability to stand-in as a lifeguard telling the inspector that if need be he'd give him the kiss of life. Blakey laughs: 'Not you mate you'd bite me tonsils out.'

Jackson, Ron

Production Manager (Holiday On The Buses)

Ron Jackson was to work on the production of many iconic films and television series in a career that spanned a quarter of a century in the industry.

His first credits were to see him work as a unit manager on the memorable comedy films from the Carry On series in the mid-1960s – Carry On Cowboy and Carry On Screaming. He progressed on to a loftier role of production manager working for Hammer Films from the early 1970s in horror films Dracula AD 1972, The Satanic Rites Of Dracula and To The Devil A Daughter. At that time Hammer were also producing a number of comedy spin-off films with Jackson working on Nearest And Dearest, That's Your Funeral, Love Thy Neighbour, Holiday On The Buses, George And Mildred and Rising Damp. The 1970s also saw him work on other films away from Hammer which included The Blood On Satan's Claw, Black Beauty and Legend Of The Werewolf. Towards the end of his career he would work on made-for-television films Jack The Ripper and A Ghost In Monte Carlo which wrapped up his career in 1990.

Jackson's television credits, beginning in the late 1960s, were to see him work as a production manager on the classic ITC series Man In A Suitcase which was followed with work in Strange Report. Other small screen credits included the hit late 1970s drama Danger UXB and the much-loved anthology series Hammer House Of Horror in the early 1980s.

Sadly, Ron Jackson has passed away in recent years.

Jagger, Mick

Mick Jagger is a British pop icon that is referred to by Stan in the Series Three episode 'The New Uniforms'.

When Inspector Blake shows Stan and Jack sketches of the proposed new uniforms and the pose of the bus driver effigy in the sketch it causes hilarity. Stan laughs: 'Look at the driver. Blimey I look like Mick Jagger.'

Mick Jagger came to prominence in the early 1960s as lead singer of the legendary British rock band The Rolling Stones. The band went on to become one of the most successful and enduring pop bands of all-time. They were at the height of their popularity in the 1960s when they had eight No.1 hits in the UK charts alone with five No.1 hits in the USA. The hits continued to flow in the 1970s and they were still registering big hits in the 1980s. The Rolling Stones have also produced some of the best-selling albums of all-time and continue to tour to this day an incredible fifty years since they formed performing to packed venues around the world. They are still a global phenomenon and rocking on to the present day.

Jaguar Car

The brand of car driven by the depot manager Mr Adams that features in the Series Three episode 'Busmen's Perks'.

As Stan contemplates taking paint from the stores at the depot, he and Jack grumble about the attention being given to the manager's Jaguar car by the maintenance worker Nobby. The car has received several coats of metallic bronze paint, has had a diesel engine fitted so it can use the same fuel as the depot's buses and had an inordinate amount of time spent repairing its cigar lighter. According to Jack all of this is paid for by the bus company and points out to the inspector that he sees this as the company's profits being squandered. However, Blakey insists the manager only uses the car when he sees fit on company business.

Jaguar cars have a long history of producing the highest quality saloon and sports cars with memorable models such as the 'E' Type, 'S' Type and XJS. The originally Coventry-based company was once the jewel in the crown of the British car industry but fell upon hard times before falling into foreign ownership. Though Jaguar still produce much sought after luxury saloon cars it is now owned by the Indian car manufacturer Tata Motors.

Jane, Melanie

TV Roles: Canteen Girl (Series 7 Episode 5 'The Football Match') and Joyce (Series 7 Episode 8 'Hot Water')

Melanie Jane was to have a brief career as an actress appearing in several television roles in the early to mid-1970s.

Aside from appearing in two episodes of On The Buses, she was also to have other comedy roles in series such as Seven Of One, Ooh La La, The Fenn Street Gang and Men Of Affairs. Jane also had credits in a range of dramas which included the award-winning The Rivals Of Sherlock Holmes, Black And Blue, Dixon Of Dock Green and Dial M For Murder.

Although a brief career as an actress was ended after a few years she managed to fit so much into such a short space of time.

Janet

Played by Lynn Dalby

A red-haired secretary of the depot manager Mr Adams who informs maintenance worker Nobby that the manager would not be needing his car until late that night as he would be doing overtime in the Series Three episode 'Busmen's Perks'.

Janet, an attractive woman in her mid-twenties, is to pop into the maintenance department to remove files from Mr Adams's Jaguar car. As she leans through the window of the car offering a glimpse of her frilly panties she is ogled by Stan and Jack that earns them a ticking off from Inspector Blake. With her posh accent and business-like demeanour she offers no encouragement to the drooling busmen before leaving the scene.

Jarvis, Mike

Wardrobe Master (Mutiny On The Buses)

Mike Jarvis worked in the film industry working in the wardrobe department from the early 1970s until the mid-1980s and was to work on several smash hit films.

His film career began when he worked as wardrobe master on Mutiny On The Buses and went on to work on Fear Is The Key, The Man Who Fell To Earth, the star-studded war film The Eagle Has Landed and The Medusa Touch in the 1970s. The following decade was to see him wind up his film career by working on the classic award-winning crime film The Long Good Friday and the Oscar-winning comedy horror and box office smash Little Shop Of Horrors.

Jelly Babies

A type of confectionary Stan takes to eating in a bid to curb his desire to smoke in the Series Six episode 'No Smoke Without Fire'.

When Stan gets involved in a bet with Jack that he can stop smoking he is determined not to have a cigarette despite attempts by Jack to weaken his resistance. 'I'd sooner have a jelly baby any day,' claims Stan as he tucks into a bagful of the sweets. 'I can believe that you've eaten three pounds of them since this morning,' jokes the toothy conductor. Stan's bid to stop smoking is to leave him moody and he later snaps at Olive calling her 'a greedy pig' when she helps herself to his jelly babies which annoys his mother as she notes his bad temper since he quit smoking. Of course jelly babies do not stop Stan from smoking as his will power wanes and he resorts to having a cigarette thus losing his bet with Jack.

Jelly Babies were first launched in 1919 by the famous Bassett's company in Sheffield, Yorkshire with the sweets first known as Peace Babies coinciding with the recent end to World War One. They were renamed Jelly Babies in 1953 and remain under that title to this day. The UK variety of the sweet comes dusted in starch and in recent years the recipe has changed and now only includes natural colouring and ingredients.

Jenkins, Mr

Played by Kevin Brennan

This tough disciplinarian takes over as general manager at the Town and District Bus Company's depot in the film Mutiny On The Buses.

Mr Jenkins, a middle-aged balding man, arrives at the depot promising sweeping changes. He quickly takes steps to smarten up his staff ordering that all staff wear the proper uniform ridding them of their sweaters and tacky t-shirts. Jenkins also looks to improve punctuality and is to introduce a radio control system to each bus and orders all bus crews to undergo a course on firefighting. His most innovative idea is to run a tour bus to major tourist attractions such as Windsor Safari Park as he pledges to run the bus company at a profit.

He runs the depot with a no-nonsense policy but his plans and ideals are constantly thwarted by Stan and Jack who he soon grows to dislike. The powerful grip he has on the staff though is to be destroyed when Stan and Jack learn he is having an affair with the flirtatious clippie known as Nymphy Norah. It gives them the upper hand in the power struggle and they are to blackmail Mr Jenkins into giving Stan the lucrative job of the tour bus driver. However, when the trial run on the tour bus goes disastrously wrong he looks to assert his influence over the manager once more but he is in for a shock. He finds that Mr Jenkins has been transferred to another depot by request of his wife who has caught him doing overtime on the office floor with a clippie. And so Mr Jenkins reign ends in shame and he fails to fulfil his promises made on arriving at the depot.

Jenkins, Mrs

Played by Damaris Hayman

This is the wife of the strict general manager who attends a darts match in the depot canteen with her husband in Mutiny On The Buses.

Mrs Jenkins is a rather sheepish woman in her early forties who speaks with a posh accent. She is appalled when a fight breaks out during a darts match in the depot canteen between a jealous Olive and the clippie Norah calling it 'disgraceful behaviour' and she wishes she hadn't attended the event. In the aftermath of the fight her husband moves to comfort a soaked Norah and he asks Inspector Blake to look after Mrs Jenkins. It later comes to light Mr Jenkins has been cheating on his wife and she is to catch him in the act with another clippie and immediately requests he is transferred to another depot. Despite how it appears it seems Mrs Jenkins is the boss in their marriage.

Jennings. Ernest

TV Role: Rag and Bone Man (Series 7 Episode 13 'Gardening Time')

Ernest Jennings career as an actor saw his credits span over twenty years through the 1960s, 70s and 80s chiefly on television with a handful of film roles.

He was to appear in a string of classic British dramas such as Doctor Who, Dixon Of Dock Green, Secret Army, Angels and most notably the BAFTA Award-winning feature-length drama The Naked Civil Servant. In comedy roles on the small screen he appeared in smash hits such as The Goodies, On The Buses, Steptoe And Son and Bless Me Father.

Jennings film roles began with The Reckoning in 1969. He also had credits in the acclaimed short comedy film Futtocks End, horror film Psychomania and The Hireling which went on to win BAFTA Awards. He was also to have an uncredited role in the quality horror film Tales From The Crypt.

Jenny

Played by Valerie Newbold

A blonde-haired clippie who is a friend of Iris and like her has a talent for darts. They take on Stan and Jack in a darts match and she is to appear in two episodes of On The Buses.

She first appears in the Series One episode 'The New Inspector' wearing broad-rimmed spectacles and a head scarf and shows a feisty side to her character. She makes catty comments towards her fellow clippie Betty who flouts the rules and is having an affair with the depot manager. Later, in the Series One episode 'The Darts Match', Jenny minus the spectacles and head scarf takes offence to Stan and Jack's sexist attitude towards her and her friend Iris playing darts on the dartboard in the canteen. A darts match ensues between the busmen and the clippies with Jenny and Iris winning comprehensively but unlike Iris she does not get an invite to join the depot's dart team.

Jeweller

An unseen character that is to lose a diamond sealed in an envelope aboard Stan's bus and offers a reward for its return in the Series Five episode 'Lost Property'.

Joan

Played by Luan Peters

An attractive blonde-haired woman who is an employee of the vending machine company that have installed an automatic food dispenser in the depot canteen in the Series Five episode 'Canteen Trouble'.

Clad rather scantily she is checking the machines are working properly but Stan complains the machine is rejecting his money. As he and Jack drool over the attractive woman she unlocks the machine and takes out two meat pies and hands them to Stan saying in a posh accent: 'Take these with the compliments of the company.' Sadly, for Stan and Jack they won't meet Joan again as the automatic food dispenser is a short-lived experiment at the depot canteen.

Joan

Played by Kate Williams

A nurse at the holiday camp who dates Chief Security Inspector Blake until Jack comes along in the film Holiday On The Buses.

Joan, a red-haired woman in her early thirties, spends her time at the holiday camp treating ill or injured holidaymakers as well as giving special treatment to Blakey's big toe which has gout. She shares the odd kiss with him and accompanies him to his old-time dance classes but that all changes when Jack arrives at the camp as a new employee. Joan is soon led astray by him and they take to having covert meetings in her treatment room for brief moments of passion. However, when Blakey discovers she has been unfaithful he is infuriated and gets involved in a heated exchange with her that gets out of hand. The camp manager witnesses it and sacks the inspector before comforting Joan who is badly shaken up by the ordeal. Her romance with Jack is to be brought to an abrupt halt soon after when the conductor is also to be sacked and moves on to pastures new.

Joe

Played by Derek Carpenter

Joe is a long-haired busman who feels the cutting edge of Stan's tongue in the Series Four episode 'Dangerous Driving'.

A young busman in his early twenties, Joe has a Birmingham accent and wears a floral shirt. He is in the canteen when he overhears Stan arranging a date with a young clippie called Pat planning to take her to a new nightclub. Joe butts in saying he doesn't understand why she wants to go out with an old man like him. Stan takes offence telling him to shut up and go away and get his mother to cut his hair. Turning to Pat, Stan jokes: 'Besides they wouldn't let you in with him love. They don't allow two girls to dance together.' Pat bursts out laughing but Joe is not amused. 'Very comical,' he sneers before walking away.

Joe

Played by Eric Francis

An elderly man employed in the depot's maintenance department who is to help Stan break the rules on two separate occasions in Series Four.

Joe, a grey-haired man in his mid-fifties who wears blue overalls, is too busy to weld snapped forks from Arthur's motorbike and tells Stan and Jack if they want it welded they'd need to do it themselves as he has to work on a bus in the Series Four episode 'Nowhere To Go'. He is willing to turn a blind eye though as they use the depot's welding equipment. However, the inspector is not so charitable and discovers they have been welding without permission and chastises them. But he cannot take the matter further as Joe reveals that he has repaired Inspector Blake's bicycle and repainted it as well as mending his mother's hairdryer all free of charge making him no better than Stan and Jack.

Later, in the Series Four episode 'Cover Up', Joe is to supply Stan with a large roll of material from the upholstery store at no cost so that he can repair his furniture at home. The material is of a new design that is to be used to cover bus seats. Joe wraps the material up in brown paper and passes it on to Stan but warns him: 'Now look it's yours, I'm off and if anything's said count me out. I don't know a thing.' Stan suddenly gets cold feet and tries to give Joe the material back but he won't accept it saying: 'What? Look I'm off to lunch. You asked for it, you've got it.' Joe is to rush away leaving Stan in a predicament.

Joe

Played by Bartlett Mullins

An ageing cleaner employed by the Luxton and District Bus Company who, whilst amidst his duty, lands Stan and Jack in trouble in the Series Four episode 'Lost Property'.

Wearing a flat cap and spectacles, Joe is a moustachioed man in his early sixties who empties the used ticket box aboard Stan's bus despite the reluctance for him to do so by Stan and Jack. He discovers the remnants of two portions of fish and chips in the used ticket box which they have eaten instead of handing them in to lost property. Inspector Blake is on hand and promises sweeping changes to the reporting of lost property by all bus crews because of Joe's discovery.

Joe (The Maintenance Man)

Played by Michael Slater

This is a balding employee who works in the maintenance department and appears in two Series Four episodes of On The Buses.

Joe, in his forties, and wearing overalls, is to help Stan and Jack to free Inspector Blake when an accident sees his head become trapped between bars on his office door knocked off its hinges in the Series Four episode 'Safety First'. Joe brings an array of tools such as a grease gun, a pair of cutters and a burning plant which eventually frees the inspector who is taken to hospital.

In a later Series Four episode called 'The Injury', Joe is willing to help Stan fake an accident at the depot in a bid to qualify for accident pay. The maintenance man weakens a wooden step by taking bolts out of it and tells Stan: 'Everything's ready Stan. Fixed the step. Now look. All you gotta do is put your foot on it and it'll go right through.' Joe reassures the concerned driver that he has tipped all the lads off so they know not to use the step but unfortunately the inspector is the one set to suffer an accident that was meant for Stan.

Joe's Fish Bar

This is an unseen fish and chip shop that briefly comes to Stan's rescue in the Series One episode 'The Canteen'.

In charge of the depot canteen, Stan runs into problems when he employs Olive and his mum to cook for the busmen as they struggle to work the equipment. In a bid to feed the impatient busmen Stan resorts to buying several portions of fish and chips from Joe's Fish Bar across the road from the depot and sells them in the canteen. This turns out to be a financial disaster as his mum sells them at a lower price than Stan has bought them in for.

Jones, Betty

Played by Juel Morrell

A trainee clippie who spends her first day at the Luxton and District Bus Company being trained by Stan and Jack in the Series Four episode 'The L Bus'.

A busty woman with long blonde hair wearing a lime green sweater, Betty is to complain to Inspector Blake that her jacket is too tight and she can't button it up. It gives Stan an excuse to flirt with her as he helps her remove her jacket much to the inspector's displeasure. Betty, trained along with three other trainees aboard the learner bus are forced into helping Stan and Jack to use the bus as a delivery van to deliver a second-hand bed to the Butler house. However, the plot is uncovered by the inspector much to Stan's cost.

Jones, Charlie and Edna

This is a married couple who work as bus crew aboard the same bus for the Luxton and District Bus Company and who are referred to in the Series Four episode 'Christmas Duty'.

The unseen couple are rostered to work on Christmas Day but when clippie Edna comes down with the flu her husband and driver Charlie has to stay at home to look after her and their children and so their shifts need covered. With Stan and Jack rostered as their replacements it means the work-shy busmen are shoe-horned into working on Christmas Day by a gleeful Inspector Blake at the last moment.

Jones, Eunice

Played by Carol Gillies

This is an employee of the Luxton and District Bus Company who works in the accounts department at the Basildon depot. She is also captain of the Basildon Bashers football team in the Series Seven episode 'The Football Match'.

Eunice Jones, a poshly-spoken woman in her early thirties wearing a hairband, is appalled when Inspector Blake, unaware that the Basildon Bashers is a ladies team bursts into their dressing room clad only in long-johns. She ridicules the Lions side and their manager Blakey saying: 'Disgraceful behaviour. What are we playing – a team of sex maniacs?' However, she is sporting enough to allow Olive to play for the Luxton Lions – a decision she won't regret.

On the pitch Eunice employs successful tactics with plans that include a novel way to score yet another goal for the Basildon Bashers. Towards the end of the match she deploys another plan after Stan accuses her team of cheating. This plan sees her team surround the complaining driver and remove his shorts. She holds his shorts aloft cheering triumphantly to end the day resoundingly for herself and her victorious team.

Jones, Tom

A hugely successful British pop singer referred to by Olive in the Series Five episode 'The Busmen's Ball'.

As Arthur ridicules Olive's unappealing figure saying that seeing her in a girdle is not a pretty sight she hits back. She snaps: 'Well you're not exactly pretty when you're standing on one leg trying to get into your yfronts.' She turns on Stan who is equally scathing of her figure and says: 'You're not exactly Tom Jones are you?'

Tom Jones is one of the most successful pop singers Britain has ever produced. Renowned for his sex appeal and powerful performances, Jones was born in Treforest, Pontypridd, Wales in 1940. He can boast two No.1 hits in the UK in the 1960s along with a string of top ten hits and to a lesser degree the hits continued to come in the 1970s, 80s, 90s and 2000s. He was also to have his own variety television shows airing both in the UK and USA where he was a huge star as well. A global star, Jones still performs to the present day and his concerts continue to draw in the fans almost fifty years after recording his first hit record.

Jones's

This is a fictional ladies clothes store that Stan is to buy his mother's new coat from in the Series One episode 'The New Inspector'.

Stan, earning more money as an assistant inspector, treats his mum to the coat of her dreams as a present with him making thirty six weekly payments to buy it. However, when she witnesses the bad treatment her son gets in his new role she decides to return the coat to Jones's herself and pleads for him to resign from his new role but she is unaware that he has just been demoted in any case.

Joyce

Played by Avril Gaynor

An attractive young trainee clippie who, along with friend and fellow trainee Liz are to receive the drooling attentions of Stan and Jack in the Series Two episode 'Self Defence'.

With long, wavy blonde hair and amidst two weeks training to become a clippie she also has a talent for martial arts having studied judo for five years. Joyce and her friend are to be chatted up by Stan and Jack but are reluctant as they hardly know the ageing busmen. The pursuit continues at self-defence classes run by Inspector Blake in the depot canteen. It is here that Joyce is chosen to demonstrate her martial arts skills giving a painful lesson to Stan and Jack. The lesson sees Stan leave the class battered and bruised and it puts him right off the idea of dating her. Joyce though, is to date Jack later that evening accompanied by her friend Liz as Stan recovers from his injuries at home.

Joyce

Played by Melanie Jane

A clippie who dates Jack and hopes to share a quiet night in at Jack's house in the Series Seven episode 'Hot Water'.

Joyce is in her twenties and has curly blonde hair. Her date with Jack, a quiet night in with a bottle of Spanish red wine is to be spoiled by a string of unwelcome visitors from the Butler house next door. She is disturbed to discover that Olive is taking a bath upstairs and is ready to walk out on the date telling Jack: 'I'm not going to be one of your harem.' The lothario conductor persuades her to stay though as he explains the Butlers are without hot water in their house. As the couple begin to kiss there is an interruption as Mrs Butler pays them a visit asking to fill up her kettle and use the toilet. Joyce is fed up and frustrated moaning: 'This room's like bloomin' Piccadilly Circus.' Once more Jack appeases his date and they begin to kiss again. However, in rushes Inspector Blake in desperate need of the toilet. This is the final straw for Joyce as she likens the room to a public convenience and despite Jack's pleas she walks out bringing a premature end to the date.

Joyce

Played by Tara Lynn

This is a holidaymaker who, on arrival at the holiday camp, agrees with her friend to go on a date with Stan and Jack in Holiday On The Buses.

Joyce pairs off with Jack and is the quieter of the two women coming across as quite shy. The date is to end miserably for Joyce and her friend Doreen as they are forced to try and push the bus that they go on the date in when it becomes stuck in wet sand on a beach. When they fail to free the bus they walk back to the holiday camp.

Joyce

Played by Ursula Mohan

This clippie is to have a long-term steady relationship with Jack and appears in three episodes of On The Buses.

She is a dark-haired clippie in her late twenties and is first seen in the Series Three episode 'Radio Control'. Joyce, along with fellow clippie Edna, is to be placed aboard Stan's bus to be trained on how to operate the new radio system installed in Luxton and District's buses. Joyce is to pair off with Jack and they share a snog aboard the bus at the Cemetery Gates. She later helps Stan and Jack to tamper with the radio system as she lends them her nail file which they use as they bid to tune into a radio station. Instead they contact a passing jumbo jet and are panicked into tuning the radio receiver back to its original settings. Later, Joyce is lucky to avoid injury as Inspector Blake boards their bus and orders them to take a detour which sees the bus crash into a railway bridge.

She next appears in the Series Four episode 'Christmas Duty' as the bus crews get into the Christmas spirit. Jack hangs a piece of mistletoe outside the ladies toilets in the bus depot and as Joyce exits they share a lingering kiss. Afterwards she walks away wishing Stan and Jack a merry Christmas and arranges to meet them in the pub later.

Joyce's final appearance, in the last episode of Series Four called 'Not Tonight', sees her excited and looking forward to a date at the pub with Jack. She and her date are joined by Stan and his date Stella in the pub but it turns into an expensive and disastrous night for Stan. The considerate side of Joyce shines through later in the episode as she tries to help Stan's ailing love life by arranging for one of her friends to go on a date with him to a nightclub. However, Stan is skint and reluctantly has to turn down her kind offer.

Joyce, Yootha

TV Role: Jessie Crawford (Series 7 Episode 11 'The Allowance')

Born in Wandsworth, London in 1927, Yootha Joyce would go on to become a successful actress renowned for starring in hit 1970s sitcoms on television as well as having a full film and stage career in acting.

She left school at the age of fifteen to join the Royal Academy of Dramatic Art where she trained to become an actress. Joyce was to then become a member of the Joan Littlewood Theatre Workshop where, in the late 1950s her career began to take off on stage. Her big break came in the West End musical production Fings Ain't Wot They Used To Be in 1960. Other stage credits included A Christmas Carol, The Good Soldier Schweik, The Londoners, a stage adaption of George And Mildred and By Candlelight amongst others.

The early 1960s saw her television career begin and she will be best remembered for her role as frustrated and neglected housewife Mildred Roper in the classic 1970s sitcoms Man About The House and its spin-off George And Mildred where she teamed up so memorably with Brian Murphy. She was also to appear in many other classic sitcoms such as Steptoe And Son, George And The Dragon, Me Mammy, The Fenn Street Gang, Seven Of One and On The Buses. Also amongst her credits were roles in comedy sketch series such as Benny Hill and The Dick Emery Show. Joyce was also a familiar face in the best of British dramas with roles in Z Cars, No Hiding Place, The Saint, The Avengers, Dixon Of Dock Green, Manhunt and Jason King amongst others.

Film roles were plentiful for her in the 1960s with a small part in the comedy Sparrows Can't Sing followed by credits in The Pumpkin Eater, the Hammer horror Fanatic, Kaleidoscope, the multi-Oscar winning A Man For All Seasons, Stranger In The House and Our Mother's House to name but a few. The 1970s saw her film career continue with roles in Fragment Of Fear, All The Right Noises, Nearest And Dearest, Burke And Hare, Steptoe And Son Ride Again and starring roles in the spin-off films Man About The House and George And Mildred.

Sadly, after a lengthy battle with alcoholism, Yootha Joyce died of hepatitis in 1980, four days after her 53rd birthday with close friend Brian Murphy at her bedside. It was a tragic loss of a great comedy talent at such a young age.

Kaiser

A derogatory name Jack calls the inspector in Stan's vivid dream about life on the buses in the 1920s in the Series Seven episode 'On The Omnibuses'.

After an accident which sees their horse drawn bus smash into a shop window Jack tells Stan that the newly-formed union will protect him from the inspector's wrath. He says: 'Come on I'm not afraid of the Kaiser.'

The name would have been a reference to Kaiser Wilhelm II – the last German emperor who ruled during World War One. His reign ran from 1888 to 1918 and he took control of the German armed forces which invaded France and set up the bloodiest war the world has ever seen. With defeat in World War One following for Germany, Kaiser Wilhelm II was forced into abdication ending centuries of royal rule in the country. The ex- Kaiser was to die in the Netherlands in 1941 at the age of eighty two but was still an important figure in Germany.

Though loathed by Adolf Hitler, the Fuhrer contemplated holding a state funeral for Wilhelm II but the ex-Kaiser's dying wish was never to return to Germany until the royal family were returned to power and so any plans for a state funeral were shelved.

Karen, Anna

TV and Film Role: Olive Rudge (On The Buses Series 1 – 7) (On The Buses, Mutiny On The Buses and Holiday On The Buses)

Born in Durban, South Africa in 1936, Anna Karen spent three years training at the South African National Theatre before moving to the UK. She was to work as an exotic dancer at the Panama Club in London before her long acting career on television, film and stage took off.

It was on the big screen that she got her first break in the early 1960s with a starring role in the short film Nudist Memories. Karen went on to appear in the star-studded comedy The Sandwich Man and the highly-rated drama Poor Cow. Alongside close friend Barbara Windsor she was to have small roles in the iconic Carry On Camping and later in Carry On Loving as well as starring in the three hit On The Buses spin-off films. Towards the end of the 1970s she was to have a small role in the sex comedy What's Up Nurse. Later in her career came further film roles in the award-winning 1990s comedy Beautiful Thing and in the 2008 horror film Flick.

Of course her best-loved role came as the put upon and frustrated housewife Olive Rudge in the classic sitcom On The Buses. Her television career as an actress started to take off in the late 1960s when she was to appear in the BBC sitcom Wild Wild Women. Other comedy roles in her career included credits in Milk-O appearing alongside Bob Grant, And Mother Makes Five, the LWT version of The Rag Trade, Goodnight Sweetheart, Boyz Unlimited and Revolver. Drama roles also came her way most notably in Dixon Of Dock Green, The Bill, The Golden Hour and she will be best remembered for her role as Aunt Sal in the BBC soap EastEnders. She has also appeared in hit children's series in the 1980s in the form of Roland Rat: The Series and Super Gran.

Also an accomplished stage actress, Karen has had a long career in that field. Her credits include Busman's Holiday which co-starred Stephen Lewis and Bob Grant and was based around On The Buses, Who Goes Bare, On The

Buses: A Fresh Start, Murder Mystery, Noises Off, When Did You Last See Your Trousers and she was, of course, a regular on the annual pantomime circuit.

Anna Karen's acting career continues to this day after more than fifty years and she also teaches drama in her spare time. A distinguished member of The Water Rats she played such an important part in the success of On The Buses and with it wrote herself a proud chapter in her life.

Anna Karen gracing the 2012 On The Buses: A Fresh Start event.

Anna shared some of her memories to John Hannam on Isle of Wight Radio.

Memories

Speaking of her early years in the UK she revealed a little known fact:- 'I went to Italy with my first husband because he was training to be an opera singer and I went out there with him and I taught English at the English consulate to the Italian employees there. It was just wonderful; it was just one big exciting adventure. Italy was beautiful absolutely beautiful.'

Anna's thoughts about On The Buses were as follows:-'We had a lot of fun and we were very, very close. I mean we were very close as a cast. We were very good friends, I think that is why it gelled so well.

The casting there was excellent. The casting was done by a man called Richard Price and with the director Stuart Allen at the time and their casting was superb and that's it working out with people who gel. Michael and I had this wonderful sort of relationship together which we did – we loved and we hated each other so that is why it worked.'

Katy

Played by Moira Foot

A young clippie ogled by Stan and Jack at the start of the film On The Buses.

Katy, who has long blonde hair and is in her twenties, is ogled by the randy busmen outside the depot as she stretches over the bonnet of a bus to change its destination board. It offers them a glimpse of her shapely legs and she naively asks the pair: 'Is it alright?' Stan encourages her to carry on altering the board as it allows them a flash of a little more than her legs saying: 'No...up a bit.' However, Stan and Jack's fun is ended as Inspector Blake arrives on the scene and rushes them onto their bus.

Keen, Peter

Sound Editor (On The Buses)

Peter Keen was to work in the sound department on a number of films and television series from the mid-1960s until the end of the 1970s in a career that spanned more than a decade in the industry.

Mainly a film-orientated career, Keen had credits in Ten Little Indians, Ned Kelly, On The Buses, the Italian comedy film What, The Homecoming, the horror classic From Beyond The Grave and Diagnosis: Murder. In the second half of the 70s he worked on bawdy sex comedy film The Bawdy Adventures Of Tom Jones, The Stud and the adult drama The World Is Full Of Married Men.

Towards the end of the 1970s Keen worked on the classic British dramas The New Avengers and The Professionals in his solitary television credits.

Keep Fit Classes

Keep fit classes are staged at Luxton's bus depot for all staff and is run by Inspector Blake and are to feature in the Series Four episode 'Dangerous Driving'.

Stan is worried about his personal health. Following a newspaper article that suggests bus drivers health is at risk due to the nature of the job and he is also keen to get fit for a date with a young clippie called Pat and so reluctantly he attends one of the keep fit classes held in the depot canteen. It turns out to be an evening to forget for Stan as he is ridiculed by the inspector for his out-dated shorts he wears and is flattened by the rotund clippie Rosie as she is pulled on top of him during an exercise. To cap it all, in a bid to stop Blakey pulling his leg about his lack of fitness he gets involved in a skipping contest with him wagering that he can outlast the scoffing inspector. However, it is Blakey that wins out leaving Stan not only exhausted but out of pocket as well.

Kennedy, Jacqueline

A famous political figure of the 1960s referred to by Stan in the Series Four episode 'The Canteen Girl'.
When it comes to light that Inspector Blake is involved in a relationship with the much younger canteen employee Molly, Stan and Jack take the opportunity to pull the inspector's leg. Jack is jokingly puzzled about why young women date older men but Stan believes he has the answer. 'It's all the rage these days innit. Well it's Jacqueline Kennedy and Onassis all over again,' explains Stan.

Jacqueline Kennedy was the wife of assassinated US president John F Kennedy. She served as First Lady until 1963 when her husband was brutally murdered. After his death she continued in a role as an unofficial ambassador for the USA until marrying the Greek shipping magnate Aristotle Onassis in late 1968. The ageing millionaire was sixty two years old when he married Jacqueline Kennedy who, herself was thirty nine, hence Stan likening Blakey and Molly's relationship to them.

Kerr, Fraser

TV Roles: TV Newsman (Series 1 Episode 1 'The Early Shift') and Pilot (Series 3 Episode 8 'Radio Control')

Born in Glasgow, Scotland in 1931, Fraser Kerr left school to study medicine at Glasgow University but was soon to move into acting via working at the Park Theatre, Glasgow as a stage manager. He would go on to have a lengthy career as actor in films, television and stage.

Stage was to see him cut his teeth in the acting profession from the mid-1950s appearing in repertory in Glasgow and Edinburgh in shows such as Miss Julie and The Spring Of Others. He went on to work for the Old Vic Company appearing in Macbeth, Romeo And Juliet and Troilus And Cressida touring Canada and USA and performing on Broadway. Kerr also appeared in the West End in Watch It Sailor, the musical Brigadoon and Night Must Fall.

His break on the big screen came in Carry On Regardless in 1961. Other film appearances came in the comedy What A Whopper, horror film Theatre Of Death and he was also to supply voice overs in the award-winning animated film The Lord Of The Rings and the 1982 horror Doll's Eye.

Kerr was to have an active television career from the early 1960s in classic dramas such as Dixon Of Dock Green, The Third Man, Dr Finlay's Casebook, Wicked Women, Kidnapped and Howard's Way. He was also to make regular appearances in hit sitcoms including Doctor In The House, On The Buses, Mind Your Language, Yes Minister and Metal Mickey.

He was also to work comprehensively on radio with hundreds of broadcasts with the BBC Drama Repertory Company. Sadly though, Fraser Kerr contracted cancer and passed away in 2000 at the age of sixty nine.

Kessler, Catherine

TV Role: The Nurse (Series 6 Episode 6 'Bye Bye Blakey')

Catherine Kessler's career as an actress spanned more than thirty years and was to see her appear in television, film and stage roles.

She was most active on the small screen in hit dramas such as Love Story, the award-winning W Somerset Maugham, The Expert, Softly Softly, Z Cars, Dixon Of Dock Green, Within These Walls, Crown Court and in the US horror series The Hunted. Kessler was to have roles in some of the best sitcoms of their time including On The Buses, The Fenn Street Gang and George And Mildred.

Her film roles were fewer and further between with a small role in the adult drama Groupie Girl and a larger part in Dyn Amo. Her most notable film appearance came in the award-winning Murder By Decree which boasted a star-studded cast.

She was also to be part of the famous Royal Shakespeare Company performing on stage in the UK and USA in the play Love's Labour's Lost in the mid-1970s. Kessler also worked on radio plays for the BBC in her varied career.

Kettlewell, Ruth

TV Roles: Nurse On Bus (Series 3 Episode 1 'First Aid') and The Nurse (Series 5 Episode 1 'The Nursery' and Series 5 Episode 5 'The Epidemic')

Born in Worcester, Worcestershire in 1913, Ruth Kettlewell enjoyed a long career as an actress. Her career began in repertory theatre and progressed on to television and films where she worked well into her 80s.

The late 1930s saw her begin work in repertory theatres but this was curtailed by the outbreak of World War Two. However, stage roles came her way after the war when she progressed on to West End performances in Paris Match, the musical The Music Man, The Killing Of Sister George and Bed at the National Theatre.

By the mid-1950s Kettlewell had broken into television and went on to appear in a string of classic British dramas in the 50s and 60s such as Emergency – Ward 10, No Hiding Place, Love Story, The Expert and W Somerset Maugham. The second half of her career saw more drama credits in The Onedin Line, Z Cars, Juliet Bravo, Tales Of The Unexpected, All Creatures Great And Small and Heartbeat. She also regularly appeared in children's series with the pick of those being Catweazle, Here Comes The Double Deckers, Boy Dominic, Just William and The Famous Five. Comedy roles came in The Likely Lads, The Dick Emery Show, All Gas And Gaiters, On The Buses, The Fenn Street Gang, The Good Life, In Loving Memory, That's My Boy and Don't Wait Up amongst others.

Kettlewell's film career began in the late 1950s with an uncredited role in the Oscar-winning Room At The Top. Other most notable film roles followed in another Oscar-winning film called Sons And Lovers, Oh What A Lovely War, Zepellin, The Black Panther, Crystalstone, Great Balls Of Fire and comedy Funny Bones.

Often typecast in bossy domineering roles such as nurses or mothers-in-law she was also to be a lifelong patron of a church-based theatrical group called The St Augustine Players.

Sadly, in 2007 at the age of ninety four, Ruth Kettlewell passed away in London.

Kidde Hi – Ex Foam Generator

This is a branded type of firefighting equipment that is installed at the bus depot by the Town and District Bus Company in the film Mutiny On The Buses.

When the foam machine is tampered with by Stan and Jack during a fire drill the depot is soon turned into a sea of foam and the inspector is to fall into an inspection pit hidden beneath the foam.

Kidde is a US-based company that manufactures fir fighting equipment. Founded by American Walter Kidde in 1917 it was first known as the Walter Kidde Company and it was to produce the world's first integrated smoke detection and carbon dioxide extinguishing system which were to be used aboard ships. Their products were to become common in the workplace producing a wide range of equipment. The company has expanded in recent years and continues to supply firefighting equipment to countries all over the world.

Kids Outing

This was an annual event run by the Luxton and District Bus Company which is to be organised by Stan in the Series Four episode 'The Kids Outing'.

Stan feels he has everything under control as he supplies balloons to keep the children entertained and has an array of sandwiches and snacks prepared by mum and Olive to feed the children. To help supervise the bus load of children he enrols mum, Olive, Arthur and Jack to help. However, he does not account for the children being so mischievous and to make matters worse one of them is the nephew of Inspector Blake and is called Harold.

The event turns into a catalogue of disasters as three troublemaking children pour a bag of sugar into the bus's petrol tank just before it leaves the depot with the children aboard which causes it's exhaust pipe to fall off en-route. The rowdy youngsters singing rowdily don't take kindly to the delay and from the upper deck of the bus they pour milk over Stan as he explains the bus will need to return to the depot for repairs.

As the bus is repaired the depot canteen has to cater for the children whose behaviour and boisterous singing leads to desperate measures to keep them entertained. Inspector Blake bids to quieten the masses with his bird impressions but leaves himself open to ridicule from Stan and Jack. Finally, the desperate driver transforms himself to perform his drag act 'Clara the Clippie' which is not a success but soon the bus is repaired which allows the kids outing to be completed.

Kildare, Doctor

This was a fictional character from a popular 1960s television series that Stan refers to in the Series One episode 'The Canteen'.

Stan scoffs at Olive's cooking ability but his mum tries to persuade him to give his sister the job of canteen cook telling him that Olive watches cooking shows on television. This makes no difference to Stan who says: 'She watches Doctor Kildare but I wouldn't let her take my appendix out.'

Doctor Kildare was a hit US television series that ran from 1961 to 1966. It followed a young doctor played by Richard Chamberlain who learns his profession at a large hospital. The series was to win a coveted Golden Globe award and was a big hit on the small screen around the world.

King, Denis

Composer (Holiday On The Buses)

Born in Hornchurch, Essex in 1939, Denis King took up music from an early age playing the banjo in public by the age of six and a pianist at thirteen in the successful band, The King Brothers. By the end of the 1960s he had moved on to study music orchestration at the Guildhall School of Music in London and soon after began composing theme music for television series, films and later went on to compose music for stage shows.

He was to compose theme music for countless television series starting in the early 1970s with the classic theme for The Adventures Of Black Beauty, The Fosters, Within These Walls, Armchair Theatre, Dick Turpin and Worzel Gummidge. The 1980s saw him write themes for Smuggler, Holding The Fort, Now And Then, Wish Me Luck and Hannay amongst others. Finally, in the 1990s he was to create the theme music for Lovejoy and Madson. On the big screen he wrote musical scores for Not Tonight Darling, the soundtrack for Holiday On The Buses, the spin-off film The Sweeney, Son Of Hitler, If You Go Down In The Woods Today and Privates On Parade to name but a few.

King has also written music for a number of stage plays such as Stepping Out – The Musical, Lost Empires, One Night A Week, A Saint She Ain't, Awakening Beauty and in 1977 his musical score for Privates On Parade (the stage adaption) won the Ivor Novello Award for best musical.

Kirby, June

Wardrobe Mistress (On The Buses)

Born in Brooklyn, New York in the USA in 1929, June Kirby was to study at the Kingston Art School in London before moving on to work in the wardrobe department chiefly in the film and television industry.

On the big screen in the early 1950s she worked on films such as The Large Rope, Meet Mr Callaghan and the sci-fi Timeslip. Around this time came her brief foray into television but she returned to films working on Assignment Redhead and Man In The Shadow towards the end of the 1950s. There after Kirby went on to credits in Lunch Hour, On The Buses, the horror film The Keep and her career in films ended with the big budget movie Supergirl in 1984. Television credits came solely in the mid-1950s in the hit BBC drama Fabian Of The Yard and The Adventures Of The Big Man.

Kiss Of Life, The

The mouth-to-mouth resuscitation technique is referred to in an episode and a spin-off film of On The Buses.

During a fire fighting course at the Luxton and District bus depot in the Series Six episode 'No Smoke Without Fire', Stan is paired off with a large clippie called Gladys who is asked to demonstrate a first aid technique that involves her lying on top of him which proves very uncomfortable. Shaken he gets to his feet and tells Inspector Blake: 'Tell you what mate by the time she's finished giving you artificial respiration you need the kiss of life.' In Holiday On The Buses, Stan and Jack are designated as lifeguards at the holiday camp's swimming pool Blakey is stunned by the decision. Jack though is adamant they are up to the job boasting: 'Ah we're both strong swimmers.' He promises he'll give the inspector the kiss of life if he falls in the pool but Blakey scoffs at such a suggestion.

The kiss of life is better known as artificial respiration. It is usually used in cases where persons have stopped breathing after almost drowning, taking a drugs overdose or suffering smoke inhalation.

Knight, Eddie

Make-Up Supervisor (On The Buses and Mutiny On The Buses)

Eddie Knight was to have a long distinguished career working in the make-up department on films and television series with spells working on Hammer Films and hit ITC series.

His career began in the late 1940s on the big screen and he would go on to work on a host of memorable films. The first half of his career were to include credits in Tommy The Toreador, Carry On Constable, Murder She Said, Double Bunk, Murder At The Gallop, Ladies Who Do and Mrs Brown You've Got A Lovely Daughter up until the end of the 1960s. It was then that he moved on to work for Hammer Films on The Devil Rides Out, Frankenstein Must Be Destroyed, On The Buses, Blood From The Mummy's Tomb, Mutiny On The Buses, Frankenstein And The Monster From Hell and Man About The House to name but a few. Other notable film credits in the second half of his career were The Blood On Satan's Claw, Doctor In Trouble, Sweeney 2, Who Dares Win, Dreamchild, Willow and Indiana Jones And The Last Crusade. However, the highlight of his career had to be the winning of an Emmy Award for make-up in 1986 on the made-for-television film The Last Days Of Patton.

Television credits came in the classic series Alfred Hitchcock Presents in 1961 before moving on to work on a plethora of hit ITC series such as Danger Man, The Prisoner, Jason King, The Protectors, Space: 1999 and Return Of The Saint. Other notable television credits included The Sweeney, the US hit drama Hart To Hart, Quatermass, Hammer House Of Horror and Reilly: Ace Of Spies.

A career spanning well over forty years ended in the early 1990s with his retirement before he sadly passed away towards the end of that decade.

Knitting

A hobby of Mrs Butler and her daughter Olive which is to interfere with Stan's love life in an episode and spin-off film of On The Buses.

As Stan entertains clippie Iris in the parlour of the Butler house in the Series One episode 'The New Conductor' they share a kiss on the sofa. However, their romantic clinch is interrupted as mum's discarded knitting needle sticks into Iris. She is concerned the damage it has done to her tights but is stunned when she sees Stan knitting with the needles. Iris is annoyed and says: 'If you're going to sit here doing your knitting I'm off.' Although Stan persuades her to stay the date is destined to end in disappointment for him.

Similarly, in the film On The Buses, Stan lies on the sofa at his house with the Irish canteen cook Bridget and as they kiss she feels a knitting needle sticking in her which belongs to Olive. However, worse is to follow as a pregnant Olive comes to collect her knitting which alarms the deeply religious Bridget who gets up quickly and says: 'A pregnant woman – it's a message. It's the lord warning me. She was a messenger come down from heaven.' Even though Stan explains it was his sister who had come down from upstairs, Bridget refuses to let him near her and she makes a quick exit from the house putting an end to their fleeting romance.

La Rue, Danny

A popular entertainer of the 1960s and onwards that Inspector Blake refers to in the Series Four episode 'The Kids Outing'.

Stan, dressed as his drag-act 'Clara the Clippie' in a bid to entertain misbehaving children in the canteen, is mocked by Inspector Blake. He ridicules the bus driver in drag saying: 'What do you think you are? The busman's Danny La Rue or something.'

Danny La Rue was a famous entertainer who came to prominence with his famous drag acts and the 1960s and 70s were to see him become one of the highest paid entertainers in Britain. He dubbed himself 'the comic in a frock' and was a regular performer on stage, television and even films throughout the 1960s, 70s, 80s, 90s and was still a big draw into the new millennium. Perhaps the most famous female impersonator of all-time was to suffer a series of strokes late in his life which was to end his career and in 2009 he passed away at the age of eighty one suffering from prostate cancer.

Labour

An abbreviated term used by Stan to describe being a jobseeker once more in the film Holiday On The Buses.

After being sacked from their jobs at the holiday camp Stan and Jack are about to enter the employment exchange. Stan, somewhat resigned, says to his friend: 'Ah well here we are back on the old labour again. Blimey that job didn't last long.'

Stan was making an abbreviated reference to the labour exchange. These were government-run establishments which served the purpose of helping to re-employ the unemployed.

Lady Doctor, The

Played by Nicolette Roeg

A doctor that carries out medical examinations of staff of the Luxton and District Bus Company in the Series Six episode 'Bye Bye Blakey'.

The posh and dark-haired doctor in her forties is to examine Inspector Blake. However, he feels the medical is pointless as he won't be around much longer. To Stan and Jack who are eavesdropping on the conversation they fear the worst but in all honesty the inspector was merely referring to a new job he has applied for away from the depot. He tells the doctor he doesn't want anyone else to know and although she feels he should tell the staff he declines.

The following day she gets a visit from a curious Stan who wants to know more details about Blakey's condition. However, she remains professional and refuses to discuss her patients with him which leaves the driver still unaware of the inspector's new job.

Lady Godiva

A historical figure referred to by Stan in the Series Two episode 'Bon Voyage'.

Stan and Jack have stripped down to their swimming trunks to sunbathe at the Cemetery Gates but as they do so a passing tramp is to steal Stan's uniform from the driver's cab on the bus. It leaves Stan in a difficult position but Jack sees no problem in him driving his bus without his uniform. 'I'm a bus driver not Lady Godiva,' says Stan.

Lady Godiva was the wife of the Earl of Mercia and lived in the eleventh century. Legend has it that in protest of unfair taxes levied on the citizens of Coventry by her husband she rode naked on a horse through the streets of the town hence Stan's reference to the historical figure.

Lady Passenger, The

Played by Ruth Holden

This is a middle-aged woman who is to have uncomfortable experiences aboard Stan's bus in the Series Four episode 'Safety First'.

An upper class woman boards Stan's bus at the depot with her shopping. When the inspector decides to travel with Stan and Jack to ensure they stick to the regulations trouble ensues. As the bus exits the depot it is forced to brake suddenly to avoid a collision and the lady passenger is flung to the floor of the bus with Inspector Blake falling on top of her, squashing her shopping and ripping her blouse open. 'You've ruined my shopping. There's a mess all over me,' complains the distressed passenger to the inspector. After the bus is reversed into the depot she disembarks and is livid declaring: 'I shall go to the manager myself this very instant and I shall demand a replacement of my shopping. Everything I've got has been squashed.' The accident is to see Inspector Blake look to cut down on accidents by implementing a new system for directing buses out of the depot but it doesn't prevent another accident.

The unfortunate lady passenger is involved once more when a similar accident befalls her when Stan brakes suddenly after the inspector's overcoat gets trapped in the bus doors which is to cause her to fall downstairs spilling her shopping. As she gets to her feet Stan, Jack and the inspector watch on as she fumes: 'I'll sue you. Just you wait.' She storms off leaving Stan to suggest Blakey gives up on his new safety regulations.

Land, Mary

TV Role: Susy (Series 6 Episode 1 'No Smoke Without Fire')

Born in 1946, Mary Land took up acting in her late teens but it was to be a relatively brief career that spanned around ten years from the mid-1960s through until the mid-70s with credits in film and television. Her career began on the big screen in the Italian western film Kill Or Be Killed in 1966. She went on to have further film roles in adult dramas Her Private Hell and Loving Feeling towards the end of the 1960s.

Land's television credits were mostly drama-based in the form of Love Story, Play For Today, Armchair Theatre and the classic prison drama Within These Walls. Her solitary comedy role was to be her fair-sized role in an episode of On The Buses.

Land Of Hope And Glory

A famous anthem sung by Stan and Jack as they mock the inspector's military background in the Series Three episode 'The Snake'.

Whilst sitting in the canteen with Stan and Jack, Inspector Blake reminisces about his military career in India saying his efforts freed the world for the likes of them. He gives them cause for hilarity when he explains he was in charge of the mules in the army adding: 'I used to lead those mules five hundred miles through jungles, mountains, monsoons, right through the swamps, aerial bombardments, through the enemy lines and I still managed to get there every month on schedule.' Immediately, Stan and Jack get to their feet and giving a mock salute they burst into song singing the first few notes of 'Land Of Hope And Glory'.

'Land Of Hope And Glory' is a patriotic British song written by the English composer Edward Elgar in 1902 with lyrics supplied by Arthur Benson. The song is now traditionally played at the close of the Last Night Of The Proms at the Royal Albert Hall and has periodically been used in many sports as England's national anthem.

Landlord

An unseen character that is to throw Inspector Blake out of his lodgings in the Series Seven episode 'Goodbye Stan'.

The landlord is to make life difficult for Blakey when he looks to increase the rent but the inspector cannot afford to pay any more money. It causes the landlord to padlock up the bathroom and put a small charge for the use of the bathroom which also contains the toilet. The situation worsens when he has to break out of the bathroom injuring his face in the process and finds the landlord's dog waiting outside which rips the seat of Blakey's trousers. The incident results in the landlord throwing him out of his lodgings forcing him to move into the Butler house as a lodger.

Lassie

This is a famous canine film star that is referred to by Stan as he ridicules Inspector Blake's raffle that he is championing in the Series Six episode 'The Prize'.

As Blakey attempts to drum up interest at the depot in a raffle in aid of a stray cats and dogs charity he boasts of the great prizes that can be won for which he is mocked by Stan and Jack. The toothy conductor jokes the top prize will be a year's supply of dog biscuits and Stan quips: 'No. It's a night out with Lassie.'

Lassie was a fictional canine character, a collie dog which featured in a number of popular films in the 1940s and 50s beginning with Lassie Come Home in 1943. Lassie was played originally by a dog called Pal who was owned and trained by Rudd Weatherwax – himself an actor and renowned animal trainer. The tales of Lassie were to be made into an award-winning television series from the mid-1950s that ran for twenty years with Lassie being played by descendants of Pal. The television series was briefly resurrected in the 1980s and 90s with a remake of the original film released in 2006. The lovable collie has the distinction of being, along with Mickey Mouse and Bugs Bunny, the only fictional animal characters to appear in a star on Hollywood's Walk of Fame.

Last Tango In Paris

A hit film indirectly referred to by Stan as he tries to persuade Arthur and Olive to join Blakey's dance team in the film Holiday On The Buses.

Stan and Jack are looking to obtain a replacement toilet from the holiday camp stores but need Inspector Blake to be occupied to do this. A planned exhibition of old-time dancing which is run by the inspector is in danger of being cancelled due to being short of a dance couple. Stan therefore asks Arthur and Olive to join the dance team so the exhibition can go ahead but Arthur is not keen on making a fool of himself in public. 'Blimey I'm only asking you to do the military two step not the last tango in Paris,' says Stan.

Last Tango In Paris was an award-winning film made in 1972. A romantic drama starring Marlon Brando and Maria Schneider, the film was to be nominated for two Oscars and attracted controversy for its strong adult content.

Late Again

Stan runs into trouble with his unpunctuality at work and is punished by Inspector Blake in the Series Two episode 'Late Again'.

Late night dates with clippie Doreen followed by early shifts don't mix for Stan. He sleeps in for another shift arriving at the depot to find that Jack has clocked him in but Inspector Blake is on the prowl. He can't find Stan and Jack tries to cover up his absence by claiming he is in the toilet which leads to Blakey awaiting his exit from the gents.

In order to back up Jack's claim, Stan is told to climb in through the toilet window at the rear of the depot in order to come out to the waiting inspector. However, Blakey is becoming impatient waiting and fumes to Jack: 'I have had to sign on two relief crews whilst he has been in there.' The matter comes to a head though when a scream is heard from inside the ladies toilet as Stan has climbed in through the wrong window and disturbs rotund clippie Ada as she applies her make-up. 'You nasty little peeping tom,' she yells at Stan. It becomes clear to the inspector that Jack has clocked Stan in and after threatening to send a full report to the Sunday papers he sends Stan home. He places the perennially late Stan on night duty which is to play havoc with his love life as an added punishment.

Launderette

These establishments were to feature in both an episode and a spin-off film of On The Buses.

In the Series Two episode 'Family Flu', Stan is attempting to do all of the housework as well as his own job as the family are bed-ridden with flu. He drops the laundry off at the launderette mid-route whilst on duty but on picking it up he lands himself in trouble. When his bus arrives back at the depot the laundry is found by the inspector and he threatens to hand it into lost property until Stan identifies it as his which earns him an ear-bashing and a reminder of rules and regulations from Inspector Blake.

A launderette causes Stan more trouble in the film On The Buses. Again he is on duty and stops his bus outside the launderette to pick up his laundry but Inspector Blake is to catch him in the act and confiscates it. Stan has the last laugh though as the laundry actually belongs to a housewife who demands its return and when the police become involved Blakey is left in an awkward and embarrassing position.

Lawrence, Andria

Film Role: Turnaround Betty (On The Buses)
TV Role: Suzy (Series 5 Episode 7 'Canteen Trouble')

This accomplished and much employed actress can boast a career spanning over twenty years on film and television in the UK, in the 1960s, 70s and on into the early 1980s.

Her film career began in the early 1960s and she was to appear in a made-for-television adventure called An Arabian Night as well as Dentist On The Job and In The Nick. The 1970s saw her with credits in a string of Hammer film productions such as horror films Countess Dracula and Frankenstein And The Monster From Hell as well as their comedy spin-off films On The Buses, Love Thy Neighbour and Man About The House. Other notable big screen roles came in For The Love Of Ada, Danny Jones and the saucy sex comedy I'm Not Feeling Myself Tonight.

Lawrence's television credits included roles in some of the best sitcoms of her generation. She appeared in Doctor

At Large, On The Buses, The Fenn Street Gang and Doctor In Charge as well as roles in memorable comedy sketch shows It's A Square World and The Goodies. She was equally at home in drama roles on the small screen. Her most notable credits were to come in No Hiding Place, Softly Softly, the award-winning historical drama The First Churchills, The Rivals Of Sherlock Holmes, Van der Valk and Dixon Of Dock Green.

By the mid-1980s Lawrence had married and became involved in the lucrative magazine publishing industry with her husband. As an executive it entailed travelling all over the world and time was so limited that she called time on her acting career. She remains active in the publishing world of glossy magazines to the present day.

Lawrence of Arabia

This is a historical figure from World War One who is referred to by Stan in the Series Five episode 'The Epidemic'.

When Stan and Jack pay a visit to Inspector Blake in his office they find him being treated for flu. With a towel over his head he looks arabesque as he has his head over a bowl of steaming hot water. On seeing him Stan jokes: 'God blimey – Lawrence of Arabia.'

Lawrence of Arabia was a title given to Lieutenant Colonel Thomas Edward Lawrence. A soldier in the British Army who, during World War One, was to act as a liaison between feuding Arab sects, uniting them and urging them to rise up and fight against the Ottoman forces at war with Britain. His actions were to see him decorated for his gallantry that also made him a legendary figure. Sadly, in May 1935 at the age of forty six, he was killed in a motorcycle accident. The legendary tale of Lawrence of Arabia was memorably retold in a 1962 film which was a multiple Oscar-winning smash hit film.

Layton, George

Scriptwriter (Series 6 Episode 2 'Love Is What You Make It', Series 6 Episode 6 'Bye Bye Blakey', Series 6 Episode 7 'The Prize', Series 7 Episode 2 'The Perfect Clippie', Series 7 Episode 9 'The Visit' and Series 7 Episode 12 'Friends In High Places')

Born in Bradford, Yorkshire in 1943, George Layton was to study at RADA on leaving school. He would go on to carve out an extensive career as an actor, scriptwriter and director on television, in films and on stage since the mid-1960s. As a scriptwriter over twenty years he supplied scripts for over a dozen sitcoms working on a number of these with his writing partner Jonathan Lynn. In the 1970s his writing credits included Doctor At Large, Nearest And Dearest, On The Buses, Doctor In Charge, Doctor At Sea, Doctor On The Go and My Brother's Keeper. His 1980s credits included Robin's Nest, Me And My Girl, Executive Stress and Don't Wait Up with his final scripts being used in the 1991 sitcom Doctor At The Top.

Layton's career as an actor is even more extensive with roles in classic television series such as The Likely Lads, Doctor Who, Z Cars, The Liver Birds, It Ain't Half Hot Mum, The Sweeney, Robin's Nest, Minder, Heartbeat and of course his role as Dr Collier in several incarnations of the Doctor comedy series penned by Richard Gordon. Film roles included a cameo in Carry On Behind and the sex comedy Stand Up Virgin Soldiers. On stage Layton has performed in the West End, on Broadway and in Australia in shows such as Chicago, Oliver, Chips With Everything and Funny Peculiar. He can also boast a career as a published author with books such as The FIB And Other Stories and The Swap And Other Stories.

Leave Rota

Inspector Blake is to refer to this on his office wall in the Series Four episode 'Christmas Duty'.

When he receives a phone call on Christmas Eve he learns a bus crew are unable to work their shift the following day. The inspector refers to the leave rota and much to his glee, but the present Stan and Jack's dismay; it tells him that the dreaded Christmas Day shift will have to be covered by the next crew on the leave rota – Stan and Jack.

Lecherous Layabouts

This less than complimentary description of Stan and Jack is frequently used by Inspector Blake in several episodes and spin-off films of On The Buses. He often uses the term when the pair of randy busmen are caught ogling or chatting up clippies or making lustful comments at inappropriate moments.

Leeside Column

This is a block of flats in the fictional town of Luxton where Jack's Aunt May lives. She is to sell her double bed to Arthur in the Series Four episode 'The L Bus'.

Legal Action

Inspector Blake threatens Stan with legal action after buying the driver's television set only for it to soon blow up leaving him injured in the Series Five episode 'The New Telly'. Whilst viewing his newly purchased television in his office it explodes and leaves him with ripped trousers and splinters in his backside. When Stan and Jack arrive on the scene Blakey exaggerates somewhat accusing Stan of trying to kill him. Shocked and angry the inspector warns: 'I'll take legal action over this Butler. I'll sue you. I'll see you get sacked for this.'

The inspector's injuries are to leave him bed-ridden for a fortnight and in a bid to appease Blakey and end any legal action, Stan visits with a brand new colour portable television set as a gift with a selection of other goods brought by Jack. Despite pleas that he just wants to be left alone, the inspector has the gifts forced upon him and the threat of legal action seems to be averted.

Lewis, Stephen

TV and Film Role: Inspector Blake (On The Buses Series 1-7) (On The Buses, Mutiny On The Buses and Holiday On The Buses)

Stephen Lewis was born in London in 1936 and began his working life as a merchant seaman in the early 1950s. In his early twenties he joined the renowned Joan Littlewood's Theatre Workshop which was to give him his break into acting. From there he would go on to have a long and successful career spanning fifty years on film, television and stage as well as being a talented script writer.

Stage roles launched his career in the late 1950s and he was soon to appear in the West End in The Hostage. He also wrote and appeared in the hit musical Sparrows Can't Sing also in the West End in 1961 which would later be made into a film. Other stage roles included credits in Intrigues And Amours, Provoked Wife and Busman's Holiday whilst also being a regular on the pantomime scene. On television his best remembered roles were as Inspector Blake in On The Buses, Harry in Oh Doctor Beeching and most recently as Smiler in the long-running sitcom Last Of The Summer Wine. Other comedy roles came most notably in Mrs Wilson's Diary where he worked alongside future On The Buses co-star Bob Grant and producer Stuart Allen, Father Dear Father, Don't Drink The Water, Rep, One Foot In The Grave, The All New Alexei Sayle Show and Revolver. Drama roles were a little less frequent but were to include roles in Manhunt and Look At It This Way. Lewis could also boast an impressive career on the big screen starting in the 1960s with roles in A Prize Of Arms, Sparrows Can't Sing, Negatives and Staircase. The 1970s saw him appear in a string of comedy films including Some Will Some Won't, On The Buses, The Magnificent Seven Deadly Sins, Mutiny On The Buses, Holiday On The Buses and The Last Remake Of Beau Geste. In the latter part of his career came roles in award-winning films Personal Services and The Krays.

Stephen Lewis also co-wrote a number of On The Buses episodes with Bob Grant and he wrote stage and screen plays for television before finally retiring from acting in 2008. He was a great talent who made Inspector Blake into a wonderful comedy character by adding in his own mannerisms and catchphrases all of which he ad-libbed.

Stephen Lewis in panto donning the inspector's uniform once more.

Memories

Speaking of his character Inspector Blake in 1971, Stephen Lewis said:- 'I came from a method acting school and I decided that the guy had been a sergeant in the army and he was used to getting his own way, yelling and screaming as they do. Of course, now in Civvy Street, he couldn't do that so he was always frustrated. He couldn't get his own way because these two blokes were skylarking about. It was an eternal battle between us.'

Speaking in 2006 at a plaque unveiling event at Pontins Prestatyn Sands camp he recalls a funny memory from Holiday On The Buses from the scene of the bus stranded on the beach:- 'When Stan and Jack looked back they saw the tide had come in and that the bus was being swamped by the sea. The director knew this was going to happen and didn't want the real bus to be destroyed so what they did was build a replica bus out of plywood. They filmed the bus being driven onto the beach and then made the switch before carrying on. Butler and Harper were larking about and as we were looking at it from a distance, the plywood bus started moving funnily, it toppled over on its side and floated away. They'd forgotten to put the weights in, so it floated out to sea and we had to call the coastguard because it was a hazard to shipping.'

Leyland Motors

A British car manufacturer referred to by Stan in the Series One episode 'Olive Takes A Trip'.

As Olive shows off her clippies uniform to the family and is praised for her smartness by her mum. Stan is not so complimentary though as he feels it looks like the uniform was made by Leyland Motors.

Leyland Motors was a successful British car manufacturer which was formed in 1896. They manufactured a wide range of vehicles such as cars, lorries, vans and buses. In the 1960s the company took over a range of other car manufacturers including Rover in 1967 and a year later it was to become the British Leyland Motor Corporation taking over more companies as it did so. The sheer size of companies within the corporation proved to be its downfall and it hit financial difficulties in the mid-1970s with the company being nationalised. However, strikes and a crippling financial crisis saw the company fragment with the Leyland name only living on in its truck division whilst British Leyland became the Rover Group in 1986. Leyland Trucks is now under foreign ownership but are still manufacturing in the UK to the present day.

Lifeguards

This is a job that Stan and Jack are to deputise at in the holiday camp in the film Holiday On The Buses.

As they have no driving duties that day they are placed on relief duty as lifeguards at the holiday camp's swimming pool. Inspector Blake is stunned but Jack insists both he and Stan are good strong swimmers. This is not to be put to the test though and they are only called upon to save Olive from embarrassment. Wearing a skimpy bikini she is pushed into the pool by Arthur and loses the bottom half of her bikini. A number of men dive into the pool to get a better look forcing Stan to blow loudly on his whistle. He shouts 'Everybody out, come on. Nobody is allowed in this pool 'til this lady's covered up.' Arthur comes to the rescue as he throws Olive a towel and tells her to cover herself up.

Lind, Gillian

TV Role: Mrs Rudge (Series 5 Episode 15 'Boxing Day Social')

Born in India in 1904, Gillian Lind was to have an extensive career as an actress on stage, film and television ranging over forty years.

She began her acting career on stage coming to prominence in the 1930s appearing in Caesar's Friend, This One Man, Clive Of India, Goodbye Mr Chips and Emma. Post-World War Two stage roles included The Step Forward and The Right Honourable Gentleman.

Her career in films was at its height in the 1930s with starring roles in Condemned To Death, The Man Outside, Open All Night and supporting roles in Dick Turpin and Death Croons The Blues amongst others. The latter part of her career on the big screen included comedy films The Oracle and Aunt Clare in the 1950s, Don't Talk To Strangers in the 1960s and ending in the 1970s with horror films Fear In The Night and also And Now The Screaming Starts.

Lind's television roles were varied with her biggest roles coming in BBC's classic 1950s dramas Pride And Prejudice and Nicholas Nickleby. Other notable drama roles came in classic series such as Dixon Of Dock Green, No Hiding Place, Man In A Suitcase, The Saint and Upstairs Downstairs. Comedy roles were to come in No That's Me Over Here, On The Buses, Now Look Here and The Dick Emery Show.

Gillian Lind retired from acting in the mid-1970s before sadly passing away in 1983 at the age of seventy nine.

Linehan, Barry

Film Role: Policeman (Mobile) (Mutiny On The Buses)

Barry Linehan was born in Ireland in 1925 and was to have a long career as an actor appearing on stage, television and in films.

His stage performances were to include roles in the 1952 stage adaption of the musical Kiss Me Kate, Ooh La La and The Odd Couple amongst others. The early 1960s was to see his small screen career begin in the Australian western Whiplash. His UK break came in the sci-fi series The Andromeda Breakthrough and he would go on to appear in many classic dramas. These included Danger Man, The Saint, Emergency – Ward 10, Public Eye, The Avengers, Adam Adamant Lives, No Hiding Place, Journey To The Unknown, Ivanhoe, Z Cars, Softly Softly, The Tomorrow People, Crown Court and the award-winning 90s drama To Play The King. Comedy roles were to come in The Likely Lads, Curry And Chips, Clochemerle, Some Mothers Do 'Ave 'Em, Love Thy Neighbour and Dad's Army.

Linehan's film roles most notably were the 1960s horror films Witchcraft and The Devil-Ship Pirates. These were followed in the 70s with credits in Suburban Wives, Mutiny On The Buses and Dark Places. His big screen career ended in 1990 with a role in the star-studded comedy film Bullseye.

Sadly, in 1996, Barry Linehan was to pass away at the age of seventy.

Lions

Big cats which are encountered by Stan and Inspector Blake as they travel through an enclosure at Windsor Safari Park in their tour bus in Mutiny On The Buses.

Safe aboard the tour bus the pair are awe struck by the ferocious lions but their safety is soon compromised. Stan brakes suddenly to avoid knocking over a lion which causes a damaged emergency door at the rear of the bus to swing open. With the bus stationery a lion leaps onto the bus through the open door and as it makes its way up the aisle it is spotted by a petrified Stan and Blakey. But when the lion backs away the pair attempt to escape by rushing upstairs and trying to exit out of the rear window but the lion follows. It attacks ripping the seat out of their trousers before retreating downstairs and off the bus. Seconds later, a furious safari guard arrives on the scene and berates Stan and Inspector Blake for disobeying the park's strict rules. He tells them: 'I shall make a full report to the manager and your company won't be sending any more buses here that's for sure. Now drive off and get out!'

The lions that appeared in Mutiny On The Buses and their off-spring remained at Windsor Safari Park until its closure in October 1992. The majority of the lions were then moved to the West Midlands Safari Park with the elderly lionesses going to a purpose-built 'retirement home' in a privately owned zoo in Kent.

Little Arthur

Played by Wayne Westhorpe and Adam Rhodes

The only son of Olive and Arthur Rudge is to cause uncomfortable moments for his dad as a baby and as he grows into a young boy his mischievous pranks are to affect his Uncle Stan's love life.

Affectionately known as little Arthur he is born into a household crippled by financial problems. It takes time for his dad to adjust to fatherhood whilst mum Olive's inexperience as a mother is evident as she rubs gripe water into her son's stomach instead of feeding it to him. In the film Mutiny On The Buses, as little Arthur grows he has a habit of breaking wind at inopportune moments which irks his dad and things get worse when he is to use his dad's new bus driver's cap as a pot. It all proves a strain for Arthur when he has the unpleasant experience of sitting on one of his son's discarded dirty nappies as well. Little Arthur is doted upon by his grandmother who is to give him more attention than she has for Stan for a time.

Little Arthur, in Holiday On The Buses, has grown into a mischievous young boy whose favourite toys are his cap gun and water pistol. He uses them to startle his uncle and likewise his dad when he fires dirty water all over his shirt from his water pistol which sees the toy being confiscated. When the family go on holiday, little Arthur is to get up to a number of mischievous pranks. He takes a leaf out of his dad's book when he ruins Stan's hopes of a romantic night in with girlfriend Sandra. Stan, who is babysitting his nephew, has his plans thwarted as little Arthur demands to be read a story then cheekily asks to watch Stan and Sandra. To keep him entertained, Stan sends his nephew to bed giving him his water pistol to play with. This proves to be a big mistake as he mischievously fills the pistol with ink and fires it at the walls and furniture leaving the room in need of redecorating. Little Arthur is chastised by his grandmother when she sees the damage he has done. He is not finished as he is also to use his cap gun in a prank that disturbs Inspector Blake as he has an afternoon nap in a deckchair. In short he is a much-loved, mischievous boy who causes problems for his family with his antics.

Little Chick

A term used to describe her son by Mrs Butler in the Series Three episode 'Going Steady'.

She laments when hearing the news that her son Stan is set to marry a clippie called Sally. Close to tears she says: 'It'll be a sad day when my last little chick flies away.' On hearing this Arthur scoffs: 'Little chick? More like a clapped-out old rooster.'

Littlewood, Frank

TV Role: The Commissionaire (Series 3 Episode 7 'Mum's Last Fling')

Frank Littlewoods's career as an actor began in the late 1940s in films but went on to work solely in bit-part television roles until the early 1970s.

His sole film roles came in Meet The Duke and the highly rated sci-fi drama Dangerous Voyage. It was on the small screen that he was most employed in supporting roles. His credits came in dramas such as The Quatermass Experiment, No Hiding Place, The Indian Tales Of Rudyard Kipling, The Power Game, The Expert, Detective, Doomwatch, Paul Temple, The Onedin Line and Dead Of Night. Littlewood's comedy roles saw him appear in several classic British sitcoms including Hancock's Half Hour, Steptoe And Son, On The Buses and Please Sir along with credits in other comedy series Frankie Howerd and The Dick Emery Show.

Livingstone, Doctor

This renowned nineteenth century explorer is referred to by Inspector Blake in the Series Five episode 'Vacancy For Inspector'.

Stan has parked his bus around a corner waiting for the next bus to come along and pick up all of his potential customers leaving him an easy trip back to the depot. However, tipped off about Stan's antics by the new acting inspector Jack Harper, Blakey creeps up to surprise Stan. As the driver looks around the corner to see if the next bus has passed he comes face-to-face with Inspector Blake who gleefully says: 'Doctor Livingstone, I presume?'

These were said to be the same words uttered by newspaper journalist Henry Morton Stanley on finding the explorer Doctor David Livingstone in a small town in Tanzania who had been missing in nineteenth century Africa for a few years. Livingstone, a Scotsman who began his time in Africa as a missionary in the 1840s, went on to become a famous explorer going on a number of expeditions. He was thought to be the first European to trek across Africa and was to search for the source of the River Nile before his death in 1873 at the age of sixty after he was struck down with malaria.

Liz

Played by Ursula Mohan

Liz was a trainee clippie at the depot who Stan takes a shine to in the Series Two episode 'Self Defence'.

Liz, with long black hair is in her twenties and a close friend of a fellow trainee clippie called Joyce. She is cautious about dating the notorious busman and when she becomes the first to sign up to attend self-defence classes followed by Joyce it encourages Stan and Jack to attend despite rubbishing the idea moments earlier. The class puts Stan off dating Liz as her friend shows her to be an expert in self-defence, injuring Stan and leaving him sure he wouldn't dare try to take advantage of Liz for fear of retribution. And so Liz is left to go on a date with Jack and her friend Joyce.

Local Secretary

A position held by Inspector Blake for a charity as revealed in the Series Six episode 'The Prize'.

As he attempts to sell raffle tickets in aid of a charity to Stan and Jack he assures them it is for a good cause as it provides stray cats and dogs with new homes with the charity being a nationwide society. The inspector, as local secretary, has the job of raising funds by promoting and selling raffle tickets for a prize draw.

Lodge, David

Film Roles: Fred (On The Buses) and Safari Guard (Mutiny On The Buses)

Born in Rochester, Kent in 1921, David Lodge got his break in acting after working in circuses as a clown and ringmaster as well as appearing in repertory. He would go on to have an extensive list of credits in films and on television.

On the big screen he would appear in around one hundred films across the genres beginning in the mid-1950s with the war film The Cockleshell Heroes. That decade brought him roles in notable films such as These Dangerous Years, The Silent Enemy, Up The Creek, Ice Cold In Alex, I Was Monty's Double, I Only Arsked and I'm Alright Jack amongst others. The 1960s were to see him appear in many classic comedy films including The League Of Gentlemen, The Bulldog Breed, Carry On Regardless, Raising The Wind, On The Beat, A Shot In The Dark and Crooks And Coronets. In drama films his most noted credits came in The Pirates Of Blood River, Captain Clegg, The Long Ships, Guns At Batasi and Oh What A Lovely War. Into the 1970s came more comedy roles in On The Buses, Hoffman, Mutiny On The Buses, Carry On Girls, Carry On Dick, The Return Of The Pink Panther, Carry On Behind and Carry On England. His other 70s film roles included Scream And Scream Again, The Railway Children, Hide And Seek and The Amazing Mr Blunden. The 1980s brought roles in Sahara, Bloodbath At The House Of Death with his final film appearance coming in 1989 in Edge Of Sanity.

Lodge was a regular face on British television with his biggest roles coming in the Thames sitcom Tottering Towers and another comedy series – Q9. His drama roles came in classic series such as Gideon's Way, The Saint, No Hiding Place, The Avengers, The Champions, Randall And Hopkirk (Deceased), Z Cars, The Persuaders, The Pathfinders, The Sweeney, Dixon Of Dock Green, Minder, Crossroads and Lovejoy. He also appeared in memorable children's series Here Comes The Double Deckers and Worzel Gummidge. In comedy roles he had credits in classic sitcoms Never Mind The Quality Feel The Width, Love Thy Neighbour, Father Dear Father, The Fenn Street Gang, Oh No It's Selwyn Froggitt, It Ain't Half Hot Mum, Bless This House, Robin's Nest and Hot Metal. He was also to have roles in comedy sketch shows such as The Reg Varney Revue and the Carry On Laughing series.

David Lodge, a long-time friend of legendary actor Peter Sellers was to work alongside him on many films and television series and was best man at Sellers wedding. He retired from acting in the mid-1990s and was to fight cancer late in life losing the battle in 2003 passing away at the age of eighty two.

Lodgers

In times of financial difficulties the Butlers often took in lodgers in a number of episodes of On The Buses.

When a clippie called Edna is thrown out of her accommodation by the landlady who doesn't like her pet dog Coco and can't abide her arriving home late after a date with Stan, the bus driver feels guilty and gives up his room for her in the Series Three episode 'On The Make'. Edna can only afford to pay three pounds a week for rent even though Arthur believes the average rent for the area to be five pounds. Her stay at the Butler house proves problematic as her large pet dog is an inconvenience. Also Stan's attempt to get overly familiar with Edna doesn't go down well with the family. After a short stay her spell as a lodger at the Butlers house comes to an end.

The next lodger to move into the house is a traffic manager called Mr Nichols in the Series Four episode 'The Lodger'. Whilst working at the depot he needs somewhere to stay and on moving into the Butler house it is Stan who suffers. He has his room stripped of its furniture which is used to decorate Mr Nichols room and Stan has to accept the situation as the lodger is paying ten pounds a week which includes bed and breakfast and an evening meal. However, the arrangement lasts one night as the following morning sees Olive take Mr Nichols his breakfast into his room where he pinches her bottom. This greatly upsets Olive and infuriates Mrs Butler who orders him to leave.

Mary, a new nurse at the Luxton and District depot, is hunting for accommodation in the area in the Series Five episode 'The New Nurse'. Stan tells her: 'My mum has done the front room up. It's nice you'll like it. We don't charge much.' Mary takes up Stan's invitation but it turns out to cause ructions in the Rudge marriage. Arthur falls for Mary and as their relationship threatens to get out of hand, the snooty nurse comes to her senses. She is to move out after telling Arthur she doesn't want to get involved with a married man.

Finally, in the Series Seven episode 'Goodbye Stan', Mrs Butler is distraught to learn that her son is leaving home for pastures new in the Midlands to take up a new job. An advert for a new lodger is put on the notice board at the depot and none other than Inspector Blake, who has recently been kicked out of his lodgings, is to move into the Butler house paying rent of four pounds a week. This turns out to be a long-term arrangement but Blakey's presence does cause problems. He soon breaks the immersion heating system at the Butler house and causes more damage when trying to repair it. More trouble arises when his mother comes to stay with the Butlers in the Series Seven episode 'The Visit' and treats the house like a hotel and Olive and Mrs Butler are treated like servants until she leaves in acrimonious circumstances. Matters aren't helped either when Mrs Butler later dates the depot's area manager Mr Simpson much to the inspector's discomfort so tensions run high. Despite these obstacles Inspector Blake remains a lodger for some time before later retiring and moving to Spain with his sister.

Lodging With Blakey

Stan is forced to lodge with Inspector Blake in a bid to break the shackles his mother has on him which constantly hampers his love life in the Series Five episode 'Stan's Room'.

Stan moves in to a spare room at Inspector Blake's house despite the strict house rules laid down by Blakey. He charges rent of eight pounds a week asking for two weeks rent in advance and tells Stan: 'I don't have any noise after eleven o'clock at night, no coming in late. I expect you to keep the place tidy and there will be no alcoholic liquor brought in the house either.' Much to Stan's frustration he is also told that no girlfriends will be allowed in the room either. The randy bus driver has other ideas though as he brings his girlfriend Doreen home after a date. It is a great physical exertion carrying her on his back up the stairs to his room without Blakey's knowledge. However, just as Stan finally thinks he has cracked it, his family led by Arthur gate-crash his romantic night in and his mum pleads for him to come home. Inspector Blake, hearing the commotion arrives on the scene to find Doreen present and he accuses Stan of trying to turn his house into a boarding house for busmen. The incident ends Stan's hopes of romance and his mum uses cunning tactics to con her son into moving back home ending his short spell as a lodger with Blakey.

Lofty

Played by John M. East

A lanky busman employed by the Luxton and District Bus Company who goes on to become a mechanic.

In the Series One episode 'The Early Shift', Lofty mocks Stan as he arrives at the depot riding Olive's bicycle laughingly welcoming Stan as a new clippie as he sits on a bench wearing a busman's uniform. Moments later, he agrees with the miffed Stan that the new schedules are murder. Later, as Jack convenes a union meeting at the depot to hold a vote for strike action, Lofty has to encourage Stan to vote in favour of a strike by pushing him firmly in the back. Lofty progresses on to become a mechanic for the company and is often seen around the depot wearing brown overalls. In the Series Five episode 'A Thin Time', Stan asks Lofty for his help complaining that his handbrake needs taken up a bit and the button on his bus used to open the doors is sticking and only works when pressed firmly so Lofty sets about working on these faults. He is called into action again in the Series Seven episode 'The Perfect Clippie' as Stan borrows his tyre pressure gauge to check the tyres of his bus as he and Jack look to wind-up Inspector Blake by going strictly by the book delaying their departure greatly. Lofty, so-called because of his great height, is keen on physical fitness and is to lend his chest expander to Stan who is bidding to get fit in the Series Seven episode 'The Football Match'.

London Philharmonic Orchestra

A famous orchestra referred to by Stan in the Series Four episode 'Christmas Duty'.

Inspector Blake has just had his teapot repaired with maintenance gluing the spout back on but Stan points out that one of the little holes is blocked up. In a bid to clear the blockage the inspector blows through the spout making a tuneful noise as he does so. Stan tells him: 'Do you know what Blakey? I believe you could play first teapot in the London Philharmonic.'

The London Philharmonic Orchestra has grown to become one of the most renowned orchestras in the world. Formed in 1932 by the famous conductor Sir Thomas Beecham, it almost folded in the late 1930s before it rose to be one of the most successful orchestras in the world performing around the globe touring Russia (then the Soviet Union) during the Cold War, India, Australia, USA, China and Europe across the decades.

Known for its performances of classical music it could also boast having played on a number of film soundtracks including, most notably, the Oscar-winning Lawrence Of Arabia and The Mission.

London Transport

A famous company that, under various guises, has supplied bus services across London for many decades which was referred to in an episode and a spin-off film of On The Buses.

As Stan suggests they paint Arthur and Olive's bedroom in green and yellow as that is the colour of Luxton and District's buses in the Series Three episode 'Busmen's Perks', Olive remarks she'd prefer red as it makes a woman look sexier. 'Well I'll give my notice in and go and work for the London Transport,' jokes Stan before the family agree on the colours of green and yellow.

The film On The Buses sees Stan undergoing a test at the London Transport's skid pan to satisfy the insurance company after having an accident in his bus. He feels it is unfair as he has to use a London Transport bus for the test as they are better than those used by Town and District. Inspector Blake is unsympathetic though and laughs that their drivers are better as well.

The London Transport body was formed in 1933 as the London Passenger Transport Board and was under public ownership providing public bus services across London. When referred to in On The Buses, the company's title was the London Transport Executive which supplied bus services in Greater London whilst routes in the outer districts of the capital were covered by London Country Bus Services. It was at this time that the company was in crisis and was not only poorly-funded but short-staffed as well. After further restructuring in 1984 and finally in 2000 the company, now privately-funded, became known as Transport for London.

London Transport Official

Played by Norman Mitchell

An employee of London Transport who shows Inspector Blake around one of the company's buses prior to Stan taking his test at the skid pan in the film On The Buses.

He authorises the inspector and Stan to use one of the London Transport buses for thirty minutes and wishes Stan the best of luck. The official also shows Inspector Blake around but Blakey is not overly impressed as he feels they are not too different from the buses used by Town and District. He encourages the inspector to look upstairs with the official boasting of more headroom on the upper deck before he disembarks to allow Blakey to examine the rest of the bus.

London Weekend Television

This ITV production company was to produce all seven series of On The Buses after it had been rejected by the BBC.

London Weekend Television was to broadcast to London at the weekends from 1968 replacing ATV London whilst Thames Television was to provide London's programming from Monday to Friday. Based originally at the former Rediffusion studios in Wembley, North London before moving to the new custom-built South Bank Studios in 1972, London Weekend Television (also known as LWT) was to produce a host of classic British television series across the genres over four decades.

Aside from On The Buses, LWT were behind many memorable sitcoms such as Hark At Barker, Doctor At Large, Please Sir, The Fenn Street Gang, Mind Your Language, Agony, Me And My Girl, The Two Of Us and comedy sketch shows The Goodies and Cannon And Ball to name but a few. As for dramas produced by LWT these included the multiple award-winning Upstairs Downstairs that was to be a huge worldwide hit, Budgie, The Gentle Touch, Dempsey And Makepeace, Poirot, London's Burning, The Charmer and Wish Me Luck.

It was also to churn out a range of hit entertainment shows spanning the decades which included It'll Be Alright On The Night, Play Your Cards Right, Game For A Laugh, Beadle's About, Surprise Surprise, Blind Date and The Gladiators. LWT were also behind many much-loved children's series such as Catweazle, The Adventures Of Black Beauty, Dick Turpin, Just William and Metal Mickey. In the sports department LWT were to produce ITV's long-running flagship sports show World Of Sport, The Big Match and the football magazine show Saint And Greavsie. Arts series such as The South Bank Show and the current affairs hit series Weekend World were also products of LWT.

London Weekend Television's reign as a broadcaster finally came to an end in 2002 after thirty four years. It was decided that all franchises across the ITV network would become known as ITV1 and so LWT were assigned to history but is still remembered with great fondness to the present day.

Long-Haired Lover From Liverpool

This was an early 1970s pop song that Olive sings badly in the Series Seven episode 'The Ticket Machine'.

Stan returns home from work to find that Olive and his mum have bought a plethora of goods from a mail order catalogue including a guitar. He is gobsmacked and can't understand the need for such an item but Olive explains that she intends to start her own pop group. She begins to strum the guitar tunelessly whilst singing terribly the song 'Long-Haired Lover From Liverpool'. The din is brought to an end as Stan shouts: 'Hold it, hold it, hold it! God the neighbours will think the cat's caught in the mangle.'

'Long-Haired Lover From Liverpool' was a smash number one hit for Little Jimmy Osmond who, at the age of nine years and eight months, remains the youngest person to record a number one hit in the UK charts. The song was the coveted Christmas number one in 1972 remaining top of the charts for five weeks and went on to sell more than a million copies in the UK alone.

Love Is A Many-Splendored Thing

A hit 1950s film referred to by Olive in the Series Six episode 'Love Is What You Make It'.

When discussing Arthur and Olive's marital problems and their courting years mum remarks that marriages are made in heaven. Stan is to disagree and says: 'This one wasn't. This was made in the back row of the stalls of The Gaumont.' Nostalgically, Olive recalls: 'Oh yes they were showing Love Is A Many-Splendored Thing.'

Love Is A Many-Splendored Thing was a triple Oscar-winning film made in 1955 starring William Holden and Jennifer Jones. The musical was a product of Twentieth Century Fox and was a box office smash around the world.

Lovegrove, Arthur

TV Role: Harry (Series 1 Episode 4 'Bus Driver's Stomach')

Born in Fulham, London in 1913, Arthur Lovegrove's career as an actor spanned the decades and the genres.

He broke into acting on stage in the 1940s with roles in Patricia's Seven Houses and The Nineteenth Hole Of Europe. Other stage credits later in his career included Red-Headed Blonde, Lucky Strike and Hindle Wakes. He was also an accomplished playwright penning several stage plays including, most notably, Goodbye Mrs Puffin.

The late 1940s was to see Lovegrove's film career get under way. The pick of these film roles saw him appear in Passport To Pimlico, Night And The City, Genevieve, The Runaway Bus, The Quatermass Experiment, A Night To Remember, Yesterday's Enemy, Crooks Anonymous, A Stitch In Time, Carry On Cowboy, The Rise And Rise Of Michael Rimmer and Eye Of The Needle.

Lovegrove was also a regular face on British television from the late 1950s primarily in drama roles. These came in hit series such as Dixon Of Dock Green, The Avengers, Gideon's Way, No Hiding Place, Softly Softly, Z Cars, Strange Report, The Onedin Line, Shoestring and the children's series Catweazle. Aside from his role in On The Buses, the majority of his notable comedy credits came in the 1970s. He appeared in The Dick Emery Show, Please Sir, And Mother Makes Five and Bless This House amongst others.

With over a hundred acting credits on film and television Arthur Lovegrove continued acting up until passing away in 1981 at the age of sixty eight.

Lowe, Eddy

Editor (Series 7 Episode 2 'The Perfect Clippie', Series 7 Episode 5 'The Football Match', Series 7 Episode 6 'On The Omnibuses' and Series 7 Episode 8 'Hot Water')

Working in the editing department at LWT, Eddy Lowe's solitary credit came in the seventh series of On The Buses in 1973. He was to edit the sequences filmed on location which featured heavily in the four episodes he worked on.

Lowestoft

A seaside resort in Suffolk where Arthur and Olive spent their honeymoon and visited again on subsequent holidays as referred to in a couple of episodes.

In the Series Two episode 'Bon Voyage' all the talk is of holidays as Stan prepares for his holiday in the Costa Brava. Arthur recalls that Olive's mum accompanied them on their honeymoon to Lowestoft and though Olive describes the town as very nice with lovely bloaters she feels that it is normally too cold for her to wear her bikini. Arthur sees this as one of the advantages of going to Lowestoft. Later, in the Series Three episode 'The Cistern', Olive voices her concerns about buying a wooden toilet seat reminding Arthur that she once got a splinter from such a seat whilst on holiday in Lowestoft.

Lowestoft is a small coastal town on the Suffolk coast and is the eastern most town in the British Isles. The resort is renowned for its top quality beaches, seaside entertainment and facilities such as The South Pier and The East Point Pavilion.

Ludski, Archie

Film Editor (On The Buses and Mutiny On The Buses)

Archie Ludski was born in London in 1929 and would go straight into the film industry from school working in the editing department on films and later on television series.

As a fully-fledged film editor he was to work on classic comedy films such as Nurse On Wheels, Carry On Cabby, Carry On Jack, Carry On Spying, Carry On Cleo, On The Buses, Mutiny On The Buses and Man About The House. He worked on many more classic films as sound and dubbing editor with the pick of those being Above Us The Waves, Man Of The Moment, Campbell's Kingdom, Carry On Cruising, Dr No, Khartoum, Ghandi, A Passage To India, Aliens and Gorillas In The Mist.

On television his credits were rare but included the classic comedy sketch series The Benny Hill Show and the hit sci-fi series Space: 1999.

Archie Ludski worked up until his retirement in 1995 meaning just short of fifty years of service to the film industry. Sadly, he passed away nine years later in 2004 at the age of seventy four.

Luigi

Played by Franco De Rosa

This is an Italian chef who works in the holiday camp canteen and is overly-protective of his sister Maria in the film Holiday On The Buses.

Luigi is a tall dark-haired, well-built man who has sworn to protect his sister's honour whilst she is in the country and resorts to violence if necessary to scare off any men showing a romantic interest in Maria much to her displeasure. When he learns of Stan having dated Maria he carries out a furious assault on the shocked bus driver in the canteen's kitchen before the camp manager comes to Stan's rescue.

Luigi is told of Stan's apparent innocence which sees him challenge Inspector Blake for spreading rumours about his sister and causes Blakey to fall against a table that collapses under his weight much to Stan and Maria's amusement. Luigi's vigilance scares Stan off pursuing Maria further and the randy driver turns his attention elsewhere.

Lumbosacral Support

This is the medical term for a corset used by Doctor Clark. He suggests Stan should wear a lumbosacral support if he insists on returning to work so soon after injuring his back in the Series Five episode 'The Injury'.

Lumkin, Tony

Recording Director (On The Buses, Mutiny On The Buses and Holiday On The Buses)

Born in 1918, Tony Lumkin was to have a lengthy career working in the sound department on film and television with credits spanning almost twenty years being based at Elstree Studios.

Beginning in the late 1950s in films he was to work on many memorable films such as Tommy The Toreador, Ice-Cold In Alex, School For Scoundrels, The Long And The Short And The Tall, The Young Ones, Summer Holiday, Crooks In Cloisters and Wonderful Life. He was also to have a long association with Hammer Films where he worked on many of their most renowned films including The Devil Rides Out, Frankenstein Must Be Destroyed, Dr Jekyll And Sister Hyde and Taste The Blood Of Dracula as well as all three On The Buses spin-off films to name but a few.

Lumkin also had television credits all of which came in the 1960s. These were the highly-acclaimed drama The Human Jungle and the hit ITC series The Avengers and The Saint.

He was also to help Dr Ray Dolby to integrate the new Dolby Noise Reduction system into films in the late 1960s at Elstree Studios with it first being used in the smash hit 1971 film A Clockwork Orange. Tony Lumkin retired in the late 1970s before sadly passing away in 1996 at the age of seventy seven.

Lumley, Sandra

Played by Sandra Bryant

This is a clippie who is to date both Stan and Jack in a number of Series Seven episodes of On The Buses.

Sandra Lumley, an attractive brunette in her late twenties has an interest in astrology and in the episode 'The Divorce' she is to date Stan. A night out at the cinema is spoiled by the presence of the newly divorced Olive and when Sandra invites Stan around to her house afterwards whilst her parents are out with hopes of romance they are to be foiled by the arrival of Inspector Blake and Olive seeking Stan to take his sister home. Sandra does go on to become a good friend of Olive when she becomes a clippie and is to be a thorn in the side of the inspector in 'The Allowance'. She unites with the other clippies as they bid to receive a public convenience allowance from the company and causes problems when she puts in a claim for a new pair of tights which were damaged in the execution of her duty.

In the last ever episode of On The Buses called 'Gardening Time' she is to be courted by Jack who showers her with stolen flowers and he tries to take the relationship to a new level when she sunbathes in his back garden. His chances of romance are later dented as Sandra labels him as being 'very mean' for allowing Inspector Blake to be arrested for attempted burglary as Jack failed to identify Blakey as being his next door neighbour to the police after the unfortunate inspector is locked out of the Butler house.

Luxton

The fictional town where the television series of On The Buses was set and was geographically placed in the near vicinity of London hence regular references to towns and suburbs in the area of the capital city.

Luxton and District Bus Company

This is a fictional bus company that featured in the television series of On The Buses.

The Luxton and District Bus Company was formed in 1873 beginning with horse-drawn vehicles before moving on to use the first motor-powered omnibuses in the early 1920s. The bus company was to implement varying innovative ideas such as relinquishing control of its depot canteen in the late 1960s allowing its staff to run the facility on their own but this is destined to end in abject failure. It was also to introduce self-defence classes for its staff, fit a radio control system to its buses, look to introduce new uniforms without much success, make a promotional push to recruit new staff using posters as adverts, at the request of female staff it introduces a public convenience allowance and also stage a number of social events at the depot for its staff. With its own depot football team and social club it also catered for its own staff 's recreational needs. Sadly, blighted by a rash of strikes in the late 1960s and early 1970s the Luxton and District Bus Company is to be absorbed in 1973 by the National Bus Company one hundred years after its formation.

Luxton and District Social Club

This fictional social club is referred to and seen in a number of episodes of On The Buses.

Known in the late 1960s as the Luxton Garage Social Club it is behind the organising of the depot's staff holiday to the Costa Brava in the Series Two episode 'Bon Voyage'. The Luxton and District Social Club is for members only and is first seen in the Series Seven episode 'The Divorce'. After an evening at the cinema Stan, Sandra and Olive visit the club for a drink bumping into Inspector Blake and Jack. The social club is also the venue for Stan's farewell drink with a number of his workmates in the Series Seven episode 'Goodbye Stan' and extends to a drunken night out for the ex-driver. There is also a night of bingo at the social club with Jack acting as bingo-caller using his own cheeky style with Olive and her mum attending along with Inspector Blake and his battle-axe of a mother in the Series Seven episode 'The Visit'. The night ends in bitter recriminations between Mrs Butler and Mrs Blake and is the last time the Luxton and District Social Club features in On The Buses.

Luxton Lions, The

This is the name of the Luxton and District's depot football team that is to take on the rival depot team from the Basildon depot called The Basildon Bashers in the Series Seven episode 'The Football Match'.

The Luxton Lions are trained, coached and managed by Inspector Blake with the team made up of largely unfit busmen from the Luxton depot but end up being short of players. In order to field a full side for the match to go ahead Olive is drafted in at the last moment leaving The Luxton Lions with an uphill task in the crunch match.

Lynn, Jonathan

Scriptwriter (Series 6 Episode 2 'Love Is What You Make It', Series 6 Episode 6 'Bye Bye Blakey', Series 6 Episode 7 'The Prize', Series 7 Episode 2 'The Perfect Clippie', Series 7 Episode 9 'The Visit' and Series 7 Episode 12 'Friends In High Places')

Born in Bath, Somerset in 1943, Jonathan Lynn began his career as an actor and writer in the early 1960s and was to write scripts for a range of television series, films and stage plays.

Lynn's script-writing career on television was to see him pen a number of episodes for hit sitcoms in partnership with George Layton in the 1970s. These included Doctor At Large, Romany Jones, Nearest And Dearest, On The

Buses, Doctor In Charge, My Name Is Harry Worth, Doctor At Sea and Doctor On The Go.

However, he is best known for co-writing with Anthony Jay the smash hit sitcoms Yes Minister and Yes Prime Minister in the 1980s for which they both won a BAFTA award. He recently re-united with Anthony Jay to co-write the hugely successful stage adaption of Yes Prime Minister and has a number of credits as actor and director on stage.

On the big screen he was to pen scripts for the 1970s thriller The Internecine Project, comedy film Clue, Suspicion and the hit British comedy film Nuns On The Run in 1990 which he was also to direct.

Jonathan Lynn, a multi-talented man, can also boast a long list of credits as an actor appearing in hit comedy series such as Doctor In The House, Doctor In Charge, The Liver Birds, The Dick Emery Show, The Good Life and in dramas such as Hadleigh, Softly Softly and Colditz amongst others. He was also to appear on hit films such as The House That Dripped Blood, Breaking Glass, Into The Night, Three Men And A Little Lady and Greedy to name but a few. With another string to his bow he has also written a number of books as well.

Into the 2010s his career is on-going after fifty years in the industry and is now largely-based in the USA.

Lynn, Tara

Film Role: Joyce (Holiday On The Buses)

This actress in the early to mid-1970s was to have a handful of film roles in what was to be a brief career in acting.

The role she is best-remembered for came in Holiday On The Buses in 1973 which was her big screen debut. She went on to appear in the sex comedy's Secret Of A Door-To-Door Salesman and Commuter Husbands. A short film called Take An Easy Ride brought an end to her acting career.

She went on to take up hairdressing and was to eventually return to work in the film industry in the make-up department thirty years after her last acting credit.

Lyons, John

TV Roles: Albert Harrison (Series 4 Episode 6 'The L Bus' and Series 4 Episode 7 'The Kids Outing'), Bill (Series 7 Episode 7 'Goodbye Stan') and Sid (Series 7 Episode 11 'The Allowance')

Born in London in 1943, John Lyons began his acting career in 1961 on leaving school when he joined the East 15 Acting School graduating on to the Theatre Workshop run by Joan Littlewood. His career has seen him work on stage, television and films for over fifty years.

On stage he has appeared in hit shows such as Oh What A Lovely War, Mrs Wilson's Diary and Intrigues And Armours – all productions of the Theatre Workshop. He'd also go on to have roles in Happy As A Sandbag, Purlie The Musical and the smash hit The Mousetrap in the late 1960s. In recent years he has made regular appearances on the pantomime circuit in Dick Whittington and Aladdin around the UK.

Lyons television career began in the mid-1960s with his biggest role coming in the award-winning ITV detective series A Touch Of Frost in which he co-starred as DS Toolan from 1992 to 2010. Other drama roles came most notably in Z Cars, Softly Softly, UFO, Follyfoot, The Onedin Line, Public Eye, Upstairs Downstairs, The Sweeney, Target, The Bill, Doctors and Shameless. As a comedy actor he appeared in a number of classic 1970s sitcoms such as Never Mind The Quality Feel The Width, On The Buses, The Liver Birds, Doctor In Charge, Sykes, Man About The House, George And Mildred and Mind Your Language. His later comedy roles included parts in Bottle Boys and The Nineteenth Hole.

On the big screen Lyons had small roles in Dr Jekyll And Sister Hyde, Yellow Dog and Sweeney 2 in the 1970s followed by Action Jackson and The Case Of The Hillside Stranglers in the 80s. Finally, in the 90s came further film roles in the star-studded comedy Bullseye and Blues Brothers 2000.

Mabs

This was a pet name that Wilf Phillips calls his girlfriend, Mrs Butler in the Series Three episode 'Mum's Last Fling'. It is an abbreviation of her Christian name Mabel in the Series Three episode 'Mum's Last Fling'.

MacGregor, Scott

Production Designer (On The Buses and Mutiny On The Buses)

Scott MacGregor was born in Edinburgh, Scotland in 1914 and shortly after World War Two he was to begin working in the film industry in the production department.

In his career he would work as a production designer for Hammer Films with credits in Taste The Blood Of Dracula, On The Buses, Blood From The Mummy's Tomb and Mutiny On The Buses. MacGregor was also extensively employed as an art director and his credits included London Calling, The Day They Robbed The Bank Of England, The Man Who Finally Died, The Vampire Lovers, The Horror Of Frankenstein, Scars Of Dracula and Vampire Circus.

On the small screen he worked on the hit 1950s BBC police drama Fabian Of The Yard, an early ITC series O.S.S and a couple of 1960s episodes of The Edgar Wallace Mystery Theatre.

Sadly, in the early 1970s, shortly after working on the first two On The Buses spin-off films, Scott MacGregor passed away at the age of fifty six in Sussex.

Machine Shop

An area of the Luxton and District's bus depot referred to by Stan in the Series Five episode 'Canteen Trouble'.

When the newly installed automatic food dispenser in the canteen rejects Stan's bent coin he receives two complimentary meat pies from the attractive representative of the vending machine company. It gives him an idea and he says to Jack: 'I tell you what mate. When we've eaten these how about going in the machine shop and start bending some coins.'

Madam Blake The Dancing Instructress

A name that Stan calls Inspector Blake as he watches him give dance lessons to holidaymakers in the film Holiday On The Buses.

As Inspector Blake gives advice to the talentless Mr and Mrs Briggs the watching Stan scoffs. He turns to Jack and amidst laughter says: 'Madam Blake the dancing instructress.'

Madden, Peter

Film Role: Mr Brooks (On The Buses)

Born in Kuala Lumpur, Malaysia in 1904, Peter Madden began his career as a drunk magician's assistant on stage and went on to become a BBC newsreader on radio also working on a number of popular radio series before breaking into acting on film and television. His career was to span over five decades in total.

Madden's film career began in the late 1930s and was to include roles in many hit films across the genres. The most notable of these were The Wicked Lady, Fiend Without A Face, Hell Is A City, Saturday Night And Sunday Morning, Oscar-winning Exodus, A Kind Of Loving, The Kiss Of The Vampire, From Russia With Love, Woman Of Straw, Dr Terror's House Of Horrors, Doctor Zhivago, Frankenstein Created Woman, On The Buses and One Of Our Dinosaurs Is Missing.

He was equally as active on television where he was to appear in a number of memorable drama series from the 1950s through until the mid-1970s. These included Ivanhoe, Dixon Of Dock Green, Zero One, Man Of The World, Danger Man, No Hiding Place, Out Of The Unknown, The Troubleshooters, Z Cars, Sherlock Holmes, The Saint, The Avengers, The Champions, Softly Softly, The Gold Robbers, Public Eye, Hadleigh and Crown Court. Comedy roles were not so prolific but did include parts in Glencannon, Steptoe And Son, Clochemerle and No Honestly.

Peter Madden continued in acting up until passing away in 1976 at the age of seventy one.

Mahoney, Janet

Film Role: Suzy (Mutiny On The Buses)

This actress was to fashion a career that would see her work with comedy legends on film, television and stage over three decades.

Janet Mahoney's forte was comedy and on the small screen she appeared in iconic series such as Howerd's Hour, The Dick Emery Show and The Two Ronnies. She also had roles in classic sitcoms including Up Pompeii and Dad's Army.

Her film career afforded her roles in much-loved features in the early 1970s. She debuted in Doctor In Trouble, appeared in Carry On Loving in a substantial role with her biggest role coming in 1972 in Mutiny On The Buses.

On stage she would appear in musicals such as Irene at the famous Adelphi Theatre in London. Mahoney was to retire from acting in the 1980s.

Maintenance

A department at the bus depot that is responsible for the upkeep and repairing of its fleet of buses that features in On The Buses on both the small and big screen. It is also a department that Stan and Jack often attempt to use to their advantage despite it being against company policy.

Maisie

Played by Iris Fry

A middle-aged brunette clippie who appears in all seven series of On The Buses though the character was never credited. Often seen in the background in the bus depot and canteen she can be seen most prominently in the Series

One episode 'The New Inspector' listening to a fellow clippie being berated as she sits on a bench in the depot. In the Series Seven episode 'The Football Match', Maisie can be seen standing alongside Mrs Butler on the touchline as the two teams take to the pitch.

Majorca

A popular Spanish resort with British holidaymakers with Stan and Aunt Maud amongst its visitors as referred to in three episodes of On The Buses.

In the Series Three episode 'The New Uniforms', Jack is confident he and Stan can pass off as airline pilots as they looks to impress two young Swedish women. He reckons Stan knows enough about flying as he flew out to Majorca on a charter holiday but the worried bus driver points out that he was drunk flying out and sick on the return flight.

His holiday to Majorca is referred to again in the Series Five episode 'The Nursery' as he recalls Spaniards drinking their wine by squirting it into their mouths and attempts to do the same with milk from a baby's bottle. Aunt Maud's holiday in Majorca sees her bring back duty free cigarettes for Stan and Jack in the Series Six episode 'No Smoke Without Fire'.

Majorca is the largest of the Balearic Islands in the Mediterranean Sea and since the 1950s has been a popular holiday destination especially with British and German holidaymakers. It has continued to grow in popularity and tourists are drawn by its several high quality beaches, hot weather and impressive facilities.

Makeover

In a bid to appear younger and impress her boyfriend Wilf, Mrs Butler undergoes a gradual makeover in the Series Three episode 'Mum's Last Fling'.

The family, much to their disdain, notice a change in their mother as she starts wearing an overly short skirt which Stan feels is so short he can see her vest. She also wears what she calls a fun wig which the family feel she can't afford but she reveals it was purchased with green stamps. Mabel is also more particular about her appearance applying mascara and perfume more often.

It does not end there as the next stage of her makeover sees her buy a new coat which she describes as her new maxi that is cavalry-style. However, Stan feels it is more like his dad's old army raincoat. She also treats herself to a pair of thigh-length leather boots paid for with housekeeping money. It all proves to be in vain as it is revealed that Wilf is in fact married leaving mum feeling heartbroken and foolish but at least the family get their devoted mother back.

Malston, Wally

Scriptwriter (Series 7 Episode 4 'The Poster')

Born in London in 1935, Wally Malston had a talent for comedy from an early age and had his own stand-up comedy act. After a spell of National Service he went into dentistry but spent his spare time writing comedy material in the 1950s when his career in television took off.

Malston (incorrectly credited in On The Buses as Malstan) wrote comedy material for hit 1950s shows Crackerjack, Sunday Night At The London Palladium and Carnival Time. Persuaded to take up writing full-time by the late, great Bob Monkhouse he went on to work on The Golden Shot, The Reg Varney Revue, Who Do You Do, On The Buses (co-writing an episode with Garry Chambers) and The Two Ronnies amongst others in the 1970s. The 1980s saw him write more material for The Jim Davidson Show, the hit quiz show 3-2-1 and the variety show Live From Her Majesty's.

In his career spanning forty years he supplied gags to comedy greats such as Bob Monkhouse, Jimmy Tarbuck, Sir Bruce Forsyth, Ted Rogers, Russ Abbott and Freddie Starr. Sadly, in 1997 stomach cancer developed and early in 1998 he lost his fight for life passing away at the age of sixty two.

Manager

Played by Paul Dawkins

The general manager in charge of the Luxton and District Bus Company's Luxton depot in the 1920s appears in Stan's dream in the Series Seven episode 'On The Omnibuses'.

A grey-haired man in his fifties, he is a strict general manager who makes life difficult for General Inspector Blake when he pays a rare visit to the depot. When the put upon inspector dares to claim it was his idea to introduce omnibuses to the Luxton depot the manager brands him an idiot as he feels it was his idea but unfairly adds that it will have been the inspector's idea should the omnibuses prove to be unsuccessful.

It is clear that the manager has no faith in Blakey as when the general inspector says he will get on his bike and follow Stan and Jack on their first trip on the omnibus to keep an eye on them the manager says he will follow Blakey in his car to keep an eye on him.

Later though the manager, in his chauffeur-driven car crashes into the side of Stan's omnibus leaving the manager fuming and it is at this point that Stan's vivid dream comes to an uncomfortable end.

Manager

Played by Frederick Hall

This manager was in charge at the Luxton depot in the early 1960s at a time when Blakey is set for promotion to inspector, Stan is set to move up from conductor to driver and Jack joins the company as a trainee conductor in the Series Six episode 'Stan's Worst Day'.

A middle-aged and dark-haired man, he is forced to chastise Blakey after catching him being pushed around the depot on a trolley by Stan and Jack. He tells an indignant and sheepish Blakey: 'You're supposed to set an example to the men Blake, not behave like an overgrown baby.' The manager storms off leaving Blakey to pledge to make Stan's life a misery once his promotion comes through.

Manager

Played by Brian Oulton

This ageing manager of the Town and District Bus Company's main depot has problems on all fronts from the staff and his inspector in the first spin-off film On The Buses.

A poshly-spoken balding man, he spends most of his time hounding Inspector Blake when the bus services fail to run smoothly. Clearly he is not an advocate for the use of women bus drivers as he holds the inspector responsible whenever they slip up and reminds Blake that it was his idea to use them. It's clear that the manager's man-management skills are fine when dealing with busmen as seen where he tells Stan in no uncertain terms that his insurance cover has been withdrawn and he'll need to undergo a test to satisfy the insurance company. However, when dealing with a woman bus driver his skills are far less polished as in when he ticks off a female driver when she follows false diversion signs he labels her a 'stupid woman' which reduces her to tears and instead of consoling her he leaves the inspector to deal with it. In the end his, and the company's patience, runs out with the women drivers and he eventually moves on to be replaced by the ambitious and tough taskmaster Mr Jenkins in the second spin-off film.

Manager

Played by Arnold Peters

In charge of the Luxton depot in the late 1960s this manager features in the Series One episode 'The New Inspector'.

A tall and slender moustachioed man in his late forties, he has his idyllic life at the depot upset by the new trainee inspector Stan Butler. As manager he enjoys an affair with an attractive clippie called Betty and he encourages her to come to work in a short skirt but a naïve Stan soon upsets the apple cart by reporting her for breaking the dress code and being cheeky as well. Of course this gets back to the manager who is flabbergasted and he orders Inspector Blake to remove Stan from his post as trainee inspector immediately labelling him 'a moron' and so Stan is demoted back to the rank of bus driver.

Manager

Played by Michael Sheard

A balding middle-aged man who is to make life uncomfortable for Inspector Blake as the depot manager in several Series Seven episodes of On The Buses.

The bespectacled man is the most intimidating and fiercest manager seen at the Luxton and District Bus Company and is somewhat highly-strung and often intimidates Inspector Blake with his short temper. He is seen in a more placid light in the Series Seven episode 'The Ticket Machine' when he rewards Stan with his much-needed efficiency bonus which he promptly loses.

Later in the series, in the episode called 'Hot Water' he berates Inspector Blake in front of Jack for arriving late for work and unshaven warning him to get a grip if he wants to remain as an inspector. The manager's threats to Blakey continue in 'What The Stars Foretell' when he finds Olive and the inspector in an innocent but uncompromising position in Blake's office. He orders Olive to get out, chastises Blakey for his behaviour and warns him that with redundancies likely as the company is amidst being taken over they could lose an inspector too. In the following episode 'The Allowance', the clippies are up in arms demanding a public convenience allowance and despite the inspector's deep reservations, he approves the idea. After a number of falsified claims by clippies and heated negotiations between staff, Inspector Blake and the manager the allowance is finally agreed. In the final episode of On The Buses called 'Gardening Time' it is his task to judge the depot's gardening competition. The main contenders for the contest are Jack and Inspector Blake but the manager awards first prize to his wife much to Blakey's displeasure as he feels that is unfair. However, the manager coldly explains: 'No you're quite right Blake it's not fair but I've got to live with her and that's not fair either, is it?'

Manager's House

The general manager's house features in Stan's vivid dream of life aboard the buses in the 1920s in the Series Seven episode 'On The Omnibuses'.

Olive, determined to work on the omnibuses, chains herself to the railings outside the general manager's house in protest at the lack of job opportunities for women. She holds up a placard chanting: 'Jobs for women. Jobs for women.' As Stan passes by in his new omnibuses he is horrified at the sight and fears the sack. He stops the bus and with Jack and his mum's help they tear Olive free and despite a section of the railings still being attached to her back she is bundled aboard the omnibus and taken away with the general manager none the wiser.

This is the only time any depot manager's house is seen in On The Buses on the small and big screen.

Manhunt

A popular British television series referred to by Stan in the Series Three episode 'The Inspector's Niece'.

Stan plans a romantic night in with clippie Sally and declines a night out with the family at the cinema. He explains to his mum that he is staying in to watch Manhunt on television but does not mention that he has invited Sally around.

Manhunt was a British drama series set during the Second World War in Nazi-occupied France centring on the French resistance movement. Starring Peter Barkworth, Alfred Lynch and Cyd Hayman, Manhunt regularly pulled in upwards of six million viewers running for two series with a total of twenty six episodes from 1969-1970. Perhaps its reference was a thinly-veiled plug as Manhunt, like On The Buses, was a London Weekend Television production.

Manifold

A part of the bus engine that Stan often uses to heat up food on both the small and big screen in On The Buses.

In the Series Three episode 'First Aid', Stan's bus sits at the Cemetery Gates and amidst an undue break he heats up sausage rolls and chips on the engine's manifold. He and Jack soon tuck into their lunch but are interrupted by the untimely arrival of Inspector Blake who is furious at the liberties taken by the pair of busmen. The film Mutiny On The Buses sees Stan heat up fish and chips on the manifold but Inspector Blake almost catches him in the act but trouble lies ahead. Stan has to drive his bus back to the depot with the burning chips still on the manifold and a fire is waiting to happen.

Marcus

Marcus was the large pet dog belonging to Aunt Maud that is to cause problems for many in the Series Two episode 'Aunt Maud'.

Marcus, a Great Dane, gives Jack an uncomfortable journey travelling aboard his bus with owner Aunt Maud on a visit to Luxton. The feisty dog rips Jack's way bill and pouch to shreds and leaves him very nervous of the troublesome pet. With Aunt Maud and Marcus coming to stay at the Butler house more problems lie ahead. Arthur's dinner of liver is scoffed by the dog leaving him with a snack of cheese and pickled onions. Stan also suffers as he has to give up his bed for Aunt Maud and he cannot sleep on the sofa as planned as Marcus has to sleep there and so he is forced into sharing a bed with Arthur – a very uncomfortable experience for them both.

More trouble beckons as Aunt Maud and Marcus have access to a taxi to the train station denied as the driver suggests they hire a horsebox instead. It is left to Stan to get his aunt and her pet to the station but when Jack refuses to allow Marcus on the bus he has to use his guile. He perches the dog alongside him in the driver's cab and manages to exit the depot with Inspector Blake powerless to stop him allowing Aunt Maud and Marcus to return home safely.

Margate

This is a long-standing holiday destination for the Butler and Rudge family which is referred to in a couple of episodes of On The Buses.

With Stan troubled with stomach pains in the Series One episode 'Bus Driver's Stomach' which are blamed on his overly-excessive diet of chips, mum reminds him of when he was sick as a child on a charabanc trip to Margate. However, Stan points out he was ill then because he had cockles, six ice creams, two plates of jellied eels, a candy floss, a ride on the big dipper and a kick in the stomach from Olive. Later, in the Series Three episode 'The Squeeze', damage to Arthur's sidecar's bodywork is blamed on Olive when on holiday in Margate a year earlier. She used the sidecar to change into her bikini damaging the bodywork in the process.

Margate is a seaside resort on the Kent coast approximately sixty four miles east of London. Renowned for its quality sandy beaches, it has long been a popular resort for Londoners seeking a day at the seaside. Its other tourist attractions include a Scenic Railway (the second oldest in the world) at the Dreamland Amusement Park and a sixteenth century Tudor house which attracts many visitors.

Maria

Played by Gigi Gatti

This is a passionate Italian waitress who is to date Stan in the film Holiday On The Buses.

Maria, in her late thirties, is employed at the holiday camp's canteen and takes a shine to the camp's newest employee Stan and shows her affection by giving him extra helpings in the canteen. They look to share a romantic evening at the camp manager Mr Coombs house whilst he spends a night at the cinema with his wife whilst Maria is left alone to clean the house. However, just as they get passionate on the settee their night is brought to an abrupt halt by the early return home by Mr and Mrs Coombs. Any hope Maria has of a romance blossoming with Stan is to be shattered by the antics of her overly-protective brother Luigi who threatens violent retribution against anyone dating her. When Stan feels the wrath of Luigi it frightens him off and, much to Maria's frustration ends any potential relationship for her.

Market Street

A fictional street referred to in the Series Three episode 'Radio Control'.

Stan receives a message on the newly-fitted radio control system from Miss Woodhall in central control. She reports a burst water main in Market Street and advises Stan to take a diversion to avoid any hold-ups.

Maroons

A delicacy offered by Joyce to Stan and Jack as she is trained aboard their bus in the Series Three episode 'Radio Control'.

As they take a break at their terminus at the Cemetery Gates, Joyce with her fellow clippie and friend Edna have a cup of tea with Stan and Jack. 'Do you want one of my maroons?' asks Joyce.

A maroon is a type of cake still popular to the present day with ingredients including chocolate, butter, apple sauce and flour.

Marriage Counsellor

Played by Aubrey Morris

A highly-strung character who is easily agitated and is to give Olive advice with regards to her troubled marriage in the Series Six episode 'Love Is What You Make It'.

Well-dressed and middle-aged the bespectacled marriage guidance counsellor has a stressful session with Olive, Stan and mum. He is bombarded by them shouting at him all at the same time with their problems and he is forced to call for quiet at the top of his voice. With them silenced he advises Olive to make herself more interesting and attractive urging her to be more exciting and sensual. He suggests she wears perfume and cooks him romantic meals. However, although Olive takes his advice and undergoes a makeover for Arthur it proves unsuccessful in breathing life back into the marriage.

Marshall, Alex

TV Role: Beryl (Series 5 Episode 14 'A Thin Time')

This actress had an acting career which revolved around many television roles from the early 1960s through to the mid-1970s.

She was more accustomed to drama roles with her biggest parts coming in the early 1970s BBC dramas Germinal and Jude The Obscure. Other such roles came in hit series such as Z Cars, Crossroads, Public Eye, Dixon Of Dock Green and Nana in the 1960s followed by credits in Coronation Street, Budgie, New Scotland Yard and Crown Court in the 70s. Marshall also appeared as a storyteller in the long-running hit children's series Jackanory with her solitary comedy role coming in On The Buses.

Martell, Philip

Musical Supervisor (On The Buses, Mutiny On The Buses and Holiday On The Buses)

Born in Whitechapel, London in 1906, Philip Martell left school and was to study at the Guildhall School of Music in the mid-1920s. On leaving he went to work as a music arranger in the film industry before forming his own orchestra to work for the BBC. However, he was destined to return to work in films in the musical department and had a long association with Hammer Films from 1963 to 1993.

As a musical supervisor and director Martell was to work on a host of memorable films such as Women Of Twilight, Trouble In Store, The Runaway Bus, One Good Turn, London Calling and Home Is The Hero in the 1950s. On into the 60s credits included The Evil Of Frankenstein, Dr Terror's House Of Horrors, Dracula: Prince Of Darkness, The Plague Of The Zombies, One Million Years B.C, Frankenstein Created Woman, To Sir With Love, Quatermass And The Pit, Frankenstein Must Be Destroyed and Run A Crooked Mile. The 1970s saw no let-up in his workload and the pick of those films being Taste The Blood Of Dracula, On The Buses, Twins Of Evil, Dr Jekyll And Sister Hyde, Vampire Circus, Mutiny On The Buses, Straight On Till Morning, Holiday On The Buses, Frankenstein And The Monster From Hell, Yanks and The Lady Vanishes. He was also to work on a handful of television series such as The Flying Doctor in the late 1950s and later in the 1980s on the Hammer House Of Horror and Hammer House Of Mystery And Suspense series.

Martell continued working up until passing away in 1993 at the age of eighty seven but he has left a wonderful legacy behind.

Martyn, Larry

TV Role: Fred (Series 7 Episode 10 'What The Stars Foretell' and Series 7 Episode 13 'Gardening Time')

Larry Martyn was born in London in 1934 and was to take up acting on leaving school in the early 1950s with his career beginning on stage in variety where he performed as a singer and comedian. From the late 1950s he was to appear regularly on television and in films chiefly in comedy roles in a career that spanned over forty years.

He was most active on television with his biggest roles coming in hit sitcoms Whoops Baghdad playing Derti Dhoti and Are You Being Served where he played Mr Mash in many episodes. The early part of his career though in the 1960s saw him appear in a number of hit dramas such as The Human Jungle, No Hiding Place, Dixon Of Dock Green, Z Cars and Man In A Suitcase. Later drama credits came in Upstairs Downstairs, Crown Court, Minder, The Gentle Touch, The Charmer, The Detectives and The Bill. Comedy though was his speciality and from the 1970s onwards he appeared in a host of classic British comedy series. Most notable of these included Up Pompeii, Six Dates With Barker, Doctor At Large, The Fenn Street Gang, For The Love Of Ada, The Liver Birds, Love Thy Neighbour, Dad's Army, On The Buses, Rising Damp and The Dick Emery Show.

The 1960s were to launch Martyn's film career. His hit films included Flame In The Streets, The Great St Trinian's Train Robbery and Up The Junction. The 70s saw him with small roles in Carry On At Your Convenience, For The Love Of Ada and Carry On Behind and in 1981 came his final film appearance in Omen III: The Final Conflict.

He remained in acting up until his death in 1994 at the age of sixty.

Mary

Played by Maxine Casson

An attractive blonde woman and player in the Basildon Bashers football team in the Series Seven episode 'The Football Match'.

Mary, with her blonde hair in ponytails and wearing the Basildon Bashers green and black striped strip introduces herself to Stan outside the changing rooms. She tells him she is Mary and is one of the forwards. In the football match that follows she scores the first goal of the match, takes part in the team's cunning plan that sees the Bashers score again and helps her team-mates to remove Stan's shorts at the end of the match.

Mary

Played by Hal Dyer

The Luxton depot gets a new nurse who moves in as a lodger at the Butler house and causes ructions in Olive and Arthur's marriage in the Series Five episode 'The New Nurse'.

Mary, a rather snobbish Scottish woman who has a low opinion of busmen, has upper class manners and snootiness which rankles with Stan but Arthur is immediately smitten. He takes to bathing, shaving and smothering himself in talcum powder in a bid to catch Mary's eye. He proceeds to upset Olive by accompanying Mary to the cinema leaving her at home. The pair get on well together. However, with Arthur intent on developing a relationship with Mary he is in for an unpleasant surprise. He presents her a box of chocolates only for her to tell him she doesn't want to get involved with a married man and Mary promptly moves out of the Butler house and out of Arthur's life.

Material

Stan uses material that the bus company uses to cover their bus seats in a bid to patch up items of furniture at home in the Series Four episode 'Cover Up'.

The sly bus driver sees using the bus seat material as a way of solving the problems the family have with their furniture in a state of disrepair. A visit to the depot's upholstery store sees Stan telling upholsterer Joe that he has two armchairs and four smaller chairs that need covering but points out he only wants bits and pieces of material. Joe shows Stan the new material being used to cover the bus seats and boasts it'll last ten years in normal service but bemoans that within a month it'll be covered in grease, muck, dogs, cats and food stains. It turns out that Stan gets more material than he bargained for as Joe gives him a roll of material which is five yards long. He has the problem of smuggling the material out of the depot without Blakey finding out and with Jack's help, in the refuge of the toilet, Stan wraps the material around his body under his overcoat and narrowly avoids being caught.

The material is used to cover armchairs, chairs and cushions as well as being made into a mat for the toilet giving the Butler's furniture a fresh look. However, when Inspector Blake pays them a visit they are given such a scare that they remove the material from the furniture and discard the material. But Stan is in for a shock when he next turns up at the depot as the inspector charges Stan forty pounds for the material which he recognised on his visit to the Butler house. He is told the company will stop the money out of his wages leaving Stan as sick as a pig at the thought of all the wasted material.

Mavis

Played by Jeanne Varney

This is a young woman who accuses Inspector Blake of stealing her friend's laundry in the film On The Buses.

Mavis, a dark-haired woman in her twenties, is to rush out of the launderette with her friend to challenge Inspector Blake who holds a laundry bag belonging to her friend. He believes it belongs to Stan and has confiscated it insisting it is evidence but Mavis proceeds to hit him time and again with her white handbag before stopping to sneeringly say: 'Ooh he must be a knicker-snatcher.'

With a policeman joining the scene she goes on to make the inspector feel even more uncomfortable as she claims: 'Yeah I reckon I seen his picture in the Sunday papers.' Mavis watches on as his details are taken down by the policeman.

Maxi

A style of coat bought by Mrs Butler as part of her makeover in the Series Three episode 'Mum's Last Fling'.

When she saunters into the living room wearing an ankle-length coat it stuns Stan who says: 'What have you got on there? Dad's old army raincoat?' She tells him it's her new maxi which is cavalry-style with Stan quipping that there is room for the horse under the coat.

Maxi-coats were to become highly fashionable in 1967 with popular designers Valentino and Yves Saint Laurent introducing the style most notably. They remained in fashion well into the 1970s and even today the maxi-coat is still marketed by leading fashion designers.

Maxted, Mary

TV Role: Iris' Mum (Series 6 Episode 3 'Private Hire')

Maxted was a bit-part actress who had a number of small roles on television spanning over twenty years from the early 1970s.

Her first credit came in On The Buses with her other comedy role coming in the less successful series Marjorie And Men. Maxted was also to have roles in hit dramas such as The Pickwick Papers, London's Burning, The Bill and Casualty. In uncredited roles she was also to appear in Upstairs Downstairs, Doctor Who and Tales Of The Unexpected amongst others.

McDonald, Mark

Director of Photography (On The Buses and Mutiny On The Buses)

Mark McDonald worked in cinematography for over twenty years primarily in the film industry and on the odd television project.

On the big screen he began by working on an Australian film called Shadow Of The Boomerang in 1960. Other film credits in that decade included Headline Hunters and Up In The Air. His most notable credits were to come in the 1970s with the likes of On The Buses, Mutiny On The Buses, Go For A Take, Secrets Of A Door-To-Door Salesman and a Children's Film Foundation productions Blinker's Spy-Spotter and Kadoyng.

His television career saw him work on the BBC drama series Theatre 625 in the mid-1960s and the early 1970s cult children's series Here Comes The Double Deckers.

McGarry, Parnell

TV Role: Gladys (Series 3 Episode 3 'The Inspector's Niece')

An actress whose career saw her appear in a number of film and television roles from the mid-1960s through until the early 1980s.

Her first break came on television in the hit BBC sitcom The Likely Lads. Further comedy roles on the small screen saw her with roles in the best of British sitcoms such as Dad's Army, On The Buses, The Fenn Street Gang and Q9 with a solitary drama role in an episode of Armchair Theatre.

She was also to have roles in films most of which were saucy sex comedies. These included Bedazzled, Up The Front, Anyone For Sex and Big Zapper. Other film roles came in the thriller Crossplot and comedy Up The Chastity Belt.

McGhee, Henry

Film Role: George Coombs (Holiday On The Buses)

Born in Kensington, London in 1928, Henry McGhee took up acting as a career in his early twenties. He went on to have a long illustrious career appearing on stage, film and television with this career spanning well over fifty years.

McGhee's first role in acting came on stage in the late 1940s and this would remain his first love as he thoroughly enjoyed performing in front of a live audience. The 1950s saw him appear in The Winter's Tale, The Taming Of The Shrew and The Egg amongst others. These were followed in the 60s with roles in Plunder, Uproar In The House and The Man Most Likely. Later in his career he'd appear in Run For Your Money, Two And Two Make Sex, Run For Your Wife, The Odd Couple, It Runs In The Family, Funny Money and The School For Wives.

On television McGhee will be best remembered for his roles in The Benny Hill Show and as Mr Pugh in the ITV sitcom The Worker which starred Charlie Drake. Other comedy roles were to come his way most notably in The Charlie Drake Show, The Goodies, Doctor In Charge, Rising Damp, The Dick Emery Show, Sykes, It Ain't Half Hot Mum and Last Of The Summer Wine. He was also an adept actor in drama roles appearing in classic series such as Ghost Squad, Z Cars, Public Eye, No Hiding Place, The Saint, Softly Softly, Gideon's Way, The Avengers, The Protectors and Q.E.D.

His career in films included roles in Sailor Beware, The Italian Job, Holiday On The Buses, Digby The Biggest Dog In The World, The Cherry Picker, Adventures Of A Taxi Driver, Revenge Of The Pink Panther and Carry On Emmannuelle.

Sadly, Henry McGhee was to suffer from Alzheimer's disease late in his life and passed away in 2006 at the age of seventy six.

McGrath, Maggie

Film Role: Gladys (On The Buses)

Maggie McGrath (also known as Maggie Rennie) was to have a career as an actress spanning thirty years chiefly on film and television. She was married to renowned film actor Michael Rennie for thirteen years until their divorce in 1960.

Her film career began in the early 1940s with small roles in Those Kids From Town and English Without Tears as well as a starring role in the comedy Schweik's New Adventures. She went on to appear in a number of hit films in the 1950s, 60s and 70s such as Nowhere To Go, The V.I.P's, Séance On A Wet Afternoon, The Great St Trinian's Train Robbery, Hostile Witness, All The Way Up and On The Buses. On the small screen McGrath had roles in the mystery series The New Adventures Of Charlie Chan, hit dramas No Hiding Place and Public Eye and the short-lived sitcom The More We Are Together.

McGregor

Played by Nicholas Hobbs

A bus driver from Burntwood depot who is a candidate in the promotional poster contest organised by the Luxton and District Bus Company in the Series Seven episode 'The Poster'.

McGregor, in his late twenties, is a body-builder who also plays for his depot's football team. He is described by Inspector Blake as having 'muscles on muscles' such is his physique. As McGregor appears in front of the judging panel he is told proudly by his chief inspector that he has put up a very creditable performance. However, he loses out in the contest to Stan and congratulates him by giving him a crushing handshake as he says coldly: 'No hard feelings Stan.'

McKillop, Don

TV Role: Harry (Series 5 Episode 4 'The Inspector's Pets')

Born in Carlisle in 1929, Don McKillop was to have a packed career as an actor with credits in film and television and he was also to work briefly with the famous Royal Shakespeare Company on stage.

From the early 1960s he was to have film roles and went on to appear in The Sinister Man, comedy film Otley, An American Werewolf In London and the made-for-television film The Hound Of The Baskervilles.

Television was to offer McKillop his widest array of roles in both drama and comedy. Drama roles in the 1960s were to include classic series such as Emergency – Ward 10, Detective, Gideon's Way, Dixon Of Dock Green and Dr Finlay's Casebook. The 1970s brought further such credits in Softly Softly, Doctor Who, Paul Temple, Doomwatch, The Onedin Line, Sutherland's Law, Z Cars and Rumpole Of The Bailey. At the tail end of his career in the 1980s came roles in Coronation Street, The Professionals, The Gentle Touch and C.A.T.S Eyes. His comedy roles came most notably in The Likely Lads and Rosie with smaller parts in The Liver Birds, On The Buses, When The Boat Comes In and Pig In The Middle.

After retiring from acting in the late 1980s, he sadly passed away in 2005 at the age of seventy six.

McManus, Mick

A famous British wrestler of the 1960s and 70s referred to by Stan in the Series Three episode 'The Inspector's Niece'.

After an uncomfortable shift training a rotund clippie called Gladys that leaves Jack glad to see the back of her Stan agrees saying: 'She'd frighten the life out of Mick McManus.' Mick McManus was a successful and famous wrestler who came to real prominence when British wrestling became cult television viewing and was covered on ITV's long-running series World Of Sport from 1965 until 1985. He was renowned as a wrestler who often resorted to breaking the rules earning him introductions such as 'The man you love to hate'. McManus was to win British and European titles over a number of weights and famously lost one of those titles through disqualification. He continued wrestling past the age of fifty and remains one of the most noted and best remembered figures from what is seen as the golden era of British wrestling.

McNab, Bob

TV Role: Bob (Series 7 Episode 5 'The Football Match')

Born in Huddersfield, Yorkshire in 1943, Bob McNab was a professional footballer whose solitary acting credit was his cameo role in an episode of On The Buses.

His football career began at his hometown club Huddersfield Town in 1963 before being signed by Bertie Mee for Arsenal three years later. A defender, McNab made his name in the famous 1970-71 Arsenal side which won the elusive League and Cup double a year after he had won an Inter-Cities Fairs Cup winners medal in European competition. Capped four times by England he finally left Arsenal in 1975 and after a brief stint at Wolverhampton Wanderers he moved further afield plying his trade in the newly-formed NASL (North American Soccer League) in the USA. He retired from playing in 1979 and was to immigrate to Los Angeles, California in the 1980s. He briefly returned to English football in 1999 as part of a consortium that took over Portsmouth Football Club where he would have a month in charge of team affairs as caretaker manager. McNab soon returned to the States and now works as a property developer in Los Angeles.

Mechanic, The

Played by John M. East

An employee of the Luxton and District Bus Company who is seen repairing Stan's bus in the Series Six episode 'Stan's Worst Day'.

When Stan's bus crashes through a row of bollards outside the town hall it suffers great damage to the undercarriage. At the depot a tall mechanic appears from beneath the bus and says to Jack: 'The sumps a complete write-off I'm afraid Jack so I've fitted another one.' With Inspector Blake witnessing the damage he orders Jack to get Stan to report to him straight away.

Medical Orderly

Played by Reginald Peters

This is a balding character in a white gown who rushes from the hospital entrance to assist Olive in the film On The Buses.

A Town and District bus pulls up outside the hospital with Olive in labour and trapped in the sidecar which sits on the rear platform of the bus. Arthur rushes to get assistance and is met by a medical orderly who tells him: 'I'll get them to prepare the delivery room then.' The worried expectant father requests a hammer and chisel and he, along with the medical orderly bring out a stretcher placing Olive in the sidecar onto it and wheeling her into the hospital as she screams out with her labour pains.

Medicals

The Luxton and District Bus Company often carried out medicals on their staff and this subject is covered in several episodes of On The Buses.

In the Series One episode 'Bus Driver's Stomach' it is announced by Inspector Blake that all bus drivers will have to undergo medicals and those that fail will be transferred to cleaning or maintenance departments.

For Stan it is inwardly very worrying as he suffers from an acute inflammation of the stomach giving him on-going stomach pains. Despite his anxiety Stan passes the medical allowing him to continue in his role as bus driver.

Staff of every grade has to undergo medicals at the depot in the Series Six episode 'Bye Bye Blakey'. Although the inspector has another job lined up he is told, much to his discomfort, that he will still have to have a medical. He is ridiculed mercilessly by Stan and Jack as he strips for his examination and as he has his medical he tells the female doctor he feels it is pointless as he won't be around much longer. With Stan and Jack eavesdropping on the conversation they mistakenly believe that the inspector is going to die and following this they go out of their way to be nice to their nemesis until they discover that he is quite healthy.

When Olive applies to become a clippie at the Luxton and District Bus Company she has to undergo a medical which is attended by her mum in the Series Seven episode 'The Perfect Clippie'. The doctor tells Olive she has excellent hearing and asks her to strip to her underwear for her examination. This concerns Mrs Butler but the doctor assures her he has sworn to the Hippocratic Oath. As it turns out Olive passes her medical enabling her to start her second spell as clippie at the depot.

Melwood

This is a bus depot that is part of the Luxton and District Bus Company and is referred to in the Series Seven episode 'The Poster'.

The Melwood depot is represented in the company's promotional poster contest. Its representative is a bus driver who plays for that depot's football team.

Mendez, Julia

TV Role: Fatima (Series 3 Episode 6 'The Snake')

Born in 1935, Julia Mendez (also known as Julie) was to have a career as an actress and was also a highly-talented dancer and choreographer. Her acting career saw her with roles in films and television usually which involved dancing. Her film career began in the early 1960s when she appeared in The Night We Dropped A Clanger, Panic, She, Devils Of Darkness, Theatre Of Death and Duffy. Mendez was also to appear as a dancer in the opening credits sequence of the James Bond film From Russia With Love in 1963.

She was also to be a choreographer in The Two Faces Of Dr Jekyll and Carry On Up The Khyber. Towards the end of the 1960s she appeared on television in the adventure series called Virgin Of The Secret Service and in the early 1970s in an episode of On The Buses.

She would continue working as a choreographer for a number of years away from film and television in many fields.

Menuhin, Yehudi

A famous violinist and conductor referred to by Arthur in the Series Three episode 'The Cistern'.

After plumbing in their new toilet, Stan prepares to demonstrate how it sounds when flushed to the family. Arthur is ticked off for not keeping quiet before Stan flexes his fingers prior to flushing the toilet. Miffed Arthur quips: 'Who do you think you are? Yehudi Menuhin?'

Yehudi Menuhin, of Russian parentage, was born in New York, USA and went on to become a famous violinist and conductor. Often regarded as the greatest violinist of the twentieth century he played with the greatest orchestras and performed on the best stages around the world for over fifty years. In 1965 he was awarded a KBE (Knight Commander of the British Empire) and was later knighted in 1985 when he became a British citizen. Other honours bestowed on him included earning the Glenn Gould Prize, he was made Ambassador of Goodwill by UNESCO in 1992 and was made a Baron of Stoke d'Abernon in Surrey a year later. Sir Yehudi Menuhin was to pass away in 1999 at the age of eighty two.

Mercer, Olive

TV Role: The Woman Passenger (Series 4 Episode 9 'Cover Up')

Olive Mercer's career as an actress was to span through the 1960s and 70s and brought roles chiefly on television.

Her biggest role came in the classic sitcom Dad's Army playing Mrs Yeatman from 1969 to 1977. Other notable comedy roles came in hit series such as Please Sir, Doctor In The House, On The Buses, Doctor In Charge, Whatever Happened To The Likely Lads and Billy Liar. Mercer was also to have roles in dramas such as Crossroads, The Pallisers, Dixon Of Dock Green, Within These Walls and Angels amongst others.

She was also to appear on the big screen solely in the 1972 sex comedy Sex And The Other Woman.

Methi Bhaji

A very spicy Indian dish served up by Mrs Sharma in the depot canteen in the Series One episode 'The Canteen'.

Stan and the rest of the busmen do not find the dish to their liking and is so hot Stan claims it has melted his fillings but Inspector Blake finds it very palatable as he spent time in India growing accustomed to it. He reveals that the dish is called methi bhaji.

Methi bhaji is a spicy dish that includes ingredients such as fenugreek leaves, garlic, onions, turmeric and green chilies with salt or sugar added depending on preference. The dish is regularly served at Indian weddings and remains appealing to those with an acquired taste for such cuisine.

Michaels, Anna

Film Role: Eileen (On The Buses)

Anna Michaels solitary credit as an actress came on the big screen in the first On The Buses spin-off film in 1971 in which she had a small role.

Middleton, Grenville

Cameraman (Series 7 Episode 8 'Hot Water')

Grenville Middleton's involvement in film and television as a cameraman and cinema-tographer was to be relatively short spanning from the late 1960s until the mid-1970s.

His film credits as a cameraman were to come in the form of foreign films One For The Pot and One Step To Hell in 1968. He would also go on to work as a cinematographer of films of an adult nature including The Stud, The Sex Thief and The Love Box.

On television he worked as a cameraman on the hit sitcom On The Buses and as a cinematographer on the documentary Hang Up Your Brightest Colours.

Once his career in film and television had ended he went on to co-found the Movingstage Marionette Company in 1979 which was to open a theatre on a river barge in 1982. This operates to the present day in the river Thames performing innovative shows featuring puppets and actors. It is now an established and unique part of the London theatre thirty years after it was formed by Middleton who is still involved with it to this day.

Midi-Skirt

This item of clothing was worn by Olive for a special anniversary meal in the Series Four episode 'The Anniversary'.

As Olive spins around showing off her new skirt mum is impressed and turns to Arthur and says: 'How do you like her midi-skirt?' He is not so keen on it and suggests that Olive should sew up the slit joking that it shows off her knickers.

The midi-skirt was first seen in the 1930s and was popular in the USA. However, it was to dip out of fashion until the late 1960s. When the highly stylish mini-skirts popularity began to wane the midi-skirt was to make a comeback in the late 1960s with the cotton variety being most popular and was often worn with platform shoes and a long coat. The midi-skirt remained in fashion until the late 1970s.

Midwinter, Dulcie

Wardrobe Supervisor (Mutiny On The Buses)

Born in the USA in 1910, Dulcie Midwinter would later move to live and work in Britain. Specialising in working in the wardrobe and costume departments on film and television from the mid-1950s she went on to work on a number of classic films in her career.

Midwinter's film credits began in the 50s working most notably on Not So Dusty, Dublin Nightmare, Serious Charge and A Touch Of Larceny. The 1960s saw her work on a string of hit films such as Tunes Of Glory, The Snake Woman, the award-winning sci-fi The Day The Earth Caught Fire, The Quiller Memorandum, The Birthday Party and The Italian Job amongst others. In the 1970s her most memorable credits came in a handful of Hammer Films productions such as Mutiny On The Buses, Captain Kronos – Vampire Hunter and Frankenstein And The Monster From Hell with other films including The Blood On Satan's Claw, Tales Of Beatrix Potter, Dulcima and the Hitchcock classic Frenzy. Her television career was far more sporadic with 60s credits coming in dramas The Sentimental Agent and The Human Jungle. Finally, in the 1970s she worked on the low budget sci-fi series Star Maidens.

After over twenty years in the industry Midwinter retired in the late 1970s before sadly passing away in 1997 at the age of eighty six.

Mike the Mechanic

Played by Michael Slater

Mike is a balding mechanic who repairs Stan's bus at the depot in the Series Four episode 'The L Bus'.

He is called upon to repair the training bus which breaks down whilst being used to train staff and covertly deliver a bed to the Butler house. The bus suffers an oil leak which Mike repairs and walks away from it carrying his toolbox telling Stan, Jack and Inspector Blake that the bus is ready.

Military Two Step

This dance is demonstrated at Inspector Blake's dance class in the film Holiday On The Buses.

The military two step is performed impeccably by the elderly couple Mr and Mrs Hodges much to Inspector Blake's satisfaction. However, the next couple Mrs Butler and Irish holidaymaker Bert Thompson are far from perfect and are accused of showing off by the inspector. Next to attempt the military two step are the cockney couple Mr and Mrs Briggs and their interpretation is clumsy and wooden. The dance is later seen being performed in the ballroom in an exhibition of old time dancing.

The military two step was devised by dance instructor James Finnigan at the start of the twentieth century in Manchester in 1900 with the help of his daughter Ethel. The dance was first part of a dance programme in 1917 and so the dance came about. It remains very popular to the current day and since 1950 has been categorised as an Old Time dance.

Milk and Slops

A diet of milk and slops is what Stan is placed on by Doctor Clark in the Series One episode 'Bus Driver's Stomach'.

Doctor Clark examines Stan who is suffering from stomach pains and the diagnosis is that he has an acute inflammation of the stomach. The doctor places the ill driver on a strict diet of milk and slops. Such a diet would have consisted of largely milk with other watery and liquid foods such as soup. The treatment is no longer prescribed with a vast array of medication now used in its place.

Milk Stout

This is a preferred drink of the inspector's mother, Mrs Blake during a night out at the Luxton and District Social Club in the Series Seven episode 'The Visit'.

Milk stout became popular as an alcoholic beverage in the late 1940s in Britain. It is a stout with the added ingredient of lactose which was sugar derived from milk which gives the beverage a somewhat sweet taste. The British government were to ban the use of the word milk from all adverts and labels for the product shortly after the Second World War. It is now a rare drink and the only famous surviving milk stout nowadays is brewed by Mackeson's.

Milkman

Played by Mike Carnell

This character calls at the Butler house in search of payment in the Series Three episode 'The Squeeze'.

When the milkman can be heard approaching the Butler house mum orders the family, who are eating breakfast, to be quiet and hides under the table. She tells the family she hasn't paid the milkman for six weeks and owes him six pounds and ten pence. On hearing this the whole family join her under the table. At this point the milkman peers through a rear window but sees nothing and leaves a note that reads no milk today on the doorstep outside the Butler house as he is fed up waiting to be paid before leaving.

Miller, Sandra

TV Role: Sally Ferguson (Series 5 Episode 3 'The Best Man' and Series 5 Episode 8 'The New Nurse')

An actress whose career was to see her gain a handful of television and film credits spread over more than twenty years. In the mid-1960s Miller's television debut came in ITV's historical drama Victoria Regina. Her other notable drama role came in the hit 1980s detective series Bergerac. Her biggest part came playing Sally in two episodes of the hit sitcom On The Buses in 1971. Another comedy role came her way in the mildly successful early 1980s mini-series Pictures and was to be her final credit in acting.

Miller's film roles were limited to a couple of adult movies in the early to mid-1980s those being Titillation and Girls Of Hollywood Hills.

Mills, Alan

Sound (Series 7 Episode 2 'The Perfect Clippie', Series 7 Episode 5 'The Football Match', Series 7 Episode 6 'On The Omnibuses' and Series 7 Episode 11 'The Allowance')

Alan Mills' career was to see him work in the sound department for London Weekend Television for almost twenty years from the late 1960s.

He would work on a wide array of television series beginning with the hit sitcom Doctor In The House. This would be followed with other comedy series such as On The Buses, Maggie And Her, Just William and A Fine Romance. Mills drama credits included LWT gems such as Budgie, Another Bouquet, the award-winning miniseries Lillie, Enemy At The Door, Blade On The Feather and Dempsey And Makepeace. Hit art series Aquarius and The South Bank Show were also amongst his credits in a career spent entirely at LWT.

Mills, Madeleine

TV Roles: Sally Ferguson (Series 3 Episode 3 'The Inspector's Niece' and Series 3 Episode 11 'Going Steady') and Christine (Series 5 Episode 13 'Vacancy For Inspector')

Madeleine Mills was an actress who had a number of credits on television crammed into a career that spanned from the early 1960s through until the mid-1970s.

Mills most notable drama roles came in the late 1960s in Doctor Who as Vana and in a handful of episodes of Softly Softly as Daphne. Other fondly remembered dramas which she appeared in included Sergeant Cork, No Hiding Place, Love Story, The Rivals Of Sherlock Holmes and Z Cars. In comedy her biggest role came in On The Buses playing Stan's girlfriend Sally and she also appeared in Please Sir, Dear Mother Love Albert and The Fenn Street Gang.

She retired from acting at a relatively early age and in recent years had fought a long battle against cancer which she ultimately lost passing away in August 2010.

Mini – The Car and Van

The Mini was an iconic motorcar which featured in both the television series and a spin-off film.

In the Series Six episode 'The Prize', as the inspector tries to encourage Stan and Jack to buy raffle tickets, they watch fellow employee Chalkie getting into his battered Mini outside the bus depot. Inspector Blake looks to impress the busmen by telling them that one of the prizes for the raffle is a Mini leading Jack to joke: 'Does Chalkie go with it?' But Blakey insists it's a new Mini that is the prize whereas Chalkie's was a model from the early 1960s.

It is a Mini Van that features in the film Mutiny On The Buses. Inspector Blake is supplied with a red Mini Van by the Town and District Bus Company so that he can check up on his bus crews when they are en-route on duty. The van, marked Traffic Control (a 1965 model), is a short-lived tool for the inspector as it soon gets crushed in the depot when Stan reverses his bus into it.

The humble Mini which was designed by Alec Issigonis was first released for sale in August 1959. Specifically designed to be economical with low fuel consumption amidst the Suez Canal fuel crisis the car would go on to be a massive success for its manufacturers (then the BMC or British Motor Corporation). The car also became something of a fashion icon in the 1960s and the sporty Mini Cooper model was a success on the sports front winning the world famous Monte Carlo Rally in 1964, 1965 and 1967. Not only were global sales huge but the car gained further fame in the cult 1969 film The Italian Job in which it featured. The classic Mini remained in production until 2000 at which point the brand came under the ownership of BMW. They were soon to release a new design, larger Mini known as the BMW Mini which remains hugely popular to the current day – proof that the legend of the Mini lives on after more than fifty years in production.

Mistletoe

The popular Christmas tradition of kissing under the mistletoe features in the Series Four episode 'Christmas Duty' with varying consequences.

Jack is to hang a piece of mistletoe above the door of the ladies toilets as he sees clippies Joyce and Edna entering and is intent on catching them as they come out. When they exit him and Stan enjoy a long, lingering kiss with the two clippies but the inspector is not impressed. He starts to remove the mistletoe as a more rotund and less attractive clippie called Rosie exits the toilets. With Inspector Blake holding the mistletoe Rosie takes it as an invitation and grabs the shocked inspector and smothers him in kisses amidst giggles much to his displeasure. A watching Stan and Jack revel in his discomfort and embarrassment. Mistletoe is seen the following day as a drunken Arthur holds some mistletoe and attempts to kiss Olive but she is put off by his drunkenness.

The tradition of kissing under the mistletoe is believed to have had its origins in Norse mythology becoming popular in Britain early in the nineteenth century. To the present day it remains a popular Christmas custom.

Mitchell, Norman

TV Roles: Nobby (Series 3 Episode 5 'Busmen's Perks' and Series 5 Episode 10 'Stan's Uniform')
Film Role: London Transport Official (On The Buses)

Norman Mitchell was born in Sheffield, Yorkshire in 1918 and would first appear in repertory theatre and was to work with the Royal Shakespeare Company prior to the outbreak of the Second World War during which he served in the famous Desert Rats. His acting career finally took off in the early 1950s and he'd go on to have one of the most active careers as an actor in history on British film and television.

On television his career began with roles in hit dramas in the 1950s such as The Adventures Of Sir Lancelot, William Tell, The Vise, The Adventures Of Robin Hood and Emergency – Ward 10. He was also to appear in hit dramas throughout the 1960s most notably including Dixon Of Dock Green, Z Cars, The Saint, No Hiding Place, Crossroads,

Dr Finlay's Casebook, Doctor Who, Coronation Street, The Prisoner, Man In a Suitcase, Softly Softly and Public Eye. The 1970s saw no let-up and he appeared in The Onedin Line, Follyfoot, Emmerdale, Crown Court, Danger UXB and Worzel Gummidge amongst others. He remained active in drama in the 80s and 90s with roles in Hammer House Of Mystery And Suspense, the award-winning Vanity Fair, All Creatures Great And Small and Casualty.

Mitchell's comedy roles began in earnest in the early 1960s and that decade saw him appear in classic comedy series such as The Rag Trade, Meet The Wife, The Dickie Henderson Show and Dad's Army. The 1970s brought him further comedy roles in hit series such as Up Pompeii, Doctor In The House, On The Buses, The Fenn Street Gang, Some Mothers Do 'Ave 'Em, Whatever Happened To The Likely Lads, The Dick Emery Show, It Ain't Half Hot Mum, George And Mildred, Robin's Nest, Sykes, The Goodies and Are You Being Served? The 80s and 90s saw him with roles in Yes Minister, Keep It In The Family, Only When I Laugh, Never The Twain, You Rang M'lord and Last Of The Summer Wine.

Mitchell could also boast an impressive film career and he was to appear in several Carry On films those being Carry On Cabby, Carry On Spying, Carry On Cleo, Carry On Screaming and Carry On Emmannuelle. Other notable film roles came in Bunny Lake Is Missing, The Great St Trinian's Train Robbery, the Oscar-winning Oliver, On The Buses, Nearest And Dearest, Bless This House, And Now The Screaming Starts, Frankenstein And The Monster From Hell, Man About The House, The Pink Panther Strikes Again and The Return Of The Soldier amongst others.

Aside from television and film, Mitchell was also active on numerous hit radio shows in a career spanning over fifty years and he continued acting until passing away in 2001 at the age of eighty two.

Mitzy

A pet dog belonging to Inspector Blake's mother is left in the care of the Butlers whilst the inspector and his mother go on a fishing trip in the Series Five episode 'The Inspector's Pets'.

Mitzy, a Dachshund, is described as a pedigree dog by Blakey who advises Stan to keep her on a leash should he take her for a walk. As it turns out Arthur's laxity is to cause consternation for Stan when his brother-in-law takes Mitzy for a walk and ends up in the Red Lion pub. He walks home in torrential rain with Mitzy and Stan frets the dog could have caught pneumonia. In a panic as he recalls that the landlord of the pub owns a large, sex-mad Dalmatian. Stan worries Mitzy may now be pregnant and tells Arthur: 'It's a pedigree dog. It's supposed to have pedigree pups not a lot of spotted dicks.' He is worrying needlessly though as, when the inspector returns from his fishing trip and takes Mitzy back he suspects nothing and merely feels Stan may have fed her a too much as she seems to have put on weight.

Mobile Policeman

Played by Barry Linehan

A stern policeman who forbids the use of the Town and District Bus Company's radio control system after a mix-up in the film Mutiny On The Buses.

The grey-haired policeman is in his late forties and is on duty in his patrol car when he receives a radio message ordering him to go to the gasworks as Inspector Blake contacts the police instead of Butler's bus after Jack has retuned the radio system to prevent Blakey pestering them. The policeman finally realises what has occurred when he is ordered to report to the bus depot. On arriving in the inspector's office he launches into a tirade on Inspector Blake warning him he could be charged with impersonating a police inspector and that he could get a five year prison sentence for it. Also for transmitting on a government frequency could earn him an eighteen month prison sentence. He promises to make out a full report and tells the inspector and Mr Jenkins that the radio system is not to be used again before he leaves the depot still fuming.

Moby Dick

This is a fictional whale that Olive is likened to in a couple of episodes of On The Buses.

In the Series Three episode 'Foggy Night', Olive ventures out into the thick fog from the bus as she needs the toilet. In order that she can find her way back to the bus she holds on to the end of a ball of wool but she runs into trouble. She rushes to find a safe spot and mum finds it tough to hang on to the wool on the bus as it is tugged violently as Olive rushes around. Stan feels it is like deep sea fishing but Arthur adds: 'More like Moby Dick.'

Later, in the Series Seven episode 'Gardening Time', Olive prepares to sunbathe in the back garden wearing a skimpy bikini whilst Inspector Blake is gardening. He likens her to a stranded great white whale as she lies down calling her Moby Dick.

Moby Dick was a fictional white sperm whale which featured in a story called The Whale written by US author Herman Melville in 1851. It told the story of a whaling ship captained by Ahab who is on a quest for revenge hunting specifically for a whale that bit his leg off which is dubbed Moby Dick. The story would go on to be made into a hit film in 1956 – over one hundred years after the book was written.

Mohan, Ursula

TV Roles: Liz (Series 2 Episode 3 'Self Defence'), Joyce (Series 3 Episode 8 'Radio Control', Series 4 Episode 5 'Christmas Duty' and Series 4 Episode 13 'Not Tonight'), Edna (Series 4 Episode 1 'Nowhere To Go') and Iris (Series 6 Episode 3 'Private Hire')

Ursula Mohan took up acting from an early age and can boast a career spanning the decades with credits on stage, television and in films.

She has had an extensive stage career which has included working with the famous Royal Shakespeare Company. From the mid-1960s she has appeared in a host of stage shows such as Tango, Love's Labour Lost, Othello, Revenge, The Good Woman, A Trip To Scarborough, The Cenci and Bloody Mary. She has also had roles in musicals including Making Tracks and Petite Rouge. In recent years stage credits have come in Children Of Hercules, The Winter's Tale, The Drowsy Chaperone and Dad's Army Marches On. Many of her stage appearances have come in the best theatres in London's West End.

On television she is perhaps best remembered for her various roles in the hit sitcom On The Buses. Her other comedy roles of note included Scott On, Agony, Bognor, Pig In The Middle and 2point4 Children. Mohan was also to appear in a number of hit dramas such as Cribb, Agatha Christie's Partners In Crime, Ruth Rendell Mysteries, London's Burning, Kavanagh QC, Casualty and Holby City. On the big screen she has had roles in Tell Me Lies and the hit 2008 film The Bank Job which was written by comedy writing legends Dick Clement and Ian La Frenais.

Aside from her variety of performances as an actress Ursula Mohan is also a tutor of drama acting at the School of Performing Arts in London but her acting career still continues apace.

Molly

Played by Gaye Brown

This is a canteen employee at the bus depot who becomes engaged to Inspector Blake in the Series Four episode 'The Canteen Girl'.

Molly, an attractive blonde-haired woman in her early thirties who speaks with a West Country accent, dates Inspector Blake. She pampers him with generous helpings in the canteen and the pair grow closer. Although marriage is planned and the couple set to leave Luxton to settle down to run a farm in the country, Stan and Jack note she has debatable morals.

Molly shares a drink with the busmen and after a few vodkas and tomato juice she has become very flirty with Stan. She tries to seduce him at home and at a social event at the depot where she finally gets passionate aboard a bus with Stan. When her furious fiancé Inspector Blake catches her in the act he is heartbroken and the marriage is cancelled but Blakey promises to remain at the depot and make Stan's life a misery leaving Molly relieved as she couldn't take the inspector not allowing her sexual freedom in their marriage.

Molly

Played by Deirdre Costello

Molly is a clippie who is unable to go on a date with Stan in the Series Four episode 'Not Tonight'.

She has long blonde hair and is described by Jack as 'a little raver' and suggests that Stan asks her out on a date. However, although keen she can't oblige as she has promised to take her granny to the bingo. A listening Inspector Blake mocks Stan as his drought of dates are set to continue. In a bid to poke fun in return Jack suggests to Molly that she dates Stan and Inspector Blake can go out with her granny. Molly points out that her gran is eighty six but Stan feels that is no problem joking that Blakey is only four years older than her. With that she apologises to Stan and promises to date him another time before leaving the canteen.

Moonlight Mystery Tour

A tour invented by Jack in a bid to lure two holidaymakers on a late night date aboard the holiday camp tour bus in the film Holiday On The Buses.

A couple of holidaymakers in their thirties called Joyce and Doreen are invited on a moonlight mystery tour which Jack describes as being by the sea and on the beach. It means Stan and Jack take the camp's tour bus without the permission of the manager and the date is destined to end in disaster.

As Stan and Jack get amorous with their dates aboard the bus parked on the beach trouble brews. Stan is to discover that the bus has become stuck in the wet sand and even Jack, Joyce and Doreen cannot push the bus out of its sand-trap.

A disgusted Joyce and Doreen decide they'll make their own way home whilst Stan and Jack are left with a problem. They need to free the bus as they have a tour to take out the following morning but Jack is confident the sand will be rock hard in the morning and will retrieve it then. However, things don't pan out like that as, a few hours later, they return to find the bus submerged as the tide comes in. It means that they lose their jobs at the holiday camp as the tour bus is lost to the sea.

Moore, Kevin

TV Role: TV Newsman (Series 1 Episode 1 'The Early Shift')

Kevin Moore's acting career stretches back to the early 1960s including roles on television, in films and on stage.

His television career saw him appear in hit dramas such as Z Cars, The Glittering Prizes, The Gentle Touch, How Many Miles To Babylon, Silent Witness, Poirot, The Bill, Heartbeat, Doctors, the feature length biography of Carry On star Kenneth Williams called Fantabulosa and most recently World Without End. Moore's comedy credits came most notably in On The Buses, Not On Your Nellie, Doctor On The Go, Yes Honestly, Ticket To Ride, Father Ted, Keeping Mum, Heartburn Hotel and the global smash hit Extras.

On the big screen Moore's film roles began in the late 1970s with an appearance in the US production Here Comes The Tigers. He'd go on to bigger and better things with roles in Ascendancy, Under Suspicion, Fierce Creatures, The Wolves Of Kromer, Fogbound, Johnny English and If Only.

As a stage actor he has appeared in London's West End and further afield. Credits include Reynard The Fox, Rough Crossing, The Duel, Singular People, The Parasol, The Resistable Rise Of Arturo U1, Take 2 and Crocodiles In Cream amongst others. Globally his most noted stage performances include Cheating Hearts (in Hong Kong and Perth, Australia), The Faith Healer (Budapest) and Twelfth Night (Barbados).

Kevin Moore continues acting to the present day.

Morgan, Garfield

TV Role: Mr Stilton (Series 6 Episode 6 'Bye Bye Blakey')

Born in Birmingham, West Midlands in 1931, Garfield Morgan broke into acting in his early twenties on stage and would go on to appear on television and in films.

His long career as an actor began in the early 1950s. Stage roles came in Macbeth, The Master Builder, A View From The Bridge, The Lion In Love, Within Two Shadows and This Savage Parade. Morgan was also to direct stage shows in the late 1950s for the Marlowe Players repertory company at a time when his acting career began to take off.

On television he will be best remembered for his role as DCI Frank Haskins in the classic hard-hitting cop series The Sweeney from 1975 to 1978. Often cast as a police officer he appeared in hit dramas such as Softly Softly, Z Cars, Dixon Of Dock Green and The Bill. Other noted drama roles were plentiful beginning in the 1960s with credits in Coronation Street, Dr Finlay's Casebook, The Saint, The Baron, Man In A Suitcase, Public Eye, The Avengers, Hadleigh and Randall And Hopkirk (Deceased) to name but a few. The 70s brought him parts in Department S, Paul Temple, The Persuaders and Follyfoot amongst others. In the 1980s more drama roles came in Dick Turpin, The Gentle Touch and Boon. The tail end of his career saw him appear in hit series including Lovejoy, Dangerfield, Heartbeat, Bad Girls, Holby City and Doctors. Comedy roles came his way in The Likely Lads, Two In Clover, On The Buses, The Dick Emery Show, The Train Now Standing, The Morecambe And Wise Show, Keep It In The Family, Shelley, Hallelujah, You Must Be The Husband and Smith And Jones being the pick of them.

Although not so extensive his film career could boast credits such as A Prize Of Arms, Perfect Friday, Henry VIII And His Six Wives, Digby The Biggest Dog In The World, The Odessa File, George And Mildred, The Englishman Who Went Up A Hill And Came Down A Mountain and the award-winning 28 Weeks Later amongst others.

Away from acting Morgan kept active riding horses in equestrian events and was also a keen golfer. Late in life he was sadly struck down by cancer and passed away in 2009 at the age of seventy eight.

Morons

A derogatory term Inspector Blake often uses to describe Stan and Jack in several episodes and a spin-off film.

In one instance in the Series Four 'The Lodger', Stan and Jack are winding up the inspector in the canteen by labelling him Dracula. He snaps back saying: 'Why don't you two shut up? You're like a couple of morons.' In Holiday On The Buses, Blakey is in for a nasty shock when Stan reverses the tour bus into the camp gates as he clings to them. Angry and pained he yells: 'You morons!'

The term moron was to be derived from the ancient Greek word moros meaning dull or foolish and was created by an American psychologist Henry H Goddard at the beginning of the twentieth century. He used the term as a type of classification for a section of people with a low IQ with other classifications being termed idiots (the lowest on his scale) followed by imbeciles then morons.

Morrell, Juel

TV Role: Betty (Series 4 Episode 6 'The L Bus') and The Clippie (Series 4 Episode 10 'Safety First')

Born in Birkenhead, Merseyside in 1935, Juel Morrell came from a family with show business in its blood. She followed suit and would appear on stage from the early 1950s and make a handful of appearances on television.

On stage she had roles in the popular pantomime Cinderella in the mid-1950s and again in the mid-1960s. She would also appear in musicals Goody Two Shoes and Hello Dolly in the early 1960s respectively. Her television roles came most notably in two episodes of the hit sitcom On The Buses in the early 1970s. These followed roles in the drama United and in the popular children's series The Tingha And Tucker Club.

Morris, Aubrey

TV Role: Marriage Counsellor (Series 6 Episode 2 'Love Is What You Make It')

Aubrey Morris was born in Portsmouth, Hampshire in 1926 and has had a full and varied career as an actor that spanned over half a century on stage, television and in films.

He made his name on stage in the 1950s appearing in the West End in Julius Caesar and later in other stage shows such as Eastward Ho! Morris was soon bound for Broadway and in the late 1950s through to the early 60s had credits in King Richard II, Romeo And Juliet, Macbeth, Troilus And Cressida and The Hostage.

On the small screen he made his debut in 1958 in the classic drama Ivanhoe. Into the 1960s his most notable drama roles came in Espionage, No Hiding Place, Z Cars, The Saint, The Avengers, Danger Man, Softly Softly, Man In a Suitcase, The Prisoner and The Champions. The 1970s brought roles in Catweazle, The Sweeney, Space: 1999, Disraeli and Return Of The Saint amongst others. On into the 1980s his drama credits included Reilly: Ace Of Spies before moving to the United States to appear in hit series such as Outlaws, Beauty And The Beast, Murder She Wrote and War And Remembrance.

The latter part of his career saw him appear in Lovejoy in the UK but the States was where he flourished appearing in Alien Nation, Tales From The Crypt, Babylon 5, Columbo and Deadwood most notably. He was also to have credits in many of British television's best-loved comedy series including The Rag Trade, The Liver Birds, On The Buses, The Fenn Street Gang, Not On Your Nellie, The Hitch Hikers Guide To The Galaxy, Metal Mickey, Chance In A Million and Hot Metal.

His film career saw him amass an impressive list of credits. The best remembered being The Quare Fellow, The Great St Trinian's Train Robbery, Up The Junction, Blood From The Mummy's Tomb, the award-winning A Clockwork Orange, The Wicker Man, Man About The House, Bordello Of Blood, Red Roses And Petrol and Visioneers.

Aubrey Morris has lived in Los Angeles, California since the mid-1980s where he now enjoys his retirement.

Morris, S F and T

A turf accountant shop that features in the Series Six episode 'Private Hire'.

Amidst taking a bus out on tests Stan and Jack use it as a removal van to earn some money. When Jack persuades the gullible Stan to gamble his earnings on a horse racing tip they park their bus outside a back street bookmakers shop called S F and T Morris. Unaware to them Inspector Blake is on their trail and when they enter the bookmakers he pounces and drives the bus back to the depot. It means that not only do they lose their money in the bookmakers they exit to find they have lost their bus as well which leaves them both with some explaining to do to Blakey.

The bookmakers shop was an actual family business and was located in Barrett's Green Road, North Acton in London but ceased trading many years ago with the site being heavily redeveloped since. The same bookmakers shop can also be seen in an episode of another hit LWT sitcom called Please Sir.

Moses, Albert

TV Role: Alf (Series 7 Episode 12 'Friends In High Places')

Born in Sri Lanka in 1937, Albert Moses can boast an acting career on stage, television and in films spanning over more than forty years.

His stage credits came at the National Theatre in The Freeway in 1974 and a year later in Phaedra Britannica. He also appeared in Long March To Jerusalem in 1977.

On television Moses will be best remembered for his role as Indian student Ranjeet Singh in the controversial hit sitcom Mind Your Language. His other notable comedy roles came in classic series such as Doctor In Charge, On The Buses, The Two Ronnies, Robin's Nest, A Sharp Intake Of Breath, Don't Wait Up, The Benny Hill Show and Never The Twain. Drama roles were also plentiful and a selection of those came in hit series including Doctor Who, Shoestring, Angels, Tales Of The Unexpected, The Chinese Detective, Juliet Bravo, Jewel In The Crown, Minder, Tenko, Murder In Mind, The Bill and Holby City.

In his film career Moses was to have a wide range of roles. He appeared in the smash hit The Man Who Would Be King, Stand Up Virgin Soldiers, The Spy Who Loved Me, Carry On Emmannuelle, An American Werewolf In London, Pink Floyd The Wall, Octopussy and East Is East.

Moses has also worked as a producer on Mind Your Language and on the 2002 film Gabriella. Additionally, he is a published author and has also written scripts for television.

Moss, Stirling

A famous motor racing driver referred to by Stan and Jack in a couple of episodes of On The Buses.

Stan injures his toe whilst home decorating in the Series Four episode 'The Injury' and he has to wear a pair of Olive's plimsolls so that he can make it in to the depot as his shoes are too painful. When Inspector Blake objects to him wearing the footwear Stan protests: 'That Moss fellow, the racing driver, he always drove in his plimsolls.' However, the inspector replies: 'Stirling Moss wasn't driving a No 11 bus to the Cemetery Gates.' Later, in the Series Seven episode 'The Perfect Clippie', Stan grovels to Inspector Blake in order to get Olive a job as a clippie and promises to get his bus out on time. He rushes to his bus urging Jack to hurry and get the bus out. A stunned Jack says: 'Alright, alright Stirling Moss. What's the hurry?'

Stirling Moss was a famous motor racing driver of the 1950s and early 60s. Although he never won the coveted Formula One World Championship his talent was unquestionable and was to finish runner-up in the title race four times. He drove for illustrious teams such as Maserati and Daimler Benz winning sixteen races in his career. Moss was to be knighted in 2000 and is still an important figure to this day in motor racing.

Moss Stores

A grocery store that feature in the Series Two episode 'Family Flu'.

With the family bed-ridden with flu it is left to Stan to shop for the invalids. Whilst on duty and mid-route he parks his bus and dashes into Moss Stores where he buys groceries such as eggs, butter, yoghurt and frozen vegetables packing them in stringed shopping bags.

Moss Stores was a genuine grocery store located in North London which remained in business until the late 1970s.

Motor Bus

A new prototype bus (also known as an omnibus) that is brought in to the Luxton and District Bus Company to replace horse-drawn buses in Stan's dream of life in the 1920s in the Series Seven episode 'On The Omnibuses'.

The introduction of the motor bus brings with it a raft of emotions at the depot and at home. The concept of a horseless bus perplexes Stan and Jack whilst Inspector Blake sees it as a chance to increase both the frequency of the services and Stan and Jack's workload much to their horror. At home Mrs Butler is sceptical of the motor bus and says the vicar feels they are the invention of the devil. Stan though warms to the idea of being a kind of pioneer as he pictures himself being one of the first to drive the motor bus. The motor bus, which runs on petroleum and has a twenty horse power engine and a top speed of twenty miles per hour, is to meet an unpleasant end. It crashes into the general manager's car at which point Stan's dream is brought to an end when Inspector Blake wakes him up back in 1973.

Motorbike Accident

Arthur's motorbike and sidecar suffers an accident in the film Mutiny On The Buses.

When Olive breaks the starter lever off of Arthur's motorbike it leaves them stranded and Stan agrees to tow the bike home on the back of his bus. However, trouble brews as Arthur reports the steering on his bike going stiff as they are towed and the motorbike veers across to the other side of the road. The rope stretches across the width of the road and it knocks a man over who is painting lines on the centre of the road causing him to fall head first into a bucket of paint before the rope wraps around a traffic island cone which rips the handlebars off the motorbike. The motorbike, untethered and out of control gathers speed as it goes down a steep road. The runaway bike with a helpless Arthur aboard and Olive in the sidecar enters a workman's tent in the middle of the road before carrying on engulfed in the tent. Olive though is left behind stuck in an open manhole cover and an instant later the bike mounts a pavement and crashes into a telephone pole. As Stan and Jack rush to their assistance Olive is pushed up out of the manhole by a miffed workman who says: 'What do you think you are doing bunging up my hole?' Arthur meanwhile, is found with another workman sprawled across him in an uncompromising position. Fortunately, nobody is injured in the accident and the motorbike is soon repaired to be made barely roadworthy once more.

Motorcycle and Combination

Arthur purchases a second-hand motorcycle and combination in the Series Two episode 'The Used Combination' it soon becomes his pride and joy. The vehicle is to feature in a number of episodes and the spin-off films.

In 'The Used Combination', Arthur buys it intending to use it to get to work and shows it off to the family but earns him ridicule from Stan and Jack. It is in such poor condition that the seatbelt snaps off the bike and the bike fails to start and when Stan attempts to start it the starter lever breaks off. When Arthur boasts that the bike came with a toolkit he doesn't realise that it holds no more than an embarrassing assortment of odds and ends. It contains a bent knitting needle, a rusty safety pin, half a tube of dried up glue and rubber bands leaving Jack to joke that they now know what is holding the bike together. With Stan's help though the motorcycle and combination is soon repaired. Later, in the same episode, on its maiden journey with Arthur, mum in the sidecar and Olive riding pillion the bike breaks down after Olive takes a call of nature. Arthur can't restart the bike as the starter lever snaps off again but luckily Stan passes in his bus and tows the bike home. However, the handlebars are ripped off and Arthur, Olive and mum are left to push the bike home and end a disastrous maiden journey.

With the Butler family stumbling through another financial crisis in the Series Three episode 'The Squeeze', Arthur is persuaded to sell his beloved motorcycle and combination to raise cash. An advert is compiled by Stan and Arthur and it has to take into account the rusty bodywork and its other failings before it is placed on the notice board at the bus depot. The ad attracts the attention of a wag who writes at the bottom of it: 'Keep death off the road.' But Stan's cunning sees him draw interest in the bike from Inspector Blake who agrees to take a look at it. This sees the family work together to give the motorcycle and combination a makeover before Blakey sees it. The sidecar has checked tape placed over the rusty bodywork and gives it a sportier look. The bike's exhaust pipe gets attention from mum who scours it with toilet cleaner whilst Stan moves to temporarily cure the noisy engine. He pours a three-in-one mixture of one part oil and three parts sawdust into the bike's gearbox to complete the makeover leaving the engine purring sweetly. Before agreeing to buy the vehicle the inspector insists on a trip in it. With Stan driving, Jack on pillion and Inspector Blake in the sidecar the journey is to turn into a catalogue of disasters. Not long after leaving the depot the bike has black smoke pouring from the exhaust as the sawdust in the gearbox catches fire and moments later the sidecar becomes detached. Blakey is left trapped and livid as the sidecar door is jammed shut. Thankfully, Stan and Jack are able to bundle the sidecar onto a passing bus and on arriving back at the depot staff rush to free the inspector. A plethora of tools are used to try to free him before a pair of pliers do the trick. Of course the ordeal means the deal is off and the motorcycle and combination remains under the ownership of Arthur.

A further accident befalls the motorcycle and combination in the Series Four episode 'Nowhere To Go'. Aboard the bike is Arthur, Olive riding pillion and mum in the sidecar as they travel to visit Aunt Maud. The front wheel, earlier repaired by Stan and Jack, snaps off on a quiet country road and Arthur ends up in a ditch whilst Olive only suffers from a soaked jumper as a hot water bottle strapped to her waist, as she has a chill on her stomach, bursts. Mum is uninjured but Arthur is not as lucky as he is left concussed. It is to be a long trek home for them and their arrival ruins a planned night of passion for Stan, Jack and their dates.

The first spin-off film On The Buses sees Arthur take a pregnant Olive for a check-up at the hospital aboard the motorcycle and combination with Stan riding pillion. With the bike newly-fitted with bus springs it proves to be a bumpy ride which sends Olive into labour. Also to make matters worse the sidecar becomes loose and Stan has to improvise but the sidecar soon breaks away running into a hedge increasing Olive's discomfort. Luckily, a passing bus is flagged down allowing Arthur and Stan to put the sidecar on the bus re-routing it to the hospital. It averts a disaster as Olive gives birth to a baby boy hours later.

Motorcycle Cop

Played by Gavin Campbell

This policeman rides a motorbike and puts Inspector Blake in his place in the film On The Buses.

False diversion signs have re-routed a Town and District bus onto a motorway. As the inspector looks to reverse the bus back up the hard shoulder and off the motorway a policeman riding a motorbike in his late twenties pulls up alongside the bus. He tells the inspector he can't reverse the bus and they'll need to carry on until the next interchange twenty miles up the road but Blakey has other ideas and moves to reverse the bus anyway. However, he stops when the policeman warns him: 'Are you moving or do you want me to book you? Now get back on your bus and drive away.' The policeman gets his way and the bus departs on its long detour.

Mould, Janet

Played by Olivia Breeze

A dark-haired trainee clippie who is to be trained by Stan and Jack aboard the training bus but ends up being embroiled in their mischief in the Series Four episode 'The L Bus'.
Janet Mould, in her early thirties, is introduced to Stan and Jack by Inspector Blake who tells them: 'I want you to pay particular attention to this young lady. She's been training all the week and she's passing her final test

tomorrow morning.' However, they soon have her breaking rules as they use the training bus to deliver a second-hand bed to Arthur and Olive. Janet is forced to help and carries the bedding onto the bus taking it onto the upper deck but things become complicated when they are all caught in the act back at the depot by Blakey. He borrows Janet's ticket machine and gleefully sets about charging Stan several parcel tickets as a punishment for carrying the bed on the bus.

Mount Road

A fictional street name mentioned in connection with an emergency diversion in the Series Four episode 'Not Tonight'.

Mountains of Mourne

A factual range of mountains likened to the bust of an attractive Irish canteen cook Bridget by Jack in the film On The Buses.

As Stan flirts with Bridget, Jack pushes her so that Stan's head nestles in her cleavage before she rushes off. Jack tells Stan he was lucky he got lost in the mountains of Mourne.

The Mourne Mountains are to be found in County Down in the south-east of Northern Ireland. The beautiful rolling hills are home to a variety of wildlife and its terrain attracts hill walkers and rock climbers. The Mourne Mountains could also soon become Northern Ireland's first national park – apt indeed for such a beautiful stretch of countryside.

Mountbatten, Lord Louis

A famous and distinguished British statesman referred to in a couple of episodes of On The Buses.

The Series One episode 'The New Inspector' sees Stan take on the poisoned chalice of a role of inspector at the bus depot. He shows off his new uniform to the family and his mum feels he looks very distinctive just like Lord Louis Mountbatten. The other reference came in the Series Three episode 'The Snake' as Inspector Blake talks of his military service in the Second World War when he spent four years in India serving under Mountbatten.

Lord Louis Mountbatten, a distant relative of Queen Elizabeth II, was a popular statesman and much-decorated naval officer. He served in the Royal Navy from 1913-1965 and rose quickly up through the ranks to hold the highest commands during the Second Ward War such as Chief of Combined Operations and latterly Supreme Allied Commander (the South East Asia Command). He would serve in India from 1943-1948 and went on to become Viceroy of India (the last man to hold that post) and the Governor-General of India. Earl Mountbatten of India as he was also known) was a popular figure in the Royal Family and a big influence on Prince Charles but his life was to end in tragic circumstances. In 1979 he was assassinated when an IRA bomb exploded aboard his private fishing boat Shadow V killing him instantly. He was seventy nine.

Mukunda, Vemu

TV Role: Vina Player (Series 3 Episode 6 'The Snake')

Primarily, a talented Indian musician, Vemu Mukunda (credited as Makunda) only had one acting role and that came in an episode of On The Buses.

Born in India in 1929, Mukunda learnt music from an early age and was to go on to study atomic physics in

Glasgow, Scotland before working in the atomic industry for a short spell. Music remained his first love and he was to become a professional musician playing concerts in his native India and beyond on various instruments. He was seen as one of the first musicians from India to bring elements of jazz into his music and introduced an innovative method to his music which he called 'Nada Brahma Tone System'. He was to spread this music around the world with his concerts in the 1980s and 90s and also taught pupils this form of music. Sadly in 2000, in London at the age of seventy, Vemu Mukunda passed away but his musical legacy lives on.

Mullard, Arthur

Film Role: Wally Briggs (Holiday On The Buses)

Born in Islington, London in 1912, Arthur Mullard was to have a variety of careers in the military, was a dance hall bouncer, a rag-and-bone man and professional boxer before turning his hand to acting. He began as an extra and bit-part actor in films and went on to appear on television and had roles on stage.

His film career began in the late 1930s and was to bring a host of uncredited roles in films such as Oliver Twist, The Blue Lamp, The Lavender Hill Mob, The Man In The White Suit, The Pickwick Papers, The Belles Of St Trinian's, The Colditz Story, The Ladykillers and Dentist On The Job. Mullard's most notable film credits came in Two Way Stretch, Crooks Anonymous, Sparrows Can't Sing, The Great St Trinian's Train Robbery, Chitty Chitty Bang Bang, Crooks And Coronets, The Vault Of Horror, Holiday On The Buses and Adventures Of A Plumber's Mate.

The mid-1950s would signal the start of his television career in the hit drama The Vise. Drama roles were rare though with notable others coming in Emergency – Ward 10, The Troubleshooters and Churchill's People. Comedy was his forte and the gruff cockney's big break came in the late 1950s with several appearances in Hancock's Half Hour and the smash hit comedy The Army Game. These were soon followed in the 1960s with roles in It's a Square World, Citizen James, Sykes And A … and a range of comedy-based sketch and variety shows. His best remembered roles came in the Ronald Wolfe and Ronald Chesney penned 1970s sitcoms Romany Jones and its spin-off Yus My Dear where he played a vulgar cockney called Wally Briggs. Also in the 1970s other comedy roles came in Oh In Colour and Who Do You Do?

Thereafter his acting career petered out somewhat but he was to write his autobiography Oh Yus, It's Arthur Mullard in 1977. A year later he had an unlikely hit in the UK pop charts recording a spoof cover of a hit song from the musical Grease called 'You're The One That I want' with comedienne Hylda Baker that reached number twenty two in the charts.

Arthur Mullard was to pass away in 1995 at the age of eighty three.

Mullins, Bartlett

TV Role: Joe (Series 5 Episode 9 'Lost Property')

Bartlett Mullins was born in Crosby, Lancashire in 1904. As an actor he would break into films in the late 1940s and television in the early 1950s.

On the big screen his career began with a string of crime-based films such as The Three Weird Sisters, The Case Of Charles Peace, Wheel Of Fate and Eight O'Clock Walk. He would go on to appear in hit films such as The Quatermass Experiment, The Curse Of Frankenstein, Frankenstein Created Woman, Half A Sixpence and Tales From The Crypt.

A television career was to offer a variety of roles in drama and comedy. The pick of his drama roles came in Douglas Fairbanks Jnr Presents, Nicholas Nickleby, No Hiding Place, Danger Man, The Saint, Maigret, Dixon Of Dock Green, Doctor Who, Dr Finlay's Casebook, The Prisoner, Z Cars and Secret Army. He also had roles in children's series including Ace Of Wands and Worzel Gummidge. Mullins comedy credits were numerous with roles in 60s classics Bootsie And Snudge, The Likely Lads and Never Mind The Quality Feel The Width.

In the 1970s he would appear in more hit comedy series such as Hark At Barker, The Goodies, The Liver Birds, On The Buses, Steptoe And Son, Sez Les, Pardon My Genie, Doctor In Charge and Some Mothers Do 'Ave 'Em.

After a career spanning well over thirty years Mullins retired from acting in the early 1980s before passing away in 1992 at the age of eighty seven.

Mum's Medical Cures

Mrs Butler holds faith in a number of medical cures and treatment some of which are unconventional and are covered in a number of episodes of On The Buses.

When Stan starts coughing in the Series One episode 'The Early Shift', his mum tries to persuade him to take some creosote for it but he isn't keen as he feels it only gets rid of dry rot. Later, in the same episode, she gives Stan a bottle of cherry linctus medicine as he goes on picket duty which later gets smashed in his pocket. The following episode 'The New Conductor' sees mum embarrassing Stan in front of his date Iris by insisting he takes his bismuth medicine before he goes to bed much to his displeasure. In the Series Two episode 'Self Defence', Stan suffers a bump on the head which mum treats by applying a cold compress on it to reduce the swelling.

Later, in Series Two, in 'Bon Voyage', Stan packs for his works holiday in Spain. Mum is insistent he takes medicines such as enteric tablets to stop him getting 'the collywobbles' and a choline mixture in case the tablets don't work.

It is revealed in the Series Three episode 'First Aid' that mum treats burns by rubbing margarine on it. Her treatment for bruises in the Series Four episode 'Safety First' is to place raw meat on them such as Olive's bruised thigh. Mum can be seen treating Stan's injured big toe in the Series Four episode 'The Injury' by putting hot compresses on it as it swells up telling him they'll do the toe good.

Of these treatments creosote, which was used to treat coughs, has long since been replaced by more effective medicines that have been developed. Cherry linctus medicine is still prescribed to this day for those with chesty coughs. Bismuth, which mum insists Stan takes every night, is a medicine still used today to treat diarrhoea, heartburn and upset stomachs. Enteric tablets and choline medicine are still used to treat stomach-related ailments. As for treating burns by applying margarine, this treatment is totally ineffective and is nothing more than an old wives tale. Also the treating of bruises by placing raw meat on them is not recommended as doing so may cause infection. Cold compresses for bumps and hot compresses for bruised toes are suitable and recommended treatment for those injuries to this day.

Munitions Factory

A place of employment for Mrs Butler during World War Two as referred to in the Series Seven episode 'Friends In High Places'.

When amidst an interview for the post of canteen cook at the bus depot Mrs Butler tells Mr Simpson that she used to work in a munitions factory during the war where she made bullets. It turns out that Mr Simpson used to be a foreman in the same factory and remembers her and her late husband, Albert. Mr Simpson and Mrs Butler get on swimmingly well together and with her becoming employed at the depot the pair soon start dating.

Munro, Alex

Film Role: Patient (Holiday On The Buses)

Born in Shettleston, Glasgow in 1911, Alex Munro made his name as a comedian progressing on to stage and had a handful of sporadic roles on television and in films.

His stage career was to take off in the 1930s when he and his brother Archie formed an act and joined Florrie Forde's music hall company working alongside the legendary entertainers Flanagan and Allen. He would go on to appear in variety shows in top theatres around the UK and later was to settle in Llandudno, Wales where he took control of the Llandudno Pier Pavilion Theatre in the 1960s. His foresight transformed the theatre and he staged his own shows there appearing in Olde Time Music Hall amongst others. In 1972 he brought pantomime to his theatre for the first time with a production of Babes In The Wood in which he appeared. Munro continued churning out shows at the theatre until the mid-1980s when ill health ended his career.

On television he was to have small roles in the hit police drama Z Cars in the early 1960s. Towards the end of that decade came a further drama role in Mr Rose.

On the big screen he was to appear in a short comedy film called Them Nice Americans in the late 1950s with his only other film role coming with a small part in Holiday On The Buses.

Alex Munro fell ill in 1985 and passed away early in 1986 at the age of seventy four. However, he is still fondly remembered in Llandudno for his big contribution to entertainment in the town.

Munsters, The

A smash hit US sitcom referred to by Arthur in the Series One episode 'The Early Shift'.

After watching a news report on the television covering the bus strike which Stan appears in the driver is mocked by Arthur. When Stan boasts at least he has been on television Arthur replies dryly: 'So have the Munsters.'

The Munsters was a hit US sitcom about a family of friendly monsters living together in an eerie house. The CBS production ran for two long series with a total of seventy two episodes from 1964 until 1966. The series, starring Fred Gwynne, Al Lewis and Yvonne De Carlo, was a huge worldwide hit and became a cult series with a future spin-off film and series being made.

Museum

This is an attraction that two Swedish students are looking to reach when visiting the bus depot in the Series Three episode 'The New Uniforms'.

Ingrid and Birgit seek help from Inspector Blake as they ask him which bus they catch for the museum. He tells them: 'Number nine due out in three minutes. Get off at Ackers Street and you'll find it on the left facing on the right.'

Mutton Stew

A dish cooked by Olive that causes problems for the Butler household in the Series Five episode 'Stan's Uniform'.

When the drains get blocked in the Butler house it is up to Stan to unblock them. It proves to be a very messy job and he asks his mum what she has been putting down the sink. 'It might have happened when I threw away the last of Olive's mutton stew,' reveals mum. Stan is shocked and worries what the stew has done to their stomachs considering the effect it has had on the drains.

My Old Man's A Dustman

This hit 1960s song is sung by a number of children aboard Stan's bus in the Series Four episode 'The Kids Outing'.

As Stan drives a bus packed with mischievous school children on what is the depot's annual children's outing the unruly kids grow restless. They can be heard raucously singing 'My Old Man's A Dustman' as the bus makes its way down the street.

The song 'My Old Man's A Dustman' was a smash hit for the singer Lonnie Donegan who was also known as 'The King of Skiffle'. It reached number one in the UK charts in March 1960 where it remained for four weeks and the song was written by Lonnie Donegan who, along with Peter Buchanan and Beverley Thorn, also wrote its highly comical lyrics.

Mystery Tour

A tour aboard an open top bus organised by the holiday camp and attended by holidaymakers and off-duty staff that featured in the film Holiday On The Buses.

The mystery tour with Stan driving the bus turns into a rushed event as he has a date lined up with holidaymaker Mavis later in the day. The tour takes in a stop at a local beauty spot where Stan is already clock-watching and is keen to hurry the passengers back onto the bus. However, this proves difficult as Olive takes the opportunity to treat herself to candy floss and crisps from a shop whilst Inspector Blake is in no mood to be rushed either as he enjoys a day out with camp nurse, Joan. As Stan frets about being late for his date Jack comes up with a solution encouraging him to take a shortcut back to the holiday camp cutting eight miles off of the journey.

The journey proves to be a perilous one fraught with hazards. Firstly, the open top bus turns a bend at speed going under a low bridge which leaves Jack hanging over the edge of the bus on the upper deck. It is chaotic as Olive gets a face full of candy floss as the bus speeds along whilst Mrs Butler has her ice cream smeared across her face and her grandson Arthur's ice cream cone ends up on his nose. As the bus continues to race along a country lane lined by over-hanging trees the branches send passengers ducking for cover on the upper deck. These branches are left scattered throughout the bus which Jack discards. The perilous mystery tour ends when the bus arrives back at the holiday camp but Stan's haste is in vain as his date's mum is on hand to thwart him again.

National Bus Company

This is the bus company that is to take over the Luxton and District Bus Company in the Series Seven episode 'What The Stars Foretell'.

Inspector Blake breaks it to the staff that the Luxton and District Bus Company have been absorbed by the National Bus Company. He warns that there will be redundancies with trainees being top of the redundancy list and he jokes he'll also get rid of staff he can't stand. He also announces that some bus routes will be lost to other bus companies. The news brings unrest but fellow busmen at the National Bus Company are to go on strike until all Luxton and District staff members are reinstated much to Blakey's chagrin.

The National Bus Company was formed in 1969 in real life and remained in operation until privatisation in 1988. It was a company that was to own a number of regional bus companies across England and Wales including Eastern National who supplied the buses and depot used for the making of On The Buses. Privatisation signalled the end of an era and the National Bus Company was broken up with the regional bus companies it owned being either fragmented into smaller companies or reinstated as a privately-owned regional bus company.

National Health Service

The government-run health service was mocked in an episode and a spin-off film of On The Buses.

In the Series Five episode 'The Strain', Stan injures his back but can't afford time off work even though he is immobilised. His doctor tells him he can get a corset to protect his back on the national health but this is of no comfort to Stan who says: 'National Health? Blimey that would take six months.' The film On The Buses sees Olive set to visit a family planning clinic. Stan jokingly tells Jack that Arthur thinks she's going to get her contraceptive pills on the National Health. Jack laughs: 'Blimey no. Not unless you're under fifteen or over sixty five.' And Stan adds: 'God blimey trust the government eh? One way's illegal the other way's impossible.'

The National Health Service was launched in 1948 in the United Kingdom and promised free health care for every British citizen. It was introduced by the Labour government led by Clement Atlee and would grow to become an invaluable service that remains in place to the present day. Although it has been blighted by a lack of funding and over-worked staff plus long waiting lists it continues to deliver free health care though a few subtle changes in recent years have seen some funding coming from the private sector.

National Insurance

A payment made in addition to wages that Stan has to pay to Mrs Sharma in the Series One episode 'The Canteen'.

When Stan is forced to dismiss Mrs Sharma from her post as canteen cook after her cooking doesn't meet with the busmen's approval he has to work out her final wage packet. Amidst doing so her husband, who is also a busman, is present and he points out to Stan that she is entitled to National Insurance on top of a week's wages.

National Insurance contributions are taken from an employee's wages and these (depending on the amount of contributions made) entitle that employee to benefits should they lose their job. It was first introduced on a small scale in the United Kingdom as part of the National Insurance Act in 1911 before being expanded by Clement Atlee's Labour government in 1946. Today, after income tax, it is the second largest tax source in the United Kingdom.

National Service

This was a mandatory conscription into the armed forces that both Stan and Jack served and which is referred to in episodes and two spin-off films of On The Buses.

Stan's spell of national service is first referred to in the Series Six episode 'The Prize' as he volunteers to peel potatoes for his mum as he bids to win favour with her. Arthur scoffs: 'The last bit of spud-bashing you did must have been in Aldershot.' Stan hits back pointing out that at least he did his national service unlike Arthur who explains that he was turned down because of his flat feet. This cuts no ice with Stan who claims Arthur dodged national service as he was a coward. In the Series Seven episode 'The Football Match', Stan prepares for football training but finds that he can no longer fit into shorts he had worn during national service and he has to find another option.

Jack's time on national service was seemingly well-spent. In the film Mutiny On The Buses, Stan and Jack's lives are made more difficult when a radio control system is introduced to the buses. Jack moves to sabotage the radio in the control centre explaining to Stan that he was on radios when he did his national service. He retunes the circuits and it proves highly successful as the radio control system falls into chaos landing Inspector Blake in hot water with the police. In Holiday On The Buses a late night date out on the tour bus ends in disaster for Stan and Jack as the bus gets stuck in wet sand on a beach. Jack boasts he studied tides whilst on national service and that they'll find the tide has gone out by the morning and they will be able to retrieve the bus. It would seem he never studied them well enough as the tide has actually come in engulfing the bus in water and ensuring Stan and Jack are sacked.

In the United Kingdom national service was compulsory as the Second World War broke out. Men aged from eighteen to fifty one were called up during the war but it was scrapped when the war was won in 1945. Compulsory national service was reinstated in 1947 until 1960 when it was scrapped for the final time.

National Stray Cats and Dogs Home

A fictional charity that Inspector Blake runs a raffle in aid of in the Series Six episode 'The Prize'.

The national stray cat and dogs home is a charity that the inspector explains provides new homes for stray cats and dogs on a nationwide scale. In a bid to raise cash for the charity he, as local secretary, is selling raffle tickets but the draw turns into a fiasco.

Neame, Christopher

Production Designer (On The Buses and Mutiny On The Buses)

Born in 1942, Christopher Neame, who would go on to become a recognised producer in film and television, came from a family steeped in tradition in the film industry and was the only son of the noted film producer Ronald Neame.

Christopher Neame spent the formative years of his career at Hammer Films where he would work as a production manager from the late 1960s. His credits included Frankenstein Must Be Destroyed, On The Buses, Blood From The Mummy's Tomb, Mutiny On The Buses, Fear In The Night, Demons Of The Mind and Frankenstein And The Monster From Hell. From production manager he progressed on to work as a producer of films later in his career with credits such as Emily, Bellman And True and Feast Of July. Neame's television career began in the late 1970s and he worked on a string of hit series as producer. These included Danger UXB, mini-series The Flame Trees Of Thika, QED, The Irish RM and the award-winning drama Soldier Soldier in the early 1990s.

Also a talented writer he was to pen his autobiography Rungs On A Ladder in 2003 with follow-up books coming in 2004 and 2005. He retired and moved to live in the South of France with his wife. Sadly, he suffered an aneurysm in June 2011 and passed away at the age of sixty eight.

Needs, James

Film Editor (Holiday On The Buses)

James Needs was born in 1919 and went straight into film editing on leaving school in the mid-1930s. Spells at Islington Studios and Shepherd's Bush were followed by a move to work at Hammer Studios in 1949 where he remained until the end of his career in the mid-1970s.

As an editor he was to work on numerous films beginning in the late 1940s with films such as Snowbound and Boys In Brown. The pick of his credits from the 1950s included The Black Widow, The Saint's Return, The Quatermass Experiment, The Curse Of Frankenstein, Quatermass 2, Yesterday's Enemy and The Mummy. On into the 1960s and Needs edited films such as Never Take Sweets From Strangers, Watch It Sailor, The Devil Shop Pirates, The Witches and many more. The 1970s were to see his long career of forty years draw to a close with him editing The Vampire Lovers, Scars Of Dracula, Dr Jekyll And Sister Hyde, Dracula AD 1972, Love Thy Neighbour, Holiday On The Buses, Captain Kronos – Vampire Hunter and Frankenstein And The Monster From Hell. He was also to work on a host of other films in a slightly different capacity in his career.

Retirement came in the mid-1970s and he was to sadly pass away in 2003 at the age of eighty three.

Nelly

This is a bus cleaner that is seen briefly in the Series Five episode 'A Thin Time'.

A dark-haired woman in her early fifties wearing a headscarf, dirty cleaning overalls and carrying a mop and bucket prepares to clean buses. Inspector Blake tells her: 'Oh Nelly. Start on that row over there and work your way down.' She looks at him and pulls a face before moving off to begin her work. This was an uncredited role in this episode.

Nerve Medicine

An item Stan is ordered to get from the chemist for Olive by his mum in the Series Four episode 'Nowhere To Go'.

Arthur, Olive and mum have a motorbike accident and return with minor injuries. Olive is upset. With Stan, Jack and their dates arriving in the hope of a romantic night in they are shocked to find the family home. Mum tells Stan: 'You got to go down to the chemist and get some of Olive's nerve medicine. She's having one of her funny turns.'

Nerve medicine is still used in the present day to treat those suffering anxiety attacks and nervous disorders.

New Inspector

Played by Bob Todd

A new inspector replaces Inspector Blake at the end of the film Mutiny On The Buses and quickly riles Stan.

Inspector Blake is demoted in rank to conductor after a trial run to Windsor Safari Park ends in disaster and the Town and District Bus Company send a replacement from head office. He is a balding man in his fifties who has very similar mannerisms to his predecessor but appears to be even stricter. The new inspector doesn't take long to berate Stan. 'Come on you get that bus out. You're due out in two minutes you know the regulations you should be carrying out your checks,' he barks. When Stan tests how far he can push him by saying they don't bother with checks he is told to carry them out or he'll report him. He later displays another trait Stan doesn't like. As he chats up, who he believes is, his new clippie Gloria she is soon whisked away from him. The new inspector introduces him to his actual new conductor – Blakey. He leads Gloria away saying: 'Come on darling I'll buy you a cup of tea.'

New Uniforms

The Luxton and District Bus Company look to introduce new uniforms in a Series Three episode of the same name.

With new uniforms on their way Inspector Blake chooses the scruffiest busmen in the depot to wear the prototypes – Stan and Jack. However, they are far from impressed especially when they see the designs as the silver grey uniforms give the busmen a camp appearance. In receipt of their uniforms Stan and Jack take the chance to mock the uniforms as they make a makeshift catwalk in the canteen and model the prototypes in front of their highly-amused colleagues. It leaves Jack promising to take the matter up with the union as he believes they're supposed to look like busmen not Peruvian postmen. For Inspector Blake he is more concerned that they keep the uniforms clean especially when he sees Stan eating a plateful of spaghetti bolognese in the canteen whilst wearing the uniform. He goes to great lengths to protect it but his efforts are in vain and Stan and Jack decide to eat elsewhere.

Later though their opinions on the new uniforms change when they prove to be a hit with the women but their earlier complaints cause great negativity amongst the rest of the staff towards wearing them and this causes the company to shelve the idea. The experiment ends and with it Stan and Jack's relationships with two attractive young Swedish women who mistook them for airline pilots in their prototype uniforms.

Newbold, Valerie

TV Roles: Jenny (Series 1 Episode 5 'The New Inspector' and Series 1 Episode 7 'The Darts Match') and The Radio Girl (Series 3 Episode 8 'Radio Control')

As an actress Valerie Newbold has had a career that has seen her appear in hit television series and in a number of stage productions. Her career began on stage and she went on to have roles in 1960s stage shows such as Photo Finish, No No Nanette and Doctor In The House. Later in her career in the mid to late 1980s she also appeared in Beyond Reasonable Doubt. For Newbold her most notable television roles came with three appearances in the smash hit sitcom On The Buses in the late 1960s and early 1970s. These were preceded by drama roles in classic series Dr Finlay's Casebook and Nicholas Nickleby.

Newbold has remained within the acting profession for forty years and continues to work on stage.

Newby Street

A fictional street referred to by Stan in the Series Seven episode 'Olive's Divorce'.

Olive is set to appear at the divorce courts accompanied by her mother and brother Stan. The driver tells Blakey they'll travel by bus saying: 'We'll catch the 10.15 to Newby Street. That's the one that goes straight past the court.'

Nichols, Mr

Played by Campbell Singer

A middle-aged transport manager who becomes a lodger in the Butler house in the Series Four episode 'The Lodger'.

The moustachioed Mr Nichols arrives at the Luxton bus depot and is to spend a few months working there having arrived from central depot. As he needs somewhere to stay and the Butlers are amidst another financial crisis he is offered a room at the Butler house. Paying ten pounds a week for bed and breakfast and an evening meal in a room furnished with Stan's bed, wardrobe, rug and bedding. Mr Nichols arrival causes friction in the family. Nichols warms to Olive immediately but the family soon find he spends overly long spells in the bathroom which forces Stan and Arthur to shave in the living room. Their noses aren't put out for long though. The morning after his arrival Mr Nichols gets his breakfast delivered to his bedroom on a tray by Olive and he is to take advantage of her by pinching her bottom. She rushes out upset and mum is outraged by the new lodger's conduct and orders him to leave.

Night Bus

This is a bus that a desperate Stan promises Inspector Blake that he'll take out as he begs him to give Olive a job as a clippie in the Series Seven episode 'The Perfect Clippie'.

Night Duty

When Stan is placed on night duty by Inspector Blake in the Series Two episode 'Late Again' it ruins his love life and alters his lifestyle.

Night duty for Stan means dating a clippie called Doreen is out of the question as she is on duty whilst Stan sleeps and when she finishes his work is about to start. His eating habits are altered as well as he eats his main meal of steak and kidney pudding and washes it down with a glass of milk stout at breakfast time after returning home from work which doesn't go down well with Arthur who has to make do with a lightly boiled egg. When Stan visits Doreen's house after breakfast he is in for a shock. His best friend Jack has taken advantage of the situation by spending the night with Doreen and so Stan's budding relationship with her ends as do his run of night duty shifts.

Nightingale, Laura

Wardrobe Supervisor (Holiday On The Buses)

Laura Nightingale was to work in the wardrobe department throughout her film and television career at Elstree Studios. She would have long associations with famous production companies such as Hammer Films and ITC (Incorporated Television Company) in her career that spanned over four decades.

She began in films in the mid-1950s with credits in hit films such as Heaven Knows Mr Allison, Another Time Another Place, The Flesh And The Fiends, The Angry Silence, The Frightened City, A Kind Of Loving, Billy Budd, Billy Liar, Nothing But The Best, The Masque Of The Red Death and The Comedy Man. In 1970 she began working for Hammer Films with credits in horror films such as The Vampire Lovers, The Horror Of Frankenstein, Scars Of Dracula, Lust For A Vampire and To The Devil A Daughter. She also worked on Hammer's many comedy productions including Love Thy Neighbour, Holiday On The Buses, Man About The House, George And Mildred and Rising Damp. On television Nightingale's career began in the mid-1960s. She had credits in a number of classic ITC series through until the early 1980s. These included The Saint, The Baron, Gideon's Way, The Champions, Department S, Randall And Hopkirk (Deceased), The Adventurer and Hammer House Of Horror.

She was to retire in the mid-1980s after more than thirty years in the industry.

Nightingale, Michael

Film Role: Pilot (Mutiny On The Buses)

Born in Brighton, Sussex in 1922, Michael Nightingale came from a theatrical family. After a spell in the Royal Navy he took up acting beginning with repertory work on stage before progressing on to television and film roles. His parts were chiefly small owing to caring for his wife who suffered from multiple sclerosis however his acting credits were impressive.

His television career began in the early 1950s with noted drama roles in Douglas Fairbanks Jr Presents, No Hiding Place, The Scales Of Justice, Danger Man, The Prisoner, The Avengers, Journey To The Unknown, UFO and Cadfael. His biggest role in drama came in Dixon Of Dock Green where he played Detective Constable Jack Cotton in over twenty episodes in the early 1960s. In comedy Nightingale had roles in Nearest And Dearest, Raffles, The Two Ronnies, The Dick Emery Show, Don't Wait Up and Victoria Wood: As Seen On TV amongst others.

On the big screen he would appear in a total of thirteen Carry On films including Carry On Cowboy, Carry On Camping and Carry On Matron. Other notable film roles came in Ice-Cold In Alex, The Young Jacobites, Watch Your Stern, Raising The Wind, Sky West And Crooked, The Raging Moon, Bless This House, Mutiny On The Buses, Clegg and The Return Of The Pink Panther.

He continued acting until retiring in 1994 before sadly passing away in 1999 at the age of seventy six.

Noakes, Barry

Cameraman (Series 7 Episode 2 'The Perfect Clippie', Series 7 Episode 5 'The Football Match', Series 7 Episode 6 'On The Omnibuses' and Series 7 Episode 11 'The Allowance')

Barry Noakes was to work as a cameraman on a number of London Weekend Television series over a spell of thirteen years in his career.

His career began in the early 1970s with credits in drama series such as The Guardians, Within These Walls, Aquarius, Another Bouquet, Enemy At The Door and the award-winning mini-series Lillie. Noakes also worked on LWT comedies On The Buses, Just William and A Fine Romance. Other credits in his career came in cinematography where he worked on the hard-hitting drama The Professionals and the mid-1990s BBC comedy The Detectives.

Noakes moved on to work at a production company in London called The Shooting Crew in the early 1990s and has gone on to train potential cameramen of the future.

Nobby

Played by Terry Duggan

This is an employee in the maintenance department at the Town and District Bus Company who frequently comes to Stan's assistance in the film On The Buses.

Nobby who is in his early forties is to help Stan and Jack to confuse the women bus drivers as he creates a number of false diversion signs which they use to great effect. Although he is later unable to repair springs from Arthur's motorbike he gives Stan bus springs to use in their place but these prove troublesome. Nobby's final assistance comes later when he repairs and refurbishes baby equipment belonging to the Butler family for the impending arrival of Olive's first baby. He was indeed a very helpful colleague.

Nobby

Played by Norman Mitchell

This is a maintenance worker at the Luxton and District Bus Company depot who Stan turns to for help in a couple of episodes of On The Buses.

Nobby is in his fifties and shows a willingness to be corrupted in the Series Three episode 'Busmen's Perks'. Stan pops into the maintenance department to obtain a couple of tins of paint and brushes and finds Nobby most obliging and it only costs the canny driver the cost of two pints of bitter. The stocky maintenance man helps Stan to smuggle the paint out of the depot by hiding it beneath sand in the fire buckets.

Later though, when a spot check is carried out in the depot stores, Nobby is in a panic fearing they will discover the two missing tins of paint and demands five pounds from Stan to replace them leaving the driver with no choice but to pay up.

The Series Five episode 'Stan's Uniform' sees Stan visit the maintenance department in the hope of assistance when his new uniform gets covered in paint. However, Nobby can be of little help as he confesses he doesn't know much about paint and the painter has gone for a cup of tea. He offers Stan and Jack some hope when he gives them a pot of paint stripper for the uniform telling them: 'You paint it on with a brush. You leave it for thirty seconds and then it softens the paint right down.' The pair of desperate busmen leave the stripper on too long though and Stan's new uniform ends up being ripped to shreds and they are forced to look elsewhere for help.

Norman the Painter

Played by Terry Duggan

Norman is a painter from the maintenance department who can be seen painting over scratches on the side of Stan's bus in the Series Six episode 'Stan's Worst Day'.

When Stan's bus gets a little too close to the town hall and gets scratched it is up to Norman, a man in his early forties and wearing overalls, to paint over the scratches before Inspector Blake finds out. However, it proves to be to no avail as the inspector arrives on the scene to discover the damaged bus. Wearing his new uniform he warns Norman to watch where he's dripping the paint as the painter stands on a step ladder looking down at Blakey.

At that point Stan rushes onto the scene bumping into the inspector which sends him crashing into the step ladder, knocking Norman off and as he falls he spills cream-coloured paint all over the inspector's new uniform. Blakey is livid and as Stan and Jack look to remove the paint from his uniform, Norman is allowed to finish his job.

Norrish, Keith

TV Roles: Brian (Series 5 Episode 5 'The Epidemic'), George (Series 5 Episode 8 'The New Nurse' and Series 5 Episode 11 'The Strain) and Busman (Series 5 Episode 12 'The New Telly')

Although Keith Norrish's acting career was to span no more than a decade from the early 1970s until the early 1980s with solely television roles he was to appear in a number of iconic series.

Drama roles were to include Doomwatch, Spyder's Web and the smash hit science-fiction series Doctor Who and Blake's Seven as well as an uncredited role in Upstairs Downstairs. He was also to appear in classic sitcoms On The Buses and had uncredited roles in Porridge and Doctor On The Go.

North Thames Gas

This is a company that Stan has to visit to pay a long overdue bill in the Series Three episode 'Mum's Last Fling'.

Whilst on duty Stan takes the opportunity to pay the gas bill and parks his bus beside a parking meter outside a building with North Thames Gas emblazoned on it. He rushes into the building and is directed to take the lift by the commissionaire. It proves to be an expensive way to pay a bill as he has received two parking tickets from a traffic warden by the time he returns to his bus.

The North Thames Gas Board was a state-owned company which was established in 1949. It supplied gas to London and surrounding areas in the Home Counties for almost a quarter of a century. In 1973 the North Thames Gas Board was dissolved when the industry was restructured with the British Gas Corporation taking over when it came into being.

Notice

When Stan contemplates handing in his notice at the Luxton and District Bus Company he is advised not to by Jack in the Series Seven episode 'Goodbye Stan'.

Stan has lined up a new job in a car factory in the Midlands and is all set to hand in his notice. However, the cunning Jack advises his long-time friend to get Inspector Blake to sack him. 'Let him sack you. Look if you chuck in your notice now your money stops straight away, right? But if he sacks you he's got to give you a week's money in lieu of notice,' explains Jack. Stan takes this advice and sets about winding up Inspector Blake much to the driver's enjoyment. He labels his nemesis a 'fish-faced twit' which eventually earns him the sack. For an instant the inspector is delighted to have finally rid himself of Stan but when he is told the troublesome driver was planning to leave for another job in any case he realises he and the bus company has been conned one last time by Stan.

Notice Board

The company's notice board is to be found in the bus depot and its canteen and is where both the Luxton and District and Town and District Bus Companies attach many important and official announcements in the form of letters, in both the television series and spin-off films. The notice board is also the place to find less formal staff notices such as the advertising of depot social events and items for sale such as Arthur's motorbike as seen in the Series Three episode 'The Squeeze'.

Nuit D'Amour

A perfume that Iris puts on prior to her darts match in the canteen in the Series One episode 'The Darts Match'.

Iris is to use the perfume to distract Stan who she is competing against in a battle of the sexes darts match. On smelling the perfume Stan calls it smashing stuff and is told it is called Nuit D'Amour which translates into English as Night Of Love. It excites him and he believes it should get an X-certificate and wouldn't get sold to a girl of sixteen. However, his mum is less impressed as she feels the place reeks of the scent and is sure Iris must have been scrubbed down in it.

Nurse

Played by Nicolette Chaffey

This character comes to Inspector Blake's assistance in the film Mutiny On The Buses.

When a fire drill at the bus depot goes badly wrong with the inspector falling into a foam-filled inspection pit a nurse in full uniform is to help the stressed Blakey out of the pit and places him in a wheelchair. She wipes some of the foam from him but before she can treat his injuries an infuriated Mr Jenkins confronts Inspector Blake and in a rage pushes him in his wheelchair back into the pit much to the nurse's shock.

Nurse, The

Played by Catherine Kessler

This nurse is to assist the doctor during the bus company's staff medicals in the Series Six episode 'Bye Bye Blakey'.

An attractive young blonde-haired nurse in her twenties is to take Stan in to see the doctor and says that she will be assisting. Sheepishly, the driver says that he doesn't allow ladies in when he is taking his trousers off but she points out that she is a trained nurse. Jack butts in and his lecherous side comes out as he welcomes the nurse to have a look when it is his medical. The nurse, seeing Stan's shyness allows him to go in alone to see the doctor whilst she leaves the scene.

Nurse

Played by Ruth Kettlewell

An employee of the Luxton and District Bus Company who is in charge of the depot's nursery and is also to treat staff members during a flu epidemic.

The nurse is a rather rotund woman in her late fifties who is to run the newly-formed nursery at the depot in the Series Five episode 'The Nursery'. She has a bullying and bossy nature and makes life very uncomfortable for Inspector Blake as she berates him for not supplying enough baby oil, chastises him for waking the babies and demands he finds her an assistant to help her. She doesn't display a great love of babies as, when another one arrives in the nursery she barks: 'Oh no not another one.'

Stan and Jack don't escape her wrath either as she orders them to put up a cot as it is not her job to do that and tells them to get out once they have finished. She is a little more pleasant to her new helper Olive but still domineering until she exits on her lunch hour.

The battle-axe of a nurse reappears in another episode later in Series Five called 'The Epidemic'. She is to attempt to combat a flu epidemic sweeping through the depot by giving anti-flu injections to the staff. In her own ruthless style she injects Inspector Blake and other staff members and later treats the inspector as he shows flu symptoms. As he suffers in his office she takes his temperature whilst he inhales from a bowl of steaming hot water with a towel over his head. She is unsure whether he has the flu describing him as a borderline case but feels it may be a touch of bronchitis and prescribes inhalation to clear his tubes.

Even though suggesting he goes home his sense of duty sees him remain at work. However, moments later he gets agitated by Stan and tips his bowl of hot water over himself scalding his legs with the nurse on hand with some burn ointment. Stan jokes that Blakey should put the ointment on himself at which point he is ordered out of the office.

Nurse, The

Played by Patricia Shakesby

A nurse employed at the bus depot who rushes to Inspector Blake's aid in the Series Four episode 'The Injury'.

When Inspector Blake has an accident when going up a flight of stairs and injures his foot it is up to Jack and Stan to help lift him over to a bench. A young blonde nurse in full uniform rushes across to the seated inspector and in a broad Irish accent says: 'I saw what happened through the window. You must have hurt your foot.' She removes his boot and examines his foot telling him he has broken his big toe. Though in pain the inspector is relieved he has witnesses to the accident and looks forward to receiving accident pay from the company.

Nurse, The

Played by Gina Warwick

This is a hospital nurse who gives Inspector Blake a blanket bath in the Series Four episode 'Safety First'.

With the inspector hospitalised after he is injured when Stan reverses his bus into Blakey's office, a nurse is to treat him to a blanket bath. She tells Stan who, out of guilt, has decided to visit him with the rest of the family that the inspector is very feverish and suffering from severe shock. At which point a drooling Arthur whispers to Stan that he'd be suffering from shock if she'd given him a blanket bath. The nurse then removes the screens around Inspector Blake's bed telling him he has visitors before she leaves.

Nurse on Bus

Played by Ruth Kettlewell

This nurse is travelling aboard Stan's bus as a passenger who is to deliver a baby on the upper deck of the bus in the Series Three episode 'First Aid'.

When a woman goes into labour on the upper deck of Stan's bus in a country lane a woman in her late fifties comes downstairs to tell Stan and Jack that she thinks she can cope with it as she is a nurse. She asks for the first aid box which Jack opens handing her a pair of tweezers causing her to snap: 'I'm trying to deliver the woman's baby not pluck her eyebrows.' Taking the first aid box she insists that Stan assists her as he is a driver and will have a good firm grip. Despite Stan's reluctance she gets her way and they succeed in delivering the baby but it all proves a bit too much for Stan in the end and he promptly faints.

Nursery

A facility introduced to the depot by the Luxton and District Bus Company in the Series Five episode 'The Nursery'.

The brainchild of Inspector Blake he sees it as an opportunity for clippies with young babies to carry on working by dropping their children off in the nursery whilst they go out on duty. With a draconian nurse in charge and Olive as her assistant things soon go awry. As the nurse takes her lunch break, Olive is left in charge and soon breaks her glasses leaving her helpless and needing to return home for a replacement pair. It means a hungry Stan and Jack are left to mind the babies but instead they help themselves to a lunch of baby food and milk fresh from a baby's bottle only to be caught in the act by Inspector Blake who promises to make out a complete report about the incident.

It can be assumed that Olive was sacked as assistant but it is unknown what became of the nursery as it never features in another episode of On The Buses.

Nye, Pat

TV Role: Mrs Blake (Series 7 Episode 9 'The Visit')

Born in London in 1908, Pat Nye was to train at RADA (Royal Academy of Dramatic Art) and had a long and distinguished career as an actress on stage, in films and on television as well as going on to manage a number of theatres.

Nye's first break came on stage in the early 1930s in Autumn Crocus. She'd go on to appear in a wide array of stage roles in shows such as Gallows Glorious, Lady Audley's Secret, East Lynne, The Bells, The Silver King and the George Bernard Shaw play Caesar And Cleopatra. She was also to work as a theatre manageress at the Theatre Royal in Margate, the Park Theatre in Hanwell, London and the Pier Theatre in Lowestoft.

In the late 1940s her film career began with a role in Mr Perrin And Mr Traill. Other notable big screen appearances included Appointment With Venus, Street Corner and The Mirror Crack'd which was to be her final film role in 1980.

On television Nye's career started in the early 1950s and included parts in classic dramas such as No Hiding Place, Sergeant Cork, Z Cars, Upstairs Downstairs, Ace Of Wands and The Bill. From the late 1960s she was also to have credits in a string of hit sitcoms such as Please Sir, The Fenn Street Gang, On The Buses, Yus My Dear and Doctor On The Go.

Pat Nye, who was to receive a military OBE in 1946 for her work in the Second World War as Chief Officer of the Wrens, continued acting up until her death in 1994 at the age of eighty six.

Nymphy Norah

Played by Pat Ashton

A highly flirtatious clippie employed by the Town and District Bus Company who takes a shine to Arthur in the film Mutiny On The Buses.
Known widely as Nymphy Norah because of her saucy and openly flirtatious nature, Norah is a busty blonde-haired clippie in her thirties. She has been engaged five times but never been married and confesses to being susceptible to seduction after a few gins. As a clippie she is happy to torment Inspector Blake as she joins forces with her male colleagues to strip down to her bare essentials after he orders them to wear nothing but their uniforms as supplied by the company to work. It is a prank that causes great embarrassment to the inspector and brings a strong rebuke from the new depot manager Mr Jenkins.

She is a woman with a reputation for wearing out her drivers even more so than the job's demands and she sets her sights on Arthur when he is appointed as her driver. She insists it is his duty to escort her to the darts match event at the depot to which he gleefully accepts. However, it turns into a riotous event as Olive is in attendance with her mum. She jealously watches on as Arthur and Norah flirt with each other and the final straw comes as he buys Norah vodka and tonics whilst she is bought less expensive drinks. A full scale argument breaks out as insults are traded between Norah and Olive before a brawl ensues with hair being pulled and dresses being ripped. The fight is eventually broken up and the incident puts Norah off pursuing Arthur further and she soon turns her attentions to the depot manager Mr Jenkins. She spends late nights at the depot with him in his office as he helps himself to the company's petty cash to pamper her. However, this brief affair ends when Mr Jenkins is caught in the act by his wife and she sees he gets transferred to another depot. And so Norah experiences another failed relationship – the story of her life.

OBE

The OBE is a coveted honour that Jack refers to in the Series Three episode 'Brew It Yourself'.

A drunken Stan is ushered into the depot canteen by Jack who orders Chalkie to get 'the cure' and the West Indian busman returns with a large plateful of mashed potatoes in an attempt to sober Stan up. 'Thanks Chalkie I'll mention it to the Queen. You'll probably get the OBE,' says Jack.

The OBE (Officer of the Order of the British Empire) is an honour given by the ruling British monarch. It is awarded to those in both military and civil service and was established in 1917 during the reign of King George V. Since then many legendary British sportsmen and women, actors and actresses and other leading figures have been bestowed with the honour some of whom would go on to be knighted.

Odeon, The

This is a cinema that Jack plans to meet Sandra at in the Series Seven episode 'The Poster'.

As Jack and Stan look to buy goods for the driver's makeover in a chemist shop the toothy conductor leaves in a hurry saying: 'I promised I'd meet Sandra at half past five outside the Odeon.'

Oh Calcutta

A popular stage show referred to in the Series Six episode 'Bye Bye Blakey'.

As a number of topless busmen sit waiting to have their medical examinations at the depot Jack likens it to a butcher's shop. Stan though describes the scene before him as the depot's answer to Oh Calcutta.

Oh Calcutta is a controversial avant-garde musical stage show which debuted on Broadway in 1969 and London's West End in 1970. Written by British writer Kenneth Tynan it courts controversy as it features fully nude male and female characters in a series of sketches covering subjects of a sexual nature. Despite the subject matter the show was to be a hit and has since had a number of revival runs around the world and it remains one of the longest running revue shows in Broadway's history. Coincidentally, On The Buses star Bob Grant was to appear in Oh Calcutta touring the UK in the show in the early 1980s.

Oh My Darling Clementine

This song is sung by holidaymakers aboard Stan's bus on the way back to the holiday camp in the film Holiday On The Buses.

As Stan speeds along a tree-lined country lane in his bus during the mystery tour passengers on the upper deck take part in a sing-song. A man standing at the front of the bus can be seen encouraging the holidaymakers to join in the singing of 'Oh My Darling Clementine'.

The song 'Oh My Darling Clementine' was written in 1884 and is an old western folk ballad popular in the USA. It tells the tale of a man's love for the daughter of a gold miner who sadly dies. The song has remained popular with it even being covered by pop idol Bobby Darin in the early 1960s which peaked at number eight in the UK charts.

Old Folks Outing

An event organised by the Luxton and District Bus Company that features in the Series Six episode 'Private Hire'.

The old folks outing to the seaside is in danger of being cancelled as the busmen are amidst a ban on overtime. However, Stan's dire financial difficulties force him into a desperate act that ensures the outing goes ahead. He and Jack sneak into the depot on a Sunday morning intending to use a coach belonging to the company without permission for the old folks outing earning money in the process. However, they don't count on Inspector Blake being on duty and with the pensioners aboard the coach he pops out from his hiding place – the boot of the coach to catch Stan and Jack in the act. He gleefully tells them that this incident will mean instant dismissal but the quick thinking Jack insists Stan was hiring the coach as permitted in the company's regulations. It saves them their jobs but leaves Stan back in dire financial straits as he has to pay the inspector for the hiring of the coach.

Old Gentleman

Played by Geoffrey Denton

This is a kind elderly passenger who shows consideration for Olive's well-being in the Series One episode 'Olive Takes A Trip'.

As Olive struggles through her first shift as a clippie for the Luxton and District Bus Company falling ill with travel sickness aboard the bus a well-spoken man in his late fifties, who is one of her passengers, offers his assistance. With the bus at a standstill he offers to fetch a glass of water for her from a nearby café claiming she'll feel a lot better for it. He returns a few moments later with a cup of tea for Olive before he departs the bus for the last time.

Old Lady

Played by Lucy Griffiths

This elderly passenger is to attack Inspector Blake angrily in the Series Seven episode 'On The Omnibuses'.

The old lady, who is in her early fifties, is seated aboard an antique bus that is no longer in service and part of a centenary exhibition at the depot. She asks Inspector Blake what time the bus leaves for Southend but is told that particular bus doesn't go there anymore and the bus she was waiting for left five minutes earlier. She is far from happy as she had been waiting all morning for the bus and when he laughs at her naivety the old lady rushes off the bus saying it's no laughing matter and hits the stunned inspector on the back with her umbrella before she hurries away.

Old Time Dancing

A style of dancing that features in the film Holiday On The Buses when Chief of Security Inspector Blake gives dance lessons and assembles a team to perform an exhibition of old time dancing at the holiday camp's ballroom.

The types of dance that falls into the category of old time dancing includes popular dances such as the military two step, the Gay Gordon, the waltz and the polka. Old time dancing is performed in ballrooms and has been a popular form of dancing since the early 1900s.

Old Woman

Played by Hilda Barry

This is an old age pensioner who is not satisfied with the Town and District's bus service in the film On The Buses.

The old woman is unfortunate enough to be aboard a bus diverted onto a motorway and arrives back at the depot two hours late. She gets off the bus and moans to the inspector: 'I've been three hours on this bus and I only wanted to go to Tesco's.' Blakey is embarrassed and apologises saying: 'Sorry madam but hurry along you'll find its still open.'

Old 666

A bus in a dilapidated state that Stan and Jack are ordered to take out to train two clippies in the Series Six episode 'No Smoke Without Fire'.

The bus in question, called 'Old 666' by Inspector Blake as that is the license plate of the bus, is in no fit state to be on the road according to Stan. He describes it as an old wreck that is only fit for the breakers yard and moans to Jack about its condition. However, Jack persuades him to take the bus out seeing it as the perfect opportunity to better acquaint themselves with two attractive clippies that they have to train.

Sadly, it proves to be the final journey for 'Old 666' as disaster strikes and Inspector Blake's life is put in danger.

Olive Courts Arthur

The chaotic and one-sided courtship of Olive and Arthur features in the Series Six episode 'Stan's Worst Day'.

In flashbacks to the early 1960s, Arthur is seen arriving in the Butler household for the first time as a hospital porter and is to lodge with the Butlers. Before long Mrs Butler acts as a matchmaker encouraging Olive to pursue Arthur insisting that they are made for each other and offers her naïve daughter advice before a planned candlelit meal for the couple. 'Well let him do the talking and then steer the conversation round to weddings, marriage and such-like,' mum says to Olive. However, the romantic meal fails to happen as Stan, Jack, Blakey and Arthur arrive home with two crates of beer to celebrate the promotion to inspector for Blakey.

Later that night a half-asleep Arthur is to make a big mistake when he returns from the toilet and gets into bed with Olive. His mistake is discovered by Mrs Butler who labels him 'a filthy swine' and gives him an ultimatum. She promises him he cannot pop in and out of bed with Olive just like that and feels Arthur now has to marry Olive. Whilst Arthur is stunned at the predicament he finds himself in Olive pleads: 'Oh Arthur say yes. It'd make me ever so happy.' As the flashback fades the rest is history as Arthur and Olive go on to get married.

Olive's Cooking

The cooking of Olive's is woefully bad and is to feature in a number of episodes and the film On The Buses.

On the small screen amongst her most notable culinary disasters are a stew that Stan jokes you need a hammer and chisel to eat it, a cake she bakes for Aunt Maud's birthday that ends up looking more like porridge to Arthur and silverside of beef which is deemed inedible when Olive needlessly adds salt to it.

In the first spin-off film she displays a distinct lack of cooking skills as she takes on the job of canteen cook in the

269

bus depot. She not only melts a saucepan but also badly burns a beef joint. Meanwhile, at home she cooks an unappetising stew and as Stan observes it he feels sure he will gain a lot more overtime with Olive cooking at the depot as bus crews will be off with food poisoning. She points out that he'll be ill as well but Stan claims he's been eating her grub for years and had become immune to it.

Olive's Clippie Career

Olive was to work as a clippie in two separate stints for the Luxton and District Bus Company each with varying degrees of success.

Her first stint as a clippie came late in 1969 in the Series One episode 'Olive Takes A Trip'. Much to Stan's discomfort she takes on a job alongside him at the bus depot but it soon becomes painfully clear that the job is not for her.

Placed under the watching and unsympathetic eyes of Stan she takes an instant dislike to the smell of diesel from the bus engine. Worse is to follow when minutes into her first journey she is felled by travel sickness rendering her useless. Clearly she is unsuited to the job and in a bid to prevent Olive being sacked Stan uses his guile telling the inspector that Olive is pregnant hence her illness and so she is released after less than a day in the job.

Three and a half years later a divorced Olive, now taking pills for her travel sickness, is forced into returning to work as a clippie with the family amidst another financial crisis.

The Series Seven episode 'The Perfect Clippie' sees her make an immediate impact with staff at the Luxton and District Bus Company. She irritates Stan and Jack as she trains aboard their bus as she quotes them the rules and regulations from the company's rule book whenever they err in their duty. This sees her being labelled a traitor when she reports their failings to the inspector who in turn commends her as a model clippie. She soon settles down in the post but is threatened with redundancy in the Series Seven episode 'What The Stars Foretell'. The bus company is absorbed by a rival bus company and redundancies are to be carried out with Olive on the redundancy list. However, her job is saved as strike action causes a rethink on the redundancy front. Olive remains in employment as a clippie until she moves on to later work in a clothing factory as featured in the late 1970s revival of the hit sitcom The Rag Trade.

Olive's Nightie

A garment Olive is seen in on many occasions in many episodes and the spin-off films of On The Buses.

A turquoise-coloured nightie that she was frequently seen wearing was of a babydoll design. These type of nightgowns came into fashion in the 1930s and became known as 'babydolls' in 1956 after actress Carroll Baker wore the garment in a film called 'Baby Doll'. They were at the height of their popularity in the 1960s and 70s but remain popular to the present day with women of varying age groups.

Olive's Transformation

In a bid to make herself more attractive to her husband Olive undergoes a makeover in the Series Six episode 'Love Is What You Make It'.

As her marriage is in danger of breaking up she seeks advice from a marriage guidance counsellor who suggests she makes herself more appealing to her disinterested husband. She dispenses with her spectacles, dons a new dress, wears perfume and restyles her hair. However, instead of compliments all poor Olive gets are insults. Arthur laughs hurtfully on seeing the new look Olive and tells her: 'I defy any man to fancy you dressed up like a dog's dinner like that.' He walks out on their candlelit dinner leaving Olive to rue having made an effort.

Omnibus

A new prototype motor-powered bus introduced to the Luxton and District Bus Company's fleet in the early 1920s that features in the Series Seven episode 'On The Omnibuses'.

Onassis, Aristotle

A famous Greek shipping tycoon referred to by Stan in the Series Four episode 'The Canteen Girl'.

Inspector Blake's relationship with a young canteen cook called Molly is mocked by Jack and Stan. Jack can't understand young women who date older men but Stan explains: 'It's all the rage these days innit. Well it's Jacqueline Kennedy and Onassis all over again.'

Aristotle Onassis, a rich shipping magnate, was born in Karatass (then a part of Greece) in 1906 and would go on to marry the widow of the assassinated US president John F Kennedy, Jacqueline Kennedy in 1968. He was twenty three years older than her and remained married for seven years until Onassis' death in 1975 amidst thier divorce.

Operation

A long running gag that runs throughout the television series and the spin-off films centres on an operation that Arthur has shortly before marrying Olive.

The operation, which Arthur has to wait eight months for is carried out at St Mary's Hospital. Although it is never revealed what the operation was it is often to cause Arthur great embarrassment and is frequently hinted at as affecting his ability to perform sexually. This is backed up in the Series Two episode 'Aunt Maud' when Aunt Maud queries why he and Olive have no kids and the conversation turns to his operation with Maud feeling that it hasn't done him any good. Later, in the Series Five episode 'Boxing Day Social' it is suggested that something was removed in the operation. As Arthur's mum scoffs that Olive and Stan have something missing from their lives with Olive having no children and Stan having no wife, Stan hits back. 'You're right love there is something missing but you're overlooking one fact. It wasn't me that had the operation, it was him,' says Stan pointing to Arthur.

It is hinted that surgery was involved in the operation in the Series Four episode 'Christmas Duty'. When Arthur holds the Christmas turkey as mum stitches it up Stan jokes: 'That reminds me Arthur. How's your operation?' Another hint is made in a later Series Four episode called 'The Injury' regarding the area of the body operated on. As Stan repositions the shower over the bath Arthur objects as it means he'll have to sit on the plug whilst having a bath. Stan teases him saying: 'No I forgot that would affect your operation wouldn't it?' Olive is puzzled but Stan explains that a shocking draft comes up through the overflow pipe.

In the film Mutiny On The Buses it is suggested that the operation was to clear an obstruction. When mum ridicules Arthur's snoring she feels he must have an obstruction up his nose which he denies. 'Oh come off it mate. What about your operation?' asks Stan. 'Oh that obstruction wasn't up his nose,' says Olive without elaborating on where the obstruction was.

Arthur's operation remained a mystery and was left open to one's imagination which helped to increase the comedic potential of what was On The Buses longest running gag.

Oulton, Brian

Film Role: Manager (On The Buses)

Born in Liverpool, Merseyside in 1908, Brian Oulton trained at RADA before going on to have a long career as an actor on stage, films and television that spanned over fifty years.

He debuted on stage in the early 1930s and that decade brought roles in We Were Dancing, Viceroy Sarah and Peril At End House amongst others before he was called up for military service in World War Two. After the war and repertory roles he'd go on to have West End roles in the 1950s and 60s in The Castle Spectre, All In The Family, National Health and The Travails Of Sancho Panza. Other notable theatre roles later in his career included The Man With Expensive Tastes, The Lovers and The Thunderbolt.

The late 1930s saw Oulton debut in films and he went on to appear in a handful of the classic Carry On films such as Carry On Nurse, Carry On Constable, Carry On Cleo and Carry On Camping. He'd also have roles in noted films such as Last Holiday, The Million Pound Note, Doctor In The House, Brothers In Law, The Silent Enemy, The 39 Steps, I'm Alright Jack, The Bulldog Breed, The Kiss Of The Vampire, The Intelligence Men, On The Buses, Gandhi and Young Sherlock Holmes.

His television career offered a plethora of roles in both classic British dramas and sitcoms. Drama roles came in a number of smash hit ITC series such as The Adventures of Robin Hood, The Saint, The Avengers, Department S, Randall And Hopkirk (Deceased) and Jason King. Other notable dramas he appeared in included Emergency – Ward 10, No Hiding Place, Coronation Street, Softly Softly, The Adventures Of Black Beauty, Crown Court, The Old Curiosity Shop and Brideshead Revisited. In comedy roles he had credits in Hancock's Half Hour, Citizen James, The Rag Trade, Steptoe And Son, Meet The Wife, George And The Dragon, The Dick Emery Show, Doctor At Large, Father Dear Father, Just William and The Young Ones amongst others.

Late in his life he turned his attention to writing plays and directing stage shows before he passed away in 1992 at the age of eighty four.

Overtime

In times of financial hardship busmen would go to any lengths to get overtime and increase their weekly wage. Stan and Jack's bids for overtime were covered in both episodes and spin-off films of On The Buses.

In the Series Five episode 'The Epidemic', as flu sweeps through the depot leaving many bus crews off sick, Inspector Blake announces that anti-flu injections are to be given to those that are fit and they will receive all the overtime they want. Stan and Jack are eager for the injections as it means they'll earn a very lucrative wage at the end of the week – thanks to overtime.

The introduction of women bus drivers to the Town and District Bus Company in the film On The Buses means Stan and his fellow male drivers will lose their overtime shifts. It infuriates them but Jack, as shop steward, is powerless to help even after taking the matter to the very top with the union as nothing can be done as it would be seen as sexual discrimination. The need for overtime is so desperate that Stan and Jack resort to a campaign of dirty tricks against the women drivers in a bid to discredit them so much so that there is a rethink in company policy and Stan and his colleagues get their way with the women drivers being dispensed with which means they get their overtime back.

Overtime Ban

When bus crews at the Luxton and District Bus Company undertake an overtime ban it threatens to force a cancellation of an old folks outing in the Series Six episode 'Private Hire'.

Bus crews launch a bid to get a pay rise by exerting pressure on the management by refusing to do any overtime. This means that an old folks outing to the seaside will have no bus crews available to operate it and so it looks set to be cancelled until Stan and Jack attempt to take advantage of the situation.

P

Page, Katherine

TV Role: Woman Passenger (Series 3 Episode 9 'Foggy Night')

Katherine Page was born in Glasgow, Scotland in 1908 and broke into acting on stage in the early 1930s and was a trained singer before a career in films and finally television eventually followed.

The 1950s brought small parts in films such as Women Of Twilight, The Intimate Stranger and the Oscar-winning film Room At The Top. She went on to have larger roles in 1960's films Identity Unknown, Gaolbreak and Design For Loving with her career thereafter being dominated by roles on the small screen.

Page, who was most active on television, appeared in a wide range of hit drama and comedy series from the late 1950s through until 2000. Her most notable drama roles included parts in The Vise, Dixon Of Dock Green, Richard The Lionheart, Z Cars, No Hiding Place, Dr Finlay's Casebook, Target, Juliet Bravo, The Citadel, Bleak House, All Creatures Great And Small and The Bill. She was also to appear in a string of hit sitcoms from the 1970s onwards such as On The Buses, Sorry, Don't Wait Up, Only Fools And Horses, One Foot In The Grave, If You See God Tell Him, Dinnerladies and Coupling.

Katherine Page carried on acting into her nineties before passing away in 2002 at the age of ninety four.

Paint Shop

An area in the bus depot referred to in the Series Six episode 'No Smoke Without Fire'.

In an unfortunate incident the paint shop in the depot was set fire to by an employee smoking and then discarded his cigarette in a can of paint thinner. A fire was to break out and was in danger of spreading to the rest of the depot until Inspector Blake put out the fire. Determined to avoid a repeat of the incident he bans smoking by all staff whilst on duty and places all staff on a fire fighting course.

Pak –A –Pet

This was a pet delivery service that features in the Series Four episode 'The Anniversary'.

When Olive and Arthur receive an anniversary present in the post via British Rail from Aunt Maud it is delivered in a box emblazoned with the company logo Pak-A-Pet. Inside is a pet poodle which Olive decides to call Scruffy but trouble lies ahead as Arthur finds the new addition to the family a nuisance.

Pallo, Jackie

This is a famous British wrestler of the 1950s, 60s and 70s who Stan likens to Arthur in the Series Six episode 'Love Is What You Make It'.

After what sounds like a violent confrontation between Olive and Arthur in their bedroom with Olive yelling in pain the couple arrive downstairs for breakfast. As Arthur walks in Stan sneers: 'Oh here he comes – Jackie Pallo without hair.'

Jackie Pallo was a professional wrestler who was one of the leading figures in British wrestling when it was at the height of its popularity in the 1960s and 70s. Famed for his long, flowing hair tied into a ponytail, Pallo would also go on to become known as 'Mr TV' as he appeared in hit television series such as Emergency – Ward 10, The Avengers, This Is Your Life and Are You Being Served? On retiring from wrestling he went on to write a revealing autobiography in 1985 which confirmed what many had suspected that wrestling was fixed with each bout carefully staged.

Jackie Pallo, a cousin of ITV's famous boxing commentator Reg Gutteridge, was to lose a fight against cancer and passed away in 2006 at the age of eighty.

Parcel Ticket

Inspector Blake issues Stan with a parcel ticket for using a company bus to deliver a bed without permission to Arthur and Olive in the Series Four episode 'The L Bus'.

When the inspector discovers that, instead of training staff, Stan has been using the training bus as a delivery van he is set to report the incident to the general manager. Jack steps in saying: 'We're allowed to carry parcels on that bus it's in the regulations. We were just showing the clippies how to handle big parcels.' Blakey is not impressed and insists he'll have to issue Stan with a parcel ticket. This shocks Stan who points out that they have got free passes so shouldn't be charged but it cuts no ice with the inspector. He proceeds to reel off a number of parcel tickets on a ticket machine and gleefully increases the charge as more items of the bed are revealed as being on the bus. It turns out to be an expensive mistake by Stan.

Parkinson, Robin

TV Role: The Vicar (Series 5 Episode 3 'The Best Man')

Born in Coventry, West Midlands in 1929, Robin Parkinson trained to become an actor in Birmingham and he would build a career on stage, television and in films.

His stage credits include an array of roles in shows such as Long Day's Journey Into Night, The Hero Rises Up and The Sea. He also had a string of appearances in London's West End in Close The Coalhouse Door, Stop It Whoever You Are, Shut Your Eyes And Think Of England and the stage adaption of the hit sitcom 'Allo 'Allo.

Parkinson's television career began in the late 1950s and was to include roles in both drama and comedy. In drama he appeared in Crossroads, Sherlock Holmes, Out Of The Unknown, Softly Softly, Z Cars, The Tomorrow People, Van der Valk, The Professionals, Juliet Bravo, QED and The Bill amongst others. His best remembered role came as Ernest Leclerc in the hit sitcom 'Allo 'Allo and he also had roles in many of Britain's best comedy series of the 1970s, 80s and 90s. These included On The Buses, The Dick Emery Show, Whatever Happened To The Likely Lads, Dad's Army, Rising Damp, Bless This House, Terry And June, It 'Ain't Half Hot Mum, The Young Ones, Hi-de-Hi and The Brittas Empire.

On the big screen Parkinson's roles included appearances in Billy Liar, The Family Way, Twisted Nerve, Alfie Darling, George And Mildred and The Asylum.

Robin Parkinson continued in acting into his late seventies before finally retiring after more than fifty years in the trade.

Parlour

This room in the Butler house is referred to and seen in a handful of episodes of On The Buses.

The parlour, a front room downstairs in the Butler house is to be the room in which Stan sleeps in when clippie Edna becomes a lodger in the Series Three episode 'On The Make'. It is also to be the room that bridegroom-to-be Bill is to sleep in on the eve of his wedding in the Series Five episode 'The Best Man'. When Bill collapses drunk at the Butler house Stan is concerned about how he's going to get him to the church on time as he is drunk himself. He tells Jack: 'The way I feel I'll be lucky to get him into the parlour tonight.' The parlour is seen for the first time in the Series Six episode 'Love Is What You Make It' when Olive tries to impress Arthur with her makeover and prepares a candlelit dinner for him. When he comes home from work in search of his dinner he is forced into the front room by mum and Stan who tell him: 'No no it's in the parlour,' before holding the door shut so he can't escape. The parlour features in the later Series Six episode 'Stan's Worst Day' when Stan, Jack, Arthur and Blakey bring two crates of beer home to celebrate Blakey's promotion to inspector in a flashback scene to the early 1960s.

Parson

Played by David Rowlands

A man of the cloth gets more than he bargained for on the upper deck of a Town and District bus in the first spin-off film On The Buses.

As he reads a bible on the upper deck he looks out of the window of the stationery bus to see Peggy, a well-built woman bus driver, relieving herself behind a bush on a country lane. A startled expression comes across the parson's face whilst Peggy is equally shocked to see she has an audience.

Party Political Broadcast

A type of short television broadcast referred to in the Series Six episode 'The Prize'.

A party political broadcast sees Arthur switching off the television saying: 'Well I think we've heard enough of that rubbish.' For once Stan is in agreement with his brother-in-law adding: 'You can say that again mate.' When mum asks what's on the other channel she is told by Arthur: 'A party political broadcast.' Stan explains that politicians feel the need to bore all viewers with their broadcasts.

Party political broadcasts were first heard on radio in the UK in 1924. It was not until 1951 that the Liberal Party held the first party political broadcast on BBC Television for that year's general election. Although it was a fiasco as it came across as poorly organised these broadcasts have become a permanent part of British television schedules. Despite negativity towards these brief broadcasts from the majority of the viewing public they remain an important advertising tool for the political parties across Britain.

Passenger, The

Played by Terry Duggan

The passenger is a well-dressed man with a large dog who boards Stan's bus at the depot in the Series Four episode 'The Anniversary'.

The man in his late thirties boards Stan's bus with his Great Dane dog and is shortly to be followed by Olive with her new pet poodle Scruffy. Moments later a fight between the two dogs breaks out and Jack exits the bus insisting that, according to the rule book, it is the inspector's job to settle disputes. When Olive calls for help, Inspector

Blake boards the bus but is to be attacked by Scruffy and he limps back off the bus seconds later. The passenger with his dog follows and is clearly unhappy as he pets his dog and snarls: 'Come on. Let's get off this bus.' He marches off leaving the inspector to examine his bitten leg.

Pat

Played by Clare Sutcliffe

Pat is a diminutive clippie bubbling with energy who forces Stan into a rethink on his own personal fitness in the Series Four episode 'Dangerous Driving'.

She is a fair-haired clippie in her twenties who lines up a date with Stan. She has a great aptitude for dancing and demonstrates the latest dance craze to Stan in the canteen which he struggles to keep up with. With the date looming at a new dance club and younger talent waiting in the wings to date Pat it forces Stan into getting fit and going on a strict diet. Later, as Stan contemplates giving up the diet, he has a rethink when Pat invites Stan back to her house after their date as her mother is away. Sadly though, it is only to be a short-term relationship between Stan and Pat.

Patient

Played by Alex Munro

A patient who is almost a part of the furniture in the nurse's waiting room at the holiday camp in the film Holiday On The Buses.

The patient is a Scottish man in his early sixties who wears a bunnet and raincoat. He waits to see the nurse but Jack comes in and queue jumps telling him: 'Do you mind mate I'm in absolute agony.' Jack pretends he has a sore leg putting on a limp as he goes in to see the nurse. Later, Jack pays the nurse another visit taking the chance to share a moment of passion with her. However, Blakey calls hoping to see the nurse as well but is told in a broad Scottish accent by the patient: 'Here here the nurse is out. You'll have to wait.' But when Blakey hears the nurse entertaining a man in her treatment room all hell breaks out.

Payne Jewellery Shop

This is the shop which Stan and Susy visit to buy her engagement ring in the film Mutiny On The Buses.

This shop was actually located on Shenley Road in the Hertfordshire town of Borehamwood around a quarter of a mile away from Elstree Studios where the film was made. The actual jewellery shop ceased trading for business many years ago.

Pearson, Alfred

Played by Reginald Stewart

He is a trainee bus driver who trains aboard the training bus under Stan and Jack with three other trainees in the Series Four episode 'The L Bus'.

Alf, as he is called by his work colleagues, has dark hair and is in his late twenties. However, he is trained in how to use the bus as a removal van rather than bus driving but when the bus breaks down and is towed back to the depot with a bed aboard it seems he'll get a chance to drive the bus. With the bus repaired Stan tells Alf that he can have a turn driving but is deprived of the chance by Inspector Blake who insists they take out another bus as theirs needs cleaning. Alf is told to get out of the drivers cab and onto another bus by the inspector. It means he has to help move the bed onto their replacement bus but they are caught in the act by Blakey. Not an ideal start to his new career as a bus driver.

Pedal Boats

A source of entertainment indulged in by the Rudge family at the holiday camp in Holiday On The Buses.

As Arthur, Olive and their son Arthur are aboard pedal boats in a man-made pond in the holiday camp Stan enters the pond being chased by a furious Inspector Blake. As Stan wades through the water he bumps into a pedal boat which has Olive and little Arthur aboard and this tips the boat causing Olive to fall into the water with her son calling for help. An amused Arthur looks on whilst Stan clambers out of the pond helped by a boy with the inspector hot on his trail.

The pedal boats have long since been removed from the Pontins camp at Prestatyn Sands where Holiday On The Buses was filmed. The pond has been drained and is currently used as a go-karting circuit.

Peggy

Played by Claire Davenport

One of a group of women bus drivers taken on by the Town and District Bus Company who suffers at the hands of Stan and Jack's pranks but she gets her revenge in the film On The Buses.

Peggy is a well-built, blonde-haired woman with a northern accent. She is one of four women drivers who round on Stan in the depot and pays him back for his bullying of a women driver. She holds his legs as he gets jets of air from a tyre pump fired up the inside of his trousers which leaves Stan writhing in agony whilst Peggy and her colleagues are in hysterics. However, she herself suffers discomfort later when she drinks tea that has had diuretic pills added to it by Stan ensuring she has an uncomfortable shift. Whilst driving her bus along a remote country lane she is forced to park it and dash from her cab and relieve herself behind some bushes much to the surprise of a parson seated on the upper deck of her bus. Although Peggy loses her position as a bus driver she is re-assigned as an inspector and soon sets about making Stan and Jack's life a misery by splitting the trouble-making bus crew up. Revenge is sweet.

Peeping Tom

Inspector Blake is mistaken for a Peeping Tom in the Series Seven episode 'The Allowance'.

When the inspector is ordered to check that clippies' visits to public conveniences whilst on duty are genuine he resorts to spying on them from behind a tree in a public park. However, a policeman noting his suspicious behaviour arrests him for being a Peeping Tom. Luckily, he is not held for too long and he rushes back to the depot where he is labelled a 'dirty old man' by Jack who asks him when his case is coming up. 'It don't. Station's sergeant turned out to be a friend of mine. He let me off with a caution. Nothing else. No apology. Nothing at all,' moans the inspector and the matter is brought to a close.

Peisley, Frederick

TV Role: Doctor (Series 7 Episode 2 'The Perfect Clippie')

Born in Finchley, London in 1904, Frederick Peisley had a long career as an actor on stage, film and television.

He began his career in repertory and stage roles in his early twenties. Stage roles would include a West End role in The Love Game at The Prince of Wales Theatre in 1931. Other credits came in The Gates Of Paradise, Ghosts, Midsummer Night's Dream, Dear Delinquent and The Flowering Cherry amongst others. He was also to show a talent for directing stage shows as well. From the early 1930s, Peisley's film career began to take off and would continue on towards the end of the 1960s. The pick of those credits were The Secret Of The Loch, Gentleman's Agreement, The Gentle Sex, The Angry Silence and Hide And Seek.

He established himself as an actor on television in 1960 and would appear in hit dramas, children's series and comedy roles. Dramas such as Emergency – Ward 10, Ghost Squad, Z Cars, Dixon Of Dock Green, No Hiding Place, Gideon's Way, The Avengers, Softly Softly, The First Churchills, Casanova, Emmerdale, The Onedin Line and The Protectors were the pick of his credits. He'd also appear in classic children's series such as Ace Of Wands, Here Comes The Double Deckers and Freewheelers. Piesley was a regular in classic sitcoms of the 1960s and 70s with his best remembered role coming in Our House where he starred alongside Carry On star Hattie Jacques. Other sitcom roles came most notably in All Gas And Gaiters, Clochemerle, Doctor In Charge, The Fenn Street Gang, On The Buses, Doctor At Sea and Sykes.

Sadly, Frederick Piesley passed away in 1975 at the age of seventy.

Pension Book

An item owned by Mrs Butler that is referred to in the Series Three episode 'Mum's Last Fling'.

Obviously, not wanting her new boyfriend Wilf to know that she is a pensioner she makes a point of hiding her pension book before he enters the room. In a flustered state she says: 'Oh my pension book. Well he needn't see that.' She quickly puts it away in a drawer in the sideboard.

Pension books for old age pensioners were introduced to Britain in 1909 and remain in use today. However, in 2005 moves were made by the Labour government to have payments paid directly into pensioners bank or building society accounts but this has proven unpopular and problematic to implement.

Perfect Driver Contest

A contest organised by the Luxton and District Bus Company in the Series Seven episode 'The Poster'.

The bus company is to release a promotional poster as part of a recruitment drive. With a bus driver being chosen to appear on the poster in the perfect driver contest the winner is also to receive one hundred pounds encouraging Stan to put himself forward for the contest. The promotional poster is just a small part of a complete reorganisation of the company which is to see a streamlining with a reduction in staff numbers and an emphasis on keeping only the efficient staff. When Inspector Blake learns that Stan is to represent the depot he is far from impressed and insists he stands no chance considering the strength of the competition which includes bus drivers from neighbouring bus depots who can boast being a part-time footballer or part-time male model or a bodybuilder. Frightened by the competition Stan undergoes a course of beauty treatment in a bid to win over the judging panel for the contest but he is not confident. At the last moment Stan tries a change of tact appearing in front of the panel in an oil-smeared uniform and puts himself across as having a responsible attitude and dedicated to helping his passengers with a clean driving record to his name. The panel, although impressed by the other contestants talents, declare Stan the winner much to the disbelief of Inspector Blake and discontent of the other contestants.

Perkins

Played by Perry Soblosky

This is a contestant in the perfect driver contest in the Series Seven episode 'The Poster'.

Perkins is a bus driver representing the Ryesburn depot that has fair hair and is in his late twenties. He is also a part-time male model but this and his good looks are not enough to win him the contest. He begrudgingly congratulates Stan on winning the contest but does not shake his hand and as he walks past him he sneers in a camp manner: 'Bitch.'

Permissive Age

A period in recent history renowned for greater sexual freedom referred to by Arthur in the Series Four episode 'Not Tonight'.

Stan's steady supply of girlfriends has dried up and he has gone without a date for a number of weeks and Arthur is keen to rub salt in the wound. He tells Stan: 'It would appear the permissive age is passing you by mate.'

The permissive age that Arthur refers to came about in the mid-1960s and was to see a large scale change in attitudes towards sex, morals and other general social standards. Acts that were once considered improper and unacceptable became part of the social norm and was also to see an increase in sexual promiscuity. This permissive age continued on into the 1970s shaping much of today's social standards.

Peters, Arnold

TV Role: Manager (Series 1 Episode 5 'The New Inspector')

Arnold Peters was born in 1925 and as an actor was to boast a career that offered credits on stage, television and in films.

On stage his most notable role came in the musical My Fair Lady in 1975 and he was also to direct stage shows from the early 1960s including an adaption of Babes In The Wood. He was also a regular on the pantomime scene with roles in old favourites such as Aladdin and Dick Whittington.

Peters television career spanned from the mid-1960s up until 2000 with roles in a range of hit series. His most noted drama roles in the 1960s came in Crossroads, Public Eye, Z Cars, Softly Softly, Dixon Of Dock Green and Hadleigh. The 70s saw him appear in the award-winning The Six Wives Of Henry VIII, Wicked Women, Jude The Obscure, War And Peace, Within These Walls, The Onedin Line, The Tomorrow People, The Duchess Of Duke Street and Secret Army amongst others. His later drama roles included appearances in Angels, The Citadel and Doctors. He was also to appear in the cream of British sitcoms over three decades including On The Buses, Doctor In The House, Please Sir, The Liver Birds, The Fall And Rise Of Reginald Perrin, Mind Your Language, Citizen Smith, Bless Me Father, It 'Ain't Half Hot Mum, To The Manor Born and Only Fools And Horses.

In films he had an uncredited role in the Oscar-winning film A Man For All Seasons but the majority of his roles were to come in made-for-television films such as Suez 1956, Why Didn't They Ask Evans, Knockback and Frankenstein.

Peters, who played Jack Woolley in the legendary long-running BBC Radio Four series The Archers from 1979 through to 2012, was also a president of Moulton Theatre in his hometown of Northampton. Sadly, after fighting Alzheimer's Disease late in his life he passed away in May 2013 in a care home at the age of eighty seven.

Peters, Luan

TV Role: Joan (Series 5 Episode 7 'Canteen Trouble')

Born in Bethnal Green, London in 1946, Luan Peters was to study at drama school amidst flirting with a career as a pop singer which failed to really take off. She went on to join the Joan Littlewood Theatre Workshop before going on to have a career in acting with roles on stage, television and in films.

After early roles in her youth at school she'd go on to appear in a number of stage roles from the late 1960s. These included A Man Most Likely To, Pyjama Tops, and in 1974 a stage show about The Beatles called John, Paul, George, Ringo and Bert. Her later theatre credits came in shows such as Dirty Linen, Shut Your Eyes And Think Of England and the farce Funny Peculiar in 1985.

On television her career as an actress began in the mid-1960s with drama roles coming in Dixon Of Dock Green, The Caesars, Z Cars, Strange Report, Public Eye, Coronation Street, Doctor Who, Target, The Professionals and The Bill to name but a few.

In comedy roles she would appear in On The Buses, Robin's Nest and Fawlty Towers most notably. Also she was to have a stint as a hostess on the hit game show The Golden Shot in the early 1970s alongside Bob Monkhouse.

On the big screen Peters had roles in Hammer Films productions such as Lust For A Vampire and Twins Of Evil. Her stunning good looks and busty figure fitted in well in the adult movie Not Tonight Darling with other film roles including Man Of Violence, The Wildcats Of St Trinian's and Pacific Banana.

Although she had no big hits as a pop singer in the 1960s her biggest moment of her pop career came when she fronted the band 5000 Volts on Top Of The Pops in 1975 singing their hit I'm On Fire which reached number four in the UK charts.

Luan Peters has now retired from acting.

Peters, Reginald

Film Role: Medical Orderly (On The Buses)

This is an actor whose career consisted chiefly of bit part roles on television and in films from the mid-1960s through until the mid-1980s.

Peters small screen drama credits included hit series such as Crossroads, Z Cars, Softly Softly, Paul Temple, Jason King, The Borgias and The Bill as well as appearances in the cult children's series Here Comes The Double Deckers. His solitary comedy role came in the controversial sitcom Never Mind The Quality, Feel The Width in the late 1960s. His film roles were to come in Inadmissible Evidence, Universal Soldier and On The Buses in the late 1960s and early 1970s.

Petty Cash

A sum of money belonging to the Town and District Bus Company which Mr Jenkins helps himself to in the film Mutiny On The Buses.

As the depot manager Mr Jenkins frolics with the notorious clippie Nymphy Norah on a sofa in his office she exclaims that she has torn her tights. The married philanderer saucily tells her to take them off and offers to help. In a care-free manner he promises: 'Oh we'll get you a new pair out of the petty cash won't we?'

Peyton Place

A famous novel referred to in the Series One episode 'The New Inspector'.

When a cheeky clippie called Betty is being reprimanded by Stan the newly-appointed assistant inspector for wearing too short a skirt on duty he asks her if she has read the rulebook. Disinterested in what he has to say she replies: 'No. Well it's hardly Peyton Place is it?'

Peyton Place was a best-selling novel written by US authoress Grace Metalious. Published in 1956 it tells the story of the lives of three women in a small New England town and their intense sexual secrets. The novel was a massive hit and within a year it was made into an Oscar-nominated film and followed by a hit US television series based on the book from 1964 to1969 that was to be a worldwide hit.

Phillips, Wilf

Played by Tommy Godfrey

A bus conductor employed by the Luxton and District Bus Company who is to date Mrs Butler in the Series Three episode 'Mum's Last Fling'.

An experienced conductor in his late forties, the balding Wilf Phillips claims to have been a widow for two years and meets Mrs Butler at the Busmen's Social event at the depot which leads to the pair dating each other. His presence sees a change in Mrs Butler's outlook on life and a change in her wardrobe but he proves to be a bad influence on her as she takes to spending the housekeeping money to pay for her nights out.

When Wilf pays the Butler house a visit he is given a chilly reception by Arthur and Stan and he shows a dark side to his nature. He is interested to hear that the new woman in his life owns the house and he suggests she moves the family out and rents the rooms out to lodgers much to the horror of Stan and Arthur. The pair, for once are united in a common cause to show Wilf up for the charlatan that he is and help comes from an unlikely source.
Inspector Blake informs Stan that Wilf is married and knows that for a fact because he has been claiming on his income tax for her for years as the inspector has had to check the code. The news breaks Mrs Butler's heart and ends their relationship just as it was getting serious.

Picket Duty

A strike over shift patterns at the Luxton and District Bus Company sees Stan and Jack forced onto picket duty in the Series One episode 'The Early Shift'.

Picket duty is no bed of roses especially when it includes starting early in the morning and having to endure freezing temperatures. Stan, Jack and a West Indian busman called George are all armed with placards forming a picket line outside the bus depot and their spirits are lifted by the arrival of Mrs Butler bearing refreshments and then a television crew arrive to report on the strike.

The busmen are buoyed by this and are grateful of the publicity. As the cameras begin to roll a bus is heard being started up inside the depot in a bid to break the strike. The bus manned by Inspector Blake is set to exit the depot and to prevent this Stan is forced to lie down in front of the bus. With the television crew catching the unfolding drama it adds more publicity and support for the strike which invariably, later that night, leads to the management exceeding to the busmen's demands to bring an end to the strike.

Picton, Don

Assistant Art Director (Mutiny On The Buses) and Art Director (Holiday On The Buses)

Don Picton could boast a career that spanned over almost forty years in the art department in films and television working on iconic film series and a number of illustrious production companies. His film credits came at Hammer Films from the late 1960s. He worked on The Lost Continent, The Horror Of Frankenstein, Scars Of Dracula, Blood From The Mummy's Tomb, Vampire Circus, Mutiny On The Buses, The Satanic Rites Of Dracula, Holiday On The Buses and Frankenstein And The Monster From Hell amongst others. Away from Hammer he had credits in Carry On Abroad and Clash Of The Titans. Picton worked in an uncredited capacity on films such as Caesar And Cleopatra, Black Narcissus, The African Queen, Sink The Bismarck, Cleopatra and For Your Eyes Only. On television he worked at Elstree Studios on hit ITC series The Saint and Danger Man.

Don Picton retired from the industry in the early 1980s.

Pictures, The

This popular form of entertainment is often referred to in On The Buses and features in the Series Seven episode 'Olive's Divorce'.

Stan takes his girlfriend Sandra to the pictures but his romantic inclinations are dashed as his mum insists that the newly-divorced and distraught Olive accompanies them. The film being screened isn't ideal for Olive as Sandra explains the plotline saying: 'It's one of them sexy foreign films. It's this woman who gets a divorce 'cos her husband goes off with another bird.' To appease his sister Stan adds: 'It ends up alright in the end. It is about this bird that gets divorced but you see she gets all the fellas chasing her. All divorced birds do.' Olive settles down to watch the film but can't help acting as gooseberry as Stan and Sandra look to share moments of passion as the film plays. She interrupts them asking Stan to put a straw in her drinks carton and also to claim that a man has put his hand on her knee. It means Stan has to postpone all romantic ideas until after their trip to the pictures.

Pill, The

The contraceptive pill is referred to in both episodes and a spin-off film of On The Buses.

As Stan returns home from work having been assaulted by hooligans in the Series Two episode 'Self Defence', mum blames the violence on the pill much to Arthur and Stan's amazement. She explains: 'If it wasn't for the pill half these louts would be at home changing nappies.' Later, in the Series Five episode 'The Strain', when Stan is bed-ridden with a back injury he is given Olive's pillow to support his back but finds it smothered in her winter green ointment. He finds the smell off-putting and realises why Arthur won't go near her. He says: 'I tell you something they ought to issue that instead of the pill.' The film On The Buses sees Olive pay a visit to a family planning clinic to get the pill but won't be getting it on the NHS, according to Jack as she is neither under fifteen or over sixty five.

The contraceptive pill was developed in the USA and is taken orally to prevent pregnancy. It became available in the UK in December 1961 and was prescribed on the NHS at a small charge. It remains the most commonly used contraceptive in the world.

Pilot, The

Played by Fraser Kerr

This pilot is contacted by mistake by Stan via the newly-installed radio control system which has been tampered with by Jack in the Series Three episode 'Radio Control'.

A moustachioed, dark-haired pilot in his late thirties who speaks with a posh accent is contacted by mistake by Stan. The pilot, flying his British Overseas Airways passenger jet to Chicago, is told by Stan believing that he is talking to another bus driver that the pilot should go to the gasworks via the High Street. The confusion leaves the pilot concerned there could be a collision but this is cleared up when Stan tells him he is using the busman's code on the radio. He orders Stan to get off his wavelength and the radio control system on the bus is promptly retuned by Jack when they realise their mistake.

Pilot, The

Played by Michael Nightingale

A pilot who is erroneously contacted by Inspector Blake and Mr Jenkins on a radio system at the depot that has been sabotaged and retuned by Jack in the film Mutiny On The Buses.

With Inspector Blake desperate to contact Stan on the Town and District's radio system having already contacted the police by mistake he is in for another disappointment. He contacts a balding pilot in his early fifties flying a Pan-American jet who responds: 'Clipper Charlie Victor two seven here. I'm receiving you…over.' Manager Mr Jenkins believing it to be a busman rages down the microphone: 'What route do you think you are on?' The pilot, quite unaware of the confusion replies that he has just come in from Calcutta. This infuriates the manager who berates Inspector Blake for having no control over his staff with them all taking the mickey.

Plaice on the Bone

The description of the fish that is lost aboard Stan's bus in the Series Five episode 'Lost Property'.

When a woman reports to Inspector Blake that she left two portions of fish and chips aboard a bus when she got off at the High Street, he is to take down her details. She demands: 'That was my old man's supper – best plaice on the bone. I want it back.' She is to be disappointed though.

Plan A

A second strategy used by the Basildon Bashers team in the Series Seven episode 'The Football Match'.

A deflated Stan accuses the captain of the Basildon Bashers of cheating and for that he pays an embarrassing penalty. The skipper Eunice Jones takes offence and says to her team-mates: 'Okay girls – Plan A.' The women surround Stan and he is held down as they pull his shorts off and she holds them up triumphantly. She and her team run away cheering leaving Stan trying in vain to cover himself up.

Plan G

A strategy used during the match by the Basildon Bashers which enables them to score a goal in the Series Seven episode 'The Football Match'.

With the second half of the football match under way the Basildon Bashers implement a plan. 'Plan G,' yells their captain. As one of their players dribble the ball the rest of the team hold hands and form an impenetrable circle around the player and they move unchallenged towards the Luxton Lions goal. The circle breaks and the player dribbling the ball is to emerge and shoots and scores from close range.

Plaster of Paris

This surprising ingredient is added to Stan's home-brewed beer in the Series Three episode 'Brew It Yourself'.

Arthur and mum are mystified to learn that Stan is to add plaster of Paris to his beer. However, he quotes from his instruction book that as they live in a soft water district he has to add the plaster of Paris to make the water used in the beer harder but mum and Arthur are still not convinced. Although surprising, plaster of Paris is indeed used in the making of home-brewed beer at times. A small amount such as a spoonful or two is added to make the water firmer.

Playboy Pyjamas

This is a brand of silk pyjamas that Stan buys as he bids to impress the new lodger Edna in the Series Three episode 'On The Make'.

The playboy pyjamas which come in a box with a slogan boasting that it is 'nightwear women can't resist' and are guaranteed crease-proof are seen by Arthur who ridicules Stan. It does not put Stan off and he later wears the silk pyjamas and tries to sneak into Edna's bedroom but is to be prevented by a vigilant Arthur.

Stan's silk playboy pyjamas or its box did not bear the famous bunny head motif so it is not thought to be the famous Playboy-branded pyjamas made by the adult entertainment company which were most popular in the 1960s and 70s. Playboy was formed in 1953 by US entrepreneur Hugh Heffner and his men's magazines would eventually become massively popular around the world. Branded merchandise, nightclubs and later television channels followed but in recent years Playboy's appeal and popularity has faced stiff competition from internet services. It is, however, fighting back by attempting to reinvent itself with the reopening of its famous London nightclub in a bid to reinforce its position.

Plaza, The

A cinema referred to as Arthur and Olive suggest a film for Stan to watch in the Series Four episode 'Not Tonight'.

After a sarcastic suggestion by Arthur, amidst a crisis in Stan's love life, Olive recommends a film. 'At The Plaza there's one called Love Swedish Style,' she says.

It is most likely that the cinema name was taken from The Plaza Theatre on Lower Regent Street in Piccadilly Circus, London. A grand theatre built in 1926 it was built for Paramount Pictures and renamed The Paramount Plaza. Decorated with lavish Italian antiques and designed in an Italian Renaissance-style it contained a grand foyer, café and a huge auditorium with three levels, a balcony, royal circle and seating for 1,896 people. In recent years the theatre has been renovated and now contains a Tesco Metro store in what was the foyer and has a small multiplex cinema still on site.

Plimsolls

A type of footwear belonging to Olive that Stan is forced to wear in the Series Four episode 'The Injury'.

Stan, sporting an injured shoulder and toe is determined to make it into work but he is unable to wear his shoes as they prove excruciatingly painful. As Olive has a bigger shoe size Stan asks to borrow her plimsolls enabling him to limp to the depot. He finds he is in for a hard time for his choice of footwear from Inspector Blake who tells him the plimsolls are inappropriate for the job. However, Jack intervenes reasoning the best racing drivers wear plimsolls but the inspector is to discover the real reason for him wearing them are that he has injured himself in an accident at home.

Policeman, The

Played by Roger Avon

A policeman on his beat whose quick action prevents a fire at the Butler house in the Series Four episode 'Christmas Duty'.

The moustachioed policeman in his late fifties sees smoke pouring out of the kitchen window of the Butler house as he passes by with the Butlers Christmas dinner burning in the oven whilst they collect Stan from work. The fire brigade are called and have to smash the kitchen window in order to extinguish the fire. When the family arrive home they find the kitchen and living room covered in foam and the efficient policeman walks in and explains what has happened. He berates them for being out enjoying themselves whilst their house could have burnt down as he is unaware that Stan was being picked up from work. 'I must be getting along I'm off duty now and my Christmas dinner'll be waiting for me. Oh by the way I think your turkey's still in the oven,' says the policeman before he makes his exit from the Butler house.

Policeman

Played by Ivor Salter

This is the policeman who arrests Inspector Blake in the Series Seven episode 'Gardening Time'.

The luckless Inspector Blake, who has decided to do some late night gardening in his striped pyjamas, gets locked out of the Butler house. As he begins to climb up a drainpipe a passing policeman in his late forties peers over the garden fence saying: 'What's the game?' Although Blakey tries to explain his predicament the policeman finds it hard to believe especially when the inspector is found to be holding his gardening tools – an axe and saw.
His fate is sealed when next door neighbour Jack arrives on the scene but instead of identifying Inspector Blake he tells the policeman he has never seen him before in his life which leads to the inspector being arrested. The following morning, the policeman brings Blakey, still in his pyjamas, into the depot and has to prevent the angry inspector from attacking Jack before he leaves the scene.

Policeman on Beat

Played by David Rowlands

This is a policeman who, whilst on his beat, is contacted on his radio by mistake by Inspector Blake in the film Mutiny On The Buses.

The dark-haired policeman in his thirties is mistaken for the number twenty three bus driver by Inspector Blake who asks him where he is. He replies: 'I'm on my way back to the station.' A stunned inspector tells him he should be going to Barley Common. When the policeman is to point out that is four miles away the inspector angrily reveals that it is his inspector speaking and orders him to get to Barley Common straight away. Believing it to be a serious situation the policeman becomes nervous and stutters: 'Yes.Yes. I'll ca-catch a bus right away.'

Policeman (Safari Park)

Played by Roger Avon

This policeman is on duty outside the safari park in the film Mutiny On The Buses.

As the tour bus from the Town and District Bus Company exits the safari park swerving viciously as Stan and a chimpanzee wrestle for control of the steering wheel, the policeman waves his arms trying to stop the bus before having to take avoiding action. When the bus screeches to a halt seconds later the policeman angrily marches across to it and opens the doors. He growls: 'What's going on here? Can't you drive this…bus,' his voice tails off as he is shocked to see a chimpanzee sitting in the driver's seat. With a puzzled expression on his face he scratches his head as he speaks.

Pontins Holiday Camp

Although never referred to in Holiday On The Buses the holiday camp that features heavily in the third spin-off film was in fact Pontins Prestatyn Sands camp in North Wales.

Serving as a self-catering holiday camp since the 1950s and the idea of entrepreneur Fred Pontin it offered affordable family package holidays. The Prestatyn Sands camp, like others in the Pontins empire, had its own form of on-site entertainment and activities available for all age groups with accommodation coming in the form of fully-furnished chalets. With an indoor swimming pool, bars, dance hall and the traditional Bluecoats entertainers the camp remains popular and in business to the current day.

Ownership of Pontins has changed hands regularly since the late 1970s and amidst administration in 2010, Pontins Holidays and it's five existing holiday camps came under the new ownership of the Brittania Hotels Group ensuring that Prestatyn Sands remained in business. The camp has since undergone a big refurbishment of chalets and other planned redevelopments are in the pipeline.

Stephen Lewis unveils a commemorative plaque at Pontins Prestatyn Sands camp.

Blakey has pulled a couple of crackers.

Pope, The

The leader of the Catholic Church across the world is referred to in a couple of episodes of On The Buses.

The Series Three episode 'Going Steady' sees Inspector Blake learn that his niece Sally plans to marry his nemesis Stan Butler and he sternly tells the bus driver he won't allow it. A miffed Stan replies: 'Blimey you're not the Pope you know.'

Later, in the Series Four episode 'Christmas Duty', mum insists that the Christmas presents will be given out at breakfast on Christmas Day as it is a family tradition. Stan agrees telling Arthur: 'Yeah like the Pope's message and the Queen's speech.'

The Pope, widely seen as the most important and powerful religious figure in the world, has an official residence in the Palace of the Vatican in the Vatican City. The first recognised Pope took up the post in the sixth century and the role, which remains hugely important, has been chosen since the sixteenth century following a meeting of cardinal electors. The Pope also, under international law, holds a diplomatic immunity given to heads of state representatives.

Poppins, Mary

A character from a smash hit Disney film that Stan gets called in the Series Four episode 'The Kids Outing'.

As Stan arrives at the bus depot for the kids outing he is organising, he holds a big bunch of balloons he hopes will keep the children entertained. 'My god. It's Mary Poppins,' jokes Inspector Blake on seeing Stan.

Mary Poppins was a character from a 1964 Disney film of the same name. A nanny who possesses magical powers she comes into the lives of two troublesome children and transforms their lives as she takes them on a number of wonderful adventures. The film (based on a novel written by Pamela Travers) was a smash hit at the box office, scooped five Oscars and remains a much-loved film to the present day.

Population Explosion

A reason that Arthur gives for he and Olive not starting a family in the Series Five episode 'Boxing Day Social'.

When Mrs Rudge and the Butler family discuss Arthur and Olive's lack of children, Arthur grows uncomfortable. He reasons: 'I mean we don't wish to rush things do we? Anyway you always have to consider the question of the population explosion.'

The population explosion that Arthur talks of was to really take off in the early 1950s. A combination of improved agriculture and food manufacturing output coupled with great medical advances has seen the world's population rocket from 2.4 billion people in 1950 to a present day figure of 6.8 billion and rising.

Port

This alcoholic beverage is drunk by mum and Olive in a number of episodes of On The Buses.

It is revealed in the Series Three episode 'Brew It Yourself' that mum owns a bottle of port that comes from Algiers. She also drinks port and lemon on social occasions along with Olive at a darts night event at the depot canteen in the Series Four episode 'The Other Woman' and again at a Boxing Day social event in the Series Five episode 'Boxing Day Social'.

Port is a fortified wine made exclusively in Portugal although similar sweet red wines are produced around the world. Made in the Douro Valley in the north of Portugal the popular drink has been in production since early in the eighteenth century.

Portable Television Set

This is an item that Stan is forced to buy for Inspector Blake in the Series Five episode 'The New Telly'.

When Inspector Blake is injured after a second-hand television set he has bought from Stan blows up he promises to take legal action to sue the bus driver. In a bid to appease the pained inspector, Stan buys him a new portable television set delivering it to him as he lies bed-ridden at home and tells him that it comes with a six month guarantee.

Blakey is not in the mood for visitors and he asks Stan to leave the television and go and he'll enjoy it later but he is in for a shock. Stan with Jack and Arthur also present make themselves at home in the inspector's bedroom and despite his protests they proceed to watch a football match on the television in a rowdy manner, swilling beer and being very vocal. If that isn't bad enough, Olive and her mum arrive hoping to watch a three-hour long film after the football. Will the inspector ever get to watch his new television set alone? It doesn't look like it.

Postman's Knock

This is a party game which Stan refers to in the Series Three episode 'Busmen's Perks'.

Arthur and Olive's bedroom has been redecorated with a new coat of paint. On finishing the job Stan warns his brother-in-law: 'If you and Olive decide to play postman's knock don't lean up against the wall mate as it's all wet.' Much to Arthur's amusement, Stan himself leans against the wall getting paint on his hand.

Postman's knock was a party game played by children that involved a child (usually a boy) going out of a room and waiting whilst the girls are allocated numbers. The boy would knock on the door and enter saying a number and proceed to kiss the girl with that given number. There are variations of the game but this is the most common form of the game.

Potter, Polly

An uncredited character and member of the Basildon Bashers football team in the Series Seven episode 'The Football Match'.

Polly Potter, a small bespectacled woman in her early fifties with greying hair who wears a green and black striped football top, is introduced to Stan, Jack and Inspector Blake by the Basildon Bashers captain Eunice Jones. Polly is a clippie at the Basildon depot and is revealed to be a full-back but her distinctly rotund figure gains her ridicule from Stan and Jack who claim she is full all round. She later goes on to play her part in her team's win over the Luxton Lions as she holds down the Lions goalkeeper as her team-mates rack up the goals.

Powell, Enoch

A highly controversial political figure referred to in the Series One episode 'The Canteen'.

The newly-appointed depot canteen cook is the Indian Mrs Sharma and she greets Inspector Blake by bowing to him. Stan jokes that with his moustache she probably thinks the inspector is Enoch Powell.

Enoch Powell was a moustachioed Conservative MP from 1950 to 1974 serving as the Minister of Health from 1960 to 1963. Later, in 1968, when he was the Shadow Defence Secretary he made a speech that shocked the nation at that time. Known as the 'Rivers of Blood' speech it warned of the overwhelming number of immigrants arriving in Britain from the Commonwealth countries and the damage this would cause if allowed to continue. It was to be seen as a racist speech and Powell was immediately sacked from his post in the Shadow Cabinet. He went on to become an Ulster Unionist MP from 1974 to 1987 when his controversial political career came to an end. In later years he was struck down by Parkinson's disease and passed away in 1998 at the age of eighty five.

Powell, Nosher

TV Roles: Bert (Series 1 Episode 4 'Bus Driver's Stomach' and Series 1 Episode 6 'The Canteen') and Vic (Series 5 Episode 11 'The Strain')
Film Role: Betty's Husband (On The Buses)

Born in Camberwell, London in 1928, Nosher Powell can boast a full career as an actor, stuntman and also an accomplished boxer. His acting roles were plentiful in film and television and equally so as a stuntman.

On the big screen from the late 1940s up until the late 1990s he made uncredited appearances in many classic films such as Oliver Twist, Demetrius And The Gladiators, A Shot In The Dark, A Fistful Of Dollars, Carry On Dick and Willow. He would also have small credited roles in Emergency Call, Circus Of Fear, School For Sex, On The Buses, The Mackintosh Man, Love Thy Neighbour and The Stick Up amongst others.

His television roles were varied ranging from the mid-1960s until the early 1990s. Powell appeared in many classic dramas such as Dixon Of Dock Green, The Baron, The Saint, The Avengers, Randall And Hopkirk (Deceased), Department S and Ellis Island. He was also frequently to appear in comedy roles in hit series including It's A Square World, On The Buses, The Benny Hill Show, Doctor At Large, Monty Python's Flying Circus, Carry On Laughing, The Comic Strip Presents, Canned Carrot and The Detectives.

As a stuntman Powell was to work on a staggering array of classic films including The Bridge On The River Kwai, Ben Hur, The Guns Of Navarone, The Longest Day, Lawrence Of Arabia, Cleopatra, Zulu, Battle Of The Bulge,

Where Eagles Dare and The Italian Job and many more. He was also to work on the majority of the James Bond series of films from 1962 to 1985. On television he'd work as a stuntman on series such as The Benny Hill Show, Blake's 7 and The Comic Strip Presents.

Powell was also a highly-talented professional boxer in the early part of his life. As a heavyweight boxer he was rated one of the best in the division in the early 1950s and later went on to be a sparring partner for legendary boxers such as Joe Louis, Sugar Ray Robinson and Cassius Clay (who went on to become Muhammad Ali). When show business took over in his life he'd go on to be a minder for legendary stars of that era such as Sammy Davis Jnr, Dean Martin, Bing Crosby, Bob Hope and the delectable actress Ava Gardener.

Nosher Powell, who retired from acting in 1998, wrote his autobiography Nosher that was published in 2001 and he enjoyed his retirement after such a long, packed and varied career but sadly passed away in April 2013 at the age of eighty four.

Pregnant

Olive finally becomes pregnant and it has repercussions for the whole family in the film On The Buses.

A visit to a family planning clinic by Olive sees her learn that she is pregnant. The news shocks Stan and Arthur is equally surprised and amazes everyone by blaming Stan saying: 'It was that Saturday night you blew the telly up.' It means that Olive has to give up her job as canteen cook and her pregnancy soon sees her developing a craving for pickled onions eating them at all times of the day. Stan's love life suffers as well as Bridget, a deeply religious Irish woman, gets passionate with him at the Butler house but she is scared off when a heavily pregnant Olive comes downstairs to collect her knitting and she sees it as a warning – a message from god in her words.

In the later stages of her pregnancy drama ensues as Olive travels with Arthur and Stan in the motorcycle combination for a hospital check-up. The bumpy ride in the sidecar sees Olive go into labour. Matters get worse when the sidecar becomes detached increasing her discomfort and it is up to Stan's quick thinking to come to the rescue as he flags down a passing Town and District bus. With Olive still trapped in the sidecar she is put aboard the bus and rushed to hospital. She later gives birth to a baby boy that weighs in at thirteen pounds twelve ounces leaving Jack to believe it must have been a baby elephant. However, Arthur describes his new-born son, later to be christened Arthur, as 'quite bonnie'.

Presents for Aunt Maud

A trip to visit Aunt Maud for the weekend by mum, Arthur and Olive in the Series Four episode 'Nowhere To Go' sees them take presents that meet with an unfortunate end.

A flowering plant and a cooked chicken wrapped in baking foil are all set to be taken to Aunt Maud. As mum gets into the sidecar holding the large plant fitting it in proves a problem. When Stan closes the sidecar roof the blooming flower buds are chopped off ruining the plant. They do still have the chicken as a present but not for much longer.

As Stan is about to hand it to mum in the sidecar it comes out of the baking foil and falls to the ground in the shed out of the family's view. He picks up the chicken and gives it a wipe down with an oily rag in a desperate bid to clean it but only makes it worse before he wraps it back up in the baking foil and gives it to mum. However, the family and the presents are destined never to reach Aunt Maud's that weekend as the motorcycle and combination suffers a couple of accidents.

Pretty Fingers

A fictional moisturising cream recommended to Stan by the chemist's assistant in the Series Seven episode 'The Poster'.

Miss Quiggly, the chemist's assistant, serves Stan and asks him what kind of skin the moisturising cream is for and is told: 'Well, eh, rather rough really. A bit on the rough side you know.' She picks up a small round container behind the counter and says: 'I can recommend this one sir. It's very good…Pretty Fingers.' Stan accepts her recommendation and later uses the product as part of his beauty treatment.

Pretty Girl on Bus

Played by Linda Regan

An uncredited character seen as the opening credits roll for the film On The Buses.

The pretty blonde girl in her twenties boards Stan's bus and as she goes upstairs she gives Jack an alluring look accompanied with a coy smile. As she nears the top of the stairs Jack catches a glimpse of her panties and he gives a lecherous grin before he rings the bell signalling for the bus to depart.

Prime Minister

The leader of the British government is referred to in the Series Seven episode 'The Visit'.

During a night at the bingo, Olive is puzzled by Jack's style of bingo-calling. She doesn't understand him labelling ball number ten – Downing Street and when he explains it is where the prime minister lives she wonders if he plays bingo too. 'Na he's too busy playing the organ isn't he?' jokes Jack which causes the inspector to call him a twit.

At the time this episode was written and aired in 1973 the prime minister of the United Kingdom was Edward Heath. Not only was he an experienced politician but he was also an accomplished musician – a very capable organist and conductor hence Jack's comment regarding the prime minister.

Prince Charming

A popular character from a number of fairy tales that Arthur is mockingly called in the Series Six episode 'The Prize'.

As Arthur reads about a pools winner scooping a fortune in the newspaper he moans: 'I think it's disgusting. I can't stand people who want something for nothing.' Seconds later, when he orders Olive to fetch his slippers she reminds him of what he had just said and he barks: 'If you don't get my slippers I'll give you a thick ear.' Mum is not impressed and remarks: 'Hark at Prince Charming.'

Prince Charming was a character in fairy tales who was a dashing young man, full of charm who sweeps women off their feet in tales such as Cinderella, Snow White and Sleeping Beauty. It later became a term used for the ideal man that women dream of marrying. Of course Arthur is neither of these hence mum's sarcastic use of the name in a mocking manner.

Probyn, Brian

Director of Photography (Holiday On The Buses)

Born in 1920, Brian Probyn was to break in to the film industry in his late thirties working chiefly as a cinematographer of films.

His credits on the big screen spanned a quarter of a century with his early film credits including Poor Cow, The

Long Day's Dying, Downhill Racer and The Revolutionary. By the early 1970s he had joined Hammer Films and would work on Straight On Till Morning, Man At The Top, The Satanic Rites Of Dracula, Holiday On The Buses, Frankenstein And The Monster From Hell and Shatter. From the mid-1970s up until the untimely end of his career Probyn worked in Australia on films such as the sex comedy Plugg, horror film Inn Of The Damned, The Mango Tree, The Little Convict and Far East.

He carried on working up until his sudden death in 1982 at the age of sixty one.

Productivity Bonus

A payment made to Jack to prevent a strike in the Series Six episode 'Union Trouble'.

With industrial action beckoning at the depot with the shop steward Jack set to call a strike when the inspector sacks the canteen employee Elsie without consultation with the union, the inspector acts quickly. Inspector Blake, with the backing of the general manager, offers Jack a productivity bonus with the understanding that the strike will be called off. The payment of thirty pounds does the trick and all strike action ceases but Stan carries on the lone fight with his own unofficial strike. He takes his action too far though and faces suspension without wages and with Jack powerless to help things look bleak for him. However, as soon as Jack receives his productivity bonus his attitude changes and he immediately calls for strike action demanding that Stan and Elsie are reinstated. It brings about capitulation from Blakey and the power of the union wins out in the end.

Professional Organiser

This is an unseen man who is brought in to run a raffle at the depot in the Series Six episode 'The Prize'.

Inspector Blake, as the local secretary of a charity for stray cats and dogs, is selling raffle tickets at the depot but faces ridicule from Stan and Jack who believe the raffle is just a fiddle. 'It's not a fiddle. As a matter of fact a professional organiser has been brought in to organise it,' explains a confident inspector. However, his confidence is to be shattered when he is badly let down and he has to explain that Mrs Butler, who has won a holiday for two in the Costa Brava in the draw, will not now get her prize. He confesses: 'I'm afraid the professional organiser who was officially brought in to help to officiate – he turned out to be fishy. Apparently, he helped himself so much to the prize money that there was no money left for the prizes. Of course, as you know, that's illegal so I'm afraid the things null and void.'

Provisional License

Olive is revealed as holding a provisional license to drive Arthur's motorcycle and combination in the Series Four episode 'Christmas Duty'.

When Arthur arrives home from the pub on Christmas Day drunk he is incapable of picking Stan up from the depot on his motorbike, Olive offers a solution. She points out that she has a provisional license and can pick up her brother but Arthur objects saying: 'Don't be so stupid you've only had two lessons.' However, as there is no other solution Olive gets her way but with disastrous consequences. With Arthur and mum aboard she crashes the motorbike and sidecar into the side of a bus parked in the depot just avoiding knocking over Inspector Blake in the process. It would seem Olive would have a very long wait to earn a full license.

PSV Badge

A PSV badge was once an essential part of a busman's uniform and is referred to in film On The Buses.

Inspector Blake is on the warpath and notices that Jack is not wearing his PSV (Public Service Vehicle) badge. He warns the conductor: 'You know the regulations. That must be worn at all times.' Jack, who claims to have lost it but knows where he can find it, is told: 'Well have it tomorrow or I'll fine ya.' It turns out that Jack has dropped it in the saucy Turnaround Betty's bedroom and it is left up to Stan to retrieve it which he manages to do at great cost.

Although worn by some bus drivers and conductors in the UK, depending on their company's policy pre-1930, the big change came when the 1930 Road Traffic Act was passed. This made it compulsory for all bus drivers and conductors to hold a public service vehicle license and wear a public service vehicle badge. The original such badges were made of enamel and were round in shape with red edges on driver's badges and green edges for the conductors. These badges had to be worn at all times whilst on duty and this remained the case until the late 1980s. Regulation changes meant it was no longer compulsory to wear PSV badges and issuing of them ceased in 1991 bringing an end to an era of PSV badges.

Pudding Club

An expression Jack uses when referring to pregnant clippies in the Series Five episode 'The Nursery'.

When Inspector Blake explains that the depot's new nursery facility will enable clippies who have had babies to return to work quicker. Jack has a sexist view on this though remarking: 'Lazy lot. Most of them got in the pudding club so they wouldn't have to work.'

The term 'pudding club' is a slang term for pregnancy and is believed to originate from the early eighteenth century when it emerged in ballads written by Thomas D'Urfey, a noted English play and song writer who was renowned for the bawdy material he wrote.

Purchase Form

This document is made out by Inspector Blake to give to Stan in the Series Four episode 'Cover Up'.

The inspector has discovered that Stan has been using company material to cover furniture in his house without anyone's authority. After a word with the manager, Blakey has a purchase form made out for Stan who is to be charged for the material costing him a total of forty pounds which he can't afford to pay. However, the inspector who is quietly satisfied with the outcome points out that it will be stopped out of his wages and explains to the deflated bus driver that they could have sacked him but that way the company would never have got their money back. It is with great reluctance that Stan has to accept the expensive purchase form.

Purchese, John

Sound Recordist (On The Buses and Mutiny On The Buses)

John Purchese's career in the film and television industry spanned over twenty years from the early 1950s through until the mid-1970s. His career began working as a producer and director on small television projects such as documentaries and short films before moving on to work in the sound department.

His career took off in the mid-1960s working on films such as The Jokers, Bedazzled and Hard Contact. He'd also work on popular short films for the Children's Film Foundation and went on to work on a handful of Hammer Films productions such as On The Buses, Mutiny On The Buses, Demons Of The Mind and Straight On Till Morning. On the small screen he was to work briefly on the cult children's television series Here Comes The Double Deckers.

QE2

This is a commonly-used abbreviation for the luxury liner, the Queen Elizabeth the Second which is referred to by Jack in the Series Two episode 'The Used Combination'.

When Stan prepares to smuggle tools out of the bus depot to repair Arthur's motorbike, Jack is surprised by the largeness of the tools. He reminds his friend that he is supposed to be repairing a motorbike not the QE2.

The QE2, the flagship passenger liner of the Cunard Line was built at the John Brown Shipyard in Clydebank, Scotland and officially launched amidst great media attention in May 1969 – around five weeks before this episode first aired on British television. Renowned for its grandeur, size and speed it could hold 1,900 passengers and had a crew compliment of 1,015. The QE2 made hundreds of transatlantic voyages between 1969 and 2008 when it was sold by Cunard and moved to its permanent home in a dock in Dubai where it was planned to turn the QE2 into a floating hotel by its new owners Nakheel Hotels. It remains in Dubai to the present day.

Incidentally, Reg Varney did travel on the QE2 and provided entertainment aboard the famous liner. He played the piano as can be seen in the photograph below of a QE2 poster kindly supplied by The Official On The Buses Fan Club.

Reg Varney tops the bill on the QE2.

Quatermass

A fictional professor famed for his experiments is referred to in a couple of episodes of On The Buses.

Stan takes up brewing his own beer in the Series Three episode 'Brew It Yourself'. As he scoops a thick layer of yeast off the top of his bucket of beer before sampling it he says: 'It's like Quatermass.' Later, in the Series Six episode 'Private Hire', Stan has the difficult task of trying to ice Olive's very runny cake which he describes as being 'like a Quatermass'.

Professor Bernard Quatermass was a fictional character created by Nigel Kneale that was to feature in three smash hit BBC television series in the 1950s, three film adaptions all of which were products of Hammer Films and a fourth television series made by Thames Television in the late 1970s. The Quatermass character was seen confronting alien life forms as a result of his experiments and developing the British space programme through his expertise in rockets.

Queen Elizabeth, The

A famous passenger liner referred to by Arthur in the Series Three episode 'Going Steady'.

With Stan's fiancée Sally coming to have tea with the Butlers, Stan is keen to make an impression. He not only washes and restyles his hair but wears a garish tie fastened with a large knot. Arthur is quick to poke fun at his brother-in-law saying: 'Well they use a smaller knot than that to tie up the Queen Elizabeth.'

The Queen Elizabeth was a luxury passenger liner owned by Cunard. Built at the John Brown Shipyard in Clydebank it was launched in 1938 and, at that time, was the largest passenger liner ever built. It could hold almost 2,300 passengers and was largely used in transatlantic voyages until it was retired from service in 1968. After being sold a number of times with various plans muted for the famous liner the Queen Elizabeth met with disaster.

Whilst being refurbished in Hong Kong harbour in 1972 a blaze destroyed the vessel causing it to partially capsize. It was to be a sad end for the Queen Elizabeth after such an illustrious history as she was destined to be scrapped.

Queens Park Rangers

This is a London football club that is referred to in the Series Two episode 'Self Defence'.

A late night shift ends with Stan and Jack being assaulted by a group of hooligans who proceed to vandalise their bus. On arriving back at the depot, Inspector Blake is shocked to see the damage caused by the hooligans who have daubed graffiti on the side of the bus which reads: 'Queens Park Rangers are a lot of…' The final word of the slogan is painted on the rear of the bus and on reading it the inspector describes it as 'disgusting'. The word is never disclosed and in true On The Buses fashion it is left up to the viewer's imagination to fill in the blank.

Queens Park Rangers are a football club that were founded in 1882 and since 1902 have played at Loftus Road, situated in Shepherd's Bush, West London. The club has spent brief and fleeting spells in England's top flight throughout its history with its proudest moment coming in 1967 when winning the League Cup. In 2011, Queens Park Rangers (also known as QPR) gained promotion to the Premier League after many years in the football wilderness but were once again relegated two years later. Incidentally, when the episode 'Self Defence' first aired in June 1969, QPR had just been relegated from the top flight finishing bottom of Division One which, at that time, was the top flight of English football.

Quid

A slang term frequently used for the British currency of a pound is heard throughout the television series and the three spin-off films of On The Buses.

It is unclear where the term originated from but a favoured theory is that it came from the Latin phrase 'quid pro quo' which translates as 'what for which' meaning to exchange something for something else. This could be construed as the act of paying money to buy a product. Another plausible theory is that it stems from the Quidhampton Paper Mill in Wiltshire, England where the first banknotes were printed in 1694 and it was around this time that the term quid originated.

Quinceharmon

Performers of 'It's A Great Life On The Buses' (On The Buses)

Quinceharmon were a noted band in Yorkshire in the 1960s and 70s where they frequented the working men's club scene. They were to be signed up by the EMI record label and it was to see them handed the task of performing the catchy theme tune song for the first On The Buses spin-off film in 1971 which was an EMI Films production in partnership with Hammer Films.

'It's A Great Life On The Buses' was written by Geoff Unwin with the lyrics penned by Roger Ferris. Quinceharmon, with Bob Holt and Ross Grant on vocals accompanied by Ivor Drawmer, Pete Jowie and Roger Harrison, recorded the track at the much-renowned Abbey Road Studios in London and it proved to be a fantastic theme tune that caught the mood of the film perfectly but sadly it did not ignite Quinceharmon's pop career. Although they were to move on to record a handful of singles with Columbia Records they never made an impact on the UK charts but continued to be a big draw in clubs around Yorkshire in the 1970s. They disbanded but in recent years reformed as Reunited and returned to the club scene that remembered them so well.

R

Radio Control

This is a radio system that is introduced to help improve the punctuality of buses in an episode and spin-off film of On The Buses.

In the Series Three episode 'Radio Control' the Luxton and District Bus Company bring in a two-way radio control system in a bid to combat unpunctuality of their buses. Inspector Blake earmarks Stan and Jack's bus to be the first in the fleet to have the system installed much to their displeasure and are also given a code to learn that will be used over the airwaves. They do benefit by having two attractive clippies placed on their bus to be trained on how to operate the radio control system but this causes the randy busmen problems. Jack tries to tamper with the radio in a bid to tune in some music for the clippies but instead they make contact with a pilot aboard a jumbo jet and the conductor hastily retunes the radio.

Worse is to follow though as the inspector boards their bus mid-route and drama beckons when they are forced to take a diversion due to a burst water main. Inspector Blake orders Stan to take a route he is unfamiliar with and it results in the bus crashing into a low bridge and they cannot radio for assistance as the radio doesn't work under a bridge. The accident, which causes ten thousand pounds worth of damage, leads to the short-lived radio control system being scrapped.

The Town and District Bus Company introduce a radio control system to their fleet in the film Mutiny On The Buses and Inspector Blake is enthusiastic that it will increase punctuality and promises Stan and Jack he won't give them a minutes peace. The early stage of the radio control system seems to go as the inspector had hoped and Stan and Jack realise something must be done to break the hold the management has over them. Jack uses his knowledge of radios gained whilst on national service to retune the circuits on the radio system in the inspector's office and feels sure that Blakey and the manager Mr Jenkins will be unable to contact them. The result is chaos as the management duo spends more time contacting policemen and pilots than their bus crews and it lands the inspector in trouble with the law. The police confiscate the radio control system and issue a stern warning to Inspector Blake. Of course it means the end of the radio control system in Town and District buses and the balance of power swings back in favour of the busmen.

Radio Girl, The

Played by Valerie Newbold

A secretary employed by the Luxton and District Bus Company who can be seen assisting Inspector Blake in the Series Three episode 'Radio Control'.

The radio girl, whose name is Miss Woodall, is a bespectacled woman in her twenties with fair hair who hands Inspector Blake the radio control set and a board with the busman's code written on it as he demonstrates the new equipment to the gathered bus crews. Miss Woodall is later seen in the radio control centre where she takes note of all incoming messages and when left in charge she can be heard over the radio warning Stan of a burst water main on his route and advises him to take a diversion.

Raffle

A raffle in aid of a local charity features in the Series Six episode 'The Prize'.

Inspector Blake is selling raffle tickets as local secretary for the National Stray Cats and Dogs Home but Stan and Jack are suspicious and are to mock him. They joke that the prizes will either be a year's supply of dog biscuits or a night out with Lassie, but the inspector counters telling them the winner could win a Mini or a holiday. When the two troublesome busmen insinuate that it's all a fiddle they are told that a professional organiser has been brought in to officiate. Raffle tickets are later sold to Mrs Butler and even Jack tries his luck and it turns out to be a winning ticket for mum who wins a holiday for two in the Costa Brava but she is in for a disappointment. The professional organiser turns out to be crooked as he helps himself to the money raised from the ticket sales which means the raffle is declared null and void with no holiday for Mrs Butler.

Rag and Bone Man

Played by Ernest Jennings

This is an ageing man with a horse and cart who is to disappoint Jack and Inspector Blake in the Series Seven episode 'Gardening Time'.

In his late fifties the scruffily dressed rag and bone man wearing a black cap, overcoat and scarf leads his horse and cart down the street before stopping outside Jack's house whilst his horse leaves a deposit on the ground. With Jack and Inspector Blake desperate for manure for their gardens they come out of their houses carrying a bucket and spade. As they argue over whose manure it is, the rag and bone man is busy shovelling up the mess to take it away and so they both miss out on the manure.

Railway Union Local Branch Meeting

An excuse Arthur uses for going down to the Red Lion pub in the Series One episode 'The New Conductor'.

When Arthur is quizzed by his mother-in-law as to why he is going to the pub she adds she hopes he isn't going drinking. He stammers: 'Eh…no…no. I've got a railway union local branch meeting.' Afterwards he hides behind the newspaper he is reading.

Ramsey, Sir Alf

This legendary football manager of the 1950s, 60s and 70s is referred to by Jack in the Series Seven episode 'The Football Match'.

The Luxton Lions are set for their first training session at the depot. As their manager Inspector Blake exits his office to take the training Jack jokes: 'Here he is – the depot's answer to Alf Ramsey.'

Sir Alf Ramsey, an ex-England international footballer, went into football management at the end of his playing career. As Ipswich Town manager he showed his potential in the late 1950s and early 1960s when he guided them from the depths of Division Three South to the top flight. In 1962 he replaced Walter Winterbottom as England manager and lifted himself into legendary status when he guided England to their finest hour in winning the 1966 World Cup Final.

This was to earn him his knighthood a year later. England, still under his management in the 1970 World Cup Finals had a turbulent tournament and despite having what was considered to be a stronger squad than in 1966, exited the tournament at the quarter-final stage at the hands of old rivals, West Germany. From this point on England's results under Ramsey became patchier with pressure mounting on him from various circles and failure to qualify for the 1974 World Cup Finals led to his sacking. However, Sir Alf Ramsey would remain a legend in the sport and sadly was to pass away in 1999 at the age of seventy nine following years of ill health.

Randy Rita

An unseen clippie said to have dated Stan in the Series Five episode 'The Inspector's Pets'.

With Inspector Blake being mocked by Stan and Jack for going on a fishing holiday with his mum he says they wouldn't understand the thrill of having the bite. 'What are you talking about? I took randy Rita out last night, look what she did to me mate,' says Stan as he pulls down his shirt collar to reveal a love bite on his neck.

Randy Ruby

This is an unseen clippie that Stan admits to eyeing up in the Series Three episode 'Brew It Yourself'.

When Stan realises that his home-brewed beer has a romantic effect on Arthur and Olive he and Jack decide to make some more and plan to ply it to the clippies. As the closing credits roll Stan tells Jack he has had his eyes on randy Ruby from Wood Green.

Rash

A stressed Olive is brought out in a rash in the Series Four episode 'The Other Woman'.

When Arthur comes home in the early hours of the morning after an evening at a darts night at the depot spent flirting with a clippie called Wendy, Olive is in a stressed state. Matters are made worse when Stan and Arthur square up to one another and as Olive nervously scratches her neck she moans: 'You're bringing on me rash.' Mum moves to take a look at her daughter's neck saying: 'Where's the ointment? Ooh she's coming all out in red splotches.' Arthur though offers no sympathy and dryly remarks: 'Well any change would be an improvement.' This sends Olive into a rage and she attempts to attack Arthur with a tin opener before being stopped by Stan.

Reader's Digest

This famous family magazine features in a couple of episodes of On The Buses.

The Series One episode 'Bus Driver's Stomach' sees Stan suffer stomach pains and Arthur is quick to point out that these are caused by his poor eating habits. He quotes from his small Reader's Digest magazine which warns of the dangers of eating fried food listing ailments that can prove fatal due to poor diet. It is enough to see Stan placed on a chips-free diet. Similarly, in the Series Four episode 'Dangerous Driving', Stan's fitness is questioned when a newspaper article claims that his occupation leaves him prone to a series of illnesses.

Although Stan is adamant he is fit, Arthur begs to differ and his Reader's Digest magazine seems to back him up. The magazine says obesity is a killer and what with his sedentary job, coupled with him being overweight it leaves Stan at risk of shortening his lifespan. Again Stan is placed on a strict diet until another newspaper article comes to light rubbishing the previous report allaying any fears Stan may have had.

The Reader's Digest is a general interest magazine which first went into print in the USA in 1922 and came to the UK in 1938. Compact in size the renowned monthly consumer magazine is sold across the globe and covers a range of topics including social matters, health issues, entertainment, travel, home decorating, holidays and family topics. It remains a popular worldwide magazine to the current day, ninety years after it was first published.

Recreation Ground

A distinctly unromantic location Stan wants to take his date to in the Series Four episode 'Nowhere To Go'.

At the end of a late night shift Stan and Jack have nowhere to take their dates Suzy and Edna to court them. A desperate Stan asks Suzy why they can't go to the recreation ground. 'What? In this weather? I'm freezing as it is,' says the surprised clippie but he jokes that he has his overcoat to keep her warm. However, their date is soon to be cut short by an intervention from Inspector Blake.

Red Indian Squaw

Arthur likens Olive to a Red Indian squaw in the Series Four episode 'The Other Woman'.

When Arthur walks out on Olive, only to return via the back door a short while later, he is greeted by a relieved Olive whose face is smeared in ointment. As she moves to give him a hug he backs away claiming that she looks like a Red Indian squaw. Stan is on hand to quip: 'Well you don't have to be afraid. You've already been scalped.'

A squaw is a term used for a native North American Indian woman.

Red Lion, The

A public house frequented by the Butler and Rudge family and busmen which is referred to in a number of episodes of On The Buses.

The Series One episode 'The New Conductor' sees Arthur in The Red Lion where he sees Stan dating his new clippie Iris despite him telling his mum he was doing an overtime shift. Arthur can't wait to land Stan in hot water and tells Mrs Butler the truth about how her son really spent his evening. The Red Lion is also the first of a long list of pubs that Stan, Jack and the bridegroom-to-be Bill and fellow bus drivers are to visit on a bachelor party in the Series Five episode 'The Best Man'. It is also the venue for the reception following Bill and clippie Sally's wedding in the same episode but Stan is unable to attend as he has an appointment with the hospital after swallowing the wedding ring. In the following episode 'The Inspector's Pets', Arthur takes the inspector's dog Mitzy for a walk and he ends up at The Red Lion. As the pub doesn't allow dogs inside, he leaves Mitzy in the yard to play with the pub dog which does not please Stan at all as he labels that dog as sex mad and fears that Inspector Blake's dog may be pregnant.

Red Sails in the Sunset

A famous hit song of the 1930s that Arthur can be heard singing in the Series Five episode 'The Inspector's Pets'.

A somewhat drunk Arthur pours himself a glass of water in the kitchen and, as he does so, he quietly sings 'Red Sails in the Sunset' before taking a seat as he prepares to take an aspirin.

The song 'Red Sails in the Sunset' was written by Wilhelm Grosz (also known as Hugh Williams) in 1935 with the lyrics, which were penned by Jimmy Kennedy, telling the tale of a yacht often seen by Kennedy off the coast of Ireland. Many great singers and groups have recorded cover versions of the song but it was Bing Crosby who had a number one hit with the ballad in 1935 in the USA. In the UK charts it was later to be Fats Domino who had the biggest hit with the song when it reached number thirty four in 1963.

Redundancies

Staff cuts are promised by Inspector Blake in the Series Seven episode 'What The Stars Foretell'.

It is Inspector Blake's job to break it to the staff that the Luxton and District Bus Company had been taken over by the National Bus Company. 'I'm awfully sorry to have to tell you but there will be certain redundancies,' announces the inspector. He warns trainee clippie Olive that she'll soon be handing in her uniform as all trainees are to be given their notice at the end of the week with other redundancies to follow. Jack, as shop steward, has other ideas and makes a stance saying: 'Hang about mate you can't make nobody redundant without prior consultation with the union and I'm the shop steward so that means me.' However, according to Inspector Blake, the redundancies have all been agreed with the union at national level and redundancies will be put into place on the basis of last in first out. The future looks bleak for a number of drivers and clippies for a while until fellow busmen at the rival bus company taking over Luxton and District come to their rescue. They go on strike until all staff at the Luxton and District Bus Company get re-instated which ends all talk of redundancies.

Redundancy Money

Inspector Blake is reluctant, for once, to sack Stan as he doesn't want the troubled driver to receive redundancy money in the Series Six episode 'Union Trouble'.

Stan, who had been on an unofficial one-man strike causing great disruption, decides to return to work without his demands being met. However, Inspector Blake prevents Stan from clocking-on and when the driver protests he is told by the inspector he is not willing to let him return to work but also refuses to sack Stan for his strike action as that would mean he would get paid redundancy money so the inspector suspends him without pay. The whole matter is soon resolved though when Jack steps in to call the busmen out on strike demanding, amongst other things, that Stan is re-instated and this brings a swift capitulation from Inspector Blake.

Regal, The

This is a cinema referred to in a couple of episodes of On The Buses.

Mrs Butler, Arthur and Olive are set for a night out at the pictures in the Series Three episode 'The Inspector's Niece' and are going to watch a film called Swedish Fanny Hill at The Regal cinema. Stan is so eager for them to go out that he gives them extra money for better seats in the circle as he has a romantic evening at home planned with a clippie called Sally. The Regal cinema gets another mention in the Series Four episode 'The Canteen Girl'.
As Inspector Blake is taking his girlfriend Molly to the pictures one afternoon, Stan and Jack take the opportunity to ridicule him. Stan jokes that he's going in the afternoon as he'll get in for half price as an old age pensioner. When Jack asks the inspector what film he is taking Molly to see, Stan butts in saying: 'Well he's gotta be taking her to The Regal isn't he to see Dracula And The Vampires. Well nice little girl that she is naturally he'll want her to meet his family.' The enraged inspector reacts by chasing the mischievous busmen out of the canteen.

Regan, Linda

Uncredited Film Role: Pretty Girl on Bus (On The Buses)

Born in London, Linda Regan entered into acting at an early age and as an actress fashioned a career with roles on television, in films and on stage. She can also boast a budding career as a highly accomplished writer of crime books later in her life.

Her television career began early in the 1970s with her most notable role coming in the hit 1980s sitcom Hi-de-Hi where she played Bluecoat, April. Other hit comedy series that she appeared in included Birds Of A Feather, The

Detectives and Hale And Pace. She was also to have credits in classic dramas such as Dixon Of Dock Green, Z Cars, Special Branch, Minder, The Gentle Touch, Bergerac, Dempsey And Makepeace, The Bill, London's Burning, Doctors and Holby City amongst others.

On the big screen she was to make a brief appearance in the film On The Buses. Other notable roles came in Adolf Hitler – My Part In His Downfall, The Hiding Place, Keep It Up Jack, Carry On England, Quadrophenia and The Last Horror Movie.

Regan was also very active on stage from the mid-1970s with credits in Straight Up and Seven Girls and the 80s brought further roles in Anthony And Cleopatra, What The Butler Saw, Last Of The Red Hot Lovers and Hayfever to name but a few. Her most recent stage appearances include Bedroom Farce, That's Show Business, The Rivals and You're Only Young Twice.

Linda Regan and her husband Brian Murphy at the 2012 On The Buses event

In 1993 Regan was to marry the great comedy actor Brian Murphy – star of memorable sitcoms such as Man About The House, George And Mildred and Last Of The Summer Wine. In recent years she has become a noted writer of crime novels with books such as Behind You, Passion Killers and Brotherhood Of Blades and has a busy schedule in her secondary career which is on-going to the present day.

Regent, The

This is a cinema that is referred to in the Series Four episode 'Not Tonight'.

With Stan moping around the house with his love life in a slump his mum suggests he goes to the pictures. Arthur, reading the newspaper ads sarcastically recommends a film for Stan to go and see. 'There's a thing here at The Regal – Hot Summer's Lust,' he jokes. But Stan doesn't see the funny side and refuses to go to the pictures.

Regulations

The rules applied by bus companies that must be adhered to by busmen are frequently referred to in episodes and spin-off films of On The Buses.

The Luxton and District Bus Company's regulations are referred to in a series of episodes. When, in the Series Two episode 'Family Flu', Stan is caught carrying his laundry aboard his bus by Inspector Blake he is told that he knows the regulations that he is not allowed to use the bus to carry his own personal effects. In the Series Three episode 'First Aid', Inspector Blake is injured aboard Stan's bus and when Jack doesn't follow correct procedures when asking Stan to depart the inspector tells him to stick to regulations and says: 'To start the bus give two distinct rings on the bell.' Jack though gets his own back on the pained inspector who has just lit up a cigarette on the lower deck of the bus as he tells him, despite his leg injury, he will have to go upstairs to smoke as per regulations or put out the cigarette. The Series Four episode 'Christmas Duty' is to see Inspector Blake berate Stan for carrying his Christmas shopping in the driver's cab. 'You know the regulations you shouldn't have a single parcel in that cab with you,' says Blakey despite Stan protesting he had to do his Christmas shopping. Parcels, it would seem are allowed inside the bus as referred to in the Series Four episode 'The L Bus'. Inspector Blake discovers that Stan and Jack have been using the training bus to deliver a bed to Arthur and he promises to report it to the general manager. However, Jack points out: 'We're allowed to carry parcels on that bus it's in the regulations. We were just showing the clippies how to handle big parcels.' The inspector is not to be fooled and charges Stan with several parcel tickets.

On the big screen, the Town and District Bus Company regulations feature in the film On The Buses as Inspector Blake reminds Jack that he must wear his PSV badge at all times and threatens Jack with a fine. Another regulation is mentioned in Mutiny On The Buses when the inspector catches Stan and fiancée Suzy kissing on the upper deck of the bus. 'How dare you. Upstairs? You know the regulations you're not even supposed to eat your lunch upstairs,' Blakey tells them. Towards the end of the same film a new inspector, brought in to replace the demoted Blakey, encounters Stan and Jack for the first time as they are minutes away from taking their bus out. He tells them: 'You know the regulations you should be carrying out your checks.' When he is told they don't bother with them he snaps that they'd better get on with their checks or he will report them both.

Rehearsal of Old-Time Dancing

When Chief Security Inspector Blake holds rehearsals of old-time dancing he is in for an uncomfortable time in the film Holiday On The Buses.

He has to contend with the mocking comments of Stan and Jack who watch on as he puts his dance team through their paces giving them lessons. An elderly couple, Mr and Mrs Hodges are first to perform the military two step and their performance is faultless impressing Blakey. The next couple to take to the floor are Mrs Butler and her dance partner – a somewhat coarse Irishman called Bert Thompson. It turns out to be a very poor dance which sees Blakey stopping them in mid-dance berating Bert for showing off and forgetting his salute – a key part of the dance. Bert responds by giving the inspector his salute – a crude two-fingered gesture. The final couple called forward are the middle-aged cockney couple Wally and Lilly Briggs. However, their performance is clumsy and wooden and is also brought to an abrupt halt as the inspector criticises Wally for having no stance at all and proceeds to give him a demonstration with some advice. In addition the inspector offers to partner Wally in a waltz, with himself being the lady. 'Here he's a bleedin' fairy,' remarks Wally. As the pair dance though there is more trouble for Blakey as the clumsy Mr Briggs stands on his injured and bandaged foot. 'You clumsy great clot,' exclaims the pained inspector. It brings a painful end to the rehearsals for him.

Relief Crews

Bus crews which are on stand-by are referred to by Inspector Blake in the Series Two episode 'Late Again'.

With Stan arriving on duty late and said to be in the toilet by Jack, Inspector Blake grows ever more impatient as he awaits his exit. He tells Jack: 'I have had to sign on two relief crews whilst he has been in there.' Moments later, a commotion breaks out in the ladies toilet as Stan climbs in through the wrong window disturbing a rotund clippie in the process. It soon becomes clear to the inspector that Stan has arrived late for work and is promptly sent home and put on night duty.

Relief crews are staff used to cover bus services should the original crew scheduled to operate the service be unable to carry out the duty due to illness, absence and unpunctuality or service disruption. To the present day this system is still applied by bus companies.

Remote Control Bus

A toy bought by Stan that features in the Series Four episode 'Christmas Duty'.

Stan reveals he has bought a small remote control bus as a Christmas present for his young nephew. He and Jack show it off to Inspector Blake in his office along with the miniature bus stop and inspector that comes supplied. It is with reluctance that Stan allows Blakey to have a chance to operate the remote control bus on the desk in Blakey's office and he enjoys himself steering the bus back and forth. However, as he talks to Stan he becomes distracted and allows the bus to crash over the edge of the desk and it lands on a teapot breaking its spout. Although the toy bus is undamaged it leaves the inspector with a teapot to repair which was intended to be a present for his mother and annoyed he tells Stan and Jack to take the toy away.

Rennison, Jan

Film Role: Gloria (Mutiny On The Buses)

Jan Rennison was born in Australia in 1947 and went on to be a beauty queen in her late teens representing Australia in the 1965 Miss World contest. She would soon embark on a career as an actress on television and in films.

Her debut on television came in 1967 in the Australian family adventure series Adventures Of The Seaspray before she furthered her career in the UK. Appearances in hit dramas such as The Persuaders and Space: 1999 came in the early to mid-1970s. She would also co-host a game show called Quick On The Draw with Bob Monkhouse. On the big screen her roles were to come in the comedy films The Magnificent Seven Deadly Sins and Mutiny On The Buses in the early 1970s.

Her career as an actress spanned ten years and she later went on to campaign for animal rights and became involved in a fight to ban fox hunting in the UK.

Request Stops

This is a type of bus stop that is referred to in a couple of episodes of On The Buses.

Stan is set to drive the coach to the airport as the depot's charter holiday gets under way in the Series Two episode 'Bon Voyage'. As he prepares to depart, Inspector Blake gives him final instructions and tells him not to stop at request stops. 'Don't worry mate I never do,' laughs Stan. The Series Four episode 'Safety First' sees Blakey give Stan and Jack an ear-bashing as a rash of complaints are received about them. Many are from passengers aggrieved that Stan failed to pick them up at request stops.

Request stops are intended only for passengers who request that the bus stops there when they first board the bus. Should a passenger wish to board a bus at a request stop they must hail the bus as it approaches by extending their arm. These types of bus stops are still in use to the present day across the UK.

Rest Room

A room at the Luxton and District bus depot referred to in the Series Three episode 'On The Make'.

The rest room is where a clippie called Edna keeps her large pet dog Coco out of the way until she brings the pet out into the depot as she prepares to move with her belongings into the Butler house as a lodger.

Reward

Inspector Blake is to receive a reward for finding a missing diamond in the Series Five episode 'Lost Property'.

He earns the reward after Stan finds the diamond at home after taking it home in an envelope which he found aboard his bus. However, when the worried bus driver fears the sack for taking the envelope home instead of handing it in to lost property it is left up to Inspector Blake to come up with a solution. He claims to have found the envelope aboard Stan's bus and that explanation saves Stan from the sack and earns the inspector a reward of ten pounds from a jeweller for the diamond's safe return. Despite Stan's pleas the inspector refuses to share the reward with him.

Rhodes, Adam

Film Role: Little Arthur (Holiday On The Buses)

Adam Rhodes career as an actor was brief after bursting into stardom as a child in the early to mid-1970s in films and on television.

Rhodes debuted in the role of little Arthur in the hit spin-off film Holiday On The Buses in 1973 in what would be his best-remembered role. On television he had credits in a Children's Film Foundation production called The Boy With Two Heads in 1974 and also appeared once more alongside Reg Varney in his popular variety show unimaginatively called Reg Varney.

A long-term career as an actor never materialised for Adam Rhodes on leaving school and he would later in life immigrate to Canada to pursue a career away from acting in real estate.

Richard, Wendy

TV Role: Elsie (Series 5 Episode 6 'The Busmen's Ball')
Film Role: Housewife (On The Buses)

Born in Middlesbrough, Teesside in 1943, Wendy Richard soon moved to London and began her working life at a fashion store whilst studying acting at the Italia Conti Stage Academy. In her late teens her acting career began and she went on to become one of Britain's best-loved actresses with roles on television, in films and on stage.

Her television career would offer a wide range of roles spanning almost fifty years. In comedy she will be best-remembered as Miss Brahms in the long running smash hit sitcom Are You Being Served and spin-off series Grace And Favour. Other hit comedy series in which she has appeared included The Likely Lads, Up Pompeii, On The Buses, Please Sir, The Fenn Street Gang, Dad's Army, Not On Your Nellie and Benidorm. Drama roles were also plentiful and she made her mark as battle-axe Pauline Fowler in the ever-popular long running soap EastEnders from its start in 1985 until her departure in 2006. She was also to have roles in Danger Man, No Hiding Place, The Newcomers, Dixon Of Dock Green, Z Cars, West Country Tales and ending her career with credits in a Miss Marple adventure called A Pocketful Of Rye. On the big screen, Richard's roles largely came in comedy films such as On The Buses, Gumshoe, Bless This House, Carry On Matron, Carry On Girls and Are You Being Served? She was also to appear in the science-fiction film No Blade Of Grass.

Her stage career was limited somewhat which, in her autobiography, she puts down to her short attention span and a tendency of boredom from going over the same lines over and over again. She would appear in stage adaptions of Are You Being Served, Blithe Spirit, No Sex Please We're British and frequent pantomime appearances in Cinderella and Dick Whittington And His Cat.

Her other achievements included having a number one hit in the UK charts in 1962 with Come Outside with Mike Sarne, penning her autobiography in the late 1990s and being awarded a MBE in 2000 for her services to television drama. Sadly though, in the latter part of her life she had a lengthy battle with breast cancer which she ultimately lost in 2009 passing away at the age of sixty five. And so a screen legend of her generation was lost to the world.

Wendy Richard
(Photo courtesy of Andrew Ruff of The Dad's Army Appreciation Society).

Richardson, David

TV Role: George (Series 5 Episode 12 'The New Telly')

David Richardson's career as an actor was to see him appear in a range of television series and films from the mid-1950s up until the early 1970s.

His television credits were to include drama series such as The Man In Room 17, Mystery And Imagination, Nicholas Nickleby, The Expert, Z Cars and Follyfoot. He was also to have comedy roles in hit series which included No That's Me Over There, On The Buses, Sez Les and The Fenn Street Gang.

Richardson's solitary film credit came in the classic Hammer film Lust For A Vampire but he did also make an uncredited appearance in the multi-Oscar winning 1956 film Around The World In Eighty Days.

Later in life, following his acting career, he was also to supply a script for a documentary called About Britain in the early 1980s.

Rickerby, Ricky

Make-Up Supervisor (Holiday On The Buses)

Ricky Rickerby was to work in the film industry in the make-up department for almost twenty years. His credits were to come in a short film called There's Always A Thursday, thriller The Last Shot You Hear, horror film Burke And Hare and the popular spin-off comedy film Holiday On The Buses.

Risky For Bus Drivers

A newspaper article with the headline 'Risky For Bus Drivers' is referred to in the Series Four episode 'Dangerous Driving'.

As Stan dines in the depot canteen, Jack reads him an interesting article from a newspaper. It claims that bus drivers are prone to many illnesses due to their stressful occupation. Stan reads the article himself but disagrees with it saying he doesn't get varicose veins driving a bus as it claims. However, Jack says: 'Oh yes you can mate. Sitting in your bus all day it restricts the blood supply to your legs and all your veins get hard and knotted up.' It cuts no ice with Stan though as he ridicules the article and resorts to showing his legs off to Jack but then Inspector Blake is to join the conversation to add fuel to the fire. He reads the article and points out that the report has been authenticated and labels Stan as unhealthy describing him as having 'floppy flab' around his waist. He promises the uncomfortable bus driver that he'll be wearing a corset before long. Although Stan remains sceptical of the report his worried mum places him on a diet and he is also to go to keep fit classes at the depot. Stan's healthy lifestyle comes to an abrupt halt though when the same newspaper writes another article rubbishing its earlier article and puts the bus driver's mind at rest.

Rita

Played by Jeanette Wild

This is an attractive young woman who plays for the Basildon Bashers against the Luxton Lions in the Series Seven episode 'The Football Match'.

Rita, a petite brunette in her twenties, first meets Stan and Jack outside the dressing rooms and introduces herself as one of the Basildon Bashers forwards. Jack is to flirt with Rita throughout the match asking her out on a date and kissing and cuddling her during the first half. Later, in the second half, when the ball rolls to Jack as he stands on his own goal-line whilst he kisses Rita, he stops the ball much to his team-mates pleasure. However, Rita says: 'Excuse me a second Jack.' She moves him to one side and kicks the ball into the net to score another goal for her side before she goes back to kissing Jack. Rita ends the match, joining in with her team-mates in removing Stan's shorts when he challenges them about their tactics.

Road Map

A road map is the only book that bus drivers are allowed to carry as stated in the Series Three episode 'The New Uniforms'.

When Inspector Blake discovers that Stan has an adult magazine tucked in a pocket inside his uniform jacket he is far from pleased. He confiscates the magazine telling Stan that the only book he is allowed to carry in his jacket pocket is a road map.

Road Safety Fund

This is a cash fund which is referred to by Inspector Blake in the Series Seven episode 'Goodbye Stan'.

Stan has tricked the inspector into paying him an extra week's wages before quitting the Luxton and District Bus Company for a new job. When Blakey tells the departing driver that there are no hard feelings that Stan conned him he explains that he got the manager to take the money out of the road safety fund. He feels it is apt as the roads will be safer without Stan driving a bus.

Robbins, Michael

TV Role: Arthur Rudge (On The Buses Series 1 – 6)
Film Role: Arthur Rudge (On The Buses, Mutiny On The Buses and Holiday On The Buses)

Michael Robbins was born in London in 1930 and began his working life as a bank clerk, becoming involved in working in theatres and soon broke into acting through amateur dramatics. He would go on to carve out a memorable career on stage, television and in films as an actor in a career spanning forty years.

Stage roles offered Robbins his break into acting in the early 1950s and he would appear in Murder At The Cathedral, Caesar And Cleopatra, Happy As Larry and The Gimmick in the 50s. For him television and film roles took precedence in his career in the 1960s but stage roles remained close to his heart and in 1972 he returned to stage to star in the West End production Time And Time Again leaving his highly successful role in On The Buses in the process. He'd also later go on to have stage roles in The School Mistress and an adaption of On The Buses: A Fresh Start which toured Canada in the 1980s as well as pantomime appearances in Dick Whittington And His Cat and Robinson Crusoe amongst others.

Towards the end of the 1950s his television career began to take off and he will always be remembered as the snobby know-it-all brother-in-law Arthur in the smash hit sitcom On The Buses in the late 1960s and early 1970s. Other notable comedy credits included Pardon The Expression, Never Mind The Quality Feel The Width, The Dick Emery Show, Thick As Thieves, How's Your Father, The Good Life, The Fuzz, George And Mildred, The Bounder, Fairly Secret Army, Hi-de-Hi and One Foot In The Grave. He was also to appear in a host of classic British dramas over thirty years. The pick of those being The Avengers, Dixon Of Dock Green, Gideon's Way, No Hiding Place, The Baron, Z Cars, The Saint, Department S, The Sweeney, Return Of The Saint, Dick Turpin, Doctor Who, Dempsey And Makepeace and The Bill.

Robbins could also boast a career as a film actor with his most notable roles coming when he reprised his role as Arthur in the spin-off films On The Buses, Mutiny On The Buses and Holiday On The Buses. He also appeared in films such as A Prize Of Arms, The Whisperers, Up The Junction, Zeppelin, Till Death Us Do Part, Man About The House, No Sex Please: We're British, The Pink Panther Strikes Again, The Great Muppet Caper and the Oscar-winning Victor Victoria amongst others.

He was also to supply voice-overs for the hugely popular PG Tips commercials featuring chimpanzees in the 1970s and was married to actress Hal Dyer who also had roles in On The Buses on the small and big screen.

Renowned as a great advocate of charity work, he was a Grand Order of Water Rats and was to be given an award in 1987 for his charity work. Sadly, early in the 1990s Robbins was to begin a battle against cancer which he finally lost in 1992 passing away at the age of sixty two.

A great talent was lost but he is still fondly remembered to this day.

Michael Robbins – The Gentleman

Michael was a key member of the On The Buses cast. With his great dry wit and wonderful facial expressions on delivery of a punch line it increased the comedic value of the man. He was much-respected as an actor and was always cautious of over-stepping the mark of decency when it came to the level of insults aimed at his screen wife Olive. An example of this came when one of the scripts required him to suggest Olive puts a paper bag over her head to improve her appearance he refused feeling the remark was too cruel and made sure the script was amended. The perfect gentleman that he was he would always make a point of apologising to co-star Anna Karen following a scene where he had to insult her.

He always held a great love of the theatre and stage work. The late Shirley Robbins (also known as Hal Dyer) told me in 2009 that the lure of a lucrative stage role prised him away from On The Buses at the end of series six in 1972. And he also admired variety actors feeling that they could only survive on their own talent. He felt they could not blame scripts, their fellow actors or the directors and could only be judged on their own skills.

Roderick, George

Film Role: Second Policeman (On The Buses)

Born in 1913, this English actor had to wait until his early forties before he got his break in acting with roles coming in films and television.

His first break came on the big screen and was to make uncredited appearances in hit films such as The Quatermass Experiment, The Ladykillers, A Night To Remember, Follow A Star, A Stitch In Time, Press For Time and Carry On Again Doctor. His credits, most notably, came in Serious Charge, Rattle Of A Simple Man, The Adding Machine, On The Buses, That's Your Funeral and Love Thy Neighbour.

Roderick's television career saw his most notable role come in the early 1960s sitcom Three Live Wires where he co-starred alongside Michael Medwin and Bernard Fox. Other hit comedy series he appeared in were to include The Larkins, Sykes And A…, The Benny Hill Show and Love Thy Neighbour. In dramas he was to have credits in classic series such as The Vise, Emergency – Ward 10, The Third Man, The Avengers, Z Cars, Ghost Squad, No Hiding Place, The Troubleshooters and The Persuaders.

After almost twenty years as an actor sadly George Roderick passed away in 1976 at the age of sixty two.

Roeg, Nicolette

TV Role: The Lady Doctor (Series 6 Episode 6 'Bye Bye Blakey')

Nicolette Roeg was born in London in 1925 and went into acting from an early age and her career brought her roles on stage and in films and television.

Her first acting roles came on stage and she would go on to have roles in West End musicals such as The Dancing Years, Belle, Fiorello, Oliver and Two Cities. Other stage roles included Careless Rapture and The Pajama Game. A talented and much under-used singer she also had roles on the pantomime scene.

In films she appeared in a handful of big screen productions in the mid-1940s. These came in musicals My Ain Folk, a starring role in Home Sweet Home and I'll Turn To You with a comedy role in Under New Management.

Television roles began to come her way from the early 1950s. Her biggest parts came in musical series such as The Passing Show and Highland Fling with drama roles coming in hit series including No Hiding Place, Dixon Of Dock Green, The Expert, The Onedin Line, Z Cars and the sci-fi series Blake's 7.

Roeg's comedy credits included Here And Now, Dear Mother Love Albert, On The Buses and a one-off special called All This And Christmas Too.

After a more than thirty years as an actress she retired in the late 1970s before sadly passing away in 1996 at the age of seventy one.

Roll – Ons

This is a type of female under-garment worn by Olive and referred to in a couple of episodes of On The Buses.

The Series Three episode 'Busmen's Perks' sees Stan joke about seeing Olive prancing around in her roll-ons in her bedroom. She objects saying it's not true and Arthur agrees as he claims she can hardly move when she has them on.

Later, in the Series Five episode 'The Strain', Stan is wearing a corset having injured his back and when he removes it in the presence of his girlfriend Doreen he scratches his sides furiously saying: 'What a relief. Now I know how you women feel when you take your roll-ons off.'

The garment known as roll-ons was an elasticated girdle with suspenders attached to it to hold up stockings and it was seen as an ideal under-garment for women to wear to maintain a good figure. The roll-ons were introduced in Britain in 1932 and were at the height of their popularity in the 1940s, 50s and 60s but as tights became popular so roll-ons became less so. Although still available to the current day the humble roll-ons are no longer a fashionable item.

Rolls Royce

An iconic luxury car referred to by Stan in the Series Two episode 'The Used Combination'.

Arthur has bought a second-hand motorbike combination and shows it off to Stan and Jack boasting it to be a quiet runner. As he attempts to start the bike without success Jack pulls his leg calling the bike marvellous saying: 'You'd hardly know it was running.' Stan adds: 'Just like the Rolls Royce.'

Rolls Royce manufactures luxury cars renowned for their style and smooth running engines. Originally formed by Henry Royce and Charles Stewart Rolls in 1906 in Crewe, Staffordshire the company known as Rolls Royce Limited went on to release a long series of memorable cars such as the Silver Shadow, Phantom VI, Silver Spirit and Corniche. All of supreme quality and style the much-sought after limousines are expensive cars only affordable by the rich and famous. Although still producing cars to the present day the company is no longer under British ownership as it is now owned by the German manufacturer BMW.

Romeo

A name often given to flirtatious men is used in a number of episodes of On The Buses.

Inspector Blake is taken aback by Stan and Jack's supreme confidence of attracting women on the works holiday to Spain in the Series Two episode 'Bon Voyage'. He fails to see what they have to offer and labels them as 'weak-kneed, washed out Romeos'. Later, in the Series Three episode 'Mum's Last Fling', Mrs Butler is dating bus conductor Wilf and as she awaits his arrival at the Butler house for the first time, Arthur offers to answer the door saying: 'I can't wait to meet Romeo.' Finally, in the Series Five episode 'Boxing Day Social', Jack flirts with Arthur's sister Linda by making eyes at her, Inspector Blake though spoils the romantic moment for them as he butts in to say to Jack: 'Oi. Oi. Come on Romeo. Get out of it.'

Romeo is a name given to a man who spends his time flirting with and courting women and comes from the Shakespeare character of the same name from his famous love story – Romeo And Juliet.

Rose and Crown, The

A public house frequented by Stan and Jack that is referred to in a number of episodes and a spin-off film of On The Buses.

In the Series Four episode 'The Canteen Girl' it is revealed that the Rose and Crown pub is located at the bottom of the road that Stan and Jack live in and there they arrange to meet Inspector Blake's girlfriend Molly. They ply her with vodka and she becomes tipsy prior to turning up at a social event at the depot.

In another Series Four episode called 'Christmas Duty', Stan and Jack set up a date with two clippies arranging to meet them at the Rose and Crown pub for a Christmas drink. In similar circumstances the two busmen have a date with clippies Sandra and Eileen in the Series Five episode 'The Epidemic' at the Rose and Crown. Stan and Jack wine and dine their dates with black velvets and oysters but when Stan starts to display flu symptoms he has to cut the date short and faces a walk home alone.

On the big screen in Mutiny On The Buses a policeman in his patrol car is contacted by mistake by Inspector Blake. Believing he is in contact with his station the policeman says: 'DS14 here. We're parked behind the Rose and Crown. We stopped here last night and picked up a couple of drunken tarts. We thought we might find a couple more here now.'

Rosie

Played by Eunice Black

A rotund clippie at the Luxton and District Bus Company who makes life uncomfortable for both Stan and Inspector Blake in a couple of episodes of On The Buses.

Rosie, a dark-haired and plump middle-aged clippie is to attend keep fit classes at the depot in the Series Four episode 'Dangerous Driving'. Inspector Blake calls her forward to pair-up with Stan in an exercise called 'The See-Saw' which doesn't impress the concerned driver. The exercise goes awry as Rosie ends up pulling him on top of her which unfairly earns Stan an ear-bashing from the inspector whilst she is left lying prostrate on the floor for a few moments. She recovers to join the rest of the keep fit class in participating in a skipping exercise. Rosie reappears in another Series Four episode called 'Christmas Duty' as Inspector Blake is amidst removing mistletoe from above the depot's ladies toilet door. She exits the toilets and gets the wrong idea and throwing her arms around the inspector's waist excitedly smothers him in kisses despite his protests. She stops to say: 'Oh lovely. Lovely. Come on give us another one for Boxing Day.' After wrapping her arms around the shocked Blakey's neck kissing him again and again amidst giggling, she finally relents. Wishing Stan and Jack a merry Christmas she saunters away across the depot.

Ross, Howard

Director (Series 3 Episode 11 'Going Steady', Series 3 Episode 12 'The Squeeze' and Series 3 Episode 13 'On The Make')

Born in Boldon, County Durham in 1940, Howard Ross would go on to have a long association with London Weekend Television directing a number of their best-loved television series from the early 1970s through until the early 1990s. He directed three episodes of On The Buses and this was quickly followed by working on the comedy special The Other Reg Varney. Ross was also to direct other LWT sitcoms such as Ours Is A Nice House, The Mating Machine, Please Sir and The Fenn Street Gang. His drama credit came in the crime drama New Scotland Yard. He was then to move on to directing a long line of current affairs series for LWT including Weekend World, The London Programme, The World This Week and the religious series Morning Worship.

Rota

The Luxton and District Bus Company's staff work to a rota system as referred to in the Series Four episode 'Christmas Duty'.

When a husband and wife bus crew call in sick for their Christmas Day shift it is with great glee that Inspector Blake refers to the rota on his office wall which tells him that Stan and Jack are next in line to cover the shift. Despite their reluctance they have no choice in the matter and they are forced to re-arrange their plans for Christmas Day.

Rotas are still widely in regular use in the workplace to the present day as a method of rotating staff shift patterns and duties.

Rowe, Bill

Dubbing Mixer (On The Buses, Mutiny On The Buses and Holiday On The Buses)

Bill Rowe was born in Crook, County Durham in 1931 and was to have a highly successful career working in the sound department on countless classic films and television series from the early 1960s in a career spanning more than thirty years.

The proudest moment of his career came in 1988 when he won an Oscar for best sound in the film The Last Emperor. He was also to win BAFTA awards for his work on Alien, The French Lieutenant's Woman and The Killing Fields. Rowe also worked on many Hammer Films productions from the mid-1960s until the mid-1970s. These included One Million Years BC, The Horror Of Frankenstein, On The Buses, Dracula Today, Mutiny On The Buses, Holiday On The Buses, Captain Kronos – Vampire Hunter and To The Devil A Daughter. Other memorable films amongst his credits were A Clockwork Orange, Digby The Biggest Dog In The World, Murder On The Orient Express, The Rocky Horror Picture Show, Death On The Nile, Escape To Athena, Watership Down, Quadrophenia, The Shining, The Mirror Crack'd, Chariots Of Fire, Local Hero, An American Tail and Batman. Rowe also had time to fashion a career on television working on hit ITC series from the late 1960s such as The Saint, The Avengers, Department S, Randall And Hopkirk (Deceased), Jason King, The Protectors and Return Of The Saint. Other television credits included a LWT documentary series All You Need Is Love looking at the growth of pop music in the twentieth century and costume drama The Last Days Of Pompeii.

A long and illustrious association with Elstree Studios was to see him made a director and head of the sound department and he was to remain in the industry up until passing away in 1992 at the age of sixty.

Rowlands, David

Film Roles: Parson (On The Buses) and Policeman On Beat (Mutiny On The Buses)

Born in Abergavenny, Wales, David Rowlands was to train at the Guild Hall School of Music and Drama in London and went on to have a career as an actor that saw him with roles on television, in films and on stage over a period of thirty years.

On television he would often be seen playing religious characters in hit sitcoms such as Bowler, Love Thy Neighbour and Rising Damp. He regularly appeared in many classic comedy series including Bless This House, Father Dear Father, Are You Being Served, The Two Ronnies, The Fall And Rise Of Reginald Perrin, Citizen Smith, The Hitch Hikers Guide To The Galaxy, Terry And June and 'Allo 'Allo. He was also to have drama roles most notably in The Wars Of The Roses, Doctor Who, Pennies From Heaven, Rumpole Of The Bailey and The Cleopatras. His film roles came in the early to mid-1970s with comedy roles in On The Buses, Bless This House, Mutiny On The Buses and Vampira. His dramatic film roles came in Assassin and 11 Harrowhouse.

Rowlands also had stage roles in shows such as Oh Clarence in the late 1960s. Other strings to his bow were that he was a qualified teacher and also had a spell as a reporter on BBC Radio Sussex. He was to retire from acting in the mid-1990s and resides on a farm in his native Wales.

Royal Garden Party

This is a famous royal event which is referred to by Inspector Blake in the Series Seven episode 'The Ticket Machine'.

When the inspector visits the Butler house in a bid to sell tickets for the Busmen's Ball event, Stan misunderstands and believes Blakey is there with regards to tickets from a stolen ticket machine which Stan has. The worried driver tells him he only did it to save Olive and his mum from the shame of a court case regarding unpaid bills. The inspector is stunned and says: 'Butler I know the Busmen's Ball is not exactly the royal garden party but I fail to see how it could shame your family.'

Royal garden parties began as long ago as the 1860s when they were started by Queen Victoria at Buckingham Palace. The tradition continues to the present day and is now used as a chance to reward and recognise members of the public service held in the gardens of Buckingham Palace and also at the Palace of Holyrood House in Edinburgh.

Royal Infirmary

A fictional hospital referred to by Stan in the Series Five episode 'The Epidemic'.

With Olive displaying flu symptoms, Arthur peers into her mouth to see if her tonsils are swollen but cannot see them and he asks where they are. 'Somewhere in the Royal Infirmary. Well that's where she had them out,' jokes Stan.

RSPCA

A famous charity which was set up to protect animals is referred to by Stan in the Series Four episode 'The Anniversary'.

When Olive and Arthur are given a pet poodle as an anniversary present it is revealed that Olive is going to cook for the dog. 'God blimey don't let her do that. We'll have the RSPCA after us,' says Stan.

The RSPCA (Royal Society for the Prevention of Cruelty to Animals) is a charity in England and Wales that, since it was founded in 1824 has looked to protect animals from mistreatment and cruelty. Funded by donations the charity, with over 1,500 employees, is one of the largest charities in the UK. Such has been its success, similar charities now exist in Ireland, Scotland, Australia, New Zealand and the USA. It is actively working to promote kindness to animals, protesting against the use of animals for scientific research, looking to protect farm animals and is calling for the end of hunting amongst many other things.

Rubber Mac

This was another term for an overcoat worn by Inspector Blake that causes him an embarrassing moment in the Series Five episode 'Lost Property'.

A passenger is in search of her two missing portions of fish and chips and feels sure she can smell something fishy around Stan's bus with the inspector, Stan and Jack in attendance. To cover up the fact that the fish and chips have been eaten by the two busmen Stan jokingly blames the inspector for the smell saying: 'It's that rubber mac he uses you see. It's like tennis shoes on a hot day only stronger.' The passenger is not amused she isn't to get her fish and chips back and barks: 'I shall write to the manager about this.' Smelling the inspector and pulling a face she adds: 'And other things.'

Ruby

Played by Pamela Cundell

She is one of the first women bus drivers to be taken on by the Town and District Bus Company in the film On The Buses.

Ruby is in her forties, has dark hair and is a woman who won't stand for any nonsense. Prior to her going out on her first shift she stands up to Inspector Blake refusing to take the bus out until he has the windscreen cleaned. She is also quick to levy out a painful punishment to Stan when he bullies a female colleague. However, underneath the tough exterior hides a mental fragility which comes to light later. She suffers at the hands of Stan and Jack's false diversion signs which direct her back to the depot moments after leaving. This sees her getting a tongue-lashing from the depot manager who labels her a stupid woman and Ruby is reduced to tears confessing that she can't stand men who shout at her. There is more suffering for her when Stan puts a diuretic pill into her tea which affects her to such an extent that she is forced to stop her bus mid-route and dash into a public house to use their toilet. Her brief career as a bus driver ends when the bus company dispenses with women drivers but the cloud has a silver-lining for her as she is to take on a new role as inspector. Ruby soon sets about upsetting Stan and Jack by putting them on separate buses which gives her and her female colleagues a little victory in the battle of the sexes with Stan and Jack.

Rudge, Arthur

Played by Michael Robbins

Arthur is a somewhat snobby booking clerk who works for British Railways. He portrays an often disgruntled figure trapped in what, for him is a loveless marriage even though Olive is a devoted and loving wife. He is also constantly at war with his brother-in-law Stan and his know-it-all attitude grates with the bus driver and often tries the patience of his mother-in-law Mabel who is offended by the way he treats Olive and disrespects her.

Arthur Rudge, in a lengthy marriage to Olive, lives in the Butler house alongside his mother-in-law Mabel and brother-in-law Stan. He often feels the bus driver gets preferential treatment but gets his own back by frequently scuppering Stan's hopes of romance with a series of girlfriends by informing Stan's mum who holds old-fashioned principles on the courting front. Aside from having a mean streak that surfaces on several occasions Arthur often berates Olive for her bad cooking, her figure and is always keen to avoid his eager wife's sexual advances to him.

Although arriving in Olive's life as a hospital porter and harbouring ambitions of studying to become a doctor, Arthur goes into employment as a booking clerk. In that post he does go on to become treasurer of the railway union for many years.

Arthur's marriage to Olive is to be a rocky one that ends in divorce in 1973 after ten years of marriage after he leaves her for another woman. His married life is blighted somewhat by him being handicapped by an operation that apparently leaves him lacking in the sexual department but this does not stop him flirting with members of the opposite sex such as clippies Wendy and Beryl. The balding, middle-aged married man also dates the depot nurse Mary whilst she lodges at the Butler house. Arthur, impressed by her upper-class mannerisms, is keen to take the relationship further but he is in for a disappointment as she has no desire to get involved with a married man.

On the big screen Arthur's life pans out somewhat differently than on the small screen. His marriage to Olive remains intact and the couple are to have a son which they christen Arthur but their relationship remains similar with Arthur still keen to avoid romantic contact with his wife and always looking to criticise her. In employment he is to be made redundant and after getting driving lessons from Stan he gets a job as a bus driver for the Town and District Bus Company. In this post he displays similar traits to Stan and Jack for which he had always criticised them for as he flirts with clippies and clowns around during a fire drill which winds up Inspector Blake.

Arthur is to flirt with his first clippie, the notorious Nymphy Norah and escorts her to a darts event at the depot but it is a relationship that fails to develop as Norah turns her attentions to the depot manager, Mr Jenkins.

In life on both the small and big screen Arthur's pride and joy is his motorbike and combination. He is also a keen darts player, enjoys watching wrestling on television, is an avid fan of the football pools and keeps fit with his yoga and breathing exercises. Although trapped in a marriage he retains a dry wit which he often uses to good effect to get under the skin of Stan. Certainly not the ideal husband though – far from it.

Rudge, Linda

Played by Helen Fraser

The younger sister of Arthur who, along with her mother, spend the Christmas period with the Butlers in the Series Five episode 'Boxing Day Social'.

Linda, a flirty brunette in her late twenties, arrives in Luxton aboard Stan and Jack's bus and attracts the attention of Jack who takes to flirting with her. He is keen that she attends the Boxing Day Social event at the depot and she is clearly attracted to the toothy-grinned conductor. However, her brother Arthur insists she is above such events and wouldn't be impressed by a lecherous person like Jack but clearly he doesn't know her very well. The Boxing Day Social event sees Linda unashamedly flirt with Jack but he is scared off by Arthur who threatens the conductor with violence and so she turns her attentions to Stan. Whilst he shows her around one of the buses in the depot she seduces him but their romantic clinch is broken up by the arrival of Inspector Blake and Mrs Rudge on the scene. Of course the blame lies firmly with Stan whilst Linda's virginal image is maintained.

Rudge, Mrs

Played by Gillian Lind

This is the elderly mother of Arthur who visits him for Christmas with her daughter in the Series Five episode 'Boxing Day Social'.

The widowed woman in her mid-sixties speaks with a posh accent and is somewhat snobby – a trait that Arthur evidently picked up from her. Mrs Rudge has a lofty opinion of her children feeling that her daughter Linda has been brought up very well and doesn't chase after men. This is soon proven not to be the case. She also feels that Arthur married too soon as he gave up a course to study to become a doctor to marry Olive.

At the Boxing Day Social event which she attends she enjoys a dance with Inspector Blake but is later in for a few shocks. Olive gets drunk and annoyed when Arthur flirts with an off-duty clippie and proceeds to make an exhibition of herself. 'I knew she wasn't right for my Arthur the day he married her,' says a bemused Mrs Rudge. Another shock comes later when she finds her daughter Linda in an uncompromising position with Stan aboard a bus but rest assured it is to be Stan's fault leaving her and her daughter able to leave Luxton with their image and dignity intact.

Rudge, Myles

Scriptwriter (Series 7 Episode 11 'The Allowance')

Born in Bristol in 1926, Myles Rudge was a multi-talented figure in the world of show business. He trained at RADA as an actor shortly after the Second World War and would go on to have acting roles on stage and in films. He was to have great success as well as a song and scriptwriter.

His acting career first saw him work on stage at the Bristol Old Vic theatre and he went on to appear in Salad Days and Angels In Love as well as appearing in repertory theatres in productions such as Great Expectations. The 1950s saw him appear in a handful of films with uncredited roles in The Mudlark and Delayed Action and later a more substantial part in You Pay Your Money.

Rudge was destined though to excel as a writer of both hit songs and sitcoms from the early 1960s through until the early 1980s. As a songwriter he'd pen hit songs for the renowned comedy actor Bernard Cribbins with Hole In The Ground and Right Said Fred becoming top ten hits in the UK charts and he was also to co-write the appealing theme song for the hit film Carry On Screaming. As well as writing scripts for popular radio shows he would also pen episodes of hit television sitcoms such as Misleading Cases, Romany Jones and On The Buses as well as less successful series including Compact and Father Charlie in the early 1980s. He continued writing scripts for stage and pantomime shows up until his retirement in 1992 as well as being a volunteer worker for the Samaritans.

Sadly, in October 2007, Myles Rudge passed away at the age of eighty one.

Rudge, Olive

Played by Anna Karen

The down-trodden, bespectacled housewife of Arthur who, despite his faults and the lack of affection he shows her, Olive remains loyal and devoted to him often defending him from criticism. She also has a fiery relationship with her brother Stan who enjoys winding her up in a good-natured manner whilst her mum is loves and supports Olive come what may.

Olive Rudge's marriage to Arthur is far from ideal and she is often to be left frustrated by her husband shunning her sexual advances and putting down her efforts to make herself more attractive. She also has to suffer criticism from Arthur and Stan about her cooking, poor eyesight, her weight and her frequent bouts of illness. However, she often gets her own back by embarrassing Arthur complaining about his lack of sexual appetite and bringing up his operation at the most inopportune moments. Her mother offers her the best support always coming to her defence when she is picked upon by Arthur or Stan.

Although chiefly a housewife, Olive frequently tries her hand at various jobs at the Luxton and District Bus Company with mainly little success. A first stint as a clippie lasts one shift as she suffers travel sickness and has to give up the job. She then takes on a job as canteen cook but her disastrous cooking and mispricing of items sees her promptly sacked after a day. A couple of years later she becomes a helper at the depot's newly-opened nursery but again this is a brief appointment as she loses her job when she leaves Stan and Jack to look after the babies when she smashes her glasses and has to return home. Finally, her second stint as a clippie for the Luxton and District Bus Company is to be more successful. She makes an immediate impact with Inspector Blake and manages to keep the job on a long-term basis.

Olive does remain devoted to Arthur throughout their marriage despite his frequent flirtations with the opposite sex. When he finally leaves her for another woman she is distraught and inconsolable during the divorce process and it takes her time to get over the heartbreak. After her divorce she reverts to her maiden name of Olive Butler and a few months' later attempts to woo lodger Inspector Blake into marriage but he is not in the least bit interested.

The life of Olive on the big screen sees her remain married to Arthur and she gives birth to their only son who is also called Arthur. She is to become pregnant again but no second baby is forthcoming for a reason that is never revealed. She takes on a job as a canteen cook at the Town and District's depot canteen and despite a series of mishaps is able to hold on to the job until she falls pregnant and has to give up the post a few weeks later.
There is only one man in her life on the big screen – her husband. The closest she gets to an extra-marital affair is when she ends up in bed with holiday-maker Wally Briggs but this is merely an accident as she mistakes his chalet for her own whilst on holiday at a holiday camp.

Olive is a character renowned for her trademark spectacles, dowdy appearance, terrible cooking, various ailments and an undying devotion to Arthur. She enjoys going to bingo with her mum, trips to the cinema with Arthur, shows an interest in knitting and dress-making, has a love of pets and is also to be a loving mother. Despite being constantly put-down by him she remains a loving wife to Arthur though terribly frustrated by a lack of sexual attention from him.

Rulebook

An essential book that has to be carried at all times by the staff at the Luxton and District Bus Company and is referred to in a number of episodes of On The Buses.

In his new role as assistant inspector, Stan ticks off a cheeky clippie for wearing a skirt he deems too short in the Series One episode 'The New Inspector'. He quotes from the rulebook: 'Appendix Three – Conductresses. Miniskirts should not be more than two inches above the knee.' However, his stance on the matter displeases the manager as he prefers the clippie dressed that way and it leads to him being demoted.

In the Series Four episode 'Safety First', an accident in the depot sees Stan reversing his bus into Blakey's office injuring the inspector which could mean the sack for Stan. Jack comes to the rescue though with help from the union secretary. According to the rulebook it was not Stan's job to manoeuvre the bus in the depot but that of the shunter and as the inspector wrongly ordered Stan to do the job it means the worried driver cannot be sacked.

The Series Five episode 'The Best Man' sees the inspector fretting that Stan and Jack are going to get the bus driver and bridegroom-to-be Bill so drunk at their bachelor party that he'll not turn up for his wedding. Jack pulls the inspector's leg and quoting from the rulebook he jokes: 'Rule sixty six – If the right man doesn't turn up it's up to you to provide a relief substitute on the job.'

The rulebook features heavily in the Series Seven episode 'The Perfect Clippie'. Olive, on her first shift as a clippie, riles Stan and Jack as she continuously pulls them up for not abiding by the rulebook. It also offends the rest of the staff at the depot but Inspector Blake defends her as a model clippie for sticking to the rules. However, bus services soon threaten to fall into chaos as the bus crews stick to the rulebook and buses are delayed by essential safety checks that have to be carried out according to the rulebook. The inspector is frustrated and has no choice but to allow the bus crews to go back to their old ways of disregarding the rulebook so that the buses can run to time. The staff members are to take great joy in ripping up the rulebook in front of the helpless inspector.

Russell, Sheridan Earl

TV Role: Harold (Series 4 Episode 7 'The Kids Outing')

Sheridan Earl Russell was to begin acting as a child in the early 1970s and his acting career was to continue up until the late 1980s appearing in television series and films.

He made his debut as an actor in the hit sitcom On The Buses on the small screen. Other notable television credits were to include small roles in award winning series such as I, Claudius and The Bill.

On the big screen he would achieve stardom with a sizeable role in the smash hit 1976 musical with a cast of children – Bugsy Malone. He'd also have credits in Jabberwocky and The Lords Of Discipline as well as in the hard-hitting made-for-television prison drama film Scum.

Russell, Tony

Composer (On The Buses Theme 'Happy Larry')

Tony Russell was a talented jazz musician who would also go on to compose music for stage shows and television series in the mid-1960s through until the early 1970s.

The late 1950s was to see Russell become a member of the famous band John Dankworth and his Orchestra which was to have chart success in the UK with top ten hits such as Experiments With Mice and African Waltz. He was to play the trombone in the successful orchestra.

He would go on to write music for stage shows such as The Match Girls at The Globe Theatre in 1966 and God Made The Little Red Apple three years later.

Surely, his best-remembered composition was the piece of music called 'Happy Larry' which was to become the theme for the hit sitcom On The Buses for the entirety of its seven series run. He also composed music for drama series Thirteen Against Fate and popular children's series such as The Herbs and its spin-off series The Adventures Of Parsley.

Russian Athletes

The newly recruited women bus drivers at the Town and District Bus Company are likened to Russian athletes in the film On The Buses.

As the well-built women drivers scoff large platefuls of food in the depot canteen Stan and Jack's conversation turns to the bane of their lives – the women drivers. 'What makes you so certain they're women? Well I mean they're like them Russian athletes aren't they. I mean technically they're women but when you go into it, it's quite different,' remarks Jack.

When the On The Buses film first aired in 1971, Russian athletes were a dominant force in many athletic field events. They were well-built women and muscle-bound competing at that time for the USSR (Union of Soviet Socialist Republics), with great success in events such as the shot put, discus and javelin.

Rusty the Cat

This is the pet cat belonging to the Butlers which is seen and referred to in a number of episodes of On The Buses.

Rusty, a grey-coloured cat, is seen curled up inside Stan's upturned cap and he complains his headwear is now fur-lined in the Series One episode 'The Early Shift'. Poor Rusty is to have a narrow escape in the Series Two episode 'Family Flu' when he is almost fed Stan's woeful attempt at a tapioca pudding which was made for his flu-ridden mother. The rubbery tapioca is so bad it is inedible and it is almost fed to the cat before Olive flushed the dish down the toilet. Later, in the same episode as Arthur, Olive and mum prepare for a visit to Aunt Maud, mum orders Stan to feed Rusty with dishes such as boiled cod and minced liver, stewed beef, minced vegetables and a piece of chopped up heart. All this after Stan thinks a drop of milk will suffice. Evidently, Rusty lives with the Butlers for a number of years as, in the Series Seven episode 'The Ticket Machine', the cat is referred to again. When Olive strums her new guitar aimlessly singing woefully out of tune Stan stops her shouting: 'Hold it! Hold it! Hold it! God the neighbours'll think the cat's caught in the mangle.'

Rye, Derek

Sound (Series 7 Episode 8 'Hot Water')

Derek Rye was to work in the sound department on both television series and films in a career spanning from the mid-1960s through until the early 1990s.

His television career began with work on several low key documentaries and public information films such as Tibetan Story and Free To Grow amongst others. His first big credit came in the hit detective drama Van der Valk. Other notable drama credits included The Sweeney, Minder, Tales Of The Unexpected, Widows and The Complete Churchill. On the comedy front his credits came in an episode of On The Buses and Canned Laughter whilst he was also to work on the classic wildlife series The Living Planet.

In films he'd work on adult-themed films from the mid-1960s with credits coming in Secrets Of A Windmill Girl, Big Zapper, The Office Party and The Love Box. However, his most noted film credit came in the late 1970s in the hard hitting spin-off film Sweeney 2.

Rye's career in the television and film industry ended early in the 1990s and he would go on to work in other areas in the sound industry.

Sack, The

Stan and Jack flirt continuously with the sack on the small and big screen in On The Buses and it is inevitable when the sack eventually comes.

Stan is finally sacked from the Luxton and District Bus Company in the Series Seven episode 'Goodbye Stan'. He manoeuvres Inspector Blake into giving him the sack when he calls him 'a fish-faced twit' because the cunning driver has another job lined up in a car factory. He deliberately gets the sack to earn himself another week's wages.

On the big screen, in the film Holiday On The Buses, both Stan and Jack are sacked from the Town and District Bus Company when Stan crashes his bus outside the depot whilst ogling a topless young woman. In the incident the depot manager is injured, his car damaged and Inspector Blake also gets injured and sacked in the process.

Stan and Jack move on to work aboard a tour bus serving a holiday camp where they are to be sacked after a few months in the job. When they use the tour bus to take two holidaymakers on a late night date to the seaside it ends in disaster. The bus gets submerged by the in-coming tide and they are promptly sacked.

Safari Guard

Played by David Lodge

A character that instructs Stan and Inspector Blake on their arrival at the safari park and goes on to ban them from future visits in the film Mutiny On The Buses.

Dressed in suitable attire, the safari guard who is in his forties and has a small moustache is to greet the trial run of the Town and District's new tour bus as it arrives at Windsor Safari Park. He gives out strict instructions before allowing Stan and the inspector entrance into the park. Of course the trial run ends in disaster when a lion enters the bus via a broken emergency door and although the beast exits the bus without harming the two petrified busmen the safari guard arrives on the scene to find the bus stationary and a door open. He furiously tells them he will make out a full report to the manager and insists that their bus company won't be allowed to return and orders them to get out.

Safety Scheme

This is a safety initiative introduced by the Luxton and District Bus Company in the Series Four episode 'Safety First'.

The safety scheme is a bid to cut down on accidents involving buses exiting the depot. It is decided that in order to prevent accidents as buses exit the front of the depot buses will instead exit via the rear exit. Stan is not amused and says: 'Who thought that out? The computer?' Inspector Blake is rather proud to say it was all his idea. However, the safety scheme flops and causes even more serious accidents which results in the scheme being scrapped.

Safety Strap

A part on Arthur's motorcycle and combination, referred to in the Series Two episode 'The Used Combination'.

As mum sits in the sidecar for the first time in Arthur's second-hand motorbike he tells her to put on the safety strap. He boasts its strength saying: 'It's been tested to a ten tonne breaking strength.' However, much to the watching Stan and Jack's amusement, the safety strap is to snap off leaving Arthur embarrassed and he mutters that he'll fix it later.

Safety straps are now universally known as seat belts.

Sally

Played by Pat Ashton

This is an attractive woman bus driver taken on by the Town and District Bus Company in the film On The Buses.

Sally, a blonde-haired woman in her mid-thirties, attracts the attention of Stan with her good looks. However, being a woman bus driver is a problem as Stan's male colleagues are strongly opposed to his budding friendship with her. A passionate woman, Sally is to date Stan and they end up snogging on the sofa at the Butler house but before things can develop further they are interrupted. Jack flanked by several angry busmen visit the Butler house and demand that Stan asks Sally to leave and they threaten him with violence if he doesn't comply. It is to leave Sally gobsmacked and disappointed when Stan carries out their orders.

The incident leads to Sally stepping down as a bus driver and takes up a role as a clippie hoping that she will now be able to have more fun. Stan pleads to be given another chance by her but she is reluctant after her previous experience. Later she is to be courted by Jack when the cunning conductor woos her with flowers and although it is not destined to be a long-term relationship Stan is left feeling hurt and betrayed by the both of them.

Salter, Ivor

TV Role: Policeman (Series 7 Episode 13 'Gardening Time')
Film Role: First Policeman (On The Buses)

Ivor Salter was born in Taunton, Somerset in 1925 and he was to have a long career as an actor on television and in films that spanned from the mid-1950s through until the late 1980s.

Perhaps his best remembered television role came in the hit long running soap Crossroads where he played farmer and religious zealot Reg Cotterill in the late 1970s and early 1980s. He was also to make a number of noted appearances in the classic sci-fi series Doctor Who as well as being cast as a policeman in many series. Notable drama roles included credits in Great Expectations, Maigret, Dixon Of Dock Green, The Saint, Dr Finlay's Casebook, The Avengers, Z Cars, Softly Softly, No Hiding Place, Jason King, The Sweeney and All Creatures Great And Small. He'd also appear in a host of hit comedy series such as Sykes And A ..., Pardon The Expression, Never Mind The Quality Feel The Width, Nearest And Dearest, The Fenn Street Gang, On The Buses, The Dick Emery Show, Don't Wait Up and Executive Stress. In addition he was a regular in the cult children's series Here Comes The Double Deckers.

Salter's career in films started in the late 1950s with credits in The Heart Within, When Strangers Meet and Be My Guest amongst others until the end of the 1960s. In the 1970s came roles in comedy On The Buses, adult films Four Dimensions Of Greta, Tiffany Jones, House Of Whipcord and horror film House Of Mortal Sin which was to be his final big screen role in 1976.

Sadly, Ivor Salter passed away in 1991 at the age of sixty five.

Sanders of the River

This is a character from a hit novel later to be made into a film that Stan is likened to in the Series Seven episode 'The Football Match'.

When Stan turns up for football training at the depot wearing knee-length shorts that are woefully out of fashion he gets mercilessly ribbed. Inspector Blake, acting as the football team manager, amidst laughs says: 'What are you going as? Sanders Of The River?'

Sanders Of The River was a novel written in 1911 by Edgar Wallace and made into a hit film in 1935. The film followed Sanders, a British colonial District Officer, in 1930s Nigeria who struggles to govern the country and turns to a native chief for support. Sanders is often attired in military uniform wearing a pith helmet and khaki-coloured knee-length shorts hence the inspector's remarks in this episode.

Sandra

Played by Sandra Bryant

An attractive woman employed at the holiday camp that has a brief fling with Stan in the film Holiday On The Buses.

A brunette with long wavy hair in her late twenties, Sandra works as a Bluecoats camp entertainer and dates Stan spending an evening with him unawares that he is babysitting for Arthur and Olive looking after his nephew, Arthur. No sooner has Sandra arrived than little Arthur as he is known creeps into the room to watch as they look to get passionate. Despite Stan reading his nephew a story with a frustrated Sandra watching on the boy ruins their chances of romance later as they snog on the sofa. He proceeds to redecorate the chalet's bedroom with his ink-filled water gun. Later Sandra and Stan's date ends by the arrival home of Mrs Butler and her date, Bert and is to see a fed-up Sandra make a hasty exit. As she leaves Bert also makes his excuses to leave as well and invites Sandra to have a beer with him as they exit the chalet.

Sandra

Played by Caroline Dowdeswell

This is a young clippie at the Town and District Bus Company who is placed aboard Stan's bus in the film On The Buses.

Sandra is a blonde-haired; somewhat naïve woman in her twenties who introduces herself to Stan as his new clippie just as he is set to resign but her appearance on the scene quickly changes his mind. 'I'm new here so you will let me know what you want me to do. I'll do everything you say,' Sandra tells Stan. He can't believe his luck and the pair get on well together and as she guides their bus out of the depot for the first time they wink at each other. This distraction causes Stan to knock over a step ladder with his bus bringing two men crashing down who are putting up a poster which crashes down onto Inspector Blake as the closing credits begin to roll.

Sandra

Played by Sharon Young

This is an attractive clippie who, despite having a boyfriend attracts the attention of Stan in the Series Five episode 'The Epidemic'.

Sandra, who is a busty long-haired blonde in her late twenties, is besotted by her boyfriend Brian who is a bus driver. The pair appear inseparable but when he becomes the victim of a flu bug sweeping through the depot she turns her attention to Stan who describes her to Jack as 'a cracker'. They go on a date with Jack and his girlfriend Eileen spending a night out at a pub. With Stan thinking his luck is in they dine on oysters and a round of drinks but he begins to come down with the flu. Sandra is disappointed and not impressed as she doesn't take kindly to him sneezing and spreading his germs around. Reluctantly, Stan has to go home ill leaving Sandra to enjoy the rest of the evening with Jack and Eileen.

Sandra the Scandinavian Stripper

An unseen character that is hired against Inspector Blake's wishes as the cabaret act in the Series Five episode 'The Busmen's Ball'.

Sandra, who performs under the stage name of Sandra the Scandinavian Stripper, charges ten pounds per performance and an extra five pounds for an X-rated show. Her act includes her doing contortions as she strips before mounting a table and doing the splits and at the end she takes off her last garment throwing it into the audience with whoever catches it allowed to go and give it back to her in her changing room after the show.

Sankeys

A shop that features in the Series Three episode 'The Cistern' when the Butler and Rudge family go shopping for a new toilet.

Sankeys sells a range of toilet cisterns and bathroom suites varying in price, colours and style. Stan, Arthur, Olive and mum bicker before agreeing to buy a pan which is listed as a frustrated export, a black plastic seat with a lid attached and a cistern which comes supplied with all the necessary pipes and fittings all for the cost of fifteen pounds. As the shop doesn't deliver goods it is left up to the family to take their new toilet and accessories home on the bus which proves troublesome especially with Inspector Blake on the prowl.

Savile Row

A famous London street renowned for its fashion and tailor shops that is referred to in the Series Five episode 'Stan's Uniform'.

Stan ruins his new uniform's jacket and trousers as they get paint-stained and in a bid to remove the paint he pays a visit to the maintenance department at the depot. However, Inspector Blake is perplexed to see Stan without his trousers on and in a bid to cover up the truth Jack explains his driver took them to the clothing store to have them altered. The inspector is not amused and says to Stan: 'If you're so particular why don't you go to Savile Row and have them fitted?'

Savile Row can be found in Mayfair, London and is famous for its high quality tailor shops. It has traditionally been the home of the best tailor establishments in Britain for well over one hundred and fifty years.

Schedules

Jack, as shop steward, is to protest about the new work schedules in the Series Seven episode 'On The Omnibuses'.

The new schedules are not to Jack's liking as they mean that he and Stan have to do more journeys per shift and they find them exhausting. However, as Inspector Blake was the man who worked them out he is adamant they will remain in place. Strike action is threatened but Jack is soon whisked away for a hastily arranged meeting with the inspector to discuss the schedules raising Stan's hopes that they will be replaced. Things don't go as he wishes though as Jack exits the meeting to announce: 'I've agreed to the management's reasonable requests.' He explains the schedules will remain in place but he will be exempt from them as he'll get time off to attend to his union duties. Stan is left fuming and realises that Jack only looked after his own interests in his discussion with the inspector and for once Blakey ended up getting his own way.

Scorpio

The star sign of Inspector Blake as revealed in the Series Seven episode 'What The Stars Foretell'.

With Olive going through a phase where she is fascinated with horoscopes she is sure that her stars say she is set to remarry. Is that man to be Inspector Blake who is lodging with the Butlers? She is eager to know when he was born so she can read his stars and he reveals he was born on the 5th of November. 'Oh you're a Scorpio. Have you got a sting in your tail?' asks Olive.

Incidentally, Stephen Lewis who played Inspector Blake was also a Scorpio having been born on the 14th of November 1936.

Scruffy

A mischievous poodle given as an anniversary present by Aunt Maud to Arthur and Olive which features in the Series Four episode 'The Anniversary'.

The poodle which Olive calls Scruffy is to prove a mischievous addition to the family and causes Arthur great discomfort. It soon becomes clear that he has an allergy to the poodle as he suffers sneezing fits when Scruffy is near but Olive loves her new pet. The little dog infuriates Arthur in other ways and he scoffs Arthur's breakfast taking a liking to his sausages whilst he is upstairs. There is yet more trouble in store later in the day when Arthur buys a 'rather expensive' box of chocolates intended to be eaten after a special anniversary dinner cooked by Olive but they are ruined when Scruffy urinates on them. Although Olive has grown attached to the poodle she is forced to return him in person to Aunt Maud due to Arthur's allergy.

However, as she boards Stan's bus on her way to her aunt's house Scruffy gets into a fight with a large dog and when Inspector Blake ventures onto the bus to stop the fight he gets bitten on the shin and his trousers get ripped. He promises to charge Olive for a pair of new trousers but Stan quickly looks to soften the blow by starting a collection asking busmen to make a contribution for the dog that bit the inspector and so Scruffy leaves Luxton a hero amongst the busmen.

Second Policeman

Played by George Roderick

This ageing policeman gets knocked to the ground in the film On The Buses.

The policeman, who is in his fifties, stands in the middle of the road halting on-coming traffic. However, a Town and District bus driven by woman driver Vera with Inspector Blake aboard runs out of control bumping into the back of a truck which in turn knocks the policeman off his feet. A panic-stricken Vera leaps from her cab which is crawling with spiders and refuses to get back in and drive away when the policeman walks over and asks sternly who is in charge of the bus? 'I am I suppose,' a sheepish inspector says and prepares to take the blame for the accident from a far from happy policeman.

Security Guard

An unseen member of staff employed by the Luxton and District Bus Company who is referred to in the Series Five episode 'Lost Property'.

A late night shift ends for Stan and Jack and they look forward to a visit to the pub but they are ordered to check their bus for lost property before they leave by Inspector Blake. As he leaves he hands them a form telling them: 'You check that bus thoroughly, fill that form in and hand it on to the security guard tonight, right?' Of course they ignore his orders which lands Stan in trouble.

See Saw

The name of a back exercise that is part of keep fit classes at the bus depot in the Series Four episode 'Dangerous Driving'.

Inspector Blake is running fitness classes and asks a busman called Harry and one of his colleagues to demonstrate the see saw which involves them rocking to and fro from a seated position to their feet and down again. The inspector then pairs Stan up with a rotund clippie called Rosie. However, their attempt at the exercise ends with the hapless driver being pulled on top of the prostrate clippie which earns him an ear-bashing from Blakey as a result before the fitness class moves on to a skipping exercise.

Self Defence Classes

A rash of assaults on the bus crews of the Luxton and District Bus Company sees self-defence classes arranged and they feature in the Series Two episode 'Self Defence'.

Stan and Jack dismiss the classes as a management ploy to appease staff but when they see two attractive clippies called Joyce and Liz sign up for lessons they soon have a change of heart. The self-defence classes give lessons in judo and karate in the depot canteen and these are given by Inspector Blake who had trained men in the army in unarmed combat. The inspector gives tips on a type of self-defence that involves finding sensitive points on the body known as atemi and demonstrates on Stan but is to receive a painful blow himself in the process.

As Stan retires to the toilet an attractive blonde clippie called Joyce takes to the floor to demonstrate her skills on Jack and does a number of throws on the conductor and is to confess she has five years' experience in judo. In addition she later demonstrates more moves on the unaware Stan when he returns from the toilet. He is in for a painful experience as she performs an array of martial arts moves such as a Japanese stranglehold, a sweeping ankle and a series of kicks and throws that leaves him prostrate on the mattress.

When he gets back to his feet he is dazed and pained. He rules out chatting up Joyce and Liz fearing for his safety if he were to try to take advantage and goes home nursing a bruised ego and a bump on the head.

Seven Year Itch

A phrase Stan uses when discussing Olive and Arthur's marital problems in the Series Four episode 'The Other Woman'.

Arthur is late returning home from a darts night event at the depot where he openly flirts with a clippie called Wendy. As Stan and mum sit up with a distraught Olive until the early hours of the morning waiting for Arthur's return Stan reflects: 'He's a fella isn't he? He's having his seven year itch.' When Olive points out they've been married nine years her brother coldly says: 'Well he must have scratched around for the other two.'

The phrase seven year itch originally stemmed from early in the nineteenth century in the USA that was used for a medical complaint which caused red pimples on the face and body and was a bacterial ailment which is now easily treatable. However, in 1955, a hit film starring Marilyn Monroe and Tom Ewell called The Seven Year Itch portrayed a man happily married for seven years who is to have his first affair and so a new meaning for the phrase was born.

Sexy Beast

Arthur is mockingly called a sexy beast by Stan in the Series Five episode 'The Best Man'.

When Olive reveals that Arthur used her talcum powder on their wedding day and now uses it every night it leaves him open to ridicule. Even though he is hung-over Stan shows he still has his quick wit as he sarcastically calls his brother-in-law a 'sexy beast'.

Shake, The

This is a fictional dance craze and hit record that is referred to in the Series Four episode 'Dangerous Driving'.

A bubbly young clippie called Pat who has a date lined up with Stan asks him if he shakes in reference to a new dance craze. She puts a record on in the canteen and proceeds to dance to the music in a dance she calls 'The Shake'. In a bid to impress, Stan joins in and the dance involves vigorous shaking of the head and arms. However, a few minutes later Stan is toiling physically and has to stop revealing to Jack that he has a stitch. It brings it home to him that he needs to get in shape for his date with Pat and decides to attend keep fit classes run by Inspector Blake at the depot.

Shakesby, Patricia

TV Role: The Nurse (Series 4 Episode 12 'The Injury')

Born in Cottingham, Yorkshire in 1942, Patricia Shakesby went straight into acting from school and fashioned a career as an actress that saw her appear on stage and have roles on television and in films.

Late in the 1950s she began on stage in a West End production called Where The Rainbow Ends. It was to be the start of a packed career in theatre with roles coming in Someone To Kill, Night of the Iguana, The Real Inspector Hound and Suddenly At Home. She has also worked on stage productions of Hamlet, Troilus And Cressida, Romeo And Juliet and La Ronde all with the famous Royal Shakespeare Company. Numerous roles in repertory theatre also came her way as well as a string of pantomime appearances.

On television she will be best remembered as Polly Urquhart in the smash hit 1980s BBC drama Howards Way and in the early 1960s played Susan Cunningham in Coronation Street. Other notable drama credits on the small screen included Z Cars, Dixon Of Dock Green, War And Peace and Sapphire And Steel. She was equally adept in comedy roles and appeared in classic sitcoms such as Hancock's Half Hour, The Likely Lads, Doctor In The House, The Liver Birds, On The Buses, The Fenn Street Gang and Yes Minister.

Her film roles came in the early to mid-1960s in the comedy film She Knows Y'Know, Offbeat and an uncredited part in He Who Rides A Tiger.

After over fifty years as an actress she still treads the boards as well as working on radio and writing plays. She is also the vice president of the Worcester Philharmonic Orchestra and resides in Tewkesbury, Gloucestershire.

Shamsi, Mohammad

TV Role: Mr Sharma (Series 1 Episode 6 'The Canteen')

Mohammad Shamsi was born in Moradabad, Uttar Pradesh in India in 1929. In his mid-thirties his acting career began to take off in the UK where he would have roles on television and in films from the mid-1950s through until the early 1980s.

His television credits were varied with roles in hit drama series such as Danger Man, Special Branch, Quiller, Z Cars and an uncredited appearance in Doctor Who. In comedy Shamsi appeared in hit sitcoms On The Buses, Sykes, Are You Being Served and a number of varying roles in It 'Ain't Half Hot Mum.

The 1970s were to see him work on a number of films that had varying degrees of success. Most notable and largest roles were to come in adventure films The Horsemen and the award-winning The Man Who Would Be King. He also appeared in comedy films The Adventures Of Barry McKenzie, The Hound Of The Baskervilles and the made-for-television film Antony And Cleopatra.

Sharma, Mr

Played by Mohammad Shamsi

This is an Indian busman who offers a solution to a problem for Stan in the Series One episode 'The Canteen'.

Mr Sharma, a rather portly, bespectacled man in his early forties is to help Stan who has to find a cook for the canteen which he is running. He offers the services of his wife who he explains has the experience necessary for working in a canteen but neglects to tell Stan that she cannot speak a word of English. When it turns out that his wife is not suitable for the job and is sacked after a day in the post, Mr Sharma is on hand to make sure his wife gets every penny entitled to her including a full week's wages and national insurance payments. He and his wife are happy with the outcome and it now means he has his wife alongside him in the UK where she has recently moved from Bombay in India.

Sharma, Mrs

Played by Shiranee Fullerton

This is a woman who takes on the job of canteen cook at the depot in the Series One episode 'The Canteen'.

Mrs Sharma who is in her forties is given the job as canteen cook by Stan as she comes with two years of experience of working in a bus depot canteen in Bombay in her native India. However, it soon becomes clear she is not suitable for the job as she cannot speak a word of English and is only able to converse with Inspector Blake who is fluent in her language. Also her spicy Indian dishes are unpalatable to the busmen whilst her cups of tea with salt added don't go down well either.

After a day in the job Mrs Sharma is dismissed by the disgruntled busmen but her husband assures that she gets a full week's wages and more. She leaves content declaring that England is a wonderful country.

Sharif, Omar

A world famous actor from the 1950s through to the late 2000s referred to by Stan in the Series Four episode 'Not Tonight'.

Stan's love life has been in crisis for a few weeks and Inspector Blake takes great pleasure in ribbing the depressed driver. 'Look mate just because you wear a moustache you're no bloomin' Omar Sharif,' says Stan hitting back at the inspector. Jack backs his driver up joking that Blakey does bear a close resemblance to Sharif's camel though.

Omar Sharif is a moustachioed Egyptian actor who shot to fame with his large supporting role in the epic war film Lawrence Of Arabia which featured camels hence Jack's remark. Sharif's other most notable film roles came in Doctor Zhivago and The Tamarind Seed and he has had a long, distinguished acting career spanning well over fifty years in which time he has won many awards as an actor.

Sheard, Michael

TV Roles: Manager (Series 7 Episode 3 'The Ticket Machine', Series 7 Episode 8 'Hot Water', Series 7 Episode 10 'What The Stars Foretell', Series 7 Episode 11 'The Allowance' and Series 7 Episode 13 'Gardening Time') and 1st Judge (Series 7 Episode 4 'The Poster')
Film Role: Depot Manager (Holiday On The Buses)

Born in Aberdeen, Scotland in 1938, Michael Sheard was to move down to England at the age of fifteen where he trained to be an actor at RADA in London and cut his teeth as an actor in repertory theatre before going on to carve out a great career on both television and in films.

His best remembered role on television came in the hit children's drama series Grange Hill from 1985 to 1989 when he played the terrifyingly tough teacher Mr Bronson. Sheard was also to feature regularly in various roles in the classic sci-fi series Doctor Who over a period of twenty two years between 1966 and 1988.

He also appeared in many classic dramas such as Crossroads, Dr Finlay's Casebook, Dixon Of Dock Green, Softly Softly, Van der Valk, The Persuaders, The Onedin Line, The Sweeney, Within These Walls, Z Cars and The Professionals. His comedy roles were to come in The Likely Lads, On The Buses, The Dick Emery Show, Not On Your Nellie, Mind Your Language, Auf Wiedersehen Pet, The Darling Buds Of May and 'Allo 'Allo to name but a few.

Sheard's film roles were to include several war films such as The McKenzie Break, England Made Me, Force 10 From Navarone, Escape To Athena and The Riddle Of The Sands. Other notable big screen roles included Holiday On The Buses, Doombeach and Another Life as well as uncredited parts in Frenzy and Indiana Jones And The Last Crusade. However, his best remembered role came in the blockbuster sci-fi sequel The Empire Strikes Back in 1980.

Renowned for his portrayals of Adolf Hitler on the big and small screen Sheard's acting career spanned well over forty years and he was also to write four autobiographies about his life and acting career. He continued working up until his death in 2005 when he sadly lost his battle with cancer passing away at the age of sixty seven.

Shop Steward

A position proudly held by conductor Jack Harper in On The Buses on both the small and the big screen.

As shop steward Jack is to use his position of power to great effect. On numerous occasions he uses his great knowledge of every rule in the book to rescue Stan and sometimes himself from the sack and he is also to instigate strike action or frequently threaten a strike unless his demands are met. This often frustrates and exasperates Inspector Blake and he is often to see himself losing out in the on-going power struggle between the union and the management.

A shop steward is an appointed Trade Union Representative in the workplace. His or her task is to act as an advisor and to represent fellow colleagues in discussions with his/her employers and management. They also act as a link between union members and the union itself and keep their members informed in any changes to their rights in the workplace.

Shopkeeper

Played by Terry Duggan

This is a character who sells the Butler family a new cistern and accessories in the Series Three episode 'The Cistern'.

The shopkeeper, an employee at the Sankeys plumbing store is in his late thirties and wears brown overalls. He displays a modicum of impatience in dealing with the family as they first opt for a wooden toilet seat and then change it for a plastic one. As he tallies up the price of the goods he is asked about delivering them to the Butler house but tells them the company doesn't deliver at the prices they charge. However, he offers to deliver the items himself in around a week's time at an extra cost but as the family need the goods immediately they decline the offer with Stan paying for the cistern and accessories before leaving the shop.

Sickness Benefit

A payment referred to by Jack in the Series Four episode 'The Injury'.

When Stan injures himself whilst decorating the bathroom he is left unfit for work. An injured right shoulder and broken big toe leaves Stan in a predicament and hearing the news Jack points out: 'Oh blimey that's bad. You know our company you won't get nothing off them. You'll only get your sickness benefit…four quid a week.'

Sickness benefit was introduced to the UK in 1948 as part of the National Insurance Act of 1946. It remained a key and important benefit for many until 1995 when it was to be replaced by Incapacity Benefit which was in turn replaced by the Employment and Support Allowance in 2008. All of these were government-subsidised payments with the money coming from employees national insurance contributions.

Sign On

A duty that all busmen have to carry out before starting their shift which features in the Series Four episode 'The Injury'.

Stan, although carrying injuries, limps in to work in a bid to have an arranged accident in order to earn accident pay. He is told to sign on for duty by Jack to make the accident official but that proves to be too painful for Stan and so he has to resort to signing on with his left hand. His signature is very tough for Inspector Blake to read and as he scrutinises it he says: 'What language is it in then? Pakistani or Arabic? You haven't changed your name to Mohammad Butler have you?' The signature suffices though but Stan's arranged accident turns into an accident for somebody else.

Silverside of Beef

A dish cooked erroneously by Olive in the Series Seven episode 'Hot Water'.

Although mum takes silverside of beef joint out of the oven declaring that it looks lovely and lodger Blakey says he loves salt beef the pair are in for a disappointment. The beef cooked by Olive turns out to be overly salty as she admits to having soaked it in a cupful of salt. A mouthful of the dish sends Blakey racing for a drink of water with Mrs Butler in pursuit of relief as well. 'You great twit! You're not supposed to soak it in salt. It is salt beef,' says the off-duty inspector berating Olive.

Silvester Method

A technique used to give artificial respiration which is demonstrated during a course on firefighting at the depot in the Series Six episode 'No Smoke Without Fire'.

Inspector Blake calls forward Stan to take part in a demonstration of the silvester method and asks him to lie down on the floor. Eagerly, the randy driver obliges believing an attractive clippie will be chosen for the exercise. However, much to his consternation and Inspector Blake's glee an overweight middle-aged clippie called Gladys is chosen as she knows the silvester method. She folds the horizontal Stan's arms across his chest and throws herself upon him pushing her weight down on his diaphragm attempting to throw his arms out wide whilst she leans back but she fails. Stan though, feels like he is being crushed and struggles to get Gladys off him. When the inspector accuses him of making a meal of the situation an exasperated Stan says: 'Tell you what mate by the time she's finished giving you artificial respiration you need the kiss of life.'

The silvester method was introduced by a British physician called Henry Robert Silvester in 1858. His technique would be in frequent use until more advanced and efficient forms of artificial respiration were developed in the second half of the twentieth century.

Simpson, Gerald

Played by Bob Todd

An area manager at the bus depot who happens to be an old flame of Mrs Butler's who features in the Series Seven episode 'Friends In High Places'.

A balding man in his sixties who is employed as an area manager by the Luxton and District Bus Company has a terse working relationship at the depot with Inspector Blake. When he appoints Mrs Butler as the new canteen cook he is delighted to discover she is an old acquaintance from World War Two when they worked in the same munitions factory.

He reveals he has been a widow for eleven years and before long he and Mabel Butler are dating each other. Gerald, being a man in a position of power soon begins to make life very uncomfortable for Blakey as he feels he is taking advantage of Mrs Butler and feels he should be paying more rent to her as a lodger and chastises him for being cruel for keeping his pet goldfish in a little bowl. Gerald's relationship with Mabel appears to be becoming serious but with his retirement approaching he reveals to her his plan to retire immediately and move to Skegness but the door is left open for romance to blossom as he invites her to visit him. His departure from Luxton is sad news for Mrs Butler but a welcome relief for Inspector Blake.

Singer, Campbell

TV Role: Mr Nichols (Series 4 Episode 11 'The Lodger')

Campbell Singer was born in London in 1909 and as an actor was to have roles in films, on television and also on stage in a career that spanned over thirty years.

Shortly after the end of World War Two, Singer's film career got under way and he went on to appear in a plethora of films. In drama roles his most notable credits included Someone At The Door, A Case For PC 49, Home At Seven, Lady In The Fog, Time Bomb, The Yellow Balloon and The Trials Of Oscar Wilde. He also appeared in fondly remembered comedy films such as The Titfield Thunderbolt, The Square Peg, On The Beat and The Fast Lady. From the early 1960s though, he would become a more television-orientated actor.

On the small screen he was to frequently appear in hit drama series such as Maigret, Danger Man, Coronation

Street, Doctor Who, The Forsyte Saga, The Saint, The Avengers, The Persuaders and Z Cars. He was also to have roles in some of the best comedy series of the 1950s, 60s and 70s including Hancock's Half Hour, Citizen James, Please Sir, On The Buses, Doctor At Large, Nearest And Dearest, Dad's Army, Sykes, The Dick Emery Show, Rising Damp and Some Mothers Do 'Ave 'Em.

On stage, Singer was to not only write stage shows but also appeared as an actor in Home At Seven (later adapted into a film) and the Agatha Christie play Spider's Web in the West End to name but a few.

He would carry on working as an actor until sadly passing away in 1976 at the age of sixty seven.

Siniawski, Petra

TV Role: The Clippie (Series 6 Episode 6 'Bye Bye Blakey')

Petra Siniawski can boast a varied career in show business spanning over forty years. She has had acting and dancing roles in film, television and chiefly on stage where she has become an experienced dance choreographer and director.

Her great dancing talent would see her have uncredited roles in smash hit films Women In Love and Fiddler On The Roof as well as in the less successful The Boy Friend and The Old Curiosity Shop. Credits did follow in The Slipper And The Rose: The Story Of Cinderella and most recently with a role in the hit musical Billy Elliot in 2000.

On television her career was limited to a role in the hit sitcom On The Buses and a small role in the children's series Jackanory Playhouse.

It was to be on stage that Siniawski would hit the big time. After roles in the stage adaption of the sitcom Are You Being Served and the musical A Chorus Line in the latter half of the 1970s bigger things lay ahead. In hit West End musicals she would have leading roles in Annie: On Your Toes and West Side Story as well as repertory theatre roles in musicals Chicago, Lulu: Bells And Ringing, Stepping Out and Blithe Spirit. As a gifted dance choreographer she would work on smash hit musicals Jesus Christ Superstar, Hair, Annie, King And I and Guys And Dolls. As a director her credits include The Sound Of Music, Sweet Charity and West Side Story.

She is still active on the West End stage scene to the present day in various roles as an actress, choreographer and director.

Sit-in Protest

Stan holds a sit-in protest in a bid to get proper canteen facilities and see that canteen cook Elsie is reinstated in the Series Six episode 'Union Trouble'.

When Jack is paid a bonus by the bus company to insure that he won't encourage strike action and Stan has no luck trying to get fellow busmen to join him in an unofficial strike he resorts to desperate measures. He stages a sit-in protest and refuses to move from the cab of his bus until his demands are met. It gives Inspector Blake a headache and he orders Jack as shop steward to resolve the issue but although he suspends Stan from the union it does not stop the sit-in protest. The inspector is left frustrated but remains determined and insists he'll starve the stubborn bus driver out though Stan counters this by claiming he is now on hunger strike. This proves all too much for Blakey to bear who resorts to trying to drag the protesting driver out of the cab but is thwarted by Stan's violent defiance as he traps the inspector's head in the cab window which forces him to retreat. As the protest drags on into the evening and night the inspector uses a different tact. He orders a jug of tea to be brought out for Stan and pretends he is leaving for the night. With Stan parched he thinks it is safe to come out of his cab and drinks the tea before paying a visit to the depot toilet. However, on his return to his bus he finds he has been out-witted by Inspector Blake who has crept across and closed the cab door before he can reach his cab thus ending the sit-in protest. He is sent home having lost his battle much to the inspector's satisfaction.

Skater's Waltz by The Foden's Motor Works Band

This is a vinyl record that is part of the Butler's collection which is referred to in the Series One episode 'The New Conductor'.

When Stan brings his new clippie Iris home after a date she asks him to put on some mood music that is non-vocal. Stan picks up a vinyl record, reading the label he says: 'Skater's Waltz by The Foden's Motor Works Band.' Iris is not impressed and gives up on the idea of having music on.

The Skater's Waltz was a classical piece of music written by the French composer Emile Waldteufel in 1882. As for The Foden's Motor Works Band they were a long-running and successful brass band formed in the early 1900s by Edwin Foden whose company manufactured trucks in Sandbach, Cheshire. In 1969 (when this episode originally aired) they released an album called Marches and Waltzes which contained the Skater's Waltz as a track and is presumably the album Stan held in the episode. The brass band, now renowned as one of the best in the world in the current day is still in existence with a new generation of musicians keeping the tradition alive.

Skeggs, Roy

Production Supervisor (On The Buses, Mutiny On The Buses and Holiday On The Buses)

Roy Skeggs has had a long and distinguished career as a producer in both film and television since the early 1970s with a long association with the Hammer Films productions company and is widely regarded as a saviour of that company when it fell on hard times.

His film career began at Hammer where he was to work as a production supervisor on all three On The Buses spin-off films, Twins Of Evil, Dr Jekyll And Sister Hyde, Vampire Circus and Captain Kronos – Vampire Hunter amongst others. He was to be elevated to role of producer at Hammer with his most notable credits being Love Thy Neighbour, The Satanic Rites Of Dracula, Frankenstein And The Monster From Hell, Man About The House, To The Devil A Daughter and Rising Damp.

He became a board member at Hammer Films but resigned in 1979 with fellow board member Brian Lawrence in amiable circumstances and they formed their own production company called Cinema Arts. However, when Hammer Films entered receivership in the same year they were asked to return to offer their assistance. They overhauled the company relocating the studios to Hapden House, Buckinghamshire where a television series was put into production and was called Hammer House Of Horror which was produced by Skeggs in 1980. It proved to be a hit in both the UK and the USA and after its completion Skeggs and Lawrence were to buy out Hammer Films. Later in the 80s came another television series called Hammer House Of Mystery And Suspense again produced by Skeggs. It is widely accepted that these changes in Hammer's production tact kept the famous company in business and Roy Skeggs must take a lot of credit for that.

Skeggs, until recently, was a managing director at Hammer and although the company is under new ownership and back in film production he has now retired from the industry. He has attended annual Hammer Films conventions occasionally as a celebrity guest amidst his retirement and is a figure held in high esteem.

Skegness

A seaside town referred to in the Series Seven episode 'Friends In High Places'.

It is revealed that area manager Gerald Simpson is to retire from his job at the Luxton and District Bus Company and move to live in Skegness. It is a move that puts an end to a budding romance between Mr Simpson and Mrs Butler though he does invite her to visit him there.

Skegness is a small seaside town on the east coast of England in Lincolnshire. Famous for being home to the first Butlins holiday camp in 1936, the town is seen as a holiday resort equipped with large, good quality beaches with a healthy supply of hotels to cater for the holidaymakers. The key tourist attractions are the pier and the long standing tall clock tower.

Skeleton

A skeleton is used by Inspector Blake during his keep fit class at the depot in the Series Four episode 'Dangerous Driving'.

The inspector, who is to use the skeleton to point out joints and parts of the body that need exercise, is left open to ridicule from Stan and Jack. They mock him claiming they can see the family likeness between him and the skeleton and they embarrass him querying the sex of the skeleton. However, the fed-up inspector hits back claiming that the skeleton was a passenger that got that way waiting for Stan's bus which puts the cheeky driver in his place.

Skidpan Test

Stan is forced to undergo a skidpan test following an accident that sees his bus destroy a telephone box and bus shelter in the film On The Buses.

The insurance company of the Town and District Bus Company withdraw their cover for Stan until he can pass a test. The test is to be carried out on London Transport's skidpan facility aboard one of their buses. With a nervous Stan full of apprehension about what waits ahead he gets into his cab and is signalled to start the test and when he sees Inspector Blake is still aboard his bus he decides that if he has to undergo the rigours of the test then so will Blakey. As his bus moves off a panicked inspector calls for him to stop but his pleas fall on deaf ears. With the bus undergoing a series of skids Blakey is flung around like a rag doll and finally as the last skid gets under way he falls from the back of the bus, sliding on his back for a number of yards before coming to a halt at the feet of the insurance company examiner Mr Brooks who says: 'Oh I thought he did very well. I'll pass him.' For Stan the ordeal is over and he gets unsteadily from his cab and staggers away.

Skipping Exercise

An exercise that is part of a keep fit class at the depot in the Series Four episode 'Dangerous Driving'.

Inspector Blake asks those at the keep fit class to line up as they prepare to do something he describes as simple – the skipping exercise. It is an exercise involving skipping with an imaginary skipping rope which Stan feels is child's play. However, it turns into an endurance test as Blakey bets Stan a pound that he can keep skipping longer than him and Jack has a laugh at their expense betting they both can't keep it up until six o'clock. Twenty five minutes later, Stan is sweating profusely and collapses into a chair whilst still pretending to skip. The triumphant inspector claims himself the winner of the contest pointing out that Stan has stopped skipping. A concerned Jack checks on the exhausted driver and jokes: 'Stopped skipping? Blimey he's stopped breathing.' Although Stan tries to claim his rope got tangled up, Blakey scoffs that it was a make believe skipping rope to which Stan says that he'll make believe his rope got tangled. It cuts no ice with Inspector Blake who expects payment of his one pound from Stan.

Slater, Michael

TV Roles: TV Newsman (Series 1 Episode 1 'The Early Shift'), Family Man (Series 1 Episode 3 'Olive Takes A Trip'), The Mechanic (Series 4 Episode 6 'The L Bus'), The Maintenance Man (Series 4 Episode 10 'Safety First') and Joe (Series 4 Episode 12 'The Injury').

Michael Slater can boast a career as an actor that was to span a quarter of a century with roles in many hit television series in the 1960s, 70s and 80s as well as countless stage roles.

He was to have a variety of roles in drama series such as Z Cars, The Champions, Dixon Of Dock Green and The Bill amongst others. His comedy roles came in several episodes of On The Buses as well as a host of other hit sitcoms including All Gas And Gaiters, Love Thy Neighbour, Romany Jones, Billy Liar and Mind Your Language.

After retiring from acting in the late 1980s, Slater was to remain involved in the acting industry. He would go on to become a member on the board of trustees of the Catholic Association of Performing Arts based in London. Slater works there to the current day where he is actively involved in hosting events and actors awards ceremonies.

Michael Slater debuting at the 2012 On The Buses event.

Sleeping Tablets

These pills are taken by Olive and are also to be offered to Stan in a couple of episodes of On The Buses.

Firstly, in the Series Three episode 'On The Make', Stan is thwarted in his attempts to have a late night rendezvous in the Butler house with the new lodger Edna. A gloating Arthur recommends that the frustrated bus driver takes a couple of Olive's sleeping tablets to help him sleep as he is determined to stop his brother-in-law from having any contact with the attractive young lodger. Later, in the Series Four episode 'Not Tonight', Stan is bored and at a loose end sitting around the house as his love life goes through a crisis. He refuses to go to the pictures and so Olive offers him one of her sleeping tablets claiming they put her to sleep as soon as her head hits the pillow. Arthur dryly agrees that they do a great job in a quietly satisfied tone of voice.

Smelling Salts

Olive is known to use smelling salts and they are referred to in a couple of episodes of On The Buses.

The smelling salts are put to good use in the Series Five episode 'The Best Man'. Prior to his wedding, busman Bill arrives at the church with Stan and he is still hung-over from his bachelor party and somewhat comatose. Olive delves into her handbag and lets Bill smell the salts which does help his condition a little allowing the wedding to go ahead. In the Series Five episode 'The Strain', Stan is desperate to make a quick return to work despite straining his back and so resorts to wearing a corset. As Arthur tightens it up Stan is left short of breath and says he feels faint. In a camp voice Arthur mockingly says: 'Here, smelling salts. Me thinks my lady has the vapours.'

Smith, Doreen

Played by Pat Ashton

This is a clippie who is to date Stan in a couple of episodes of On The Buses.

Doreen is a bubbly blonde employed clippie employed by the Luxton and District Bus Company who is in her thirties and is very flirtatious. She works aboard the number fourteen bus at the depot and is to date Stan but it is another romance destined for failure. The Series Five episode 'Stan's Room' sees Doreen left frustrated and annoyed when her attempts for privacy and moments of passion with Stan are thwarted by constant interruptions at the Butler house. Even a bid to sneak upstairs into Stan's room is to fail and Doreen storms home in a huff. When she dates him again he has become a lodger at Inspector Blake's house and they face more frustration when Stan manages to carry her on his back up to his room only to be tracked down by his family. Their appearance alerts the inspector and Doreen once more leaves in a fury and is fed-up.

In a later Series Five episode called 'The Strain', Doreen who is now slimmer, dates Stan once more but is unaware he has injured his back and has to wear a corset to date her. This injury comes back to haunt Stan when he looks to snog her on the sofa at the Butler house. Sadly, he only succeeds in aggravating his back injury as they kiss and he is left incapacitated. As he struggles to move she pleads to take him up to bed but there will definitely be no romance that night for the pair of them. Doreen and Stan's relationship is no more after this episode.

Smoking Ban

A ban on smoking in the workplace is put in place at the bus depot in the Series Six episode 'No Smoke Without Fire'.

When the paint shop at the bus depot is set fire to by an employee who throws a lit cigarette into a can of paint thinner it is left up to Inspector Blake to put the fire out and as a result drastic action is taken. The Luxton and District Bus Company puts in place a smoking ban at the depot and the inspector warns Stan and Jack: 'In future anyone caught smoking whilst they're on duty is going to be sacked on the spot.' However, the ban turns out to be short-lived.

Snake

A pet snake is to create havoc in the Butler household in the Series Three episode 'The Snake'.

The snake is owned by the depot's canteen cook Fatima who is to perform an exotic dance with the snake at an Indian social event at the depot with Stan and Jack watching on enthralled. It doesn't take Jack long to line up a date with Fatima after the event but she is keen to take the snake with her. The canny conductor has other ideas though and places the large snake in his laundry bag and asks an unaware Stan to take it home with him.

Later that evening a quiet night in turns into a nightmare for the Butler and Rudge family when the snake escapes from the laundry bag and they are forced to take refuge in the toilet as the reptile slithers along the landing. Things look desperate for them until Jack calls around to collect his bag with Fatima. She manages to charm the snake back into the bag to avert the danger and the couple beat a hasty retreat before an angry Stan can confront them.

Snake in the Grass

A term Stan uses to describe his brother-in-law Arthur in the Series Five episode 'A Thin Time'.

Arthur purchases some expensive wigs as the family stumble through another financial crisis but is pressurised into returning them by the family. However, despite promising otherwise he proceeds to keep a wig and is seen wearing it by an angry Stan at the depot. 'You snake in the grass,' exclaims the bus driver as he berates Arthur for going back on his word.

A snake in the grass is a term for a deceitful person who is not trustworthy.

Snob

Arthur is often labelled as a snob and on a number of occasions his snobbery comes to the surface.

The Series Three episode 'Radio Control' sees Arthur berating Stan for mispronouncing words as he bids to learn the newly-created busman's code. Stan tries to show he can speak properly by reciting an old poem he learnt at school but he is ridiculed for mispronouncing again. 'You're a snob,' barks Stan. In a Series Five episode called 'The Epidemic', Olive has come down with the flu and reveals that she wears a vest under her nightgown. A disgusted Arthur shows the snob in him again as he sneers: 'How working class.' Later in the same series, in the episode 'The New Nurse', Arthur warms to a new lodger in the house. Mary, the new depot nurse, speaks with a posh accent and has a snobbish attitude which appeals to Arthur. He looks to impress her by changing his eating and bathing habits and improving his etiquette. He also tells her a white lie pretending he and Olive always travel home by taxi rather than by bus. The snobbishness is a trait that Arthur portrays in many episodes and the spin-off films.

Snoring

Arthur's snoring causes problems for Stan on the small screen and Olive on the big screen in On The Buses.

Forced to share a bed together in the Series Two episode 'Aunt Maud', Stan and Arthur are soon at each other's throats. Stan complains about his brother-in-law's snoring describing it as sounding like a stuffed pig. It is so bad that he claims he hasn't heard anything like it since the silencer fell off his bus.

In the film Mutiny On The Buses, Arthur gets berated by Olive when his snoring wakens up their son but he is adamant he does not snore. Later in the film his snoring continues to annoy Olive and in a bid to turn him over to stop him snoring she pushes him out of bed. The furore brings mum and Stan onto the scene to offer their opinion on Arthur's snoring. Mum feels that there must be something wrong with his tubes to which an indignant Arthur disagrees. She goes on to suggest his nasal passages have tightened, shrivelling up a bit with age but he insists: 'I have not shrivelled up.' Fed up being ridiculed he asks mum and Stan to leave the room. Olive is to bid to counter her husband's snoring by sewing tennis balls onto the back of his pyjama jacket, in order to stop him from lying on his back, which causes him to snore. Arthur angrily refuses to wear the jacket though and so his snoring will have to be tolerated.

Soblosky, Perry

TV Role: Finalist (Series 7 Episode 4 'The Poster')

Perry Soblosky was to have a brief career as an actor in the early to mid-1970s which was to see him in a handful of roles on television and in films.

He was to specialize in bit-part roles appearing in dramas The Adventurer, Special Branch and the BBC sci-fi series

Moonbase 3. His solitary comedy role was to come in the hit sitcom On The Buses. His final acting credit came in 1974 on the big screen in the Hammer film Captain Kronos – Vampire Hunter.

Social Club Committee

A body involved with the organising and running of events at the Luxton and District Bus Company's depot that is referred to in a couple of episodes of On The Buses.

In the Series One episode 'The Canteen' it becomes clear that the busmen themselves make up the social club committee with Jack appointed the representative of the committee. He liaises with the management and it is arranged that the busmen will run the depot canteen themselves. Later, during a Boxing Day social event in a Series Five episode, Jack flirts with Arthur's sister Linda but is frightened off when Arthur threatens him. She is not to be put off though and when she approaches Jack he makes an excuse saying that the social committee have asked him to help out behind the bar at the event.

Son of Dracula

A fictional film poster on the side of Stan's bus which is used to ridicule Inspector Blake in the Series Two episode 'Bon Voyage'.

Stan and Jack have an instant camera in the depot which they intend taking on the depot's charter holiday to Spain. They see an opportunity to have a laugh at Inspector Blake's expense offering to take a photo of him standing next to Stan's bus. He is lined up next to a poster advertising a film called Son of Dracula and as he is asked to show off his teeth Jack takes his picture. The photo has Stan and Jack in stitches though the inspector is less pleased and doesn't think the photo is him but Stan points out it must be him as it says so beside him where it reads Son of Dracula. Although there was a Universal Pictures production called Son of Dracula in 1943 this is not the film mimicked in the episode. The poster on the side of Stan's bus gave starring roles to a pair of fictional actors called Vincent Greene (presumably based on the legendary actor of horror films Vincent Price) and Karina Froblin. The fictional production company had a tongue-in-cheek title – Veriorible Films Limited.

Sound and Vision

This is the name of a fictional magazine seen being read by Mrs Butler as the family contemplate renting a new colour television set in the Series Five episode 'The New Telly'.

South Bank Studios

This was the new home to London Weekend Television from 1972 where the seventh and last series of On The Buses was filmed.

The South Bank Studios were a newly-built custom-made studio complex on the banks of the River Thames and LWT moved into their new home from their Wembley Studios base in North London. The new complex housed three studios, dressing rooms, rehearsal rooms, wardrobe departments, a restaurant, clubroom and a host of staff amenities. However, the studios were to have one slight disadvantage over those in Wembley in that the studio doors were not big enough to allow the double decker Lodekka buses into the studios for the filming of On The Buses. Another solution was found with single deck buses having a mock upper deck fitted once in the studios. Aside from On The Buses other hit LWT comedy series filmed at the South Bank Studios included Not On Your Nellie, Doctor At Sea, Maggie And Her, Candid Camera, The Rag Trade, Mind Your Language, Agony, Cannon And Ball, Metal Mickey, Game For A Laugh and The Two Of Us. Dramas filmed at the studios were Upstairs Downstairs, Within These Walls, Bouquet Of Barbed Wire, The Gentle Touch, London's Burning and memorable current affairs, sports and arts series. These included World Of Sport, The South Bank Show, Weekend World and Saint And Greavsie.

In 2002, LWT (along with other regional franchises) were rebranded ITV1 and the South Bank Studios would go on to become the home of the complete range of ITV channels 1, 2, 3 and 4. The studios were renamed The London Studios and since then many hit series have been churned out with the studios now more than forty years old.

Southend

A seaside town referred to in a couple of episodes of On The Buses.

As Stan prepares to take a coach out of the depot as the works charter holiday sets out for the airport he receives final instructions from Inspector Blake in the Series Two episode 'Bon Voyage'. The inspector says: 'Southend via Basildon. Don't go stopping at request stops.' In the Series Seven episode 'On The Omnibuses', an elderly passenger sits aboard a long out-of-service bus at the depot's special exhibition and she asks Inspector Blake when it leaves for Southend. She doesn't like his answer that the bus she is on doesn't go to Southend anymore and that she has missed her bus and so angrily she thumps him with her umbrella.

Southend-on-Sea as it is also known is forty miles east of London in Essex and is a seaside resort. The town is most noted for having the longest leisure pier in the world and a diesel-powered railway runs the length of it. The town also boasts a number of festivals based around the sea front and has a funicular railway that scales a cliff in the town which is popular with tourists.

Spaghetti Bolognese

This is a dish eaten by Stan in the depot canteen much to the consternation of Inspector Blake in the Series Three episode 'The New Uniforms'.

With Stan chosen to trial a new prototype uniform he sits down to eat a plateful of spaghetti bolognese in the canteen with the new uniform on. Blakey is horrified to see Stan eating the messy dish with such care-free abandon and steps in to try to prevent the uniform getting dirty. He tries to tuck a tea cloth under Stan's chin but only succeeds in making matters worse with strands of spaghetti trapped behind the tea cloth dirtying Stan's shirt and tie. Fed up the driver asks Jack to get him a spoon and pusher for him and begins to mockingly wail like a baby. After further interference from the inspector the pair of harassed busmen decide to eat elsewhere.

This is an Italian dish made with spaghetti mixed with minced beef and a bolognese sauce.

Spiders

Olive's fear of spiders is to give Stan an idea as he looks to discredit the women bus drivers in the spin-off film On The Buses.

Stan collects a tin container full of spiders and lets them loose in woman driver Vera's cab at the depot prior to her boarding her bus. The trouble starts once the bus leaves the depot as the spiders begin to crawl up Vera's legs causing her to itch. When she finally sees the spiders she lets out a scream as she takes her hands off the steering wheel, losing control of her bus which bumps into the back of a lorry and knocks a policeman off his feet. Inspector Blake who is also aboard her bus has an awkward fall and injures his wrist. Moments later, Vera races out of her cab in a panic refusing to get back in and drive away despite the inspector's orders. 'I can't, I can't! There's spiders in my cab,' screams Vera. 'I don't care if you've got ants in your pants. You get in that cab,' yells the unsympathetic inspector. The bus eventually arrives back at the depot to find a manager who is beginning to lose patience with the women bus drivers.

Spot Check

A random check of paint stock levels in the maintenance department at the depot carried out by the management proves costly for Stan in the Series Three episode 'Busmen's Perks'.

Stan has taken two tins of paint, a paintbrush, hardener and spirits from the stores for some home decorating. Soon, however, Nobby an employee in the maintenance department, is in a panic when he sees the management carrying out a spot check of the stock. He tracks Stan down asking him for five pounds for the two tins of paint in order to cover up for the missing stock which Stan has already used. The peeved busman has no choice but to pay up.

St Barnabas Church

This is the church where busman Bill is to marry the inspector's niece Sally in the Series Five episode 'The Best Man'.

St Luke's Maternity Hospital

This is the hospital where Olive is to give birth to her son Arthur in the first spin-off film On The Buses.

St Mary's Hospital

The hospital where Arthur has his infamous operation as referred to in the Series Six episode 'Stan's Worst Day'.

Stan looks back on when Arthur first moved into the Butler house as a lodger and announced a delicate matter. Arthur was about to undergo an operation which he describes as being surgical in nature but refuses to go into details. The operation is to be carried out at St Mary's hospital.

St Michael's Church

The name of the church that Stan mistakenly believes Bill and Sally are to be married at in the Series Five episode 'The Best Man'.

He tells Inspector Blake not to worry and promises him as best man that he'll get the bridegroom Bill to St Michael's church on time for the wedding. However, the inspector has to remind Stan that the wedding is to be held at St Barnabas and it sets him off fretting about the competence of Stan as the best man.

Staff Pass

This is a type of pass that Inspector Blake is travelling on in the film Holiday On The Buses.

When Blakey is asked for his ticket as he boards the tour bus he reminds the cheeky conductor that he has a staff pass. This pass entitled free travel aboard the tour bus to employees at the holiday camp.

Staff Shortage

This problem affects the Town and District Bus Company in the film On The Buses.

A staff shortage at the depot sees the canteen unable to offer hot food due to a lack of a canteen cook which also leaves them short of bus crews. For Stan and Jack though this isn't a problem as it means they get all the overtime they want and allows them to act as layabouts without fear of the sack as they see themselves as indispensable. However, they are in for a shock as Inspector Blake resolves the staff shortage issue by introducing women bus drivers to the depot.

Staff Social and Darts Match

An event held in the depot canteen referred to as the busmen versus the management darts match on a poster and features in the film Mutiny On The Buses.

The event sees a darts match in which Stan and Jack resort to dirty tricks to distract Inspector Blake as an attractive clippie flaunts herself as he is about to throw his darts. The ploy works as Blakey's dart hits a light above the dartboard earning him an ear-bashing from his manager and team-mate Mr Jenkins and leaves the busmen in prime position to win the darts match.

Later in the evening the event descends into a brawl as Olive takes offence to the saucy clippie Norah openly flirting with Arthur. After trading catty insults and drinks being thrown at each other a fight ensues between the women. As the pair wrestle with each other, pulling hair and dresses getting torn Stan tries to stop the fight but ends up being struck on the head with a tray. Finally though, Olive is hauled away kicking and screaming whilst Mrs Butler cools Norah down by pouring a jug of water over her. As Norah lets out a scream, Mr Jenkins steps in to comfort the dishevelled clippie promising her a towel and a brandy to warm her up in his office. It is a chaotic end to the event leaving Olive and Arthur embarrassed and Stan nursing a headache.

Stalin's Purge

This is a historic event that is referred to by Jack in the Series One episode 'The New Inspector'.

As the bus company searches for a new inspector conversation turns to Inspector Blake's predecessor. Jack mockingly claims: 'The old inspector went to Russia to carry out Stalin's purge.' However, Blakey corrects him saying he went to Bognor to grow roses.

Stalin's purge was carried out by the then Russian leader Joseph Stalin from 1936 to 1938. He had become alarmed by a growing percentage of the population of the Soviet Union who were seeking reforms and a more democratic running of the country. Stalin was to authorise a ruthless repression of those not willing to fully support him and his policies. The purge, as it became known as, saw hundreds of thousands of people either imprisoned or executed and whilst it kept him in power it blackened his name and reputation all around the world.

Stan's Career as Conductor

Prior to becoming a bus driver Stan was employed as a conductor by the Luxton and District Bus Company and he reminisces about this in the Series Six episode 'Stan's Worst Day'.

In the early 1960s Stan is a conductor aboard the bus driven by Cyril Blake. Their relationship is far more amiable but with Blakey set for promotion to inspector that is all set to change. Stan clowns around with his driver Blakey in the depot by pushing him around on a trolley but when it bumps into the manager it lands them in trouble.

The manager gives Cyril an ear-bashing and warns him that with promotion comes responsibility and so he should not be acting like a baby. It causes Blakey to turn to Stan and give him a chilling warning that once he is inspector he will make Stan's life a misery. Days later Cyril is promoted to inspector and Stan moves on to become a bus driver and his new conductor is new to the job and is called Jack Harper. A new friendship is formed.

Stan's Dream

An exhausted Stan falls asleep at work and has a vivid dream in the Series Seven episode 'On The Omnibuses'.

Stan dreams of life in the 1920s at the Luxton and District Bus Company as the first motor-powered buses are brought into service. Meanwhile, Jack is bidding to start up a union in a bid to get better work conditions but a tyrannical Inspector Blake will have none of it. At home, his sister Olive campaigns for women's rights whilst his mother runs the house and also washes the depot manager's laundry.

His dream takes a frightening twist as Olive later chains herself to railings outside the manager's house demanding a job aboard the omnibuses. Worse is to follow as the manager's laundry gets strewn all over the road as it is blown from mum's grasp as she travels on Stan's bus. It invariably leads to Stan crashing the new motor-powered bus into the manager's car and as he is yelled at by the inspector for the accident he is awoken from his dream by Blakey shouting at him to waken up in the present. A startlingly real dream is over.

Stan's Uniform

Stan is to ruin two uniforms in a short space of time in the Series Five episode 'Stan's Uniform'.

When the drains need unblocking at home Stan sees no harm in doing the job whilst still wearing his uniform. However, the uniform ends up covered in remnants of what was blocking the drains such as bacon rinds, tea and paint.

When he turns up at the depot in the filthy uniform his hopes are dashed that he will receive a new one and in fact all he receives is an ear-bashing from the inspector and cleaning vouchers. But Jack's cunning comes into play as they take the uniform to be dry-cleaned and retextured. This leaves the uniform in tatters and Inspector Blake is left with no option but to allow Stan to have a new uniform.

Later, he proudly shows off his new uniform at home and as Arthur paints furniture at the time a disaster is about to strike. Stan sits down at the table in a chair coated in wet paint and shortly after receiving the uniform it is left paint-stained. Bleach and detergent can't remove the paint at home and so in a desperate bid he and Jack call in to the maintenance department at the depot. They try using paint stripper and a wire brush to remove the paint but only succeed in ripping the trousers and jacket to shreds and so another uniform bites the dust. All that is left for Stan to do is scavenge a replacement old uniform from the clothing store and though it saves his job he is lambasted for his appearance once more by Inspector Blake.

Station Hotel, Grimsby

A hotel in which Olive and Arthur spent their honeymoon as revealed in the Series Five episode 'Canteen Trouble'.

Steedman, Shirley

TV Role: Eileen (Series 5 Episode 12 'The New Telly')

Born in Glasgow, Scotland in 1949, Shirley Steedman was to break into acting in her early teens progressing from stage onto television and films. Her career as an actress spanned two decades during which time she was very active.

She had her first acting roles in her native Glasgow in the mid-to late 1960s. These roles came in plays Six Characters In Search Of An Author and The Visions Of Simone Manchard before making her break into television.

Steedman's television career was highlighted by her portrayal of Princess Alice in the award-winning costume drama Edward The Seventh in the mid-1970s. Other notable drama roles came in Dr Finlay's Casebook, East Lynne, A Man Called Intrepid and Penmarric. She was also to appear in hit sitcoms of the 1970s such as On The Buses, Whatever Happened To The Likely Lads and Open All Hours. Her film roles were fewer and further between but she was to appear in the Oscar-winning film The Prime Of Miss Jean Brodie in the late 1960s. She would also have credits in made-for-television films such as Jane Eyre and Jonah And The Whale.

Steedman quit acting in the early 1980s and has since gone on to working in reflexology.

Stella

Played by Charlotte Howard

This is an attractive new employee in the depot canteen who catches the eye of Stan in the Series Four episode 'Not Tonight'.

Stella, an opportunistic blonde in her late twenties, feels restricted by the low wages she gets paid in the depot canteen. She catches Stan's eye and takes advantage of his vulnerability as he is amidst a crisis in his love life and the pair go out on a date. His generosity sees her treated to drinks, cigarettes and he even pays for a pair of tights for Stella. When she goes home with him he thinks his luck is in. However, she cons him out of the remainder of his wages claiming she needs money for her rent and once she has it she excuses herself to go to the toilet and makes a swift exit out of the house. Naively, Stan hopes to date Stella again but on their next meeting he is in for a shock and a blow to his already low self-confidence. Dressed in costly new attire she has a new job as a receptionist for the manager at the depot and in a newly-acquired posh accent she snootily rejects a date with Stan saying it wouldn't be right for a woman of her standing to be seen dating a busman. On this painful note the brief relationship ends.

Stensgaard, Yutte

TV Role: Ingrid (Series 3 Episode 10 'The New Uniforms')

Born in Thisted, Denmark in 1946, Yutte Stensgaard was to move to the UK in 1963 and worked as a stenographer, au pair and model before her acting career took off in the late 1960s with roles coming in films, television and on stage.

On the big screen she is best-remembered for her role in the Hammer production Lust For A Vampire in 1971. Other roles in horror films came in Scream And Scream Again and Burke And Hare. Comedy roles came her way in Zeta One, Some Girls Do, Doctor In Trouble, A Promise Of Bed and an uncredited part in Carry On Again Doctor amongst others. Her television roles were varied with her biggest role coming in the hit sitcom Doctor In The House where she played a student called Helga. This would be followed by other comedy roles in On The Buses, The Adventures Of Don Quick and The Marty Feldman Comedy Machine. She was also to appear in hit dramas such as The Saint, Special Branch, Jason King, The Persuaders and Dead Of Night. Stensgaard was also to co-host the smash hit game show The Golden Shot alongside Bob Monkhouse from 1970 to 1971 in another string to her bow, so as to speak.

The early 1970s were to see her flirt with a stage career as she appeared in Christmas pantomime Red Riding Hood and in a comedy production called Boeing Boeing.

Stensgaard, fed up with her somewhat limited and typecast roles, quit acting and immigrated to the USA in the mid-1970s. She became a devout Christian and was to go on to become a director for a major radio network in the States. In recent years she has begun to embrace her past occupation as an actress by appearing at a number of Hammer conventions although still living in the USA.

Stewart, Mr

Played by Alan Curtis

An inspector who is set to take over from Inspector Blake in the Series Four episode 'The Canteen Girl'.

Mr Stewart, in his early forties, is a chief inspector at number two depot that is brought in to replace Inspector Blake who is set to leave and set up home with his potential wife-to-be Molly. He is quick to make an impact with Stan and Jack, addressing them with a stern face he berates their personal appearance quoting the regulations and is encouraged to report them by Inspector Blake.

On checking their bus Stewart is horrified to find cigarette ends in the driver's cab and a cheese roll in the first aid box and promptly suspends them both and promises they will be sacked the next time they infringe the rules. Mr Stewart's strictness shocks Stan and Jack and encourages them to scupper Inspector Blake's budding relationship with Molly in a bid to keep the less strict inspector at the depot.

Stewart, Reginald

TV Role: Alf (Series 4 Episode 6 'The L Bus')

Reginald Stewart's career as an actor spanned a quarter of a century from the early 1970s up until the mid-1990s. Primarily, his roles came on television and less so in films.

He debuted in an episode of On The Buses and would go on to appear in hit sitcoms such as The Fenn Street Gang and Love Hurts and the less successful comedies About Face and Perfect Scoundrels. Drama was his forte though and he was to have parts in the hit 70s series Law And Order and Secret Army. In the 1980s his most notable drama roles came in The Gentle Touch, The Adventures Of Sherlock Holmes, The Bill, London's Burning and Miss Marple followed in the 90s with credits in Cracker, Heartbeat, The Governor and Bramwell.

Aside from made-for-television films, Stewart's solitary big screen role came with a small part in the 1972 production Bleak Moments.

Stilton, Mr

Played by Garfield Morgan

This is the depot manager who orders Inspector Blake to take his medical in the Series Six episode 'Bye Bye Blakey'.

Mr Stilton is in his early forties, has a receding hairline and holds Inspector Blake in high esteem. With the inspector revealing his intentions to take another job offering promotion away from the depot, Mr Stilton admits he'll be sorry to see him go. His departure is seemingly imminent and Blakey requests he be excused from the upcoming mandatory staff medicals feeling it leaves him open to ridicule from the busmen and undermines his authority. Mr Stilton is far from pleased and though he asks the doctor if Blake can be excused he is unsuccessful. His final say on the matter comes when he orders the inspector to get a grip of himself and take the medical.

Stopcock

The stopcock that services the Butler house is referred to in a couple of episodes of On The Buses as well as a larger version outside the house in the street.

In the Series Three episode 'The Cistern', Stan fails in a bid to successfully plumb in a new toilet and is soaked as a pipe springs a leak showering him in water. He yells at Arthur to turn the stopcock off but it is far too late to prevent him being soaked. Later, in the Series Seven episode 'Hot Water', Jack steals a stopcock from the bus depot's washroom and fits it in at the Butler house as he and Inspector Blake look to install an immersion heater and restore hot water to the house. Of course things don't go to plan and when Jack attempts to turn the water back on in the street a large stopcock comes off in his hands and water is sent shooting high into the air and soon the street is awash with water.

Stores

This is an area in the holiday camp that Stan and Jack raid for paint and a toilet in the film Holiday On The Buses.

When little Arthur shoots ink from his water gun all over the chalet's bedroom walls the family are left with a room that needs redecorating. Stan and Jack pay a visit to the stores and help themselves to a couple of tins of paint and two paintbrushes. They smuggle the items back to the chalet by hiding them in little Arthur's pram but their problems aren't over. Later they need to revisit the stores to get a replacement toilet after blowing up the toilet in the family's chalet. They sneak the new toilet out of the stores and back to the chalet under the cover of darkness late in the summer evening.

Strikes

The Luxton and District Bus Company is frequently to see strikes taking place or being threatened and feature in a number of episodes.

The very first episode of On The Buses called 'The Early Shift' sees Stan and Jack deprived of the canteen facilities due to a new set of shifts brought into place. With the problem exasperated by the inspector refusing to allow Stan to eat his lunch in the warmth of his cab, Jack convenes a meeting with his fellow busmen and they vote to strike. The strike gets a welcome boost when a television crew cover the story and catch what looks like Stan being injured whilst on picket duty which leads to capitulation from the management and sees a return of their canteen facilities.

An unofficial strike is instigated by Stan in the Series Six episode 'Union Trouble' and when Jack is paid a bonus by the management to not back the strike; Stan is forced to go it alone. His grievance is with the reduction of canteen opening hours and the sacking of the canteen employee Elsie. With no support from his colleagues, who want nothing to do with a strike that has no union backing, Stan is forced into desperate measures. He stages a sit-in protest which he is forced to abandon and when he sheepishly looks to return to work a few days later Inspector Blake is intent on keeping him suspended without wages. However, by this time Jack has received his bonus and his attitude changes. He immediately calls on his fellow busmen to go on strike until Stan is reinstated and the inspector is forced to back down by re-instating Stan, restoring all-day canteen facilities and keeping Elsie in employment.

Strike action is threatened in the Series Seven episode 'On The Omnibuses' as Jack is unhappy with the new schedules worked out that sees him and Stan doing more journeys per shift leaving them exhausted. When the inspector refuses to discuss the schedules further Jack rallies his colleagues and announces a strike which sees Inspector Blake take the shop steward up to his office for discussions. These avert strike action as Jack arranges for himself not to work the full schedules as he gets time off for his union duties but for the other busmen the arduous schedules remain in place.

Once again in the Series Seven episode 'Friends In High Places', a strike is narrowly avoided at the depot. Jack protests about the terrible standard of cooking in the canteen and demands changes from Inspector Blake otherwise there will be a strike. However, the canteen cook Mrs Webb solves the problem as she resigns which appeases the busmen but gives the inspector a position to fill.

Stripper, The

This is a piece of music that Stan and Jack hum along to in the Series Six episode 'Bye Bye Blakey'.

As the inspector reluctantly shows up for his medical Stan and Jack urge him to strip off. As he starts to undress they, accompanied by other busmen, mockingly hum 'The Stripper'' music most famously associated with a strip-tease act.

'The Stripper' is a piece of jazz music which was composed and recorded in the USA by British-born musician David Rose in 1962 and was to be a number one hit in the US charts. The song would go on to feature in many hit television series and films of varying genres and was often used at concerts to introduce bands such as The Sweet and Motley Crue.

Stupid Great Lump

This is Arthur's derogatory description of his long suffering wife Olive. He often uses the term when she either embarrasses him or does something foolish and it is heard in both the episodes and spin-off films of On The Buses.

Suffragettes

A famous woman's rights group that Mrs Butler refers to in the Series Six episode 'On The Omnibuses'.

Amidst Stan's dream of life in the 1920s, Olive complains that it is wrong that women aren't allowed to do the same jobs as men. Her mum ticks her off for having such thoughts saying: 'You've been listening to them suffragettes again.'

The suffragettes were part of a woman's movement founded at the end of the nineteenth century that campaigned for various rights to be granted to women. These included women to have the right to vote and to work. Gradually, for a number of reasons, the suffragette movement would become practically obsolete by the late 1920s. During World War One, women were called upon to take up jobs normally reserved for men who were fighting a savage war giving them a chance to prove their worth in the workplace whilst from 1918 they were granted the right to vote. With more bills passed in parliament in preceding years a woman's suffering was all but over in Britain and the suffragette movement was assigned to history.

Sugar Bertie

This is the call sign of Stan Butler using the busman's code when a radio control system is installed in the buses of the Luxton and District Bus Company in the Series Three episode 'Radio Control'. Aboard his number eleven bus though Stan is referred to as Sugar Bertie 11 by Inspector Blake across the airwaves.

Sugar Daddy

This is Arthur's description of the depot manager Mr Jenkins in the film Mutiny On The Buses.

Miffed that his clippie, the notorious Nymphy Norah, no longer has any interest in him he labels her a 'gold digger'. He tells a very interested Jack: 'She's found herself a sugar daddy.' Arthur reveals it to be Mr Jenkins and insists she stays back late in the depot with him every night.

Sugar daddy is a slang term describing an ageing man in a position of power or who has wealth who courts a younger woman by showering them with favours or gifts in return for their friendship or more.

Sump

A part on Stan's bus that, when damaged, lands him in trouble in a couple of episodes of On The Buses.

The Series Four episode 'The L Bus' sees Stan and Jack use the depot's training bus as a delivery van to deliver a bed to Arthur and Olive. However, with four trainees aboard, the bus breaks down en-route with oil leaking from the sump. The bus has to be towed back to the depot where Inspector Blake is to discover the bed aboard the bus and takes great satisfaction in charging Stan a large sum of money for using the bus to transport the bed in the form of several parcel tickets. Later, in the Series Six episode 'Stan's Worst Day', Stan writes off the sump of his bus when ogling a pretty, young woman. He drives his bus up onto a kerb and over bollards which leaves the sump a complete write-off. It earns Stan a dressing down from Inspector Blake with the mechanic left to fit a new sump to the bus.

The sump is a basin-like part that sits below the engine which is filled with oil. This oil lubricates the moving parts of the engine and is a vital part that ensures a smooth running engine.

Sunshine

This is a slang term of endearment that Arthur often calls his wife Olive in both the episodes and spin-off films of On The Buses. He often uses the term either when on amiable terms with her, requesting a favour or on occasions when he is drunk.

Supersonic Concorde

This is an iconic passenger jet which is referred to by Arthur in the Series One episode 'The Darts Match'.

When playing darts at home, Stan uses his favourite feather-flighted darts but when barged by Olive a dart ends up in a stew prepared for dinner. After fishing it out of the stew Stan feels the dart is ruined as the centre of gravity will have been altered and will affect the angle of flight. 'That's a six penny dart not the supersonic Concorde,' scoffs Arthur.

The Concorde was a supersonic passenger aeroplane developed jointly by Britain and France. It flew for the first time in 1969 just a month and a half before the episode 'The Darts Match' originally aired on British television. Concorde entered service in 1976 and would reach speeds of Mach 2 enabling it to fly from London and Paris to New York in around four hours (twice as fast as conventional jets). Operated by British Airways and Air France, Concorde was an expensive means of travel and financially it turned out to be an unsustainable project. Following a disastrous crash in 2000 in France which killed over a hundred passengers and crew the Concorde's days were numbered. It was retired from flight in 2003 after many years running at a massive economic loss but to this day it remains a remarkable feat of engineering which is still remembered fondly today.

Supplementary Public Convenience Allowance

A payment introduced by the Luxton and District Bus Company and paid to the clippies in the Series Seven episode 'The Allowance'.

The clippies, led by new arrival Jessie, are up in arms and furious at having to pay to use public conveniences whilst on duty unlike the men. With a threat of strike action looming the general manager is happy enough to authorise a supplementary public convenience allowance which causes Inspector Blake a headache as he is left to deal with all the paperwork.

It becomes clear to him that a lot of dishonesty leads to some clippies putting in false claims and so the inspector is obliged to check up on the clippies' visits to toilets. This lands him in trouble as a policeman arrests him believing him to be a Peeping Tom.

The allowance is deemed unworkable by the manager and is to be replaced by a flat weekly rate payment of fifty pence which is agreed by all parties. However, newspapers are soon to break the news that the town clerk is to make all public conveniences free of charge for both men and women and this news buoys Inspector Blake as he realises it signals the end of the public convenience allowance payment.

Surgery

This is an area of the holiday camp which features in the film Holiday On The Buses.

The surgery is where the camp nurse Joan treats her patients – both holidaymakers and staff. She is to treat Inspector Blake who has gout in his foot, Stan's injuries following an attack by the Italian chef Luigi and she also has a few passionate meetings with Jack in her surgery.

Surplus Ticket Machine

Amidst another financial crisis Stan is encouraged by Jack to obtain a surplus ticket machine in the Series Seven episode 'The Ticket Machine'.

Stan is in desperate need of money to pay for goods bought from a mail order catalogue by his mum and Olive which are soon broken and with his efficiency bonus denied him his options are limited. Jack offers him a dishonest solution suggesting Stan pays five pounds to obtain a ticket machine claimed to be surplus to requirements but has actually been stolen from the depot stores by one of Jack's friends. He tells Stan he can use the machine to sell tickets, keeping the money to pay off his debts. Although Stan has grave misgivings he agrees but when the ticket machine is found to have been stolen by the management the police are called. The petrified driver narrowly avoids being caught as he smuggles the stolen machine out of the depot. However, the whole caper is to be uncovered when the inspector visits the Butler house to sell tickets for the Busman's Ball and discovers a ticket from the stolen machine. With the threat of the sack hanging over him he receives his efficiency bonus of fifty pounds but soon loses it. The cunning Inspector Blake confronts Stan with the ticket he found at the Butler house and offers to sell it to Stan for fifty pounds. He has no choice but to accept or he will be sacked and his efficiency bonus ends up being donated to the busman's benevolent home by the inspector.

Susie

Played by Sally Douglas

This is a busty clippie that a drunken Stan makes a pass at in the Series Three episode 'Brew It Yourself'.

Susie, a young brunette in a mini-skirt is in for a shock at the depot. As she walks past Jack and Stan the tipsy driver pulls her on top of him and despite her protests attempts to kiss her. His unwanted attentions don't go unmissed by Inspector Blake and as she escapes his clutches she complains before making an exit. The inspector moves to chastise Stan for his behaviour and discovers the driver is drunk and orders him to take a breathalyser test.

Suspension

Stan and Jack often live with the fear of suspension from the Luxton and District Bus Company for their mischievous behaviour and the punishment is covered in a number of episodes of On The Buses.

The Series Three episode 'First Aid' sees the busmen tested on their first aid knowledge. Inspector Blake warns Stan and Jack that if they aren't ready to sit the test they will be suspended but thankfully for them they are ready and get a pass mark. The pair are not so lucky in the Series Four episode 'The Canteen Girl'. The replacement inspector Mr Stewart suspends Stan and Jack when he finds a cheese roll in the first aid box and cigarette ends in the driver's cab aboard their bus. They are suspended for one shift with loss of pay. In the Series Six 'Union Trouble', Stan looks to return to work after his failed one-man strike but Inspector Blake has other ideas. He is intent on suspending Stan without wages for what he calls gross industrial misconduct but the suspension is never implemented. Jack threatens to call a strike unless Stan is reinstated which leads to capitulation from the inspector.

Sutcliffe, Clare

TV Role: Pat (Series 4 Episode 3 'Dangerous Driving')

Clare Sutcliffe's career as an actress spanned over almost twenty years and included roles on television, in films and on stage.

She first appeared on television in the mid to late 1960s and went on to have roles in classic dramas such as Z Cars, Softly Softly, Manhunt, Coronation Street, Country Matters and Thriller. On the comedy front her credits included On The Buses, Happy Ever After and Dear Mother Love Albert. On the big screen she had a starring role in the psychological drama I Start Counting in the late 1960s. She was also to appear alongside On The Buses star Reg Varney in The Best Pair Of Legs In The Business and her final credit in films came with a bit-part role in the 1983 drama The Ploughman's Lunch.

Her stage career included roles in stage shows such as The Finest Family early in the 1970s.

By the mid-1980s Sutcliffe's acting career was at an end and she was to pursue a career elsewhere.

Suzy

Played by Suzanne Heath

A clippie who is to date Stan but is ultimately to be left disappointed in the Series Four episode 'Nowhere To Go'.

A small, blonde-haired clippie in her twenties, Suzy dates Stan but they find they have nowhere to go at the end of the evening. Going back to her house is ruled out as her mum would be up watching television and Stan rules out taking her back to his house as his family would switch off the telly and watch them.

As they embrace in the depot, Inspector Blake interrupts them and chases them out of the depot as it is time to lock up meaning they'll have to wait until the following night for a chance of romance. With Arthur, Olive and mum set to visit Aunt Maud for the weekend, Stan plans to entertain Suzy at home with Jack and his date Edna to join them. Suzy looks forward to the evening but is in for a disappointment. After their double date the foursome arrive back at the Butler house for a romantic evening in but are to find Arthur, Olive and mum back home. They have had a motorbike accident on their way to Aunt Maud's and are in a state and so Suzy's hopes are dashed again leaving her to go home disgruntled.

Suzy

Played by Mary Land

A clippie who pairs off with Jack as she and her friend Frieda are placed on Stan and Jack's bus in the Series Six episode 'No Smoke Without Fire'.

Suzy, who is slender and has long blonde hair, is a trainee clippie who attends a course of instruction on firefighting at the depot during which she enjoys a lingering kiss with Jack as Inspector Blake demonstrates how to give the kiss of life. She is suitably impressed describing his kissing as perfect. Later, she and Frieda are placed aboard Stan and Jack's bus to be trained but the old bus designated to them breaks down on a country lane. The two randy busmen take the chance to get to know their trainees better. Suzy gets taken upstairs on the bus for a snog by Jack but their fun is interrupted by the arrival on the scene of Inspector Blake. He orders Suzy and Frieda to get on the bus behind them as he insists on boarding Stan and Jack's bus and escorting them back to the depot. For Suzy it spells the end of her brief flirtation with Jack in the process.

Suzy

Played by Andria Lawrence

This is a canteen employee who is a little too generous for her own good in the Series Five episode 'Canteen Trouble'.

Suzy has short blonde hair and is in her thirties and is a close friend of Stan and Jack. On nights out with them she is kept supplied with vodkas and in return in the depot canteen she offers them overly-generous helpings of food far beyond what they have paid for. Also she gives Stan food to take home free of charge during another of his financial hardships. However, a suspicious Inspector Blake is determined to see the canteen run at a profit and, realising Suzy's generosity to Stan and Jack, he sacks her from the post replacing her with what he hopes will be a less corruptible member of staff.

Suzy

Played by Janet Mahoney

This is a clippie who is to be engaged to Stan in the film Mutiny On The Buses.

Suzy, a brunette in her late twenties, is a clippie at the Town and District Bus Company. She cons Stan into engaging her and proves herself to be headstrong and determined in the relationship. Suzy is intent on moving into a flat with her new fiancé but when he suggests she moves into the Butler house she refuses saying: 'Oh no I'm not having that. I'm not getting married until we've got a place of our own.' Their attempts to rent a flat are frequently thwarted by lack of funds, rising prices and family commitments tying Stan to the Butler household. Suzy grows increasingly frustrated and is to finally call off the engagement after Olive falls pregnant again with Stan being called upon again to financially support the family.

Suzy

Played by Jeanette Wild

This young clippie is left disappointed after a date with Stan in the film On The Buses.

Suzy is a brunette with shoulder-length hair who Stan describes as 'a right little raver'. He takes her on a date to a Wimpy bar until eleven o'clock but it becomes clear the date was a disappointment for her as nothing happened. When Stan asks her out on another date the following day she gives him a cold stare and says: 'Eh? You must be joking.' She marches away leaving Stan a little mystified.

Sweeney, Maureen

Film Role: Mavis (Holiday On The Buses)

Maureen Sweeney's career as an actress consists of almost forty years of credits including roles in films, on stage and television.

Her first big break in acting on the big screen came in 1973 with a sizeable role playing holidaymaker Mavis in Holiday On The Buses. Other film credits in her career included a small part in the crime drama The Squeeze and most recently in the thriller Sorted.

On stage she was to perform under the direction of Joan Littlewood at the renowned Stratford East Theatre Royal. Sweeney also appeared in A Natural Cause and later in A Bit Of Business at the National Theatre.

She was most active though on television with roles in hit sitcoms such as Romany Jones, That's My Boy, Only Fools And Horses, Love Hurts and Believe Nothing. Her drama credits are impressive with credits in 1970s classic series including The Sweeney, Within These Walls, The Duchess Of Duke Street and Crossroads. In the 1980s she would appear in Dempsey And Makepeace and the 90s saw her with a starring role in the ITV mini-series She's Out and a smaller role in The Bill followed in the 2000s with a part in Casualty.

Her acting career continues on stage to the present day.

Swimming Pool

A facility at the holiday camp that is a source of entertainment for holidaymakers but is to cause more embarrassment for Olive and Arthur and sees Stan and Jack stand in as lifeguards at the swimming pool in the film Holiday On The Buses.

T

Tabla Player

Played by Austin Baptiste

An Indian musician with sideburns and a moustache dressed in Indian attire. He plays the drum-like instrument at the Indian social event as Fatima performs a snake dance in the Series Three episode 'The Snake'.

Tabla is a pair of hand drums usually played in accompaniment with Hindustani classical music. Different tones and sounds are obtained depending on the area of the hand that makes contact with the drum.

Tapioca Pudding

A type of dessert Stan tries, and fails miserably, to make for his bed-ridden mum in the Series Two episode 'Family Flu'.

Under doctor's orders mum has flu and is restricted to bed with Stan left to cook for her. His attempts to make her a tapioca pudding have disastrous results as the dessert is extremely tough and waterproof. Arthur feels the last time he saw something like that they were building the M1 and he suggests that Stan should patent it. When he serves his mum the dish she finds it inedible but tries to put a brave face on it to avoid hurting Stan's feelings. As soon as he leaves she tries giving the dish to the pet cat Rusty but even he refuses to eat it. The tapioca pudding ends up being flushed down the toilet by Olive.

Tarzan of the Buses

A name Inspector Blake calls Stan when he finds a pair of leopard skin y-fronts amongst the driver's laundry aboard his bus in the Series Two episode 'Family Flu'.

When Stan confesses that the y-fronts and laundry bag is his, Inspector Blake lifts up the embarrassing item of underwear and once he has finished laughing he jokes: 'Tarzan of the buses.' He goes on to ask Stan if he swings from the chandeliers at home making monkey noises.

This was a clear reference to the popular Edgar Rice Burroughs novel which told the story of an orphan boy brought up by apes in the jungle and was called Tarzan of the Apes. The book and its sequels were adapted into a series of hit films and television series.

Tattoo

Inspector Blake is revealed as having a tattoo on his left arm in the Series Five episode 'The Epidemic'.

As staff members at the Luxton and District Bus Company prepare to have their anti-flu jabs at the depot the inspector is found to have a tattoo on his left arm as he is asked to roll up his sleeve. The tattoo is of a heart with an arrow through it and inside it is written 1941 whilst above the heart are the words Cyril loves Elsie. Blakey is clearly embarrassed by the tattoo as Stan and Jack rib him mercilessly about it giving them much hilarity. The inspector explains the tattoo away as being done at a time when he was a young foolish soldier in love. Sadly, he found that when he returned from Burma after the Second World War she had not waited for him and had found herself another man.

Taxi Driver

Played by Terry Duggan

A cockney character who is to take Inspector Blake to the train station from the Butler house in his taxi in the Series Five episode 'The Inspector's Pets'.

The taxi driver has picked the inspector up from his house, stopping off at the Butler house on the way to the train station as Blakey has to drop off his pets for Stan to look after whilst he is away on a fishing holiday. The taxi driver brings in the inspector's aquarium and with a hint of impatience says: 'You better hurry up if you want to catch that train guvnor.' Moments later, the pair depart for the train station.

Tea Leaves

Mum displays a talent for reading tea leaves in the Series Seven episode 'What The Stars Foretell'.

When Olive asks her mum to read her tea leaves Mrs Butler is reluctant. She had promised never to read them again after she claims to have seen the ghost of her husband in the dregs but relents. Mum prepares to do her reading by asking Olive to switch the light off and tells Blakey to draw the curtains before asking Olive to swirl her tea-cup around three times and then turn it upside down on a saucer. Her cup shows what appears to be two wedding bells in the tea leaves and mum foresees a tall, thin man coming into Olive's life and says she's very happy for her. On a roll she reads her own cup's tea leaves and sees wedding bells again and believes she is going to be married as well. When she throws away Blakey's tea she looks at the leaves in the bottom of his cup and again sees wedding bells. Whilst Inspector Blake is adamant he has no intention of marrying, mum claims the leaves say he is going to marry a fair lady. It soon leads to Mrs Butler and Olive vying for him to be their husband – much to his horror.

The art of reading tea leaves is also known as tasseography and has its origins in the seventeenth century.

Tea with the Butlers

When Stan mistakenly believes Inspector Blake to be dying he invites him around to his house for tea in a bid to be nice to him in his last few days alive in the Series Six episode 'Bye Bye Blakey'.

The Butlers prepare for his visit with Mrs Butler visiting the florist for flowers but ends up buying a wreath which Stan feels is inappropriate but that they can save it for the funeral. Mum is also to cook a special meal which she feels will be easy to digest – white boiled fish and semolina. However, the whole event turns out to be an uncomfortable occasion, with the Butler family clumsily making references to death as they entertain the inspector. When Blakey thanks them for their kindness and admits to being overcome, Arthur makes a point of wanting to shake the inspector's hand as he admires the inspector's courage. In the following days it becomes clear that Stan has made a mistake as Inspector Blake reveals he is fit and well and death is not on the cards. Here the goodwill to the inspector ends at the depot.

Ted

A barman who serves Stan and Jack on their date with Stella and Joyce in the Series Four episode 'Not Tonight'.

Ted, who is in his fifties, is asked by Stan what cigarettes he has for sale. He replies: 'Only king-size Stan.' He proceeds to collect their empty glasses and brings the busmen and their dates another round of drinks. His small role in this episode was uncredited.

Temple, Shirley

This was a successful child film star who Stan is mockingly called in the Series Seven episode 'The Football Match'.

Stan wears a pair of knee-length shorts to football training at the depot and has his leg pulled by Inspector Blake and Jack. His conductor is to line up for training and says to Stan: 'You can stand next to me Shirley Temple.'

Shirley Temple was born in Santa Monica, California in the USA in 1928 and shot to fame as a child in the 1930s starring and singing in a number of hit films. With her angelic looks and curly hair she was destined to become a huge worldwide star in the 1930s and 40s before retiring from acting in 1950 at the age of just twenty two. Although she would return to act on television in the late 1950s and early 1960s her future career lay elsewhere. As well as being an important board member for iconic companies such as Walt Disney Company and the National Wildlife Foundation she would go on to have a number of ambassadorial roles for the US government. She retired from these roles in 1992 and continues to enjoy her retirement.

Terry's

This is a florist shop that Jack rushes into to buy a bouquet of flowers for the attractive clippie Sally in a bid to impress her in the Series Three episode 'The Inspector's Niece'.

This florist was an actively trading shop no doubt located in North London in relatively close proximity to the Wembley Studios where On The Buses was filmed at that time.

Tests

When Inspector Blake asks Stan and Jack to take a bus out on tests the mischievous busmen take the opportunity to make money out of the situation in the Series Six episode 'Private Hire'.

Stan, needing to raise money to pay off debts, is encouraged by Jack to use the bus as a removal van to move furniture for Iris who is a secretary at the bus depot instead of taking the bus out on tests. However, with the job almost complete the inspector catches them in the act and the pair end up with another ear-bashing. To make matters worse Stan is persuaded to gamble away the money he has earned at the bookmakers. With the pair in the betting shop a cunning Blakey drives the bus back to the depot and on their exit they believe their bus has been stolen. Panic-stricken and fearing the sack they return to the depot on foot and uncomfortably try to explain away the loss of their bus unaware that the inspector has it in his possession. He enjoys watching the two busmen squirm and worry about their jobs but uses it as a chance to team them a lesson that they cannot treat the bus as if it were their own. When they finally realise that the bus is safe back at the depot they are not amused by the inspector's craftiness but at least they aren't sacked as they had feared they would be.

Third Canteen Lady

Played by Shirley English

An uncredited character, she is a blonde-haired woman in her early thirties with her hair tied back. She serves tea to Jack in the depot canteen in the spin-off film On The Buses.

Thompson, Bert

Played by Wilfrid Brambell

This Irish holidaymaker has a holiday romance with Mrs Butler in the film Holiday On The Buses.

Bert is a widow in his fifties who is looking for female company whilst on holiday at the holiday camp. He is a catholic who fancies himself as a bit of a dancer although he does not impress Inspector Blake as he is prone to showing off. He takes a shine to Mrs Butler and she is not to be put off by his coarseness and randy mannerisms even when he makes a pass at camp employee Sandra. The ageing couple enjoy several dates as their relationship develops. Even though he tries plying her with gins and vodkas and visits her chalet the relationship is destined to go no further as the holiday comes to an end. However, he does pledge to keep in touch with Mabel as he departs the holiday camp for the last time.

Thompson, Gladys

The deceased wife of Bert Thompson referred to in the film Holiday On The Buses.

Gladys is described by Bert as being a 'lovely, warm person' who was hard to control after she had drunk a couple of gins. He remarks that Mabel reminds him of his late wife, Gladys but she insists he won't get her going after a couple of gins.

Thorpe Bay

This small seaside town is referred to by Stan in the Series Two episode 'Family Flu'.

With the family down with the flu Stan tells Jack that he is sending them off down to his mum's sister at Thorpe Bay for a few days during their recovery.

Thorpe Bay is located in Essex and is four miles east of the bigger resort of Southend-on-Sea. Although it lacks major attractions it is well-served by leisure facilities and is populated by many people employed in London who make the daily commute to the capital city.

Three Horseshoes, The

A public house referred to by Jack in the Series Five episode 'The Best Man'.

Jack and Stan plan a pub crawl for fellow busman Bill's bachelor party. The Three Horseshoes is to be visited at 9.15 pm where they are to meet employees from the maintenance department. It is to be the second stop on the pub crawl.

Three-in-One Mixture, The

A three-in-one mixture poured into the gearbox of Arthur's motorbike in a bid to make the engine run quieter as he looks to sell the motorcycle in the Series Three episode 'The Squeeze'.

Stan tells Arthur of the trick which involves adding what he calls a 'three-in-one mixture' into the gearbox. The mixture is three parts sawdust and one part oil and Stan insists the engine will run quieter for about half an hour – long enough for Arthur to sell the bike. Although the mixture does the trick initially it all goes wrong whilst Stan and Jack take Inspector Blake out for a run in the bike as he shows an interest in buying it. The sawdust in the gearbox catches fire causing plumes of thick black smoke to pour out of the exhaust and so the mixture fails to convince the inspector to buy the bike.

This mixture is still in use today by a few unscrupulous unlicensed car dealers looking to sell cars and motorbikes that are in poor condition. It is thought that the sawdust has a temporary effect of deadening the noise of loose fittings in the engine but this is only a short-term solution to the problem.

Tibbles

Played by Tiberius Grant

A white, long-haired Persian cat belonging to Jack that features in the Series Seven episode 'Gardening Time'.

Jack is determined to win the depot's gardening competition and is to use Tibbles in a bid to sabotage the inspector's hard work on the garden next door at the Butler house. Even though Inspector Blake warns Jack that he'll chop Tibbles up for mouse meat if the cat ventures into the garden, the crafty conductor waits until the inspector departs the scene before letting his cat loose in the Butlers back garden. He encourages the cat to relieve himself in Blakey's treasured flowerbeds but little damage is done but it encourages the inspector to resort to dirty tricks himself in a bid to win the depot's gardening competition.

Tilbury

A small town in Essex referred to by Mrs Butler in the Series Two episode 'Aunt Maud'.

She arrives at the depot with Olive and lands Stan in trouble with the inspector when she lets slip that he has taken the number eleven off-route to Tilbury to pick up his Aunt Maud at the train station. This information interests a bemused inspector.

Tilbury is a relatively new town located on the outskirts of London on the River Thames and is best known for its deep water port and docks.

Tiller Girls, The

This is a famous dance troupe which is referred to by Jack in the Series Two episode 'The Used Combination'.

As Stan pretends to have cramp whilst attempting to smuggle tools out of the depot, Inspector Blake labels him as being unhealthy. Blakey puts it down to bad circulation and he suggests the driver does an exercise to alleviate the problem. He proceeds to show Stan one he learnt in the army that involves lifting one's legs high. A watching Jack jokes: 'What regiment were you in? The Tiller Girls?'

The Tiller Girls were formed in 1890 in Manchester by John Tiller. His dancers performed with their arms linked as he felt it would ensure a disciplined routine where they danced as one. Their dance was characterised by high kicking movements and was to become hugely popular being performed all over the world. Despite the death of its founder in 1925 the dance troupe remained in the public eye and is still performed to the current day although its popularity has waned somewhat.

Time and Motion Survey

This is a survey which Inspector Blake refers to in the Series Three episode 'Radio Control'.

Fed up with Stan and Jack's continued unpunctuality the inspector announces that their bus will be the first to be fitted with a two-way radio system. They feel they are being picked on but Blakey points out that a time and motion survey shows Stan and Jack's bus to be the slowest and most unpunctual in town and shows that the hearses are getting to the Cemetery Gates quicker than them.

Time and motion studies began towards the end of the nineteenth century and were a detailed observation of the time taken for a particular task to be carried out at work. It came into being in a bid by companies to maximise efficiency in the workplace.

Time Sheets

Paperwork filled out by inspectors is referred to by Jack in the Series Five episode 'Vacancy For Inspector'.

Jack, to Stan's disgust, has become an acting inspector and so in an attempt to appease his former driver and friend he says: 'Look the inspector makes up the time sheets doesn't he? I can put you down for all the overtime you want and you won't have to work it.'

Time sheets are official documents filled in detailing the hours worked in a week by an employee which in turn determines their weekly wage earned.

Tino's Club

This is a nightclub that is referred to in the Series Four episode 'Not Tonight'.

Stan is skint and with his love life in crisis he is down in the dumps. Jack though, pays him a visit on a Saturday night inviting him to a night out at Tino's Club with clippie Joyce accompanying Jack with her friend ready to date Stan. However, to Jack's disappointment his depressed friend has to turn down the offer as Stan doesn't even have enough money to cover the date despite being told it would cost him less than three pounds.

Tiny Tim

This is a famous US singer and musician that Olive is likened to in the Series Three episode 'The Snake'.

When the family become trapped in the bathroom with a snake on the loose on the landing there is no means of escape and Olive resorts to shouting for help out of the bathroom window. Her pathetic high-pitched effort is ridiculed by Stan who remarks: 'You sound like Tiny Tim on one of his off days.'

Tiny Tim was a famous US singer who was at the height of his popularity in the 1960s and early 1970s. Renowned as a singer capable of hitting all of the high notes with his vibrato voice he was relatively short in stature hence his stage name. Tiny Tim appeared regularly on US television and had a number of hit records in the USA. With the added talent for being a ukulele player and a bit-part actor he was to remain popular until the mid-1970s. Tiny Tim (born Herbert Khaury) carried on performing until suffering a fatal heart attack whilst singing at a charity music event in 1996. He was sixty four.

Todd, Bob

Film Role: New Inspector (Mutiny On The Buses)
TV Role: Gerald Simpson (Series 7 Episode 12 'Friends In High Places')

Born in Faversham, Kent in 1921, Bob Todd was a late arrival on the acting scene. After serving in the RAF in the Second World War, training in dentistry and having a failed career in cattle breeding he turned to acting as he entered his forties with roles following on television, in films and on stage.

On television Todd will be best-remembered for playing the straight man role alongside comedy legend Benny Hill from 1968 to 1981. He'd also play similar parts in hit comedy sketch series such as It's A Square World, The Dick Emery Show, The Marty Feldman Comedy Machine and Q9. The pick of his sitcom credits included Sykes And A…, Citizen James, Hancock's, Please Sir, Doctor In Charge, On The Buses, The Fenn Street Gang, Doctor At Sea and he was also to appear in the 1970 Christmas special Carry On Again Christmas. He also featured in two episodes of the cult early 1970s children's series Here Comes The Double Deckers.

His film career saw him with mainly small roles in comedy films such as The Intelligence Men, Hot Millions, Carry On Again Doctor, Mutiny On The Buses and Adolf Hitler – My Part In His Downfall. Todd also appeared in a range of other films including The Flying Sorcerer, Digby The Biggest Dog In The World, Scars Of Dracula, The Four Musketeers, Superman III and his final role in The Return Of The Musketeers in 1989.

Stage roles were varied for Todd appearing in the John Antrobus comedy The Bed-Sitting Room and he would go on to have a part in the 1981 adaption of Hamlet. He was also a regular on the pantomime circuit with credits including Cinderella and Emu In Pantoland.

Sadly, after an acting career spanning almost thirty years, Bob Todd passed away in 1992 at the age of seventy.

Tough Passenger

Played by Peter Davidson

This is an aggressive passenger who causes trouble aboard Stan's bus in the Series Seven episode 'The Perfect Clippie'.

A well-built, bearded Scottish passenger is annoyed when trainee clippie Olive brings the bus to an abrupt halt. In a broad Scottish accent he says: 'What's going on?' Jack has no idea what is happening and this angers the passenger who turns on the unnerved conductor and shouts: 'You're the bloody conductor.' When Olive complicates matters Jack tells her to shut up but the passenger thinks he is talking to him and sneers: 'What did you say?' Without waiting for an answer he sits back down and proceeds to open a bar of chocolate and throws the wrapper onto the floor littering the bus. When Stan arrives and demands to know who has caused the mess the Scot squares up to him saying: 'It was me.' The driver's tone changes when he sees the size of the passenger who pushes him and calls him a little tramp. As a consequence Stan falls backwards knocking over Jack and Olive which brings an uncomfortable end to the conflict.

Town and District Bus Company, The

This fictional bus company with red-liveried buses features heavily in the three On The Buses spin-off films.

The Town and District Bus Company is a troubled company running at a loss and blighted by disputes between staff and management. Disharmony in the workplace comes about with the introduction of women bus drivers to the depot but it is an experiment that fails and the women drivers end up as inspectors. A management change sees a new hard-line boss take over and makes bold pledges to run the depot and the company at a profit. In a bid to improve punctuality a radio system is fitted into the buses but this is sabotaged by Jack and is soon removed.

The Town and District Bus Company also places its staff on a course of firefighting and invests in a range of firefighting equipment and another innovation is to bring great expectations. The company plans to run tour buses to popular tourist attractions however more staff incompetence sees the promising idea fail resulting indirectly in another management change. It means that the Town and District Bus Company is destined to continue to run at a loss.

Town's End

This is a destination for buses of the Town and District Bus Company which is referred to verbally and visually in the three spin-off films.

In the first spin-off film On The Buses, Stan and Jack's number thirteen bus terminates at the Town's End. It is situated directly across the road from the infamous Turnaround Betty's house and features in many scenes in the film. In the following two films Mutiny On The Buses and Holiday On The Buses, a number of buses can be seen with Town's End on their destination boards.

Trade Disputes Act of 1909

This is a legal act that is referred to in the Series Seven episode 'On The Omnibuses'.

Amidst a vivid dream, Stan and Jack are busmen in the early part of the twentieth century threatening to go on strike. Inspector Blake warns them of the consequences saying they'd be sacked. He adds: 'And under the trade disputes act of nineteen hundred and nine you'll get six months hard labour.'

Although such an act did exist it did not allow those involved in industrial action to be sentenced to hard labour or to be sacked.

Traffic Warden

Played by Eunice Black

This is a jobs worth of a character that causes problems for Stan in the Series Three episode 'Mum's Last Fling'.

A rotund and bespectacled, dark-haired woman in her fifties, the traffic warden comes across Stan's bus parked beside two parking meters outside an office block. As he is inside paying an overdue gas bill she issues his bus with two parking tickets despite pleas from an intimidated Jack. She shows no mercy applying one ticket beneath the windscreen wiper and another to the rear of the bus before exiting the scene. As Stan returns to the bus he is told he has parking tickets by Jack but he shrugs it off in a carefree manner, screws up one of the tickets and throws it away before driving off. However, that is not the end of the matter. The determined traffic warden retrieves the discarded ticket and hands it over to Inspector Blake at the depot leaving Stan with fines to pay and an ear-bashing to take from Blakey as well.

Trainee Clippie

Played by Parnell McGarry

This is an overweight trainee aboard Stan's bus who gives Jack an uncomfortable time in the Series Three episode 'The Inspector's Niece'.

The trainee clippie is in her late thirties with curly blonde hair and proves to be a clumsy student whose flirtatiousness is not welcome either. Jack is glad to see the back of her and he moans that he is covered in bruises from where she kept bumping into him. Her chances of getting a favourable report from him are nil as he describes her as 'a dead loss' to Inspector Blake. Later in the episode she offers Stan and Jack a useful piece of information though. She rushes up to inform them that their new trainee Sally is actually the inspector's niece and she makes a swift exit sniggering to herself as she goes.

Training

Stan is forced into training and getting fit as he bids to take his place in the depot's football team the Luxton Lions in the Series Seven episode 'The Football Match'.

He begins his fitness regime at home borrowing a fellow employee's chest expander which he hopes will lose him a couple of inches off his waist and build up muscles but instead he ends up embarrassing and injuring himself. More embarrassment waits at the depot as he lines up for football training wearing knee-length shorts that belonged to his late dad. He has to suffer ridicule from all quarters before training gets under way. As coach the inspector puts the team through its paces with a series of basic training routines and exercises but Stan and Jack are very confident that with star player Bob in the side the Luxton Lions can't lose. However, disaster strikes as Stan clowns around during an exercise. He collides with Bob leaving their most talented player injured with a suspected broken ankle ruling him out of their big match against the rival depot team – the Basildon Bashers. It is a disastrous end to the training and leaves Stan very unpopular with his team-mates.

Training Bus

A bus used at the Luxton and District Bus Company to train staff which features in the Series Four episode 'The L Bus'.

It is Stan and Jack's turn to take out the training bus and they are to have the task of training two clippies called Janet and Betty and trainee drivers Albert and Alfred. The first day of training goes off without incident but the following day is quite different. Stan and Jack are to use the training bus as a delivery van as they look to transport a second-hand bed from Jack's aunt's house to the Butler residence as Arthur and Olive have purchased it. Disaster strikes though as the bus breaks down mid-route when the engine suffers an oil-leak and has to be towed back to the depot with the bed still aboard. Although Stan and Jack desperately try to move the bed onto their next bus with the reluctant help of their four trainees they are to be discovered by Inspector Blake. He promptly sets about charging Stan a hefty fee for using the bus to deliver a bed which gives him great satisfaction. It is a costly end to Stan's spell on the training bus.

Transport Manager

A post held by Mr Nichols who spends a short time at the Luxton depot and is briefly to lodge at the Butler house in the Series Four episode 'The Lodger'.

Traps Lane

This road is referred to by Stan in the film On The Buses.

When he and Arthur are aboard the motorcycle and sidecar with Olive as passenger as she goes into labour Stan makes a suggestion. He advises Arthur to take a shortcut to the hospital by going down Traps Lane and they'll be at the hospital in five minutes. However, Traps Lane turns out to have a hump-backed bridge which ensures a very uncomfortable journey for Olive and not ideal for a woman in her condition.

Travel Sickness

This is a condition that Olive suffers from which handicaps her chances of holding down a job as a clippie in the Series One episode 'Olive Takes A Trip'.

In an effort to combat her travel sickness Olive takes pills but they tend to have a side effect of making her sick. However, the pills do alleviate the problem and enable her to hold down a position as clippie a few years later at the second attempt.

Treasurer of the Railway Union

A position held by Arthur and referred to in the Series One episode 'The Early Shift'.

Arthur criticises Stan for not attending union meetings and warns that the unions are being infiltrated. With a sense of self-satisfaction he says: 'I pride myself on the fact that I've never missed a union meeting. Twelve years I've been treasurer of the railway union and every member comes to every meeting.' Stan though is unmoved and quips: 'With you as treasurer I'm not surprised.'

Trial Run to Windsor Safari Park

The Town and District's new tour bus manned by driver Stan and Inspector Blake without passengers aboard goes on a trial run to Windsor Safari Park in the film Mutiny On The Buses.

Prior to departing, Inspector Blake is warned about the price of failure by the manager whilst a moment of carelessness sees Stan damage the emergency exit door of the bus and this will later prove costly. Spirits are high though, as the bus first departs the depot and is cheered on its way by a crowd of excited staff but trouble is around the corner.

On arrival at the safari park the bus is met and welcomed by the park's safari guard, and the bus enters taking in the sight of elephants the size of the bus and baboons resembling the inspector according to Stan. Before entering the lion's enclosure they are given strict guidelines and warned that all doors and windows must be kept shut at all times by the safari guard.

They are allowed to proceed but when Stan has to brake suddenly to avoid knocking down a lion the damaged emergency exit door pops open at the rear of the bus and a lion leaps aboard. It ventures up the aisle towards the unaware busmen until they realise the danger but fortunately the ferocious beast retreats. However, when they see the lion approach again they escape to the upper deck of the bus and even contemplate climbing out of the rear window to escape but are put off by the sight of a pack of lions waiting down below. The lion aboard the bus follows them upstairs and rips the seat of Stan and Blakey's trousers before it retreats and exits the bus much to their relief. They nervously creep downstairs only to be greeted by the enraged safari guard who tells them they will not be allowed back to the park and orders them to get out. A glum Inspector Blake fears the sack and blames Stan for the disastrous trial run but the drama is not over.

As the bus makes its way out of the park a pair of chimpanzees enter the bus via the open rear window on the upper deck before making their way downstairs. One leaps onto the steering wheel and takes control of the bus and the other leaps onto the inspector and the bus races out of the park almost knocking over a policeman. It runs out of control around in circles in a car park before coming to a halt. At which point the policeman opens the door of the bus and begins to berate the driver but is shocked to see a chimpanzee in the driver's seat with Stan and Inspector Blake attempting to look innocent. The disastrous trial run results in the planned tour bus project being scrapped with the inspector being demoted for his part in the fiasco.

Turnaround Betty

Played by Andria Lawrence

This is a housewife who causes trouble for both Jack and Stan in the film On The Buses.

Betty is a very flirtatious married woman in her thirties with blonde hair who is always seen scantily clad in a skimpy nightie. She lives in a house across the road from the Town's End terminating bus stop which leads to her striking up a relationship with Jack who is to spend his time cavorting with her in her bedroom whilst her husband is out.

Betty refers to a Town and District book of timetables to plan their all too brief moments of passion but when she errs reading it Jack is in trouble. He is late getting back to his bus and is caught by an awaiting Inspector Blake as he exits Betty's house in a state of undress earning him a tongue-lashing. Betty is later to be visited by Stan who is searching for Jack's lost PSV badge and lures him up to her bedroom where she uses her charm to seduce the driver. However, her suspicious husband arrives home unexpectedly and almost catches them in the act but Stan somehow escapes leaving a trail of damage behind him. Betty's infidelity remains unproven and when Jack is placed on a new route their relationship ends.

Turnaround Point

A term used in the public transport industry that is used chiefly in the film On The Buses.

When reminding Jack of the perils of the in-coming women drivers Stan says: 'No woman bus drivers gonna get you to the turnaround point early so you can have it off with your bird.' The turnaround point on their route comes at the Town's End stop opposite which lives Betty – a housewife that Jack has a brief affair with hence her nickname – Turnaround Betty.

The term describes the point of a journey in public transport when a vehicle has reached its destination and will thus stop before turning and proceeding back the way it came to its depot or point of origin.

TV Commentator

Played by Peter Cockburn

This unseen character can be heard commentating on a football match on Inspector Blake's television in the Series Five episode 'The New Telly'.

TV Interviewer

Played by Fraser Kerr

This television reporter is to visit the bus depot to report on a strike by the busmen in the Series One episode 'The Early Shift'.

The moustachioed reporter, in his late thirties, speaking with a posh accent and wearing a sheepskin coat arrives at the depot with a film crew which is much to Jack's pleasure as the strike needs the publicity. When the inspector looks to break the strike by taking a bus out of the depot the reporter and his crew are on hand to capture the drama and their report is aired on television later that evening. Acting as the newsreader, the reporter ends the bulletin with a late newsflash announcing that the management have agreed to meet the busmen's demands to end the strike.

Twiggy

This is a famous fashion model, actress and singer who is referred to by Arthur in the Series Four episode 'The Kids Outing'.

In a desperate bid to entertain unruly children in the depot canteen, Stan appears in drag dressed as a clippie and prepares to sing a song. A surprised Olive says: 'Oh look it's Stan.' An unimpressed Arthur replies: 'Well I didn't think it was Twiggy.'

Twiggy, whose real name was Lesley Lawson, was to be an iconic figure in Britain during the swinging sixties. The petite blonde was voted British Woman of the Year and a national newspaper named her 'The Face of 1966'. She shot to fame as a model appearing on famous glossy magazines such as Vogue and would go on to model all over the world. Her career took a new turn in the 1970s when she took up acting appearing in film, television and stage roles and was also to become a singer recording a number of songs but failed to have any hits. It is still modelling she is best-remembered for and still models to the present day for noted companies such as Marks and Spencer.

Tyre Pump

This is a piece of equipment in the depot that is used by women bus drivers to punish Stan in the film On The Buses.

After harassing a woman driver once too often Stan gets his come-uppance. A band of well-built women drivers round on their male counterpart and carry him over to the depot's tyre pump as he wrestles furiously to get free but it is to no avail. The pump is placed up his trouser leg and turned on to send blasts of air rocketing up his leg causing him to yell out in pain. The punishment is carried out again before the women walk away amidst hysterics leaving Stan writhing in agony on the ground. More pain comes his way when Jack goes to remove the pump but accidentally sends another blast of air to the stricken driver's nether regions.

U

Ultra

The manufacturer of the Town and District Bus Company's new radio control system fitted into their fleet of buses that features in the film Mutiny On The Buses.

Ultra was formed in 1920 and manufactured quality headphones and the London-based company expanded into manufacturing radio and television receivers that were to be used by the emerging broadcaster the BBC in the late 1930s. The company split into two in the late 1950s when one sector manufactured radios and televisions whilst the other built other electrical products.

In 1961 the former came under the ownership of Thorn Electrical Industries which would go on to be part of the production company (Thorn-EMI) behind all three On The Buses spin-off films hence, most probably, the appearance of the radio system made by Ultra. During the 1960s, Ultra were to build radio systems in the transport industry and continued to operate under the Ultra name until 1974. In the late 1970s it became Ultra Electronics and although it was to change ownership it continues to produce a wide range of electrical and radio equipment to various transport outlets and aviation industries around the world to the present day.

Uncle Herbert

This is an unseen relative in the Butler family who is referred to in a couple of episodes of On The Buses.

Uncle Herbert is discussed by Mrs Butler and her sister Maud in the Series Two episode 'Aunt Maud'. Stan's aunt is puzzled that he is still a bachelor and she is suspicious when she hears he goes out with Jack most nights and remarks that she hopes he isn't going to turn out like Uncle Herbert. Stan though, is curious and although his mum is reluctant to talk about Herbert she hints that he was homosexual but assures Stan that it is alright now as it is legal.

The uncle's sexual orientation is referred to again in the Series Seven episode 'The Poster'. As Stan has purchased a range of beauty products for himself mum is concerned that he might turn out like Uncle Herbert. She goes on to reveal that he once borrowed her nightdress at Christmas and also ended up in court for an undisclosed reason. It is her opinion that he had trouble with his hormones as she claims that is what the magistrate said.

Uncle Willie

By coincidence both Stan and Jack had an Uncle Willie who is referred to in a couple of episodes of On The Buses.

Jack's Uncle Willie is mentioned in the Series Four episode 'The Injury' with him recalling when they dressed him for his funeral. He jokes, as the Butler family struggle to dress an injured Stan for work, that the driver is stiffer than his deceased uncle. He also feels that the dead Willie looked better than the injured Stan does as well.

In the Series Five episode 'Lost Property', it is revealed that Stan's dad was to inherit a pair of second-hand false teeth from Uncle Willie when he passed away. These teeth were lost aboard a bus but were handed in and he was to get them back.

Union

The influence of the union is to feature heavily in both the episodes and spin-off films of On The Buses often portraying the power struggle between the workforce and the management.

When On The Buses aired from 1969 to 1973, trade unions in the workplace held a great deal of power over management with the threat of industrial action always a powerful weapon. Such was the power of the unions it is widely accepted that wide scale strike action, in 1978 through into 1979 known as the 'Winter of Discontent' brought about the downfall of James Callaghan's Labour government.

A change was just around the corner though when, in the 1980s, Margaret Thatcher's Conservative government brought laws into place that made strike action more difficult to stage legally which rested a great amount of power away from the unions which they have never managed to fully regain.

Union Agreement

This is an understanding between the union and the Town and District Bus Company which is referred to by Jack in the film On The Buses.

The union agreement is that all busmen are entitled to the option of a hot meal in the depot canteen at all times. However, a staff shortage deprives the canteen of a cook and cold food is only available which sees Jack remind the troubled inspector of the agreement and says himself and Stan are going home for dinner. Although Inspector Blake protests otherwise he is powerless to stop them.

Union Meeting

A gathering of union members in the depot canteen features in the Series Seven episode 'The Poster'.

Jack is intent on seeing that Stan is nominated as depot representative for a promotional poster contest and sharing the prize money that goes with it. He calls a union meeting to persuade the attending busmen to vote for his driver and friend and gets his way much to the consternation of Inspector Blake.

Union Secretary

An unseen member of the union who Jack is to visit in a bid to defend charges made against Stan in the Series Four episode 'Safety First'.

With Stan being accused of dangerous driving and attempted manslaughter after his bus reverses into Inspector Blake's office injuring him, Jack visits the union secretary. He learns that the inspector is to blame for the accident as he ordered Stan to manoeuvre the bus in the depot when, in fact, that is the job of the shunter and so all charges are subsequently dropped.

Unwin, Geoff

Composer ('It's A Great Life On The Buses' – Theme From 'On The Buses')

Geoff Unwin had a background in show business that would lead to him composing music.

In the late 1950s he and his wife were to perform on stage for the Argyle Theatre for Youth in productions of Alice In Wonderland and David Copperfield. He was to tour schools performing the productions in a mobile theatre. Into the early 1960s and Unwin pioneered the world's first music sampler – a keyboard instrument which brought a new sound to pop music. He was to introduce it to the greatest musicians of that generation including The Beatles, Dusty Springfield and Stevie Wonder. However, his claim to fame came in 1971 when he was to compose the theme song 'It's A Great Life On The Buses' that was to feature in the first of the On The Buses spin-off films. He based the tune around the popular cockney song 'Knees Up Mother Brown' and it was to suit the film perfectly. It was to be his most noted composition and is a noteworthy contribution to the film.

Unwin moved on from composing film theme music but has remained involved with music in other capacities to the present day.

Up The Junction

This popular 1960s film is referred to by Arthur in the Series One episode 'The Darts Match'.

As the Butler family discuss an upcoming darts match with two clippies, mum says she never knew the busmen played games with the clippies. Arthur points out they play games all the time but not darts and goes on to say to mum: 'You want to go round the back of the depot one Saturday night. Makes 'Up The Junction' look like a prayer meeting.'

Up The Junction was a 1968 film based on a novel written by Neil Dunn which is about life in a run-down area of London. It tells the story of a woman from an upper class lifestyle in Chelsea who starts a new life in Battersea working in a factory as she searches for her own independence. Her life descends into an affair with a young man and when she becomes pregnant she has to seek an illegal abortion. Directed by Peter Collinson, the film starred Dennis Waterman, Suzy Kendall and Liz Fraser. Coincidentally, in the cast in supporting roles were a number of actors and actresses who went on to appear in On The Buses on the small or big screen those being Michael Robbins, Doreen Herrington, Aubrey Morris, Queenie Watts and Larry Martyn.

Up the Wooden Hill to Bedfordshire

This is a song from the 1930s that is sung by a drunken Mrs Butler in the Series Three episode 'Brew It Yourself'.

Stan is bemused to find that the family have drunk all of his home-brewed beer and finds Arthur, Olive and his mum drunk. He points his tired mum in the direction of the stairs and as she makes her way towards them she starts to drunkenly sing 'Up the Wooden Hill to Bedfordshire.'

The song and its lyrics were adapted from an old nursery rhyme with it being recorded in 1936 by Vera Lynn who was soon to go on to become a forces sweetheart in World War Two.

Upholstery Store

This is an area in the bus depot that is seen in the Series Four episode 'Cover Up'.

Stan and Jack visit the depot's upholstery store to obtain some material that is used to cover the bus seats from the upholsterer Joe. The desperate driver needs the material to repair an armchair at home and seeks a supply free of charge. A short time later, as Stan and Jack are set to take their bus out, Joe rushes from the store to hand Stan a large wrapped package containing the material before nervously making a hasty exit.

Uplifts

This is a device worn in his shoes by Stan in the Series Seven episode 'The Poster'.

As Stan bids to win the promotional poster contest he is encouraged by Jack to wear uplifts in his shoes to make him appear taller. He tells the driver that all of the film actors wear them and it helps to attract women and so Stan fits the wedge-like uplifts into his shoes. However, he finds walking in them awkward and it is to earn him great ridicule from Inspector Blake and a couple of busmen. This persuades Stan to rid himself of the uplifts and face the judging panel for the contest on his own terms.

Varney, Jeanne

Film Role: Mavis (On The Buses)

As an actress Jeanne Varney had a solitary film role before she took up a career away from acting.

Her role came in the first On The Buses spin-off film in 1971 when she appeared in one of the best scenes in the film alongside her father Reg who was star of the show and other comedy legends Stephen Lewis, Bob Grant and Wendy Richard.

She remained very close to her father throughout his long life and in his later years was to care for him when he fell ill.

Varney, Reg

TV Role: Stan Butler (On The Buses Series 1-7)
Film Role: Stan Butler (On The Buses, Mutiny On The Buses and Holiday On The Buses)

Born in Canning Town, London in 1916, Reg Varney was to begin in show business at the age of seven. After a number of years performing on the working men's club circuit he'd progress on to roles on stage, in films and on television in a career that was to span over fifty years.

After serving with the Royal Engineers in the Second World War he demobbed and his stage career began to take off. In the late 1940s he would have a starring role in the comedy Gaytime where he appeared alongside a young star of the future – his name was Benny Hill. Aside from pantomimes he'd have stage roles in The Marquis Trio, Sky High, This Is The Show and Showtime in the 1950s. Roles in films and on television would then supersede his stage career but he was to tour New Zealand and Canada and in 1988 toured Australia as On The Buses was adapted into a stage show.

In the early 1950s, Varney broke into films with a role in the comedy Miss Robin Hood which boasted a quality cast. He'd go on to have credits in the 1960s in Joey Boy and the classic The Great St Trinian's Train Robbery. The following decade brought further comedy roles in On The Buses, Mutiny On The Buses and Holiday On The Buses as well as starring roles in Go For A Take, The Best Pair Of Legs In The Business and a small role in the short film The Plank – a remake of the 1967 comedy classic at the end of the 1970s.

On television Reg Varney will always be best remembered as the cheeky bus driver Stan Butler in the hit sitcom On The Buses which ran from 1969 to 1973 and he would reprise the role in spin-off films and on stage. He had, however, shot to fame in the early 1960s sitcom The Rag Trade playing Reg Turner which was, like On The Buses, written by Ronald Wolfe and Ronald Chesney. Other notable comedy roles came in Beggar My Neighbour, Reg Varney and Down The Gate. In drama he'd appear in Emergency Ward – 10 and ITV Playhouse which featured a dark comedy play called The Best Pair Of Legs In The Business which was later to be adapted into a film.

Varney had been blighted by heart attacks in 1965 and in 1981 a more serious one would see him cut back his workload and by the early 1990s he had retired from acting. During this time he developed a great talent as an artist painting landscapes which today are much sought after. Sadly, in November 2008, after developing a chest infection, Reg Varney passed away in a nursing home in Budleigh Salterton, Devon at the age of ninety two. A multi-talented man, a great comedy actor, entertainer, talented pianist and artist was lost to the world.

Reg Varney makes his final television appearance in 2005.

Picture courtesy of the private collection of Of The Official On The Buses Fan Club.

Reg Varney – The Consummate Professional

Aside from holding a bus driver's license, Reg Varney prepared meticulously for his role as Stan Butler in On The Buses. He was a fabulous character actor and to learn more about being a bus driver he would often take time out during filming episodes in the Wood Green depot's canteen. He would sip tea and mingle with real life bus drivers learning some of their tricks of the trade, picking up the banter and their experiences so that he could incorporate all that he had learnt into his character.

The price of fame that came with playing Stan Butler meant that Reg became a household name. Any mundane trips to the shops would result in him being mobbed by hordes of fans pleading for autographs. These were unsettling experiences for Reg though he certainly enjoyed being known by everyone. It got to such a stage that he left his beloved wife Lily to do his shopping. His ventures out of his Georgian house in Enfield were largely confined to trips to the studios for filming and nights out at his local pub – the Rose And Crown.

Vasey, Suzanne

TV Role: First Aid Clippie (Series 3 Episode 1 'First Aid')

Born in 1945, Suzanne Vasey broke into acting on leaving school in the early 1960s and until the early 1970s would have credits on stage and television.

Her first roles came on stage in the early 1960s with small parts in a number of Old Vic Theatre productions such as A Flea In Her Ear, Love For Love, The Dance Of Death, Rites, The Way Of The World and Macrunes's Guevara amongst others. She also appeared in other stage shows including The Diplomatic Baggage and Bird Of Paradise.

Vasey's television roles were largely in hit dramas such as The Man In Room 17, Softly Softly, Department S and Wicked Women. On the comedy front she had credits in Mrs Thursday and On The Buses.

Veil

Olive is to wear a veil over her face to her divorce hearing in the Series Seven episode 'Olive's Divorce'.

The veil being worn is an idea of her solicitor who believes it will impress the judge. Jack sees the sense in that and offers Stan some advice. He says: 'She better keep that veil over her face when she's in court or the judge'll find Arthur had every justification.'

Vera

Played by Pat Coombs

This diminutive figure of a woman in her mid-forties is one of the first women drivers to be taken on by the Town and District Bus Company in the film On The Buses.

Although she has a fear of spiders, Vera is not afraid to stand up to Stan and Jack's bullying. This is evident when Stan parks his bus in the depot leaving her unable to exit her driver's cab. As Stan and Jack laugh at her predicament she clambers out of her cab over the bonnet of her bus giving them a glimpse of her pink knickers. In fits of laughter Jack describes them as 'a pair of passion killers'. To heighten her discomfort she burns herself on the hot bonnet but she is set to get her revenge. Her fellow women drivers arrive on the scene and, rolling her sleeves up and glaring at Stan she says: 'Come on girls let's sort this little boy out.' With that she and her friends corner Stan and use a tyre pump to teach the cheeky driver a lesson.

Stan is to get his own back as he places a number of spiders in the driver's cab of her bus prior to her boarding in a bid to discredit the women drivers. With Inspector Blake aboard to monitor her disaster awaits. Not long after leaving the depot the spiders are soon crawling up Vera's legs and when she sees them she screams, losing control of her bus which crashes into the back of a lorry which in turn knocks a policeman to the ground. Vera exits her cab and despite an injured Blakey telling her to get back in her cab and drive off the panicked woman screams: 'I can't. I can't. There's spiders in my cab.' It is an incident that lands the inspector in trouble with the manager who begins to doubt opting to use women drivers. Vera again suffers at the hands of Stan and Jack when they put diuretic pills into her tea. The pills cause her to need frequent visits to toilets whilst on duty which throws the bus services into chaos.

The accumulative effect of Stan and Jack's actions towards Vera and her female colleagues sees the bus company dispense with women bus drivers. However, she benefits from this misfortune as she is to become one of four new inspectors at the depot. She moves quickly in the role to split Stan and Jack up as a bus crew. She feels they are troublemakers and should be kept apart so she does have the last laugh in her conflict with Stan and Jack.

Vesuvius

This is a famous volcano that Jack is likened to by Inspector Blake in the Series Seven episode 'The Football Match'.

Amidst enrolling for the depot's football team Inspector Blake points out that neither Stan nor Jack are fit enough for a place on the team. As Jack stands, taking another puff of his cigarette the inspector says: 'Look at Vesuvius here.'

Mount Vesuvius is an active volcano in south west Italy just east of the city of Naples. The volcano famously erupted in AD 79 burying the city of Pompeii and is still regarded as one of the most active volcanos in mainland Europe although its last major eruption came in 1944. When erupting, clouds of smoke and ash are sent spewing hundreds of feet into the air hence the inspector likening the chain-smoking Jack to the volcano.

Vic

Played by Nosher Powell

A bus driver who helps Stan and Jack guess the weight of a clippie in the Series Five episode 'The Strain'.

Vic is a tall, well-built bus driver with sideburns who is dining in the canteen. In a cockney accent he offers to guess the weight of Doreen and walks over, spits on his hands before rubbing them together and lifts the clippie effortlessly up to the level of his shoulders and puts her back down. He pauses in thought and then says: 'About nine stone ten and a half.' He takes a seat in the canteen leaving Stan to attempt something similar but the slighter driver only succeeds in injuring his back in the process.

Vicar, The

Played by Robin Parkinson

A character who conducts the wedding ceremony which sees the inspector's niece Sally wed the busman Bill in the Series Five episode 'The Best Man'.

The bespectacled, blonde-haired vicar is frustrated in dealing with the late running busman's wedding and ticks the inspector off for cursing whilst in church. He is keen to rush the ceremony along and criticises Stan for arriving late with the bridegroom and points out in a frustrated manner that he has a busy schedule to keep. However, when a further delay occurs when Stan can't remove the wedding ring from his finger, the vicar loses his patience and yells for them to hurry up. Finally, the wedding is completed and the vicar watches on unimpressed as the wedding party leave the church and board a waiting bus.

Villiers Road

The street in which a clippie that Stan is dating lives in which is referred to in the Series Two episode 'Late Again'.

A clippie called Doreen, who is on early shifts, is looking forward to a date with Stan but when he is placed on night shifts he has to cancel the date. He asks Jack to go around to her house in Villiers Road to tell Doreen he can't make the date but the crafty conductor ends up taking advantage of the situation.

Vina Player

Played by Vemu Mukunda

A bearded Indian who wears spectacles and sits on the floor of the canteen playing the traditional Indian-stringed instrument as Fatima performs her entertaining snake dance in the Series Three episode 'The Snake'.

Virgo

The star sign of Olive as revealed in an episode and spin-off film of On The Buses.

In the Series Seven episode 'What The Stars Foretell', Olive and her friend Sandra discuss horoscopes with Jack in the depot canteen. 'I read my stars every day and they always come true. I'm a Virgo,' Olive tells Jack.

The film On The Buses sees Olive fall pregnant and her mum reminisces about when Olive was born. She recalls that she was in labour for so long that her daughter was born under two birth signs with the top half being born under Leo and the bottom half was born under Virgo.

Actress Anna Karen, who played Olive, was born on the 19th of September 1936 and herself is a Virgo by birth. Obviously, this was taken into account when the scripts were written.

Waiting Room

This part of the bus depot is referred to by Jack in the Series Four episode 'Nowhere To Go'.

Jack and Stan have a problem as, after a late shift, they have nowhere to take their dates – a pair of clippies and so they resort to snogging them aboard their bus. When the inspector catches them in the act he orders them to leave but cheekily Jack asks him to open up the waiting room so they can take their dates there. Of course Blakey refuses pointing out that the waiting room is only there for people legitimately waiting for a bus. This scuppers any hopes the busmen had for a night of passion meaning they must wait for another opportunity.

Walker, Rudolph

TV Role: George (Series 1 Episode 1 'The Early Shift')

Born in Trinidad, West Indies in 1939, Rudolph Walker moved to the UK in 1960 and was soon to build a successful career as an actor that would span fifty years including roles on television, in films and on stage.

It was on television that he shot to fame in the controversial 1970s sitcom Love Thy Neighbour playing Bill Reynolds and more recently has spent over a decade in the hit soap EastEnders in the role of Patrick Trueman. Another notable role came in the popular 1990s sitcom The Thin Blue Line with other comedy credits including On The Buses, The Fosters, The Lenny Henry Show, Mr Bean and A Perfect State. He was equally at home in dramas over the decades with credits in Adam Adamant Lives, Emergency Ward – 10, The Champions, Doctor Who, Paul Temple, Black Silk, Rules Of Engagement, The Bill, Lovejoy, Casualty, Bugs and Doctors to name but a few.

On the big screen his career began with an uncredited role in the 1966 Hammer film The Witches. In the early 1970s came credits in All The Right Noises, Universal Soldier, 10 Rillington Place, Man About The House and a starring role in the spin-off film Love Thy Neighbour. His other notable film roles came in the 1990s in Let Him Have It, Bhaji On The Beach and The House Of Angelo and in the 2000s in Ali G Indahouse and perhaps his greatest big screen performance in the 2007 cricket drama Hit For Six.

Walker was also to have a number of stage credits from the early 1970s onwards. That decade saw him with roles in classic plays such as The Tempest and Othello along with parts in One Night, Play Mas and a stage adaption of Love Thy Neighbour. The 1980s and 9's brought further roles in Pericles, Prince Of Tyre, Elektra and Timon Of Athens amongst others.

In 2006, Walker was awarded the OBE for his services to drama and he remains active in the acting profession after fifty years in the industry.

Walker, Sue

TV Role: Ada (Series 2 Episode 5 'Late Again')

Sue Walker had a short career as an actress in the late 1960s until the mid-1970s with credits in television and films.

She debuted on television as an angry clippie in On The Buses in the late 1960s. This would be followed by other small comedy roles in Oh Father and the hit sitcom Steptoe And Son. In drama she was to have an uncredited part in the hit prison drama Within These Walls
.

Her solitary film role was to come in the 1972 production The Trouble With 2B.

Waller, Kenneth

TV Role: Busman (Series 5 Episode 15 'Boxing Day Social')

Born in Huddersfield, Yorkshire in 1927, Kenneth Waller was to arrive late to acting in the mid-1950s with roles on stage before appearing in films and on television in a career that spanned over forty years.

After many repertory roles he'd progress onto stage making his West End debut in the musical Free As Air in 1957. He'd go on to appear in several more London stage productions such as Salad Days, The Solid Gold Cadillac, Anne Of Green Gables and The Importance Of Being Earnest. His later stage credits included a touring production of Entertaining Mr Sloane where he appeared alongside Barbara Windsor.

In the late 1950s, Waller's film career began with an uncredited role in the Oscar-winning Room At The Top. Other memorable films that he appeared in were to include Chitty Chitty Bang Bang, Scrooge, Fiddler On The Roof and Carry On Behind.

Although his first television role didn't come until the mid-1960s it is for his small screen roles that he will be best-remembered. His biggest role came in the hit 1980s sitcom Bread where he played Grandad and he also had sizeable roles in the light drama Big Deal and the hit sitcom Are You Being Served? Outwith these roles he appeared in several hit British dramas such as Crossroads, Softly Softly, The Onedin Line, Z Cars, Dixon Of Dock Green, Doctor Who, All Creatures Great And Small, Ellis Island and Coronation Street. His comedy credits included On The Buses, Doctor In Charge, The Top Secret Life of Edgar Briggs, The Liver Birds, Doctor On The Go, Boon, Never The Twain and children's series The Queen's Nose.

He continued in acting up until he sadly passed away in early 2000 at the age of seventy two. Also a talented pianist who played with leading orchestras the noted actor is still missed today.

Walter, Jules

TV Role: Chalkie (Series 7 Episode 5 'The Football Match' and Series 7 Episode 7 'Goodbye Stan')

Born in Antigua, West Indies, Jules Walter (actual name Walters) was to move to the UK and carved out a career as an actor from the early 1970s through until the mid-1980s with credits coming chiefly on television but he also appeared in films and on stage. He was also a talented artist.

On television he would appear in a string of hit sitcoms that included On The Buses (taking over the role as Chalkie from Glen Whitter), Sykes, Some Mothers Do 'Ave 'Em and Metal Mickey. In dramas he would have credits in classic series such as The Onedin Line and The Professionals with a number of uncredited roles in Doctor Who and Blake's 7. His film roles were few and far between and were limited to a small part in the sex comedy Can You Keep It Up For A Week in the mid-1970s. A few years later came a bigger role in the classic war film The Wild Geese.

Walter returned home to his native Antigua in the late 1980s to live. His talent for art and his recognition of fine artwork saw him become Vice President of the Antigua Art Society before moving on to the role of director of a small art gallery in Antigua.

Walters, Hugh

TV Role: Bill (Series 5 Episode 3 'The Best Man')

Born in Mexborough, Yorkshire in 1939, Hugh Walters broke into acting in his early twenties with roles on stage which were to be followed by roles on television and in films.

His stage debut came in 1962 and he'd appear alongside comedy legends Peggy Mount, Max Wall, Richard Briers and Ronnie Barker in stage productions such as The Beaver Coat, Ubo Roi and The Real Inspector Hound amongst others. More recently he has had credits in My Three Angels, Ten Little Indians and Bedroom Farce.

A year after his stage debut his television career began. He would appear in classic comedy sketch shows Six Dates With Barker, The Dick Emery Show and The Russ Abbott Show. He'd also appear in a host of hit sitcoms over four decades which included The Likely Lads, Doctor At Large, On The Buses, A Fine Romance, Shine On Harvey Moon and The Brittas Empire. His drama roles came in Nicholas Nickleby, Ivanhoe, Jason King, Doctor Who, Survivors, The New Avengers, Z Cars, The Agatha Christie Hour, Rumpole Of The Bailey, Casualty, All Creatures Great And Small, The House Of Eliott, Heartbeat and Doctors to name but a few. He'd also have roles in much-loved children's series Here Comes The Double Deckers and The Ghosts Of Motley Hall.

On the big screen his first role came in the musical comedy Catch Us If You Can in 1965. He would go on to have credits in Rocket To The Moon, Alfie Darling, George And Mildred, Brimstone And Treacle, The Missionary, 1984, Firelight and he also portrayed Charles Hawtrey in the made-for-television film about the Carry On cast – Cor Blimey.

Walters, also a talented writer, supplied scripts for the early 1970s sitcom The Train Now Standing and has worked on radio as well. He continues to act into the 2010s more than fifty years since his first acting role.

Wapping

A borough of London that is where Inspector Blake is from as referred to in the Series Seven episode 'Friends In High Places'.

When the inspector takes offence to Jack making himself at home in the Butler house he tells him: 'Remember that an Englishman's home is his castle.' The miffed conductor hits back saying: 'Look you're not English. You're from Wapping and this isn't your home, you're only the lodger here.'

Wapping is a borough of London in the Docklands on the banks of the River Thames. It has been home to some of Britain's most popular tabloid newspapers since the mid-1980s and the area has undergone great redevelopment in recent decades. Old warehouses in the Docklands have been refurbished and transformed into luxurious flats and rich clientele have been attracted to the area.

Ward, Dervis

Film Role: Angry Passenger (Mutiny On The Buses)

Born in Dowlais, Wales in 1923, Dervis Ward was to have a career spanning well over thirty years as an actor with roles on stage, in films and finally on television.

Ward's career began on stage at the end of the Second World War with roles in Lady Windermere's Fan and Zoo In Silesia. He'd continue on with frequent stage roles into the 1960's appearing in Ross and Saint Joan Of The Stockyards amongst others.

His film roles from the late 1940s onwards included credits in critically-acclaimed films such as The Long Haul, The World Of Suzie Wong, The Loneliness Of The Long Distance Runner and To Sir With Love. Other big screen roles saw him have an uncredited role in the multiple Oscar-winning Ben Hur and credits in Gorgo, The Violent Enemy, The Vengeance Of She, Dad's Army, Mutiny On The Buses and The Prince And The Pauper to name but a few. Towards the end of the 1950s he was to appear in television roles in smash hit dramas such as The Adventures Of Robin Hood. Ward would later appear in hit series that included No Hiding Place, Z Cars, Dixon Of Dock Green, Gideon's Way, The Avengers, The Champions and The Protectors. Comedy roles though were less frequent but he had credits in The Charlie Drake Show, For Amusement Only and the children's cult series Here Comes The Double Deckers.

Dervis Ward passed away in 1996 at the age of seventy two.

Warwick, Gina

TV Role: The Nurse (Series 4 Episode 10 'Safety First')

Gina Warwick's brief career as an actress brought her roles in films and on television from the mid-1960s through until the early 1970s.

On the big screen she would have credits in the comedy film Mister Ten Per Cent and had a sizeable role in the late 1960s Amicus horror production The Haunted House Of Horror. In an uncredited capacity she also made appearances in the multi-Oscar-winning film A Man For All Seasons and Carry On Follow That Camel. Her biggest television role came in the LWT comedy sketch show We Have Ways Of Making You Laugh and she went on to appear in On The Buses. Warwick's most noted drama credit came in an episode of the hit series Department S.

She was to quit acting in the early 1970s and was to sadly pass away in 2003.

Washroom

An area in the bus depot referred to by the general manager in the Series Seven episode 'Hot Water'.

The manager tells Jack and the inspector that an immersion heater and stopcock have been stolen from the depot's washroom.

Watts, Gwendolyn

TV Role: Iris (Series 1 Episode 2 'The New Conductor' and Series 1 Episode 7 'The Darts Match')

Born in Carhampton, Somerset in 1932, Gwendolyn Watts was to have a long career as an actress with roles on stage, television and in films from the mid-1950s.

She made her first appearance as an actress on stage and was to have roles in Hot And Cold In All Rooms and The Boyfriend. In the 1960s her credits included parts in the Lionel Bart musical Blitz and in DH Lawrence plays such as A Collier's Friday Night and The Widowing Of Mrs Holroyd. Towards the end of her career came a role in the musical Stepping Out in 1996. The late 1950s saw Watts make her television debut in an episode of the classic series Alfred Hitchcock Presents. She would have further drama roles in Walk A Crooked Mile, The Avengers, Maigret, Z Cars, No Hiding Place, Coronation Street and her final small screen credit in The Final Cut in 1995. Her comedy roles were plentiful and came in some of the best of British comedy series in the 1960s and 70s. These included It's A Square World, The Rag Trade, Steptoe And Son, The Benny Hill Show, Pardon The Expression, On The Buses, Love Thy Neighbour and a starring role in Sorry I'm Single. On the big screen from 1960 into the early 1970s she was to appear in a range of films. Her credits included the Oscar-winning Sons And Lovers, Billy Liar, The System, Fanatic, The Wrong Box, Carry On Doctor, Carry On Again Doctor, The Games and Carry On Matron. An uncredited role also saw her appear in the smash hit musical My Fair Lady which scooped eight Oscars in 1965.

Sadly, in 2000, Gwendolyn Watts passed away at the age of sixty seven.

Watts, Queenie

Film Role: Lily Briggs (Holiday On The Buses)

Born in London in 1926, Queenie Watts was to break into acting in films in the early 1960s and progressed on to stage and television roles.

She debuted in the hit 1963 musical film Sparrows Can't Sing directed by the famous Joan Littlewood and penned by Stephen Lewis (later of On The Buses fame). Other credits came in gritty dramas such as Poor Cow, Up The Junction and All Coppers Are… . She'd also have a small role in the hit musical Half A Sixpence, Holiday On The Buses, Schizo and an uncredited part in the classic film Alfie. Watts was also to have a number of stage roles appearing regularly in the Royal Court Theatre, London in stage productions such as Saved, Early Morning and Come Together in the late 1960s and early 1970s. From the late 1960s she began a successful television career. Her best-remembered role was as Lily Briggs in the Wolfe and Chesney sitcom Romany Jones and it's spin-off series Yus My Dear. Comedy was her forte and she'd appear in a range of hit comedy series such as Dad's Army, Up Pompeii, The Goodies, Never Mind The Quality Feel The Width, Steptoe And Son, Sykes, The Dick Emery Show and George And Mildred. She was no stranger to drama roles though with the pick of those coming in Dixon Of Dock Green, Doomwatch, Callan and Country Matters.

Aside from her career as an actress Queenie Watts was a talented pianist and ran a number of East End pubs with her husband. She would attract punters to her pub by playing the piano at nights. Sadly though, in 1980, she lost a fight against cancer passing away at the age of fifty three.

Waybill

This is a document to be filled in by the conductor and which is referred to in a number of episodes and spin-off films of On The Buses.

A waybill was a document which was used to note ticket sales on each bus journey. These would be filled in and handed in to the inspector whose job it was to check and sign the waybill at the end of each shift. Even in today's modern age the humble waybill is still in use by some select bus companies.

Wayne, John

A legendary US film actor referred to in a couple of episodes of On The Buses.

In the Series Three episode 'Foggy Night', trapped on a fog-bound bus, Inspector Blake is forced into going out into the night to find a phone box so he can report their situation to the depot. He makes a long goodbye speech to the passengers promising them he'll get through. After he exits Stan jokes: 'There he goes – the Luxton and District Bus Company's John Wayne.' Jack adds: 'One hundred percent true grit.' When Stan completes his final ever journey aboard his bus in the Series Seven episode 'Goodbye Stan', he nostalgically speaks warmly of his bus and the many journeys they have done together. A listening Inspector Blake moans: 'It's like John Wayne saying goodbye to his horse.'

John Wayne (born Marion Morrison in 1907) was to become one of the most famous actors of all-time. In a career in films spanning fifty years he was to appear in well over a hundred films and was renowned for his hard man roles in westerns and war films. His nickname was 'The Duke' and he would win an Oscar for his role in the classic western True Grit in 1969. Sadly, he was to pass away ten years later in 1979 after losing a battle against stomach cancer. He was seventy two.

We Shall Not Be Moved

A song that is sung by rowdy children aboard Stan's bus as it arrives back at the depot in the Series Four episode 'The Kids Outing'.

The song 'We Shall Not Be Moved' was initially an American folk song from the nineteenth century. It would be adapted into a pop song recorded by the US artist Pete Seeger in 1955 and around ten years later by the Australian folk band The Seekers. Also in the 1960s the song was to become popular amongst British football supporters who would use their own lyrics in their adaptions.

Webb, Mrs

Played by Claire Davenport

A canteen cook employed by the Luxton and District Bus Company seen in two Series Seven episodes of On The Buses.

Mrs Webb is a blonde-haired woman in her early forties, who comes across as being a little ignorant and speaks with a northern accent. Her lack of cooking talent first becomes apparent in the episode 'The Allowance' when Jack and his driver Sid complain that her tea is undrinkable and they suggest that she puts her tea urn in for a de-coke. She doesn't take kindly to the remarks and suggests they drink the coffee instead but Sid points out that her coffee is even worse.

In the following episode 'Friends In High Places' unrest grows about Mrs Webb's cooking. The terrible standard of cuisine in the depot canteen is so bad that even Olive can't eat the food and Jack feels it is time to make a stand. He threatens industrial action unless changes are made but Mrs Webb makes for a daunting figure when she brandishes a meat cleaver when confronting Jack about his criticism. When Inspector Blake tries to sort out the dispute he only makes matters worse when he hints that her cooking isn't great. Mrs Webb sees this as the last straw and taking off her apron she declares she is quitting and leaves the inspector with the difficult task of finding a replacement cook.

Wedding Anniversary

Arthur and Olive's wedding anniversary features in two episodes of On The Buses and much like their marriage the celebrations are marred by insults, arguments and mishaps.

The couple celebrate their tenth wedding anniversary in the Series Four episode 'The Anniversary' and they receive a present from Aunt Maud – a pet poodle that they call Scruffy. The day starts with Arthur giving Olive a card that turns out to be the same card from the previous year. Stan sees it as meanness but Arthur insists he used the card again for sentimental reasons. Later that evening, Olive cooks a special anniversary meal and undergoes a makeover. She wears a new midi-skirt and hair extensions for the occasion whilst Arthur buys a bottle of sherry and a box of expensive liqueur chocolates to go with the dinner. He is less than complimentary about Olive's skirt and lambasts her when her hair extensions end up in his soup. The dinner turns into a disaster when the main course of chicken ends up being eaten by Scruffy leaving the family forced to dine on an omelette made by Mrs Butler. To round off the evening Arthur's box of chocolates is ruined when Scruffy leaves a deposit on them and so ends a tenth wedding anniversary littered with mishaps.

The deterioration in their marriage is evident the following year. In the Series Six episode 'Stan's Worst Day', Arthur arrives home drunk and as he enters his bedroom Olive throws a vase at him. She is upset that he has forgotten that it is their wedding anniversary but Arthur argues that he hadn't forgotten and quips: 'Why do you think I went out and got drunk.' This is the last straw for Olive who tells him to get out and amidst an argument a pillow is ripped sending feathers flying everywhere. They do finally patch up their differences and go shopping for an anniversary present the following day with Arthur claiming he needs a new cap.

Weedon, Ray

Editor (Series 7 Episode 11 'The Allowance')

Ray Weedon was to work in editorial departments for London Weekend Television and Channel Four in a career that spanned over thirty years.

At LWT from the early 1970s until the early 1990s, Weedon edited a range of television series such as hit comedy series that included The Stanley Baxter Picture Show, On The Buses, Metal Mickey, The Goodies and Hale And Pace. Also in drama he was editor for a number of episodes of A Married Man and Dempsey And Makepeace. Other credits came in the mystery documentary Strange But True and the long-running arts series The South Bank Show. Weedon moved on to work on Channel Four productions early in the 2000s which were less successful projects to end his career.

Welding

Stan and Jack are forced into trying their hand at welding at the bus depot in the Series Four episode 'Nowhere To Go'.

In a bid to repair Arthur's motorbike after the fork snaps on the front wheel, Stan and Jack seek help from Joe in the maintenance department. However, he is too busy repairing a bus and says they'll have to do it themselves and shows them the welding torch. Whilst Stan is adamant they cannot weld, Jack reassures him saying he knows all about welding as he watched someone do it once. Placing the snapped fork of the front wheel in a vice, Stan dons a pair of asbestos gloves whilst Jack puts on a pair of protective goggles as he begins to start up the blow torch. They suffer a series of mishaps with the fork being welded at the wrong angle; Stan's gloves get set on fire and a pair of tongs gets welded to the fork but finally the job is completed much to their satisfaction. However, the welding job turns out to be a little less successful than they thought.

Wells, Elaine

TV Role: Chemist's Assistant (Series 7 Episode 4 'The Poster')

Elaine Wells was to have a career as an actress that spanned around thirty years. Her acting roles were largely to be television-based.

From the mid-1950s she had a number of roles on the small screen in hit dramas. Her biggest role came in the hard-hitting 1970s prison drama Within These Walls where she played Prison Officer Spencer from 1975 to 1978. Her other drama credits included Crossroads, Dr Finlay's Casebook, Coronation Street, Edward and Mrs Simpson, Lillie and Partners In Crime amongst others. Comedy roles were sparser and the most notable came in an episode of On The Buses.

Aside from a number of made-for-television film credits, Wells sole big screen role came in the late 1950s in a thriller called Kill Her Gently.

Welch, Raquel

This famous actress is referred to by Stan in the Series Four episode 'The Injury'.

As Stan redecorates the bathroom with tiled wallpaper he gets criticised by Arthur. The know-it-all brother-inlaw describes the wallpaper as 'cheap and nasty' and a 'cheap imitation'. 'I always say if you can't have the real thing settle for something completely different,' says Arthur. Stan feels Arthur is being a hypocrite and hits back saying to his mum: 'Just because he couldn't marry Raquel Welch he didn't go out and become a monk did he?'

Raquel Welch, born in Chicago, USA, is an actress famed for her beauty and stunning figure who shot to fame with a role in the classic 1966 sci-fi film Fantastic Voyage. This was soon followed by a role that cemented her place as a global sex symbol when she appeared as a prehistoric bikini-clad woman in the Hammer production One Million Years BC. In 1973 she was to win the Golden Globe award for best motion picture actress for her part in The Three Musketeers and she has continued as an actress and model up to the present day.

Wembley Studios

This was the first home of London Weekend Television where the first six series of On The Buses were filmed from 1969 until 1972.

Initially, Wembley Studios in London were opened in 1926 as film studios by British Talking Pictures and were taken over by Fox Films (later to become 20th Century Fox). Films to be made there included Wedding Rehearsal, Death At Broadcasting House and the final film to come out of Wembley Studios before television productions took over was The Ship That Dies Of Shame in 1954.

The future of the studios lay in television though and early in 1955 they underwent renovations after being bought by Associated Rediffusion – an ITV broadcasting company for London on weekdays. The studios also had a massive new studio built called Studio 5 which opened in 1960. Associated Rediffusion used Wembley Studios to film hit series such as Double Your Money, Opportunity Knocks, Take Your Pick, Ready Steady Go, The Dickie Henderson Show and classic 1960's dramas which included No Hiding Place.

The studios were to change hands again in May 1968. Rediffusion (having dropped the Associated from their name) lost the franchise as London's weekday broadcaster which went to new company Thames and after lengthy discussions London Weekend Television (London's new weekend television broadcasting company) leased Wembley Studios from Redifussion. LWT would put Studio 5 to good use as buses could enter and it would double ideally as the inside of the bus depot in the hit sitcom On The Buses. Also filmed at Wembley Studios was a mixture of hit comedy, drama and light entertainment series including Hark At Barker, Doctor On The Go, Please Sir, The Fenn Street Gang, Upstairs Downstairs, Aquarius and World Of Sport. However, in 1972, LWT moved to their new home – the new custom-built South Bank Studios.

The Wembley Studios were to be left unoccupied until being bought by Lee International Film Studios in 1978. The studios were reconverted into film studios with much of the television equipment being removed with films such as Quadrophenia, The Elephant Man and Brazil being filmed there. However, when the company bought the larger Shepperton Studios they were to leave their Wembley home in 1986.

Three years later, Limehouse Television bought Wembley Studios with the film studios on the site being demolished and replaced by a retail park. Studio 5 remained and was re-equipped with further improvements made to the facilities. It was to see popular television series such as Food And Drink, The Word, Whose Line Is It Anyway, You Bet and a number of music videos and shows were also filmed here. Sadly, Limehouse Television were to be made bankrupt late in 1992 and the studios were again to change ownership.

In 1993 Wembley Studios came under the ownership of Fountain Television with the studios later to be renamed Fountain Studios. More renovations and upgrades of the site were carried out and the studios were to become highly active once more. It produced hit series such as Hearts Of Gold, Pop Idol, The X Factor, The Cube and Test The Nation amongst others.

Another owner change in 2006 saw the company InvestinMedia buy the studios and they have continued to put the studios to good use to the present day almost ninety years since they first opened.

Wendy

Played by Nina West

This young clippie is seen discussing horoscopes in the depot canteen in the Series Seven episode 'What The Stars Foretell'.

Wendy is a blonde-haired clippie who, like her fellow clippies Sandra and Olive, shares a belief and an interest in horoscopes printed in a magazine. Sharing a cup of tea with her colleagues she insists the horoscopes are right when Jack pours scorn on the idea.

Wendy

Played by Kate Williams

This is a clippie who is wrongly accused of having an affair with Arthur in the Series Four episode 'The Other Woman'.

Wendy, an off-duty clippie in her late twenties wearing a short, tight skirt attends a darts night event in the depot canteen. Arthur seems more interested in chatting her up than playing darts and plies her with gin whilst cruelly neglecting Olive who is present. It bothers her to such an extent that she returns home early complaining of a headache which leaves Arthur to continue to flirt with Wendy until the end of the evening.

With Arthur arriving home in the early hours of the morning and with Wendy having a reputation as a maneater the family jump to conclusions that causes unrest in Arthur and Olive's marriage. It sees him rethink his position in the family and the following morning he prepares to catch a bus at the depot as he plans to go and stay with his sister. The family arrive on the scene but things look bad when Wendy turns out to be the clippie aboard the bus that Arthur boards. Mrs Butler demands that Inspector Blake sacks Wendy for immoral behaviour whilst Olive accuses her of seducing Arthur. However, the clippie is gobsmacked and turns to them and says in a cockney accent: 'Just because he bought me a few gins he spread it around? Who'd fancy him? I wouldn't be seen dead with him Shrivelled up little weed.' It clears Wendy of any blame and Olive is all too willing to forgive her husband once more.

West, Nina

TV Role: Wendy (Series 7 Episode 10 'What The Stars Foretell')

Nina West's career as an actress would see her with acting credits on television, in films and on stage from the early 1970s through until the early 1980s.

Her television roles all came in the early 1970s. These came in the hit drama The Rivals Of Sherlock Holmes and in LWT sitcoms On The Buses and The Fenn Street Gang.

Towards the end of the 1970s she was to have a small role in the sex comedy film Adventures Of A Plumber's Mate – her solitary big screen role.

On stage West's most notable role came in the early 1980s production Ten Times Table.

Westhorpe, Wayne

Film Role: Olive's Baby aka Little Arthur (Mutiny On The Buses)

Born in 1970, Wayne Westhorpe's first acting role came playing little Arthur in the 1972 film Mutiny On The Buses. For the following spin-off film Holiday On The Buses the same role was played by Adam Rhodes.

This was to be Westhorpe's only acting credit and on leaving school he took up a career away from show business.

Whitehurst, Derek

Assistant Director (On The Buses)

Derek Whitehurst was to have a long distinguished career in the film and television industry. He began in the mid–1940s in the camera department and would go on to make his name as an assistant director from the late 1950s on both the big and small screen.

It was at Hammer Films that he worked for a large part of his career, working on some of their best-loved horror films of the 1950s, 60s and 70s. These began with The Curse Of Frankenstein and went on to include Taste The Blood Of Dracula, The Vampire Lovers, Scars Of Dracula, Vampire Circus and Frankenstein And The Monster From Hell amongst others. He'd also work on Hammer's comedy productions which included On The Buses and Man About The House. Away from Hammer he had credits in other films the pick of which were Inadmissible Evidence, The Virgin And The Gypsy, And Now The Screaming Starts and Friend Or Foe.

He was also to have impressive credits on television such as Journey To The Unknown, hard-hitting classic dramas The Sweeney and The Professionals and finally, in the early 1980s in the popular children's series Terrahawks.

In the late 1980s, after more than forty years in the industry, Whitehurst was to retire. Sadly, in 2006, after a long illness he was to pass away.

Whitter, Glen

TV Role: Chalkie (Series 3 Episode 4 'Brew It Yourself', Series 3 Episode 10 'The New Uniforms', Series 3 Episode 12 'The Squeeze', Series 5 Episode 6 'Busmen's Ball', Series 5 Episode 7 'Canteen Trouble', Series 5 Episode 13 'Vacancy For Inspector', Series 6 Episode 3 'Private Hire' and Series 6 Episode 5 'Union Trouble')

Born in the West Indies, Glen Whitter was to move to the UK to build an acting career that brought him roles on television and in films from the mid-1960s until the early 1980s.

He made his small screen debut with an uncredited role in the classic sci-fi series Doctor Who and he went on to appear in a total of three episodes. He'd also have credits in drama The Troubleshooters and played a bus conductor in the hit sitcom Doctor In The House. Whitter's biggest role of his career came in On The Buses where he played the West Indian bus conductor Chalkie in several episodes as well as making numerous uncredited appearances in the hit sitcom as well.

On the big screen his solitary credit was to come with a small part in the 1980 cult sci-fi film Flash Gordon.

When his acting career came to an end he was to return to the West Indies and would go on to run a chain of restaurants in Tobago.

Why Are We Waiting

This is a song that is to be sung in a couple of episodes of On The Buses.

Firstly, in the Series One episode 'The Canteen', the busmen grow impatient waiting to be served their food in the canteen by new employees Olive and Mrs Butler. They loudly sing 'Why Are We Waiting' thumping the tables as they do so. Later, in the Series Four episode 'The Kids Outing', Stan's bus breaks down with a bus full of children aboard. They are restless and bemused and start singing 'Why Are We Waiting'. When Jack ordersthem to shut up and tells them they will be going back to the depot he ends up getting food flung at him by the troublesome children.

The song 'Why Are We Waiting' is sung to the tune of the Christmas carol 'Oh, Come All You Faithful' which was written in 1751. It has been sung for generations by groups of people who grow frustrated either waiting for someone or something to arrive.

Wild, Jeanette

Film Role: Suzy (On The Buses)
TV Role: Rita (Series 7 Episode 5 'The Football Match')

Jeanette Wild was to have a career as an actress that saw her appear in both hit films and television series from the mid to late 1960s through until the early 1980s.

She had her first roles on the big screen with credits in Her Private Hell, Zeta One, On The Buses and Dr Jekyll And Sister Hyde amongst others. Uncredited roles also came her way in the Morecambe and Wise comedy film The Magnificent Two and Chitty Chitty Bang Bang. On television, Wild could boast credits in classic comedy series such as Up Pompeii, Monty Python's Flying Circus, On The Buses and the less successful sitcoms Leave It To Charlie and How's Your Father.

She was equally active in dramas with her most notable credits coming in Z Cars, The Troubleshooters, Softly Softly and Coronation Street.

Wilkins, Miss

An ex-teacher of Stan's who is referred to by his mum in the Series One episode 'The New Conductor'.

As Stan gets very nervous, feeling ill at the prospect of having a new conductor aboard his bus, his mum recalls how he used to be the same at school when he used to get a new teacher. She remembers when he first had Miss Wilkins as his teacher and every morning he used to feel sick and she would put a hot water bottle on his stomach but Stan points out he was only eight-years-old at the time. When she offers him the same treatment he refuses claiming if he turns up at work with a hot water bottle up his jacket they will think he is a pregnant clippie.

Williams, Kate

TV Roles: Doreen (Series 2 Episode 5 'Late Again') and Wendy (Series 4 Episode 4
'The Other Woman').
Film Role: Joan (Holiday On The Buses)

Born in London in 1941, Kate Williams was to study drama at the East 15 Acting School and graduated before going on to build an impressive career as an actress with roles coming on stage, television and in films.

She debuted on stage in the mid-1960s with a string of credits at the Royal Court Theatre, London appearing in Their Very Own And Golden City, Live Like Pigs and The Dragon. The pick of her 1970s stage roles came in the 1975 Sir Noel Coward play Tonight At 8:00 followed a year later by Liza Of Lambeth. In the 1980s she remained active with credits in Keeley's Mother, Chorus Girls and Break Neck at Stratford East's Theatre Royal.

Williams was still treading the boards in the 1990's with roles in What A Bleedin' Mystery, She Stoops To Conquer and Cockroach Who? She remains active on stage to the present day.

Kate Williams.

Williams made her television debut in the late 1960s and her best-remembered role came in the controversial 1970s sitcom Love Thy Neighbour where she played Joan Booth – wife of the bigoted Eddie Booth. She would also appear in several other hit comedy series such as On The Buses, Doctor At Large, Please Sir, Shine On Harvey Moon, Just Good Friends, Only Fools And Horses and May To December. Drama roles were plentiful and she most memorably played Audrey Withey in Widows and its sequels Widows 2 and She's Out. She also appeared in a long line of classic British dramas such as Dixon Of Dock Green, The Gentle Touch, Murder Most Horrid, The Bill, Berkeley Square, Holby City and in recent years was to have a long stint in the hit soap EastEnders.

Film roles began for her in the late 1960s with a leading role in Poor Cow and she also had a small role in the spin-off film Till Death Us Do Part. The 1970s brought further notable credits in Melody, Love Thy Neighbour, Holiday On The Buses and Quadrophenia. A small role in the award-winning Little Dorrit in 1988 was followed in the 1990s with credits in The Mystery Of Edwin Drood as well as a string of appearances in a number of made-for-television films.

Williams remains active as an actress to the present day and also teaches drama at the noted Italia Conti Academy of Theatre Arts in London.

Wilmot, Sid

Played by John Lyons

The bus driver aboard Jack's bus who is not impressed when the clippies insist on stopping their buses at each public toilet on their route in the Series Seven episode 'The Allowance'.

Sid Wilmot is in his early thirties, has long wavy hair and is employed as a bus driver by the Luxton and District Bus Company. He is always ready to voice his opinion complaining about the canteen tea to Mrs Webb and later is far from impressed when the clippies protest at having to pay to use public toilets whilst on duty by insisting on stopping at all public toilets on their routes. Sid complains vehemently to Jack in the depot and is so fed up with the late running buses that he wants Inspector Blake to stand up to the clippies and get the buses running on time again. However, he does revel in the inspector's later discomfort when he is arrested for being a Peeping Tom and he jokingly asks Blakey when his case is coming up. Sid is a driver with a conscience for good timekeeping but still happy to wind up the inspector.

Wilson, Harold

This was a British Prime Minister during the 1960s and 70s who is referred to by Mrs Butler in the Series One episode 'The Early Shift'.

As a television crew prepare to start filming Stan who is on picket duty his mum feels he should have some make-up on like other famous people on television such as Harold Wilson. Stan jokes that he probably borrows Barbara Castle's powder puff.

Harold Wilson was Prime Minister of the Labour government in the UK from 1964 to 1970 and so was in power when this episode originally aired on British television. However, his party lost power when the Conservatives led by Edward Heath won the 1970 General Election but he found himself back at 10 Downing Street in 1974 becoming Prime Minister for the second time. Two years later, in 1976 Wilson was to resign at the age of sixty describing himself as being mentally and physically exhausted. Soon afterwards he was diagnosed as having Alzheimer's disease and James Callaghan took over as Prime Minister. Wilson thereafter was to regularly attend sittings at the House of Lords up until his death in 1995 at the age of seventy one due to colon cancer and Alzheimer's disease.

Wimpy Bar

This popular UK restaurant chain was referred to by Stan in the film On The Buses.

Stan enthuses over a date he had with an attractive young clippie called Suzy and tells an envious Jack that he never got home until after eleven o'clock. Jack is surprised but Stan tells him: 'The Wimpy Bars don't close 'til then you know.'

Wimpy restaurants (named after the character from the popular Popeye cartoons that had a love for hamburgers) were established in the UK by the American businessman and entrepreneur Eddie Gold. By the 1950s he had a dozen such restaurants in the UK when a large British food manufacturer J Lyons and Company took over the brand, expanding it and by the early 1970s there were over a thousand Wimpy restaurants all around the world. However, from the mid-1970s stiff competition had arrived on the scene in the form of fast food chains from the USA such as McDonald's, Burger King and Kentucky Fried Chicken which was to hit Wimpy's custom. The company was sold to United Biscuits in 1977 but their market share continued to dwindle and a number of their restaurants closed. After a number of ownership changes, Wimpy under South African ownership is now under-going a rebranding and massive refurbishment as it looks to re-establish itself in the UK some sixty years after they first came to prominence.

Window Cleaner

Played by Johnny Briggs

This is a character who mistakenly becomes embroiled in Arthur and Olive's marital problems in the Series Six episode 'Love Is What You Make It'.

A handsome man in his mid-thirties who visits the Butler house looking to clean their windows but Olive believes him to be the man who is attracted to her that Stan has told her about. She looks to bring him into the house but Jack steps in to chase him off as he has already arranged for Inspector Blake to visit and be seduced by Olive as they look to make Arthur jealous. The miffed window cleaner agrees with Jack's claim that Olive is entertaining and as he tells her he'll see her tomorrow he is shoved out of the door by Jack. He does indeed return the following day as promised and makes it into the parlour where he is served a cup of tea by Olive when Arthur and Stan enter the room. The window cleaner is startled by their arrival and slowly gets up from his seat with a nervous look on his face before dashing out of the house never to be seen again.

Windsor Safari Park

A popular tourist attraction that features in the film Mutiny On The Buses as Stan and Blakey visit the park in the Town and District's new tour bus in a trial run with future plans to run tours to the attraction.

Windsor Safari Park, located on the outskirts of the historic Berkshire town of Windsor, was opened for business in 1969 by the Billy Smart family famed for their circus. It contained a range of wild animals including chimpanzees, elephants and lions all of which could be seen at close quarters by driving through the various enclosures. The park was an immediate success and in the 1970s and 80s the park was expanded in size and facilities improved. A new range of animals, a boat trip, children's rides and eateries made it a highly popular tourist attraction despite a number of new owners over the years. With Themes International running the park, expansions continued with an impressive new aquatic area and dolphinarium added.

However, in 1992, shortly after more expensive refurbishment and a fall in visitor numbers, Themes International was in financial peril and Windsor Safari Park went into receivership and closed for the last time in January 1992. The animals were relocated to zoos and safari parks around the world and the site was bought by the Lego Group. After a complete renovation of the site, in 1996, a Legoland theme park opened and remains in business to the present day.

Winnie

Played by Winifred Braemar

This ageing canteen employee appears in three Series Four episodes of On The Buses.

Winnie is a red-haired canteen employee in her fifties who is first seen in the episode 'The Kids Outing'. With the canteen full of misbehaving children it is up to Stan to think of a novel way to entertain them. He decides to perform a drag act in which he sings a song with Winnie accompanying him on the piano. She briefly appears in the episode 'The Lodger' as she can be seen answering the telephone behind the counter in the canteen and tells Inspector Blake the phone call is for him as he is about to sit down to lunch.

Finally, in the episode 'Not Tonight', Winnie takes a new employee called Stella under her wing and tells her that Stan, who has been eyeing the attractive Stella up, is not married which interests the new employee as she watches him counting his wages.

Wintergreen Ointment

An ointment used by Olive and referred to in the Series Five episode 'The Strain'.

When Stan is left bed-ridden when he injures his back, Arthur brings him Olive's pillow to support his back. However, it is covered in wintergreen ointment and the smell in unbearable to Stan but Olive explains she puts the ointment on to keep her catarrh away.

Wintergreen ointment is still used to the present day and is used to treat a range of medical ailments. It can be used to treat dry and cracked skin, aching joints and muscles and a range of cold symptoms including blocked noses and sore throats.

Wolfe, Ronald

Co-creator and Co-writer of On The Buses
Producer (On The Buses, Mutiny On The Buses and Holiday On The Buses)

Born in Stoke Newington, London in 1922, Ronald Wolfe was to start writing scripts for radio in his late teens. He would go on to form a partnership with Ronald Chesney in the early 1950s and from radio scripts they progressed on to write a number of smash hit television sitcoms, films and stage shows over the next forty years.

Wolfe's biggest hits came with The Rag Trade in the early 1960s and On The Buses in the late 1960s into the early 1970s. The Wolfe and Chesney success story had begun in the mid-1950s when they wrote Educating Archie. Their other notable writing credits on the small screen included Meet The Wife, Romany Jones and Yus My Dear. They were also to write sitcoms that aired on Norwegian, Australian and US television in the 1960s, 70s and 80s.

On the big screen he and Ronald Chesney wrote their first film script for the 1966 musical I've Gotta Horse. This was followed in the early 1970s with the three On The Buses spin-off films which they also produced. Their final foray onto the big screen came in the mid-1990s with the Norwegian version of The Rag Trade – Fredriksson's fabrikk.

He would also write scripts for a number of stage shows such as a 1962 adaption of The Rag Trade and in the 1980's a comedy revue called A Little Bit On The Side. In 1987, Anna Karen, Doris Hare and Michael Robbins reunited to tour Canada in the stage show On The Buses – A New Life.

Wolfe was to retire in the late 1990s but was a staunch supporter of the annual On The Buses events in Borehamwood and went on to write a book about his life in show business called Ronnie Wolfe: A Life In Memoirs. Sadly, late in his life he suffered ill health and whilst in a nursing home he suffered serious head injuries after falling downstairs in 2011 and died at the age of eighty nine. This was a tragic end for a man who has brought so much laughter to people all over the world.

Ronnie Wolfe (left) and Ronnie Chesney in 2008.

Ronnie Wolfe at the 2009 On The Buses event.

The late Ronald Wolfe was a special man. Not only was he a superbly-talented comedy writer but he was also a man who saw the cast of On The Buses as a sort of additional family who he cared for greatly. In later years as annual On The Buses events were organised he was an ever-present and always had time for the fans – young or old. Even when in deteriorating health his desire and enthusiasm to mingle with the fans never diminished and that is something those fans greatly appreciated.

At one of those events Wolfe disclosed how the idea was inspired by another classic sitcom of the late 1960's. He and his writing partner Ronald Chesney recognised that men in uniforms were always going to get a laugh as proven by the smash hit Dad's Army which hit the TV screens in 1968. A year or so later and Wolfe and Chesney brought the uniforms of busmen onto our screens in On The Buses and the rest is history. He was also to reveal that many of the plotlines they used were inspired by similar experiences in their own lives.

Woman

Played by Amelia Bayntun

This is a disgruntled passenger who loses her husband's supper aboard Stan's bus in the Series Five episode 'Lost Property'.

The ageing housewife in her fifties reports the loss of two portions of fish and chips in a visit to Inspector Blake's office and demands the return of the items. However, when a search is carried out of the bus nothing is found as Stan and Jack have already eaten the fish and chips. The woman is far from happy as she is sure she can smell the fish and promises that she will write to the manager to complain before she storms off.

Woman And The Stars

A fictional woman's magazine that clippies are seen reading in the Series Seven episode 'What The Stars Foretell'.

Olive and her friends Sandra and Wendy are to eagerly read their horoscopes from a magazine called Women And The Stars. The magazine also contains fashion items and cooking recipes. Jack though, is sceptical of the horoscopes and is surprised that the clippies believe in them.

Woman Getting off Bus

Played by Shirley English

A woman who gets off Stan's bus and hands money to Jack for her ticket as the opening credits roll on Mutiny On The Buses. This was an uncredited role.

Woman Passenger, The

Played by Olive Mercer

A passenger who believes she has lost an ear-ring aboard Stan's bus in the Series Four episode 'Cover Up'.

As the inspector is set to go for his lunch an ageing woman holding a wicker basket waylays him in the depot and says she has lost an ear-ring aboard Stan's bus. She recognises it as Stan's bus describing Jack to Inspector Blake as having 'a shifty looking face and big teeth' much to the eaves-dropping Jack's annoyance. As the inspector searches the bus parked in the depot she calls him off the bus telling him she has found her ear-ring in her basket amidst her brussel sprouts. Apologising for the inconvenience she makes a hasty exit.

Woman Passenger, The

Played by Katherine Page

A woman stranded aboard Stan's fog-bound bus in the Series Three episode 'Foggy Night'.

The dark-haired woman in her sixties is seated to the rear of the bus on the lower deck. When the bus comes to an abrupt hall she asks Blakey: 'Is anything wrong inspector?' He assures her it is just a routine stop and boasts that all of their drivers are highly-trained and know the route but then Stan enters the bus to declare that he is lost. Later, when the bus arrives back at the depot early the next morning she is the first to disembark carrying a parcel with a disgruntled look on her face.

Women Bus Drivers

The introduction of women bus drivers by the Town and District Bus Company causes great friction at the depot in the film On The Buses.

The decision, which Inspector Blake claims was all his own idea, is brought about due to a shortage of bus crews which the inspector believes Stan and Jack are exploiting. The male bus drivers are up in arms about the decision as they see it as a threat to their livelihood and a huge financial blow as they fear losing their overtime. When the union is unable to come to their rescue and rid them of the women bus drivers, Stan and Jack begin a dirty tricks campaign in a bid to discredit the women. After a number of incidents involving the women, the management capitulate and dispense with women bus drivers but Stan and Jack needn't feel so smug as a number of the displaced women end up being made in to inspectors where they set about making the pair of busmen's lives a misery.

Wreck of the Hesperus, The

A poem which Stan used to recite at school is mentioned in the Series Three episode 'Radio Control'.

When Arthur ridicules Stan for mispronouncing his words as he tries to learn the busman's code his mum comes to his defence. She reminds Stan of a poem he used to recite at school called 'The Wreck of the Hesperus' but when Stan mentions it he is ridiculed once more for dropping his aitches by Arthur.

The Wreck of the Hesperus was a poem written by the US poet Henry Wadsworth Longfellow in 1842. It tells of a captain of a ship who ignores a seaman who warns of an approaching storm. It is a disastrous move as his ship is to hit a reef in the storm and sinks with the captain losing his life after managing to save the life of his daughter.

X Certificate

A term Stan uses to describe the perfume that Iris wears in the Series One episode 'The Darts Match'.

As Stan flirts with Iris in the depot canteen just before their darts match starts she sprays herself with perfume. Smelling it, Stan describes it as smashing stuff and feels sure they don't issue it to girls whilst Iris insists that she doesn't waste it on little boys. With that Stan adds it smells so good it should get an X certificate.

The X certificate was a rating issued by the British Board of Film Censors from 1951 until 1982. It deemed a film to be suitable only for those aged 16 and over and this was extended to 18 and over in 1970. In 1982, the X certificate was replaced by the 18 certificate which, in turn, in 1990 was changed to PG (Parental Guidance).

Yarmouth

A seaside town which Stan and Jack holidayed in as referred to in the Series Two episode 'Bon Voyage'.

When Stan and Jack tell Inspector Blake of their ploy to attract women by pretending to be professional photographers during their upcoming holiday in Spain, the inspector is highly- sceptical and feels sure the women won't fall for it. Stan though, is confident and says: 'They fell for it at a wet weekend in Yarmouth last year.'

Yarmouth (better known as Great Yarmouth) is located on the Norfolk coast and the town is a small seaside resort. It is best known for its Britannia and Wellington piers with the Britannia Theatre on the pier being one of only very few theatres found on piers in England. The town is also home to the Winter Gardens – a multi- purpose venue which is now a nightclub and also in Yarmouth since 1819 has been a large monument to Admiral Nelson.

Yoga

A form of exercise which Arthur partakes in as revealed in the Series Five episode 'The Nursery'.

When Arthur ridicules Olive when she practices putting nappies on a doll and ends up twisting the doll's legs into an awkward position she quickly hits back. She mentions that he also gets into peculiar positions in the bedroom but he clears up the confusion by confessing to Stan: 'It just so happens I was practising my yoga.'

Yoga, which originated in ancient India, is a disciplined form of exercises that uses meditation to achieve physical, spiritual and mental discipline. It dates back as far as the 2nd century BC and has grown to be a popular practice all over the world.

Young, Jimmy

A famous singer and disc jockey referred to by Stan in the Series One episode 'The Early Shift'.

When Stan prepares for another early shift he receives his shoes from his mother who has been heating them in the oven. However, when he steps into the shoes he finds them far too hot and says to his mum: 'Next time give 'em five minutes at number six and send the recipe to Jimmy Young'.

Jimmy Young is best-remembered as a BBC Radio Two disc jockey but he originally shot to fame as a singer in the early 1950's having a string of top ten hits in the UK and also two number one hits, those being Unchained Melody and The Man From Laramie. He went on to become a disc jockey in the early 1960's at Radio Luxembourg before moving on to become one of the first BBC Radio One presenters in 1967. By 1973 he moved on to Radio Two to present his own mid-morning show where he remained for almost thirty years. It was to contain a pleasant mix of music, chat, recipes, current affairs and a wide range of celebrity guests ranging from royalty to Prime Ministers and actors to pop stars amongst others. Jimmy Young would be awarded an OBE in 1979; a CBE in 1993 and in 2002 was knighted and became Sir Jimmy Young. He finally left the BBC at the end of 2002 at the age of eighty one and is now enjoying his retirement.

Young, Sharon

TV Role: Sandra (Series 5 Episode 5 'The Epidemic')

Sharon Young was to have a brief career as an actress that was to span from the mid-1960s into the early 1970s and consisted of roles in films and on television.

She debuted on the big screen in a science fiction film that was a spin-off of the cult television series Doctor Who. Young had a small role in Doctor Who And The Daleks which starred Peter Cushing and Roy Castle in 1965. This was to be her only film role.
On television she was to appear in the BBC sci-fi series Adam Adamant Lives, followed in the late 1960s with another drama role in the hit series The Troubleshooters. Her final acting credit came in the classic sitcom On The Buses in 1971 with her biggest role where she played the attractive clippie Sandra.

Acknowledgements

I would like to thank a number of people for making this book possible. As you read the book you will notice a few quotations from the scripts of On The Buses so thanks to the late Ronnie Wolfe (co-copyright holder) for the permission to use those. A handful of photographs in this book were kindly supplied by Steve Holden who runs The Official On The Buses Fan Club so a big thanks to Steve as well as my sister Michelle Walker and photographer Cliff Harris. Bus enthusiast David Sheppard as well deserves thanks for use of his photo and information on his wonderfully restored Lodekka. Also there are a handful of memories of working on either episodes or spin-off films of On The Buses supplied by actors, actresses and crew members which I am highly grateful for so Stuart Allen, Olivia Breeze, Ronnie Chesney, the late Hal Dyer, Harry Fielder and Damaris Hayman I thank you all. Some rare interviews with the late Bob Grant reveal more about the man which I am sure all fans will enjoy so a big thank you to John Murray at VRFM Radio and John Hannam at Isle of Wight Radio for the use of this material – it is much appreciated. Research came about through various avenues such as books, websites and close first-hand information so many of them to mention that I collectively thank them all. The support of families and friends has also been great during the long road through research, writing, editing and moving through the publication phases. The book cover design is the artwork of Steve Lilly a noted professional artist and so much appreciation goes to him. Finally, publication came about thanks to Mirador Publishing so a final and big thank you to Sarah Luddington and all of those that made this book possible.